THE THERAVĀDA ABHIDHAMMA

THE

THERAVĀDA ABHIDHAMMA

Inquiry into the Nature *of* Conditioned Reality

Y. KARUNADASA

Wisdom

Wisdom Publications
199 Elm Street
Somerville, MA 02144 USA
wisdompubs.org

First published by the Centre of Buddhist Studies,
The University of Hong Kong, 2010, second printing 2014.
Reprint 2019 Wisdom Publications

LIBRARY OF CONGRESS CATALOGING-IN-PUBLICATION DATA

Names: Karunadasa, Y., author.
Title: The Theravāda Abhidhamma: inquiry into the nature of reality / Y. Karunadasa.
Description: Somerville, MA: Wisdom Publications, [2019] | "First published by the Centre of Buddhist Studies, The University of Hong Kong, 2010, second printing 2014"— Title verso. | Includes bibliographical references and index. |
Identifiers: LCCN 2018040474 (print) | LCCN 2019010187 (ebook) | ISBN 9781614294696 (ebook) | ISBN 9781614294535 (hardcover: alk. paper)
Subjects: LCSH: Abhidharma. | Reality. | Tipiṭaka. Abhidhammapiṭaka. | Theravāda Buddhism. | Buddhist philosophy.
Classification: LCC BQ4200 (ebook) | LCC BQ4200 .K37 2019 (print) | DDC 294.3/42041—dc23
LC record available at https://lccn.loc.gov/2018040474

ISBN 978-1-61429-453-5 ebook ISBN 978-1-61429-469-6
23 22 21 20 19 5 4 3 2 1

Cover and interior design by Graciela Galup. Set in Diacritical Garamond Pro 11.25/15.

Wisdom Publications' books are printed on acid-free paper and meet the guidelines for permanence and durability of the Production Guidelines for Book Longevity of the Council on Library Resources.

♲ This book was produced with environmental mindfulness.
For more information, please visit wisdompubs.org/wisdom-environment.

Printed in the United States of America.

To Malathi

Bhariyā' va paramā sakhā

PUBLISHER'S ACKNOWLEDGMENT

The publisher gratefully acknowledges the generous help of the Hershey Family Foundation in sponsoring the production of this book.

CONTENTS

FOREWORD BY BHIKKHU BODHI ix

PREFACE xv

Introduction 1

1 The Real Existents 17

2 The Nominal and the Conceptual 55

3 The Two Truths 71

4 The Analysis of Mind 83

5 Consciousness 93

6 Classes of Consciousness 103

7 The Ethically Variable Mental Factors 121

8 The Unwholesome Mental Factors 141

9 The Beautiful Mental Factors 155

10 The Cognitive Process 169

11 The Analysis of Matter 187

12 The Great Elements of Matter 201

13 The Real Dependent Matter 211

14 The Nominal Dependent Matter 229

15 The Material Clusters 249

16 The Time and Space 271
17 Momentariness 283
18 The Conditional Relations 317

APPENDIX: THERAVĀDA AND VIBHAJJAVĀDA 341
ABBREVIATIONS 357
NOTES 361
BIBLIOGRAPHY 409
INDEX 419
ABOUT THE AUTHOR 451

FOREWORD

During his long ministry of forty-five years, the Buddha consistently taught a practical path to liberation that unfolded in three successive stages: moral behavior (*sīla*), concentration (*samādhi*), and wisdom (*paññā*). The Buddha himself emphasized the pragmatic ramifications of the path, and thus in his discourses he had to treat each major division in relatively broad terms. In the generations following his death, however, each of these three divisions of the path underwent an extensive process of elaboration, which resulted in a vast enrichment of Buddhist thought and literature.

The training in moral behavior was expanded into the detailed body of disciplinary rules and regulations known as the Vinaya. While the fundamental rules and procedures of the Vinaya probably stemmed from the age of the Buddha himself, it seems likely that their expansion according to technical methods of analysis and adjudication occurred during the first century or two after his passing. The training in concentration, which involves the refinement of attention, was expanded by giving detailed consideration to the various objects of meditation and the higher states of consciousness attained by dedicated practice. In the Theravāda tradition, the end product of this process of elaboration is the treatment of concentration that we find in such works as the fifth-century *Visuddhimagga*, translated by Bhikkhu Ñāṇamoli as *The Path of Purification*. This influential treatise pulls together the methods of meditation taught in the Nikāyas into a framework of forty meditation subjects, each treated in extensive detail.

The culmination of the Buddha's path, however, was the training in wisdom, and it was on this that he laid the greatest emphasis. The Pāli word *paññā*, translated here as "wisdom," is used in Buddhist literature in a precise technical sense. In this context, it means knowing and directly seeing the constituents of experience as they actually are. These constituents of experience, in the Nikāyas, are explained by way of such categories as the five aggregates (*khandha*), the six or twelve sense bases (*āyatana*), and the six or eighteen elements (*dhātu*). All these categories were comprised under the more general term *dhammā*, a plural form that here refers not to the Buddha's teachings as such but to the factors into which experience was dissected and laid bare for investigation by the practitioner of insight meditation. Thus the training in wisdom came to be understood as the effort to analyze, discern, and penetrate the constituent factors of experience. It is this penetrative insight that culminates in liberation (*vimutti*), the final goal of the teaching.

This training in wisdom, as an intellectual discipline, gave rise to the first great wave of Buddhist philosophical thought in the period following the demise of the Buddha. The exact process by which this development came about is not entirely clear, but we can sketch in broad strokes the course it probably followed. At a certain point in time the Saṅgha, the community of ordained disciples, may have started to give increasing attention to the analysis and classification of the factors of experience that served as the objects of wisdom. Specialist monks would have compiled ever longer lists of elements, proposing various schemes of analysis and classification and determining their connections and relationships. In time, these efforts spawned several complex systems, similar in conception but different in execution. It is these systems that were given the designation Abhidhamma (in Pāli), or Abhidharma (in Sanskrit). The word *abhidhamma* itself already occurs in the Nikāyas, where it is used in relation to discussions held by the disciples. In this context, the word probably meant the methodical exploration of the teachings through inquiry, dialogue, and debate. As the new methods of collecting and classifying dhammas were articulated with greater precision, the word *abhidhamma* came to be extended to the imposing intellectual edifices that started to emerge from such undertakings. Subsequently, the word was also transposed to the texts that advanced these classificatory schemes, which were originally oral compositions.

With the spread of Buddhism across northern India, the ancient unified monastic community was divided into different schools, probably in the earliest phase simply on account of geographical separation and slightly different approaches to interpretation. But over time, it is likely that they each developed their own distinctive way of systematizing the dhammas recognized as the constituents of experience. Thus by the third or fourth century after the Buddha's demise, a variety of Abhidharma systems must have adorned the Buddhist landscape in northern India. However, the records of Indian Buddhism at our disposal testify to the survival of only three major systems of Abhidharma, which prevailed in different parts of the Buddhist world. One, which seems to have gained prominence in the northwest in the area known as Gandhāra (corresponding to parts of present-day Pakistan and Afghanistan), is ascribed to a school called the Dharmaguptakas. This system is represented by a large work in four sections preserved solely in Chinese translation, called the **Śāriputra-abhidharmaśāstra* (舍利弗阿毘曇). The extent of this work's influence cannot be gauged with any degree of certainty, but the fact that it spread to China testifies to its importance during a particular phase of Buddhist history. Probably from a fairly early period, with the virtual disappearance of the Dharmaguptakas as an independent school, interest in its Abhidharma system also faded away, leaving the field to the other two Abhidharma systems.

These two systems have had greater longevity and exerted a more potent influence on Buddhist thought and practice over the centuries. The Buddhist school that prevailed in Kashmir, known as the Sarvāstivāda, "the School [holding that] All Exists," had a collection of seven canonical Abhidharma texts originally preserved in Sanskrit. In the early centuries of the Common Era this school became highly influential throughout northern India and beyond. Although, with the destruction of Buddhism in India, the Sarvāstivādins eventually disappeared, the system itself retained its prestige. Their seven canonical Abhidharma books, as well as various treatises of the school, had been translated into Chinese and engaged the interest of Chinese scholars in the early dynasties when Buddhism flourished in the Middle Kingdom. The Sarvāstivāda Abhidharma, as codified in a work known as the *Abhidharmakośa*, continued to be studied and formed a philosophical basis for later Indian Buddhist schools representing Mahāyāna Buddhism. Such schools as the Madhyamaka and Yogācāra schools took the Abhidharma of the Sarvāstivāda as their point of departure, regarding it as a valid exposition of conventional truth. Even today the *Kośa* is studied in Tibetan monastic universities and in both academic and monastic circles in Taiwan and Japan. However, while the Sarvāstivāda Abhidharma still plays an important role in these traditions as an object of academic study, it no longer functions as the wellspring of a living tradition of practice and meditation.

The third system of Abhidhamma has enjoyed quite a different fate. This is the Abhidhamma system of the Theravāda school, which flourished in the countries of southern Asia where Theravāda Buddhism took root, especially Sri Lanka and Burma. Here, even up to the present, it serves as an important branch of learning as well as a guide to meditation practice and realization. The Theravādin Abhidhamma system, like its Sarvāstivāda cousin, is grounded in a collection of seven canonical texts, but all quite different from their northern counterparts. These are preserved in Pāli, the ecclesiastical language of Theravāda Buddhism. The canonical texts in turn have given rise to commentaries and subcommentaries, and these in turn have generated summary manuals with their own commentaries and subcommentaries. Thus today the Theravāda Abhidhamma is represented by a huge body of literature preserved both in Pāli and in the indigenous languages of the lands of Theravāda Buddhism.

The most influential Abhidhamma text in the Theravāda tradition is a little manual known as the *Abhidhammatthasaṅgaha*, composed in Sri Lanka perhaps in the twelfth century. This work has been the subject of influential commentaries and has appeared in several English translations. It is on the basis of this work that, with the assistance of the late Burmese elder Venerable Rewata Dhamma Sayadaw, I composed *A Comprehensive Manual of Abhidhamma*, of which it forms the nucleus. Although I provided the *Manual* with a detailed explanatory guide, as well as with charts and tables, I have also recognized the need for an independent work in fluent English explaining the basic contours of the Theravāda Abhidhamma system for the serious, scholarly student of Buddhist thought.

Now, with the publication of the present book, that need has been met. The author, Professor Y. Karunadasa, is the ideal person to write such a work. He is perhaps the most erudite Sri Lankan scholar of Abhidhamma who combines breadth of learning with fluency in the English language. He is acquainted with almost the entire body of Abhidhamma literature in both Pāli and Sinhala, as well as works by contemporary Sri Lankan expositors of Abhidhamma. He knows the Sarvāstivāda Abhidharma and thus can draw comparisons between the Theravādin and Sarvāstivādin systems. He is also acquainted with Western philosophy and psychology, and thus can build bridges between the frameworks of Western thought and classical Abhidhamma, both Theravādin and Sarvāstivādin. To add to this, he has long experience teaching the Abhidhamma in English. Presently, as a visiting professor at the University of Hong Kong, he is helping to make the Theravāda Abhidhamma better known to followers of Mahāyāna Buddhism, who in recent years have shown keen interest in the thought world of their southern co-religionists.

Professor Karunadasa has based this book on the *Abhidhammatthasaṅgaha*, and he often refers to the edition I published, *A Comprehensive Manual of Abhidhamma*. But he does not merely explain an established system in the traditional manner, as more conservative monks from Sri Lanka, Burma, or Thailand generally do. Having been exposed to various strains of contemporary thought, he is able to draw out the relations between the ancient Buddhist Abhidhamma systems and modern ways of thinking. He also does not hesitate to explore various "meta-questions" that pertain to the Abhidhamma, questions that arise not from within the system itself but from an external perspective regarding its underlying premises and purposes. His book therefore offers a wealth of insights that can stimulate the readers' interest and enrich understanding.

My own dear teacher, the late Venerable Nyanaponika, himself a formidable Abhidhamma scholar, had long ago written a collection of essays called *Abhidhamma Studies* (Boston: Wisdom Publications, 1997). In his preface to this work, he wrote:

> Abhidhamma is meant for inquiring and searching spirits who are not satisfied by monotonously and uncritically repeating the ready-made terms, even if these are Abhidhamma terms. Abhidhamma is for imaginative minds who are able to fill in, as it were, the columns of the tabulations, for which the canonical Abhidhamma books have furnished the concise headings. (xxviii)

With this book, Professor Karunadasa has shown that he is one of those "inquiring and searching spirits" who contribute to the exploration and elucidation of the Abhidhamma. I am happy to welcome this work to the growing body of literature on the Abhidhamma available in English and hope that it will promote a better understanding and appreciation of this important expression of Buddhist wisdom.

Venerable Bhikkhu Bodhi

PREFACE

The first chapter of this volume is an expanded version of my *Dhamma Theory: The Philosophical Cornerstone of the Abhidhamma*, which was published by the Buddhist Publication Society in 1985. Five other chapters are revised versions of five articles on the Theravāda Abhidhamma that I contributed to the *Journal of Buddhist Studies* of the Centre of Buddhist Studies, Sri Lanka, from 2003 to 2009. I am grateful to its editorial board for their permission to reproduce them here.

In presenting this work I must first record here my deep sense of gratitude to the late Dr. W. S. Karunaratne, Professor of Buddhist Philosophy at the University of Ceylon (1952–73), for introducing me to Abhidhamma studies, and to the late Dr. D. Friedman, Reader in Indian Philosophy at the School of Oriental and African Studies of the University of London (1960s), under whose watchful eyes I pursued my doctoral research on a subject mainly relating to Theravāda Abhidhamma.

I am most grateful to Venerable Dr. Bhikkhu Bodhi, former president and editor in chief of the Buddhist Publication Society, for taking out time from a tight schedule to write the Foreword to this work and for his perceptive comments on my Introduction to this work.

Venerable Dr. K. L. Dhammajoti, the Glorious Sun Professor of Buddhist Studies at the University of Hong Kong, evinced a deep and abiding interest in this work ever since I began it some years ago. I have benefited much from his numerous publications on the Sarvāstivāda Abhidharma in tracing parallel doctrinal interpretations in the Theravāda and the

Sarvāstivāda exegesis. To the venerable professor I would like to offer my grateful thanks.

Venerable Dr. Guang Xing, Assistant Professor at the Centre of Buddhist Studies of the University of Hong Kong, has been a constant supporter of this project from the start, tracking the draft closely and critically, and finally ensuring that it was ready for publication. Many are the occasions when he came to my help to ensure that what I had word-processed did not collapse. All I need to say in this regard is that if not for his prompt and timely assistance, this work would not have seen the light of day. To Venerable Guang Xing I would like to offer my grateful thanks.

I must also record here my grateful thanks to Venerable Dr. Jing Yin, Director, Centre of Buddhist Studies, the University of Hong Kong, and Dorothy Ho, administration manager, Centre of Buddhist Studies, for their continuous support in getting this work completed as early as possible and for providing me with all the necessary wherewithal for preparing the manuscript.

Venerable Dhammika, the Australian-born monk who is currently in Singapore; Coray Bill, my former pupil at the University of Hong Kong; and Venerable Huifeng, PhD candidate at the Centre of Buddhist Studies, read through the first chapter of this work and made some suggestions to improve its presentation. To all of them I must express my grateful thanks.

Rebekah Wong and So Hau-Leung, the former volunteer administrators of the Centre of Buddhist Studies, evinced a keen interest in this work and it was they who initially suggested that I should write a book on Theravāda Abhidhamma for the benefit of the students reading for the MBS degree at the University of Hong Kong. To both of them I would like to express my grateful thanks.

I must also express my sincere thanks to Venerable Pilesse Chandaratana, Liza Cheung, Terence Chan, Irene Lok, and Susan P. S. Wong, all PhD candidates at the Centre of Buddhist Studies, and Sandra Lam and Bryce Neilsen, both alumni of the University of Hong Kong, for their many acts of kindness and generosity while I was preparing this work. However, it is to Aosi Mak and Paul Law, both graduate students at the University of Hong Kong, that I owe a special debt of gratitude for devoting much of their precious time to the arduous task of formatting the manuscript and for proofreading and generating the index, thus preparing the whole manuscript for the press.

In conclusion, I must express my sincere thanks to Professor C. F. Lee, Venerable Dr. Jing Yin, Venerable Hin Hung, and other members of the Li Chong Yuet Ming Buddhist Studies Fund of the Li Ka Shing Foundation for accepting this book to be included in the Centre of Buddhist Studies publication series.

Finally I would like to offer my grateful thanks to Wisdom Publications, a nonprofit publisher of Buddhist books, for sponsoring this publication as its American edition. This edition will certainly ensure a wider circulation of the book.

Dr. Mary Petrusewicz of Wisdom Publications carefully went through the whole manuscript and made many valuable suggestions to improve the quality of the book. I benefited much from her critical mind and sound sense. My grateful thanks to Dr. Petrusewicz.

Y. Karunadasa
Centre of Buddhist Studies, the University of Hong Kong
Hong Kong
August 2018

INTRODUCTION

THE PRESENT WORK, as its subtitle clearly indicates, is an inquiry into the Abhidhamma perspective on the nature of conditioned reality. Therefore observations in the Abhidhamma on the nature of nibbāna, the one and only unconditioned reality according to Theravāda Buddhism, do not come within the purview of this work.

Although the main focus of this work is on the Theravāda Abhidhamma, wherever it was deemed necessary, some parallel data in other schools of Buddhist thought have also been taken into consideration. This has been done for two main reasons. One is to bring the subject into a wider perspective and to present it with a greater measure of precision. The other is that the postcanonical Abhidhamma exegesis that was compiled mainly in Sri Lanka cannot be properly understood unless we take into consideration parallel doctrinal interpretations in other schools of Buddhist thought. Despite the geographical separation from India, Buddhist thought in Sri Lanka did not develop in complete isolation from Buddhist thought on the mainland. There is overwhelming evidence in the relevant sources that the Theravādin exegetes were well acquainted with the doctrinal interpretations and developments in the Buddhist schools on the mainland, and sometimes explicitly responded to them.

It is obvious from an overview of the sources that the Theravāda Abhidhamma shows signs of historical growth, but our interpretation of this process of growth has to be approached with caution. In this connection, we would like to quote an observation made by Venerable Bhikkhu Bodhi in his *Comprehensive Manual of Abhidhamma*:

> While it is tempting to try to discern evidence of historical development in the Commentaries over and beyond the ideas embedded in the Abhidhamma Pitaka, it is risky to push this line too far, for a great deal of the canonical Abhidhamma seems to require the Commentaries to contribute the unifying context in which the individual elements hang together as parts of a systematic whole and without which they lose important dimensions of meaning. It is thus not unreasonable to assume that a substantial portion of the commentarial apparatus originated in close proximity to the canonical Abhidhamma and was transmitted concurrently with the latter, though lacking the stamp of finality it was open to modification and amplification in a way that the canonical texts were not.[1]

This is a very pertinent observation because the laconic definitions of various dhammas (real existents) given in the *Dhammasaṅgaṇi*, for example, presuppose the commentators' exegetical framework within which they assume significance. Unless we read the text and the commentary carefully, we may come across instances that seem to show a tension between the text and the commentary. To give one specific example: in the *Dhammasaṅgaṇi*, "material nutriment" is defined by enumerating some types of solid material food. In its exegesis, the Pāli commentary says that this is a definition by way of embodiment (*vatthuvasena*) of the material nutriment.[2] Apparently this looks like a new interpretation on the part of the commentator. However, it is fully vindicated by the fact that elsewhere in the *Dhammasaṅgaṇi* itself "material nutriment" is subsumed under the heading *dhammāyatana*, the sphere of the objects of mind.[3] This means that it cannot be known by any of the sense faculties other than the mind.

We can identify several stages in the historical development of the Theravāda Abhidhamma. Probably the first stage was the emergence of an expository methodology that exhibits features of the Abhidhamma but precedes the body of thought formally embodied in the Abhidhamma literature. Several Pāli suttas—for example, the Saṅgīti and the Dasuttara of the *Dīghanikāya*—explain doctrinal terms in the framework of a catechism. Here we find doctrinal tenets explained by an impersonal technical terminology without literary embellishments or reliance on similes, metaphors, and stories to illustrate them. It is possible to consider such suttas as representing the earliest stage in the development of the Abhidhamma. One book in the Sutta Piṭaka that comes very close to the Abhidhamma, both in terms of content and methodology, is the *Paṭisambhidāmagga*.

Next comes the canonical Abhidhamma with its seven treatises. These are *Dhammasaṅgaṇi*, *Vibhaṅga*, *Dhātukathā*, *Puggalapaññatti*, *Kathāvatthu*, *Yamaka*, and *Paṭṭhāna*. We could even include the postcanonical but precommentarial *Peṭakopadesa* and *Nettippakaraṇa*, two works on Buddhist hermeneutics, in the Abhidhamma tradition.

Next in chronological order come the Pāli commentaries on the Abhidhamma. These are *Atthasālinī*, the commentary to the *Dhammasaṅgaṇi*; *Sammohavinodanī*, the commentary to the *Vibhaṅga*; and *Pañcappakaraṇaṭṭhakathā*, the combined commentary to the other five treatises. To this same class of literature belongs the *Visuddhimagga*. For although it is not formally recognized as an Abhidhamma work, chapters 14–17 can be considered a summary of the Theravāda Abhidhamma. Each of the three commentaries gave rise to its own subcommentary (*mūlaṭīkā*), and each subcommentary in turn to its own subcommentary (*anuṭīkā*).

The final phase of the Abhidhamma literature is represented by nine compendiums on the Abhidhamma, what the Burmese tradition calls *let-than*, or "little finger manuals." These are *Abhidhammāvatāra*, *Abhidhammatthasaṅgaha*, *Nāmarūpapariccheda*, *Paramatthavinicchaya*, *Rūpārūpavibhāga*, *Saccasaṃkhepa*, *Mohavicchedanī*, *Khemappakaraṇa*, and *Nāmacāradīpaka*. These, in turn, gave rise to their own subcommentaries—for example, *Abhidhammatthavikāsinī*, the subcommentary to the *Abhidhammāvatāra*.

It is not only in the Abhidhamma commentaries that we find Abhidhamma exegesis. We find it in the commentaries to the Sutta Piṭaka as well. In these, the material in the Pāli suttas too came to be interpreted in the light of the Abhidhamma. We must bear in mind, however, that the exegesis we find in the Pāli commentaries was not a completely original contribution on the part of the Pāli commentators but was mainly based on a vast corpus of exegetical material that grew over many centuries and had been preserved at the Mahāvihāra in Anuradhapura. As the Abhidhamma ascended in importance, the commentaries on the suttas must have come more and more under its influence. Through the Pāli commentarial exegesis, the boundaries of Theravāda Buddhism became more clearly demarcated and its position more firmly entrenched.

In the whole range of the Pāli Buddhist literature we can, in a way, identify two layers of thought. One is early Buddhism, which is presented in the Pāli Sutta Piṭaka and to a lesser extent in the Vinaya Piṭaka. The other is the distinctly Theravāda Buddhism, which makes use of both the literary sources of early Buddhism and the texts of the Pāli Abhidhamma to evolve a very comprehensive system of thought. Both early Buddhism and the Buddhism of the Abhidhamma period share the same ultimate goal, the realization of nibbāna, but they delineate the nature of wisdom in somewhat different ways. The earlier form uses broad strokes to depict the fundamental principles that one has to contemplate with wisdom, whereas the later form uses minutely defined analysis.

That the suttas were commonly accepted by all the early Buddhist schools is seen from the *Kathāvatthu* of the Pāli Abhidhamma Piṭaka. This polemical work, as is well known, contains arguments and counterarguments by the Theravādins and non-Theravādins over the interpretation of a wide range of Buddhist doctrines. What is interesting to note here is that as recorded in this work, both Theravādins and non-Theravādins quote from the same suttas in support of their doctrinal interpretations. This shows that all early Buddhist schools recognized the authority and authenticity of the suttas. This particular situation also suggests that as a formal doctrinal systematization, the Theravāda Abhidhamma arose after the first division of the Saṅgha into Theravāda and the Mahāsaṅghika, which later gave rise to the emergence of many other schools.

It is probable that all early Buddhist schools had their own Abhidharma treatises, embodying the particular perspectives they had adopted in interpreting what the Buddha taught. Some of these treatises are now forever lost. However, the Chinese Tripiṭaka has preserved to this day canonical books belonging to two other Abhidharma systems. One is the Sarvāstivāda Abhidharma with its seven treatises. These are *Jñāna-*

prasthānaśāstra, *Dharmaskandhaśāstra*, *Saṃgītiparyāyaśāstra*, *Prajñaptiśāstra*, *Vijñānakāyaśāstra*, *Prakaraṇapādaśāstra*, and *Dhātukāyaśāstra*. The other is the *Śāriputrābhidharmaśāstra*, which some modern scholars attribute to the Dharmaguptaka school.

Among the Buddhist schools in India, it was the Sarvāstivāda and the Sautrāntika that attracted the special attention of the Theravādins. These were two of the leading schools with whom the Theravādins had much in common. Both subscribed to a realistic view of existence, but with this difference: whereas the former had a tendency to an extreme form of realism, the latter had a propensity, but certainly not a commitment, to idealism.

Among the Sarvāstivādins the tendency for reification is more evident. This is shown by their elevating to the level of dharmas (real existents) items that appear to be nominal constructions or pure denominations. Thus, for example, they believed that the conditioning characteristics of that which is conditioned are also conditioned and therefore real. This interpretation is partly based on a sūtra that mentions the three characteristics of the conditioned as the arising, the passing away, and the change-in-continuance.[4] In the Pāli version of the corresponding sūtra, which occurs in the *Aṅguttaranikāya*, these are introduced as "*saṅkhatassa saṅkhata-lakkhaṇāni*,"[5] which when translated literally reads, "the conditioned characteristics of the conditioned." Understood in this literal sense, it means that the characteristics of the conditioned are also conditioned. It is in this literal sense that the Sarvāstivādins seek to understand the phrase.

Why exactly the term *saṅkhata* (conditioned) is repeated is worth examining here. If we go by the Pāli commentary, the repetition is not due to any idiomatic peculiarity of the language but is absolutely necessary. Why? Because if the term is not repeated, it gives the very wrong impression that what is conditioned has only three characteristics. However, it has many other characteristics, as for example the characteristic of non-self (*anattā*). The repetition is meant to show that these are the three specific characteristics on the basis of which what is conditioned can be recognized as conditioned. Perhaps as a critical response to the Sarvāstivādins' literal interpretation of the phrase, a Pāli commentary refers us here to two other sentences of the same genre, which also occur in the *Aṅguttaranikāya*.[6] One is: "there are these three wise characteristics of the wise" (*tīṇ'imāni paṇḍitassa paṇḍita-lakkhaṇāni*). The other is: "there are these three foolish characteristics of the fool" (*tīṇ'imāni bālassa bāla-lakkhaṇāni*).[7] Surely just because "wise" and "foolish" are repeated, it does not necessarily follow that the characteristics themselves are as wise and foolish as the wise man and the fool. The very purpose of the repetition is to show the specific characteristics that enable us to identify the wise man as wise and the fool as foolish. For both the wise man and the fool have an enormous number of characteristics besides the ones mentioned here.

The repetition of the term *saṅkhata* shows the immense care taken in the Pāli suttas to explain terms in such a way as to forestall any kind of misunderstanding. In this connection, we would like to cite another example here. As we all know, Buddhism rejects the notion of "self." Then obviously, it logically and inevitably follows that from the Buddhist perspective we cannot cling to a self, for how can we cling to a thing that does not really exist? This is precisely why in the Pāli suttas we find the expression *atta-vāda-upādāna*, "clinging to the notion of 'self,'" and not *atta-upādāna*, "clinging to self."[8] When one realizes nibbāna, what disappears is not self, for there is no self to disappear, but the erroneous belief in a self.

The Sautrāntikas, as is well known, recognized only the authority of the sūtras and rejected the authenticity of the śāstras (*ye sūtra-prāmāṇikā na tu śāstra-prāmāṇikāḥ*).[9] In their analysis of empirical existence they were guided by the principle of parsimony: entities should not be multiplied beyond necessity. Through this strategy they were able to ensure ontological minimalism. The net result is a reduction in the number of dharmas recognized by other schools of Buddhism.

As we shall see in the chapters that follow, there are signs of Sautrāntika influence on the Theravāda. What appears to be a specific instance could perhaps be seen in the definition of what is visible, the objective sense field corresponding to the eye organ. In the *Dhammasaṅgaṇi* of the Abhidhamma Piṭaka this is defined as consisting of both color and figure.[10] However, in commenting on this the Pāli commentary says that only color constitutes what is visible and that "figure" is a conceptual construct superimposed on the differentiation of color.[11] This exactly is the Sautrāntikas' stance on this matter, over which they had a sustained argument with the Sarvāstivādins.[12] It is in the context of this new interpretation that we need to understand why in some Pāli subcommentaries we find the more specific term *vaṇṇāyatana*, the sense sphere of color, instead of the more general term *rūpāyatana*, the sense sphere of the visible.[13]

As indicated above, some points in the Theravāda exegesis can be understood better in the light of parallel interpretations in other schools of Abhidharma. We would like to give one specific example. Now according to the Theravāda theory of the cognitive process, after the moment of adverting to the object, there arises a type of consciousness determined by the object. If the object is color, there arises eye consciousness; if sound, ear consciousness and so forth. What we need to note here is that this particular eye consciousness is described as "mere seeing" (*dassana-matta*).[14] As Venerable Bhikkhu Bodhi clarifies, it is the consciousness "by which the sense datum is experienced in its bare immediacy and simplicity prior to all identificatory cognitive operations."[15]

The accuracy of this clarification of "mere seeing" is clearly borne out by an observation made in the *Abhidharmakośabhāṣya* and its *Vyākhyā*. Here it is said: "Through visual consciousness one knows 'blue' (*nīlaṃ vijānāti*), but one does not know 'it is blue.' Through mental consciousness one knows 'blue' (*nīlaṃ vijānāti*) and one [also] knows 'it is blue' (*nīlaṃ iti ca vijānāti*)."[16] If mental consciousness recognizes blue as blue, this, as the *Abhidharmakośabhāṣya* clearly indicates, involves some kind of judgment and verbalization at a very subtle level in the act of recognizing the object.[17] It is very likely that it is for these very same reasons that the Theravādins, too, describe eye consciousness as "mere seeing." In the same way, we can understand the other four: "mere hearing," "mere smelling," "mere tasting," and "mere touching."

It is also worth noting here that the Pāli Buddhist exegetes were acquainted not only with non-Mahāyāna but with Mahāyāna Buddhist schools as well. Venerable Ñāṇamoli draws our attention to a statement in the subcommentary to the *Visuddhimagga*, which runs as follows: "And some misinterpret the meaning of the dependent origination thus,

'Without arising, without cessation (*anuppādaṃ anirodhaṃ*)' instead of taking the unequivocal meaning in the way stated."[18] It is obvious that here the allusion is to the Madhyamaka philosophy of Nāgārjuna.

Nor did geographical separation from Sri Lanka prevent Buddhist exegetes on the mainland from noticing doctrinal developments in the Theravāda Buddhist exegesis. One example concerns the theory of *bhavaṅga* consciousness. The term *bhavaṅga* occurs in the *Paṭṭhāna* of the Abhidhamma Piṭaka and in the *Milindapañha*. However, it is in the Pāli Buddhist exegesis that we find a detailed account of it. Taking this account into consideration, some scholars assumed that it was modeled on *ālaya-vijñāna*, the storehouse consciousness of the Idealistic school of Buddhism.[19]

However, the situation is just the opposite. In *Karmasiddhiprakaraṇa,* Ācārya Vasubandhu, while adducing reasons for recognizing a special kind of consciousness called *ālaya-vijñāna* in addition to the six groups of consciousness (*ṣad vijñānakāya*), says:

> In the sūtras of the Tāmraparṇīyanikāya this particular consciousness is called *bhavāṅga-vijñāna,* in the sūtras of the Mahāsāṃghikanikāya it is called *mūla-vijñāna* (the root consciousness), and the Mahīśāsakanikāya calls it *āsaṃsārika-skandha* (the aggregate that endures until the end of *saṃsāra*).[20]

In the above quotation "Tāmraparṇīyanikāya" means the Theravāda Buddhist school in Sri Lanka. As pointed out by Étienne Lamotte, in the Tibetan version of the *Karmasiddhiprakaraṇa* the term occurs as "the venerable Tāmraśāṭīyas."[21]

This reference in the *Karmasiddhiprakaraṇa* clearly shows that the *bhavaṅga* consciousness as we find it in the Theravāda exegesis is earlier than *ālaya-vijñāna.* It also shows that *bhavaṅga* consciousness of the Theravādins as well as the *mūla-vijñāna* of the Mahāsāṃghikas and the *āsaṃsārika-skandhaka* of the Mahīśāsakas inspired Ācārya Vasubandhu to justify the need for recognizing the *ālaya-vijñāna.*

In the Pāli Buddhist exegesis we also find a number of critical observations made in respect to non-Buddhist schools of Indian philosophy. However, it is mostly the doctrinal tenets of the Sāṃkhya and the Vaiśeṣika systems that attracted the special attention of the Pāli exegetes. The Sāṃkhya is referred to as Kāpilā, the followers of Kapila, the founder of the system, and also as Pakativādino, the Exponents of Primordial Nature, because in their view what is called *prakṛti* (Pāli: *pakati*) is the ultimate causal nexus of the world of non-self.[22] The Vaiśeṣika is referred to as the theory of Kaṇāda because he was the founder of this school.[23] However, in the precommentarial *Milindapañha* we find Saṅkhyā and Visesikā used in referring to these two schools.[24]

As we shall see in detail, dhamma theory provides the ontological foundation for Abhidhamma philosophy. Briefly stated, it means the resolution of the world of experience into a number of basic factors called dhammas, together with an explanation as to their interconnection and interdependence on the basis of conditional relations. One misconception that has gained currency about this theory is that it amounts to some kind of pluralism. As we have shown in the first chapter, dhamma theory is based not only on analysis (*bheda*) but on synthesis (*saṅgaha*) as well. Analysis, when overemphasized, leads to pluralism. Synthesis, when overemphasized, leads to monism. What we find in the Theravāda Abhidhamma is a combination of both. This has enabled it to transcend the binary opposition between pluralism (*sabbaṃ puthuttaṃ*) and monism (*sabbaṃ ekattaṃ*), or as one Pāli commentary says, the binary opposition between the principle of plurality (*nānatta-naya*) and the principle of unity (*ekatta-naya*).[25]

As to the two complementary methods of analysis and synthesis, it is necessary to make one observation here. The Sarvāstivādins overemphasized the analytical method. This led to their theory of tri-temporality (*trai-kālya*), according to which the substance of the dharmas persists in the three divisions of time—future, present, and past. What we should not overlook is that even the very expression *sabbatthivāda* (*sarvāstivāda*), by which this school is known, amounts to an admission by it of the notion of *sabbaṃ atthi* (all exists). *Sabbaṃ atthi*, it should be noted, is one of the four extremist philosophical positions mentioned in the Pāli suttas—the position of extreme realism. Its polar opposite is "nothing exists" (*sabbaṃ natthi*), which is the Buddhist expression for extreme nihilism. As explicitly stated in the Pāli suttas, the Buddha keeps equally aloof from all such extremist positions through his doctrine of dependent origination.[26]

Another issue that requires our attention concerns the relationship between dhamma theory and the concept of "emptiness" (*suññatā*). For this purpose, it is necessary to clarify what exactly Pāli Buddhism means by emptiness. In the words of the Buddha as recorded in a Pāli sutta, the world is empty in the sense that it is empty of a self or of anything pertaining to a self (*attena vā attaniyena vā suññaṃ*).[27] Here the world means the world of experience, the only world that Buddhism recognizes. And it is precisely this world that early Buddhism analyzes into five *khandhas* (aggregates), twelve *āyatanas* (bases of cognition), and eighteen *dhātus* (elements of cognition), and which the Abhidhamma analyzes into eighty-one (conditioned) dhammas. What all this amounts to saying is that the khandhas, āyatanas, and dhātus, as well as the dhammas, are all empty of a self or of anything pertaining to a self. Thus "empty" and "non-self" become mutually convertible expressions: what is empty is non-self and, likewise, what is non-self is empty. Therefore, from the Theravāda perspective, we are at full liberty to restate the well-known statement *sabbe dhammā anattā* (all dhammas are non-self), which is common to both early Buddhism and the Theravāda Abhidhamma, as *sabbe dhammā suññā* (all dhammas are empty).

It is of course true that each dhamma, both mental and material, is defined as "own nature" (*sabhāva*).[28] However, what we need to remember is that this so-called own nature arises and exists in dependence on a multiplicity of impermanent conditions. As the Pāli commentaries clarify, strictly speaking, a dhamma is not "that which bears its own nature" but "what is being borne by its own conditions."[29] It is also observed that "own nature" (*sabhāva*) does not mean "own sway" (*vasavattitā*).[30] It will thus be seen that although the term *sabhāva* is used as a synonym for *dhamma*, it is interpreted in such a way that it means the very absence of sabhāva in any sense that implies a substantial mode of being. In other words, none of the dhammas is a self-entity (*atta*) or anything pertaining to a self-entity (*attaniyena*). It is in this sense that we need to understand why the dhammas are "empty" (*suñña*).

Of equal significance is the distinction drawn between two truths, the consensual (*sammuti*) and the ultimate (*paramattha*). In almost all other Buddhist schools, one truth is considered higher and the other lower. Their very use of the term *saṃvṛti* for the relative truth clearly indicates this, for saṃvṛti means not that which reveals but that which conceals. For the Theravāda, on the other hand, there is no hierarchical difference between the two, despite the fact that one is called "conventional" and the other "ultimate." This situation is fully consonant with the distinction drawn in the Pāli suttas between *nītattha*, a statement whose meaning is already drawn out, and *neyyattha*, a statement whose meaning has to be drawn out.[31]

It is to this twofold distinction that most Buddhist schools trace their double truth. However, it must be emphasized that the relevant sutta passage does not say that one statement is higher or lower than the other. All it says is that a *nītattha* statement should not be understood as a *neyyattha* statement, and vice versa. One who disregards this distinction, the sutta goes on to say, misrepresents the Tathāgata.[32] Here, it is worth noting the well-known saying that the Dhamma is a means to an end and not an end in itself. As an extension of this idea, it came to be recognized that the Dhamma as a means can be presented in many different ways, from many different perspectives. As recorded in the Bahuvedanīya Sutta of the *Majjhimanikāya*, when two disciples of the Buddha, a monk and a layman, had an unstoppable argument as to the number of feelings, Ānanda reported this matter to the Buddha. Then the Buddha told Ānanda that both of them were correct, because they looked at the issue from two different perspectives. The Buddha told Ānanda that he had presented feelings not only as two or three but also as five, six, eighteen, thirty-six, and one hundred and eight.[33] It was on this occasion that the Buddha told Ānanda: *pariyāya-desito ayaṃ Ānanda mayā dhammo*, meaning that the Dhamma has been presented in many different ways, from many different perspectives (*aneka-pariyāyena*).[34] The clear message is that what accords with actuality, and therefore what is true, can be restated from many different perspectives and need not be repeated in the same way as a holy hymn or a mantra.

The Dhamma, it may be noted, is not actuality as such but a description of actuality. It is a conceptual model that describes the nature of actuality through a series of propositions. We find this idea formally expressed in a Pāli commentary: *paññattiṃ anatikkamma paramattho pakāsito*.[35] That is, it is by not going beyond *paññatti* that the nature of actuality has been presented. Here the term *paññatti* means both word (*nāma-paññatti*) and meaning (*attha-paññatti*).[36] Therefore the nature of actuality has been presented within a conceptual framework through the symbolic medium of language. Thus we see that here, as elsewhere, Buddhism avoids absolutism. There is no one absolutist way of presenting the Dhamma that is valid for all times and climes.

There could be more than one conceptual model encapsulating the nature of actuality. The validity of each will be determined by its ability to take us to the goal—that is, from bondage to freedom, from ignorance to wisdom, from our present predicament to final emancipation. It is instructive to note that the Pāli suttas themselves give us a clear indication as to how we should distinguish the Dhamma from what is not the Dhamma. Whatever leads to the cessation of passion (*rāga*), aversion (*dosa*), and delusion (*moha*) is the Dhamma and whatever leads away from it is not the Dhamma. Thus the criterion is not textual, although of course it occurs in the Buddhist texts.

That the Dhamma has been presented from many different perspectives can be seen from the Pāli suttas themselves. To give one example, the noble truth of suffering is usually defined as "birth is suffering, decay is suffering," and so on, until we come to the last item: "in brief, the five aggregates of grasping are suffering." However, in one passage in the *Saṃyuttanikāya* where the four truths are formally presented, we find the first truth defined as "the five aggregates of grasping."[37] Here the last item in the usual definition of suffering, the one that is most comprehensive, is presented as the meaning of suffering.

What we need to remember is that "the five aggregates of grasping" is a different way of referring to individual existence in its saṃsāric dimension. Individual existence, from the Buddhist perspective, is an impersonal congeries of dependently arising psychophysical factors that we grasp as "this is mine" (*etaṃ mama*), "this I am" (*eso' ham asmi*), and "this is my self" (*eso me attā*). But what we grasp in this manner is constantly changing (*anicca*) and therefore not under our full control (*anattā*). This is what Buddhism means by the suffering at the very core of our existence (*saṅkhāra-dukkha*).[38]

Thus it is not the five aggregates but the five aggregates of grasping that become a source of suffering. If "the five aggregates of grasping" is another expression for life in saṃsāra, then it can be concluded that what Buddhism is saying is not simply that there is suffering in saṃsāric life but that saṃsāric life itself is suffering. What we should not overlook here is that by "suffering" Buddhism means conditioned experience, any experience dependent on impermanent conditions. Any conditioned experience, whether it is extremely pleasant or otherwise, is suffering because of its dependent nature. This should explain why even *jhāna* experience, which represents higher levels of mind's unification and therefore higher levels of happiness, is also brought under the category of "suffering." For, in the final analysis, even jhāna experience is impermanent and therefore conditioned.[39] As a matter of fact, Buddhism does not deny the possibility of sensual indulgence and sensual pleasure (*kāmasukhallikānuyoga*), as is very well shown by Buddhism's reference to sensuality as one of the two extremist practices that should be avoided. What Buddhism questions is not its impossibility but its validity as a means to emancipation.

There are other examples of presenting the Dhamma in different perspectives. For instance, in the *Saṃyuttanikāya* one who has entered the stream (*sotāpanna*) is described in more than one way.[40] In the same Nikāya we also find the path leading to the unconditioned (nibbāna) described in eleven different ways.[41]

By taking these and other similar cases into consideration, we should not hasten to conclude that they represent different historical stages in the development of Buddhist thought, unless of course there is clear evidence to the contrary. Rather, they should be understood in light of the statement that the Dhamma can be presented from different perspectives.

It is in light of these observations that we need to understand the significance of the commentarial statement that the Buddha sometimes teaches the Dhamma according to conventional truth, sometimes according to ultimate truth, and sometimes through a combination of both.[42] As one Pāli commentary says, it is like a teacher choosing different dialects to teach his pupils who speak different dialects.[43] There is absolutely no implication here that one dialect is either higher or lower than another.

Closely associated with the distinction drawn between two truths is the development by the Abhidhamma of a logical apparatus for defining the dhammas. The first is called agent denotation (*kattu-sādhana*), the second is called instrument denotation (*karaṇa-sādhana*), the third is object denotation (*kamma-sādhana*), the fourth is locative denotation (*adhikaraṇa-sādhana*), and the fifth is nature denotation (*bhāva-sādhana*). Their implications in the context of the dhamma theory will become clear from the chapters that follow. However, it is necessary to focus our attention on the first. Here, what is sought to be defined occurs in the nominative case. It exactly corresponds to what we call today the subject-predicate sentence. One example given is: cognition cognizes (*viññāṇaṃ vijānāti*).[44] This kind of definition, it is said, is made by superimposing a distinction where there is no such distinction (*abhede bheda-parikappanā*).[45] Such a superimposition creates a distinction between the agent and the action. For this very reason, the Abhidhamma says that this kind of definition is tentative and provisional and not valid in an ultimate sense (*nippariyāyena*).[46] It is resorted to only as an aid to understanding. Thus all such innocent-looking sentences as "I see," "My eyes see," "I see with my eyes," and "eye consciousness sees" are not valid in an ultimate sense. To make them valid we have to rephrase them in the language of causality. When so rephrased, they all mean: "Depending on the eye and the eye object arises eye consciousness." When we say "it happened" or "it occurred," from the Buddhist perspective we mean "there was a happening" or "there was an occurrencing."

In fact, this is not an Abhidhamma innovation. We find this idea expressed in the Pāli suttas as well. When a monk asked the Buddha, "Who is it, Venerable Sir, that feels," the Buddha replied, "It is not a fit question (*na kallo pañho*). I am not saying (someone) feels. If I were saying so, the question would be a fit one. But I am not saying that. If you were to ask thus: 'Conditioned by what, Venerable Sir, does feeling arise,' then the proper answer would be: Conditioned by sensory contact, feeling arises."[47]

As will be noticed, what made the Ābhidhammikas evolve this system of definition is their awareness that the structure of actuality does not exactly correspond to the structure of language. We tend to believe that there is an ontological subject corresponding to the grammatical subject. Language is also based on the recognition of a dichotomy between substance and quality (*ādhāra-ādheya*). This dichotomy, as one Pāli commentary says, is usually expressed through what is called the genitive expression (*sāmi-vacana*),[48] as for example the color of the rainbow. Buddhist philosophy of almost all schools begins with the abolition of this distinction.

Another important aspect of the Theravāda Abhidhamma concerns paññatti, the category of "the nominal and the conceptual." According to dhamma theory, only the dhammas are real; all things besides the dhammas are conceptual constructs or logical abstractions with no objective counterparts. However, there surfaced a trend in certain Buddhist schools toward reversing this process by way of reification. As recorded in the *Kathāvatthu*, some Buddhist schools maintained that "there is an immutable something called 'thusness' in the very nature of things, material or otherwise," which is unconditioned. Thus, distinct from matter there is materiality of matter (*rūpassa rūpatā*), distinct from feeling there is feelingness of feeling (*vedanāya vedanatā*), and so forth.[49] Some other Buddhist schools elevated the principle of dependent origination to the level of an unconditioned entity.[50]

The Theravāda held that this process of reification overstepped the bounds of paññatti (*paññattiṃ atidhāvitvā gaṇhanti*).[51] As one Pāli commentary says in this regard, there is no separate entity called "dependent origination" distinct from the factors that arise in dependence on other factors.[52] The same is true, for example, of impermanence. There is no separate entity called "impermanence" additional to what is subject to impermanence. If it were otherwise, so runs the argument, then this impermanence would require another impermanence to make it impermanent, and this in turn would require still another, thus resulting in a process of interminability (*anupaccheda*) or infinite regress (*anavaṭṭhāna*).[53]

In the Appendix there is a discussion on why the Theravāda came to be known as Vibhajjavāda, the Doctrine of Analysis. This designation, it seems to us, has to be understood in the context of the doctrinal controversy between the Theravādins and the Sarvāstivādins on the tri-temporality (*trai-kālya*) of the dharmas. In the course of this discussion an attempt will be made to show that the Third Buddhist Council was an historical event and not "a pious fabrication" on the part of Theravāda Buddhist historiography. At the early stages of Buddhist academic studies, it was thought by some scholars that the name of Venerable Moggallāna (Tissa Moggaliputta), who, according to Theravāda tradition, presided at the Third Buddhist Council, occurs only in the commentaries and chronicles compiled in Sri Lanka. However, as pointed out by Louis de La Vallée Poussin, the Venerable Elder's name occurs in the Chinese version of the *Vijñānakāya*, one of the seven books of the Sarvāstivāda Abhidharma Piṭaka.[54] As he has pointed out further, the first chapter of this Sarvāstivāda work is named "Maudgalyāyana-Skandhaka" after Venerable Moggallāna because its sole purpose is to refute from the Sarvāstivāda perspective the evidence adduced by the Theravādin Elder against the theory of tri-temporality.[55] In fact, in the sixth chapter of the *Kathāvatthu*, which is said to have been compiled at the Third Council by the Theravādin Elder, we find a criticism of the Sarvāstivāda theory from the Theravāda perspective.

I

THE REAL EXISTENTS

IN THE ENTIRE VOCABULARY of the Abhidhamma no other term is as central to defining its theory of reality as *dhamma*. In its characteristically Abhidhammic sense, it embraces not only the basic factors into which the whole of phenomenal existence is resolved but also that which transcends phenomenal existence—namely, the unconditioned reality of nibbāna.[56] This rendering of dhamma in an all-inclusive sense is nevertheless not without antecedence. In the early Buddhist scriptures (Pāli suttas) too, we find it used in a similar sense. A case in point is the well-known statement *sabbe dhammā anattā* (all things are non-self).[57] There is, however, a difference to be noted here. In the earlier texts *sabbe dhammā* means "all things" in a general sense, whereas the Abhidhamma uses it in a technical sense to mean "the basic factors into which all things can be resolved." In this shift of the term's meaning from a general to a technical sense we can trace most of the methodological differences between early Buddhism and the Abhidhamma. For it is within a framework where dhamma is postulated as the basic unit of reference that the Abhidhamma seeks to present all its doctrinal expositions. In this methodological difference we can also observe a shift in emphasis from an empiricist to a rationalist approach.

The dhamma theory of the Abhidhamma is based on the philosophical principle that all the phenomena of empirical existence are made up of a number of elementary constituents, the ultimate realities behind manifest phenomena. It is this principle that provides the rationale for all the modes of analysis and classification found in the Abhidhamma systematization. The dhamma theory is, however, not merely one principle among others in the body of Abhidhamma philosophy. It is the base on which the entire system rests. It would thus be quite fitting to call this theory the cornerstone of the Abhidhamma. Yet the dhamma theory was intended from the start to be much more than a mere hypothetical scheme. It arose from the need to make sense out of experiences in meditation and was designed as a guide for meditative contemplation and insight. The Buddha had taught that to perceive the world correctly is to see not self-entities and substances but bare phenomena arising and perishing in accordance with their conditions. The task the Abhidhamma specialists set themselves was to specify exactly what these bare phenomena are and to show how they interact with other bare phenomena to make up our commonsense picture of the world.

The dhamma theory was not peculiar to any one school of Buddhism but penetrated all the early schools, stimulating the growth of their different versions of the Abhidharma. Of these, the Sarvāstivāda version of the theory, together with its critique by the Madhyamaka, has been critically studied by a number of modern scholars. The Theravāda version, however, has received less attention. There are sound reasons for proposing that the Pāli Abhidhamma Piṭaka contains one of the earliest forms of the dhamma theory, perhaps even the oldest version. This theory, after all, did not remain static but evolved over the centuries as Buddhist thinkers sought to draw out its implications and respond to problems it posed for the critical intellect. Thus the dhamma theory was repeatedly enriched, first by the Abhidhamma commentaries and then by the later exegetical literature and the medieval compendiums of Abhidhamma, the so-called little finger manuals, such as the *Abhidhammatthasaṅgaha*, which in turn gave rise to their own commentaries and subcommentaries.

The present chapter seeks to trace the main stages in the origin and development of the dhamma theory and to explore its philosophical implications. The first part will discuss the early version of the theory as represented by the Abhidhamma Piṭaka. At this stage, the theory was not yet precisely articulated but remained in the background as the unspoken premise of Abhidhamma analysis. It was during the commentarial period that an attempt was made to work out the implications of early Abhidhamma thought, and it is this development that will be treated in the subsequent parts of this chapter.

The Early Version of the Dhamma Theory

Although the dhamma theory is an Abhidhammic innovation, the antecedent trends that led to its formulation and its basic ingredients can be traced to the early Buddhist scriptures that seek to analyze empiric individuality and its relation to the external world. In the discourses of the Buddha there are five such modes of analysis. The first is that into *nāma* and *rūpa*.[58] This is the most elementary analysis in the sense that it specifies the two main components, the mental and the corporeal aspects, of the empiric individuality. However, what we must not overlook here is that *nāma-rūpa*, when it occurs in the twelve-factored formula of dependent arising, conveys a more specific sense. In this specific sense, *nāma* means five mental factors that invariably arise with consciousness—namely, feeling (*vedanā*), perception (*saññā*), volition (*cetanā*), contact (*phassa*), and attention (*manasikāra*). *Rūpa* in *nāma-rūpa* means the four great material elements and the materiality that depends on them.[59] In this specific sense, therefore, we cannot consider *nāma-rūpa* as an exhaustive definition of empiric individuality. *Nāma-rūpa* represents only a part of the individuality, the other part being represented by *viññāṇa*, which is consciousness. That *viññāṇa* is not part of *nāma* is shown not only by the statement that *nāma-rūpa* has *viññāṇa* as its condition (*viññāṇa-paccayā nāma-rūpaṃ*) but also by the other statement that *viññāṇa* has, in turn, *nāma-rūpa* as its condition (*nāma-rūpa-paccayā viññāṇaṃ*).[60] What both statements show is the reciprocal conditionality of *viññāṇa* and *nāma-rūpa* and not that one could be subsumed under the other. What has been observed so far should show that it is not correct to translate indiscriminately *nāma-rūpa* as mind and matter, or to define the psychophysical personality as consisting of *nāma* and *rūpa*. The textual or the doctrinal context should be taken into consideration to determine whether the two terms are used in the general or in the specific sense.

The second mode of analysis is that into the five *khandhas* (aggregates): corporeality (*rūpa*), feeling (*vedanā*), perception (*saññā*), mental formations (*saṅkhāra*), and consciousness (*viññāṇa*).[61] The third is that into six *dhātus* (elements): earth (*paṭhavī*), water (*āpo*), temperature (*tejo*), air (*vāyo*), space (*ākāsa*), and consciousness (*viññāṇa*).[62] It will be noticed that in the second analysis attention is focused more on mental aspects, for while they are represented by four aggregates, what is nonmental is counted as one. In the third, on the other hand, attention is focused more on nonmental aspects, for while they are represented here by five elements, what is mental is counted as one. It is very likely that the two analyses were made to supplement each other. The fourth analysis is that into twelve *āyatanas* (bases of cognition): the eye, ear, nose, tongue, body, and mind, and their corresponding objects: the visible, sound, smell, taste, touch, and mental objects.[63] The fifth analysis is that into eighteen *dhātus* (elements of cognition). It is an elaboration of the immediately preceding mode obtained by the addition of the six kinds of consciousness that arise from the contact between the sense organs and their objects. The six additional items are the visual, auditory, olfactory, gustatory, tactile, and mental consciousnesses.[64]

Now the purposes for which Buddhism resorts to these different modes of analysis are varied. For instance, the main purpose of the khandha analysis is to show that there is no ego either inside or outside the five khandhas that go to make up the empiric individuality. None of the khandhas belongs to me (*n'etaṃ mama*), they do not correspond to "I" (*n'eso' ham asmi*), nor are they my self (*n'eso me attā*).[65] Thus the main purpose of this analysis is to prevent the intrusion of the notions of "mine," "I," and "my self" into what is otherwise an impersonal and egoless congeries of mental and physical phenomena. The analysis into twelve āyatanas shows that what we call individual existence is a process of interaction between the internal (*ajjhattika*) sense organs and the external (*bāhira*) sense objects. The analysis into eighteen dhātus shows that consciousness is neither a soul nor an extension of a soul substance but a mental phenomenon that comes into being as a result of certain conditions.[66] There is no independent consciousness that exists in its own right.

In similar fashion, each analysis is used to explain certain features of sentient existence. It is, in fact, with reference to these five modes of analysis that Buddhism frames its fundamental doctrines. The very fact that there are at least five kinds of analysis shows that none of them is taken as final or absolute. Each represents the world of experience in its totality, yet represents it from a pragmatic standpoint determined by the particular doctrine it is intended to illuminate.

The purpose of our referring to the five types of analysis is to show that the dhamma theory of the Abhidhamma developed from an attempt to draw out their full implications. It will be seen that if each analysis is examined in relation to the other four, it is found to be further analyzable. That the first, the analysis into nāma and rūpa, is further analyzable is seen by the second, the analysis into the five khandhas. For in the second, the nāma component of the first is analyzed into feelings, perceptions, mental formations, and consciousness. That the analysis into khandhas can be further analyzed is shown not only by the use of the term *khandha*, which means "group," but also by the next analysis, that into six dhātus. For, in the latter, the rūpa component of the former is analyzed into five—namely, earth, water, temperature, air, and space. That the analysis into six dhātus is also further analyzable is seen from the fact that consciousness, which is reckoned here as one item, is made into four in the khandha analysis. That the same situation is true of the analysis into twelve āyatanas is shown by the next analysis, that into eighteen dhātus, because the latter is an elaboration of the former. This leaves us with the last, the dhātu analysis with eighteen items. Can it be considered final? This supposition too must be rejected, because although consciousness is here itemized as sixfold, its invariable concomitants, such as feeling (*vedanā*) and perception (*saññā*), are not separately mentioned. It will thus be seen that none of the five analyses can be considered exhaustive. In each case one or more items is further analyzable.

This, it seems to us, is the line of thought that led the Ābhidhammikas to evolve still another mode of analysis that in their view is not amenable to further analysis. This new development, which is more or less common to all the systems of Abhidharma, is the analysis of the world of experience into what came to be known as *dharmas* (Sanskrit) or *dhammas* (Pāli). The term *dhamma*, of course, looms large in the discourses of the Buddha, found in a variety of connotations that have to be determined by the specific context. In the Abhidhamma, however, the term assumes a more technical meaning, referring to those items that result when the process of analysis is taken to its ultimate limits. In the Theravāda Abhidhamma, for instance, the aggregate of corporeality (of the khandha analysis) is broken down into twenty-eight items called *rūpa-dhammas* (material dhammas). The next three aggregates—feeling, perception, and mental formations—are together arranged into fifty-two items called *cetasikas* (mental factors). The fifth, consciousness, is counted as one item with eighty-nine varieties and is referred to as *citta*.[67]

Thus the dhamma analysis is an addition to the previous five modes of analysis. Its scope is the same, the world of conscious experience, but its divisions are finer and more exhaustive. This situation in itself does not constitute a radical departure from the earlier tradition, for it does not as yet involve a view of existence that is at variance with that of early Buddhism. There is, however, this situation to be noted: since the analysis into dhammas is the most exhaustive, the previous five modes of analysis become subsumed under it as five subordinate classifications.

The definition and classification of these dhammas and the explanation of their interconnections form the main subject matter of the canonical Abhidhamma. The Abhidhammikas presuppose that to understand any given item properly is to know it in all its relations, under all aspects recognized in the doctrinal and practical discipline of Buddhism. Therefore, in the Abhidhamma Piṭaka, they have classified the same material in different ways and from different points of view. This explains why, in the *Dhammasaṅgaṇi* and other Abhidhamma treatises, we encounter innumerable lists of classifications. Although such lists may appear repetitive, even monotonous, they serve a useful purpose, bringing into relief not only the individual characteristic of each dhamma but also its relations to other dhammas.

One widespread misunderstanding of the dhamma theory of the Theravāda Abhidhamma is that it amounts to some kind of radical pluralism. As the Venerable Nyanaponika Thera observes, "It has been a regular occurrence in the history of physics, metaphysics, and psychology that when a 'whole' has been successfully dissolved by analysis, the resultant 'parts' themselves come in turn to be regarded as little 'wholes.'"[68] This is the kind of process that culminates in radical pluralism. As we shall soon see, about a hundred years after the formulation of the dhamma theory such a trend surfaced within some early schools of Buddhist thought and culminated in the view that the dhammas exist in all three divisions of time—future, present, and past. Such a situation is certainly not true of the Theravāda Abhidhamma for the simple reason that the whole edifice of its dhamma theory is based not only on analysis (*bheda*) but also on synthesis (*saṅgaha*). The analytical method dominates in the *Dhammasaṅgaṇi*, which according to tradition is the first book of the Abhidhamma Piṭaka; here we find a complete catalogue of the dhammas, each with a laconic definition. The synthetical method is more characteristic of the *Paṭṭhāna*, which according to tradition is the last book of the Abhidhamma Piṭaka; for here we find an exhaustive catalogue of the conditional relations of the dhammas. The combined use of these two methods shows that, according to the methodological apparatus employed in the Abhidhamma, a true picture of the nature of reality must be based on both analysis and synthesis.

In this connection, we find the following verse in the *Nāmarūpa-pariccheda*, an Abhidhamma compendium of the medieval period, which draws our attention to the importance of the two complementary methods of analysis and synthesis:

> Analysis and synthesis are praised by the wise,
> liberation in the *Sāsana* [comes from] analysis and synthesis,
> the purpose of the method of analysis and synthesis is ultimate,
> [here] is explained the heading of analysis and synthesis.[69]

Bheda is the commentarial term for "analysis." It is sometimes paraphrased as "the resolution of the compact" (*ghana-vinibbhoga*) into its component parts, or "of the aggregation (*samudāya*) into its constituents (*avayava*)."[70]

Thus if analysis plays an important role in the Abhidhamma's methodology, no less important a role is played by synthesis. Analysis shows that what we take to be one is really many, what appears to be a unity is only a union of several factors. Its purpose is to dispense altogether with the notion of "self" or "substance," the belief that there is an inner and immutable core in our objects of experience. However, analysis can achieve this objective only partially, for when it dispels the notion of "substance" from what is analyzed, all that it does is to transfer the notion of "substance" from one locus to another, from the whole to the parts, from the thing that is analyzed to the factors into which it is analyzed. The notion of the "substantial forest" vanishes, yielding place to a multiplicity of equally substantial trees. This inadequacy of the analytical method could be remedied when it is supplemented by synthesis (*saṅgaha*)—that is, the interrelating of the factors obtained through analysis. Synthesis shows that the factors into which a thing is analyzed are not discrete entities existing in themselves but interconnected and interdependent nodes in a complex web of relationships, so that none of them could be elevated to the level of a substance or discrete self-entity. Thus both analysis and synthesis combine to demonstrate that what is analyzed and the factors into which it is analyzed are equally nonsubstantial.

It is only for purposes of definition and description that things are artificially dissected and presented as discrete entities. The truth of the matter is that the phenomenal world of experience exhibits a vast network of relational categories where nothing can exist in splendid isolation. As the subcommentary to the *Visuddhimagga* observes, if the Abhidhamma resorts to analysis it is "because the nature of things that are amenable to analysis can be elucidated only through analysis."[71] We find more or less the same idea in the subcommentary to the *Abhidhammāvatāra*, when it says: "Whatever distinguishable characteristic there is among the dhammas that have come into oneness as dhammas, it is but proper to hold it out as a separate entity, because it results in the clear understanding of the meaning."[72]

In fact, the Theravāda commentarial exegesis was not unaware of the possibility of misrepresenting the dhamma theory as some kind of pluralism. The commentary to the *Itivuttaka* says that one could mistakenly transgress the bounds of the dhamma theory (*atidhāvanti*) by ignoring the causal relationship of the dhammas and by focusing only on the principle of plurality (*nānattta-naya*), a situation that, it says, could lead to the extremist view of annihilation (*uccheda*): "This self and the world indeed get annihilated with no prospect of causal continuity."[73] The subcommentary to the *Dīghanikāya* has a similar observation to make: "The erroneous grasping of the principle of plurality (*nānatta-nayassa micchāgahaṇa*) is due to the undue emphasis on the radical separateness (*accanta-bheda*) of the dhammas. This is the cause of the dogmatic adherence to the notion of 'annihilation' (*ucchedābhinivesassa kāraṇaṃ*)."[74] What both subcommentaries seek to show is that the dhamma theory is not a reductionist view of existence leading to nihilism. Reductionism is the binary opposition of substantialism. The Abhidhamma view of existence sets itself equally aloof from both extremes.

If the dhamma theory is not radically pluralist, it does not represent some kind of monism either. Any such interpretation, as the Pāli commentaries say, is due to overstressing the principle of unity (*ekatta-naya*) and undue focusing on the absolute nondistinctness (*accantaṃ abhedagahaṇa*) of the dhammas. This necessarily paves the way to the wrong view that the dhammas constitute an unanalyzable absolute unity.[75]

The rejection of both alternatives means that dhammas are not fractions of a whole indicating an absolute unity, nor are they a concatenation of discrete entities. They are a multiplicity of interconnected but distinguishable coordinate factors. They are not reducible to, nor do they emerge from, a single reality, which is the fundamental postulate of monistic metaphysics. If they are to be interpreted as phenomena this should be done with the proviso that they are phenomena with no corresponding noumena. For they are not manifestations of some mysterious metaphysical substratum but processes taking place due to the interplay of a multitude of conditions.

In thus evolving a view of existence that cannot be interpreted in either monistic or pluralistic terms, the philosophy of the Abhidhamma accords with the "middle doctrine" of early Buddhism. This doctrine avoids both the eternalist view of existence, which maintains that everything exists absolutely (*sabbaṃ atthi*), and the opposite nihilistic view, which maintains that absolutely nothing exists (*sabbaṃ natthi*).[76] It also avoids, on the one hand, the monistic view that everything is reducible to a common ground, some sort of self-substance (*sabbaṃ ekattaṃ*), and, on the other, the opposite pluralistic view that the whole of existence is resolvable into a concatenation of discrete entities (*sabbaṃ puthuttaṃ*).[77] Transcending these two pairs of binary extremes, the middle doctrine explains that phenomena arise in dependence on other phenomena without a self-subsisting noumenon that serves as the ground of their being.

The interconnection and interdependence of these dhammas are not explained on the basis of the dichotomy between substance and quality, what the Pāli Buddhist exegesis calls "the distinction between the support and the supported" (*ādhāra-ādheya-bhāva*).[78] A given dhamma does not inhere in another as its quality, nor does it serve another as its substance. The so-called substance is only a figment of our imagination. The distinction between substance and quality is denied because such a distinction leaves the door open for the intrusion of the theory of a substantial self (*attavāda*) with all that it entails.

It is with reference to conditions that the interconnection of the dhammas should be understood. The conditions are not different from the dhammas. The dhammas themselves constitute the conditions. As one Pāli exegetical work observes, "Here is found neither a self nor a nonself; it is the dhammas that generate dhammas."[79] How each dhamma becomes a condition (*paccaya*) for the arising of another (*paccayuppanna*) is explained on the basis of the system of conditioned genesis (*paccayākāra-naya*). This system, which consists of twenty-four conditions, aims at demonstrating the interdependence and dependent origination of all dhammas in respect to both their temporal sequence and their spatial concomitance.[80]

The Dhamma Theory and the Buddhist Controversy on the Concept of "Person"

The foregoing was a brief summary of the earlier phase of the dhamma theory as presented in the books of the Abhidhamma Piṭaka. About a hundred years after its formulation, it gave rise to one of the most important controversies in the history of Buddhist thought relating to the question of determining the validity of the concept of "person" in relation to the reality of the dhammas. If dhammas are the basic factors of sentient existence, what exactly is the position of the person (*puggala*) in relation to the dhammas? Is the person as real as the dhammas? If so, is the person known in a real and ultimate sense (*saccikaṭṭha-paramaṭṭhena*)? This in brief is the issue that led to the controversy, and its relevance to our subject is that it led to a further clarification of the nature of the dhammas.[81]

As background, let us first clarify the early Buddhist teaching on the concept of "person." Strictly speaking, early Buddhism does not deny the concept of "person" as such, if by "person" is understood not an enduring entity distinct from the five khandhas, nor a substance persisting in time, nor an agent within the khandhas, but simply the sum total of the five causally connected and ever-changing khandhas. From the point of view of the dhamma analysis, this definition can be restated by substituting the term *dhamma* for the term *khandha*, for the dhammas are the basic factors obtained by analyzing the khandhas.

Is there then no difference between early Buddhism and Abhidhamma as to the status of *puggala*, the person? The answer is both yes and no. Yes, because both early Buddhism and Abhidhamma do not recognize the person as an entity, separate and distinct from the mental and physical factors (khandhas/dhammas) into which "person" is analyzed. No, because as we shall soon see, the Abhidhamma introduces two levels of reality, one consensual (*sammuti*) and the other ultimate (*paramattha*)—a distinction that we do not read in the early Buddhist scriptures (Pāli suttas), despite their containing identifiable antecedent trends. It is in the context of the schema of two levels of reality that the Abhidhamma's stance regarding this question is clarified. The position held here is that while the dhammas constitute the ultimate reality, the person is subsumed under consensual reality. Therefore, strictly speaking, the controversy is not whether the person exists or not but whether the person exists in a real and ultimate sense (*saccikaṭṭha-paramaṭṭhena*).[82]

The main argument of the Pudgalavādins, those who believed in the ultimate reality of the person, is that in order to give a rational explanation to concepts such as "moral responsibility" and "rebirth" it is necessary to postulate a constant factor besides the constantly changing dhammas. This constant factor, which they call "person," is neither the same as the five aggregates nor different from them. The first part of this definition shows where the Pudgalavādins differ from other Buddhists, and the second where they differ from non-Buddhists who admit a soul entity. The Theravāda position is that if the concept of "person" is of this nature, it cannot be described either as conditioned (*saṅkhata*) or as unconditioned (*asaṅkhata*) and that what is not so describable (person) does not exist in a real sense.[83]

The Pudgalavādins resort to scriptural authority as well in defense of their theory. One scripture they cite in this connection is the "Discourse on the Bearer of the Burden" (*Bhārahāra Sutta*). It speaks of a burden (*bhāra*), the bearer of the burden (*bhārahāra*), the taking up of the burden (*bharādāna*), and the laying down of the burden (*bhāra-nikkhepana*).[84] This discourse, it is claimed, recognizes the person (bearer) distinct from the five aggregates (burden).[85] Another discourse of the same genre is the one on "What Does Not Belong to You" (*Na Tumhākaṃ Sutta*). It says that what does not belong to you, you should abandon. "What does not belong to you" is identified as the five aggregates.[86] This also seems to suggest that there is a person besides the things that do not belong to him.

However, this kind of discourse need not be understood in a literal sense. Early Buddhism, it may be noted here, makes a clear distinction between two kinds of statement. One has its meaning already drawn out (*nītattha*) and thus made "explicit," and the other has its meaning yet to be drawn out (*neyyattha*) and thus by extension made "implicit."[87] The allusion is to definitive and nondefinitive statements. The two discourses mentioned above do not appear to be definitive statements. For if they are understood in a literal sense, they contradict a vast majority of other discourses that deny the reality of the person distinct from the sum total of the five aggregates.

For the Theravādins "personalism" (*pudgalavāda*) amounts to a veiled recognition of the soul theory (*ātmavāda*). In fact, the *Kathāvatthu* makes no distinction between "person" (*puggala*) and "self/soul" (*atta*) in its refutation of personalism. Even the *Vijñānakāya* of the Sarvāstivāda Abhidharma presents the opponent of personalism as one who advocates emptiness (*śūnyavādin*).[88] For early Buddhism as well as for Abhidhamma, "emptiness" means "absence of self." They are mutually convertible expressions. It is no matter for surprise, therefore, that no Buddhist school came under the severe criticism of other Buddhists as did the Pudgalavādins. They were rather derisively referred to as "heretics in our midst" (*antaścara-tīrthaka*).[89]

One question that arises here is whether in denying the ultimate reality of the person, the Theravādins have overstressed the reality of the dhammas. Does the description of dhammas as *saccikaṭṭha* (exist in a true sense) and *paramaṭṭha* (exist in an ultimate sense) mean that they are real and discrete entities existing in their own right? Has the Abhidhamma veered toward an absolutist interpretation of the dhamma theory? This question is important because an affirmative answer is found in some contemporary scholarly writings. This is particularly so in those writings that seek to extol the merits of the Madhyamaka at the expense of the Abhidhamma.

Such a conclusion, it appears to us, is not tenable. For if the dhammas are described as real and ultimate, this means not that they partake of the nature of absolute entities but that they are not further reducible to any other reality, to some kind of substance that underlies them. That is to say, there is no "behind the scenes" substance from which they emerge and to which they finally return. This means, in effect, that the dhammas represent the final limits of the Abhidhammic analysis of empirical existence. "Without having been the dhammas come into being (*ahutvā sambhonti*), and having been they disappear [without any residue] (*hutvā paṭiventi*)." As one Pāli commentary says, "existence in an ultimate sense" (*paramatthato vijjamānatā*) means "the fact of having arisen due to conditions" (*paccaya-sambhūtatā*).[90] How could one say that what exists due to conditions exists in an absolutist sense?

If the dhammas are described as ultimately real (*paramattha*), this also means that none of them is a substance or a quality. This will become clear if we consider parallel theories in the substantialist schools of Indian philosophy. According to the Vaiśeṣikas, for instance, color, sound, odor, and savor are qualities of the elemental substances (*mahābhūtas*). For the

Abhidhamma, on the contrary, they are not qualities inhering in some kind of substance. Rather, they are some of the basic factors into which material existence is resolved. This is precisely why they are called dhammas.

As mentioned above, the Abhidhamma recognizes two levels of reality, the ultimate (*paramattha*) and the consensual (*sammuti*). If the dhammas come under the first, it is because they are not further analyzable, and thus they become the objects of the highest level of cognition. If composite things, like tables and chairs, come under the second, it is because they are analyzable and are therefore known as objects of conceptual thought. Analyzability is the mark of things composite, and nonanalyzability is the mark of things elementary. This distinction between two levels of reality is of course implicit in the very notion that all phenomena of conditioned existence are resolvable into a number of basic constituents. However, it was in the Theravādins' response to the Pudgalavādins that this distinction came to be formally articulated.

In the early Buddhist discourses we do not see such a distinction explicitly stated. It is of course true that analysis plays an important role in them. But its purpose is not so much to validate two levels of reality. The purpose of the khandha analysis, for instance, is to show that individuality as well as the aggregates into which it is analyzed are equally unsubstantial and that nothing can be identified as one's own self. Its purpose is to evolve a rational psychology to explain the totality of the human experience without resorting to unverifiable entities. What is more, in the early Buddhist discourses, unlike in the Abhidhamma, the term *paramattha* is not used in an ontological sense to mean that which really exists. The term is exclusively used as another expression for *nibbāna* to emphasize the fact that nibbāna is "the highest good," "the highest ideal."[91]

The Dhamma Theory and the Buddhist Controversy on the Concept of "Tri-temporal Existence"

Another doctrinal controversy the dhamma theory gave rise to was whether the dhammas exist in the three divisions of time. If the dhammas, as generally accepted, exist only in the present, how could one satisfactorily explain Buddhist teachings that involve both past and future phenomena? The doctrine of *karma*, for instance, says that past karma can have its effect either in the present or in the future. The phenomenon of memory involves remembering of thoughts and images that have already ceased to exist. It is said that two or more consciousnesses cannot exist at one and the same time.[92] It follows, then, that when we examine our own thought it is really our past consciousness that becomes the object of our present consciousness. The same consciousness cannot examine itself, just as a fingertip, which can touch many a thing, cannot touch itself.[93] It is said that a person who has developed the faculty of retrospective cognition (*pubbenivāsānussati-ñāṇa*) can recall past births. Another case in point is the theory of cognition. An instance of cognition requires a series of thought moments to culminate in full cognition. Accordingly, if both mind and matter are of equal duration, it follows that the object of perception is always inferred and not directly perceived. For when the cognitive process culminates in full cognition, the original sense datum that has impinged on the sense organ has already ceased to exist. In view of these and other Buddhist doctrines that involve both past and future phenomena, the speculation arose as to whether past and future dhammas too really exist in some manner.

There were in fact some antecedents that served as a background to such speculations. The early Buddhist discourses often allude to past and future things in order to stress the kind of impact they could have on the present. It is true the past is defined as that which has already lapsed (*yad atītaṃ . . . pahīṇaṃ taṃ*) and the future as that which has yet to come (*appattañ ca anāgataṃ*).[94] But in a sense past and future are as real as the present. The ordinary worldling is said to be often engrossed in memories of the past and in expectations of what is yet to come. When feelings of attachment to things pleasant and feelings of repulsion to things unpleasant arise, they are said to arise in respect to things belonging to the past and the future as well. "And, how, monks, is this desire generated for things in the past? One remembers and turns over in one's mind thoughts about things based on desire in the past. As one does, so desire is generated. Becoming desirous, one is fettered by those things. I call this a fetter, monks—that heart full of lust. That is how desire is generated for things in the past based on desire."[95] The same holds true for the future and the present.

We find this idea in the early Buddhist statement on sense perception as well. It shows how at the end of a perceptual process the ordinary individual comes to be assailed and overwhelmed by his own conceptual proliferations. These relate not only to things present but to things past and future as well. When it comes to mental culture what matters is not whether things exist objectively or not. It is the impact they could exert on the individual that matters.[96]

This seems to be the reason why early Buddhist discourses define the idea of "all" or "totality" (*sabba*) with reference to the three divisions of time. "All that is corporeal" (*sabbaṃ rūpaṃ*) means not only that which is corporeal now but all instances of corporeality of the past and the future (*atītānāgatapaccuppanna*).[97] The totality of the other four aggregates is defined in the same way. This tri-temporal denotation is in fact extended to include many other categories, mostly those that come under Buddhist ethics and psychology.[98] As the Pāli commentaries observe, their purpose is to stress the idea that the description is "all comprehensive" (*anavasesa-pariyādāna, sabbasaṅgāhaka*).[99]

We find the same situation in the books of the Abhidhamma Piṭaka as well. Thus in the *Vibhaṅga* we read: "(Among the eighteen *dhātus*) seventeen *dhātus* could be (*siyā*) past, future, or present. [On the other hand] *dhamma-dhātu*, the sphere of mental objects, could be past, future, present, or not describable as past, future, or present."[100] The four noble truths are also described in a similar way: "Whereas three noble truths are either past, future, or present, the noble truth of the cessation of suffering [nibbāna] is not to be so described."[101]

Equally interesting is the fact that even the respective functions of the dhammas are similarly described. To give an example from the *Vibhaṅga* again: "Here what is the eye sphere? That eye, which is invisible and reactive, sensitive and dependent on the four great elements, constituting a part of the individual, [and] through which invisible and reactive eye one saw, sees, will see, or may see materiality that is visible and reactive. This is eye, the eye sphere, the eye element, the eye faculty."[102]

This is why the Pāli commentaries describe all conditioned dhammas as "belonging to the three times" (*tekālika*) and the unconditioned nibbāna as "time free" (*kāla-mutta*).

What we have cited above does not in any way suggest that either early Buddhism or the Theravāda Abhidhamma recognized the reality of the past and the future in an ontological sense. It is purely in a psychological sense that they are real. However, the doctrinal controversy we are discussing relates to the ontological status of the past and future dhammas/dharmas. In what manner are they real in relation to the present dhammas/dharmas?

The issue led to another doctrinal controversy and resulted in the emergence of a new sect called the Sarvāstivādin school. What separated them from the Theravādins was their theory that dharmas exist in all the three divisions of time. The theory is based on a distinction made between the actual being of the dharmas as phenomena and their ideal being as noumena. It assumes that the substance of dharmas persists in all the three divisions of time. It is their manifestation as phenomena that is impermanent and subject to change. A dharma actualizes only in the present moment, but its essence continues to persist. This development comes into focus with the use of *sabhāva* (own nature, own being) as another expression for *dharma*.

A qualified version of the theory (*vibhajyavāda*) came to be espoused by a dissident group of the Sarvāstivādins known as Kassapikas/Kāśyapīyas. According to this version, only the present and part of the past exist, whereas the future and a part of the past do not exist. The basis of the distinction is karmic effect. The past karma that has not borne fruit (*adatta-phala, avipakka-vipāka*) exists; the past karma that has borne fruit (*datta-phala, vipakka-vipāka*) does not exist anymore.[103]

Another qualified version of the theory is attributed to the Andhakas. In their view the dhammas belonging to the three divisions of time (*atītādibhedā dhammā*) exist by way of material and other aggregates as past, present, or future. However, each temporal division does not represent the other two either potentially or actually. There is no past that is at once future and present, nor any future that is at once present and past. The past, the future, and the present "exist only as thus" (*heva atthi*).[104] The theory thus appears to be a compromise between the two positions taken up by the Theravādins and the Sarvāstivādins.

A detailed critique of the Sarvāstivādins' theory of tri-temporality (*traikālya*) and its two qualified versions is found in the *Kathāvatthu*. This critique could very well be the work of the Venerable Moggaliputta Tissa Thera, who presided at the Third Buddhist Council. It could also be the earliest extant account of the subject. As shown by Louis de La Vallée Poussin, a Sarvāstivāda rejoinder to the Theravāda view is found in the first chapter of the *Vijñānakāyapāda* of the Sarvāstivāda Abhidharma Piṭaka, whose authorship is attributed to the Venerable Devaśarman. The chapter is named after the Venerable Moggaliputta Tissa Thera (Maudgalyāyanaskandhaka), and its contents clearly show at whom the rejoinder is made.[105]

In the *Kathāvatthu* controversy the Sarvāstivādins cite the tri-temporal denotation of the five aggregates, noted above, as scriptural authority for their theory. The Theravādins, for their part, quote from the *Niruttipatha Sutta* of the *Saṃyuttanikāya*, where it is said that there are "three pathways of language, designation, and description" that are mutually exclusive and therefore never mixed: "was" applies only to "whatever has passed, has ceased"; "will be" applies only to "what has not been born, has not become manifest"; and "is" applies only to "whatever has been born, has become manifest." This sutta goes on to say that even Vassa and Bañña, who rejected causality, did not deny the distinction between the three temporal divisions for fear of being condemned by others.[106]

Apart from scriptural authority, the *Kathāvatthu* adduces the following arguments:

> The very definition of past as "something that has ceased, that is departed, changed, gone away," and the very definition of future as "something that is not yet born, not yet come to be, not yet come to pass, not happened, not befallen, is not manifested" excludes every possibility of the past and the future being consid-

> ered as "existing." If the term "to exist" is predicable of all the three divisions of time, the attributes of one become applicable to the other two as well. The pastness of the past, the presentness of the present, and the futureness of the future become equally applicable and hence mutually convertible, resulting in the complete obliteration of all distinctions between the three divisions of time.
>
> It is contended by the Sarvāstivādins that when a "present thing" ceases to exist, it loses its "presentness" but not its "thingness," just as a "white cloth" when dyed gives up its "whiteness" but not its "clothness." The counterargument of the Theravādins is that in an expression such as "present material aggregate" (*paccuppanna-rūpakkhandha*), in whichever order the two terms "present" and "material aggregate" are used, if no distinction is made between them and thus if they are considered "as identical, as of one import, as the same, as of the same content and origin," then when one says that the "present material aggregate" has ceased to exist, one must admit that the material aggregate has given up not only its "presentness" but also its "materiality." To admit the cessation of one and to deny the cessation of the other is not valid, as they are not two distinct entities. If, as the Sarvāstivādins assert, the material aggregate retains its materiality, then it becomes something persistent, permanent, and eternal—an idea that even the Sarvāstivādins are averse to admit.[107]

As the *Kathāvatthu* shows, the Sarvāstivāda theory amounts to: "having existed (in the future), it exists (in the present, and) having existed (in the present), it exists (in the past)" (*hutva hoti, hutvā hoti*). The transition is from future existence to present existence and from present existence to past existence. The Theravāda position amounts to: "having not been, they come into being, after having been, they cease to be" (*ahutvā sambhonti, hutvā paṭiventi*).[108] Here the transition, if it could be called so, is from nonexistence to existence and from existence to nonexistence.

As the Pāli commentators elaborate on this theme, when a dhamma arises in the present moment, it is not the case that its future own being (*sabhāva*) becomes manifest in the present; when it ceases to be it is not the case that its own nature continues to persist in the past.[109] There is no store (*sannidhi*) from which they come and there is no receptacle (*sannicaya*) to which they go.[110] When the violin is played, so runs the illustration, the sound that arises does not come from a preexisting store, and when it disappears it does not go to any of the directions or subdirections to be deposited. It is because of the violin, the bowstring, and the appropriate effort on the part of the player that the sound arises without having first existed, and when it disappears it disappears without a residue.[111]

In the case of dhammas, one cannot speak of an arrival (*āgamana*) or a departure (*nigamana*), because they have no existence either before their appearance or after their disappearance.[112] If they appear it is not that they come from somewhere (*na kuto ci āgacchanti*); if they disappear it is not that they go anywhere (*na kuhiñ ci gacchanti*). With no preexistence (*pubbanta*) and postexistence (*aparanta*), they have their existence only in the present and that, too, in dependence on conditions (*paccayāyattavutti*).[113] If it is necessary to speak of a past and a future existence of the dhammas, then it is a dhamma's nascent and cessant phases that must be so considered, for a dhamma does not exist before its genesis and after its cessation.[114] An Abhidhamma manual adds that if anything can be predicated of the past and the future dhammas, it is none other than their absolute nonexistence (*sabbena sabbaṃ natthi*).[115] For in the case of past and future dhammas, one cannot speak even of an inkling of existence (*vijjamānatā-lesa*).[116] Each temporal division is devoid (*suñña*) of the other two and distinct (*vivitta*) from one another.[117]

These observations appear to have been made for two purposes. One is to criticize the theory that dhammas exist in all the three divisions of time. The other is to clarify the Theravāda position in relation to this theory.

There is another aspect that needs clarification here. It relates to the Theravāda's response, if there is any, to the four well-known theories developed within the Sarvāstivāda system on the subject of tri-temporality. Each theory seeks to provide an answer to the very natural question that if a dharma has two aspects, the permanent essence and its phenomenal manifestation, what exactly is their difference and what precisely is their relationship? How do they differ and unite in the same dharma?

Among the four theories, the first is attributed to Bhadanta Dharmatrāta. It is known as *bhāva-anyathātva* (change in the mode of being) because it says that while the mode of being (*bhāva*) of a dharma becomes different (*anyathā*), its underlying substance (*dravya*) remains unchanged. When a future dharma transits from the future to the present it abandons its future mode of being and acquires the present mode of being; in the same way, when it transits from the present to the past it abandons its present mode of being and acquires the past mode of being. In all these temporal transitions the substantial essence (*dravya*) of the dharma remains unchanged. It is just as when a golden vessel is broken, its form changes but not its color; or when milk is turned into curd, its savor and so on undergo change but not its color.[118] The theory obviously involves the notion of a permanent substance persisting through time and, in this regard, as its critics say, it amounts to a veiled recognition of the Sāṃkhya theory of evolution: change is only an alteration of a persistent substance.[119]

A theory almost identical with the above is cited in a Pāli subcommentary. While criticizing the Jaina theory of sevenfold predication (*sattabhaṅgavāda* = *saptabhaṅgavāda*) the subcommentary says: "There are those who say, just as when a golden pot is made into a crest, potness disappears and crestness appears, while the gold remains the same, even so, in the case of all existents (*bhāva*), one aspect (*ko ci dhammo*) disappears, another aspect appears, while their own nature (*sabhāva*) remains unchanged."[120] In criticizing this theory, the subcommentary says that the gold that remains unchanged in the example cited must be either a basic factor (*dhamma*) or an aggregation of basic factors (*samūha*). If it is of the first kind, then it cannot persist but can only exist in time, and that too in the present moment. If it is of the latter kind, then being something analyzable it is not real. Therefore the notions of existence (*atthitā*), nonexistence (*natthitā*), permanence (*niccatā*), and impermanence (*aniccatā*) do not apply to it.[121]

For the Theravāda no dhamma can become different from what it is (*na ca sabhāvo aññathā hoti*). What really takes place is not *bhāvaññathā*, that is, alteration of the dhamma, but *bhāva-vigamana*, that is, the displacement of the dhamma.[122] In the case of a dhamma, a change of aspect amounts to its complete disappearance.

Although the Theravāda rejects the theory of *bhāvānyathātva*, we find the corresponding Pāli term *bhāvaññathatta* in the Pāli commentaries, but in a different sense. It means the varying degrees of intensity (*ussada*) the four great material elements assume when they enter into the composition of material compounds (*omattādhimattatā-saṅkhātaṃ bhāvaññathattaṃ nāma*).[123] When, for example, solid gold becomes liquidized due to the earth element's loss of intensity, what becomes different is the earth element's previous level of intensity and not the characteristic peculiar to the earth element. In the same way, when sweet cane syrup becomes solidified into molasses due to the water element's loss of intensity, what becomes different is the water element's previous level of intensity and not the characteristic peculiar to the water element. In both cases it is the alteration of the intensity that takes place (*bhāvaññathattaṃ paññāyati*) and not the loss of the characteristics peculiar to the earth and water elements (*na lakkhaṇaṃ pana vigacchati*).[124]

The second Sarvāstivāda theory is attributed to Bhadanta Ghoṣaka. It is known as *lakṣaṇa-anyathātva* (change in the characteristic) because it says that although the characteristic (*lakṣaṇa*) of a dharma changes, its substance remains the same. Accordingly, when a dharma appears at different times, the past dharma retains its past characteristic without being completely dissociated from its future and present characteristics. Likewise the present and the future have the present and the future characteristics, respectively, without being completely deprived of the other two characteristics.[125] Just as a man who is passionately attached to one particular woman is "not altogether deprived of his capacity of love toward other females (but this capacity is not prominent)."[126] This theory, as generally observed, has the defect of obliterating the temporal distinctions, because it says that the three characteristics of the past, present, and future exist simultaneously, though in varying degrees of intensity.

Lakkhaṇa-aññathattta, which is the Pāli for *lakṣaṇa-anyathātva*, is also found in the Pāli commentaries.[127] However, it is not used in the same sense as *lakṣaṇa-anyathātva*. Nor is the term ever used as an allusion to Bhadanta Ghoṣaka's theory. For the Theravāda, the characteristic (*lakkhaṇa*) is not different from what is characterized by it—that is, the dhamma.[128] They are mutually convertible terms. Therefore, for the Theravāda, *lakkhaṇa-aññathatta* (alteration of the characteristic) means the same as *dhamma-aññathatta*, the alteration of the dhamma. This, as explained above, is an impossibility.[129] For in the case of dhammas, the irreducible data of existence, to change means to cease to be. As one subcommentary says: "No dhamma will abandon its own nature (own characteristic) when in union with any other dhamma, because to admit this possibility is to admit the very nonexistence (*abhāvappatti*) of the dhamma."[130] In this context, it is also observed that a dhamma is what it is irrespective of time distinctions, for a dhamma does not assume different characteristics corresponding to the three divisions of time.[131] It is in this sense that Theravādins understand *lakkhaṇa-aññathatta* and it is in this sense that they deny its possibility.

The third theory was advocated by Bhadanta Vasumitra. It says when a dharma is in transit through time it does not change its substance but only its state—*avasthānyathātva*, the state being determined by the dharma's causal efficiency (*kāritra*)—that is, the potency to project results (*phalākṣepa*). When a dharma is in a state when it does not produce its function, it is called "future." When it produces its function it is called "present." When, after having produced its function, a dharma does not produce its function anymore, it is past. In all these three phases the substance of the dharma remains the same.[132] "It is just as in an abacus the same ball receives different significations according to the place it is thrown in. If it is thrown in the place of units it means one; if in the place for hundreds it means a hundred, and if in the place for thousands it means one thousand."[133]

The Theravāda position in relation to this theory is similar to the Sautrāntikas'. Both schools make no distinction between the dhamma and its function. As one subcommentary says: "There is no function/activity apart from the dhamma" (*dhammato aññā kiriyā nāma natthi*).[134] If the dhamma and its function (*kiriyā*) are not different, then the question of whether the dhamma persists in the three temporal divisions while its function manifests in the present time does not arise.

The fourth theory on tri-temporality is attributed to Bhadanta Buddhadeva. It is known as *anyathā-anyathātva*, the change of contingency, or *apekṣānyathātva*, the change of mutual dependence. It says that a dharma in its transit in time is called future, present, and past in relation to its preceding and succeeding moments. It is just as the same female is called "mother" in relation to her child and "daughter" in relation to her own mother. Accordingly, when a dharma has something before it but nothing after it, it is called "future"; when it has something both before and after it, it is called "present"; when it has something after it but not before it, it is called "past."[135]

One criticism against this theory is that, according to it, the three mutually exclusive temporal determinations occur simultaneously: since "anterior" and "posterior" are relative terms, the anterior and posterior moments of the past will have to be called "past" and "future," and the intermediate moment, the "present." In the same way, future too will be tri-temporal. The present dharma, although momentary, will belong to all the three periods in relation to what precedes and succeeds.[136]

The Definition of Dhamma as Own Nature

The Theravādins, as noted above, reject all versions of tri-temporality. However, they seem to have been influenced by the Sarvāstivāda in one important aspect: the use of the term *sabhāva* (own being, own nature) as another expression for *dhamma*. *Sabhāva* in the sense of *dhamma* does not seem to occur in any of the books of the Abhidhamma Piṭaka. It is in the Abhidhamma exegesis that we find the term used in the above sense.

The term occurs in the *Paṭisambhidāmagga* where the five aggregates are described as *sabhāvena suññaṃ*, devoid of own nature or own being.[137] We will understand its significance in the course of this chapter. More relevant to our subject here is its occurrence in the *Nettippakaraṇa*, a work on Buddhist hermeneutics. There in a discussion on dependent arising we find a distinction made between *hetu* as cause and *paccaya* as condition. In the case of a plant, for example, seed is the *hetu*, earth and water are its *paccayas*. Both perform two generative functions, but with a difference. The first is specific and the second generic. *Hetu* has a characteristic not shared by others (*asādhāraṇa-lakkhaṇa*) and *paccaya* has a common characteristic (*sādhāraṇa-lakkhaṇa*). *Hetu* is an internal (*ajjhattika*) quality and *paccaya* an external (*bāhira*) quality. Thus *hetu* is the thing that is proper to a given dhamma. Hence it is called *sabhāva*, "own nature." Since *paccayas* are the things that help it externally, they are called *parabhāva*, "other nature."[138]

This seems to be the first-ever explicit reference in a Theravāda work to the idea that a given thing has its "own nature." Whether this led to the use of the term *sabhāva* in the sense of *dhamma* is difficult to ascertain. It is very likely, however, that the Pāli commentators were influenced by the Sarvāstivāda. For *sabhāva* was used in the Sarvāstivāda as another term for *dharma* long before the Pāli commentaries were compiled.

The question that arises is, in which sense do the Theravādins use *sabhāva* as another expression for *dhamma*? This will become clear if we examine the commentarial definition of dhamma, which is as follows: dhammas are so called because they bear their own nature (*attano sabhāvaṃ dhārentī ti dhammā*).[139] This definition at once implies that dhamma and sabhāva are two different things. Dhamma is the bearer and sabhāva is that which is borne by the dhamma. Does this amount to the admission that there is a duality between the dhamma and its sabhāva, between the bearer and the borne, a dichotomy that goes against the grain of the Buddhist doctrine of *anattā*?

This situation has to be considered in the context of the logical apparatus used by the Ābhidhammikas in defining the dhammas. This involves three main kinds of definition. The first is called agency definition (*kattu-sādhana*) because it attributes agency to the thing to be defined. Such, for example, is the definition of cognition (*viññāṇa*) as "that which cognizes" (*vijānātī ti viññāṇaṃ*). The second is called instrumental definition (*karaṇa-sādhana*) because it attributes instrumentality to the thing to be defined. Such, for example, is the definition of cognition as "that through which (the mental factors) cognize." The third is called definition by nature (*bhāva-sādhana*), whereby the abstract nature of the thing to be defined is brought into focus. Such, for example, is the definition of cognition as "the mere act of cognizing is cognition" (*vijānana-mattam eva viññāṇaṃ*).[140]

The first two kinds of definition are said to be provisional and, as such, are not valid from an ultimate point of view. For the attribution of agency and instrumentality invests a dhamma with a duality when it is actually a unitary and unique phenomenon. Such attribution is called "the assumption of a distinction where there is no such distinction" (*abhede bheda-parikappaṇā*).[141] It is this kind of assumption that leads to the wrong notion that a given dhamma is a substance with inherent qualities or an agent that performs some kind of action. Such definitions are based on tentative attribution (*samāropaṇa*) and thus are not ultimately valid.[142] It is as a matter of convention (*vohāra*) and for the sole purpose of facilitating the grasp of the idea to be conveyed (*sukha-gahaṇatthaṃ*) that a duality is assumed by the mind in defining the dhamma, which is actually devoid of such duality.[143] Both agency and instrumentality definitions are resorted to for the convenience of description, and as such they are not to be understood in their direct literal sense. On the other hand, what is called definition by nature (*bhāva-sādhana*) is the one that is admissible in an ultimate sense (*nippariyāyato*). This is because this type of definition brings into focus the real nature of a given dhamma without attributing agency and instrumentality to it, an attribution that creates the false notion of a duality within a unitary dhamma.[144]

It is in the context of these implications that the definition of dhamma as that which bears its own nature has to be understood. Clearly, this is a definition according to agency (*kattu-sādhana*), and hence its validity is provisional. From this definition, therefore, one cannot conclude that a given dhamma is a substantial bearer of its qualities or "own nature." The duality between dhamma and sabhāva is only an attribution made for the convenience of definition. For in fact both denote the same actuality. Hence it is categorically stated that apart from sabhāva there is no distinct entity called dhamma (*na ca sabhāvā añño dhammo nāma atthi*),[145] and that the term *sabhāva* signifies the mere fact of being a dhamma (*dhamma-*

matta-dīpanaṃ sabhāva-padaṃ).[146] Elaborating on this, a Pāli subcommentary says that apart from the fact of being molested (*ruppana*), which is the characteristic of matter, there is no separate entity called matter, and in the same way, apart from the fact of hardness (*kakkhaḷatta*), which is the characteristic of the earth element, there is no separate entity called the earth element.[147]

If dhamma and sabhāva denote the same actuality, why is the dhamma invested with the function of bearing its own nature? For this implies the recognition of an agency distinct from the dhamma. This, it is observed, is done not only to conform with the inclinations of those who are to be instructed[148] but also to stress the fact that there is no agent behind the dhamma.[149] The point being emphasized is that the dynamic world of sensory experience is not due to causes other than the selfsame dhammas into which it is finally reduced. It is the interconnection of the dhammas through causal relations that explains the variety and diversity of conditioned existence and not some kind of transempirical reality that serves as their metaphysical ground. Nor is it due to the fiat of a Creator God, because there is no divine creator over and above the flow of mental and material factors.[150]

In other words, the definition of *dhamma* as that which bears its sabhāva means that any dhamma represents a distinct fact of empirical existence that is not shared by other dhammas. Hence *sabhāva* is also defined as that which is not held in common by others (*anañña-sādhāraṇa*),[151] as the nature peculiar to each dhamma (*āveṇika-sabhāva*),[152] and as the own nature not predicable of other dhammas (*asādhāraṇa-sabhāva*).[153] If the dhammas are said to have "own nature" (*saka-bhāva, sabhāva*), this is only a tentative device to drive home the point that there is no "other nature" (*parabhāva*) from which they emerge and to which they finally lapse.[154]

Now this commentarial definition of dhamma as sabhāva poses an important problem. It seems to go against an earlier Theravāda tradition recorded in the *Paṭisambhidāmagga*. This text specifically states that the five aggregates are devoid of own nature (*sabhāvena suññaṃ*).[155] Since the dhammas are the basic factors of the five aggregates, this should mean that the dhammas, too, are devoid of own nature. What is more, does not the very use of the term *sabhāva*, despite all the qualifications under which it is used, give the impression that a given dhamma exists in its own right? And does this not amount to the admission that a dhamma is some kind of quasi-substance?

The Pāli commentators were not unaware of these implications and they therefore took the necessary steps to forestall such a conclusion. This they sought to do by supplementing the former definition with another that actually nullifies the conclusion that the dhammas might be quasi-substances. This additional definition states that a dhamma is not that which bears its own nature but that which is borne by its own conditions (*paccayehi dhārīyantī ti dhammā*).[156] Whereas the earlier definition is agent denotation (*kattu-sādhana*) because it attributes an active role to the dhamma, elevating it to the position of an agent, the new definition is object denotation (*kamma-sādhana*) because it attributes a passive role to the dhamma and thereby downgrades it to the position of an object. What is radical about this new definition is that it reverses the whole process, which otherwise might culminate in the conception of dhammas as substances or bearers of their own nature. What it seeks to show is that, far from being a bearer, a dhamma is being borne by its own conditions.

Consonant with this situation, it is also maintained that there is no other thing called a dhamma than the "quality" of being borne by conditions.[157] The same idea is expressed in the oft-recurrent statement that what is called a *dhamma* is the mere fact of occurrence due to appropriate conditions.[158] In fact, in commenting on the *Paṭisambhidāmagga* statement that the five aggregates and, by implication, the dhammas are devoid of own nature (*sabhāva*), the commentator observes that since the aggregates have no self-nature, they are devoid of own nature.[159] It will thus be seen that although the term *sabhāva* is used as a synonym for *dhamma*, it is interpreted in such a way that it means the very absence of sabhāva in any sense that implies a substantial mode of being. "Own nature" (*sabhāva*) does not mean "own sway" (*vasavattitā*). In the case of dhammas that exist depending on impermanent conditions, none has the power to exercise any kind of sway (*natthi kā ci vasavattitā*).[160] In this connection, a subcommentary observes that the meaning of *sabhāva* is, therefore, the same as the meaning of "emptiness" (*sabhāvattho nāma suññattho*).[161]

When a dhamma/sabhāva is sought to be characterized as "empty" (*suñña*), what is intended to show is not that it is void but that it is devoid—devoid of a self or substance (*attena*), or of anything pertaining to a self or substance (*attaniyena*).[162] In fact, this is the meaning given to the concept of "emptiness" in the Pāli suttas as well. When Ānanda asked the Buddha in what sense the world is empty (*suñña*), the Buddha replied: "It is, Ānanda, because it is empty of self and of what belongs to self that it is said, 'Empty is the world.'"[163] Thus for early Buddhism "empty" (*suñña*) is another expression for "non-self" (*anattā*). They are mutually convertible terms: what is "non-self" is "empty" and, likewise, what is "empty" is "non-self." Understood in this context, we have the liberty of restating the well-known statement *sabbe dhammā anattā* (all things are non-self) as *sabbe dhammā suññā* (all things are empty). It is in this sense that the Abhidhamma, too, says that "all dhammas"—that is, the basic factors into which the conditioned reality is resolved and also the unconditioned reality of nibbāna—are "*anattā*" (non-self). In the same sense are used the words "hollow" (*tuccha*), "devoid" (*ritta*), "essenceless" (*asāra*), and "devoid of essence" (*sāra-vajjita*).[164]

One Pāli commentary also refers to a prevalent misconception, namely, that when the *Paṭisambhidāmagga* says "the material form (and the other aggregates) that is born is devoid of own nature" (*jātaṃ rūpaṃ sabhāvena suññaṃ*), it means the nonexistence of material form in an ultimate sense and not that it is devoid of any substance or of anything substantial.[165] Refuting this view, the commentary points out that the very use of the term "born" (*jāta*), which means "arisen," falsifies this interpretation: For how can the material form that has arisen (*jātaṃ rūpaṃ*) be nonexistent?[166] The equation of emptiness and nonexistence, it is said, "is contradicted by the general agreement of the world at large, by the word of the Buddha, by logic, by word meaning, by textual evidence, and by many forms of proper reasoning."[167]

The Definition of Dhamma as Own Characteristic

According to this definition, dhammas are so called because they bear their own characteristics (*salakkhaṇa*).[168] This means that own nature and own characteristic are the same. Visibility, for instance, is the own characteristic of color. Although color is divisible as blue, yellow, and so on into an innumerable number, the characteristic peculiar to all varieties of color is their visibility (*sanidassanatā*), their susceptibility to be seen (*daṭṭhabbatā*), the possibility of their becoming an object of visual consciousness.[169] Hence it is also called "individual characteristic" (*paccatta-lakkhaṇa*), "special characteristic" (*visesa-lakkhaṇa*), "the characteristic that separates it from other characteristics" (*asādhāraṇa-lakkhaṇa*), and "intrinsic characteristic" (*āveṇika-lakkhaṇa*).[170] As in the case of dhamma and sabhāva, in the case of dhamma and salakkhaṇa, too, the duality is only an assumption made for the convenience of definition. To define earth element (*paṭhavī-dhātu*) as "that which has the characteristic of solidity" (*kakkhaḷatta-lakkhaṇā*)[171] is therefore not valid from an ultimate point of view because it assumes a duality between the earth element and the characteristic of solidity. The correct definition is the one that states that solidity itself is the earth element (*kakkhaḷattam eva paṭhavī-dhātu*).[172] This does not assume a distinction between the characteristic and what is characterized by it.

The question is raised that if the characteristic (*lakkhaṇa*) and what is characterized by it (*lakkhitabba*) were the same, would it not amount to saying that "a thing is its own characteristic" (*sayam eva attano lakkhaṇaṃ*)?[173] The answer is that in the case of dhammas where each represents one particular characteristic, no fallacy is involved in saying so (*nāyaṃ doso*). For the distinction is not in the dhamma itself. It is a distinction constructed by our own mind (*buddhi-parikappita*) corresponding to the distinction between the meanings of two words where one is used to explain the other.[174] The term "earth element" (*paṭhavī-dhātu*), for example, means the same thing as "solidity" (*kakkhaḷatta*). Therefore to explain what "earth element" means, one could say that "it has the characteristic of solidity." The distinction is assumed to help our understanding of its distinct meaning (*atthavisesāvabodha*).[175]

This definition too could give the wrong impression that a dhamma bears its own characteristic. This explains why it is supplemented by another that is intended to nullify any substantial implications. According to it, a dhamma is not that which bears its own characteristic. Rather, it is that which is characterized [by others] (*lakkhīyati, lakkhīyamāna*).[176] Here "to be characterized" means that the characteristic of a dhamma is brought about by and is therefore dependent on other dhammas. "To be characterized" (*lakkhīyanti*) is therefore paraphrased as "to be borne" (*dhārīyanti*) or "to be upheld" (*upadhārīyanti*).[177]

While the own characteristic (*salakkhaṇa*) is peculiar to each dhamma, the universal characteristic (*sāmañña-lakkhaṇa*) is applicable to *all dhammas*.[178] The former is individually predicable and the latter universally predicable. Hence the universal characteristic is defined as that which brings together those that are differentiated in many ways (*anekabhedasaṅgāhaka*).[179] The difference goes still further. As own characteristic is another name for dhamma, it has objective counterpart. On the other hand, the universal characteristic is a mental construct having no objective reality. On this interpretation, the three characteristics of conditioned reality (*saṅkhata-lakkhaṇa*)—namely, arising (*uppāda*), cessation (*vaya*), and change-in-continuance (*ṭhitassa aññathatta*)—become universal characteristics. They are not elevated to the level of dhammas. If they were to be so elevated that would undermine the very foundation of the dhamma theory. If, for instance, origination (*uppāda*), existence (*ṭhiti*), and dissolution (*bhaṅga*) are postulated as real and discrete entities, then it would be necessary to postulate another set of secondary characteristics to account for their own origination, existence, and dissolution, thus resulting in an infinite regress (*anavaṭṭhāna*). This is the significance of a commentarial observation: "It is not correct to assume that origination originates, decay decays, and cessation ceases, because such an assumption leads to the fallacy of infinite regress."[180]

Corresponding to the individual and universal characteristics are two kinds of understanding. The first is known as *ñāta-pariññā*, "full understanding as the known." It arises by observing the specific characteristics of the dhammas: "materiality (*rūpa*) has the characteristic of being molested (*ruppana*), feeling (*vedanā*) the characteristic of being felt (*vedayita*), and so on."[181] The second is known as *tīraṇa-pariññā*, "full understanding as investigating." It arises by attributing universal characteristics to the same dhammas: "materiality is impermanent (*anicca*), unsatisfactory (*dukkha*), and not-self (*anattā*), and so are feeling and other aggregates."[182] Both kinds of full understanding pave the way for the emergence of another. It is the most important from the point of view of emancipation and is known as *pahāna-pariññā*, "full understanding as abandoning." It is to be accomplished by abandoning the three basic misconceptions: perception of permanence in what is impermanent, perception of pleasure in what is painful, and perception of self in what is not-self.[183]

This shows the relevance of the dhamma theory to Buddhist mental culture. As mentioned at the beginning of this chapter, the dhamma theory was intended from the start to be more than a mere hypothetical scheme. Its purpose is to serve as a guide for meditative contemplation and insight.

The Definition of Dhamma as Ultimately Real

In what sense the dhammas represent the final limits into which empirical existence can be analyzed is another question that drew the attention of the Theravāda exegetes. It is in answer to this question that the term *paramattha* came to be used as another expression for *dhamma*. It was noted earlier that the use of this term in this sense was occasioned by the Theravādins' response to the Pudgalavādins' assertion that the person exists in a real and ultimate sense. In the Abhidhamma exegesis the term *paramattha* is defined to mean that which has reached its highest (*uttama*), implying thereby that the dhammas are ultimate existents with no possibility of further reduction. Hence "own nature" (*sabhāva*) came to be further defined as "ultimate own nature" (*paramattha-sabhāva*).[184]

The term *paramattha* is sometimes paraphrased as the actual (*bhūtattha*). This is explained to mean that the dhammas are not nonexistent like an illusion or mirage or like the soul (*purisa*) and primordial nature (*pakati*) of the non-Buddhist schools of thought. The evidence for their existence is not based either on conventions (*sammuti*) or on mere scriptural authority (*anussava*). On the contrary, their very existence is vouchsafed by their own intrinsic nature. The very fact of their existence is the mark of their reality. As the *Visuddhimagga* observes: "It [dhamma] is that which, for those who examine it with the eye of understanding, is not misleading like an illusion, deceptive like a mirage, or undiscoverable like the self of the sectarians, but is rather the domain of noble knowledge as the real unmisleading actual state."[185] The kind of existence implied here is not past or future existence but present actual and verifiable existence (*saṃvijjamānatā*).[186] This emphasis on their actuality in the present phase of time rules out any association with the Sarvāstivādins' theory of tri-temporality.

The description of dhammas as paramattha means not only their objective existence (*paramatthato vijjamānatā*) but also their cognizability in an ultimate sense (*paramatthato upalabbhamānatā*).[187] The first refers to the fact that the dhammas obtain as the ultimate, irreducible data of empirical existence. The second refers to the fact that the dhammas are known not as objects of conceptual thought but as objects of the highest knowledge. It is in fact in order to emphasize the cognizability of the dhammas that they are sometimes described as *ñeyya-dhamma* (knowable dhammas). The use of the term *ñeyya* (knowable), so runs a commentarial observation, is to rule out the view that dhammas are not cognizable, and the use of the term *dhamma* is to exclude from the domain of actuality such concepts as the "soul" postulated in sectarian philosophies.[188]

If the term *paramattha* brings into focus the irreducibility of the dhammas, the term *aviparītabhāva* shows their irreversibility.[189] This term means that the essential characteristic of a dhamma is nonalterable and nontransferable to any other dhamma. It also means that it is impossible for a given dhamma to undergo any modification of its specific characteristic even when it is in association with some other dhamma.[190] The same situation remains true despite the differences in the time factor, for there is no modification in the nature of a dhamma corresponding to the divisions in time.[191] Since a dhamma and its intrinsic nature are the same (for the duality is only posited for purposes of explanation), to claim that its intrinsic nature undergoes modification is to deny its very existence.

The Nature and Range of Dhammas

In the course of this chapter we saw that the Abhidhamma uses a number of terms to describe the basic constituents into which it analyzes the world of experience. Among them are *dhamma* (basic factor of actuality), *bhāva* (being), *sabhāva* or *sakabhāva* (own being, own nature), *salakkhaṇa* (own mark, own characteristic), *paccatta-lakkhaṇa* (individuating characteristic), *paramattha* (ultimate), *saccikaṭṭha* (true existent), and *bhūtattha* (actual being). These different terms bring into focus two important characteristics of the dhammas. One is that they exist in a real and ultimate sense, thus representing a category that truly exists independently of the cognitive act. The second is that each dhamma represents a particular characteristic that is peculiar to it and that thus sets it apart from all other dhammas.

If these and other words are used as different expressions for dhamma, they are not intended to show that a dhamma is something complex and therefore that it has different aspects. As a datum of actuality, a constituent of conditioned reality, a dhamma is a unitary fact with no possibility of further resolution. This is a situation on which the Pāli exegetes focus much attention: Hence it is said: "In the ultimate sense, a dhamma has but one own nature although it is sought to be expressed in many ways that are superimposed on it. This is like using a string of synonyms to express the same thing in an easily understandable manner."[192] The reference to superimposition for purposes of description is very significant. For as we saw in the course of this chapter, description necessarily involves dualities and dichotomies, such as the characteristic and the characterized, the agent and the action, the bearer and the borne, the possessor and the possessed. But all such dualities and dichotomies have no corresponding objective counterparts. They are mind-made and mind-based attributions made for the convenience of definition and description.

Although a given dhamma represents one own nature, as Rupert Gethin observes, each dhamma should be understood as representing a broad class. If a given instance of any one class of dhamma is grouped together with other instances, this means that they all share one common nature. The fact that they constitute one class does not mean that they are identical in all respects, that they are "phenomenologically indistinguishable."[193] This observation is important because it is made as a correction to a view expressed by P. J. Griffiths—namely, that all instances of a given class "share the same essential existence and the same individuating characteristic" and therefore "they can be distinguished one from another only in terms of their spatio-temporal locations."[194]

In this connection, Rupert Gethin has also drawn our attention to a very pertinent observation made in the *Abhidhammāvatāra*, a medieval compendium on the Theravāda Abhidhamma. This refers to the fact that although the Abhidhamma formally recognizes eight kinds of morally wholesome consciousnesses that operate in the sphere of sense (*kāmāvacara*), "if other variables are taken into account there are 17,280 kinds."[195]

Relative Position of the Dhammas

The relative position of the dhammas is another aspect that requires clarification. Do they harmoniously blend into a unity or do they divide themselves into a plurality? We may do well to examine two of their important characteristics. One is their actual inseparability (*saṃsaṭṭhatā*, *avinibhogatā*), the other their conditionedness (*sappaccayatā*).

The first refers to the fact that in a given instance of mind or matter, the basic constituents (= dhammas) that enter into its composition are not actually separable one from another. They exist in a state of inseparable association forming, so to say, a "heterogeneous unity." In the case of mental dhammas, we find this idea expressed in the early Buddhist discourses as well. For example, in the *Mahāvedalla Sutta* it is said that the three mental states—namely, feeling (*vedanā*), perception (*saññā*), and consciousness (*viññāṇa*)—are blended (*saṃsaṭṭha*) so harmoniously that it is impossible to separate them from one another and thus establish their identity.[196] The same idea finds expression in the *Milindapañha*. When Nāgasena Thera is asked by King Milinda whether it is possible, in the case of mental factors that exist in harmonious combination (*ekato bhāvagata*), to separate them out and establish a plurality, such as "this is contact, and this sensation, and this mentation, and this perception," and so on, the Elder answers with a simile:

> Suppose, O king, the cook in the royal household were to make a syrup or a sauce and were to put into it curds, and salt, and ginger, and cumin seed, and pepper and other ingredients. And suppose the king were to say to him: "Pick out for me the flavors of the curds and of the salt, and of the ginger, and of the cumin seed,

> and of the pepper, and of all the things you have put into it." Now would it be possible, great king, separating off one from another those flavors that had thus run together, to pick out each one, so that one could say: "Here is the sourness, and here the saltiness, and here the pungency, and here the acidity, and here the astringency, and here the sweetness?"[197]

In like manner, it is maintained, we should understand the position of the mental dhammas in relation to one another.[198]

This situation is true of the material dhammas too. The commentary to the *Dhammasaṅgaṇi* says that the material dhammas, such as color, taste, odor, and so on, cannot be separated from one another like particles of sand.[199] The color of the mango, for instance, cannot be physically separated from its taste or odor. They remain in inseparable association. This is what is called positional inseparability (*padesato avinibhogatā*).[200]

The basic principle recognized is that "strictly speaking, no material dhamma subsists in another" (*aññaṃ rūpaṃ aññasmiṃ rūpe paramatthato nevatthi*).[201] Savor, for instance, is not found inside color. If it were otherwise, so runs the argument, then with the apprehension of color one should be able to apprehend savor as well. What is intended to show is that no dhamma inheres in another dhamma, as does quality in substance. If the dhammas support one another, this should be understood purely with reference to the principles of causality and conditionality. In fact, it is maintained that apart from conditionality even the material dhammas do not exhibit the principle of "supporting and being supported"—that is, the distinction between substance and quality (*na hi paccayabhāvaṃ antarena rūpadhammānam' pi ādhārādheyabhāvo atthi*).[202]

If the dhammas, both mental and material, are not separable, one from another, why are they presented as a plurality? The answer is that although they are not actually separable, yet they are distinguishable (*vibhāgavanta*) one from another.[203] It is this distinguishability that serves as the foundation of the dhamma theory. Hence it is often mentioned in the Abhidhamma subcommentaries that the real nature of the things that are distinguishable can be brought into focus only through analysis.[204]

The other characteristic pertaining to the relative position of the dhammas is their conditionedness (*sappaccayatā*). This is akin to the conception discussed above, for it also seeks to explain the nature of the dhammas from the point of view of synthesis. As we shall see in detail,[205] five postulates are recognized as axiomatic, either implicitly or explicitly: The first is that nothing arises fortuitously (*adhicca-samuppanna*) without any reference to causes and conditions. The second is that nothing arises from a single cause (*ekakāraṇavāda*). The third is that nothing arises as a single effect (*ekassa dhammassa uppatti paṭisedhitā hoti*).[206] The rejection of these three views means that according to Abhidhamma it is always the case that a plurality of conditions gives rise to a plurality of effects. Applied to the dhamma theory, this means that a multiplicity of dhammas brings about a multiplicity of other dhammas.

One implication that follows from this principle of conditionality is that the dhammas invariably arise as clusters. This is true of both mental and material dhammas. Hence whenever consciousness (*citta*) arises, together with it there arise at least seven mental factors (*cetasika*)—namely, sensory contact (*phassa*), feeling (*vedanā*), perception (*saññā*), volition (*cetanā*), one-pointedness (*ekaggatā*), psychic life (*arūpa-jīvitindriya*), and attention (*manasikāra*). These seven are called universal mental factors (*sabba-citta-sādhāraṇa*) because they are invariably present even in the most minimal unit of consciousness.[207] Thus a psychic instance can never occur with less than eight constituents—namely, consciousness and its seven invariable concomitants. Their relationship is one of necessary conascence (*sahajāta*). We thus can see that even the smallest psychic unit or moment of consciousness turns out to be a complex correlational system. In the same way, the smallest unit of matter, which is called the basic octad (*suddhaṭṭhaka*), is in the ultimate analysis a cluster of (eight) material dhammas—namely, the four great elements of matter: earth (solidity and extension), water (viscidity and cohesion), fire (temperature of cold and heat), and air (mobility, motion), and four items of dependent matter: color, odor, taste, and nutritive essence (*ojā*). None of these eight material dhammas arises singly because they are necessarily co-nascent (*niyata-sahajāta*) and positionally inseparable (*padesato avinibhoga*).[208]

It will thus be seen that in the sphere of mind as well as in the domain of matter there are no solitary phenomena. This situation is equally true whether we examine the dhammas as causes (conditions) or as effects (the conditioned).

It is in light of these observations that the question posed earlier as to whether the dhammas exhibit a unity or a plurality has to be discussed. The answer seems to veer toward both alternatives, although it appears paradoxical to say so. Insofar as the dhammas are distinguishable, one from another, to that extent they exhibit plurality. In so far as they are not actually separable, one from another, to that extent they exhibit unity. The reason for this situation is the methodological apparatus employed by the Ābhidhammikas in explaining the nature of empirical existence. As mentioned earlier, this consists of both analysis (*bheda*) and synthesis (*saṅgaha*). Analysis, when not supplemented by synthesis, leads to pluralism. Synthesis, when not supplemented by analysis, leads to monism. What one finds in the Abhidhamma is a *combined use* of both methods. This results in a philosophical vision that beautifully transcends the dialectical opposition between monism and pluralism.

2

THE NOMINAL AND THE CONCEPTUAL

What emerges from the dhamma theory is best described as dhamma realism, for as we have seen, it recognizes only the ultimate reality of the dhammas. What is interesting about this view of existence is that it involves more denials than affirmations. We have already noted how it denies the notion of "substance and quality" and, as we shall see in the sequel, it also denies the objective reality of time, space, motion, physical contact, and the notion of "gradual change." Only the ultimate reality of the dhammas is affirmed; whatever cannot be subsumed under the heading "dhamma" is deprived of its ultimate reality. We can observe here the principle of parsimony in the analysis of empirical existence and an attempt to ensure ontological minimalism. Then how does the dhamma theory interpret the "commonsense" view of the world, a kind of naïve realism in the sense that it tends to recognize realities more or less corresponding to all linguistic terms? What relation is there between the dhammas, the basic factors of existence, on the one hand, and the objects of commonsense realism, on the other? What degree of reality, if any, could be bestowed on the latter?

It is in their answers to these questions that the Ābhidhammikas formulated the theory of *paññatti*—concepts or designations[209]—together with a distinction drawn between two kinds of truth, consensual (*sammuti*) and ultimate (*paramattha*). This theory assumes significance in another context. In most of the Indian philosophies that were associated with the *ātma* tradition and subscribed to a substantialist view of existence, such categories as "time" and "space" and such notions as "unity," "identity," and "universality" came to be defined in absolute terms. The problem for the Ābhidhammikas was how to explain such categories and notions without committing themselves to the same metaphysical assumptions. The theory of *paññatti* was the answer to this problem.

The term *paññatti* conveys such meanings as making known, laying down, manifestation, designation, appellation, notion, and concept. The term occurs both in the Suttas and the Vinaya, sometimes in a general and sometimes in a somewhat technical sense.[210] Its use in the Abhidhamma in a technical sense to mean concept or designation could, however, be traced to the *Poṭṭhapāda Sutta* of the *Dīghanikāya*, where we find the well-known saying of the Buddha on the use of language: "These, Citta, are names (*samaññā*), expressions (*nirutti*), turns of speech (*vohāra*), and designations (*paññatti*) in common use in the world. And of these the Tathāgata makes use indeed but is not led astray by them."[211] This saying assumes significance in the context of the Buddha's use of the word *atta-paṭilābha* (obtainment of self) in order to designate the three kinds of obtainment of self: the gross self, the mental self, and the formless self. The point emphasized is that the use of the phrase "obtainment of self" does not in any way imply the recognition of a self-entity that persists in the three different obtainments. There is no permanent substantial entity that could be observed to correspond to the term "self" (*atta*). Here the term *atta* is a paññatti, a designation in common use in the world, which the Buddha uses without clinging to it (*aparāmasaṃ voharati*).[212]

The earliest reference to paññatti as used in the Abhidhamma is found in the *Niruttipatha Sutta* of the *Saṃyuttanikāya*. Here it is said that the division of time into past, present, and future and the designation of time as "was," "is," and "will be" are three pathways of expression (*nirutti*), designation (*adhivacana*), and concept-making (*paññatti*).[213]

What may be described as the first formal definition of *paññatti* occurs in the *Dhammasaṅgaṇi*. Here the three terms, *paññatti*, *nirutti*, and *adhivacana*, are used synonymously and each term is defined by a number of appropriate equivalents:

> That which is an enumeration, that which is a designation, an expression (*paññatti*), a current term, a name, a denomination, the assigning of a name, an interpretation, a distinctive mark of discourse on this or that dhamma.[214]

Immediately after this definition, it is said that all the dhammas are the pathway of paññattis (*sabbe dhammā paññattipathā*). What this amounts to saying is that all the dhammas can be designated by linguistic terms. Thus one distinction between paññatti and dhamma turns out to be that between expression and reality.

In elaborating on this, the Pāli commentary says that paññatti means the process of predicating: "What is it that is predicated? It is 'I,' 'mine,' 'another,' 'another's,' 'a person,' 'a state,' 'an individual,' 'a man,' 'a youth,' 'Tissa,' 'Datta,' 'a conch,' 'a chair,' 'a mat,' 'a pillow,' 'a monastery,' 'a cell,' 'a door,' 'a window'—these are the various ways of predicating."[215] This miscellany of examples is so designed as to include any kind of predication through the symbolic medium of language. Elaborating on this further, the commentary observes that there is no such thing that does not constitute the object of being named, in other words, that nothing can escape the possibility of being named. There is one thing, it is said, that coincides with all things and all things in one thing. This one thing is the act of naming (*nāma-paññatti*), which is said to be applicable to anything in the four spheres of existence (*catubhūmaka-dhammesu nipatati*).[216]

In this regard, the commentary makes this interesting observation: "There is no living being or phenomenon that may not be called by a name. The trees in the forests and the mountains are the business of the country folk. For they, on being asked 'what tree is this?' say the name they know, as 'Cutch,' 'Butea.' Even of the tree the name of which they know not, they say, 'It is the nameless tree.' In addition, that stands as the established name of that tree. And the same with fishes, tortoises, etc., in the ocean."[217] This all-embracing role, which the commentary assigns to name or naming (*nāma*), reminds us of two stanzas in the *Saṃyuttanikāya*:[218]

> What has weighed down everything?
> What is most extensive?

What is the one thing that has
all under its control?
Name has weighed down everything;
nothing is more extensive than name.
Name is the one thing that has
all under its control.[219]

Since paññatti represents name and meaning as concepts, it has to be distinguished from dhammas, the category of the real. And since the term *paramattha* is used in the Abhidhamma as a description of what is ultimately real, the above distinction is also presented as that between *paññatti* and *paramattha*, or that between *paññatti* and *dhamma*, because *paramattha* and *dhamma* are mutually convertible terms. Thus we have the category of *paññattis* on the one hand, representing that which exists as name and concept, and the category of *dhammas* on the other, representing that which exists as ultimate constituents of existence. The two categories imply two levels of reality as well. These two levels are the conceptual and the real. It is the distinction between that which depends on the operation of mind and that which exists independently of the operation of mind. While the former owes its being to the act of cognition itself, the latter exists independently of the cognitive act.

These two categories, the *paññatti* and the *paramattha*, or the "conceptual" and the "real," are said to be mutually exclusive and together exhaustive of the whole of the knowable (*ñeyya-dhamma*).[220] Thus what is not paramattha is paññatti. Similarly, what is not paññatti is paramattha. Hence the *Abhidhammāvatāra* makes this assertive statement: "Besides the two categories of *paramattha* (the real) and *paññatti* (the conceptual), a third category does not exist. One who is skillful in these two categories does not tremble in the face of other teachings."[221]

Although the theory of *paññatti* is formally introduced in the works of the Abhidhamma Piṭaka, it is in the Abhidhamma exegesis that we find more specific definitions of the term along with many explanations on the nature and scope of paññattis and how they become objects of cognition.

In the first place, what is called *paññatti* cannot be subsumed under *nāma* (the mental) or *rūpa* (the material). Hence the *Nāmarūpa-*

pariccheda describes it as "*nāma-rūpa-vinimmutta*"—that is, distinct from both mind and matter.[222] This is another way alluding to the fact that paññattis are not dhammas. Both paññatti and nibbāna are excluded from the domain of the five aggregates.[223] Since paññatti refers to that which has no corresponding objective counterpart, it is also called *asabhāva-dhamma*—that is, dhamma without own nature.[224] This description distinguishes it from the real factors of existence. Since sabhāva, the intrinsic nature of a dhamma, is itself the dhamma, from the point of view of this definition what is qualified as *asabhāva* (absence of own nature) amounts to an *abhāva*, a nonexistent in the final sense. It is in recognition of this fact that the three salient characteristics of empirical reality—namely, arising (*uppāda*), presence (*ṭhiti*), and dissolution (*bhaṅga*)—are not applied to them. These three characteristics can be predicated only of those things that answer to the Abhidhamma's definition of empirical reality.[225] Again, unlike the real existents, paññattis are not brought about by conditions (*paccayaṭṭhitika*).[226] For this same reason, they are also defined as "not positively produced" (*aparinipphanna*). Positive production (*parinipphannatā*) is true only of those things that have their own individual nature (*āveṇika-sabhāva*).[227] Only a dhamma that has an own nature, with a beginning and an end in time, produced by conditions, and marked by the three salient characteristics of conditioned existence, is positively produced.[228]

Further, paññattis differ from dhammas in that only the latter are delimited by rise and fall. Unlike the paññattis, the dhammas come into being having not been (*ahutvā sambhonti*), and, after having been they cease (*hutvā paṭiventi*).[229] Paññattis have no own nature to be manifested in the three instants of arising (*uppāda*), presence (*ṭhiti*), and dissolution (*bhaṅga*). Since they have no existence marked by these three phases—the nascent, present, and cessant—such temporal distinctions as past, present, and future do not apply to them. Consequently they have no reference to time (*kāla-vimutta*).[230] For this selfsame reason, paññattis have no place in the traditional analysis of empirical reality into the five khandhas, for what is included in the khandhas should have the characteristics of empirical reality and be subject to temporal divisions.[231] Nor can paññattis be assigned a place in any of the four planes of existence recognized in Buddhist cosmology (*paññatti bhūmi-vinimmuttā*).[232] Another noteworthy characteristic of paññattis is that they cannot be described either as conditioned (*saṅkhata*) or as unconditioned (*asaṅkhata*), for they do not possess their own nature (*sabhāva*) to be so described.[233] Since the two categories of the "conditioned" and the "unconditioned" comprise all realities, the exclusion of paññattis from these two categories is another way of underscoring their unreality.

What the foregoing observations amount to saying is that while a dhamma is a thing established by own nature (*sabhāva-siddha*), a paññatti is a thing merely conceptualized (*parikappa-siddha*). The former is an existent verifiable by its own distinctive intrinsic characteristic, but the latter, being a product of the mind's synthesizing function, exists only by virtue of conceptual thought.

In the Theravāda Abhidhamma we find two kinds of paññatti. One is called *nāma-paññatti*, concept-as-name, and the other *attha-paññatti*, concept-as-meaning. The first refers to names, words, signs, or symbols through which things, real or unreal, are designated. "Nāma-paññatti is the mere mode of recognizing (*saññākāra-matta*) by way of this or that word whose significance is determined by worldly convention."[234] It is created by worldly consent (*lokasaṅketa-nimmitā*) and established by worldly usage (*lokavohārena siddhā*).[235] The other, called *attha-paññatti*, refers to ideas, notions, or concepts corresponding to the names, words, signs, or symbols. It is produced by the interpretative and synthesizing function of the mind (*kappanā*) and is based on the various forms or appearances presented by the real existents when they are in particular situations or positions (*avatthā-visesa*).[236] Both *nāma-paññatti* and *attha-paññatti* thus have a psychological origin and, as such, both are devoid of objective reality.

Nāma-paññatti is often defined as "that which makes known" (*paññāpanato paññatti*) and *attha-paññatti* as "that which is made known" (*paññāpiyattā paññatti*).[237] The former is an instance of agency definition (*kattu-sādhana*) and the latter of object definition (*kamma-sādhana*). What both attempt to show is that *nāma-paññatti*, which makes *attha-paññatti* known, and *attha-paññatti*, which is made known by *nāma-paññatti*, are mutually interdependent and therefore logically inseparable. This explains the significance of another definition that states that *nāma-paññatti* is the term's relationship with the ideas (*saddassa atthehi sambandho*) and that *attha-paññatti* is the idea's relationship with the terms (*atthassa saddehi sambandho*).[238] These two pairs of definition show that the two processes of conceptualization and verbalization through the symbolic medium of language are but two separate aspects of the same phenomenon. It is for the convenience of definition that what really amounts to a single phenomenon is treated from two different angles, which represent two ways of looking at the same thing.

The difference is established by defining the same word, *paññatti*, in two different ways. When it is defined as subject, it is *nāma-paññatti*—the concept-as-name. When it is defined as object, it is *attha-paññatti*—the concept-as-meaning. If the former is that which expresses (*vācaka*), the latter is that which is expressed (*vacanīya*).[239] In the same sense, if the former is designation (*abhidhāna*), the latter is the designated (*abhidheya*).[240] The two kinds of paññatti thus condition each other like subject and object. Since *attha-paññatti* stands for the process of conceptualization, it represents more the subjective and dynamic aspect, and since *nāma-paññatti* stands for the process of verbalization, it represents more the objective and static aspect. For the assignment of a term to what is constructed in thought—in other words, its expression through the symbolic medium of language—invests it with some kind of relative permanence and objectivity. It is, so to say, crystalized into an entity.

According to its very definition, attha-paññatti exists by virtue of its being conceived (*parikappiyamāna*) and expressed (*paññāpiyamāna*). Hence it is incorrect to explain attha-paññatti as that which is conceptualizable and expressible, for its very existence stems from the act of being conceptualized and expressed. This rules out the possibility of its existing without being conceptualized and expressed.

As noted above, names (*nāma-paññatti*) can also be assigned to dhammas that constitute the category of the "real." However, what should not be overlooked is that names given to dhammas do not have corresponding attha-paññattis, concepts-as-meanings. The subcommentary to the

Visuddhimagga observes: "A dhamma having its own nature is profound (*gambhīra*), but a paññatti is not."[241] What this seems to mean is that objects of conceptual thought like tables and chairs are easily recognizable, whereas the dhammas are difficult to be grasped.

That names given to dhammas do not have corresponding attha-paññatti, concepts-as-meanings, is also shown by the identification of attha-paññatti (also called *upādā-paññatti*) with what is called *sammuti* or consensual reality.[242] Thus the denotation of attha-paññatti includes only the various objects of conceptual thought, which constitute the consensual reality (*sammuti*) and not the constituents of ultimate reality (*paramattha*). Accordingly, we can have the following sequence: attha-paññatti (meaning-concept) = upādā-paññatti (derivative concept) = sammuti (consensual reality).

It is, in fact, not by resorting to paññattis but by transcending them at the higher reaches of mind's unification that one should be able to go beyond the conceptual and establish one's own mind directly on the real (dhammas). This is what is called the transcendence of the conceptual level (*paññatti-samatikkamana*). The meditator should first go beyond such concepts as "earth element," "water element," and so on, and establish her mind directly on the individuating characteristics that correspond to them, such as solidity, viscidity, and so on. It is when one is continuing to focus one's uninterrupted attention on them that the individuating characteristics become more and more evident, more and more clear, and one's whole material body appears in its true form as a mere mass of elementary material constituents, all empty (*suñña*) and impersonal (*nissatta, nijjīva*).[243]

The logical conclusion that is thrust upon us by the Buddhist doctrine of *paññatti/prajñapti* is that all hypostatized entities and all objects of reification are nothing but conceptual constructions, or logical abstractions, or pure denominations with no corresponding objective realities. Only the dhammas are real. A dhamma, as noted earlier, is defined as that which has its own nature (*sabhāva, saka-bhāva*) or own characteristic (*sa-lakkhaṇa, saka-lakkhaṇa*). The characteristics common to all the dhammas are known as universal characteristics (*sāmañña-lakkhaṇa*).

Three of the best examples of universal characteristics are impermanence (*aniccatā*), suffering (*dukkhatā*), and selflessness (*anattātā*), which are known as the three signs (marks) of sentient existence (*tilakkhaṇa*). Although these three characteristics are fundamental to the Buddhist view of phenomenal existence, in the final analysis they too turn out to be conceptual constructions. As the *Abhidhamma Mūlaṭīkā* says, when we consider them as separate abstractions they too share the nature of conceptual constructs (*paññatti-gatika*) with no objective reality (*paramatthato avijjamāna*).[244] For in addition to, and distinct from, what is subject to impermanence, there is no separate independent entity called "impermanence." The same situation is true of the other two characteristics as well.

Even the principle of "dependent origination," which is set forth as the central conception of Buddhism, turns out to be a conceptual construction. Because in addition to, and distinct from, the dhammas that arise in dependence on other dhammas, there is no independently existing entity called "dependent origination." However, some Buddhist schools had a tendency to reverse this process. We learn from the *Kathāvatthu* that some Buddhists, the Pubbaseliyas and Mahīśāsakas according to the commentary, wanted to elevate the principle of dependent origination to the level of an unconditioned entity. In refuting this idea, the Pāli commentary observes: "Besides and in addition to such factors as ignorance there is no separate entity called 'dependent origination.'"[245]

We find a similar situation recorded in the *Kathāvatthu* in respect to the four noble truths as well.[246] Since the four truths are described in the early Buddhist discourses as *tathāni* (true, real) and *avitathāni* (not otherwise), some Buddhists, the Pubbaseliyas according to the commentary, argued that they are a set of unconditioned realities. Here a distinction is made between truth as concrete base (*vatthu-sacca*) and truth as characteristic (*lakkhaṇa-sacca*). The former refers, for example, to the actual experience of suffering. The latter refers to the abstract characteristic of suffering. While the former is conditioned (*vatthu-saccaṃ saṅkhataṃ*), the latter is unconditioned (*lakkhaṇa-saccaṃ asaṅkhataṃ*).[247] Here the Theravāda position is that the abstract characteristic of suffering has no objective existence distinct and separate from the actual experience of suffering.

We find another interesting attempt at reification attributed to a Buddhist school called the Uttarāpathakas. They held that "there is an immutable something called such-ness (or that-ness) in the very nature of all things, material or otherwise [taken as a whole]."[248] Since this suchness cannot be brought under any of the particular conditioned realities such as materiality, it is therefore reckoned to be unconditioned. Thus, distinct from matter, there is materiality of matter (*rūpassa rūpatā*). In the same way, there is feelingness of feeling (*vedanāya vedanatā*), perceptionness of perception (*saññāya saññātā*), and so on.[249]

In this regard, the Theravāda position is that all these hypostatized entities and attempts at reification are due to overstepping the bounds of paññatti (*paññattiṃ atidhāvitvā gaṇhanti*). Therefore they are to be understood as conceptual constructs, pure denominations with no objective counterparts.

Now let us examine the different kinds of attha-paññatti (= *upādā-paññatti*). In the *Abhidhammatthasaṅgaha* we find them arranged into six groups:

> There are [1] such terms as "land," "mountain," and the like, so designated on account of the mode of transition of the respective elements; [2] such terms as "house," "chariot," "cart," and the like, so named on account of the mode of formation of materials; [3] such terms as "person," "individual," and the like, so named on account of the five aggregates; [4] such terms as "direction," "time," and the like, so named according to the revolution of the moon and so forth; [5] such terms as "well," "cave," and the like, so named on account of the mode of non-impact and so forth; [6] such terms as *kasiṇa* signs and the like, so named on account of respective elements and distinguished mental development.[250]

The six kinds of paññatti mentioned here are concepts of continuity (*santāna-paññatti*), collective concepts (*samūha-paññatti*), local concepts (*disā-paññatti*), temporal concepts (*kāla-paññatti*), and sign concepts (*nimitta-paññatti*). What follows is Lama Anagarika Govinda's arrangement of the six kinds:

1. Inorganic material forms, based on physical laws of nature—e.g., "land," "mountain."
2. Organized material forms, based on constructive intelligence—e.g., "house," "chariot."
3. Organic forms, based on the five psychophysical aggregates (*pañcakkhandha*)—e.g., "man," "individual."
4. Immaterial forms of locality (*disā*) and time (*kāla*), based on the revolutions of celestial bodies (like the moon).
5. Immaterial forms of spatial quality (*asamphuṭṭhākāra*, lit. "noncontact")—e.g., "pit," "cave."
6. Immaterial forms of visualization, based on spiritual exercises (*bhāvanā*, meditation)—e.g., the after-image (*paṭibhāga-nimitta*) of hypnotic circles (*kasiṇa*).[251]

All instances of attha-paññatti can also be brought under two main headings—namely, collective concepts (*samūha-paññatti*) and noncollective concepts (*asamūha-paññatti*). A collective concept is due to grasping a group as one (*samūhekattagahaṇa*)—that is, imposing unity on diversity, grasping manyness as oneness. The best example of such grasping is the wrong belief in a living being as a self-entity (*satta-sammosa*).[252] The correct position is that "distinct from the group" (*samūha-vinimmutta*), there is no living being as a self-entity.[253] It is by the resolution of the compact (*ghana-vinibbhoga*) that the true position becomes evident.[254] Two examples of noncollective concepts are "time" and "space."

Besides the six main kinds of attha-paññatti mentioned above, the Abhidhamma commentaries and compendiums refer to many other kinds. The *Puggalapaññatti Aṭṭhakathā* is the most informative. It mentions several classifications of paññattis. Some of them are from the canonical texts (*pāḷi*), some are according to the methods of the commentaries (*aṭṭhakathā-nayena*), and others are from neither the canonical texts nor the commentaries but according to the methods of celebrated exegetes. What follows is a brief description of each of them.

Apositional Concept (*Upanidhā Paññatti*)

This refers to ideas based on mutual reference (*aññam aññam upanidhā*) or juxtaposition (*sannivesa*). Many varieties are listed, namely: (1) Apposition of reference—for example, "second" as against "first," "third" as against "second," or "long" as against "short" and vice versa. "It is with reference to what is short that 'long' is so called as being higher (*uccatara*) than that; 'short' is so called as being lower (*nīcatara*) than long; and a thing smaller than that is 'little,' with reference to which a greater thing is 'big.'" (2) Apposition of what is in hand—for example, *Chattapāṇi*, one who carries an umbrella in his hand; *Satthapāṇi*, one who carries a knife in his hand. (3) Apposition of association—for example, earring wearer, topknot wearer, crest wearer. (4) Apposition of contents—for example, corn wagon, ghee pot. (5) Apposition of proximity—for example, Indasāla Cave, Piyaṅgu Cave. (6) Apposition of comparison—for example, golden-colored person, a person with a bull's gait. (7) Apposition of majority—for example, lotus pond, so called because of the preponderance of lotuses; Brāhmaṇa village, so called because of the majority of Brahmins. (8) Apposition of distinction—for example, jewel ring, diamond ring.[255]

Concept of Nonexistence (*Abhāva-Paññatti*)

That abhāva or "nonexistence" has no objective reality corresponding to it may appear too obvious a thing to be recognized by a separate paññatti. However, it assumes much significance when it is remembered that the substantialist schools of Indian philosophy, particularly the Vaiśeṣikas, consider it as an independent category (*padārtha*). For the Buddhists abhāva is not a real entity but a mere notion dependent on *bhāva* (existence) (*abhāvo bhāvaṃ nissāya pavattati*).[256] What is abhāva (nonexistence) has no sabhāva (own nature).[257] From the Buddhist perspective, one could argue that if abhāva is an independent category, then it should in turn have another abhāva, and thus this would lead to what many Buddhist schools refer to as *anavaṭṭhā/anavasthā*, the fallacy of infinite regress.[258]

Concepts Established through Adherence to Wrong Views (*Abhinivesa-Paññatti*)

This particular paññatti seems to have been mentioned only in the *Paramatthavinicchaya*.[259] It embraces all substantial entities and categories postulated in non-Buddhist schools, as for example soul, self (*atta*), primordial nature (*pakati*), and so on.[260] It is called "adherence concept" because some dogmatically adhere to the wrong view that these entities and categories exist, although they do not really exist (*abhāve'pi pavattite*).[261] It is further observed that if others believe in things that do not really exist, it is because they overstep the bounds of paññatti and believe that they exist in an ultimate sense (*paññattim atidhāvitvā gaṇhanti paramatthato*).[262] The *Siṃhala Sanne* to the *Abhidhammatthasaṅgaha* observes:

> What we call continuity concept (*santāna-paññatti*) corresponds to what others postulate as substance in which quality inheres (*guṇī-dravya*). In like manner, collective concept (*samūha-paññatti*) corresponds to what others postulate as union or association (*saṃyoga*), limb or part (*avayava*), body or whole (*avayavī*). Concept of direction (*disā-paññatti*) and concept of time (*kāla-paññatti*) correspond to their direction substance (*diśā-dravya*) and time substance (*kāla-dravya*). What others consider as space substance (*ākāśa-dravya*) is what we call concept of space (*ākāsa-paññatti*).[263]

As to nāma-paññatti, there are six kinds. They are distinguished on the basis whether the term in question represents: (a) something that exists, (b) something that does not exist, (b + a) something that does not exist by something else that exists, (a + b) something that exists by something else that does not exist, (a + a) something that exists by something else that exists, or (b + b) something that does not exist by something else that, likewise, does not exist.[264] What follows is an explanation of the six kinds:

a. *Vijjamāna-paññatti* is a term that represents something that exists, where "exists" is understood in a real and ultimate sense (*saccikaṭṭha-paramaṭṭhena*). It is also called *tajjā-paññatti* or "verisimilar concept" because it refers to names and designations given to real existents (= dhammas), such as *vedanā* (feeling) and *paṭhavī-dhātu* (earth element).[265] It is also called *sabhāva-paññatti* because it designates dhammas that have their own nature. Although the real existents (dhammas) can be given names and designations (= *nāma-paññatti*), their existence does not depend on their being named and designated. Since they have their own nature (*sabhāva*), they exist independently of conceptual ascription.

b. *Avijjamāna-paññatti* represents something that does not exist in a real and ultimate sense. This is in direct opposition to the first, for it represents not things having their own nature (*sabhāva*) but things dependent on the interpretative and synthesizing function of the mind (*kappanā-siddha*). To this category belong such terms as "person" and "living being," when understood as self-entities, and "table," "sun," "moon," and so forth; in other words, all instances of consensual reality (*sammuti*). In this category are also included such terms as primordial nature (*pakati/prakṛti*), cosmic soul (Brahman), and the like, which from the Buddhist perspective do not exist.[266]

c. *Vijjamānena-avijjamāna-paññatti* is a term that represents a nonexistent on the basis of another term that represents an existent. An example is *tevijja*, "possessor of the three higher levels of knowledge." Only the higher levels of knowledge exist in a real sense, but there is no self-entity behind them. To the same category belongs *chaḷabhiñña*, "one with the six kinds of direct knowledge."[267]

d. *Avijjamānena-vijjamāna-paññatti* is a term given to a real existent on the basis of a term expressive of a nonexistent. An example given is *itthi-sadda*, "woman's voice." Here the sound of the voice is ultimately real, but not the woman as a self-entity.[268]

e. *Vijjamānena-vijjamāna-paññatti* is a term given to a real existent on the basis of another term, which also represents a real existent. An example given is *cakkhu-samphassa*, "eye contact." Here *cakkhu*, the eye, represents one of the dependent material dhammas, and *samphassa*, contact, one of the mental factors (*cetasika*)—both of which are recognized as real existents.[269]

f. *Avijjamānena-avijjamāna-paññatti* is a term that signifies a nonexistent on the basis of another term that also signifies a nonexistent—for example, *khattiya-putta*, "warrior's son." Here since both terms refer to persons as self-entities, both are expressive of nonexistent entities.[270]

3

THE TWO TRUTHS

If the doctrine of *dhammas* led to its ancillary theory of *paññatti* as discussed above, both in turn led to another development—that is, the distinction drawn between two kinds of truth as *sammuti-sacca* (conventional truth) and *paramattha-sacca* (ultimate truth). Although this distinction is an Abhidhammic innovation it is not completely dissociated from the early Buddhist teachings. For the antecedent trends that led to its formulation can be traced to the early Buddhist scriptures themselves.

One such instance is the distinction drawn in the *Aṅguttaranikāya* between *nītattha* and *neyyattha*. The former refers to those statements that have their meaning "drawn out" (*nīta-attha*)—that is, to be taken as they stand, as explicit and definitive statements. The latter refers to those statements that require their meaning "to be drawn out" (*neyya-attha*).[271] The distinction alluded to here may be understood in a broad way to mean the difference between the direct and the indirect meaning. The distinction is so important that to overlook it is to misrepresent the teachings of the Buddha: "Whoever declares a discourse with a meaning already drawn out as a discourse with a meaning to be drawn out and [conversely] whoever declares a discourse with a meaning to be drawn out as a discourse with a meaning already drawn out, such a one makes a false statement with regard to the Blessed One."[272]

What is most important to remember here is that this sutta passage makes no preferential value judgment in respect to the two statements. One statement is not singled out as higher or lower than the other.

It seems very likely that this distinction between *nītattha* and *neyyattha* has provided a base for the emergence of the subsequent doctrine of double truth, not only in Theravāda but also in other Buddhist schools. In fact, the commentary to the *Aṅguttaranikāya* seeks to establish a correspondence between the original sutta passage and the Theravāda version of the two truths.[273] It must also be noted that in the schools of Sanskrit Buddhism *nītārtha/nītattha* is evaluated as higher than *neyārtha/neyyattha*. As F. Edgerton observes, in Buddhist hybrid Sanskrit literature, "a *nītārtha* text . . . is recommended as a guide in preference to one that is *neyārtha*." As he further observes, "In Pāli neither is *ipso facto* preferred to the other; one errs only in interpreting one as if it were the other."[274]

Another important link between the Abhidhamma theory of double truth and early Buddhism is found in the *Saṅgīti Sutta* of the *Dīghanikāya*, where four kinds of knowledge are mentioned: (1) the direct knowledge of the doctrine (*dhamme ñāṇa*), (2) the inductive knowledge of the doctrine (*anvaye ñāṇa*), (3) knowledge of analysis (*paricchede ñāṇa*), and (4) knowledge of (linguistic) conventions (*sammuti-ñāṇa*).[275] That there is a close parallelism between the latter pair of knowledge referred to here and the Theravāda theory of the two truths as ultimate (*paramattha*) and conventional (*sammuti*) is fairly obvious. For what is called *paramattha* is obtained by analyzing what is amenable to analysis (*pariccheda*). So knowledge of analysis (*paricchede ñāṇa*) could be understood to mean the ability to resolve what appears as substantial and compact into its basic constituents. This exactly is what the dhamma theory is. On the other hand, *sammuti-ñāṇa*, which is the knowledge of linguistic conventions, could be understood to mean the ability to know that what appears as substantial and compact, yet analyzable, is not ultimately real and therefore that it is a part of consensual reality (*sammuti*). As we shall see in the sequel, this exactly is what *sammuti* is all about. Thus what the sutta passage refers to as the third and fourth kinds of knowledge anticipates not only the dhamma theory but also the theory of double truth, which is a logical extension of the dhamma theory.

One interesting feature in the Theravāda version of the theory is the use of the term *sammuti* for relative truth. For in all other schools of Buddhist thought, the term used is *saṃvṛti*. The difference between *sammuti* and *saṃvṛti* is not simply that between Pāli and Sanskrit, for the two terms differ both in etymology and meaning. The term *sammuti* is derived from the root *man*, to think, and when prefixed with *sam* it means consent, convention, or general agreement. On the other hand, the term *saṃvṛti* is derived from the root *vṛ*, to cover, and when prefixed with *sam* it means covering, concealment. This difference is not confined to the vocabulary of the theory of double truth alone. That elsewhere, too, Sanskrit *saṃvṛti* corresponds to Pāli *sammuti* gets confirmed by other textual instances.[276] Since *sammuti* refers to convention or general agreement, *sammuti-sacca* means truth based on convention or general agreement. On the other hand, the idea behind *saṃvṛti-satya* is that which covers up the true nature of things and makes them appear otherwise.

In introducing the double truth, a number of Pāli commentaries cite two stanzas. According to the first, the Buddha himself proclaimed two kinds of truth as conventional and ultimate, and a third does not exist.[277] This emphasis on two kinds of truth to the exclusion of a third reminds us of the Yogācāra school of Buddhism, which advocates a theory of triple truth. It also reminds us of a verse occurring in the *Pitāputrasamāgama Sūtra*, stressing the fact that besides the relative (*saṃvṛti*) and the absolute (*paramārtha*), a third truth is not to be found.[278]

The second stanza sets out the validity of the two kinds of statement corresponding to *sammuti* and *paramattha* as follows:

> Statements referring to convention-based things (*saṅketa*) are valid because they are based on common agreement; statements referring to ultimate categories (*paramattha*) are valid because they are based on the true nature of the real existents.[279]

As shown here, the distinction between the two truths depends on the distinction between *saṅketa* and *paramattha*. Now, *saṅketa* includes things that depend for their being on mental interpretations superimposed on the category of the real. For instance, the validity of the term "table" is based not on an objective existent corresponding to the term but on mental interpretation superimposed on a congeries of material dhammas organized in a particular manner. Although a table is not a separate reality distinct from the material dhammas that enter into its composition, nevertheless the table is said to exist because in common parlance it is accepted as a separate reality. On the other hand, the term *paramattha* denotes the category of real existents (dhammas) that have their own objective nature (sabhāva). Their difference may be stated as follows: When a particular situation is explained on the basis of terms indicative of the real existents (dhammas), that explanation is *paramattha-sacca*. When the selfsame situation is explained on the basis of terms indicative of things that have their being dependent on the mind's synthesizing function, that explanation is *sammuti-sacca*. The validity of the former is based on its correspondence to the ultimate data of empirical reality. The validity of the latter is based on its correspondence to things established by conventions.

In the Sarvāstivāda Abhidharma the difference between *saṃvṛti* (relative) and *paramārtha* (ultimate) is explained in a similar manner. It is sought to be based on the principle of physical reducibility and mental analyzability. Thus in the *Abhidharmakośabhāṣya* we read that if the notion of a thing disappears (*na pravartate*) when it is physically reduced into pieces, then that particular thing exists relatively (*saṃvṛti-sat*). The idea of a pitcher, for instance, disappears when it is reduced to pieces. Again, if the notion of a thing disappears when it is analyzed by mind, then that particular thing, too, is to be regarded as existing relatively. Water, for example—if the material dharmas such as color, which constitute what is called water, are separated mentally from one another, then the notion of "water" disappears. It is to be understood therefore that such things as pitcher, cloth, water, fire, and so on, are called so according to conventional practice and from the point of view of relative truth. Hence from the point of view of relative truth, if one says, "There is a pitcher," "There is water," one speaks truthfully and not wrongly.[280]

The *Abhidharmakośa-vyākhyā* observes that the two examples given here refer to two kinds of reducibility (*bheda*): the pitchers, and so on, can be broken by means of a physical apparatus (*upakrama*), whereas water, and so on, can be analyzed by mind (*buddhi*). Stated otherwise, what exists relatively is of two kinds: (a) that which exists on the basis of another that is also relative (*saṃvṛtyantara-vyapaśraya*), and (b) that which exists on the basis of something that is real (*dravyāntara-vyapaśraya*). In the case of the former, it is physically breakable and mentally analyzable. Both possibilities can be there at one and the same time. A pitcher, for example. It can not only be reduced to pieces by another physical object but can also be analyzed by mind into its constituent atoms and elements. In the case of the atoms, they can be analyzed only by mind. An aggregate atom (*saṃghāta-paramāṇu*), for example, can be analyzed only by mind into its constituent unitary atoms (*dravya-paramāṇu*), and not physically.[281]

In the opinion of Bhadanta Śrīlāta, a celebrity of the Sautrāntika school, the difference between the two truths consists in this: that which exists in a number of objects (*dravya*) is *saṃvṛti*; that which exists in a single object is *paramārtha*. In other words, if the thing in question loses its original name when it is analyzed, it is *saṃvṛti*; if it does not, it is *paramārtha*.[282] Although this explanation appears to be different from the ones we have already discussed, here too analyzability is taken as the criterion in distinguishing the two kinds of truth.

One important question that concerns the two truths is the status of one truth in relation to the other. Are the two truths coordinate? Or is one truth higher than the other in the sense that it is more valid? Obviously the use of the term *paramattha/paramārtha*, which means the ultimate, absolute, or the highest, to describe one truth seems to show that what is so described represents a higher level of truth. This in fact seems to be the position taken up by almost all Buddhist schools. But not so with Theravāda. As pointed out by K. N. Jayatilleke in his *Early Buddhist Theory of Knowledge*, one misconception about the Theravāda version of double truth is that *paramattha-sacca* is superior to *sammuti-sacca* and that "what is true in the one sense, is false in the other."[283] This observation that the distinction in question is not based on a theory of degrees of truth will become clear from the following free translation of the relevant passages contained in three Pāli commentaries:

> Herein references to living beings, gods, Brahma, and so on, are *sammuti-kathā*, whereas references to impermanence, suffering, egolessness, the aggregates of the empiric individuality, the bases and elements of sense perception and mind cognition, bases of

> mindfulness, right effort, and so on, are *paramattha-kathā*. One who is capable of understanding and penetrating to the truth and hoisting the flag of arahantship when the teaching is set out in terms of generally accepted conventions, to him the Buddha preaches the doctrine based on *sammuti-kathā*. One who is capable of understanding and penetrating to the truth and hoisting the flag of arahantship when the teaching is set out in terms of ultimate categories, to him the Buddha preaches the doctrine based on *paramattha-kathā*. To one who is capable of awakening to the truth through *sammuti-kathā*, the teaching is not presented on the basis of *paramattha-kathā*, and, conversely, to one who is capable of awakening to the truth through *paramattha-kathā*, the teaching is not presented on the basis of *sammuti-kathā*.
>
> There is this simile: Just as a teacher of the three Vedas who is capable of explaining their meaning in different dialects might teach his pupils by adopting the particular dialect which each pupil understands, even so the Buddha preaches the doctrine adopting, according to the suitability of the occasion, either the *sammuti-* or the *paramattha-kathā*. It is by taking into consideration the ability of each individual to understand the four noble truths that the Buddha presents his teaching either by way of *sammuti* or by way of *paramattha* or by way of both (*vomissaka-vasena*). Whatever the method adopted, the purpose is the same: to show the way to immortality through the analysis of mental and physical phenomena.[284]

As seen from the above quotation, the penetration of the truth is possible by either teaching, the conventional or the ultimate, or by the combination of both. One method is not singled out as superior or inferior to the other. It is like using the dialect that a person readily understands, and there is no implication that one dialect is either superior or inferior to another. What is more, as the commentary to the *Aṅguttaranikāya* states specifically, whether the Buddhas preach the doctrine according to *sammuti* or *paramattha*, they teach only what is true, only what accords with actuality, without involving themselves in what is not true (*amusā'va*).[285]

The statement "the person exists" (= *sammuti-sacca*) is not erroneous, provided one does not imagine by the term "person" a substance enduring in time. Convention requires the use of such terms, but as long as one does not imagine substantial entities corresponding to them, such statements are valid. On the other hand, as the commentators observe, if for the sake of conforming to the ultimate truth one would say, "The five aggregates eat" (*khandhā bhuñjanti*), "The five aggregates walk" (*khandhā gacchanti*), instead of saying, "A person eats," "A person walks," such a situation would result in what is called *vohārabheda*—that is, a breach of convention resulting in a breakdown in meaningful communication.[286]

Hence in presenting the teaching, the Buddha does not exceed linguistic conventions (*na hi Bhagavā samaññam atidhāvati*)[287] but uses such terms as "person" without being led astray by their superficial implications (*aparāmasaṃ voharati*).[288] Because the Buddha is able to employ such linguistic designations as "person" and "individual" without assuming corresponding substantial entities, he is called "skilled in expression" (*vohāra-kusala*).[289] The use of such terms does not in any way involve falsehood (*musāvādo na jāyati*).[290] As one commentary says: "Whether the buddhas speak according to conventional truth or whether the buddhas speak according to absolute truth, they speak only what is true and only what is actual."[291] Skillfulness in the use of words is the ability to conform to conventions (*sammuti*), usages (*vohāra*), designations (*paññatti*), and turns of speech (*nirutti*) in common use in the world without being led astray by them.[292] Hence in understanding the teaching of the Buddha, one is advised not to adhere dogmatically to the mere superficial meanings of words (*na vacanabhedamattam ālambitabbaṃ*).[293]

The foregoing observations should show that according to the Theravāda version of double truth, one kind of truth is not held to be superior or inferior to the other. In this connection, one important question arises. If no preferential evaluation is made in respect to the two truths, what is the justification for calling one the absolute or ultimate truth and the other the conventional truth? Here what should not be overlooked is that if one truth is called absolute or ultimate it is because this particular kind of truth has for its vocabulary the technical terms used to express what is ultimate—that is, the dhammas into which the world of experience is ultimately resolved. Strictly speaking, the expression *paramattha* (absolute/ultimate) does not refer to the truth as such, but to the technical terms through which it is expressed. Thus *paramattha-sacca* really means the truth expressed by using the technical terms expressive of the ultimate factors of existence. In like manner, *sammuti-sacca* or conventional truth means the truth expressed by using conventional or transactional terms in common parlance.

Another thing that needs mention here is the obvious fact that sammuti is not the same as sammuti-sacca. So is the relationship between paramattha and paramattha-sacca. Sammuti is that which is based on general agreement or common consent—for example, "table," "chair," "sun," "moon," "living being *in the sense of a self-entity*." All these exist by way of being designated by words (*nāma-paññatti*). In other words, all forms of sammuti or what is consensually real are different kinds of attha-paññatti (meaning-concepts).[294] They are all objects of conceptual thought. On the other hand, paramattha means that which is ultimate, that which is not further resolvable or divisible. The reference is to the dhammas, the ultimate data of existence. Accordingly, sammuti and paramattha are not on par.

On the other hand, sammuti-sacca and paramattha-sacca are on par. For as two ways of explaining what is true, they are of equal status. One is not superior or inferior to the other. No preferential value judgment is introduced here.

The position taken up by the Theravādins as to the relative position of the two truths is very faithful to the distinction drawn in the *Aṅguttaranikāya* between two ways of presenting the Dhamma—that is, the distinction drawn between nītattha and neyyattha, to which we have already drawn attention. For, as we saw earlier, no preferential evaluation is made in respect to them. One statement is not considered higher or lower than the other. All that is emphasized is that they should not be confused. This precisely is the situation with the Theravāda version of double truth as well.

In fact, the *Abhidhammāvatāra* says that if one were to understand the true implications of the two truths, one should not make a confusion between the two (*asaṅkarato ñātabbāni*).[295] What this really means is that we should not interpret one truth as if it were the other. They are two different but parallel contexts.

This situation also reminds us of the particular context in which the four noble truths should be understood. Although the four noble truths represent four different facts, no preferential evaluation is introduced in respect to them. As four statements or propositions, they are all coordinate. One particular truth is not held out as superior or inferior to another. That is precisely why they are all introduced as noble truths (*ariya-saccāni*). All are equally noble (*ariya*) and all are equally true (*sacca*). But this does not mean that suffering (*dukkha*) and cessation of suffering (*dukkha-nirodha*) in themselves are of equal status. It is only as two propositions or as two statements of truth that they are coordinate.

Thus there is one important feature common to the four noble truths, the distinction between nītattha and neyyattha, and the Theravāda version of double truth. It is that in none of them do we find a hierarchical presentation. This situation is very much in consonance with how early Buddhism presents various modes of analysis: The factors obtained through analysis, such as the five aggregates, the twelve sense bases, and the eighteen elements of cognition, are never presented in such a way as to show that one factor is higher or lower than another. They are always presented not one above another or one below another but one besides another in order to show that they are parallel factors. What is salutary about this method is that it prevents the intrusion of the distinction between substance and quality, a distinction that paves the way for the intrusion of the notion of a "substantial self" (*attavāda*) with all that it entails.

On the other hand, to the best of our knowledge, in all other schools of Buddhist thought belonging to the two main traditions, the absolute truth (*paramārtha-satya*) is considered superior to relative truth (*saṃvṛti-satya*). This becomes all the more obvious by the use of the term *saṃvṛti* to express the conventional or relative truth. Saṃvṛti means that which covers, hides, or conceals the true nature of reality. If saṃvṛti means that which conceals, it is clearly implied that paramārtha means that which reveals the true nature of reality. Thus the very use of the term *saṃvṛti* to express one of the truths shows that particular truth is less truthful and therefore inferior to what is called *paramārtha-satya*, the absolute truth.

Another interesting conclusion to which the foregoing observations lead us is that as far as the Theravāda is concerned, the distinction between sammuti-sacca and paramattha-sacca does not refer to two kinds of truth as such but to two ways of presenting what accords with actuality. They are in fact two ways of understanding the same thing. Although they are formally introduced as two truths, they are explained as two modes of expressing what is true. They do not represent two degrees of truth of which one is superior or inferior to the other. This explains why the two terms *kathā* (speech) and *desanā* (discourse) are sometimes used when referring to the two kinds of truth.[296] The great advantage in presenting sammuti- and paramattha-sacca in this way is that it does not raise the problem of reconciling the concept of a plurality of truths with the well-known statement in the *Suttanipāta*: "Truth is indeed one, there is no second" (*ekaṃ hi saccaṃ na dutīyam atthi*).[297] What this seems to mean is shown in the *Bodhisattvabhūmi* when it says that "truth is one in the sense of being non-contradictory" (*avitathārthena tāvad ekam eva satyaṃ na dvitīyam*).[298]

The Theravāda version of double truth also provides us with a clear clue as to how we should understand the statement in the Pāli commentaries that the teachings in the Sutta Piṭaka and the Abhidhamma Piṭaka correspond respectively to conventional teaching (*vohāra-desanā*) and absolute teaching (*paramattha-desanā*). The Sutta Piṭaka is said to contain teachings mostly based on conventional terms (*vohāra-desanā*), because therein the Blessed One, who is skilful in the use of conventions, has taught the doctrines with a preponderance of conventional terms. In contrast, the Abhidhamma Piṭaka is said to contain teachings mostly based on paramattha-desanā because therein the Blessed One, who is skilful in the use of absolute terms, has taught the doctrine with a preponderance of absolute terms.[299]

This does not mean, as some are inclined to think, that the teachings in the Abhidhamma Piṭaka represent a higher set of doctrines. The distinction drawn should be understood in the same way as that between the two kinds of truth. Understood in that way, it does not in any way refer to two kinds of doctrines of which one kind is higher than the other. All that it does is to bring into focus two different ways of presenting the same set of doctrines. In the Sutta Piṭaka more use is made of conventional and transactional terms in ordinary parlance, whereas in the Abhidhamma Piṭaka more use is made of specific, technical terms that directly refer to the ultimate categories of empirical existence. It is a question pertaining to methodology and not a question pertaining to content.

Another distinction drawn in presenting the Dhamma is that between *pariyāya-desanā* and *nippariyāya-desanā*. The first refers to the discursively applied method or illustrated discourse employing stories, similes, metaphors, and other figures of speech, which we find in the Suttas (*suttanta-bhājanīya*). The other refers to the presentation of the Dhamma in a precise, technical, and impersonal terminology, which we find in the Abhidhamma (*abhidhamma-bhājanīya*). In the *Milindapañha* we find a string of synonyms for the *nippariyāya* method: *sabhāva-vacana* (words expressive of own nature of dhammas), *asesa-vacana* or *nissesa-vacana* (words expressive of that which is all-inclusive), *bhūta-vacana* (words expressive of what is actual), *taccha-vacana* (words expressive of what is true), *yāthāva-vacana* (words expressive of what is exact), and *aviparīta-vacana* (words expressive of that which is not distorted).[300]

As noted above, sammuti refers to what is conventional, and paramattha to what is ultimate. However, what should not be overlooked here is that not only sammuti but also paramattha, when they serve as two kinds of truth, have to be communicated through a common medium—namely, nāma-paññatti or name concepts. This is the significance of the commentarial statement: "It is without going beyond (the parameters) of paññatti that the ultimately real is presented" (*paññattim anatikkamma paramattho pakāsito*).[301] This means that both truths are subsumed under paññatti, the category of the nominal and the conceptual.

4

THE ANALYSIS OF MIND

IT WAS THE EARLY Buddhist teaching on the nature of mind that determined the scope, methods, and orientation of the psychology that we find in the Abhidhamma. Therefore it is necessary to begin this chapter with a brief introduction to the basic principles of the early Buddhist analysis of mind.

Early Buddhism recognizes three basic psychological principles. The first is the dependent arising of consciousness, expressed in the well-known saying: "Apart from conditions, there is no arising of consciousness."[302] Consciousness is not some kind of potentiality residing in the heart and becoming actualized on different occasions. Nor is it a static entity that runs along and wanders without undergoing any change, a kind of permanent soul entity that transmigrates from birth to birth.[303] Consciousness always springs up in dependence on a duality. "What is that duality? It is (in the case of eye consciousness, for example) eye, the visual organ, which is impermanent, changing, and becoming other and visible objects, which are impermanent, changing, and becoming other. Such is the transient, fugitive duality (of eye-cum-visible objects), which is impermanent, changing, and becoming other. Eye consciousness, too, is impermanent. For how could eye consciousness, arisen by depending on impermanent conditions, be permanent?"[304] The coincidence (*saṅgati*), concurrence (*sannipāta*), and confluence (*samavāya*) of these three factors, which is called sensory contact, and those other mental phenomena arising in consequence are also impermanent.[305] Just as the friction of two sticks produces fire, even so consciousness springs up from the interaction of sense organs and sense objects. Depending on whether it springs up in respect to the eye, or the ear, or any other sense organ, it is named accordingly.[306]

The second basic principle of early Buddhist psychology is that consciousness does not exist as an isolated phenomenon. It always exists in conjunction with the other four aggregates into which the empiric individuality is analyzed. Hence the Buddha says: "Bhikkhus, though someone might say: 'apart from corporeality, apart from feeling, apart from perception, apart from volitional formations, I will make known the coming and going of consciousness, its passing away and rebirth, its growth, increase, and expansion,' that is impossible."[307] Thus consciousness cannot be separated from the other four aggregates. However, it can be distinguished from the other four aggregates, and it is this circumstance that makes it definable and describable.

The third basic principle of early Buddhist psychology is the mutual dependence of consciousness and nāma-rūpa.[308] *Nāma* is a collective name for five mental factors—namely, feeling (*vedanā*), perception (*saññā*), volition (*cetanā*), sense impression (*phassa*), and mental advertence (*manasikāra*).[309] These are the basic mental factors that necessarily arise together with any kind of consciousness. For as that which constitutes the knowing or awareness of an object, consciousness cannot arise in its solitary condition. It must be accompanied at least by five mental factors known as *nāma*. *Rūpa* means the four great elements of matter (*mahābhūta*) and the materiality that is dependent on them (*upādārūpa*).[310] It refers to the organic matter that enters into the composition of a living being. The reciprocal dependence of consciousness and nāma-rūpa means that just as much as consciousness cannot exist without nāma-rūpa, even so nāma-rūpa cannot exist without consciousness. Since *rūpa* in nāma-rūpa means the material components of a living being, the reciprocal dependence of consciousness and nāma-rūpa shows how Buddhism understands the nature of the mind-body relationship.

Buddhism avoids the dualistic theory that maintains that mind and matter are strictly separate entities. It also avoids the monistic theory that maintains that mind and matter are finally reducible to one, either to mind (idealism) or to matter (materialism). Setting itself equally aloof from these two positions, Buddhism explains the mind-body relationship as one of reciprocal dependence.

The three psychological principles that we have discussed so far combine to dispense with the notion of a mental substance. There is no thing-in-itself beneath or behind the mental phenomena into which the mental continuum is analyzed. Consciousness is in no way a self or an extension of a self-substance:

> It would be better, bhikkhus, for the uninstructed worldling to take as self this body composed of the four great elements rather than the mind. For what reason? Because this body composed of the four great elements is seen standing for one year, for two years, for three, four, five, or ten years, for twenty, thirty, forty, or fifty years, for a hundred years, or even longer. But that which is called "mind" and "mentality" and "consciousness" arises as one thing and ceases as another by day and by night. Just as a monkey roaming through a forest grabs hold of one branch, lets that go and grabs another, then lets that go and grabs still another, so too that which is called "mind" and "mentality" and "consciousness" arises as one thing and ceases as another by day and by night.[311]

It was this radically dynamic nature of early Buddhist psychology that gave direction to its Abhidhamma version. The Abhidhamma psychology begins by analyzing the apparently continuous stream of consciousness into a number of cognitive acts. Each cognitive act is, in turn, analyzed into two component parts. One is bare consciousness, called *citta*, and the other a constellation of mental factors, called *cetasikas*. The conception of a cognitive act in this manner can be traced to the early Buddhist analysis of the individual being into five aggregates. Among them the four mental aggregates are always inseparably conjoined.[312] While citta corresponds to the aggregate of consciousness (*viññāṇakkhandha*), the cetasikas represent the other three mental aggregates. Citta as the knowing or awareness of an object is generally counted as one, while cetasikas, which function as concomitants of citta, are fifty-two in number.

Their position in relation to the well-known twelve *āyatana*s and eighteen *dhātus* is as follows: While *citta* corresponds to *manāyatana*, the *cetasikas* come under *dhammāyatana*, the sphere of mental objects. This shows that cetasikas are directly apprehended by citta without the intermediate agency of any of the physical senses. Since *manāyatana* is internal (*ajjhattika*) and *dhammāyatana* external (*bāhira*), this shows, as Th. Stcherbatsky observes, that the principle of externality of one element in relation to another is recognized in the mental sphere as well.[313] For in the āyatana division, while citta (*manāyatana*) becomes the subjective part, the cetasikas are placed in the objective part (*dhammāyatana*). This distinction, it may be noted here, does not correspond to the modern distinction between the subjective and the objective. This is, perhaps, traceable to the Buddhist denial of a self-entity as the agent of experience.

In the dhātu analysis citta is represented by seven items—namely, mind (*mano*) and the six kinds of consciousness based on the five physical sense organs and the mind. Among the seven items, the first is the mental organ as bare consciousness. The next five refer to this same mind (*mano*) when based on the five physical sense organs—namely, eye consciousness, ear consciousness, nose consciousness, tongue consciousness, and body consciousness. The sixth is mind consciousness—that is, consciousness having nonsensuous objects. This shows that mind (*mano-dhātu*) in its capacity as a cognitive faculty performs two functions. The first is its function as that which cognizes nonsensuous objects—that is, as the sense organ sensitive to ideas. The second is its function as the *sensus communus*—that is, as that which organizes and integrates the individual experiences of the physical sense organs. We find this twofold function recognized in the earlier scriptures as well, when they say that while each separate sense is active in its own sphere the mind is the resort of them all.[314]

However, on the definition of mano-dhātu there is no unanimity between Theravāda and Sarvāstivāda, the two major schools of Abhidharma. The Sarvāstivāda position is that mano-dhātu is not a separate entity, distinct from the six kinds of consciousness. It is the name given to the consciousness that has ceased immediately before the emergence of the next.[315] In this sense *mano-dhātu* is the *āśraya*, the *point d'appui* of the consciousness that immediately follows it. In view of this causal function, it receives the name mind (*manas*), mind element (*mano dhātu*), and mind faculty (*manendriya*). It is only as an explanatory device that it is counted as a separate entity.[316] The Theravāda too says that the immediately preceding consciousness is a condition for the immediately succeeding one. However, because of this circumstance the preceding consciousness is not defined as mano dhātu. For the Theravāda, mano dhātu is distinct from the six kinds of consciousness.

As noted above, although the cetasikas are external to citta, their relationship is one of inseparable association and invariable concomitance. Citta as bare consciousness can never come into being as a solitary phenomenon in its true separate condition. It necessarily arises together with cetasikas. Nor can the cetasikas arise unless in conjunction with the arising of citta. Sometimes we read, "the citta has arisen," with no mention of the cetasikas. It is like saying the king has arrived, for he does not come alone without his attendants but comes attended by his retinue. Even so citta always appears together with a set of cetasikas. There is, however, this difference to be noted. Whenever citta arises with some cetasikas, there are other cetasikas that do not arise together with it at the same time. This means that while citta can arise leaving aside some cetasikas, no cetasika can arise without the citta. Hence the cetasikas are described as "occurring by leaning on the citta" (*cittāyattavutti*).[317] It is, in fact, citta that coordinates the cetasikas and thus functions by way of dominance (*adhipatibhāvena*).[318]

The distinction between citta and cetasikas as separate psychic events is said to be very subtle. Just as it is not possible—so runs the illustration—to separate off the different flavors in a syrup or soup and say here is the sourness and here the saltiness and here the sweetness, even so both citta and cetasikas blend together harmoniously in such a manner that one cannot be separated from the others. This is true of a series of such psychic moments as well.[319]

Their relationship is therefore described in the *Kathāvatthu* as one of *sampayoga*, con-yoked-ness. *Sampayoga* implies the following characteristics: concomitance (*sahagata*), co-nascence (*sahajāta*), and con-joined-ness (*saṃsaṭṭha*).[320] This means that citta and cetasikas arise together, run together, cease to exist together, and thus exhibit a harmonious unity. We find this same idea in the Pāli commentaries when they refer to four characteristics common to both citta and cetasikas. The first is simultaneous origination (*ekuppāda*). The second is simultaneous cessation (*eka-nirodha*). The third is that they have a common object of attention. In the case of eye consciousness, for instance, a datum of visibility functions as an object common to both. The fourth is that they have a common physical base (*eka-vatthuka*). In the case of eye consciousness, for instance, both citta and cetasikas arise with eye as their common physical base.[321]

Commenting on these characteristics, the commentaries raise this question. Since the lifespan of all mental dhammas is the same, why is simultaneous origination mentioned in addition to simultaneous cessation? For if citta and cetasikas arise together, they should necessarily cease together. The answer is that this is in order to exclude material dhammas that, sometimes, arise together with mental dhammas. In such a situation, the material dhammas do not cease together with the mental dhammas, because the lifespan of matter is longer than that of mind. Hence the need to mention both characteristics. Again there are two mind-originated material phenomena, called bodily and vocal intimations, which arise and cease together with consciousness.[322] Where these two (and all other material dhammas) differ from citta and cetasikas is in their inability to experience an object. Therefore if only the first two characteristics are mentioned, it can give the wrong impression that mind-originated matter too can experience an object of cognition. It is in order to avoid such a wrong impression that the third characteristic—that is, having a common object (*ekārammaṇa*)—is mentioned. If the fourth characteristic is mentioned, it is in order to recognize that in whichever plane of existence a material aggregate is found (the sensuous and the fine-material spheres), citta and cetasikas have the same physical base, either one of the five material sense organs or the heart base.[323]

Sometimes we find the relationship between citta and cetasikas explained under eight aspects—namely, simultaneous arising (*ekuppāda*), simultaneous cessation (*ekanirodha*), having the same object (*ekālambana*), having the same physical base (*ekavatthuka*), concomitance (*sahagata*), co-nascence (*sahajāta*), con-yoked-ness (*saṃsaṭṭha*), and simultaneous occurrence (*sahavutti*).[324] This is an attempt to combine what the *Kathāvatthu* and Pāli commentaries say on their relationship.

In the Sarvāstivāda Abhidharma too we find more or less the same idea. In a given instance of cognition, both consciousness and mental factors have the following characteristics: (a) an identical sense organ as their base (*āśraya*); (b) an identical object of cognition (*ālambana*), because the function of both is to grasp their respective domain (*viṣaya-grahaṇa*); (c) an identical form (*ākāra*), because both take their characteristic form after the object; (d) an identical duration (*kāla*), because both arise and cease together; and (e) identical number of *dravyas*—that is to say, in a given instance of cognition, there has to be only one consciousness and it should be accompanied only by one of each of the kind of concomitants that should arise together with that particular consciousness.[325]

On the citta-cetasika relationship we find a dissent view recorded in the *Kathāvatthu*. It says that mental states do not pervade each other (*anupaviṭṭha*) as oil pervades sesame seeds or sugar pervades sugarcane.[326] This seems to be based on the assumption that if some mental states pervade other mental states, they are like qualities inhering in substances, a distinction that all Buddhist schools reject. The Theravāda counterargument is that the close association between mental states is not a case of one inhering in another. Rather, it is a case of describing the relationship between mental states when they exhibit such characteristics as concomitance, coexistence, con-joined-ness, a simultaneous genesis and a simultaneous cessation, and all having a common physical base and a common object.[327]

Both citta and cetasikas show how a multiplicity of mental states combines to produce a single unit of cognition. What we call an instance of cognition is neither a single isolated phenomenon nor a substantial unity. Rather, it is a complex of multiple mental states, each representing a separate function and all combining toward the cognition of the object. Their internal combination is not based on the substance-quality distinction. Citta is not some kind of mental substance in which the cetasikas inhere as its qualities. As mental dhammas or basic factors of psychological experience, they are coordinate. They are neither derivable from one another nor reducible to a common ground. Their relationship depends entirely on the principles of conditionality. In this connection, the *Paṭṭhāna* enumerates six conditional relations.

The first is by way of co-nascence (*sahajāta*). This means that each mental state, citta or cetasika, on arising causes the other mental states to arise together with it. The second is by way of reciprocity (*aññamañña*), which is a subordinate type of the first. In this relationship each mental state is at the same time and in the same way a conditioned state in relation to the very states that it conditions. The third is by way of support (*nissaya*). It refers to something that aids something else in the manner of a base or foundation. The condition by way of support can be pre-nascent (*purejāta*) or co-nascent (*sahajāta*) in relation to what it conditions. Here, the reference is to the latter kind because each mental state supports the others that are co-nascent with it. The fourth condition is by way of association (*sampayutta*). In this relationship each mental state causes the other mental states to arise as an inseparable group, having the four characteristics that we mentioned above. The fifth and sixth conditional relations are by way of presence (*atthi*) and nondisappearance (*avigata*). Both are identical and differ only in the letter. Here one mental state helps another to arise or to persist in being by its presence or nondisappearance. In view of the broad definition given to this conditionality, the previous four conditional relations become subsumable under it.[328]

What we have discussed so far highlights only the multiple internal relations within a single unit of cognition. However, a single unit of cognition is not an isolated event that could be understood only with reference to the present moment. It has a past as well as a future as it becomes a conditioned and a conditioning state in relation to the preceding and succeeding cognitive acts. These relations, as Venerable Nyanaponika Thera says, can be described as its "multiple external relations."[329] We find them explained in the *Paṭṭhāna* under four aspects of conditionality. The first and second, called proximity (*anantara*) and contiguity (*samanantara*), are identical in meaning and differ only in the letter. Formally defined, they refer to a relationship where one mental state causes another mental state to emerge immediately after it has ceased, thus preventing the intervention of another mental state between them. Between the preceding and the succeeding cognitive acts there is no gap. This is precisely what *anantara* and *samanantara* mean. The other two conditions, called absence (*natthi*) and disappearance (*vigata*), are also identical in meaning but differ only in the letter. The first refers to a mental state that by its absence provides the opportunity for the presence of another. The second refers to a mental state that by its disappearance provides the opportunity for the appearance of another. Both describe the relationship between the preceding and succeeding mental states.[330] What we find here is a continuous, uninterrupted, incessant flow. As one Pāli subcommentary says: "As long as the preceding cognitive act does not disappear, so long does the succeeding cognitive act not appear. Due to their incessant appearance without any gaps in between them, they appear as one."[331]

Cognitive acts, unlike material clusters (the minimal units of matter),[332] do not arise in juxtaposition. They necessarily arise in linear sequence. Here one can speak of only temporal sequence and not spatial concomitance. As we shall see in the sequel, in the Pāli Buddhist exegesis, matter is defined as that which is extended in three-dimensional space. The same situation is not true of mind. As one Pāli subcommentary observes, strictly speaking, mental dhammas have no spatial location of genesis (*uppatti-desa*), although it is possible to speak of physical sense organs and their objects as their places of arising (*sañjāti-desa*). At a given moment there can be only one cognitive act. What is more, the present cognitive act cannot cognize itself. It is just like the same sword cannot cut itself, or the same fingertip cannot touch itself.[333] This amounts to a rejection of what is called "*taññānatā*"—that is, the idea that the same consciousness has knowledge of itself.[334]

5

CONSCIOUSNESS

Definition of Consciousness

IN THE ABHIDHAMMA psychology, bare consciousness, that which constitutes the knowing or awareness of an object, is called *citta*. It can never arise in its true separate condition. It always arises in immediate conjunction with mental factors, the factors that perform more specialized tasks in the act of cognition. In the books of the Abhidhamma Piṭaka the individual nature of consciousness is often sought to be described by positioning it in relation to other basic factors (dhamma) into which individual existence is analyzed. This perhaps explains why we do not find in them a formal definition of consciousness.

In the Abhidhamma exegesis we find consciousness being defined in three different ways. The first is by way of agent (*kattu-sādhana*): "Consciousness is that which cognizes an object" (*ārammaṇaṃ cintetī ti cittaṃ*).[335] It is of course true that apart from the object (*ārammaṇa*), there are other conditions, such as immediate contiguity (*samanantara*) and support (*nissaya*) necessary for the genesis of consciousness. However, if they are not mentioned here it is because even if they are present, consciousness cannot arise without the object condition. The importance given to the object is also shown by the fact that consciousness is also defined as "that which grasps the object" (*ārammaṇika*).[336] This definition is intended to refute the wrong notion that consciousness can arise without an object (*nirālambaṇavāda*).[337]

The second definition is by way of instrument (*karaṇa-sādhana*): "Consciousness is that through which the concomitant mental factors cognize the object" (*etena cintetī ti cittaṃ*).[338] In this definition, while consciousness becomes the instrument, the concomitant mental factors become the agent. The third definition is by way of activity or mode of operation (*bhāva-sādhana*): "Consciousness is the mere act of cognizing the object" (*cintanamattam'eva cittaṃ*).[339]

It is only the third definition that is valid from an ultimate point of view (*nippariyāyato*),[340] because, strictly speaking, consciousness is neither that which cognizes (agent) nor that through which cognition takes place (instrument), but is only the process of cognizing an object. As a basic factor of actuality (dhamma), consciousness is the mere occurrence due to conditions.[341] It is not an entity but an activity, an activity without an actor behind it. The point being emphasized is that there is no conscious subject behind consciousness. Therefore the two definitions by way of agent and instrument are to be understood as provisional defining devices. Their purpose is to facilitate our understanding (*sukha-gahaṇatthaṃ*) of the nature of consciousness and, more important, to refute the wrong belief that a permanent self-entity is the agent or instrument of cognition.[342] If there is an agent or an instrument of cognition, it is not beneath or behind the mental phenomena into which the mental continuum is analyzed.

Another defining device adopted in the commentaries in delimiting consciousness or any other ultimate existent (dhamma) is to specify the following: (a) its characteristic (*lakkhaṇa*)—that is, the own characteristic or own nature that sets it apart from other existents; (b) its function (*rasa*)—that is, the task (*kicca*) it performs; (c) its manifestation (*paccu-paṭṭhāna*)—that is, the way it presents itself within experience; and (d) its proximate cause (*padaṭṭhāna*)—that is, the immediate condition of its dependence.[343] In the case of consciousness, its characteristic is the cognizing of an object. Its function is to serve as a forerunner (*pubbaṅgama*) of the mental factors (*cetasikas*), which necessarily arise together with it. Its manifestation is as a continuity of dependently arising process (*sandhāna*). Its proximate cause is nāma-rūpa, the mental factors and corporeal phenomena without which consciousness cannot arise as a solitary phenomenon.[344]

Physical Bases of Consciousness

The most well-known classification of consciousness is into six types according to their respective cognitive faculties—namely, eye consciousness (*cakkhu-viññāṇa*), ear consciousness (*sota-viññāṇa*), nose consciousness (*ghāna-viññāṇa*), tongue consciousness (*jivhā-viññāṇa*), body consciousness (*kāya-viññāṇa*), and mind consciousness (*mano-viññāṇa*). The first five faculties are physical and the sixth mental. They are also called doors (*dvāra*) because each of them serves as a channel through which consciousness and its concomitants of a cognitive process gain access to the object.

Although the six cognitive faculties are called doors, in one important respect the first five differ from the sixth, the mind. While the first five serve as the physical bases (*vatthu*) of the five kinds of consciousness named after them, obviously the mind cannot function as a physical base of the consciousness named after it. This means that door (*dvāra*) is not the same as base (*vatthu*). A door is an avenue through which consciousness and its concomitants gain access to the object, whereas a base is a physical support for the occurrence of consciousness and its concomitants.

If the first five types of consciousness have their respective physical bases, is there a physical base for mind and mind consciousness as well? If mind has a physical seat, what exactly is the relationship between the two?

In the context of Buddhism as a religion that gives a preeminent place to mind, this is a delicate problem to be resolved. For if mind is assigned a physical base, how is the possibility of matter determining the mind to be avoided?[345]

Within the Abhidharma tradition, we find two different solutions to this problem. The Sarvāstivādins dispensed altogether with the notion of a physical seat of mental activity. In their view, what is called mind (*manas*) or the mental organ is not a separate entity distinct from the six kinds of consciousness. It is a name given to the consciousness that has ceased immediately before the emergence of the present moment of consciousness. In this sense, it is the *āśraya*, the *point d'appui* of the consciousness that immediately succeeds it.[346] Thus here we have a situation where the immediately preceding consciousness functions as a base for the immediately succeeding consciousness. If mind (*manas*) is none other than the immediately preceding consciousness, why is it assigned a status as a separate entity? The answer is that since the first five kinds of consciousness have as their bases the five physical sense organs, it is necessary that a similar base (but not physical) be assigned to mind consciousness as well.[347]

The Physical Base of Mind and Mind Consciousness

The Theravādins took an entirely different position. It is true that they too maintain that the immediately preceding moment of consciousness serves as a condition for the immediately succeeding moment of consciousness. This conditional relationship is called one of immediate contiguity, or one of linear sequence (*anantara*, *samanantara*). However, the Theravādins do not consider the immediately preceding consciousness as the base (*vatthu*) of the immediately succeeding consciousness. For the Theravādins the base of mind and mind consciousness is physical and not mental.

This position seems to be closer to the Pāli suttas, where consciousness and nāma-rūpa are described as dependent on each other. As noted in chapter 1, nāma-rūpa refers to certain mental and material phenomena that arise together with consciousness. The material phenomena in question could mean the five physical sense organs on which the fivefold sense consciousness depends and whatever kind of other organic matter on which mind and mind consciousness depend as their physical support. This gets further confirmed by a sutta statement, according to which "this body of mine, made of material form, consisting of the four great elements . . . is subject to impermanence, to being worn and rubbed away . . . and this consciousness of mine is supported by it and bound up with it (*ettha sitaṃ ettha paṭibaddhaṃ*)."[348]

The first-ever reference within the Theravāda tradition to the physical base of mind and mind consciousness is found in the *Paṭṭhāna*, the Abhidhamma Book of Conditional Relations. This work, first, specifically mentions that eye (*cakkhu*) is a condition by way of base (*nissaya-paccaya*) for eye consciousness (*cakkhu-viññāṇa*). Likewise the ear, the nose, the tongue, and the body are mentioned as base conditions for the four kinds of consciousness named after them. But when it comes to mention that which forms a base condition for mind and mind consciousness, the language becomes less specific:

> That materiality based on which the mind element and the mind consciousness element occur, that materiality is a condition by way of base for the mind element and mind consciousness element and the mental phenomena associated with them (*yaṃ rūpaṃ nissāya mano-dhātu ca mano-viññāṇa-dhātu ca vattanti, taṃ rūpaṃ mano-dhātuyā ca mano-viññāṇa-dhātuyā ca taṃ sampayuttakānañ ca dhammānaṃ nissaya-paccayena paccayo*).[349]

It will be seen that in the excerpted sentence the physical base of mind and mind consciousness is not specified. It is alluded to in a circuitous way as "*yaṃ rūpaṃ . . . taṃ rūpaṃ*" (whatever materiality on which mental activity depends). The term, as Mrs. Rhys Davids observes, is "guarded," but we cannot agree with her when she further observes that "the evasion is quite marked."[350] What we find here is not evasion but caution, a case of leaving the matter open. One possibility as to why the *Paṭṭhāna* took the above position is that the physical seat of mental activity was thought to be very complex and pervasive, and therefore that its location was not limited to one particular part of the physical body.

In fact, we find a similar theory attributed to the Mahāsāṃghikas. It says that consciousness penetrates the entire physical body and, depending on its object (*viṣaya*) and support (*āśraya*), it can contract or expand. The subtle (*sūkṣma*) mind consciousness (*manovijñāna*) resides in the entire body that constitutes its support.[351]

However, when we come to the Pāli commentaries we meet with a different situation. What the *Paṭṭhāna* has left unspecified the commentaries have identified as the heart base (*hadaya-vatthu*). The *Visuddhimagga* says: "The heart base has the characteristic of being the [material] support for the mind element and for the mind-consciousness element. Its function is to subserve them. It is manifested as carrying of them. It is to be found in dependence on the blood . . . inside the heart. It is assisted by the primaries (earthness, waterness, fireness, and airness) with their functions of upholding, and so on; it is consolidated by temperature, consciousness, and nutriment; it is maintained by life [faculty]; and it serves as physical base for the mind element and mind-consciousness element, and for the states associated with them."[352]

Elsewhere in the *Visuddhimagga* the heart base is mentioned as a pre-nascence condition for the mind consciousness and for the states associated with it. A pre-nascence condition is a thing that arises first and becomes a condition to something else that arises later. This is based on the view that the lifespan of matter is longer than that of mind. At the time of rebirth-linking, however, the heart base is a condition by way of co-nascence to the mind consciousness element and the states associated with it. A co-nascence condition is a thing that serves as a condition to another that also arises at the same time.[353]

The commentators' interpretation of the words, "whatever materiality on which mental activity depends (*yaṃ rūpaṃ . . . taṃ rūpaṃ* of the *Paṭṭhāna*)" as the heart base can neither be supported nor refuted with reference to that statement. For it is an answer to a question left unanswered. However, as S. Z. Aung observes, had the *Paṭṭhāna* regarded the heart to be the seat of mental activity, it would have certainly mentioned it so, without alluding to it in such a guarded and cautious manner.[354]

What is called the heart base (*hadaya-vatthu*) is not absolutely identical with the heart as such. Like the physical sense organs, it is a subtle and delicate species of matter and is located inside the heart (*hadayabbhantare*). Like the physical sense organs, it also comes into being through the action of kamma.[355] But in one important respect the heart base differs from the physical sense organs. Unlike the latter, the heart base is not elevated to the level of an *indriya* or faculty. What is called *indriya* in Abhidhamma psychology is that which exercises a dominating influence on other mental and material phenomena that are associated with it. Thus the eye organ is called an *indriya* (= *cakkhu-indriya*) because its relative strength or weakness influences the consciousness that is named after it.[356] This appears to be the reason why each of the first five kinds of consciousness is named not after its object as visible consciousness, sound consciousness, and so on, but after its organ as eye consciousness, ear consciousness, and so on.

The nonrecognition of the heart base as a faculty (*indriya*) has many important implications. The most important is that it clearly shows that mental activities are not controlled and determined by the heart base, although they depend on it as their physical base or support.

It is also very important to notice here that it is the mind that depends on the heart base that is recognized in the Abhidhamma as a faculty (*manindriya*). Through this strategy, the preeminence of the mind is maintained although it is said to rest on a physical base. The classic example given is the boatman and his boat. Although the boatman has the boat as his physical support, it is the boatman who controls the boat. The mind is like the boatman and the physical base on which the mind depends is like the boat. Another example is the case of a man born blind and a stool-crawling cripple who wanted to go on a journey. The blind man made the cripple climb up on his shoulders and made the journey following the instructions given by the cripple. The cripple who can see is like the mind, and the blind man who can walk is like the physical base of the mind.[357]

In recognizing the heart as the seat of mental activity, the commentators have followed an ancient Indian tradition recorded not only in the religious literature but also in the medical tradition, as for example Caraka and Suśruta. However, as Mrs. Rhys Davids notes, the term *hadaya* (heart) finds a place in the Buddhist popular psychology, but in the sense of "inmost," "inwardness," and also of "thorough." Thus we have *hadaya-sukha* (inward happiness), *hadayaṅgama* (going deep into the bosom of the heart), *dhammassa hadaya* (the heart of the doctrine).[358] In the Abhidhamma Piṭaka the term *hadaya* is sometimes used as synonymous with mind (*mano*) and mind consciousness (*mano-viññāṇa*).[359] References such as these, too, may have encouraged the commentators in arriving at their conclusion.

However, the commentators seek to provide some empirical evidence in support of the cardiac theory of the seat of consciousness. It is said that when someone thinks of anything, bringing it to mind intently and directing his whole mind to it, he experiences exhaustion (*khijjana*) in his heart. Therefore it is to be inferred that the seat of mental activity is inside the heart (*hadayabbhantare*).[360]

As noted above, there is no evidence in the antecedent Buddhist literature to justify the cardiac theory of the seat of mental activity. Nor is there evidence to suggest that this new theory was shared by any of the other schools of Buddhist thought. This becomes all the more evident from a passing comment made by Ācārya Yaśomitra in his *Abhidharmakośavyākhyā*—namely, that Buddhists in Sri Lanka (Tāmraparṇīyā) imagine (*kalpayanti*) that heart base (*hṛdaya-vastu*) is the support (*āśraya*) of mind consciousness. This work goes on to say that according to them the heart base exists even in the immaterial sphere, for they claim that materiality exists even in the immaterial sphere. In justifying this interpretation, it is said that "āṅ" in the word *ārūpya* has to be understood in the sense of "little" (*īṣad-arthe*) and not as indicating complete absence of materiality, just as the word *āpiṃgala* means not completely non-yellow-brownish.[361]

The latter part of Ācārya Yaśomitra's observation does not faithfully represent the Theravāda position. The correct Theravāda position is that *arūpa-loka*, the immaterial plane of existence with its four realms, is where materiality has been totally transcended. Here only consciousness and its concomitants remain.

Classification of Consciousness

Consciousness (*citta*) has a single characteristic as that which constitutes knowing or awareness of an object. However, it divides itself into a variety of types, based on its possible combinations with various mental factors. These types, according to one method of differentiation, are eighty-nine, and according to another, one hundred and twenty-one.[362] It will thus be seen that the term *citta* (consciousness) occurs in two separate senses. One is the bare phenomenon of consciousness as one of the eighty-one conditioned dhammas. The other is a given combination of consciousness and its concomitant mental factors. It is the particular context that determines the exact sense.

The different classes of consciousness are again made into several groups according to different criteria of classification. There are two main classifying criteria. One is based on the Buddhist teaching on *jhāna* experience and Buddhist cosmology, and the other on Buddhist ethics—more particularly, the Buddhist doctrine of *kamma*.

The first classification yields four classes that correspond to the four planes of existence—namely, the sense sphere (*kāma-bhava*), the fine-material sphere (*rūpa-bhava*), the immaterial sphere (*arūpa-bhava*), and the supramundane (*lokuttara*). The four classes are not mutually exclusive, as the criteria of classification are somewhat overlapping. For example, the fine-material and the immaterial-sphere consciousnesses could occur in the sensual plane of existence as well. This means that although there is a close relationship between the first three classes of consciousness and the three planes of existence, they are not identical. The three planes provide the classifying principles but they are not three "groups of consciousness." They are the three realms that Buddhist cosmology recognizes. There is a close correspondence, however, between the three classes of consciousness and the three planes of existence. One class of consciousness subsumes the types that are typical of the plane after which it is named. They have a tendency to arise more often there than in the other two planes.

The fourth class of consciousness is supramundane (*lokuttara*). It directly leads to the realization of nibbāna, the reality that transcends the world of conditioned experience. It is in contrast to this class of consciousness that the other three classes are called mundane (*lokiya*).

In this fourfold classification we can see an ascending order of sublimation, where the succeeding consciousness is subtler and more sublime than the preceding. The sense-sphere consciousness that is related to the sensuous and is subject to the sway of passion is placed at the bottom. The consciousness that transcends the world of conditioned experience is placed at the top.

The second classification, as mentioned above, is based on Buddhist ethics, or more particularly, on the Buddhist doctrine of *kamma*. On this basis, too, consciousness divides itself into four classes as skillful (*kusala*), nonskillful (*akusala*), resultant (*vipāka*), and functional (*kiriya*). The first class is kammically wholesome and the second kammically unwholesome. The third class is the results of kammically wholesome and unwholesome consciousness. The fourth class is neither kamma nor results of kamma. The third and fourth classes are kammically neither wholesome nor unwholesome. They are therefore classified as *abyākata*—that is, indeterminate. They cannot be determined in terms of the dichotomization as kammically wholesome and unwholesome.[363]

6

CLASSES OF CONSCIOUSNESS

We begin our discussion of the different classes of consciousness according to three planes by examining the sense sphere, proceding from there to the fine-material sphere and the immaterial sphere.

Sense-Sphere Consciousness

Sense-sphere consciousness divides itself into many kinds depending on its ethical quality. We begin our discussion with unwholesome consciousness.

Unwholesome Consciousness

The analysis of unwholesome consciousness of the sense sphere is based on the three roots of moral evil: greed (*lobha*), hatred (*dosa*), and delusion (*moha*). On this basis the unwholesome consciousness divides itself into three groups: consciousness rooted in (1) greed, (2) hatred, and (3) delusion. The first group is then divided into eight types according to three principles of dichotomization. The first is its emotional value—that is, the tone of the feeling that is concomitant with the consciousness. The second is whether it is associated with or dissociated from wrong view. Here wrong view (*diṭṭhi*) could mean any belief or ideology in conformity with which the consciousness arises, thus providing an ideological justification for the consciousness rooted in greed. Or, as Venerable Bhikkhu Bodhi observes, "the view itself may be an object of attachment in its own right."[364] The third is whether the consciousness rooted in greed occurs spontaneously (*asaṅkhārika*) or is induced by an external factor or by one's inclination or habit (*sasaṅkhārika*).

The eight classes of the consciousness rooted in greed:[365]

1. accompanied by joy, associated with wrong view, spontaneous
2. accompanied by joy, associated with wrong view, induced
3. accompanied by joy, dissociated from wrong view, spontaneous
4. accompanied by joy, dissociated from wrong view, induced
5. accompanied by equanimity,[366] associated with wrong view, spontaneous
6. accompanied by equanimity, associated with wrong view, induced
7. accompanied by equanimity, dissociated from wrong view, spontaneous
8. accompanied by equanimity, dissociated from wrong view, induced

The second class of unwholesome consciousness is rooted in hatred (*dosa*). It is always accompanied by displeasure (*domanassa*), because hatred that is its root can never be accompanied either by joy or by equanimity. Therefore, unlike the one rooted in greed, it cannot be differentiated into two types on the basis of feeling. Nor does it arise in association with wrong view. Wrong view can certainly give rise to acts of hatred. But it cannot exist together with hatred in one and the same consciousness. By its very nature hatred excludes the possibility of any view, whether it is right or wrong. In view of these reasons, the consciousness rooted in hatred can be differentiated only into two types, as spontaneous or induced:[367]

9. accompanied by displeasure, associated with aversion, spontaneous

10. accompanied by displeasure, associated with aversion, induced

The third class of unwholesome consciousness is rooted in delusion (*moha*). Delusion is one of the three unwholesome roots and, as such, is present in every type of unwholesome consciousness. However, in the class of unwholesome consciousness under consideration, only delusion is present as an unwholesome root. The sheer intensity of delusion here excludes both greed and hatred. It is therefore described as one involving sheer delusion (*momūha*). It has two types, one accompanied by doubt (*vicikicchā*) and the other by restlessness (*uddhacca*).[368] The emotional value of both is not one of either pleasant or unpleasant feeling but one of equanimity. This is because when the mind is overwhelmed with sheer delusion it is not in a position to evaluate the object as agreeable or disagreeable. And this prevents its being associated with pleasant or painful feeling.

The usual dichotomization as spontaneous and induced, too, does not appear here. Since these two types do not have natural acuteness (*sabhāva-tikkhatā*), they are not spontaneous (*asaṅkhārika*). And since they are rooted in sheer delusion, the question of deliberately arousing them does not arise. Hence they cannot be described as induced (*sasaṅkhārika*) either.[369]

The two types of consciousness rooted in delusion:

11. accompanied by equanimity, associated with doubt
12. accompanied by equanimity, associated with restlessness

Thus the Abhidhamma analysis of unwholesome consciousness yields three classes and twelve types. As noted above, delusion (*moha*) is present in every type of unwholesome consciousness, because all such consciousness is due to ignorance or a deluded state of mind that clouds the true nature of the object of cognition. If the first two classes of consciousness are described as rooted in greed and hatred, it is because greed and hatred dominate in them and not because delusion is absent in them. In fact greed and hatred can never arise unless in combination with delusion.

On the other hand, delusion can arise in isolation from the other two unwholesome roots, as is shown by the eleventh and twelfth types of unwholesome consciousness.

Again, greed and hatred cannot arise in combination. Their mutual exclusion is shown by the first two classes of unwholesome consciousness. Greed operates as attachment in relation to something agreeable and palatable. Hatred operates as aversion in relation to something disagreeable and unpalatable. Since attachment and aversion are mutually exclusive, the presence of one implies the absence of the other.

It will be noticed that among all states of unwholesome consciousness, only two are accompanied by displeasure (*domanassa*). These are the two kinds of consciousness rooted in aversion (*paṭigha-sampayutta*). The other states of unwholesome consciousness, whether rooted in greed or delusion (*moha*), are accompanied either by a feeling of joy (*somanassa*) or indifference (*upekkhā*), but not displeasure. This leads us to the interesting conclusion that among the eighty-nine classes of consciousness, only two are associated with displeasure.

From this circumstance it does not necessarily follow that according to Abhidhamma there are more pleasures in life than displeasures. What matters here is not the number of the types of consciousness accompanied by displeasure but, more important, their frequency, how often they occur and recur.

Rootless Consciousness

The term "root" (*hetu*), as noted earlier, denotes those mental factors that determine the ethical quality of volitional acts. These are greed (*lobha*), hatred (*dosa*), and delusion (*moha*), and their opposites—namely, nongreed (*alobha*), nonhatred (*adosa*), and nondelusion (*amoha*). Rootless consciousness is that which is devoid of roots. Unlike the rooted (*sahetuka*) consciousness, it is comparatively weak because it represents a consciousness that is not motivated by any of the six roots. It divides itself into eighteen types: fifteen are resultant (*vipāka*) and the other three functional (*kiriya*).

The term "resultant" (*vipāka*) describes the types of consciousness that arise as results of kamma. They are the results of volitional activity (*kamma*), both wholesome and unwholesome. However, they, in turn, are not kammically differentiated as wholesome and unwholesome. If they can be so differentiated, then this would mean that results of kamma are also kamma. This would result in a situation where one kamma gives rise to another kamma, and the latter in turn to yet another, and thus to an interminable process of kammic determinism.

We find the same idea in the *Abhidharmakośabhāṣya*, where it compares vipāka to food and drink that once consumed do not produce themselves into food and drink again. Similarly, from one vipāka does not proceed another vipāka, for if this hypothesis were true, then deliverance from all suffering would not be possible.[370]

There are in all fifteen types of sense-sphere resultant consciousnesses, divided into two groups. The first group consists of seven types of consciousness, called unwholesome resultant consciousness (*akusala-vipāka-citta*). The use of the term "unwholesome" is to show that they are resultants produced by unwholesome kamma. It does not mean that the resultants themselves are unwholesome (or wholesome). Of the seven types, the first five are the fivefold sense consciousnesses based on the eye, the ear, the nose, the tongue, and the body. Since these are results of unwholesome kamma, their objects are undesirable (*aniṭṭha*). There is, however, a difference to be noted. In the case of the first four sense consciousnesses, the object is weak and therefore the associated feeling is neutral. On the other hand, in the case of body consciousness, the impact of the object is strong and therefore the associated feeling is painful (*dukkha*).[371]

The other two types of resultant consciousness are (1) receiving consciousness (*sampaṭicchana-citta*) accompanied by equanimity and (2) investigating consciousness (*santīraṇa-citta*) accompanied by equanimity. The first is so called because, in a cognitive process, it "receives" the object that has impinged on the sense organ. The second, which arises immediately after the first, is so called because it investigates the object of cognition received by the first.[372]

The second group of resultant consciousnesses arises as results of wholesome kamma. It includes eight types, and seven of them correspond to the seven types mentioned above. However, since these are results of wholesome kamma, their objects are desirable (*iṭṭha*) or extremely desirable (*ati-iṭṭha*), but the accompanying feeling, except in the fifth, is one of equanimity—that is, neutral feeling. The fifth, which is body consciousness, is accompanied by pleasure (*sukha*) because the impact of the object on the body is strong. The eighth resultant due to wholesome consciousness has no counterpart in the corresponding class of resultants due to unwholesome kamma. It is called investigating consciousness (*santīraṇa-citta*) accompanied by joy (*somanassa*). Thus the investigating consciousness resulting from wholesome kamma has two types: one is accompanied by neutral feeling (*upekkhā*) and the other is accompanied by joy (*somanassa*). The first arises when the object of cognition is comparatively desirable, and the second when the object of cognition is especially desirable.[373]

The last three types of rootless consciousness, as noted earlier, belong to a category called *kiriya*. When a consciousness is described as kiriya, it means that it is neither the result of kamma nor does it have kammic potency. Of the three types of rootless kiriya, the first two play an important role in the series of mental events that constitute a cognitive process. One is called "five sense-door adverting consciousness" (*pañca-dvāra-āvajjana-citta*). Its function is to advert (*āvajjana*) to an external sense object that has impinged on any of the five physical sense organs. It is after this function of adverting to the object that the appropriate sense consciousness arises. The second is called "mind-door adverting consciousness" (*mano-dvāra-āvajjana-citta*). Its function is to advert to an object that appears at the mind door and that thus sets in motion a process of mental events leading to the cognition of a mental object. This same consciousness performs another function when it appears in a cognitive process based on any of the five physical sense organs. Here its function is to determine the object that has been apprehended by sense consciousness. When it performs this role it is called *votthapana-citta*, the consciousness that determines the object of cognition.[374]

The third type of kiriya consciousness that is devoid of both wholesome and unwholesome roots pertains exclusively to the experience of the Buddha, the Pacceka Buddha, and the arahant. It is called *hasituppāda-citta*, the smile-producing consciousness, because its function is to cause them to smile about sense-sphere phenomena. There are four other types of consciousness (to be examined below)—namely, the four beautiful sense-sphere kiriya consciousnesses, with which the Buddha, the Pacceka Buddha, and the arahant may smile.[375]

Wholesome Consciousness

Buddhism traces all moral wholesomeness to the three roots of nongreed or generosity (*alobha*), nonhatred or loving-kindness (*adosa*), and non-delusion or wisdom (*amoha*). Any consciousness that is accompanied by them is evaluated as skillful or wholesome (*kusala*).

The use of the two terms *kusala* (skillful) and *akusala* (unskillful) to denote what is morally good and evil, respectively, shows the close affinity between Buddhist ethics and Buddhist psychology. If what is morally wholesome is called skillful, it is because when the mind has such wholesome qualities as generosity and compassionate love, it experiences mental health (*ārogya*), mental purity (*anavajja*), and skillfulness (*kosalla*), all resulting in mental felicity.[376] On the contrary, if negative mental dispositions such as greed, aversion, and delusion are called unskillful, it is because they impair our mental health and reduce the mind's skill. Thus, the Buddhist evaluation in terms of *kusala* and *akusala* is based on psychology, on a distinction made between positive mental dispositions that enhance our mental health and efficiency on the one hand, and negative mental dispositions that impair our mental health and mental efficiency on the other.

There are in all eight types of sense-sphere wholesome consciousness. In differentiating the eight types, three classifying criteria are adopted. The first is the emotional value (tone) of the consciousness. This means the tone of feeling (*vedanā*), which, as we shall see, is concomitant with every type of consciousness. The second is whether the consciousness is associated with knowledge (*ñāṇa-sampayutta*) or dissociated from knowledge *ñāṇa-vippayutta*). Here knowledge means knowledge of things as they are. It is the mental factor of wisdom (*paññā*) or the absence of delusion (*amoha*). The third classifying criterion is whether the consciousness is spontaneous (*asaṅkhārika*) or nonspontaneous (*sasaṅkhārika*), whether it is unprompted or prompted. If consciousness occurs without being prompted by external influence or "by the force of one's own inclination or habit," it is spontaneous (*asaṅkhārika*). If it occurs owing to inducement by another or by one's own deliberation, it is nonspontaneous (*sasaṅkhārika*). Here the volitional effort is induced by oneself or by another.

The eight types of consciousness as differentiated above are as follows:[377]

1. accompanied by joy, associated with knowledge, spontaneous
2. accompanied by joy, associated with knowledge, induced
3. accompanied by joy, dissociated from knowledge, spontaneous
4. accompanied by joy, dissociated from knowledge, induced
5. accompanied by equanimity, associated with knowledge, spontaneous
6. accompanied by equanimity, associated with knowledge, induced
7. accompanied by equanimity, dissociated from knowledge, spontaneous
8. accompanied by equanimity, dissociated from knowledge, induced

It will be seen that none of the wholesome consciousnesses are accompanied by displeasure (*domanassa*). They are accompanied either by joy (*somanassa*) or by equanimity (*upekkhā*). Of the eight classes, four are dissociated from knowledge. This means that such consciousness is not accompanied by the mental factor called wisdom (*paññā*). But this does not involve delusion (*moha*), which mental factor occurs only in unwholesome consciousness. However, the question arises whether wholesome consciousness dissociated from knowledge could really be called wholesome. The commentarial explanation is that it is called wholesome only in an indirect way: "As a fan made not of palmyra leaves but of mats, and so on, is called, figuratively, a palmyra fan from its resemblance to it, so consciousness dissociated from knowledge is called wholesome."[378] It is further observed that from an ultimate point of view (*nippariyāyena*) consciousness associated with knowledge is called wholesome in the three senses of mental health (*ārogya*), mental purity (*anavajjatā*), and skill (*kosalla*). Whereas consciousness dissociated from knowledge is called wholesome only in respect to the first two senses.[379] This shows that skill associated with consciousness is due to the presence of the knowledge factor.

Resultant Consciousness with Roots

There are eight rooted resultants. These eight and the rootless eight resultants, examined above, are the kammic results of the eight types of wholesome consciousness. Content-wise there is no difference between the eight wholesome and the eight rooted resultants. However, there is a difference to be noted: the former are wholesome and the latter indeterminate.

Functional Consciousness with Roots

We have already examined three types of functional (*kiriya*) consciousness that are rootless. The category to be examined now consists of eight types, all with roots. The eight in question are the exact counterparts of the eight types of sense-sphere wholesome consciousness. There is, however, this important difference to be noted. The eight wholesome types are experienced only by worldlings and trainees, that is, those who have not yet realized nibbāna, whereas the eight types of kiriya consciousness arise only in those who have realized nibbāna. This is because they have transcended the kammic order (*kamma-niyāma*). And this is precisely why nibbāna is described as *kamma-nirodha*, the cessation of kamma.

There is one question that arises here. If the eight kinds of kiriya consciousness contain, among others, nongreed (generosity), nonhatred (compassionate love), and nondelusion (wisdom), is not the arahant then conditioned by them? Obviously the answer is a categorical no. In fact, it is their very opposites—greed, hatred, and delusion—that condition our psychological experience. This seems to be the reason why these three roots of moral evil are described as *pamāṇa-karaṇa*: that which restricts, that which sets limits to.[380] If nibbāna is described as *appamāṇa* (without *pamāṇa*), it is in this context that we should understand it—that is, as free from the limiting factors of greed, hatred, and delusion. The three roots of moral evil are also described as *nimittakaraṇa*, that which leads to "taking signs."[381] What this seems to mean is that one who is conditioned by them converts objects of perception to objects of pleasure (greed) or displeasure (hatred, aversion) through delusion. The one who has realized nibbāna is also described as *sīmātiga*—that is, one who has gone beyond (transcended) all defilements that function as limiting factors (*sīmā*).[382] The liberated one is also described as one who lives with a mind in which all barriers have been broken asunder (*vimariyādikata-cetasā viharati*).[383]

What all this amounts to saying is that when nongreed (generosity), nonhatred (compassionate love), and nondelusion (wisdom) transcend the kammic order they operate at the highest level. In the nibbānic experience they function not as conditioning but as deconditioning factors. This is why nibbāna is singled out as the only unconditioned dhamma. In this particular context, therefore, the rendering of kiriya as "functional" does not seem to be very appropriate. It gives the wrong impression of "mere doing," "doing for its own sake." The real position is quiet otherwise. It is not that the arahant has withdrawn from all activities. Rather, the arahant has withdrawn from all self-centered and egocentric activities. If the nibbanic experience is kammically neither wholesome nor unwholesome, this means that it represents the highest wholesomeness, a wholesomeness that transcends the kammic order (*kamma-niyāma*).

Fine-Material-Sphere Consciousness

In the foregoing pages, we discussed the types of consciousness experienced in the sense sphere. All those types, as we have noted, amount to fifty-four and are classifiable as unwholesome, wholesome, resultant, and functional, or as unwholesome, rootless, and, as we shall see soon, beautiful. Now we come to the types of consciousness that obtain in the two meditative attainments called rūpajjhāna and arūpajjhāna and in the two planes of existence called rūpa-loka and arūpa-loka. If they are called exalted (mahaggata) it is in relation to the consciousness of the sense sphere. For in contrast to the latter they represent a higher level of experience where consciousness becomes more and more centered and more and more unified until it reaches the point of complete unification and quietude.

The jhāna concentration needs to be preceded at least by a temporary suspension of five mental impediments (*nīvaraṇa*). These are sensual desire (*kāmacchanda*), ill will (*vyāpāda*), sloth and torpor (*thīna-middha*), restlessness and worry (*uddhacca-kukkucca*), and doubt (*vicikicchā*). The five hindrances are so called because they defile the purity and serenity of mind (*cetaso upakkilesa*) and weaken the intellectual faculty (*paññāya dubbalīkaraṇa*). "Sensual desire is compared with water mixed with manifold colors, ill will with boiling water, sloth and torpor with water covered by moss, restlessness and worry with agitated water whipped by the wind, and skeptical doubt with turbid and muddy water. Just as in such water one cannot perceive one's own reflection, so in the presence of these five mental hindrances one cannot clearly discern one's own benefit, nor that of the other, nor that of both."[384]

Once the mind is freed from these inhibiting factors, it becomes a fertile ground for the emergence of the five basic factors of *rūpajjhāna*, the exalted consciousness of the sphere of fine materiality. These are: *vitakka* (thinking in its initial state), *vicāra* (reflecting or sustained thought), *pīti* (zest), *sukha* (happiness), and *ekaggatā* (one-pointedness of mind). The last factor is present in every kind of consciousness (*sabba-citta-sādhāraṇa*). But in the case of jhāna consciousness this factor is intentionally elevated to a definite level of intensity.

The jhāna experience of fine materiality (*rūpajjhāna*) consists of five stages arranged according to an ascending order of mind's unification. The first jhāna differs from the rest by the presence therein of all the five jhāna factors—namely, vitakka, vicāra, pīti, sukha, and ekaggatā. The progress upward through the other stages consists in the successive elimination of the first four factors. Thus in the second jhāna, vitakka is eliminated, in the third vitakka and vicāra are eliminated, in the fourth vitakka, vicāra, and pīti are eliminated, while in the fifth even sukha (happiness) is abandoned and is substituted by *upekkhā* (equanimity). The net result of the successive elimination of jhāna factors is that ekaggatā, one-pointedness of the mind, gets more and more intensified until it reaches the highest point of intensity in the fifth jhāna. In this jhāna, with the substitution of happiness with equanimity, a hedonically neutral stage of pure concentration is created. The five stages of the jhāna consciousness are as follows:

1st stage: vitakka, vicāra, pīti, sukha, ekaggatā
2nd stage: vicāra, pīti, sukha, ekaggatā
3rd stage: pīti, sukha, ekaggatā
4th stage: sukha, ekaggatā
5th stage: upekkhā, ekaggatā

Each jhāna is identified by the jhāna factors assigned to it. But this does not mean that it consists only of those factors. They are among many mental factors contained in each jhāna.

Of the five jhānas, it is the fifth that is characterized by "the supreme perfection of equanimity and mindfulness." It is the foundation jhāna (*pādakajjhāna*) for the realization of the six kinds of higher knowledge (*chaḷabhiññā*). These are psycho-kinesis (*iddhividha*), clairaudience (*dibba-sota*), telepathic knowledge (*cetopariya-ñāṇa*), retrocognitive knowledge of past existences (*pubbenivāsānussati-ñāṇa*), knowledge of the decease and survival of beings (*cutūpapāta-ñāṇa*), and knowledge of the destruction of defiling impulses (*āsavakkhaya-ñāṇa*). Among them, the first five are mundane because they are attained through the utmost perfection in mental concentration. The knowledge they yield is helpful for emancipation, but in themselves they do not constitute the liberating knowledge. On the other hand, the last is supramundane (*lokuttara*) because it is attained through insight (*vipassanā*) and it is the means whereby deliverance from all suffering is realized.

The jhāna consciousness divides itself into fifteen types under the three aspects of kammically wholesome (*kusala*), resultant (*vipāka*), and functional (*kiriya*). The kammically wholesome are experienced by worldlings and trainees (*sekha*) who develop jhānas here in this world. The kammically indeterminate resultant consciousness arises only in the fine material sphere (*rūpa-loka*)—that is, in the beings who have been born there as a consequence of developing the jhānas. The kammically indeterminate five kiriya types are experienced only by the Buddha, the Pacceka Buddha, and the arahant when they attain the jhānas.

Immaterial-Sphere Consciousness

The five jhānas of fine materiality, as noted above, differ according to the progressive elimination of their constituent factors (*aṅgātikkama*). The four jhānas of nonmateriality, on the other hand, differ according to the elimination of their objects of concentration (*ārammaṇātikkama*).[385] Their identification is therefore based not on their constituent factors but on the objects of their concentration. Accordingly, the exalted consciousness of the sphere of nonmateriality becomes fourfold and appears in the following order:

1. the base of infinite space (*ākāsānañcāyatana*)
2. the base of infinite consciousness (*viññāṇañcāyatana*)
3. the base of nothingness (*ākiñcaññāyatana*)
4. the base of neither perception nor non-perception (*n'evasaññānāsaññāyatana*)

Each succeeding jhāna arises by surmounting the object of the preceding one. Therefore, in terms of subtlety and refinement, the succeeding one is higher than the preceding one. However, as to the number of jhāna factors, there is no difference among them. They all have in common the two jhāna factors of equanimity and one-pointedness. Since these are the two jhāna factors that constitute the fifth jhāna of fine materiality, the four immaterial jhānas are considered as a further extension of it.

The four types of immaterial jhāna consciousness become twelve under the three aspects of wholesome (*kusala*), resultant (*vipāka*), and functional (*kiriya*). The kammically wholesome are experienced by worldlings and trainees (*sekha*) who develop immaterial jhānas here in this world. The kammically neutral resultants arise only in the immaterial planes of existence—that is, in the beings who have been born there as a consequence of developing the jhānas. The kammically neutral five kiriya types are experienced only by the Buddha, the Pacceka Buddha, and the arahant when they experience jhāna.

This brings us to an end of our discussion of jhāna consciousness, both of the fine material and immaterial types. One conclusion that we can draw is that jhāna experience as understood by Buddhism does not lend itself to interpreting in terms of mysticism. What the different stages of jhāna show is the progressive elevation of ordinary sensuous consciousness to higher levels of mind's unification and refinement. They are not spontaneous occurrences but must be realized through practice in concentration. They have to be brought about by individual effort and strictly according to the methods laid down in Buddhist psychology. Their content is fully analyzable according to the psychological categories and principles recognized in Buddhism. The analysis does not leave any residue to be interpreted in terms of mysticism or theology.

As Venerable Nyanaponika Thera observes, similar experiences are sometimes interpreted by others as some kind of absorption or union with a transcendental reality or as its manifestation within the meditator. They are said to provide evidence for the existence of a transempirical reality in the form of a personal God or impersonal godhead. Such an interpretation is certainly not consonant with the Buddhist view of existence.[386] The Buddhist doctrine of *anattā* means that it does not recognize a noumenon in its microcosmic or macrocosmic sense. In fact, as Venerable Nyanaponika Thera observes further, Buddhism recognizes the likelihood of falsely interpreting the content of jhāna experience in a manner not warranted by facts. This seems to be the reason why the meditator on rising from his jhāna experience is advised to review its content in light of the three marks of sentient existence—namely, impermanence (*anicca*), liability to suffering (*dukkha*), and absence of an abiding ego or a persistent substance (*anattā*).[387] Such a practice has the salutary effect of preventing the jhāna experience from being interpreted in metaphysical or theological terms.

In fact, the Abhidhamma presents an exhaustive psychological analysis of the jhāna experience purely in empirical terms. We give below quotations from the *Dhammasaṅgaṇi* and its commentary, which is an analysis of the first jhāna of the sphere of fine materiality:

> "Whenever one is developing the way to the attainment of the sphere of pure form (fine materiality) and, being detached from sensual things and unwholesome states of mind, one has entered into the first absorption produced by the earth *kasiṇa*, which is

> accompanied by thought conception (*vitakka*) and discursive thinking (*vicāra*) born of detachment, and one is filled with rapture (*pīti*) and joy (*sukha*), at such a time there is contact, feelings. . . . " The list includes the same fifty-six mental factors that constitute the first kind of wholesome consciousness of the sphere of sense.[388] However, as the Pāli commentary observes, in the case of jhāna the mental factors operate at a higher level.[389]

Thus the jhāna consciousness is analyzable in the same way as any other type of consciousness. The factors into which it is analyzed do not have among them any unverifiable, mysterious entities. The transition to higher reaches of mind's unification is a causal process, a process of dependent origination. The jhāna experience does not represent a stage where the world of mind and matter is transcended. Therefore, in the final analysis, the jhāna experience is also conditioned (*saṅkhata*) and dependently arisen (*paṭiccasamuppanna*). For Buddhism "suffering" means any kind of "conditioned experience," whether it is pleasant or painful. And since jhāna experience is also conditioned, it does not represent complete emancipation from suffering.

Supramundane Consciousness

The supramundane consciousness pertains to the process of transcending the world. World means the totality of our experience, consisting of the five aggregates of clinging, corporeality (*rūpa*), feelings (*vedanā*), perceptions (*saññā*), mental formations (*saṃkhāra*), and consciousness (*viññāṇa*). The consciousness under consideration transcends the world and leads to the attainment of nibbāna.

There are eight types of supramundane consciousness, distinguished into two groups as path consciousness (*magga-citta*) and fruition consciousness (*phala-citta*). These eight types of supramundane consciousness pertain to the four stages of stream-entry (*sotāpatti*), once-returning (*sakadāgāmi*), nonreturning (*anāgāmi*), and arahantship (*arahatta*). Each stage involves two types of consciousness. Path consciousness (*magga-citta*) is so called because it eradicates defilements and gives access to each stage. Fruition consciousness (*phala-citta*) is so called because it experiences the stage of liberation made possible by the corresponding path. Fruition consciousness arises as a result of and in immediate succession to path consciousness. For in supramundane consciousness, unlike the mundane, the effect of wholesome consciousness takes place immediately after its occurrence.[390]

To transcend the world means to gradually eliminate the fetters that tie beings to saṃsāra. There are ten such fetters: (1) the belief in an ego entity (*sakkāya-diṭṭhi*), (2) skeptical doubt (*vicikicchā*), (3) clinging to mere rites and ritual as a means to emancipation (*sīlabbata-parāmāsa*), (4) sensual desire (*kāma-rāga*), (5) ill will (*vyāpāda*), (6) craving for fine-material existence (*rūpa-rāga*), (7) craving for immaterial existence (*arūpa-rāga*), (8) conceit (*māna*), (9) restlessness (*uddhacca*), and (10) ignorance (*avijjā*). Of the four types of path consciousness, the first (stream-entry) has the function of cutting off the first three fetters. The second (once-returning), while not eliminating any fetters, attenuates the grosser forms of sensual desire and ill will. The third (nonreturning) eradicates the fourth and fifth fetters. The fourth (arahantship) destroys the remaining five fetters. The four types of fruition consciousness, as noted above, have the function of experiencing the stage of liberation made possible by the corresponding path consciousness.[391]

The eight types of supramundane consciousness are sometimes counted as forty by taking into consideration the five stages of *rūpajjhāna*. Any of these five jhāna stages could be made the basis for the realization of the four stages of enlightenment. It is on this basis that the eight types of supramundane consciousness are arranged into forty types. This explains why the Abhidhamma refers to all types of consciousness sometimes as eighty-nine and sometimes as one hundred and twenty-one.

Beautiful Consciousness

In the preceding pages we examined the different classes of consciousness according to the three planes: the sense sphere, the fine-material sphere, the immaterial sphere, and the supramundane, which transcends the three planes of existence. What is called "beautiful consciousness" is a category that cuts across all four classes in the sense that it includes some classes of consciousness belonging to all of them. "Beautiful consciousness" (*sobhana-citta*) is an expression for all types of consciousness other than the twelve unwholesome and the eighteen rootless. The category is so called because it is invariably accompanied by beautiful mental factors (to be examined below). It will be seen that the denotation of "the beautiful" is wider than that of "the wholesome." The former refers not only to all wholesome consciousness but also to resultant and functional types accompanied by beautiful mental factors. The category of "the beautiful" thus includes twenty-four types of sense-sphere consciousness as well as the fifteen and twelve types of consciousness experienced in the second and third planes of existence, plus the eight types of supramundane consciousness.

7

THE ETHICALLY VARIABLE MENTAL FACTORS

As we have seen in chapter 2, consciousness (*citta*) does not arise in its true separate condition. It always arises together with a set of mental factors called *cetasikas*. Consciousness is the basic awareness of an object. Therefore it has to be supported by a set of concomitant mental factors, which exercise more specialized tasks in the act of cognition. It is these mental factors that we propose to discuss in the present and next two chapters.

There are in all fifty-two mental factors. They are usually subsumed under four broad headings, as follows:

1. Seven universals—that is, ethically variable mental factors "common to all types of consciousness" (*sabba-citta-sādhāraṇa-cetasika*).
2. Six occasionals—that is, ethically variable "miscellaneous" (*pakiṇṇaka*) mental factors found only in particular types of consciousness, not in all. (These two categories are brought under the common designation *añña-samāna* to show their ethical variability.)
3. Fourteen unwholesome (*akusala*) mental factors.
4. Twenty-five beautiful (*sobhana*) mental factors.

In this chapter we propose to examine the ethically variable mental factors—that is, the universals and the occasionals.

The Seven Universals

The seven universals are *phassa* (contact), *vedanā* (feeling), *saññā* (perception), *cetanā* (volition), *ekaggatā* (one-pointedness), *arūpa-jīvitindriya* (psychic life faculty), and *manasikāra* (attention).[392] These are the basic nonrational elements invariably present in every type of consciousness, whatever be its ethical quality, whether wholesome (*kusala*), unwholesome (*akusala*), resultant (*vipāka*), or functional (*kiriya*), or in whichever plane of existence it is experienced. The sequence of their enumeration does not correspond to a chronological sequence in their occurrence. They all occur simultaneously with the genesis of every consciousness.

Although the Pāli term used to designate this category—namely, *sabba-citta-sādhāraṇa* (common to all consciousness)—occurs only in the commentaries, the conception is not without precommentarial history. The idea behind this is that bare consciousness can never be separated from mental factors, among which the seven universals are the most rudimentary. They perform the most essential cognitive functions without which no unit of consciousness can become a cognitive act.

The idea of the universals has its counterpart in the Sarvāstivāda Abhidharma as well. Here the corresponding category is called *mahābhūmika-dharma*, universal mental factors. It consists of not seven, as in Theravāda, but ten mental factors. They are *vedanā* (feeling), *saṃjñā* (perception), *cetanā* (volition), *sparśa* (contact), *chanda* (inclination/predilection), *prajñā* (understanding), *smṛti* (mindfulness), *manaskāra* (attention), *adhimokṣa*/*adhimukti* (determination), and *samādhi* (concentration).[393] It will be seen that six of the items in the Theravāda list—namely, *phassa* (contact), *vedanā* (feeling), *saññā* (perception), *cetanā* (volition), *ekaggatā* (one-pointedness) and *manasikāra* (attention)—are represented here. (*Ekaggatā* of the Theravāda list corresponds to *samādhi* of the Sarvāstivāda list.) The only exception is *arūpa-jīvitindriya* (psychic life faculty). This is because the Theravādins recognize two faculties of life, one psychic (*arūpa*) and the other material (*rūpa*).[394] They are the vitalizing factors of mental and material dhammas. On the other hand, the Sarvāstivādins recognize only one life faculty, which they include in a category called *citta-viprayukta-saṃskāra*.[395] What is included in this category is neither mental nor physical but common to both mental and material factors. Hence there is no need to duplicate the life faculty as one mental and the other material. This explains why it does not find mention in the Sarvāstivāda list of universals. There are thus four items in the Sarvāstivāda list—*chanda* (inclination), *prajñā* (understanding), *smṛti* (mindfulness), and *adhimokṣa* (determination)—that do not occur in the Theravāda list. However, these four are accommodated in the Theravāda Abhidhamma, but under different categories. *Chanda* and *adhimokkha*, as we shall see, come under the heading *pakiṇṇaka*, the miscellaneous mental factors. This shows that like the universals, these two mental factors are ethically variable but, unlike the universals, they do not occur in every type of consciousness. As we shall see, the other two, *smṛti* and *prajñā*, are for the Theravādins two beautiful (*sobhana*) mental factors. As such, they are ethically wholesome and not ethically variable, as the seven universals are.

What led to the theory of the universals can be traced to early Buddhist discourses, where it is said that consciousness (*viññāṇa*) and *nāma-rūpa* are dependent on each other. While *nāma-rūpa* is dependent on consciousness (*viññāṇa-paccayā nāma-rūpaṃ*), consciousness in turn is dependent on *nāma-rūpa* (*nāmarūpa-paccayā viññāṇaṃ*). *Nāma* in *nāma-rūpa* is explained to mean five mental factors—namely, feeling (*vedanā*), perception (*saññā*), volition (*cetanā*), contact (*phassa*), and attention (*manasikāra*). *Rūpa* in *nāma-rūpa* means material phenomena consisting of the four great elements of matter and the matter that is dependent on them.[396] The mutual dependence of consciousness and *nāma-rūpa* is compared to the position of two bundles of bamboo reeds kept standing but leaning against each other. When one falls, the other falls as well.[397] Then in the *Mahānidāna Sutta* of the *Dīghanikāya* we are given to understand that the analysis of the world of experience cannot go beyond the mutual reciprocity of consciousness and *nāma-rūpa*.[398] If we overlook for the moment the material factors represented by *rūpa*, what is of importance for us to note is that consciousness and the five mental factors (*nāma*) are necessarily co-nascent and mutually dependent. Let us also note here that the five mental factors that the Pāli suttas bring under *nāma* occur in the list of mental factors that the Abhidhamma calls universals, although the Abhidhamma adds two more to raise the number to seven.

The next stage in the history of this idea is seen in a group of five mental states mentioned in the *Dhammasaṅgaṇi* to which the commentary gives the name *phassa-pañcaka*, the pentad (beginning) with sense contact.[399] However, the pentad is not completely identical with the five mental factors mentioned under *nāma*. While four items—*phassa*, *vedanā*, *saññā*, and *cetanā*—are common to both groups, in place of *manasikāra* in the *nāma* group we have *citta* (consciousness) in the other group (pentad). Thus what the pentad is intended to show is the same principle, that consciousness and *nāma* are conascent. The only difference is that the pentad does not include *manasikāra* (attention). As pointed out by Venerable Nyanaponika Thera, the pentad of mental states is called *phassa-pañcamā* in the *Theragāthā* and this, as he says, seems to be the only instance in the Sutta Piṭaka where the group's name appears.[400] Again, as pointed out by him, the (five) items in the pentad are mentioned seriatem in the *Mahāsatipaṭṭhāna Sutta*,[401] *Rāhula Saṃyutta*,[402] and *Anupada Sutta*.[403] Very significant is a passage in the *Nettippakaraṇa* where the pentad is referred to as *phassa-pañcamakā dhammā* (the things having sense contact as their fifth). This work refers to the five items as "associated with consciousness" (*viññāṇa-sampayutta*).[404]

Since *viññāṇa* is mentioned separately, it is very probable the term *manasikāra* takes its place here.[405] For the five items in question are mentioned elsewhere in the same work. Thus what the *Nettippakaraṇa* refers to as *phassa-pañcamakā dhammā* are identical with the five factors mentioned in the Pāli suttas as *nāma*. These five mental factors thus represent the earlier stage of the Abhidhamma theory of the universals. It is also interesting to note that in Ācārya Vasubandhu's *Pañcaskandhaprakaraṇa* the relevant list has only five mental factors. These five factors are exactly identical with what the Pāli suttas mention as *nāma* of the compound *nāma-rūpa*.[406] The earliest work where the seven universals are mentioned without the technical designation "common to all consciousness" attached to them is *Milindapañha*: "The origin of visual consciousness, O King, is dependent on the sense organ of sight and visual objects, and such things as arise simultaneously—namely, contact (*phassa*), feeling (*vedanā*), perception (*saññā*), volition (*cetanā*), one-pointedness (*ekaggatā*), psychic life faculty (*arūpa-jīvitindriya*), and attention (*manasikāra*)."[407]

Thus the theory of universals has a continuous antecedent history. Where the category differs from the list given in the Pāli suttas is in the addition of two new items—namely, *ekaggatā* (one-pointedness) and *arūpa-jīvitindriya* (psychic life faculty). Where it differs from the *phassa-pañcaka* is in the absence in it of *citta* (consciousness) and the presence instead of *manasikāra*, *ekaggatā*, and *arūpa-jīvitindriya*. The list with the largest number of items, as we have seen, is the Sarvāstivāda list, containing as many as ten.

The universals perform the most essential cognitive functions in every act of cognition. This will become clear if we examine their individual functions.

Let us take *phassa* first. *Phassa* literally means touch or contact, and connotes sensorial or mental impression. Its precedence over the other six should be understood not in a chronological but in a logical sense. If it is given priority of place it is because it stands as the *sine qua non* for the inception of consciousness and mental factors. For all mental factors arise simultaneously with consciousness. This idea is very much emphasized in the Theravāda exegesis because some other Buddhist schools, such as the Mahāsāṃghika and the Sautrāntika, maintained that mental factors arise in sequence (*pubbāparakkama*). The Mahāsāṃghikas, according to a Pāli subcommentary, say: "first sensory contact touches the object, what is thus touched, feeling feels; what is touched and felt, perception perceives; what is thus touched, felt, and perceived, volition co-ordinates."[408]

Phassa is defined in the Pāli suttas as the correlation (*saṅgati*) that is set up between the sense organ, the sense object, and the sensory awareness (*tiṇṇaṃ saṅgati phasso*).[409] Sometimes it is more elaborately defined as "the coincidence, concurrence, and confluence of these three factors is sensory contact."[410] Whether this means that *phassa* is another expression for "the correlation of the three" (*tiṇṇaṃ saṅgati*) or whether it implies that *phassa* is something besides the correlation is a question that came to be discussed in the Buddhist schools.

The Theravāda position is that phassa is not the mere correlation of the three (*na saṅgati-mattam'eva phasso*) but what actually results from it.[411] Hence phassa is a mental factor distinct and separate from the relationship. The same idea is found in the Sarvāstivāda Abhidharma as well. In defending this position the Sarvāstivādins quote the *Ṣaṭṣaṭka Dharmaparyāya* (*Chachakka Sutta* in *Majjhimanikāya*), which enumerates, among other things, six types of internal sources of consciousness (*ajjhattika āyatana*), six types of external sources of consciousness (*bāhira āyatana*), six types of consciousness (*viññāṇakāya*), six types of sensory contact (*phassakāya*), six kinds of feeling (*vedanākāya*), and six kinds of craving (*taṇhākāya*). The fact that the six kinds of sensory contact are mentioned besides the first three groups is said to confirm that sensory contact is not the same as the correlation of the three groups. It is also contended that any other interpretation would mean that the sūtra is repeating the same item under different names.[412]

The Sautrāntikas take a different position. Sensory contact (*sparśa*) is not a separate mental factor but another expression for the correlation of the sense organ, the sense object, and the sense consciousness. If the sūtra passage does not repeat, so they argue, why is it that sensory contact and craving are mentioned in addition to the six external sources of consciousness, since the sixth external source, which is *dharmāyatana*, includes both sensory contact and craving? The counterargument of the Sarvāstivādins is that if the sūtra passage mentions the six external sources of consciousness besides the six kinds of sensory contact, it is in order to recognize other mental factors, such as perception, which also come under it.[413]

The precommentarial *Nettippakaraṇa* shows that on this issue the earlier Theravāda position is the same as that of the Sautrāntikas. In this work phassa is defined as having, for instance, the union between the eye, the visible, and visual consciousness as its characteristic (*cakkhu-rūpa-viññāṇa-sannipāta-lakkhaṇo phasso*).[414] According to Theravāda Buddhism, the characteristic is not different from that which is characterized. Hence the above definition should mean that phassa is not different from the union between the three items in question.

What led to this issue could perhaps be understood in light of the dhamma theory. A dhamma, as noted earlier, is a basic factor that is not amenable to analysis. If phassa is the "union of the three," then it becomes something analyzable and hence not real. This is how the Sautrāntikas came to their conclusion. It is in line with their tendency to cut down the number of dharmas. The Theravāda and the Sarvāstivāda took the opposite position in order to retain its reality as a separate dhamma: phassa is not the "union of the three" but what results from it.

If phassa is listed as a mental factor (*cetasika*), then obviously it does not refer to the physical collision between the sense organ and the sense object. However, in the *Milindapañha* we find phassa described as being similar to the butting of two rams, or the clashing of two cymbals, or the clapping of two hands.[415] Referring to this, E. R. Sarachchandra says that here the meaning of phassa "has got more and more narrowed down to stand for the physical reaction alone."[416] However, as clarified by the commentaries, when the *Milindapañha* uses the term "eye" (*cakkhu*), in this particular context, it refers not to eye but to eye consciousness (*cakkhu-viññāṇa*).[417] This explanation appears more plausible. In the sentence "Having seen a visible form through the eye" (*cakkhunā rūpaṃ disvā*), "eye" means not the physical eye but eye consciousness. "The eye sees," when rephrased in the language of causality, means "depending on the eye and the eye object, arises eye consciousness" (*cakkhuñ ca paṭicca rūpe ca uppajjati cakkhu-viññāṇaṃ*).

The Abhidhamma term for "physical impact on occasion of sensory stimulation" is not *phassa* but *pasāda-ghaṭṭana*, the striking of the sensitive portion of the sense organ with the object. Although phassa is not physical impact, it is something similar to it. While it is nonmaterial, it behaves as if it were "touching the object."[418] Although phassa does not impinge on the object, it brings about a sort of collision between the consciousness (in the sense organ) and the object.[419] This is described as the "initial descent of consciousness" (*cittassa paṭhamābhinipāto*) on the object.[420] What is hinted at is that phassa is the mental factor throuch which consciousness mentally touches the object.

In fact, one Pāli subcommentary anticipates the question: If contact is a mental dhamma, how can it be described as having the characteristic of touching? The answer is revealed in the following illustrations: when a person sees another person eating a sour mango, saliva arises in his mouth; or when a compassionate person sees another person being tortured, her body begins to tremble; or when a person standing on the ground sees another person precariously standing on the branch of a tree, his lower legs begin to shake; or when a person sees a fearful goblin, her thighs begin to stiffen.[421] In the same way, phassa does not touch the object in a physical sense. Nevertheless, it helps consciousness to mentally touch the object of cognition.

Phassa is also "the initial awareness of the objective presentation,"[422] and in this sense it initiates the entire cognitive process. This justifies its position as a universal mental factor.

Considered in relation to the three factors whose union (*saṅgati*) results in phassa, phassa divides itself into six types as eye contact, ear contact, nose contact, tongue contact, body contact, and mind contact. Already in the Pāli suttas we find the six types distinguished into two groups as *paṭigha-samphassa* (compact contact) and *adhivacana-samphassa* (verbal or designation contact). *Paṭigha-samphassa* refers to impressions that occur as the result of external stimuli, such as sights and sounds. The term *paṭigha* implies impact, resistance, or the ability to react. Hence the five physical sense organs and their sense objects are called *sappaṭigha-rūpa*, materiality having the characteristic of *paṭigha*.[423] However, in this particular context, the commentaries take into consideration only the sense organs. Accordingly, *paṭigha-samphassa* is so called because it arises with the fivefold physical sensory apparatus as its basis (*vatthuṃ katvā*).[424] On the other hand, *adhivacana-samphassa* is so called becauses it arises with the noncorporeal four khandhas as its base.[425] Thus *adhivacana-samphassa* is the same as *mano-samphassa*—that is, mind contact.

But why is mind contact called *adhivacana-samphassa*, designation contact? This is a question to which there seems to be no clear answer in the Pāli commentaries. In the *Abhidharmakośabhāṣya* we find two somewhat similar explanations. According to one, *adhivacana* is another expression for name (*adhivacanam ucyate nāma*). "Speech bases itself on names; it illuminates the meaning of names. Therefore *adhivacana* means name."[426] "Name is the object par excellence of contact associated with mental consciousness. In fact, it is said: Through visual consciousness one 'knows blue' (*nīlaṃ vijānāti*), but one does not know 'this is blue.' Through mental consciousness one 'knows blue' (*nīlaṃ vijānāti*) and also knows 'this is blue' (*nīlam iti ca vijānāti*)."[427]

According to the other explanation, only the mental consciousness is activated with regard to its objects or applies itself to its objects by reason of expression or speech. Therefore mental consciousness is called *adhivacana* and the contact associated with it is called *adhivacana-saṃsparśa*.[428]

What both explanations seek to show is the intimate association between language and mental consciousness. If mental consciousness recognizes blue as blue (= this is blue), this involves some kind of judgment and the participation of language in the act of recognizing the object. This, in other words, means that language has no role to play in the five kinds of contact associated with the physical sense organs. We find a similar idea recognized in the Theravāda Abhidhamma as well. As we shall see, in a cognitive process—eye consciousness, for example—does not identify the object of sight. Its function is described as "mere seeing" (*dassana-matta*). At this stage the object "is experienced in its bare immediacy and simplicity prior to all identificatory cognitive operations."[429] It is best described as seeing without knowledge of what is seen. Perhaps what the Pāli commentaries mean by "mere seeing" is not different from what the *Abhidharmakośabhāṣya* says in this regard.

The second universal mental factor is *vedanā* (feeling). Contact, as we have noted above, is the initial descent of consciousness on the object, "the encounter between consciousness and object."[430] There is a close connection between contact and feeling. "Conditioned by contact, arises feeling" (*phassa-paccayā vedanā*). Feeling means the affective tone that necessarily and simultaneously arises with contact. This affective tone could be pleasant (*sukha*), painful (*dukkha*), or neutral (*adukkhama-sukha*). The third species of feeling indicates the line that divides the hedonic quality into pleasant and painful. However, this hedonic neutrality is not the same as equanimity or balance of mind (*tatramajjhattatā*). The latter implies a higher intellectual state. There cannot be any cognitive act that is not hedonically affected by the object of cognition. Hence, in the same way as contact, feeling too becomes a universal mental factor.

"Feeling is that which feels. It has the fact of being felt as its characteristic, experiencing as its function, relishing of the associated mental states as its manifestation, and tranquility as its proximate cause."[431] When it comes to experiencing the "flavor" of the object, all other mental factors experience it partially and derivatively. In the case of contact, there is mere touching; in the case of perception, there is mere noting/perceiving; in the case of volition, there is mere coordinating; and in the case of consciousness, mere cognizing. But in the case of feeling, it alone experiences the object directly and fully. The other mental factors are like a cook who, after preparing a number of dishes for the king, tastes each only to test them, whereas feeling is like the king who partakes of whichever dish he pleases.[432]

In terms of its affective quality, feeling divides itself into three, as pleasant, painful, and neutral. And since feeling has contact as its immediate condition, it is also divisible into six, as feelings born of eye contact, ear contact, nose contact, tongue contact, body contact, and mind contact. The feelings based on the first four physical senses are always neutral. On the other hand, feelings based on the sense of touch are either pleasant or painful and never neutral.

We need to understand this difference in light of the Abhidhamma teaching on the physiology of sense perception. As we shall see later, the first four physical sense organs and their objects are a species of dependent material dhammas. Therefore their impact is not strong enough to produce physical pain or pleasure. It is as if a piece of cotton were placed on an anvil and struck with another piece of cotton. The impact is not strong enough to affect the gross, great material elements of the physical body. In the case of the sense of touch, the situation is different. Although the organ of touch is a species of dependent matter, the object of touch consists of three great material elements. Therefore, here, gross matter (great material elements) itself comes in contact with gross matter and produces a severe impact. What happens is that when the external gross elements strike the body sensitivity they come in contact with the internal gross elements of the physical body. In this case, the impact is illustrated by the analogy of a piece of cotton placed on an anvil and struck with a hammer. The hammer comes in contact with the piece of cotton and imparts its shock to the anvil as well.[433]

Feelings associated with mind contact can be pleasant, painful, or neutral. Feeling is reckoned as a faculty (*indriya*) as well—that is, as a phenomenon exercising control over its associated phenomena. When analyzed as a faculty, the threefold feeling (pleasant, painful, and neutral) becomes fivefold. The pleasant feeling of the threefold division is here arranged into two as pleasure (*sukha*) and joy (*somanassa*). The first is bodily and the second mental. Similarly the painful feeling of the threefold division is arranged here into two as pain (*dukkha*) and displeasure (*domanassa*). The former is physical and the latter mental. Feeling that is neither painful nor pleasant is arranged here as a faculty called equanimity (*upekkhā*).[434]

The connection between feeling and the next universal—namely, *saññā* (perception)—is shown by the saying: What one feels, that one perceives (*yaṃ vedeti taṃ sañjānāti*). Here saññā means the perceiving of the object appearing at any of the sense doors or at the mind door. It has the characteristic of noting an object as blue, green, and so on (*sañjānana-lakkhaṇa*), and the function of recognizing (*paccabhiññāṇa-rasa*) what has been previously noted. This is likened to a carpenter's recognizing a piece of wood by the mark he had made on it; or to our recognizing a man by the sectarial mark on his forehead, which we have noted and say, he is so-and-so; or to a treasurer's specifying certain articles of jewelery by the ticket on each.[435] Thus the role of saññā as a universal is to isolate and recognize the object of cognition.

As Venerable Nyanaponika Thera observes, the characteristic of saññā and the function assigned to it shows the vital role it plays in the arising of memory. Memory, it may be noted here, is not listed as a separate mental factor. As the Venerable Thera observes, the reason is that memory "is a complex process" and as such it cannot be represented by a single dhamma: "Remembering, which is connecting with the past, is a function of perception in general. However, among the many mental factors involved in a process of perception it is saññā that plays the initial role in this complex process. And therefore saññā has to be considered as cognition as well as recognition."[436]

Cetanā (volition) is the next universal. It is the most dynamic mental factor, being the driving force, the motivating factor that leads to the realization of goals. As a mental factor, it is cetanā that organizes the other mental states associated with itself on the object of cognition. For it represents the conative or volitional aspect of cognition. Therefore its role in this respect is likened to an energetic farmer bustling about his laborers to get in the harvest, or to the leader of a warrior band, fighting and inciting.[437]

What is the role of cetanā as a universal and cetanā as kamma? We need to understand this in light of the Abhidhamma teaching on *kamma-paccaya*, the conditional relation by way of kamma. It is of two kinds. One is co-nascent (*sahajāta*) and the other asynchronous (*nānākhaṇika*). In the former, the conditioning state is cetanā, which arises with every type of consciousness. The conditioned states are consciousness and mental factors that arise together with it. As a universal mental factor, its function is to organize and coordinate the associated mental states to act on the object.[438]

In the case of the asynchronous, the condition is a past cetanā and the conditioned states are mental and material dhammas that arise as a result. This shows that cetanā as kamma and its results as vipāka do not arise at one and the same time. There must always be a temporal difference between them.[439]

As a universal mental factor, cetanā is found in all types of consciousness, including the resultant. In the resultant it is not motivated and has no accumulative power.

The next in the list of universals is *ekaggatā*, "the one-peaked" condition or one-pointedness of mind on the object. It is the focusing of the mind on the object. Its role as a universal shows that some level of concentration is present in varying degrees of intensity in every consciousness. For it is the factor that fixes the mind on the object. It prevents the conascent mental states from dissipating. Absence of wandering (*avisaraṇa*) and distraction (*vikkhepa*) is its characteristic. Its function is to bring together (*sampiṇḍaṇa*) the mental states that arise with it. As water kneads bath powder into a paste, so does it weld together coexistent states and thus prevents them from dissipating.[440]

The sixth universal mental factor is *arūpa-jīvitindriya*, the psychic faculty of life. In its role as a faculty it controls its co-nascent mental states. Its role is to infuse life into its coassociates and to sustain them. Its characteristic is its ceaseless watching and controlling the mental states in a cognitive act. Its function is to be seen in the uninterrupted continuity of the mental process (*pavattana-rasa*).[441]

This brings us to *manasikāra*, the last universal. *Manasikāra* literally means "making in the mind" (*manasmiṃ kāro ti manasikāro*),[442] because it is by virtue of this mental factor that the object is "made present to consciousness." Thus its usual translation as "attention" coincides with its literal meaning as well. Attention "has the characteristic of driving associated mental states toward the object, the function of joining associated mental states to the object, and it manifests itself as facing the object."[443] It is attention that regulates the object, and in this sense it should be regarded as the charioteer of associated mental states.[444] As a cognitive factor, attention has to be present in all consciousness.

That attention on the object is indispensable for any perception to arise is recognized in early Buddhist teachings as well. It is said that three conditions are necessary for perception to take place. The first is that the sense organ must be unimpaired—that is, it must have the faculty of sight or hearing, as the case may be. The second is that external objects must come within its range. The third is that there must be an appropriate act of attention (*tajjo samannāhāro*).[445] Where any one of these conditions fails to operate there will be no resulting consciousness. Here the term used for "attention" is not *manasikāra* but *samannāhāra*.

The Occasionals

This group consists of six mental factors—namely, *vitakka* (initial application), *vicāra* (sustained application), *adhimokkha* (resolve), *viriya* (energy), *pīti* (zest), and *chanda* (desire to act). Like the universals, these mental factors are also ethically variable. They become ethically qualifiable according to the kind of consciousness with which they are associated. Unlike the universals, they are not found in every type of consciousness. The use of the term "occasional" brings out their difference from the universals. A parallel group is not found in the Sarvāstivāda Abhidharma. The one that comes closest to it is a category called *aniyata-bhūmi-dharma* (the indeterminate), consisting of eight elements. However, only vitarka and vicāra are common to both and the rest are mutually exclusive.[446]

Let us take the first two occasionals together, as they are closely related. *Vitakka* is defined as "the disposition, the fixation, the focusing, the (initial) application of the mind," and *vicāra* is "the (continuous) adjusting or focusing of thought."[447] That they represent two levels of a single process is clear. Vitakka has as its characteristic the lifting (*abhiniropaṇa*) of the consciousness and its concomitants to the object, and vicāra the further binding (*anumajjana*) of the consciousness and its concomitants to the object.[448] As when a drum is struck, it goes on reverberating and emitting a continuous sound, so initial application of mind should be looked on as the initial state and sustained application of the mind as the after-reverberation and continuous emission of sound.[449] Vitakka represents the initial incidence of the mind on the object, "as it were the striking of a bell, because it is grosser than, and runs before, the latter. The latter is the consequent binding of consciousness on the object, as it were the reverberation of the bell, because it is more subtle and of the nature of repeated threshing of the object."[450] These commentarial observations show that *vitakka* is at the inception of a train of thought, representing the deliberate movement of voluntary attention. However, *vitakka* has to be distinguished from *manasikāra*, which, as we saw above, is a universal. Their difference seems to be that whereas manasikāra represents a rudimentary cognitive factor that must combine with every type of consciousness, vitakka represents a more complex form of attention that is not indispensable for an act of cognition. Vicāra as the continued exercise of the mind maintains the voluntary thought continuum initially set up by vitakka.

The vitakka-vicāra combination, it may be noted here, has a causal connection with vocal expression. In fact, in the Pāli suttas they are defined as *vacī-saṅkhāra*—that is, verbal constructions, or subconscious operations of the mind preceding vocal utterance. Hence it is said: "Having first had initial thought [*vitakka*] and discursive thought [*vicāra*] is activity of speech."[451] The close connection between vitakka and verbal expression is also indicated in the *Madhupiṇḍika Sutta* where we get the earliest Buddhist theory of perception. Here in a thought process leading to perception we find vitakka (but not vicāra) appearing immediately before *papañca*. Papañca, it may be noted here, is a very complex psychological stage characterized by a proliferation of concepts associated with language.[452]

As to why vitakka and vicāra are defined as vocal constructions (*vacī-saṅkhāra*), the *Abhidharmakośavyākhyā* refers to some comments made by the ancient teachers (*pūrvācārya*). In their opinion vitarka is an indistinct murmur of the mind that has inquiry as its aim (*paryeṣaka-manojalpaḥ*). It is dependent on volition (*cetanā*) or knowledge (*prajnā*) and is the gross state of mind. Vicāra is also an indistinct murmur of the mind, but it has as its aim the attempt to fix (*pratyavekṣaka*) its object and it represents a refined state of the coarser vitarka.[453] Accordingly, vitarka and vicāra are almost identical. They differ in that whereas the former refers to the state of inquiry of the mind, the latter refers to the state of judgment. Both precede all vocal utterance.

Another important role assigned to vitakka and vicāra is as two factors of jhāna consciousness. In this role they operate at a higher level of intensity. Hence in jhāna experience vitakka has the capacity to inhibit the hindrances of sloth and torpor (*thīna-middha*), and vicāra the capacity to inhibit the hindrance of doubt (*vicikicchā*). Both vitakka and vicāra are present in the first jhāna, but in the second vitakka gets eliminated. Neither has a role to play in the other three higher jhānas, and hence their absence in them as jhāna factors.[454]

As to these two mental factors, the Sautrāntikas take a different position. In their view, what is said in the sūtras on vitarka and vicāra is clear enough: *Vitarka* and *vicāra* are vocal *saṃskāras* that immediately precede as causes of verbal utterance. They are not two separate dharmas but are two names given to a collection of dharmas that function as a necessay condition for verbal utterance. Vitarka represents a coarser stage, vicāra a refinement of the same stage.[455]

After vitakka and vicāra comes *adhimokkha* as the third occasional. It literally means "a releasing on" (*adhimuñcana*) of the consciousness and its concomitants toward the object. Adhimokkha is decision or resolve. It has determination (*saṇṇiṭṭhāna*) as its characteristic, resistance to slinking along (*asaṃsappana*) as its function, unshakableness as its manifestation, and an object fit to be decided (*saṇṇiṭṭhātabba-dhamma*) as its proximate cause.[456] Thus adhimokkha represents a positive state of the mind, a state free from doubt and indecision due to the presence of an object calling for increased attention.

For the Sarvāstivāda *adhimokṣa* (*adhimokkha*) is not an occasional but a universal (*mahābhūmika*). As to why it is so, there are two opinions. Ācārya Saṃghabhadra says that since all consciousness arises with an element of approval, it is to be concluded that adhimokṣa is a universal mental factor.[457] Another explanation is that it is by virtue of adhimokṣa that consciousness exercises sovereignty without obstacles over the object.[458] For the Sautrāntika adhimokṣa is not a separate dharma because it does not distinguish itself from knowledge (*jñāna*): the characteristic of adhimokṣa is to make the consciousness determined (*niścita*) with regard to the object. This characteristic is not different from the characteristic of knowledge.[459]

Ācārya Yaśomitra refers to three other interpretations given to adhimokṣa. The first is that it is the consideration of the object from the point of view of its qualities (*guṇato avadhāraṇa*). The second is that it is the mind's compliance (*ruci*) with the object. The third is that it is the contemplation of an object in conformity with the decision already made.[460]

To make the Theravāda position clear: Adhimokkha, as the Sautrāntikas maintain, is not an expression for a complex of dharmas. It is a separate item having the status of a dhamma. It is not, as the Sarvāstivādins maintain, a universal but a mental factor that arises only with some types of consciousness. But for both Theravāda and Sarvāstivāda it is an ethically variable factor.

The many interpretations given to adhimokkha/adhimokṣa show its importance in the Abhidharma psychology. However, it is not found among the mental factors mentioned in the *Dhammasaṅgaṇi*. It was the commentaries that introduced it as one of the "whatsoever other" (*ye-vā-panakā*), or supplementary factors. The Pāli suttas use the term more or less as synonymous with *chanda* and *viriya* (*chando adhimokkho viriyaṃ*).[461] In the *Vibhaṅga*, adhimokkha is said to be conditioned by craving (*taṇhā-paccayo adhimokkho*).[462] Here the meaning seems to be firm resolve or decision. What all this suggests is that the recognition of adhimokkha as a separate mental factor is a postcanonical development.

The next item in the list of occasionals is *viriya* (energy). Its inclusion in this category shows that it is an ethically variable factor; it could be wholesome or unwholesome depending on the kind of consciousness with which it is associated. Thus viriya can be directed for the realization of goals either wholesome or unwholesome.

However, we find elsewhere viriya being defined and recognized as something invariably wholesome and desirable. Numerous in fact are the references in the Pāli suttas extolling the virtues of viriya. Equally numerous are the references blaming its opposite quality, indolence (*kosajja*).

Viriya as ethically variable seems to be confined to the Theravāda Abhidhamma. The Sarvāstivāda, for instance, includes it among the ten universal wholesome factors (*kuśalamahābhūmika*). This obviously means that it is always associated with wholesome consciousness. It is defined as "endurance of the mind" (*vīryaṃ cetaso'bhyutsāhaḥ*) in morally wholesome actions.[463]

Why the two Abhidharma schools took two different positions on this matter is worth examining. It is true that for Theravāda viriya is ethically variable. But the emphasis is on the indispensability and desirability of wholesome viriya in pursuing spiritual goals. It was this aspect, more than its opposite aspect, that was often brought into focus. This, it seems, is the early Buddhist position as well, although the Pāli suttas extol energy without qualifying it as wholesome. It is unlikely that they have overlooked the possibility of misdirected energy. In fact, its possibility is clearly recognized in describing desirable energy as *sammappadhāna* (right endeavour) and *sammā vāyāma* (right effort). At least these two contexts thus acknowledge the moral variability of viriya. For the Sarvāstivādins misdirected energy is not energy proper but is in fact indolence. They seek to justify this interpretation with reference to a sūtra passage where vīrya of those outside the religion is called *kauśīdya* (indolence).[464] This sūtra passage, in our view, need not be understood in such a literal sense. What it seems to suggest is that misdirected energy, which the Theravādins call *micchā-vāyāma* (wrong effort), is as futile as indolence. If vīrya is invariably wholesome, this gives rise to the question whether vīrya is not involved in realizing unwholesome goals as well. It is perhaps as an answer to this question that the Sarvāstivādins include chanda (explained below)—that is, the desire to act (*kattukamyatā*)—in the category of ethically variable universal factors. Accordingly, chanda can corporate both with wholesome and unwholesome consciousness. Since the Sarvāstivādins recognized vīrya as invariably wholesome they had to recognize its opposite, which is *kauśīdya* (indolence), as a separate mental factor, a factor that is invariably unwholesome.[465] A factor parallel to this is not found in the Theravāda list of unwholesome mental factors. The reason seems to be that for the Theravādins indolence is not a separate mental factor but the relative absence of energy. For energy can have different levels of intensity, ascending upward to its highest pitch or descending downward to the zero point. As we shall see later, we find a similar situation in how the two schools defined the phenomena of heat and cold. For the Sarvāstivādins cold is the opposite of heat and therefore these are counted as two separate elements, whereas for the Theravādins, cold is not a separate element but the relative absence of heat, and heat is represented by the fire element.

Wholesome viriya plays a vital role in Buddhist ethical teachings. It is one of the five spiritual faculties (*indriya*) and it is described in the *Dhammasaṅgaṇi* as "the mental inception of energy, the striving and the onward effort, the exertion and endeavour, the zeal and ardour, the vigour and fortitude, the state of unfaltering effort, the state of sustained desire, the state of unflinching endurance, the solid grip of the burden."[466] Wholesome viriya is also one of the five spiritual powers (*bala*). It is counted as one of the four means of accomplishing *iddhi*. It is wholesome viriya that appears again as right effort (*sammā vāyāma*) or as the four modes of supreme effort (*sammappadhāna*) in the noble eightfold path. It is again this same mental factor that we find elevated to the sublime position of a factor of awakening (*bojjhaṅga*). And as one Pāli commentary says, "right energy should be regarded as the root of all attainments."[467]

The next item in the list of occasionals is *pīti*—that is, zest or pleasurable interest. Pīti has satisfaction (*sampiyāyana*) as its characteristic, the thrilling of body and mind as its function (*kāyacitta-pīnanarasa*), and elation (*odagga*) as its manifestation.[468]

Pīti and sukha appear to be closely connected, but there is a difference between the two. Pīti is a conative factor included in the aggregate of mental formations. Sukha is a variety of feeling and is therefore included in the aggregate of feeling. What the Theravādins mean by pīti is not pleasant feeling but pleasurable interest or zest. It is a conative factor dissociated from any hedonic content. A commentary explains the difference as follows: Pīti is delight that results in attaining a desired object (*iṭṭhārammaṇa-paṭilābhe tuṭṭhi*) and sukha is the enjoyment of "the flavor" of what is acquired (*paṭiladdha-rasānubhavanaṃ sukhaṃ*). Where there is pīti there is bound to be sukha (*yattha pīti tattha sukhaṃ*). Where there is sukha, there pīti is not necessarily present (*yattha sukhaṃ tattha na niyamato pīti*).[469]

Because pīti is an ethically variable factor it can be developed as a wholesome mental factor of jhāna experience (*jhānaṅga*). At this level, as Venerable Bhikkhu Bodhi observes, it is best translated not as "zest" but as "rapture."[470] The commentaries mention five grades of pīti that can be experienced when developing concentration. To quote from Venerable Bhikkhu Bodhi's rendering:

> Minor zest, momentary zest, showering zest, uplifting zest, and pervading zest. Minor zest is able to raise the hairs on the body. Momentary zest is like flashes of lightening. Showering zest breaks over the body again and again like waves on the sea shore. Uplifting zest can cause the body to levitate. And pervading zest pervades the whole body as an inundation fills a cavern.[471]

The last occasional mental factor is *chanda*. Chanda is defined as the desire to act (*kattukamyatā*).[472] It has to be distinguished from *kāmacchanda*, the sensual desire that is one of the five mental hindrances (*nīvaraṇa*), and also from *lobha*, which is greed. Chanda is ethically variable, whereas kāmacchanda and lobha are invariably unwholesome. Chanda finds no mention in the *Dhammasaṅgaṇi* list of mental factors. It is introduced in the commentaries as one of the supplementary factors (*ye-vā-panakā*). In the suttas, chanda is often mentioned as more or less synonymous with effort (*vāyāma*), exertion (*ussāha*), and striving (*ussaḷhi*). Although chanda is thus closely connected with viriya (energy), the two are not identical. Chanda is the desire to act, the desire to accomplish. The great potentiality of both chanda and viriya in realizing wholesome goals is shown by their elevation to the level of *adhipati*.[473] An adhipati is a predominant mental factor that has a dominating impact on the consciousness to which it belongs, facilitating it to accomplish difficult tasks. Unlike chanda, viriya could function as a faculty (*indriya*) as well. Where a faculty differs from a predominant is that whereas the former has its range of control limited to its respective sphere, the latter's range of control applies to the whole consciousness. A predominant is likened to a king who has lordship over all his ministers, whereas the faculties are like ministers who govern their own respective districts.[474]

In the Sarvāstivāda chanda is listed not as an occasional but as a universal. This means that for both schools chanda is an ethically variable factor.

8

THE UNWHOLESOME MENTAL FACTORS

THIS CATEGORY CONSISTS of fourteen mental factors—namely, (1) *moha* (delusion), (2) *ahirika* (moral shamelessness), (3) *anottappa* (moral fearlessness), (4) *uddhacca* (restlessness), (5) *lobha* (greed), (6) *diṭṭhi* (wrong view), (7) *māna* (conceit), (8) *dosa* (hatred), (9) *issā* (envy), (10) *macchariya* (avarice), (11) *kukkucca* (worry), (12) *thīna* (sloth), (13) *middha* (torpor), and (14) *vicikicchā* (doubt).

Among these fourteen factors, the first four—moha, ahirika, anottappa, and uddhacca—differ from the rest in one important respect. Unlike the rest, they are invariably associated with every unwholesome consciousness. They are therefore called universal unwholesome factors (*sabba-akusala-sādhāraṇa*).[475]

Moha, which is delusion, is defined as mind's blindness (*cittassa andhakārabhāva*). Its function is nonpenetration (*asampaṭivedha*) or concealment of the true nature of the object (*ārammaṇa-sabhāva-chādana*). It is manifested as improper conduct (*asammā-paṭipatti*) and its proximate cause is unwise attention (*ayoniso manasikāra*).[476] Its sway over unwholesome states of mind is more extensive than that of lobha and dosa, although these three items together constitute the three radical roots of moral evil. For as we have seen, while moha is present in all the twelve types of unwholesome consciousness, lobha is present in eight and dosa in two. This means that it is only in a mind overcome by moha, a mind that cannot see the real nature of the object, that lobha and dosa can arise. In this sense moha, which is the same as avijjā, is more primary than lobha and dosa. Hence as a Pāli commentary observes, moha should be seen as the root of all that is unwholesome.[477] If lobha and dosa cannot arise together it is because of their mutual exclusivity. Lobha is attachment to what is agreeable and attractive, and dosa is repulsion to what is disagreeable and repulsive.

The next two mental factors coexisting with every unwholesome consciousness are ahirika (absence of moral shame) and anottappa (absence of moral fear). The first is defined as absence of disgust (*ajigucchana*) and absence of shame (*alajjā*) at bodily and verbal misconduct, and the second as moral recklessness or absence of dread for such misconduct. Both manifest as not shrinking away from evil. The proximate cause of ahirika is lack of respect for one's own self, and that of anottappa is lack of respect for others.[478]

These two mental factors play a vital role in the Buddhist teaching on the causality of moral evil. This is clearly seen in their opposites, moral shame (*hiri*) and moral fear (*ottappa*), being defined as guardians of the world (*lokapālā dhammā*).[479] As one Pāli sutta says, if moral shame and moral fear were not to protect the world, the world would descend down to the lowest level of moral depravity, where "one would respect neither one's mother, nor one's mother's sister, nor one's brother's wife, nor one's teacher's wife."[480] Thus the lack of moral shame and moral fear are the two primary causative factors for the deterioration of the average moral standard of humankind.

The Sarvāstivāda, too, recognizes this situation by listing them as universal unwholesome mental factors (*akuśala-mahābhūmika-caitasikas*). The Sautrāntikas do not recognize them as two separate mental dharmas. This does not mean that they have dispensed with the notion of moral shame and moral fear. In their view, they are two names given to a complex of mental dharmas when they operate in a particular manner.

The fourth mental factor arising with every unwholesome consciousness is uddhacca, agitation or restlessness. It has "mental excitement as its characteristic, like wind-tossed water; wavering as function, like a flag waving in the wind; whirling as manifestation, like scattered ashes struck by a stone; unsystematic thought owing to mental excitement as proximate cause."[481] It is the distraction of the mind, the state of being distrait. However, uddhacca is not a mental property that is antithetical to attention. For as we have noted, attention is present in varying degrees of intensity in all consciousness, irrespective of their ethical quality. For without some degree of attention to the object, no thought complex could arise at all. Uddhacca as mind's agitation is therefore the opposite of vūpasama, mental calm. The presence of uddhacca in all unwholesome consciousness shows that a mind overcome by it is not a fertile ground for the emergence of wholesome qualities. Uddhacca is also one of the five impediments (*nīvaraṇas*), because it distorts the clarity of mind and weakens the capacity for proper understanding.

Auddhatya (*uddhacca*) as a universal unwholesome mental factor is found in the Sarvāstivāda as well. It is defined as a mental factor antithetical to mental calm. At its other extreme is *kauśīdya*, mind's lassitude or sluggishness. A mind in which kauśīdya dominates and auddhatya is reduced is sluggish (*līna*). Whereas a mind in which auddhatya dominates and kauśīdya is reduced is excited (*uddhata*). Both states of mind are equally injurious to mental health and for the cultivation of spiritual qualities.[482]

The four mental factors discussed so far are invariably present in all unwholesome consciousness. This does not mean that they are the only conditioning factors of moral evil. As unwholesome universals, they have to combine with other unwholesome factors to produce a given unwholesome consciousness.

Among them the first is lobha (greed), which is one of the three cardinal roots of moral evil. It stands for all degrees of passionate clinging to both sensuous and nonsensuous objects. It is the self-centered desire to possess and gratify. It has "the characteristic of sticking to an object like bird lime, the function of adhering to like fresh meat in a hot pan, the manifestation of not letting go like a taint of lampblack, the proximate cause as enjoyment of things that leads to bondage."[483] An intensified state of lobha is *abhijjā* (covetousness), the obsessive desire to acquire what others possess (*para-sampatti*), to make others' property one's own. It is the outstretched hand of the mind for others' prosperity.[484] On the role played by lobha in the genesis of unwholesome states of mind, all schools of Buddhism agree. It combines with dosa and moha to form the triad of unwholesome roots.

The next unwholesome mental factor is *diṭṭhi*. It literally means view. However, here it means wrong view, although the term is not qualified by *micchā* (wrong). It stands for all forms of wrong perspectives, views, opinions, speculations, and ideologies. As a mental factor diṭṭhi means "seeing wrongly." It has the characteristic of interpreting things unwisely and its function is to preassume. It is manifested as wrong belief and erroneous interpretations.[485]

It is interesting to note here that diṭṭhi in the sense of wrong view arises only in a consciousness that is primarily conditioned by lobha (greed) and not, as might be expected, in a consciousness that is motivated only by moha (delusion or ignorance). Why this is so will become clear if we take into consideration the role assigned to psychology in the Buddhist critique of views and ideologies. Buddhism is aware of the impact of our desires on the kind of beliefs and views we tend to entertain. There is a tendency on our part to believe in what is agreeable and palatable and to reject what is disagreeable and unpalatable. Hence Buddhism takes into consideration the psychological motivation of ideological positions. Nowhere is this so clearly stated as in the well-known phrase *taṇhā-paccayā upādānaṃ*—that is, grasping has craving as its condition. Now grasping is said to be of four kinds, among which two are concerned with views. One is called *diṭṭhi-upādāna*, the grasping of views, and the other *attavāda-upādāna*, the grasping of the belief in a self.[486] Since Buddhism does not believe in a self, it is not the self but the belief in a self that can be grasped. This is why the second type of grasping is called "grasping of the belief in a self" and not "grasping of the self."

What is relevant to us here is the fact that, as shown above, Buddhism identifies craving as the causative factor of all speculative views and the belief in self. It is in conformity with this situation that Buddhism seeks to trace the origin of the eternalist (*sassatavāda*) and the annihilationist (*ucchedavāda*) views to psychological factors. The first is the Buddhist expression for all spiritual views of existence that are based on the duality principle, the duality of the permanent self (soul, spirit) and the temporary physical body. The second is the Buddhist expression for all materialist views that are based on the identity principle, the identity of the self and the physical body. The first is called eternalism (*sassatavāda*) because it believes in a metaphysical self that is permanent and that survives death. The second is called annihilationism (*ucchedavāda*) because it believes in a temporary physical self that gets annihilated at death. According to their Buddhist diagnosis, both views have a psychological origin. The first is due to *bhava-taṇhā*, the desire for eternal life, the desire to perpetuate ourselves into eternity. The second is due to *vibhava-taṇhā*, the desire for eternal death, the desire to see ourselves completely annihilated at death with no prospect of postmortem existence.

Thus when the Abhidhamma says that diṭṭhi arises only in a consciousness that is mainly motivated by lobha, it is in conformity with the early Buddhist teaching on the origin of speculative views and beliefs. Yet one question remains: Why is the genesis of wrong view excluded from all consciousness that is motivated by moha, which, as we saw above, stands for delusion or ignorance? Is not wrong view due more to ignorance than to desire or craving (lobha)?

As we have noted earlier, there are two types of consciousness motivated by moha (delusion). One is associated with vicikicchā (skeptical doubt) and the other with uddhacca (restlessness). As to the first, a mind that is obsessed with vicikicchā means that it is overwhelmed with perplexity, indecisiveness, and vacillation due to moha. Such a consciousness is not capable of forming any view, whether it is right or wrong. For the formation of any view requires some form of positive or negative evaluation of the object. As to the second, a mind that is obsessed with restlessness means that it is in a state of turbulence due to distraction and disquietude. Such a consciousness, too, is not capable of forming any view, whether right or wrong, because the mind's turbulence prevents any positive or negative evaluation of the object. This is not to overlook the fact that, as already noted, the mental factor of uddhacca (restlessness) is common to all unwholesome consciousness. However, in this particular consciousness it is more pronounced than in others. Thus the two types of consciousness motivated by delusion and obsessed with doubt and restlessness, respectively, lack natural acuteness to evaluate and judge. It is for this very reason, as we have noted earlier, that the description in terms of prompted (*sasaṅkhārika*) and unprompted (*asaṅkhārika*) is not applicable to these two types of consciousness.

There are two main reasons for Buddhism's concern with wrong views. One is that dogmatic attachment to views (*diṭṭhiparāmāsa*) gives rise to ideological perversion that prevents us from seeing things in their proper perspective. Second, wrong views can be a source of wrong and evil aspirations, resulting in wrong and evil conduct. Ideologies could at times bring a human being to the lowest levels of moral depravity. Hence the Buddha says: "No other thing than evil views do I know, O monks, whereby to such an extent the unwholesome things already arisen are brought to growth and fullness. No other thing than evil views do I know whereby to such an extent the wholesome things not yet arisen are hindered in their arising, and the wholesome things already arisen disappear."[487]

That diṭṭhi as wrong view plays a complex role in the causality of unwholesome states of mind is shown by its being considered under a number of aspects. It is one of the latent proclivities (*anusaya*) that becomes patent (*pariyuṭṭhāna*) when the appropriate conditions for its arising are there.[488] As one of the mental intoxicants (*āsava*), it muddles the mind and causes the loss of mind's clarity, the clarity that is necessary for seeing things in their proper perspective.[489]

In the Sarvāstivāda the position of *dṛṣṭi* (*diṭṭhi*) in relation to consciousness is rather complex. Here dṛṣṭi is not counted as a separate mental factor (*caitasika*). It is an aspect of *prajñā/mati*, which in the Sarvāstivāda is one of the ten universals (*mahābhūmika*). Here dṛṣṭi is defined as *tīraṇa* or *santīraṇa*—that is, judgment preceding the consideration of the object (*upanidhyāna*). By judgment is meant the preconceived framework within which the object is cognized. It is a subjective factor wrought by the synthesizing function of the mind and superimposed on the object. Dṛṣṭi is not an invariable aspect of prajñā. However, whenever dṛṣṭi arises, it arises as an aspect of prajñā. Prajñā can exist without dṛṣṭi but dṛṣṭi cannot exist without prajñā. In this particular context prajñā means the misdirected and defiled version of it.[490]

In passing we would like to note here that in the Sarvāstivāda wrong views are classified in a somewhat different manner. All wrong views, defined as a misdirected variety of prajñā, are of five kinds. The first is *satkāya-dṛṣṭi*, the wrong belief that the so-called self-entity is identical with one or more of the five aggregates of clinging. The second is *mithyā-dṛṣṭi*, the belief that consists of denying (*apavāda*) that which really exists, as for instance the fact of suffering and so on. It is of course true that all forms of erroneously conceived views are different versions of mithyā-dṛṣṭi. However, this particular variety of wrong view receives the name *mithyā-dṛṣṭi* because it represents "the most false" of all false beliefs. It is in fact this variety of view that is based on negation (*apavāda*), whereas all other wrong views depend on affirmation and erroneous attribution (*samāropikā*). The third is *antagrāha-dṛṣṭi*, the wrong belief in the two extremes of eternalism (*śāśvatavāda*) and annihilationism (*ucchedavāda*). The fourth is the wrong view that considers as exalted (*ucca*) that which is lowly and unwholesome. The reference is to *dṛṣṭi-parāmāsa*, clinging to wrong beliefs and views. The fifth is the wrong view through which one considers as cause that which is not the cause, as path that which is not the path. The reference is to *śīlavrata-parāmāsa*, clinging to mere rules and rituals, which has as its ideological basis all wrong beliefs and ill-grounded speculations as to the nature of sentient existence.[491]

The next unwholesome mental factor is *māna* (conceit). Like diṭṭhi, it arises only in a consciousness primarily motivated by lobha (greed).[492] For māna in the sense of conceit is closely associated with attachment to the notion of a "separate selfhood." Although diṭṭhi and māna are primarily motivated by lobha, by nature they are mutually exclusive. They do not arise together in one and the same consciousness. They are compared to two fearless lions who always live in the forest but who cannot live in the same den. If diṭṭhi is due to self-deception, māna is due to self-comparison.

Māna is "conceit at the thought 'I am the better man'; conceit at the thought 'I am as good [as they]'—all such sort of conceit, overweening, conceitedness, loftiness, haughtiness, flaunting a flag, assumption, desire of the heart for self-advertisement."[493] The threefold conceit based on the notions of "superiority," "equality," and "inferiority" is in the Pāli suttas called *tisso vidhā*, "the three modes of comparison," and their origin is attributed to ignorance of the true nature of reality.[494]

According to the commentarial definition, māna has haughtiness as its characteristic, self-exultation as its function, and is manifested as vainglory. Its proximate cause is greed dissociated from wrong view[495] because, as mentioned earlier, conceit and wrong view are mutually exclusive although both have to be motivated by greed.

Māna is closely connected with *mada*, which is self-infatuation. However, in the Theravāda Abhidhamma there is no separate mental factor called *mada*. This seems to suggest that it was understood as a variety of māna. In fact in the *Vibhaṅga* mada is paraphrased by māna.[496] On the other hand, in the Sarvāstivāda māna and mada are two separate mental factors. Here māna means self-elevation due to self-comparison. Mada means self-elevation due to self-obsession with what one possesses, whether it is material or spiritual. It gives rise to thoughts of haughtiness, arrogance, and excessive pride.[497]

The next four unwholesome mental factors—namely, dosa (hatred), issā (envy), macchariya (avarice), and kukkucca (worry)—are closely associated, as they occur only in the two types of consciousness primarily motivated by aversion (*paṭigha*).[498] They do not arise in the consciousness rooted in greed because none of them exhibits any sign of attraction to the thing in relation to which they arise as their object. What is common to all four mental factors is not their empathy with but their repugnance to the object.

Dosa is "the vexation of spirit, resentment, repugnance, hostility, ill temper, irritation, indignation, antipathy, abhorrence, mental disorder, detestation, anger, fuming, irascibility, hate, hating, hatred, disorder, getting upset, derangement, opposition, hostility, churlishness, abruptness, disgust of heart."[499] It is the annoyance at the thought of harm, actual or imagined, either to oneself or to those who are near and dear to one, or at the thought of benefit to those whom one does not like. It could even arise groundlessly (*aṭṭhāne*), without any reason. One gets annoyed, saying, "it rains too much," "it does not rain," "the sun shines too much," "it does not shine."[500]

What is peculiar to dosa is that a consciousness rooted in it is always accompanied by a feeling of displeasure (*domanassa*). For when one is confronted with things offensive, distasteful, and contrary to one's expectations, the general mood is one of sullenness.

Closely connected with dosa is issā (envy), the next unwholesome factor. It is the "resentment at the gifts, the hospitality, the respect, the affection, reverence, and worship accruing to others."[501] Issā has the characteristic of jealousy (*usūyana*) at another's success, dissatisfaction with it (*anabhirati*) as its function, aversion (*vimukhabhāva*) toward it as its manifestation, and others' success (*parasampatti*) as its proximate cause.[502]

The next mental factor that goes with dosa (hatred) is macchariya (avarice). It is "meanness, niggardliness, selfishness, want of generosity, the inability to bear the thoughts of sharing with others."[503] Its characteristic is concealing one's own prosperity, already obtained or to be obtained. Its function is the reluctance to share what one has with others. It is manifest as shrinking away from sharing. Its proximate cause is one's own success and not others' success, as in the case of envy.[504] "Let it be for me only and not for another"[505] sums up the nature of avarice. It is ugliness of the mind (*cetaso virūpabhāva*).[506]

There are two varieties of avarice. One is the soft variety (*mudu*) called *veviccha* (to be obsessed with too many wants). It manifests as: "Let it be mine, not another's." The other is the hard variety (*thadda*) called *kadariya* (covetousness). It prevents another from giving to others, which therefore is more ignoble than the soft variety.[507] Both varieties of avarice can occur not only in relation to things material but in relation to things spiritual as well. The latter is called *dhamma-macchariya* (spiritual avarice).[508]

The last mental factor that arises in the two consciousnesses mainly rooted in dosa is kukkucca. It literally means "wrongly done act" or "what is wrongly done." However, as the *Abhidharmakośabhāṣya* points out, it refers not to the act wrongly done but to scruples, remorse, uneasiness of conscience, and worry that results from such acts. It is a case of naming the effect by its cause.[509] It is precisely in this way that kukkucca is understood in the Theravāda as well. It is not only remorse over the evil that is done but also remorse over the good that is not done. It is "consciousness of what is lawful in something that is unlawful; consciousness of what is unlawful in something that is lawful; consciousness of what is immoral in something that is moral; consciousness of what is moral in something that is immoral—all this sort of worry, fidgeting, over-scrupulousness, remorse of conscience, mental scarifying—this is what is called worry."[510] "Mental scarifying" is so called because "when reproach of conscience arises over deeds of commission and omission, it scales the mind as the point of an awl does a metal bowl."[511]

Together with uddhacca, kukkucca is one of the five mental impediments (*nīvaraṇa*). While uddhacca, as we have noted, occurs in every unwholesome consciousness, kukkucca is limited to the two types of unwholesome consciousness rooted mainly in dosa. This shows that uddhacca can occur without kukkucca, but kukkucca cannot occur without uddhacca.

On the ethical quality of kaukṛtya/kukkucca, the Sarvāstivādins take a different position. For them it is not invariably unwholesome. It could also be wholesome in certain occasions. Regret or remorse in relation to a good action omitted and bad action committed is wholesome. Regret or remorse in relation to a bad action omitted and good action committed is unwholesome.[512]

Where kukkucca becomes commendable according to Theravāda is when it means healthy doubt with regard to the transgression of Vinaya rules. However, it is specifically stated that this kind of praiseworthy *vinaya-kukkucca* should not be confused with kukkucca when it means a mental hindrance.[513]

The next two unwholesome mental factors, *thīna* (sloth) and *middha* (torpor), always occur together as two species of mental sickness (*gelañña*). Thīna is "indisposition or unwieldiness of consciousness" or "sluggishness or dullness of consciousness."[514] Its characteristic is lack of driving power. Its function is to remove energy. It is manifested as subsiding of the mind.[515] Middha as torpor is the morbid state of the mental factors (*cetasika*). "Its characteristic is unwieldiness. Its function is to smother. It is manifested as laziness or as nodding and sleep."[516] Thīna refers to sickness of the consciousness (*citta-gelañña*), whereas middha to sickness of the mental factors (*cetasika-gelañña*).

When consciousness is overcome by the morbid state called thīna, it becomes inert and "hangs down like a bat from a tree and like a pot of raw sugar hung to a peg. It is a form of mental density with no possibility of expansion, like a lump of butter too stiff for spreading."[517] "It is the shrinking state of the mind like a cock's feather before fire."[518] Middha, the morbid state of the mental factors, shuts in mental factors and prevents them from issuing forth by way of diffusion.[519]

One characteristic that combines both thīna and middha is their inability to combine with the types of consciousness that are unprompted (*asaṅkhārika*). This is because these two factors represent "psychological fatigue" or "psychological inertia." By their very nature they are opposed to adaptability and the necessary drive for action. They are therefore compelled to arise only in the types of unwholesome consciousness, five in all, that are prompted or induced by external factors (*sasaṅkhārika*).

As to the nature of middha, the Abhayagiri Fraternity of the Theravādins took up a different position. In their view middha is not unwieldiness of the mind; it is unwieldiness of the physical body. Because of this unorthodox interpretation of middha, members of the Abhayagiri were called *middhavādino* by the orthodox Theravādins.[520] The term literally means those who advocate torpor (of the physical body). But it seems to have been intended in a derogatory sense to mean "those who profess in a state of torpor."

In his commentary to the *Dhammasaṅgaṇi*, Ācariya Buddhaghosa criticizes the above view without identifying its advocates. His main argument is as follows: In the *Dhammasaṅgaṇi* definition of *middha*, *kāya* means not physical body but the "body" of mental factors. If kāya in this particular context means the physical body, then such mental factors as *kāyassa lahutā* (lightness of *kāya*), *kāyassa mudutā* (malleability of *kāya*), and so on will have to be understood in a similar way—that is, as referring to the lightness and malleability and so on of the physical body. In such a situation, how are we to understand such physical factors as *rūpassa lahutā* (lightness of materiality) and *rūpassa mudutā* (malleability of materiality), and so on, which specifically mean lightness and malleability of the physical body?[521]

In the suttas, for instance, one encounters such statements as: "He experiences bliss by kāya, realizes the ultimate truth by kāya." If *kāya* here means the physical body, then one will have to believe that the experience of bliss and the realization of the truth are made through the physical body. It may, of course, be contended that the use of the words *soppa* (sleep) and *paccalāyikā* (drowsiness) in the *Dhammasaṅgaṇi* definition of *middha* proves that the reference is to physical and not mental torpor. Our answer to this contention is that sleep and drowsiness are not middha as such but its causes. It is a case of describing the effect through its cause (*phalūpacāra*), just as the two faculties of masculinity and femininity are sometimes described as the two sexes, though in fact they are what result from the two faculties. Again, together with thīna, middha constitutes one of the mental impediments (*nīvaraṇa*). And since impediments are defined as that which "causes the weakening of knowledge and corruption of mind," middha surely cannot be understood as something material.[522]

The last unwholesome mental factor is *vicikicchā*, often rendered as "doubt." Its various nuances can be seen in the *Dhammasaṅgaṇi* definition: "The doubt, the hesitating, the dubiety, which on that occasion is puzzlement, perplexity; distraction, standing at cross-roads, uncertainty of grasp, evasion, hesitation, incapacity of grasping thoroughly."[523] Vicikicchā, as one commentary says, is the inability to decide which is which (*idam ev'idanti nicchetuṃ asamatthabhāvo ti vicikicchā*).[524] Vicikicchā has doubting as its characteristic, vacillation as its function, indecisiveness as its manifestation, and unwise attention as its proximate cause.[525] Thus vicikicchā combines doubt as well as the inability to decide.

The nature of vicikicchā can be further clarified if we position it in relation to *adhimokkha*. Adhimokkha, it may be recalled here, is decision or resolve having the characteristic of conviction and manifesting as decisiveness. In this sense adhimokkha represents a position opposed to vicikicchā. In fact, in the Pāli commentaries we often find the two verbs *vicikicchati* (doubts) and *na adhimuccati* (does not resolve) used as synonymous expressions.[526] And in the *Visuddhimagga* we read, "with the absence of vicikicchā there arises adhimokkha."[527] That vicikicchā also refers to a position opposed to *sampasāda* (serenity, tranquility, faith) is shown by the use of the words *na sampasīdati* (is not tranquilized) as an expression for *vicikicchati*.[528]

Vicikicchā is also defined as a state of denseness and rigidity in a psychological sense. For when one is overcome by perplexity due to indecision, one's mind becomes stiff and dense, a condition that impedes effective thinking. This is why it is counted as a mental impediment, for vexation due to indecision and the mind's vacillation is an impediment to mental culture and spiritual progress.

9

THE BEAUTIFUL MENTAL FACTORS

THIS CATEGORY OF MENTAL FACTORS has to be understood in relation to beautiful consciousness (*sobhana-citta*). "Beautiful consciousness," as we have noted earlier, is the Abhidhamma's expression for all consciousnesses, excluding the kammically unwholesome (*akusala*) and the rootless (*ahetuka*). The "beautiful" category includes not only all kammically wholesome consciousnesses but also the resultant (*vipāka*) and functional (*kiriya*) consciousnesses that are kammically indeterminate (*abyākata*) but possess "beautiful" mental factors—the mental factors that we propose to examine here.

The category of the "beautiful" includes twenty-five mental factors. This means that it is larger than either of the two categories that we have discussed so far—the ethically variable and the unwholesome. Among the beautiful mental factors, nineteen occur in all beautiful consciousnesses (*sobhana-sādhāraṇa*): (1) *saddhā* (faith), (2) *sati* (mindfulness), (3) *hiri* (moral shame), (4) *ottappa* (moral fear), (5) *alobha* (nongreed), (6) *adosa* (nonhatred), (7) *tatramajjhattatā* (neutrality of mind), (8) *kāya-passaddhi* (tranquility of mental factors), (9) *citta-passaddhi* (tranquility of consciousness), (10) *kāya-lahutā* (lightness of mental factors), (11) *citta-lahutā* (lightness of consciousness), (12) *kāya-mudutā* (malleability of mental factors), (13) *citta-mudutā* (malleability of consciousness), (14) *kāya-kammaññatā* (wieldiness of mental factors), (15) *citta-kammaññatā* (wieldiness of consciousness), (16) *kāya-pāguññatā* (proficiency of mental factors), (17) *citta-pāguññatā* (proficiency of consciousness), (18) *kāyujjukatā* (rectitude of mental factors), and (19) *cittujjukatā* (rectitude of consciousness).

The others are those mental factors that do not necessarily arise with every beautiful consciousness. There are six: (1) *sammā-vācā* (right speech), (2) *sammā-kammanta* (right action), (3) *sammā-ājīva* (right livelihood), (4) *karuṇā* (compassion), (5) *muditā* (appreciative joy), and (6) *amoha* (nondelusion).

Let us examine first the factors in the first group. Among them the first is *saddhā*, a term often translated as faith. It could be understood as trust, faith, or confidence which one reposes on someone or something as to result in certitude of mind and a sense of self-assurance in relation to what one wants to undertake. Although saddhā is confidence in someone or something external, it could generate self-confidence as well. It removes perplexity of mind resulting from self-doubting. In the Buddhist context saddhā is faith in the Buddha, the Dhamma, and the Saṅgha.

The main function of saddhā is to purify (*sampasādana*) the mental states associated with it. "[Just as] the purifying gem of a universal monarch thrown into water causes solids, alluvia, water weeds, and mud to subside and make the water clear, transparent, and undisturbed, so faith when it arises discards mental obstacles, causes the corruptions to subside, purifies the mind, and makes it undisturbed."[529] We find a similar definition in the Sarvāstivāda Abhidharma as well. "Śraddhā is the clarification of the mind. It is the mental factor through which the mind, disturbed by defilements and subdefilements, becomes clarified, just as polluted water becomes clear in the presence of the water-purifying gem (*udaka-prasādaka-maṇi*)."[530] Thus the main function of saddhā is to bring about clarity and perspicuity of mind by removing the defects and stains of both emotional and intellectual instability. Saddhā thus paves the way for the arising of positive states of mind. It is the precursor and forerunner (*pubbaṅgama, purecārika*) for all acts of charity and virtue.[531]

Saddhā also functions as a spiritual faculty (*saddhindriya*) and as a spiritual power (*saddhā-bala*). Its elevation to these two levels shows that saddhā is not only a prerequisite but also a corequisite in mental culture, leading to the realization of the final goal.

The next beautiful mental factor is *sati*. In its literal sense it means memory, but in Buddhist psychology it means not memory regarding the past but mindfulness, presence of mind, to be attentive and watchful of the present. Its characteristic is "not wobbling, that is, not floating away from the object (as of a pumpkin in a stream), its function is to maintain unforgetfulness, it manifests as the state of facing the object, its proximate cause is firm perception."[532] Sati is the presence of mind in relation to the object as opposed to mere superficiality. It is this quality that enables sati to plunge directly into the object, unlike, as the commentary says, pumpkins and pots that float on water.[533] Although it is not the same as attention (*manasikāra*), both are closely connected. Without some degree of attention to the object no cognitive act will take place. But the same is not true of mindfulness. There can be a cognitive act without mindfulness. So while attention is reckoned as a universal, a factor common to all consciousness, sati is reckoned as a universal beautiful factor, a factor shared only by beautiful consciousness. However, when mindfulness is present—that is, when the consciousness is beautiful—the quality of attention enhances and therewith the quality of the whole act of cognition. This is the salutary role mindfulness plays in a cognitive process.

Sati has the ability to discriminate between good and bad and it thus enables one to do the right thing and avoid what is wrong. Hence the Venerable Nāgasena tells King Milinda: "As mindfulness springs up in one's heart, O King, one searches the categories of good qualities and their opposites, saying to himself: such and such qualities are good, such and such qualities are bad, such and such qualities are helpful and such and such qualities are just the opposite. Thus does the recluse make what is evil in himself to disappear and keep up what is good."[534]

The proximate cause of mindfulness is solid perception (*thira-saññā-padaṭṭhāna*), or the four foundations of mindfulness.[535] The first shows the close connection between *saññā* as perception and *sati* as mindfulness. It implies that the relative strength of mindfulness corresponds to the relative strength of perception. For mindfulness to be properly established it should have a strong perceptual foundation. The second refers to the proximate cause of mindfulness from a different angle: here it takes into consideration the well-known four bases of mindfulness as its proximate cause.

For the Sarvāstivādins *smṛti* (*sati*) is a universal factor of consciousness. It could become wholesome or unwholesome depending on the consciousness with which it is combined. For the Theravādins it is invariably beautiful and therefore it does not occur in unwholesome consciousness. Why the Theravādins exclude mindfulness from all unwholesome consciousness is clear. According to them, all unwholesome consciousness is necessarily accompanied by *uddhacca*, a mental factor that, as we have already noted, represents restlessness, agitation, and disquietude, and whose function is to make the mind unsteady, "as wind makes a banner ripple."[536] Such a mind is not a fertile ground for the emergence of right mindfulness. But do not the Pāli suttas sometimes refer to wrong mindfulness as the opposite of right mindfulness? For the Sarvāstivāda, of course, mindfulness can branch off on the right direction as right mindfulness and on the wrong direction as wrong mindfulness. It is very unlikely that the Theravāda Abhidhamma has overlooked this situation. The Theravāda position in this regard seems to be that some kind of mental state similar to mindfulness is not entirely absent in unwholesome consciousness, as when, for example, someone is stealing someone else's property. But this kind of mental state is not mindfulness but attention to the object (*manasikāra*) due to other mental factors such as greed. It is best described as some kind of attention (*manasikāra*) with agitation and excitement (*uddhacca*) at the background.

Mindfulness occupies a pivotal position both in Buddhist ethics and psychology. Its importance and its influence on other mental factors can be seen by its being presented under different ethico-psychological categories: mindfulness is a spiritual faculty (*indriya*), a spiritual power (*bala*), a factor of awakening (*bojjhaṅga*), and the seventh factor of the noble eightfold path.

The next two mental factors, *hiri* and *ottappa*, are always presented as a pair. Hiri is moral shame and ottappa moral fear—both in relation to bodily and verbal misconduct. "To be ashamed of what one ought to be ashamed of, to be ashamed of performing evil and unwholesome things: this is called moral shame. To be in dread of what one ought to be in dread of, to be in dread of performing evil and unwholesome things: this is called moral dread."[537] They combine to act as restraining forces against their opposites, shamelessness and fearlessness at evildoing.

Moral shame has its origin within (*ajjhatta-samuṭṭhānā hiri*), whereas moral fear has its origin without (*bahiddhā-samuṭṭhānaṃ ottappaṃ*), because the former is influenced by oneself (*attādhipati hiri nāma*) and the latter by society, the world at large (*lokādhipati ottappaṃ*).[538] In the case of moral shame, what is of decisive significance is one's own self, one's own conscience, one's own moral sense, which acts as an inner mentor directing one's actions in the right direction. In the case of moral fear what is of decisive significance is public opinion, what the world at large says and thinks about what one does. Moral shame is therefore said to be rooted in the intrinsic nature of shame (*lajjā-sabhāva*) and moral fear in the intrinsic nature of fear (*bhaya-sabhāva*).[539] By public opinion Buddhism means neither the opinion of the majority nor the opinion of the minority but the opinion of the wise people (*viññū purisā*) of a society. Hence what is morally rewarding is described as "praised by the wise" (*viññuppasattha*) and what is morally reprehensible is described as "censored by the wise" (*viññū-garahita*).[540]

Thus self-control due to moral shame is a case of controlling oneself by one's conscience (*attādhipateyya*), and self-control due to moral dread is a case of controlling oneself by taking public opinion into consideration (*lokādhipateyya*).[541] Their difference is illustrated as follows: "If there were two iron balls, one cold but smeared with dung, the other hot and burning, a wise man would not catch the cold one because of his loathing of the dung nor the hot one for fear of getting burned. Even so a wise man should avoid bodily and verbal misconduct through moral shame and moral dread."[542]

If Buddhism considers these two moral qualities as highly commendable, it also considers their absence as equally reprehensible. Their absence, as we noted earlier, is recognized as two separate mental factors—namely, *ahirika* (absence of moral shame) and *anottappa* (absence of moral dread)—which are invariably present in all unwholesome consciousness. In Buddhism's view moral shame and moral dread are of decisive importance for protecting and stabilizing the moral foundation of society.

They are the very foundation of moral governance. Their absence leads to the erosion and collapse of the social fabric, resulting in anarchy in moral life. As we have noted earlier, the Buddha identifies moral shame and moral dread by describing them as "guardians of the world" (*lokapālā dhammā*).[543]

The next two beautiful universal factors are *alobha* (nongreed) and *adosa* (nonhatred). Together with *amoha* (nondelusion) they constitute the three roots that may be either kammically wholesome or indeterminate. They are wholesome when they occur in wholesome consciousness and indeterminate when they occur in resultant (*vipāka*) and functional (*kiriya*) consciousness. When they are described as beautiful, they include both the wholesome and the indeterminate. Of these three factors, only alobha and adosa occur in all beautiful consciousness. Amoha, the third, is a variable adjunct not necessarily found in all beautiful consciousness. Hence only the first two roots are reckoned as beautiful universals. However, we will be referring here to the third as well because of its close connection with the other two.

Alobha and adosa can be understood both negatively and positively. In the negative sense they mean absence of greed and hatred, respectively. In the positive sense the former signifies such wholesome qualities as charity, liberality, and renunciation, and the latter amity, goodwill, gentleness, friendliness, benevolence, and loving-kindness (*mettā*). This should explain why mettā is not mentioned as one of the four illimitables (*appamaññā*) in the list of beautiful factors. For the sublime quality of loving-kindness is the same as nonhatred (*adosa*) when it is elevated to the highest level as a positive factor. On the other hand, as the Venerable Nyanaponika Thera observes, the negative term *amoha* has always a positive significance, for here the reference is to knowledge and understanding and its higher reaches as insight, wisdom, or an immediate vision into the nature of actuality. As he observes further, "if the other two roots provide the volitional impetus and the emotional tone required for wholesome consciousness, this particular root represents its rational or intellectual aspect."[544]

Alobha has the characteristic of not clinging (*agedha*) or not adhering (*alaggabhāva*) to the object, like a drop of water on a lotus leaf. Its function is not to lay hold and is manifested as detachment.[545] Adosa has the characteristic of absence of churlishness or resentment, the function of destroying vexation or dispelling distress, and it is manifested as agreeableness.[546] And when adosa is elevated to the level of a *brahmavihāra*, one of the four divine abodes, it is called mettā, the sublime quality of loving-kindness toward all living beings. In this capacity it has the characteristic of promoting the welfare of all living beings (*hitākārapavatti*). Its function is to prefer their welfare (*hitūpasaṃhāra*). Its manifestation is the removal of ill will. Its proximate cause is seeing beings as lovable.[547] The allaying of aversion is its attainment (*byāpādupasamo etissā sampatti*); the arising of selfish affection is its collapse (*sinehasambhavo vipatti*).[548]

As noted above, alobha and adosa together with amoha are the triad of wholesome roots (*kusalamūla*). On their multifaceted role, we find some interesting observations made in the commentary to the *Dhammasaṅgaṇi*:

> Nongreed is the cause of giving, nonhatred is the cause of virtue, and nondelusion is the cause of mental culture. Through nongreed one avoids the overestimates of the covetous, through nonhatred the partiality of the hateful, and through nondelusion the perversions of the deluded. Through nongreed one acknowledges a fault as a fault, although one continues to be with that fault. For unlike the greedy, such a one does not conceal his own faults. Through nonhatred one recognizes one's own virtue as virtue and continues to cultivate that virtue. Through nondelusion one knows what is really true as really true and continues to be in conformity with what is really true. Unlike the deluded person, one does not mistake what is true as false and what is false as true. Through nongreed one overcomes the suffering due to dissociation from what is agreeable, and through nonhatred the suffering due to association with what is disagreeable. Through nondelusion one overcomes all suffering due to not getting what one desires. For unlike the deluded, the nondeluded one knows the nature of things as they truly are. Through nongreed one overcomes the suffering associated with birth, because craving

(*taṇhā*) is the cause of birth. Through nonhatred one conquers suffering due to old age, since one who is overcome with keen hatred becomes quickly aged. Through nondelusion one conquers the suffering due to death, for verily to die with the mind baffled is suffering that does not come over the nondeluded.

Nongreed prevents birth in the sphere of *petas*, for it is mainly due to craving that beings are born there. Nonhatred prevents birth in purgatories, for it is due to hatred associated with ferocity that beings are born there. Nondelusion prevents birth in the animal kingdom, for it is due to delusion that beings are born among animals, who are always in a state of delusion.

By nongreed one gains insight into impermanence, for the one who is greedy owing to his obsession with his wealth and prosperity does not regard impermanent things as impermanent. By nonhatred one has insight into suffering, for one inclined to amity, while possessing things, has abandoned the basis of vexation and can therefore consider conditioned things as a source of suffering. By nondelusion one gains insight into soullessness, for the nondeluded person can grasp the nature of actuality. Through insight into impermanence arises nongreed, through insight into suffering arises nonhatred, and through insight into soullessness arises nondelusion.

Absence of greed is the cause of good health, for the nongreedy man does not resort to what is attractive but unsuitable. Absence of hate is the cause of youthfulness, for the man of no hate, not being burned by the fire of hate, which brings wrinkles and gray hairs, remains young for a long time. Absence of delusion is the cause of long life, for the nondeluded man knows what is advantageous and not advantageous and, avoiding what is not advantageous and practicing what is advantageous, lives a long life. Again, absence of greed is the cause of the production of wealth, for wealth is obtained through liberality. Absence of hate is the cause of the production of friends, for through love friends are obtained and not lost. Absence of delusion is the

> cause of personal attainments, for the nondeluded man, doing only that which is good for himself, perfects himself. Again, absence of greed brings about life in *deva* heavens, absence of hate brings about life in Brahma heavens, and absence of delusion brings about the Aryan life. Moreover, through absence of greed one is at peace among beings and things belonging to one's party, inasmuch as, if disaster befall them, the sorrow that depends on excessive attachment to them is absent. Through absence of hate one is happy among beings and things belonging to a hostile party, inasmuch as in the man of no hate inimical thoughts are absent. Through absence of delusion one is happy among beings and things belonging to a neutral party, inasmuch as for the nondeluded there is no excessive attachment to all beings and things belonging to a neutral party.[549]

Again, "through nongreed one gives up the addiction to sensuality and through nonhatred the commitment to self-mortification."[550] Here we find an insightful observation on the psychological origin of self-inflicted austerities. The practice of mortifying the flesh in order to purify the self is said to be motivated by hatred, a subtle form of hatred, which we suspect is directed toward one's own self over its spiritual lapses and inadequacies. Or it could be an externally directed hatred toward those who gloat in sensual indulgence.

The next beautiful factor is *tatramajjhattatā*. The term literally means "middleness there," with "there" meaning in relation to all objects of cognition. This literal meaning holds for the term in a technical sense as well. For it signifies a balanced state of mind resulting from an impartial view of all objects of experience. So tatramajjhattatā means "equipoise," "equanimity," "even-mindedness," or "neutrality of mind." It is also called *upekkhā*, which means equanimity. However, upekkhā could also mean neutral feeling, the zero point between painful and pleasant feelings. This is not the meaning intended here. Upekkhā, as another expression for tatramajjhattatā, means not the affective mode in which the object is experienced but a balanced state of mind in relation to the object. This is the one that is referred to as *tatramajjhattupekkhā*, equanimity-neutrality.[551] It is a neutral attitude, an intellectual, not hedonic, state of mind that enables one to maintain a balanced attitude.

The characteristic of tatramajjhattatā (neutrality of mind) is the evenness of consciousness and its mental factors. Its function is to avoid deficiency and excess and to prevent partiality (*pakkha-pātupacchedana*). It is manifested as neutrality (*majjhattabhāva*). It is this neutrality of mind that can be elevated to the level of equanimity to all living beings, when it is called one of the four "divine abodes" or "immeasurables," the other three being loving-kindness (*mettā*), compassion (*karuṇā*), and appreciative joy (*muditā*). Equanimity in this higher sense has the characteristic of promoting the aspect of neutrality toward all living beings. Its function is to see equality in living beings. It is manifested as the allaying of resentment. It succeeds when it makes resentment subside (*paṭighānunaya-vūpasamo tassā sampatti*).[552] "It fails when it produces worldly-minded indifference due to ignorance" (*gehasitāya aññāṇupekkhāya sambhavo vipatti*).[553] Equanimity enables one to transcend, among other things, all preferences and prejudices based on color, caste, race, ethnicity, gender, and beliefs.

Next in the list of universal beautiful factors we find twelve items arranged into six pairs. They represent six different qualities, each made twofold (= pair) by extending it to *kāya* and *citta*. Here kāya, which literally means body, refers to the "body" of mental factors that arise together with consciousness. Citta, as we already know, means consciousness. Each pair signifies a quality shared both by consciousness and its concomitants. These twofold six qualities are closely interconnected. Therefore they always arise together.

The first pair consists of *kāya-passaddhi* (tranquility of mental factors) and *citta-passaddhi* (tranquility of consciousness). It is "the serenity, composure, tranquility" of the mental factors and consciousness.[554] "Taken together these two states have the characteristic of pacifying the suffering of both mental factors and of consciousness, the function of crushing the suffering of both, the manifestation of an unwavering and cool state of both, and they have mental factors and consciousness as proximate causes."[555]

The second pair is *lahutā* in its twofold aspect. Lahutā is lightness or buoyancy, the opposite of sluggishness and inertia. Its characteristic is the absence of heaviness (*garubhāva*) and its function is to destroy heaviness. It is manifested as absence of rigidity and its proximate cause is the body of mental factors and consciousness. It is opposed to such defilements as sloth (*thīna*) and torpor (*middha*), which bring about rigidity and inertia.[556] This quality of lightness (*lahutā*) is the "mind's capacity for quick transformation or modification" (*sīghaṃ sīghaṃ parivattana-samattha*),[557] a quality useful for moral training and spiritual development.

The third pair is *mudutā* in its twofold aspect. Mudutā is malleability, plasticity, the absence of rigidity. Its characteristic is the absence of stiffness (*thaddhabhāva*) and its function is to destroy stiffness. It manifests as nonresistance and has mental factors and consciousness as its proximate cause. Its presence means the absence of such defilements as wrong view (*diṭṭhi*) and conceit (*māna*), which give rise to stiffness and rigidity.[558]

The fourth pair is *kammaññatā* in its twofold extension to mental factors and consciousness. Kammaññatā literally means "workableness or serviceableness." It is wieldiness, tractableness, or pliancy as a quality of consciousness and mental factors. Its characteristic is the subsiding of unwieldiness and its function is to destroy unwieldiness. It is manifested as success in making something as the object of consciousness and mental factors. It is opposed to all mental hindrances that make consciousness unwieldy.[559]

The fifth is the pair of *pāguññatā*. It means fitness, ability, competence, or proficiency as a quality of mind. Its characteristic is healthiness of the mental factors and consciousness and its function is to eradicate the twofold unhealthiness. It is manifested as absence of disability. It is opposed to defilements such as absence of faith, which gives rise to mental unhealthiness.[560]

The last pair is *ujjukatā*, defined as rectitude, straightness, or the absence of deflection, twist, and crookedness. Its characteristic is uprightness and its function is to eradicate the mind's crookedness. It is manifested as absence of crookedness and is opposed to such defilements as craftiness, which creates crookedness in the body of mental factors and consciousness.[561]

Among these six pairs only the twofold *passaddhi* is mentioned in the Pāli suttas. However, as Venerable Nyanaponika Thera says, the other five, except *pāguññatā*, are traceable to Pāli suttas, although they are not formally introduced there as in the Abhidhamma.[562] The use in the Pāli suttas of such terms as *lahu*, *mudu*, *kammañña*, and *uju* in describing the kind of mind that is necessary for moral development shows the antecedent trends that led to the formulation of the six pairs. It is also interesting to notice that in the Sarvāstivāda Abhidharma we find parallel factors only for the first, which incidentally is the pair specifically mentioned in the Pāli suttas as well. However, the Sarvāstivāda definition of the pair takes a different form: here *citta-praśrabdhi* is defined as tranquility of the mind (*citta-karmaṇyatā*) and *kāya-praśrabdhi* as tranquility of the five physical sense organs.[563]

When the six pairs occur together they represent a state of mind that is tranquil, agile, malleable, wieldy, proficient, and upright. Their presence ensures the absence of the five mental hindrances of sensual desire, ill will, sloth and torpor, restlessness and worry, and skeptical doubt. They prepare the mind to its deliverance from all suffering. The Abhidhamma does not ignore the importance of physical health either as a necessary instrument for mental development. As we shall see in a future chapter, there are three material properties corresponding to three of the six pairs that we have discussed so far. The three are lightness (*lahutā*), malleability (*mudutā*), and wieldiness (*kammaññatā*) of the physical body (*rūpassa*). These three physical properties, as the six pairs of mental properties, always arise together (*na aññam aññaṃ vijahanti*)[564] and their simultaneous presence represents the kind of physical health and bodily ease necessary for the practice of mental culture.

The nineteen mental factors that we have examined so far are the universal beautiful factors, those that occur in all beautiful consciousness. There remain six more beautiful factors. They are not universals but variable adjuncts not necessarily occurring in all beautiful consciousness. Among them the first three are called *virati* or abstinences. They are called so because they are the three mental factors responsible for the deliberate abstinence from wrong speech, wrong action, and wrong livelihood. They refer to the three mental factors corresponding to right speech (*sammā-vācā*), right action (*sammā-kammanta*), and right livelihood (*sammā-*

ājīva). Right speech is abstinence from four types of wrong speech: false speech, slander, harsh speech, and frivolous talk. Right action is abstinence from the three types of wrong bodily action: killing, stealing, and sexual misconduct. Right livelihood is abstinence from wrong livelihood: dealing in poisons, intoxicants, weapons, slaves, and animals for slaughter, or any other means of livelihood that is morally reprehensible though materially rewarding.

If the three abstinences represent three factors of the noble eightfold path, what about the other five path factors? To state briefly, right view (*sammā-diṭṭhi*) is represented by nondelusion or wisdom, which is the last in the list of beautiful factors. Right thought (*sammā-saṃkappa*) and right effort (*sammā-vāyāma*) are represented by *vitakka* and *viriya*, which, as noted earlier, are two of the ethically variable occasional factors. Right mindfulness (*sammā-sati*) is represented by the mental factor *sati*, which is the second in the list of beautiful factors. Right concentration (*sammā-samādhi*) is represented by *ekaggatā*, which is one of the seven universals. Thus the (eight) factors of the noble eightfold path are represented in the list of mental factors in four of its subdivisions: universals, occasionals, beautiful universals, and beautiful occasionals.

The next two occasional adjuncts of beautiful consciousness are *karuṇā* and *muditā*, compassion and appreciative joy. They are two of the four sublime states called illimitables (*appamaññā*), or divine abodes (*brahmavihāra*), the other two being *mettā* and *upekkhā*, loving-kindness and equanimity. The latter two are not mentioned here because, as we have seen, they are two modes of the two mental factors called *adosa* (nonhatred) and *tatramajjhattatā* (neutrality of mind), respectively. This does not mean that nonhatred and neutrality of mind always arise as two of the sublime states. It does mean that the two mental factors in question have the potentiality to be elevated to the sublime states of *brahmavihāras*. On the other hand, karuṇā and muditā are not elevated states of other mental factors. They appear as mental factors in their own right. While adosa and tatramajjhattatā occur in all beautiful consciousness, karuṇā and muditā are present only on occasions.

Karuṇā (compassion) has the characteristic of promoting the allaying of suffering in others. Its function lies in not being able to bear others' suffering. It is manifested as noncruelty. Its proximate cause is to see helplessness in those overwhelmed by suffering. Its success lies in the quieting of cruelty. Its failure lies in the arising of sorrow.[565] Compassion associated with feelings of sorrow for others' suffering is not genuine compassion. It is some kind of sentimentalism. When the mind is overcome by sentimentalism it fails to correctly assess the situation and to take the right measures to help others.

Muditā (appreciative joy) has the characteristic of gladness when others succeed. Its function lies in being not envious. It is manifested as the absence of aversion. Its proximate cause is when one sees others' success. Its success lies in the subsidence of aversion. Its failure lies in the production of merriment.[566] Appreciative joy is not merrymaking and it is not accompanied by excited feelings of elation or outbursts of emotional excitement over the success of others.

The last in the list of beautiful mental factors is *amoha* (nondelusion), also called *paññā* (wisdom) or *ñāṇa* (knowledge). It means knowing things as they actually are (*yathābhūta*), or knowledge in conformity with the nature of actuality. This particular mental factor, as we have seen, combines with nongreed (*alobha*) and nonhatred (*adosa*) to form the well-known triad of the wholesome roots. Its mention here as an occasional adjunct of beautiful consciousness shows that, unlike the other two, it does not necessarily occur in all beautiful consciousness. For, as we have noted in chapter 6, among the eight types of sense-sphere wholesome consciousness, four are "dissociated from knowledge" (*ñāṇa-vippayutta*) and four are "associated with knowledge" (*ñāṇa-sampayutta*). Therefore the recognition of nondelusion or wisdom as an occasional adjunct of beautiful consciousness conforms to this situation.

Paññā has the characteristic of illuminating (*obhāsana*) or understanding (*pajānana*). "As when a lamp burns at night in a four-walled house the darkness ceases, [and] light manifests itself, so understanding has illuminating as its characteristic. There is no illumination equal to the illumination of understanding."[567] Further, "Understanding (*paññā*) has unfaltering penetration as its characteristic, like the penetration of an arrow shot by a skilled archer; illumination of the object as its function, as it were a lamp; nonperplexity as its proximate cause, as it were a good guide in the forest."[568]

10

THE COGNITIVE PROCESS

THE ABHIDHAMMA THEORY of cognition is based on two basic ideas of early Buddhist psychology. One is that mind is a process without an enduring substance. The other is that all psychological experience is a continuum of mental events. Accordingly, cognition is not the immediate result of the contact between the sense organ and the sense object. Rather, it is the cumulative result of a continuum of cognitive events. The process begins from a simple sensory contact and proceeds gradually to the apprehension of the object. There is no self or subject behind the cognitive process as an enduring entity experiencing the object or as an agent directing the various mental activities. They take place naturally according to the principles of psychological order (*citta-niyāma*), each stage in the continuum being conditioned by the immediately preceding one (*laddha-paccaya-citta-santāna*).[569] Ācariya Buddhaghosa, after describing the process of cognition, makes this interesting observation: "There is no agent or director who, after the object has impinged on the sense organ, says: 'You perform the function of attention or you perform the function of cognition.'"[570] Each of the various acts, such as adverting attention to the object, functions according to its own law and the whole process is recognized as the law of the operation of the mind (*citta-niyāma*). The momentary mental events do not occur in the mind. Rather, the momentary mental events themselves are the mind.

The cognitive process, as described in the Abhidhamma, is mainly based on a formulated theory of moments and the conception of *bhavaṅga* consciousness. What is called *bhavaṅga* is not a kind of consciousness additional to the eighty-nine or one hundred and twenty-one types mentioned earlier. It is a name given to one of the resultant consciousnesses when it performs a particular function. In this technical sense, the term occurs first in the *Paṭṭhāna* of the Abhidhamma Piṭaka and then in the *Milindapañha*.[571] However, it was in the Pāli exegetical works that the idea came to be fully developed. The term literally means "constituent of becoming," but what it means as a technical term will become clear if we refer here to the two streams of consciousness recognized in the Pāli exegesis.

One is called *vīthi-citta*. *Vīthi* means a pathway or a process. Hence what is called *vīthi-citta* refers to mind when it is active—that is, when consciousness occurs in a cognitive process. The other is called *vīthi-mutta*. This refers to mind when it is free from cognitive processes—that is, when it is in its passive condition.[572] These two processes could be referred to as process consciousness and process-free consciousness, respectively.

The process-free consciousness performs three different functions. The first is its function as bhavaṅga. In this capacity it ensures the uninterrupted continuity of individual life through the duration of any single existence. For whenever the process consciousness is interrupted, as for example in deep dreamless sleep, it is immediately followed by the process-free consciousness, thus preventing the possibility of any gap arising in the continuous flow of consciousness. Whenever a cognitive process subsides, the bhavaṅga consciousness supervenes. In other words, it intervenes between every two cognitive processes and thus separates them as two different cognitive units. The second function of the process-free consciousness is its function as death consciousness (*cuti-citta*), the last consciousness to occur in any individual existence. The third function of the process-free consciousness is as rebirth-linking consciousness (*paṭisandhi-citta*), the first consciousness to occur at the moment of rebirth. Immediately after rebirth-linking consciousness has arisen and fallen away, it is followed by bhavaṅga consciousness, which performs the function of preserving the continuity of individual existence.[573]

The process-free consciousness, too, has its object. It is identical with the object an individual has experienced in her last cognitive process in the immediately preceding existence. When a person is almost near death, some object will present itself to the last cognitive process of that person. This object can be one of three kinds: (1) an act of good or evil kamma committed earlier, (2) a sign or image of the kamma (*kamma-nimitta*) that will determine the kind of rebirth awaiting her, (3) a sign of the plane of existence (*gati-nimitta*) where the dying person is destined to be reborn.

Whenever the process-free consciousness performs the three functions of death, rebirth-linking, and life-continuum, in all these instances it has its own object—that is, an object that is identical with what an individual has experienced in her last cognitive process in the immediately preceding existence. This situation conforms to the early Buddhist teaching that there is no such thing as an uncaused consciousness. Therefore the process-free consciousness should not be understood as an unrelated entity existing by itself. As E. R. Sarachchandra observes, it is also a cognizing consciousness although it does not cognize the external world. Nor is the process-free consciousness an undercurrent persisting as the substratum of the process consciousness. It does not function like a self-conscious soul, nor is it the source of the process consciousness.[574] The two streams of consciousness are not parallel movements functioning concurrently. The placid flow of the process-free consciousness must be interrupted if the active process consciousness were to operate. In the same way, it is only when process consciousness consisting of a cognitive process subsides that the process-free consciousness supervenes. There is thus an alternative flow of the two streams of consciousness.

A cognitive process, as mentioned above, is called *citta-vīthi* and the activity set in motion is called *visayappavatti*, a process having reference to an object. However, it is after the sense organ, and not after the sense object, that each cognitive process is named. The six cognitive processes are referred to as those based on eye door, ear door, nose door, tongue door, body door, and mind door. "Door," *dvāra* in Pāli, is the word used for the sense organs because it is through them as media that the mind interacts with the objects and it is through them that the objects enter the range of the mind.

Of the six doors of cognition, the first five are the five physical sense organs. The reference is not to the visible sense organs, what in common parlance are known as the eye, the ear, and so on, but to their sentient organs (*pasāda*). Based on the six doors of cognition, there are six cognitive processes. The first five, which involve the physical senses, are together called the five-door processes (*pañca-dvāra-vīthi*) and the sixth the mind-door process (*mano-dvāra-vīthi*). The mind door is the channel from which even the five-door processes emerge. Therefore they are sometimes called mixed-door processes (*missaka-dvāra-vīthi*), as they involve both the mind door and a physical sense door. Accordingly, the ideational processes that occur solely at the mind door are also called bare mind-door processes (*suddha-mano-dvāra-vīthi*).[575]

The five-door cognitive processes follow a uniform pattern although they are based on five different sense organs. The objects presented at each sense door could differ on their degrees of intensity. These objects accordingly are classified into four grades: very great (*ati-mahanta*), great (*mahanta*), slight (*paritta*), and very slight (*ati-paritta*). The words "great" and "slight" do not indicate the size or grossness of the object. They refer to the force of the impact the objects can have on the consciousness. In this particular context "great" and "slight" should be understood as strong and feeble, respectively.[576] One question that arises is why the strength or weakness of the sense organs is not taken into consideration here. As faculties, it is the sense organs that determine the degrees of intensity of the five kinds of consciousness, and this is precisely why each consciousness is named not after its object but after its sense organ. However, if only the relative intensity of the sense object is taken into consideration here, this is to recognize the force of the stimulus as determined at a given moment by all possible factors. If the object is "very great," it will give rise to the maximum number of cognitive events, and if "great," "slight," or "very slight," this will reflect in the number of cognitive events that the object will generate.

A cognitive process with a very great object will give rise to a full cognitive process whose temporal duration will consist of seventeen mind moments. When computed in relation to mind, the lifespan of a moment of matter is equal to seventeen mind moments. Therefore if the cognitive process lasts for seventeen mind moments, this also means that it lasts for one moment of matter. The cognitive process with a very great object is the one where the object that enters the avenue of sense door remains until it is fully grasped by that cognitive process.

A process of cognition begins when the placid flow of the bhavaṅga begins to vibrate owing to the impact of the sense object entering a sense door. This initial stage is called the vibration of the bhavaṅga (*bhavaṅga-calana*). In the second stage the flow of the bhavaṅga gets interrupted. This is called the arrest of the bhavaṅga (*bhavaṅga-upaccheda*). These two stages are, strictly speaking, not part of the cognitive process. Rather, they pave the way for its emergence. It is at the third stage that there arises the five-door adverting consciousness, so called because it adverts attention to the object at the sense door. This is the beginning of the stream-of-process consciousness that launches into the cognitive process (*vīthi-pāta*). The next stage could be one of the five types of sense consciousness that cognizes the impinged object. If it is a visible object, eye consciousness will arise performing the function of seeing (*dassana-kicca*), and if it is sound, ear consciousness will arise performing the function of hearing (*savaṇa-kicca*) and so forth. In this particular context, sense consciousness (*viññāṇa*) is defined as the mere awareness of the presence of the object. If it is eye consciousness, it is the mere act of seeing (*dassana-matta*), if it is ear consciousness, it is the mere act of hearing (*savaṇa-matta*), and so forth. It does not produce knowledge of any sort. It represents the initial level of consciousness when the impinging object "is experienced in its bare immediacy and simplicity" prior to its discriminative functions by the succeeding cognitive events. As clarified in chapter 7, at this stage eye consciousness is a form of nonverbal awareness. Through it one knows "blue," but not "this is blue." "This is blue" is re-cognition that involves some form of verbalizing. It is known only by mind consciousness.

Next in the order of succession are the three types of consciousness (*citta*) performing the functions of receiving (*sampaṭicchana*), investigating (*santīraṇa*), and determining (*votthapana*) the object. It is at these three successive stages that the object comes to be gradually comprehended by the discriminative and selective functions of the mind.[577]

Immediately after the stage of determining (*votthapana*) comes the most important cognitive event in the cognitive process. This is called *javana*, a technical term whose meaning is "running swiftly." Javana "runs swiftly over the object in the act of apprehending it." It is at this stage that the object comes to be fully comprehended. For this purpose it is necessary for javana to have seven swift "runnings" over the object.

Javana has three main aspects: the first is cognitive, the second affective, and the third volitional. Its cognitive aspect is defined as "experiencing the object" (*anubhavana*). As to the affective aspect of javana, we find two divergent views in the Theravāda exegesis. One is that javana does not produce any emotional reaction toward the object cognized. It is only after the end of the cognitive process that any feeling tone arises. After the seven acts of cognition have arisen and fallen one by one in succession, there arises an emotion of attraction or aversion toward the object. One reason given for the nonemotive nature of javana is that the preceding cognitive events remain emotionally neutral and therefore the javana in itself is not in a position to initiate any feeling tone. Another reason given is that both javana and the cognitive events preceding it arise and perish in such quick succession that they cannot develop any inclination either to be attracted or repelled by the object.[578]

This explanation does not clarify how the emotive reaction could occur after the cognitive process is over. What this perhaps means is that the emotive reaction arises among the ideational processes that arise in response and consequence to a cognitive process based on any of the physical sense organs.

The opposite view is that javana has an affective dimension as well. Depending on the attractive or repulsive nature of the object, the javana is either attracted to or repulsed by it.[579]

Javana, as noted above, has a volitional aspect as well. It is the only stage in the cognitive process that is associated with volition (*cetanā*). Unlike any of the preceding stages, javana has thus the ability to make an act of volition, and since all volitional activities can be morally qualified as wholesome and unwholesome, the javana is the only stage that has an ethical aspect as well.[580]

The final stage in a full process of cognition is called *tadārammaṇa*, a term that literally means "having that object." It is so called because it takes as its object the object that has been apprehended by the javana.[581]

What we have examined so far are the different stages in a full cognitive process occasioned by a "very strong" stimulus (*balavārammaṇa*). Such a cognitive process necessarily culminates in registration (*tadāram-*

maṇa) and is therefore called *tadārammaṇa-vāra*, a process ending in registration. If the stimulus is "strong," it will set in motion a cognitive process leading only up to javana. Such a process is called *javana-vāra*, a process leading to javana. If the stimulus is "slight," the cognitive process will end in *votthapana*, the determining consciousness. Such a process is called *votthapana-vāra*, a process ending in determining consciousness. If the stimulus is "very slight," it will result only in the vibrations of the bhavaṅga. It will not ensue a cognitive process and is therefore called *moghavāra*, a sensory stimulation without effect.

A full cognitive process ending in registration contains nine different stages, but to make it complete another stage called the past bhavaṅga (*atīta-bhavaṅga*) is added at the very beginning of the process. The past bhavaṅga is the mind moment that occurs in the process-free consciousness immediately before its vibration (*bhavaṅga-calana*) due to the impact of the object at the sense door. The entire process beginning with past bhavaṅga and ending with tadārammaṇa takes place within seventeen mind moments. The calculation is made by assigning a definite number of moments to each stage of the process, in the following manner:

Stages of the cognitive process	Moments assigned
1. past bhavaṅga (*atīta-bhavaṅga*)	1
2. bhavaṅga vibration (*bhavaṅga-calana*)	1
3. bhavaṅga arrest (*bhavaṅga-upaccheda*)	1
4. five-door adverting (*pañca-dvāra-āvajjana*)	1
5. sense consciousness (*viññāṇa*)	1
6. receiving/assimilating (*sampaṭicchana*)	1
7. investigating (*santīiraṇa*)	1
8. determining (*votthapana*)	1
9. javana	7
10. registration (*tadārammaṇa*)	2
Total number of mind moments	17

It will be noticed that although the past bhavaṅga is assigned one mind moment, apparently it does not play a role in the cognitive process. Why it is introduced needs explanation. According to the Abhidhamma theory of moments, matter is weak and lethargic at the submoment of arising but strong and efficient at the submoment of existence.[582] Therefore a material object must pass its submoment of arising and arrive at the submoment of existence in order to have an impact at the sense door. It must also be noted that in terms of temporal duration the submoment of the arising of matter is exactly equal to a mind moment.[583] This situation should show that the mind moment called past bhavaṅga coincides exactly with the submoment of arising of the material object. It is in order to recognize the arising moment of the material object that the past bhavaṅga is added to represent the initial stage of the cognitive process.

The addition of past bhavaṅga makes the cognitive process one that consists of seventeen mind moments. As noted above, seventeen mind moments are exactly equal to the lifespan of one matter moment because the mind is said to change rapidly and break up more quickly than matter.[584] Accordingly, a matter moment that arises simultaneously with a mind moment perishes together with the seventeenth mind moment in a given series.[585] When it is said that a complete cognitive process lasts for seventeen mind moments, it also means that a complete cognitive process lasts for one matter moment.

Why the cognitive process is calculated in this manner can be understood in a wider perspective if we examine here the Vaibhāṣika-Sautrāntika controversy on the causality of cognition. Any act of cognition involves the participation of at least three things: the sense object, the sense organ, and the sense consciousness. According to the theory of moments, however, these three items are equally momentary. (For, with regard to lifespans, the Vaibhāṣikas and the Sautrāntikas do not make a distinction between mind and matter.) Since causality demands a temporal sequence between the cause and the effect, how can a causal relationship be established between three equally momentary things?

The Vaibhāṣikas seek to solve this problem by their theory of simultaneous causation (*sahabhū-hetu*), according to which the cause need not precede the effect. Both cause and effect can be coexistent and therefore, as far as this situation is concerned, causality can be defined as the invariable concomitance of two or more things.[586] Accordingly, the object, the organ, and the cognition can arise simultaneously and operate as cause and effect, as in the case of the lamp and its light or the sprout and its shadow.

The Sautrāntikas take strong exception to this interpretation. They reject the Vaibhāṣika theory of simultaneous causation on the ground that the cause must necessarily precede the effect and therefore to speak of a causality when the cause and the effect are coexistent is meaningless. The example of the lamp and the light makes no sense because the lamp is not the cause of light, both the lamp and the light being results of a confluence of causes belonging to a past moment. Hence they maintain that object is the cause of cognition and therefore the object must precede the act of cognition. The two cannot arise simultaneously and yet activate as cause and effect. The whole situation is clearly brought into focus by the following objection raised by the Dārṣṭāntikas:

> The organs and the objects of the sense consciousness, as causes of sense consciousness, belong to a past moment. When (for example) a visible object and the eye exist, the visual consciousness does not exist. When the visual consciousness exists, the eye and the visible object do not exist. In their absence during the moment of (visual) consciousness, there is no possibility of the cognition of the object. Therefore all sense perceptions are indirect.[587]

This is what led the Sautrāntikas to establish their theory of the inferability of the external object (*bāhyārthānumeyavāda*).[588] What is directly known is not the object but its representation. The existence of the object is inferred from its correspondence to the impression perceived. The causal relationship between the object and its cognition is determined by the peculiar efficiency of the sense object. This is also known as the theory of representative perception (*sākāra-jñāna-vāda*).[589]

This is a brief statement of how the Vaibhāṣikas and the Sautrāntikas solved the problem posed by the theory of moments to the causality of cognition. The Vaibhāṣika position is that the external object, though momentary, can be directly cognized as it activates simultaneously with the act of cognition. The Sautrāntika position is that the momentary object can never be cognized directly but has to be inferred, since the object as cause has to arise before the act of cognition.

The Theravādins' solution to the problem takes a form different from both. What enabled them to solve the problem is their theory that the lifespan of a moment of matter is longer than that of a moment of mind. The theory makes it possible for a given material thing to arise before the arising of consciousness, at least before the occurrence of one mind moment, and yet be the object of that very same consciousness. The fact that a material object lasts as long as seventeen mind moments means that it allows itself to be fully cognized by a series of seventeen cognitive events. Thus the Theravādins were able to establish the theory of direct perception of the external object despite their recognizing the theory of momentariness.

However, this explanation was not acceptable to the members of the Abhayagiri fraternity. The theory they presented was similar to that of the Sautrāntikas. It says that the physical objects of sensory consciousness are not only momentary but atomic in composition, and therefore they disappear as soon as they appear, "just as drops of water falling on a heated iron ball." As such they cannot come within the range of the respective consciousnesses based on the physical sense organs. They become objects of mind consciousness, but not objects of sensory consciousness. The clear implication is that they are inferred as objects of mind consciousness.[590] It is not possible to say more about this theory of the Abhayagiri fraternity, as there is only a passing reference to it in one of the Pāli subcommentaries.[591]

If the Theravādins retain the theory of direct perception, this does not mean that conceptual activity does not contribute anything to the original bare sensation. It is of course true that as far as one single cognitive process is concerned the mind does not edit the raw data of perception in such a way as to falsify the true nature of the external object. The mind only performs the function of selective discrimination so that the external object is more clearly seen as the result of mental activity. A commentary gives this simile to illustrate the situation. As several children are playing on the road, a coin strikes the hand of one of them. The child asks the other children what it is that hit his hand. One child says that it is a white object. Another sees it with dust on it. Another describes it as a broad and square object. Another says that it is a *kahapana*, a square copper coin. Finally they take the coin and give it to their mother, who makes use of it.[592] Just like the kahapana in the simile, the original stimulus that comes to the attention of the mind is gradually identified until it finally comes to be fully experienced at the javana stage of the cognitive process.

What is said above is true only of a single cognitive process based on any one of the physical sense organs. However, each single cognitive process is not only repeated several times but is also followed by several sequels of mind-door or ideational processes, which exercise a synthesizing function on what is cognized. It is only then, and then only, that a distinct recognition of the object occurs. This will become clearer when we discuss toward the end of this chapter the cognitive processes that occur exclusively at the mind door.

Another issue that divided Buddhist schools concerned the agent or instrument of perception. In the case of visual consciousness, for example, what is it that really sees the object. In this connection, Venerable K. L. Dhammajoti refers to four different views as recorded in the *Abhidharmamahāvibhāṣāśāstra*: The Vaibhāṣikas maintain that it is the eye, the visual organ, that sees. But it can do so only when it is associated with visual consciousness. It is the visual consciousness that cognizes the object. However, it can do so only when it relies on the force of the eye. What this seems to mean is that while the eye sees the object, visual consciousness is aware of it. Here a distinction is made between seeing (*paśyati*) and discerning or cognizing (*vijānāti*). The second view is the one held by Ācārya Dharmatrāta, according to which it is the visual consciousness that sees the object. According to the third view, held by Ācārya Ghoṣaka, it is the understanding (*prajñā*) conjoined with consciousness that really sees the object. The fourth view, held by the Dārṣāntikas, is that it is the confluence (*sāmāgri*) of consciousness and its concomitants that acts as the agent of seeing.[593]

The Theravādin view in this regard is similar to the one held by Ācārya Dharmatrāta. It is the visual consciousness, the consciousness dependent on the eye, that sees the visible object. One reason given by those who say that it is the eye that sees is based on the sutta saying "On seeing a visible object with the eye" (*cakkhunā rūpaṃ disvā*). According to the Theravādins, this saying is only an idiomatic expression, what is called an "accessory locution" (*sasambhāra-kathā*), like "He shot him with the bow." It is a case of metaphorically attributing the action of that which is supported (visual consciousness) to that which is the support (visual organ), as when one says "The cots cry" when in fact what one means by that is that the children in the cots cry (*nissitakriyaṃ nissāye viya katvā*). Therefore the sentence has to be rephrased as, "On seeing a visible object with visual consciousness" (*cakkhu-viññāṇena rūpaṃ disvā*).[594]

In this connection, the Ancients say: "The eye does not see a visible object because it has no mind (*cakkhu rūpaṃ na passati acittakattā*). The mind does not see because it has no eyes (*cittaṃ na passati acakkhukattā*)."[595] It is argued that if the eye sees, then during the time a person is having other (nonvisual) consciousnesses, too, he should be able to see visible things, which really is not the case. This is because the eye is devoid of volition (*acetanattā*). On the other hand, were consciousness itself to see a visible object, it would be able to see things lying behind a wall as well, as it cannot be obstructed by resistant matter (*appaṭighabhāvato*).[596]

Apparently the controversy on whether the eye sees or eye consciousness sees seems to be a semantic issue. As one subcommentary observes, when it is maintained by some that it is the eye that sees, they do not mean every instance of the eye but the eye that is supported by consciousness. Likewise, when others maintain that consciousness sees, they do not mean every instance of consciousness but consciousness supported by the eye. Both groups recognize the cooperation of both eye and consciousness.[597] However, there is this difference to be noted between the Vaibhāṣika and Theravāda positions: according to the former, it is the eye supported by consciousness that sees, whereas according to the latter, it is the consciousness supported by the eye that sees.

This whole controversy, according to the Sautrāntikas, is a case of devouring the empty space. Depending on the eye and visible objects arises eye consciousness. Therefore the question as to what it is that sees and what it is that is seen does not arise. There is no agent or action here.

What we really see here is the play of impersonal dhammas, the dhammas appearing as causes and effects. It is merely as a matter of conforming to worldly expressions that it is said "the eye sees," "the consciousness cognizes."

This interpretation can easily be accommodated within the Theravāda Abhidhamma as well. For although it is said that consciousness cognizes (*viññāṇaṃ vijānāti*), it is a statement made according to agent denotation (*kattu-sādhana*)—that is, on the model of subject-predicate sentence. It implies that there is an agent accomplishing a certain action. Therefore this statement is not valid in an ultimate sense (*nippariyāyato*). To be valid, it has to be restated in terms of activity denotation (*bhāva-sādhana*) as: "Cognition is the mere phenomenon of cognizing" (*vijānana-mattam'eva viññāṇaṃ*). And when this statement is rephrased in the language of causality, it means: "Depending on the eye and the visible, visual consciousness arises."[598]

Another problem that engaged the attention of Buddhist schools is what exactly constitutes the object of perception. The problem arose in the context of the theory of atoms, what the Theravādins call material clusters (*rūpa-kalāpa*). According to this theory, all physical objects of perception are atomic in composition. The question is how an atomically analyzable physical object becomes the object of sensory consciousness. In this regard there are two views. The one maintained by the Vaibhāṣikas is that an assemblage or agglomeration of atoms becomes the object of sensory consciousness. It is the atoms assembled together in a particular manner that is directly perceived.

This is what they call immediate perception. It is the succeeding mental consciousness that synthesizes the raw data of perception into a synthetic unity that determines whether the object is a jug or a pot. This theory ensures that the object of direct and immediate perception is not an object of mental interpretation but something that is ultimately real.[599] The Sautrāntikas object to this view on the ground that if a single atom is not visible, a collection of atoms, too, cannot become visible. In their opinion, it is the unified complex or the synthetic unity of the atoms that becomes the object of sensory consciousness. The Vaibhāṣikas reject this view because the synthetic unity of the atoms is not something real but a product of mental interpretation. It is a case of superimposing a mental construct on the agglomeration of atoms. This makes the object of sensory consciousness something conceptual (*prajñapti-sat*) and not something real (*paramārtha-sat*).[600]

The Theravādins' explanation on this matter is similar to that of the Vaibhāṣikas. It first refers to two alternative positions, both of which are not acceptable. The first alternative is to suppose that one single atom (material cluster) impinges on the organ of sight. Here the actual reference is to the color associated in a single material cluster (*eka-kalāpa-gata-vaṇṇa*). On the impossibility of a single atom generating sensory consciousness, all Buddhist schools agree, for the obvious reason that a single atom is not visible. The second alternative is to suppose that several atoms impinge on the organ of sight. Here the actual reference is to the color associated with several material clusters (*katipaya-kalāpa-gata-vaṇṇā*). This possibility too is rejected.[601] This does not amount to a rejection of the Vaibhāṣika view. What it seems to mean is that the object of sensory consciousness is not a mere collection of atoms, but a conglomeration of atoms assembled together in a certain manner.[602] In this connection, one anticipatory objection is raised. If one single atom is not visible, even a multitude of them are not visible. It is just like assuming that although a single blind person cannot see, a group of them is capable of seeing.[603] It is interesting to notice that this same objection in almost identical terms is raised by Ācārya Śrīlāta against the Vaibhāṣika view as well.[604] The Theravādin response to this objection is that the above illustration is not all-conclusive (*nayidaṃ ekantikaṃ*). There is enough empirical evidence to support the view. For instance, although a single person cannot draw a [heavily laden] palanquin or a cart, a number of people joining together and gathering sufficient strength are in a position to do so. Or it is like many strands of hair becoming visible as each strand contributes to the total visibility of the hair.[605]

What we have discussed so far relates to the five-door cognitive processes—that is, those that occur with the five physical sense organs as their bases. What is called a mind-door cognitive process is one that occurs when ideas or images come into the range of the mind. It is an ideational process that operates independently of the physical sense organs. Hence it is introduced as bare mind-door process (*suddha-mano-dvāra-vīthi*).[606] There are four conditions necessary for an ideational process: (1) the mind must be intact (*asambhinnattā manassa*), (2) mental objects must come within the mind's focus (*āpāthagatattā dhammānaṃ*), (3) dependence on the heart base (*vatthusannissita*), (4) attention (*manasikāra-hetu*).[607] The stimulus in a five-door process, as we have noted, is graded into four according to its intensity. On the other hand, the stimulus at the mind-door process is graded into two as clear (*vibhūta*) and obscure (*avibhūta*).[608] However, there is this important difference to be noted: While the objects of the five-door processes belong strictly to the present moment, the objects of the mind-door process could belong to any period of time—past, present, or future. They could even be free from any temporal reference (*kāla-vimutta*), as in the case of conceptual constructs (*paññatti*) and nibbāna, the unconditioned.[609]

A mind-door process with a clear object (*vibhūtālambana*) has the following sequence of events: (a) vibration of the bhavaṅga when an object enters the avenue of the mind door, (b) the arrest of the bhavaṅga, (c) mind-door adverting consciousness, (d) seven moments of javana, and (e) two moments of registration, after which the cognitive process subsides into the bhavaṅga. In the case of a mind-door process occasioned by an obscure object (*avibhūtālambana*), the two moments of registration do not occur.[610] Thus in a mind-door process the stages of receiving, investigating, and determining do not occur because they are mental activities that operate only in relation to an object that is external.

As to how an object enters the range of the mind door, two occasions are identified. The first is the occasion when mind-door processes arise in response to and in consequence of a cognitive process based on any of the physical sense organs. They are called consequent (*tad-anuvattaka*) or consecutive (*anubandhaka*) mind-door processes. Their genesis is due to the circumstance that when a five-door process has just ceased, its past object comes to the mind's focus and sets off many sequences of mind-door processes.[611] It is these mind-door processes that contribute to the distinct recognition of a sense object. For as we have already noted, such recognition of a given object depends on a number of thought processes that grasp, among other things, its shape, name, and so on, supplemented with an overall process of synthesizing the disparate elements into the perception of a unity. All these functions are performed by the mind-door processes that arise as a sequel to a five-door process.

The other occasion when mind-door processes take place is when an object enters the range of the mind door entirely on its own or "naturally" (*pakatiyā*)—that is, without being occasioned by an immediately preceding five-door process. These are ideational processes that take place without the antecedent of sensory impingement. The commentaries identify three occasions for the revival of such ideational processes. The first is when one revives in memory what one has actually experienced with the five senses of seeing, hearing, smelling, tasting, and touching. The processes of reflection occasioned by such revival are called experience-based processes (*diṭṭhavāra*). The second type occurs when one revives in memory what one has reflected on from information or knowledge gathered from a secondary source different from firsthand experience, and the processes of reflection occasioned by such revival are called *sutavāra* or information-based processes. The third occasion when ideational processes could occur is when one imaginatively constructs an object on the basis of what one has actually experienced and also on what one has learned from information gathered from a secondary source. The processes of reflection occasioned by such imaginative construction are called processes based on both (*ubhayavāra*).[612]

In the Burmese tradition we find a slightly different classification of the occasions of ideal revival. When one revives in memory what one has actually experienced, it is called *diṭṭhavāra*. But when one constructs in imagination fresh things based on one's own experience, it is called *diṭṭha-sambandha* (associated with experience). When objects are constructed out of and connected with information gained either by listening to others or reading books, it is *suta-sambandha* (associated with things heard). "Any apparently a priori object that may enter the field of presentation from any other sources except the last two is classed as things 'cogitated' (*viññāta*)."[613]

As E. R. Sarachchandra observes, the third category is not found in the Abhidhamma commentaries, and as he further observes, what seems to be included in the category of the cogitated (*viññāta*) are "abstract concepts, judgments and all forms of thinking that cannot be regarded as being based on sensory experience."[614] The absence of this third category in the Pāli commentaries is not without significance. It clearly shows that according to the mainstream Theravāda view, the third category is not acceptable. What is ideally revived should be based on past experience. Accordingly, only what has been experienced through the five physical senses of seeing, hearing, smelling, tasting, or touching can be revived as an image in the mind.

11

THE ANALYSIS OF MATTER

THE DHAMMA THEORY, as we have seen, is intended to provide an exhaustive catalogue of the components of actuality. We have discussed so far the components resulting from the analysis of mind into its basic constituents. The analysis of matter in the Abhidhamma, too, follows a similar pattern. For it is within the framework of the dhamma theory that both analyses are presented.

Definition of Matter

In the Abhidhamma Piṭaka we do not get a formal definition of matter (*rūpa*). What we get instead are individual definitions given to the material dhammas into which the whole of material existence is resolved. The commentaries define *rūpa* in the sense of matter as that which has the characteristic of *ruppana*.[615] *Ruppana* refers to mutability of matter, its susceptibility to being "deformed, disturbed, knocked about, oppressed, and broken."[616] The use of the term in this sense is traceable to a sutta passage where the Buddha says: "And why, monks, do you say material form (*rūpa*)? It is deformed (*ruppati*), therefore it is called material form. Deformed by what? Deformed by cold, by heat, by hunger, by thirst, by flies, mosquitoes, wind, sunburn, and creeping things."[617]

The characteristic of *ruppana* is often paraphrased as *vikāra*. Vikāra is the alteration matter undergoes owing to such adverse physical conditions as cold and heat.[618] Vikāra in the sense of alteration is again paraphrased as *visadisuppatti*—that is, genesis of dissimilarity.[619] What this means becomes clear in the context of the theory of moments, according to which all material dhammas (as well as mental dhammas) are of momentary duration. They disappear as soon as they appear without having time to undergo change. Therefore change came to be interpreted, not as the alteration between two stages in the same dhamma but as the disappearance of one dhamma and the immediate emergence in its place of another.[620] Understood in this manner, what is called *visadisuppatti* (genesis of dissimilarity) is not the dissimilarity between two stages of the same material dhamma but the dissimilarity brought about by the disappearance of one and the emergence of another. The reference is to the appearance of a series of momentary material dhammas, where the succeeding dhamma is dissimilar to the immediately preceding one. This phenomenon of "becoming dissimilar" is due to the impact of such adverse physical conditions as heat and cold (*sītādi-virodha-paccaya-sannidhāne visadisuppatti yeva*).[621] Obviously the reference here is not to the empirically observable change in material things, what the commentaries call "evident decay" (*pākaṭa-jarā*).[622] Rather, it refers to the never-stopping, infinitely graduated, incessant change in matter, what is called "incessant decay" (*avici-jarā*).[623]

In the Sarvāstivāda Abhidharma we find a somewhat different definition: matter is that which has the characteristic of *pratighāta*. *Pratighāta* is resistance or impenetrability.[624] This characteristic of matter is due to its extension in space (*yad deśam āvṛṇoti*): "Where there is an object with the characteristic of resistance (impenetrability), there cannot be [at the same time] another object that also has the same characteristic of resistance (impenetrability)" (*yatraikaṃ sapratighaṃ vastu tatra dvitīyasyotpattir na bhavati*).[625] This definition thus highlights the characteristic of spatial extension (*āvaraṇa-lakṣaṇa*), which makes matter resistant and impenetrable.

What is interesting to note here is that the Theravāda, too, recognizes this definition in an indirect way. This will become clear if we examine the definitions given in the Theravāda to the four great elements of matter (*mahābhūta*): earth (*paṭhavī*), water (*āpo*), fire (*tejo*), and air (*vāyo*). The first represents solidity (*kakkhaḷatta*) and spatial extension (*pattharaṇa*), the second fluidity (*davatā*) and cohesion (*bandhanatta*), the third temperature of cold and heat (*sīta, uṇha*), and the fourth distension (*thambhitatta*) and mobility (*samudīraṇa*).[626] These four material elements are necessarily coexistent (*niyata-sahajāta*) and positionally inseparable (*padesato avinibhoga*). They are therefore present in all instances of matter, beginning from the smallest material unit (*rūpa-kalāpa*) to anything bigger than that.[627] The fact that the earth element that represents solidity and spatial extension is said to be present in every instance of matter is another way of saying that every instance of matter is characterized by solidity—whatever be the degree and, by extension, whatever be the extent. This is another way of saying that every instance of matter has the characteristic of resistance/impenetrability (*pratighāta*).

Material Dhammas

Material dhammas are the basic constituents into which the whole of material existence is reduced. Their aggregation and interaction explains the variety and diversity of the physical phenomena of our world of experience. Apart from these material dhammas, no other matter is recognized. What is called "material substance" is explained away as a product of our own imagination. Any given instance of matter is therefore resolvable into these material dhammas without leaving any residue to be interpreted in a substantial sense. The dichotomy of substance and quality has no role to play in the Abhidhamma's analysis of matter (or of mind). No material dhamma is either a substance or a quality of any other material dhamma.

A material dhamma is normally postulated as if it were a discrete entity. However, this does not mean that it has an independent and isolated existence. It is entirely for the convenience of definition and description that it is so postulated. For it always exists in inseparable association with a set of other material dhammas. Even when the analysis of matter "ended" in atomism (theory of *rūpa-kalāpa*), this principle of positional inseparability was not abandoned. For even the so-called atom (*paramāṇu*) is, in the final analysis, a cluster of material dhammas (*rūpa-kalāpa*), one physically inseparable from another, all forming a "heterogeneous" unity.[628]

In the course of this chapter we shall notice that some of the material dhammas represent certain phases, modalities, and characteristics of what really amounts to rūpa in the sense of matter. Strictly speaking, to introduce them as material dhammas is in a way to misrepresent their true nature. However, there is this justification for our doing so: the Pāli commentators themselves observe that they are not true material dhammas but nominal entities. Yet as a matter of convention (*rūḷhiyā*), the commentators themselves refer to them by the same term.[629] Hence if we, too, keep introducing them as material dhammas, this, be it noted, is done as a matter of convention (*rūḷhi*).

Although the Abhidhamma Piṭaka refers in all to twenty-seven material dhammas, the Pāli commentaries have increased the number to twenty-eight by adding heart base as the physical seat of mental activity. The final list is as follows. Four great material elements: (1) earth (*paṭhavī*), (2) water (*āpo*), (3) fire (*tejo*), and (4) air (*vāyo*); five sense organs: (5) organ of sight (*cakkhu*), (6) organ of hearing (*sota*), (7) organ of smell (*ghāna*), (8) organ of taste (*jivhā*), and (9) organ of touch (*kāya*); the objective sense fields, with the exception of the tangible: (10) the visible (*rūpa*), (11) sound (*sadda*), (12) smell (*gandha*), and (13) taste (*rasa*); three faculties: (14) faculty of femininity (*itthindriya*), (15) faculty of masculinity (*purisindriya*), and (16) material faculty of vitality (*rūpa-jīvitindriya*); (17) heart base (*hadaya-vatthu*), (18) nutriment (*āhāra-rūpa*), (19) and space element (*ākāsa-dhātu*); two modes of self-expression: (20) bodily intimation (*kāya-viññatti*) and (21) vocal intimation (*vacī-viññatti*); three characteristics of matter: (22) lightness of matter (*rūpassa lahutā*), (23) malleability of matter (*rūpassa mudutā*), and (24) wieldiness of matter (*rūpassa kammaññatā*); four phases of matter: (25) production of matter (*rūpassa upacaya*), (26) continuity of matter (*rūpassa santati*), (27) decay of matter (*rūpassa jaratā*), and (28) impermanence of matter (*rūpassa aniccatā*).

Material Dhammas Included among the Objects of Mind (*Dhammāyatana-Rūpa*)

These twenty-eight material dhammas are represented in the list of twelve āyatanas as follows: The five physical sense organs (nos. 5, 6, 7, 8, 9) constitute the first five internal āyatanas. (The sixth internal āyatana, that is, *manāyatana*, is mental). The four objective sense fields (nos. 10, 11, 12, 13) constitute the first four external āyatanas. The four great material elements, with the exception of the water element (nos. 1, 3, 4) constitute the fifth external āyatana. All the remaining material dhammas (nos. 2, 14–28) constitute a part of *dhammāyatana*, the sixth external āyatana representing objects of mind.

Ajjhattika (Internal)	*Bāhira (External)*
Cakkhāyatana= no. 5	*Rūpāyatana*= no. 10
Sotāyatana= no. 6	*Saddāyatana*= no. 11
Ghānāyatana= no. 7	*Gandhāyatana*= no. 12
Jivhāyatana= no. 8	*Rasāyatana*= no. 13
Kāyāyatana= no. 9	*Phoṭṭhabbāyatana*= nos. 1, 3, 4
(Manāyatana)	*Part of Dhammāyatana*= nos. 2, 14–28

It will be seen that sixteen material dhammas are included in the dhammāyatana. They are cognized not through any of the physical sense organs but by mind, through a process of inference. The five physical sense organs are also of this nature. For they refer not to the visible (gross) sense organs but to their subtle counterparts.[630] They are known only as objects of mind cognition. Hence, strictly speaking, they can also be included in the dhammāyatana. However, since they are already represented by five separate āyatanas, they are not designated as dhammāyatana-rūpa. We shall be using the term *dhammāyatana-rūpa*(*s*) to mean only those sixteen items that in the Abhidhamma are so designated.

There is general agreement among Buddhist schools that the first five internal and the first five external āyatanas are rūpa in the sense of matter. From the point of view of early Buddhism, too, this is so. It is in regard to the category of *dhammāyatana-rūpa* that Buddhist schools differ. As we have seen, for the Theravāda it consists of sixteen items. For the Sarvāstivāda, on the other hand, there is only one dharmāyatana-rūpa, called *avijñapti-rūpa*.[631] However, seven of the items in the Theravāda list have their counterparts in the Sarvāstivāda as well, but not as part of dharmāyatana-rūpa. They are the water element (no. 2), the two faculties of sex (nos. 14, 15), nutriment (no. 18), the space element (no. 19), and the two modes of self-expression (nos. 20, 21). These seven items, with the exception of nutriment, appear as subdivisions of other āyatanas. On the other hand, nutrition appears as a combination of three other āyatanas.[632] Such a difference as to the relative position of these seven items and the āyatanas presupposes a difference as to their interpretation. But this needs not concern us here.

The Theravādins do not recognize under any guise the avijñapti-rūpa, which for the Sarvāstivādins is the one and only dharmāyatana-rūpa. The Dārṣṭāntikas and the Sautrāntikas strongly criticize the very notion of *avijñapti-rūpa*, and oppose its elevation to the status of a dharma. For these two schools, it is only a mental construct with no objective counterpart. There is no evidence to suggest that the Sautrāntikas recognized any dharmāyatana-rūpa. For them all that is material can be subsumed under the first five internal and the first five external āyatanas.

Two things emerge from the foregoing observations. One is that some Buddhist schools did not recognize dhammāyatana-rūpa. The other is that two leading schools that recognized it did not agree on what it should constitute. Both seem to suggest that the inclusion of some material dhammas in dhammāyatana is an innovation on the part of the Abhidharma/Abhidhamma.

However, the Theravāda Abhidhamma seeks to establish a link between dhammāyatana-rūpa and early Buddhist teachings. This it does on the basis of a sutta passage where we find material form (*rūpa*) defined in its totality:

> Whatever material form there is, past, present, or future, internal or external, gross or subtle, inferior or superior, far or near, all that material form. . . .[633]

It will be seen that this passage uses some pairs of words to embrace components of corporeality in their entirety. Two of them are: gross or subtle (*oḷārika* and *sukhuma*) and far or near (*dūre* and *santike*). These two pairs, according to the Abhidhamma, are meant to distinguish dhammāyatana-rūpa from the rest.[634] The five physical sense organs and the five physical sense objects are called gross (*oḷārika*) because their presence is easily apprehended through sensory impingement. The other material dhammas included in dhammāyatana are called subtle (*sukhuma*) because they are not easily apprehended (*dupparīññeyya*). They have to be known as objects of mind cognition only through a process of inference.[635] The distinction between gross and subtle is thus not based on the relative size of the object but on how its presence can be observed.

Likewise the other pair, far and near (*dūre* and *santike*), in this particular context does not signify spatial distance or proximity. The five physical sense organs and the five physical sense objects are called "proximate" because their contact (*ghaṭṭana*), resulting in visual consciousness and so on, witnesses to their very presence. Because of their being thus easily known (*gahaṇassa sukarattā*), they are called "proximate" (*santike*). "Far" signifies the dhammāyatana-rūpas because in contrast to the rest they are not easily apprehended (*duviññeyya*).[636]

We find the two terms gross (*audārika*) and subtle (*sūkṣma*) used in a similar sense in the Sarvāstivāda as well.[637] Here "subtle" refers to avijñapti, the dharmāyatana-rūpa, and "gross" to all other material dharmas. An alternative explanation is that the pair does not indicate an absolute dichotomization but are of relative application (*āpekṣikam*). What is subtle in relation to something could be gross in relation to something else.[638] However, the Sarvāstivādins interpret "near" (*antika*) and "far" (*dūra*) in a different context to justify their theory of tri-temporality. The material dharmas that exist now (present) are "near." The material dharmas that will be (future) and those that were (past) are "far."[639]

It is very unlikely that the sutta passage has used the two pairs of words in such a technical sense. We can understand them in a direct and literal sense. What it seeks to lay stress on is the totality of material phenomena (*sabbaṃ rūpaṃ*), first with reference to time (past, present, or future), second with reference to a given individual (internal or external), third with reference to the nature of material form (gross or subtle), fourth with reference to its quality (inferior or superior), and finally with reference to its location (far or near). We find the same formula, with the necessary changes, applied to the other four aggregates as well, quite obviously to stress the idea of "all."

The original sutta meaning of the two terms is, in fact, retained in the *Vibhaṅga* of the Abhidhamma Piṭaka: "Whatever other material form there is that is not proximate (*anāsanne*), not in the vicinity (*anupakaṭṭhe*), far (*dūre*), and not near (*asantike*)—this is called material form that is 'far.' Whatever material form there is that is in proximity (*āsanne*), in near vicinity (*upakkaṭṭhe*), not far (*avidūre*), and near (*santike*)—this is called material form that is 'near.'"[640]

Equally significant is the explanation given by Bhadanta Śrīlāta, a celebrity of the Sautrāntika School: material dharmas that exist in a visible locality (*dṛśya-deśa*) are near (*antika*); those that exist in an invisible locality (*adṛśya-deśa*) are far (*dūra*).[641] The criterion is not whether the material dharmas are visible or not, for such a criterion would bring the sphere of visibility (*rūpāyatana*) under one heading and the remaining material dharmas under the other.

Another link the Abhidhamma establishes between *dhammāyatana-rūpa* and early Buddhist teachings is the *Saṅgīti Sutta* of the *Dīgha-nikāya*. This sutta says that all materiality is of three kinds: (1) visible and impinging (*sanidassana-sappaṭigha*), (2) nonvisible and impinging (*anidassana-sappaṭigha*), and (3) nonvisible and nonimpinging (*anidassana-appaṭigha*).[642] The sutta does not identify what and what material form is subsumed under each heading.

"Visible" (*sanidassana*), as the Abhidhamma says, is an exclusive adjective reserved for *rūpāyatana* because of the obvious reason that it signifies "the visible," the sense field of the organ of sight. "Impinging" (*sappaṭigha*) or "with impact" describes the five physical sense organs and their sense objects.[643] For their contact is necessarily associated with some impact and is therefore grosser than that between mind and mind objects. The other material dhammas (= *dhammāyatana-rūpa*), which are objects of mind consciousness, are therefore nonvisible (*anidassana*) and nonimpinging (*appaṭigha*).[644]

Accordingly, the twenty-eight material dhammas can be subsumed under the three headings, as follows:

1. visible and impinging = the sense field of the organ of sight (no. 10)

2. nonvisible and impinging = the five physical sense organs and their sense fields, except the visible (nos. 1, 3, 4 = tangible, 5–9, 11–13)
3 nonvisible and nonimpinging = material dhammas included in dhammāyatana (nos. 2, 14–28)

Among the sixteen material dhammas that come under dhammāyatana, only five can be traced to the Pāli suttas. These are the water element (*āpo-dhātu*), faculty of femininity (*itthindriya*), faculty of masculinity (*purisindriya*), edible food (*kabaḷīkāra-āhāra*), and space element (*ākāsa-dhātu*).[645] Among these five items, the water element and edible can certainly be included in rūpa in the sense of matter. However, it is very unlikely that the Pāli suttas understood them in such a way as to justify their inclusion in the dhammāyatana—that is, as two items of materiality that can be cognized only by the mind (*mano*). As to the two faculties of sex, what is important to remember here is that the suttas do not present them as two material dhammas cognizable only by the mind.[646] This leaves us with only one item—namely, space element (*ākāsa-dhātu*). This, it seems to us, is the only item that we can subsume under the heading "nonvisible and nonimpinging." As we shall see in the sequel, when the Abhidhamma includes space element among material dhammas, it means void region, the space bound by matter. This is the meaning it seems to assume in the suttas as well. We find the term "space element" (*ākāsa-dhātu*) used in the suttas when they analyze the living being into six components: the four great material elements, space element, and consciousness element.

One question that arises here is why the Sarvāstivādins and the Sautrāntikas do not recognize space element as a dharmāyatana-rūpa. As we shall see, for the Sarvāstivādins, too, it means void region (space delimited by matter), but for them it is something visible (*sanidarśana*). Hence they include it in the sense field of the visible and not in dharmāyatana.[647] The Sautrāntikas take an entirely different position: space element is a mental construct with no objective counterpart (*prajñapti-sat*).[648]

If we go by the *Saṅgīti Sutta's* division of material form into three groups, it is only space element that qualifies as a dhammāyatana-rūpa. Where the Abhidhamma shows a development in this regard is when it adds fifteen more items to this category. When we go through these items we will not fail to notice that most of them are not on par with other material dhammas. They merely signify certain modes, characteristics, and phases of other material dhammas. Then the question that arises here is why they are presented as separate material dhammas.

There seem to be two main reasons for this situation. One is the felt need to make the catalogue of material dhammas as exhaustive as possible so as to represent all material phenomena in our world of experience. The second is that in doing so, not to introduce any distinction between substance and quality into the catalogue of material dhammas. Hence the real material dhammas as well as some of their modalities and characteristics are all presented under the common designation of *rūpa-dhamma* (material factors). When Buddhism analyzes a thing into its basic constituents, those basic constituents are always presented as coordinate parallel factors and not as exhibiting a hierarchy. Through this strategy, it avoids the substance-quality distinction intruding into the lists of factors. The factors are presented not as one above or below another but as one besides another. The idea is to show that the factors into which a composite thing is resolved are not fractions of a whole, but coordinate factors, all connected according to the principles of conditionality.

The Real and the Nominal Material Dhammas

It was noted above that some material dhammas represent certain characteristics or modalities of other material dhammas. The difference between the two groups of material dhammas became more apparent in light of two new developments found in the commentaries. One is the definition of *rūpa* in the sense of matter, as that which has the characteristic of mutability (*ruppana*). The other is the definition of *dhamma* as that which has its own nature (*sabhāva*). These two defining characteristics of rūpa and dhamma could not be applied to all material dhammas because of the obvious reason that some of them are merely indicative of certain properties of other material dhammas. Hence in order to make this distinction explicit the commentaries make a division of all material dhammas into two groups as *nipphanna* and *anipphanna*.

The positive term *nipphanna* with the intensive prefix *pari* (*parinipphanna*) occurs in three of the *Kathāvatthu* controversies in a more or less technical sense. If a given thing is parinipphanna, it should have the following characteristics: it is conditioned (*saṅkhata*), dependently arisen (*paṭicca-samuppanna*), subject to decay (*khaya-dhamma*), to waning away (*vaya-dhamma*), in the nature of producing dispassion (*virāga-dhamma*), subject to cessation (*nirodha-dhamma*), and change (*vipariṇāma-dhamma*).[649] From this it follows that the term *parinipphanna* can be used to describe all conditioned dhammas, mental as well as material. The Pāli commentaries, too, use the term, both in its ordinary and intensive forms, to carry the same implications.[650]

Accordingly, the category of *nipphanna* (concretely produced) includes material dhammas produced by the four generative conditions of matter—namely, kamma, consciousness (*citta*), temperature (*utu*), and nutriment (*āhāra*).[651] This means that the opposite term *anipphanna* (nonconcretely produced) refers to material dhammas that are not so produced. Nevertheless, they are reckoned as material dhammas because they exist as modalities or attributes of other material dhammas, which have a real and concrete genesis due to the four generative conditions of matter. Only the latter have their own natures (*attano sabhāvena siddhā*)[652] and therefore they alone can be apprehended through their own natures (*sabhāvena pariggahetabba*). The rest are contrary thereto (*tabbiparīta*).[653] Therefore another name for the *nipphanna* category is "matter having its own nature" (*sabhāva-rūpa*).[654] They are also called "matter having its own characteristic" (*salakkhaṇa-rūpa*) because they are marked by the three characteristics of impermanence, suffering, and non-self. Or else they alone have the three characteristics of the conditioned—namely, arising (*uppāda*), presence (*ṭhiti*), and dissolution (*bhaṅga*).[655] A yet another name for the *nipphanna* category is "matter to be comprehended by insight" (*sammasana-rūpa*) because they can be made the objects of insight contemplation.[656]

The *nipphanna* category is also called "material matter" (*rūpa-rūpa*). The reason given for coining this term is that as a matter of convention, the term *rūpa* has also been used to denote things devoid of the nature of materiality and thus its meaning has become unduly stretched. Hence the need arises to reduplicate the term.

What this amounts to saying is that the opposite group, the *anipphanna* category, does not represent real material dhammas. Rather, they represent certain modalities and attributes of matter. In this sense they are said to go together with the other group (*taggatika*). Strictly speaking, they have to be excluded from the list of twenty-eight material dhammas. This is why some subcommentaries fix the total number of conditioned dhammas at seventy-one and not at eighty-one. It is by excluding the ten items included in the *anipphanna* category.[657]

Great Elements of Matter and Dependent Matter

Another well-known division of the twenty-eight material dhammas is the one into *mahābhūta*, the four great elements of matter, and *upādā-rūpa*, dependent matter. This division is often mentioned in the Pāli suttas as well. However, they do not say what and what constitute the category of *upādā-rūpa*.

As to the relative position of the two categories, we have a clear statement in the *Paṭṭhāna* of the Abhidhamma Piṭaka. As mentioned here, the four mahābhūtas are conditions by way of conascence (*sahajāta*), support (*nissaya*), presence (*atthi*), and nondisappearance (*avigata*) in relation to upādā-rūpas.[658] The first means that the mahābhūtas, as they arise, serve as a condition for the arising, simultaneously with them, of the upādā-rūpas. Thus both groups arise at one and the same time. However, it is the mahābhūtas that function as the condition, while the upādā-rūpas become what is conditioned by them. Although the upādā-rūpas are conascent with the mahābhūtas, the upādā-rūpas are not a condition by way of co-nascence in relation to the mahābhūtas. The next relationship between them is based on the condition by way of support (*nissaya*). This means that the mahābhūtas serve as a necessary support or foundation for the upādā-rūpas to depend on. The two conditions by way of presence (atthi) and nondisappearance (avigata) mean the same kind of condition. Here it means that the presence and nondisappearance of the mahābhūtas ensures the presence and nondisappearance of the upādā-rūpas.

The above conditional relations show that the upādā-rūpas are dependent on the mahābhūtas. The mahābhūtas are also dependent, not, of course, on the upādā-rūpas, but on themselves. Each mahābhūta depends on the other three and therefore none of them can arise in isolation from the other three. This difference between the mahābhūtas and the upādā-rūpa is summed up in a subcommentary: "That which clings to the mahābhūtas while being clung to by others is not upādā-rūpa; that which clings to the mahābhūtas while being not clung to by another is upādā-rūpa."[659]

In contemporary writings upādā-rūpa has often been rendered as "derived materiality/matter." Such a rendering does not seem to represent the true position. Upādā-rūpa is not a variety of matter that is derived or evolved from the mahābhūtas. The notion of "derivation" or "evolution" is not consonant with Buddhist philosophy because it presupposes a dichotomy between substance and quality. The moment we understand upādā-rūpa as a derivative from mahābhūtas, the former become qualities and the latter substances, a distinction categorically rejected by the Abhidhamma.

There is another important reason why we should not render upādā-rūpa as "derived matter/materiality." As we have observed, dhammas are the basic constituents of mental and material existence. Therefore none of them is further reducible to any other reality. If upādā-rūpas are derived from mahābhūtas, then the former are reducible to the latter. In such a situation, they forfeit their right to be designated as dhammas, for the simple reason that they are no more irreducible. If this were so, then the list of twenty-eight material dhammas would get reduced to four—that is, the four mahābhūtas.

12

THE GREAT ELEMENTS OF MATTER

FROM ITS VERY BEGINNING Buddhism has recognized only four mahābhūtas as the great elements of matter. Many other Indian religions and philosophies have recognized five mahābhūtas as elemental substances. These are earth (*pṛthivī*), water (*ap*), fire (*tejas*), air (*vāyu*), and space/ether (*ākāśa*). The fifth differs from the other four in many respects. It is a noncorporeal substance devoid of tactility and is characterized by ubiquity, absolute continuity, and infinite magnitude. Therefore, unlike the other four, it is not atomic in composition.[660] In recognizing only four mahābhūtas, Buddhism agrees with Jainism, where "the elemental tetrad" (*dhādu-catukka*) consists of the same four items.[661] It is of course true that, as observed by Mrs. Rhys Davids, in the Pāli suttas space is sometimes mentioned immediately after, and apparently as coordinate with, the four mahābhūtas.[662] But this does not mean that space is the fifth mahābhūta, just as much as consciousness (*viññāṇa*), which is also mentioned after the five items in question,[663] is not the sixth mahābhūta. It is true that Buddhist schools differ when they explain the nature of space, but they all agree in not recognizing it as one of the mahābhūtas.

The Pāli suttas describe the mahābhūtas in simple and general terms and illustrate them mostly with reference to the constituents of the human body: Earth element is that which is hard (*kakkhaḷa*) and rigid (*kharigata*)—for example, hair of the head or body, nails, teeth, skin, flesh, and so on. Water element is water (*āpo*), or that which is watery (*āpogata*)—for example, bile, phlegm, pus, blood, sweat, tears, and so on.

Fire element is fire or heat (*tejo*), or that which is fiery (*tejogata*)—for example, heat in the body that transmutes food and drink in digestion. Air element is air (*vāyo*), or that which is airy (*vāyo-gata*)—for example, "wind discharged upward or downward, wind in the abdomen or belly, vapors that traverse the several membranes, the inhaling and exhaling of breath."[664]

These are concrete instances of the mahābhūtas. Their description seems to suggest that early Buddhism did not make a departure from their popular conception. However, the use of the term *dhātu* to describe them implies that they represent some material properties rather than material entities. What the suttas seem to explain is how four material properties manifest themselves in concrete form. When we come to the Abhidhamma we find this situation more clearly explained. The Abhidhamma, too, defines the earth element as that which is hard (*kakkhaḷa*) and rigid (*khara*). The first is said to represent its characteristic (*lakkhaṇa*) and the second its mode (*ākāra*). But this is only a provisional definition. Strictly speaking, the earth element is not that which is hard but hardness itself. Hence we find it defined as that which has the characteristic of hardness (*paṭhavīdhātu kakkhaḷatta-lakkhaṇā*).[665] Even this definition is provisional because it creates the wrong impression that the earth element is different from the characteristic of hardness. It shows a duality between the characteristic and what is characterized by it. For the Abhidhamma the characteristic and the characterized are the same. If it assumes a duality it is in order to facilitate our understanding of the specific meaning (*atthavisesāvabodha*).[666] We need to understand the definitions given to other mahābhūtas in the same way.

If the earth element represents hardness, it represents softness as well. For softness is the relative absence of hardness. The use of such words as hard (*kakkhaḷa*), soft (*muduka*), smooth (*saṇha*), rigid (*pharusa*), heavy (*garuka*), and light (*lahuka*) is to bring out the varying degrees of intensity the earth element assumes.[667]

The earth element is also defined as that which extends (*pattharatī ti paṭhavī*).[668] Extension is occupation in space. "Tri-dimensional extension gives rise to our idea of a solid body. As no two bodies can occupy the same space at the same time, Buddhists derive their idea of hardness (*kakkhaḷatta-lakkhaṇa*) from *paṭhavī*."[669] Thus extension and hardness (solidity) are mutually convertible terms: what is extended is hard and what is hard is extended. The earth element's function is to act as a sort of fulcrum or foundation for all other material dhammas. Hence it is said to manifest as receiving (*sampaṭicchana*).[670] Its function of supporting can be seen in all instances of matter, whether they are hardy, watery, fiery, or airy. As the Sarvāstivādins say, if the ocean supports ships, it is not due to the water element but to the earth element present in water. If things remain aloft on air, it is not due to the air element but to the earth element present in air.[671]

The water element represents fluidity (*davatā*), sometimes referred to as trickling (*paggharaṇa*) or oozing (*nissanda*) and viscidity (*sineha*). Its function is to intensify or agglutinate coexisting material dhammas. It manifests as binding together or as cohering material phenomena.[672] "For the water element binds together iron, and so on, in masses, makes them rigid. Because they are so bound, they are called rigid; similarly in the case of stones, mountains, palm seeds, elephant tusks, ox horns, and so on. All such things the water element binds and makes rigid; they are rigid because of its binding."[673] The water element's function of binding together, like the function of the earth element, is present in all instances of matter. This function of the water element, as the Sarvāstivādins say, can be seen even in a blazing fire. For the nonbroken continuity in a blazing fire is due to the presence therein of the water element.[674]

The fire element (*tejo-dhātu*) represents the phenomenon of heat (*usma*, *usuma*, *uṇhatta*). What, then, is the position of cold? This is a question to which the Theravāda and the Sarvāstivāda give two different answers. The Sarvāstivāda position is that cold is represented not by the fire element but by the water element.[675] This reminds us of the Vaiśeṣikas, who maintain that heat is the peculiar quality of the fire substance (*tejasa uṣṇatā*) and that cold is the quality of the water substance (*apsu śītatā*).[676]

On this issue the Theravāda Abhidhamma takes an entirely different position. As noted earlier, for the Theravādins the water element is not a part of the sense object of touch. The tangible consists of the other three mahābhūtas. This shows that cold cannot be associated with the water element. If it could be so associated, then the water element would become an object of touch. An Abhidhamma subcommentary observes: "Although cold (*sītatā*) is known by the sense of touch, it is really the fire element. The sensation of cold (*sīta-buddhi*) is obtained when the heat is less, for there is no distinct quality (*guṇa*) called cold. Hence it is that during the summer season when people enter the shade, having first stayed in the sun, they experience the sensation of cold. And when they stay there for a long time they (in turn) experience the sensation of heat."[677]

Thus according to Theravāda Abhidhamma, cold is not the peculiar characteristic of the water element. Rather, it is the relative absence of heat. And it is the fire element that represents heat. Cold and heat are two different modes in which the fire element is experienced.

The function of the fire element is ripening, maturing (*paripācana*).[678] This is the element that heats, matures, sharpens, and imparts heat to all other material dhammas.

The air element refers to distension (*thambhitatta*) and fluctuation (*chambhitatta*).[679] Unlike the other three mahābhūtas, it represents the more restless and dynamic aspects of material existence. The Pāli commentaries define it as motion (*samudīraṇa*). However, when the theory of momentariness was developed this definition could not be retained in the same form. For one logical corollary of momentariness is the denial of motion: Momentary material dhammas have no time to move from one point in space to another. They disappear wherever they appear. Therefore "motion" came to be redefined to mean "the arising of momentary material dhammas in adjacent locations" (*desantaruppatti*).[680] It is this situation that creates the appearance of "motion." Accordingly, the air element is not motion as such but the cause of the arising of material dhammas in adjacent locations (*desantaruppatti-hetu-bhāvena . . . gametī ti*).[681]

To sum up our discussion of the four mahābhūtas, the earth element signifies solidity and extension, the water element viscidity and cohesion, the fire element heat and cold, and the air element distension and motion, or (according to the later interpretation) the cause of "motion." They are not qualities or attributes of what is called *bhūta-rūpa*. They are its coordinate constituents. They represent four distinct forces or phenomena in the sphere of matter.

The characteristic (*lakkhaṇa*), function (*rasa*), and manifestation (*paccupaṭṭhāna*) of one mahābhūta differ from those of another.[682] However much one mahābhūta is influenced by the other three, it never abandons its essential characteristic. A Pāli commentary cites this sutta passage: "The four mahābhūtas might alter their characteristics sooner than it were possible for the Aryan disciple, endowed with assured faith in the Buddha, to alter."[683] The clear implication is that both are equally impossible. A given mahābhūta is identically the same as its own characteristic (*salakkhaṇa*). Therefore to say that its own characteristic has altered is to admit that it does not exist anymore. Such a situation would certainly lead to the collapse of the theory of the four mahābhūtas. What all this means is that the four mahābhūtas, which represent four distinct basic characteristics of matter, are neither transmutable into one another nor reducible to a common ground.

Another characteristic of the four mahābhūtas is their coexistence. They arise, exist, and cease together. For, as noted earlier, their conditional relationship is one of reciprocal co-nascence (*aññamañña-sahajāta*). This means that they are related in such a way that they assist each other to arise and be together. Their cessation is of course not due to conditions. Any dhamma, mental or material, that arises necessarily comes to an end without the intervention of any external causes.[684]

The *Visuddhimagga* explains the mutual conditionality of the four mahābhūtas under all possible combinations and permutations:

> Taking each one beginning with "earth" there are three others whose occurrence is due to that one, thus with three due to one, their occurrence takes place in four ways. Likewise each one, beginning with "earth," occurs in dependence on the other three, thus with one due to three, their occurrence takes place in four ways. But with the last two dependent on the first two, with the second and fourth dependent on the first and third, with the first and third dependent on the second and fourth, with the first and fourth dependent on the second and third, with the second and third dependent on the first and fourth, they occur in six ways with two elements due to two.[685]

Reciprocal co-nascence (*aññamañña-sahajāta*) means when the conditioning state arises it causes to arise together with it what is conditioned by it. It is this principle that is elaborated here. It shows how each mahābhūta becomes a condition as well as the conditioned in relation to the other three at one and the same time.

Closely connected with the mutual conditionality of the mahābhūtas is their positional inseparability (*padesato avinibhoga*). They exist in inseparable association and therefore they are not positionally resolvable.[686] As to their relative position, the *Visuddhimagga* says: "And just as, whomsoever the great creatures such as the spirits grasp hold of (possess), they have no standing place either inside him or outside him and yet they have no standing independently of him, so too these elements are not found to stand either inside or outside each other, yet they have no standing independently of one another."[687] Thus they have no thinkable standing place relative to each other.

This explanation is justified on the following grounds: "If they were to exist inside each other, then they would not perform their respective functions. If they were to exist outside each other, then they would be resolvable and in such a case the theory of inseparability (*avinibbhuttavāda*) would fail to establish its validity."[688]

The relative position of the four mahābhūtas is thus neither one of inclusion nor one of exclusion. If both alternatives are not valid, it is because the mahābhūtas are not discrete material entities but material properties, representing, as we saw, solidity and extension, liquidity and viscidity, heat and cold, and distension and "mobility." Hence their relative position is not one of spatial juxtaposition. In a given instance of matter, all are present and obviously not in four different places. As material properties, they can be distinguished from one another, but they cannot be positionally separated from one another.

Each mahābhūta assists the other three by performing the function peculiar to it:

> The earth element which is held together by water, maintained by fire and distended by air is a condition for the other three primaries by acting as their foundation. The water element which

> is founded on earth, maintained by fire and distended by air is a condition for the other three primaries by acting as their cohesion. The fire element which is founded on earth, held together by water and distended by air is a condition for the other three primaries by acting as their maintaining. The air element which is founded on earth, held together by water and maintained by fire is a condition for the other three primaries by acting as their distension.[689]

Since the four mahābhūtas exist together, and since they are not separable, one from another, how they enter into the composition of various material aggregates is clear: in every instance of matter, they are all present. To give an example from the Sarvāstivāda Abhidharma, which very well accords with the Theravāda stance as well: the presence of water, fire, and air elements in an earthy substance (*pṛthivīdravya*) is inferred from its cohesion, maturing, and expansion, respectively; the presence of earth, fire, and air elements in water is shown by its support of ships, its heat and motion; the presence of earth, water, and air elements in a blazing fire is shown by its solidity (*sthairya*), cohesion or unbroken continuity, and mobility; and the presence of earth, water, and fire elements in the air is shown by its action of holding up, its touch of cold, and its touch of heat.[690]

The fact that Buddhism does not recognize the mahābhūtas as elemental substances is also relevant to how it explains the composition of material aggregates. A lump of ice, according to Buddhism, is composed of all the four mahābhūtas. Its solidity, cohesion, temperature, and so on, are witness to their presence in it. For the Vaiśeṣikas, for instance, ice is essentially a watery (*ap*) substance. In their view, all matter is ultimately reducible to the four kinds of eternally existing atoms: the earthy, the watery, the fiery, and the airy. In their view no substance is destroyable and therefore decomposition of a compound means its reversal to the original position. When ice melts it becomes water and water is ultimately composed of watery atoms.[691] For Buddhism, whether ice remains as it is, or whether it becomes water when melted or vapor when excessively heated, in all these different states the four mahābhūtas are present.

Moreover, although the four mahābhūtas are present in every instance of matter, they do not exhibit a quantitative difference. It is in equal proportion that they enter into the composition of material things.[692] "There is as much water element in a blazing fire as the fire element. There is as much fire element in a cascading waterfall as the water element." If there were a quantitative difference, so runs the argument, then the notion that they are not separable from one another would not be logical (*na yujjeyya*).[693] This idea is not confined to Theravāda. This is what other Buddhist schools call "the equal presence of the mahābhūtas" (*tulya-bhūta-sadbhāva*).[694]

If the four mahābhūtas are present in equal proportion, how are we to understand the variety and diversity of material aggregates? It is a matter of common experience, for instance, that in many respects a solid stone is different from a piece of snow, and both are different from a blazing fire. Or to put it another way: If the sense of touch consists of earth, fire, and air elements, what accounts for the diversity in tactile sensations? One surely does not get the same tactile sensation when one touches, say, an icicle and a blazing fire.

The diversity, it is maintained, is not due to a difference in quantity but to a difference in intensity (*ussada*) or capability (*sāmatthiya*).[695] In a given material aggregate, one mahābhūta can have a higher degree of intensity than any of the other three. In a hard object, although all four are present in equal proportion, yet the earth element has more intensity than the other three. So does the water element in water, the fire element in fire, and the air element in air.

As objects of touch, the mahābhūtas (except the water element) reach the sense avenue simultaneously. However, bodily cognition of them does not arise at once. For the object of touch is determined by one of two alternative factors. One is deliberate attention (*ābhuñjita-vasena*). The other is the extrusion of one element over the others (*ussadavasena*).[696]

The first alternative is illustrated as follows: "When the bowl is filled with food and brought, one who takes up a lump [of food] and examines whether it is hard or soft is considering only the element of extension (earth element), though there may be heat and mobility present. One who investigates by putting the hand in hot water is considering only the element of heat, though extension and mobility are present. One who lets the wind beat upon the body by opening the window in the hot season is considering, while the wind beats gently and softly, only the element of mobility, though extension and heat are present."[697]

The second alternative is illustrated as follows: "But he who slips or knocks his head against a tree, or in eating bites on a stone, takes as his mental object only the element of extension on account of its extrusiveness, though where he slipped, and so on, heat and mobility were present. One treading on fire makes only the element of heat his object owing to its extrusiveness, although extension and mobility are present therein. When a strong wind blows, striking the ear as if to make one deaf, although extension and heat are present therein, the element of mobility alone is made the object owing to its extrusiveness."[698]

We find the intensity principle in other Buddhist schools as well. The *Abhidharmakośabhāṣya* poses the question of why all the mahābhūtas do not become the object of touch simultaneously. The answer given is similar to the one we have mentioned as the second alternative: "One perceives in a given aggregate that particular element that is the most intense (*paṭuma, sphuṭatama*) and not others."[699] According to the Sautrāntikas, the mahābhūtas that are not perceived in a given aggregate exist there in a state of seeds, or as energy, or as potentiality (*bījatas, śaktitas, sāmārthyatas*) and not in a state of activity.[700]

As noted above, one cannot speak of material objects as earthy (*paṭhavī*), watery (*āpo*), fiery (*tejo*), and airy (*vāyo*). For in every instance of materiality all the four mahābhūtas are present. However, if in a given material object the earth element has a higher degree of intensity (*ussada*) or capability (*sāmatthiya*), then as a matter of convention that material object is called earth (*paṭhavī*). Similarly, the names of the other three mahābhūtas are used.[701] This is only a concession to their popular conception.

Why the Theravāda Abhidhamma excludes the water element from the sense of touch needs explanation. It is partly explained by what we have mentioned about the position of cold in relation to the mahābhūtas. The water element, as we have seen, represents fluidity and viscidity. But the Theravāda position is that both fluidity and viscidity are not felt by the sense of touch. S. Z. Aung illustrates this situation as follows: "When one puts his hand into cold water, the softness of water felt is not āpo, but *paṭhavī*; the cold felt is not āpo, but *tejo*; the pressure felt is not āpo, but *vāyo*."[702] The water's fluidity and viscidity, whatever be their degree of intensity, are not felt by the sense of touch. It is known only as an object of mind consciousness.[703]

We may now consider the position assigned to the mahābhūtas as four basic material dhammas. What we want to maintain here is that Buddhism assigns them a comparatively primary position. In Sāṃkhya, for instance, mahābhūtas are not irreducible constituents of matter. They are said to evolve immediately from the *tanmātras* and ultimately from *prakṛti*, the first cause of the world of non-self.[704] According to Vedānta, the mahābhūtas are produced from the corresponding *sūkṣma-bhūtas* (subtle elements). The former are a species of gross matter and the latter a species of subtle matter.[705] For Jainism the ultimate constituents of matter (*puggala*) are not the four mahābhūtas (*dhādu-catukka*) but the homogeneous atoms (*paramāṇu*).[706] The Nyāya-Vaiśeṣika postulates four kinds of atoms corresponding to the four elemental substances—earth, water, fire, and air.[707] This is an attempt to reconcile the older theory of the mahābhūtas with the later atomic theory. It prevents the four elemental substances getting reduced to a secondary position.

In Buddhism the four mahābhūtas are assigned a truly primary position. As four material dhammas, they represent four basic factors of all material phenomena. They are not reducible to the level of four qualities of an underlying material substance. Nor are they derivatives or evolutes from any kind of primordial matter. It is of course true that a given instance of matter consists not only of the four mahābhūtas. It consists of a set of upādā-rūpas as well, such as color, smell, savor, and so on. But what are called upādā-rūpas are dependent on the mahābhūtas. Even the theory of material clusters (*rūpa-kalāpa*), which is the Theravāda version of atomism, did not reduce the four mahābhūtas to a secondary position. For in every material cluster (*rūpa-kalāpa*), defined as the minimal unit of matter (*sabba-pariyantima*), all the four mahābhūtas are present.[708] However, as components of phenomenal existence, they are subject to all laws of conditioned existence.

13

THE REAL DEPENDENT MATTER

We have examined how the Abhidhamma divides the material dhammas into two groups as "concretely produced" (*nipphanna*) and "nonconcretely produced" (*anipphanna*), in order to separate the real from the nominal. In this chapter we propose to examine the dependent material dhammas included in the first group, which consists of fourteen items distributed as follows: five sense organs, four sense fields, three faculties, material nutriment, and the physical base of mental activity.

Sensitive Matter

Pasāda-rūpa, "sensitive matter," is the term used in the Abhidhamma to refer to the five material sense organs: the organs of sight (*cakkhu*), hearing (*sota*), smell, (*ghāna*), taste (*jivhā*), and touch (*kāya*). The Pāli suttas refer to them very often. The purpose, however, is not so much to describe their nature as a species of matter, rather it is to draw attention to the role they play in the causality of sense perception and in the gratification of sensual pleasures.[709] In the Abhidhamma, on the other hand, we find more attention focused on them as a species of matter.

Pasāda literally means clearness, brightness, serenity, or faith. As a descriptive term for the material sense organs, it had not been used in the Pāli suttas. "Taken causatively," says Mrs. Rhys Davids, "it may conceivably have meant either that which makes clear—a revealer as it were—or that which gratifies or satisfies."[710] It is infact suggestive of both meanings. While the first indicates their receptivity and reactivity to external sense data, the second brings into focus the part they play in the gratification of sensual pleasure.

In Sanskrit Buddhism, too, we find the term *prasāda* used in the same sense. The sense organs are suprasensible (*atīndriya*) and translucent (*accha*). Because of their translucence, like the luminosity of a gem (*maṇiprabhāvat*), they cannot be burned or weighed.[711] Nor can they be cut into two. When a part of the body is chopped off, the body sensitivity (*kāya-prasāda*) does not thereby multiply itself. The part that is cut off is devoid of body sensitivity. This is inferred from the fact that on the basis of the part that is separated, tactile sensation does not arise.[712] On this point, Ācārya Yaśomitra makes this interesting observation: "How then could there be tactile sensation with the tip of the nose when it is cut but not separated from the nose? It is connected with the nose. Therefore body sensitivity arises again. But how is it that when the tails of the house lizards, and so on, are chopped off, they begin to vibrate if they are devoid of body sensitivity? This is due to the alteration (*vikāra*) of the air element and not to body sensitivity."[713]

The sense organs should not be understood according to their popular conception. The very purpose of using the term *pasāda* is to dismiss such a conception. Each sense organ consists of two parts: the composite or peripheral organ (*sasambhāra*) and the sentient organ (*pasāda*). The first is what we ordinarily mean by eye, ear, nose, tongue, and body. The second is the real sense organ and has the first as its basis (*vatthu*).[714] The difference between the peripheral (gross) and the sensitive sense organs is as follows:

> The peripheral or the compound eye (*sasambhāra-cakkhu*) is white from the abundance of phlegm, black from that of bile, red from that of blood, rigid from that of the element of extension, fluid from that of cohesion, hot from that of heat, and oscillating from that of mobility. The sensitive eye (*pasāda-cakkhu*) is located in the centre of the compound eye. It permeates the oc-

> cult membranes as sprinkled oil permeates seven cotton wicks. It is served by the four elements doing the functions of sustaining, binding, maturing, and vibration, just as a princely boy is tended by four nurses doing the functions of holding, bathing, dressing, and fanning him. It is not bigger in size than the head of a louse. The organ of hearing is situated in the interior of the compound organ, at a spot shaped like a finger-ring and fringed by tender tawny hairs, and is tended by the four primary elements. The organ of smell is in the interior of the compound organ, at a spot shaped like a goat's hoof. The organ of taste is above the middle of the compound organ, at a spot shaped like an upper part of a torn lotus leaf. The organ of touch is to be found everywhere in this physical body, like a liquid that soaks a layer of cotton.[715]

Thus unlike the other four sense organs, the body sensitivity is not located in a particular locus but is diffused all over the organic body. This situation, it is maintained, does not lead to confusion (*saṅkara*) in the respective functions of the different sense organs. For the characteristic (*lakkhaṇa*), function (*rasa*), manifestation (*paccupaṭṭhāna*), and the proximate cause (*padaṭṭhāna*) of one sense organ are different from those of another. The organ of sight, for instance, has the characteristic of being sensitive only to the visible and not to the other sense objects; its function is to draw attention to its respective objective field only and it manifests itself as the physical base of visual consciousness but not as the physical base of any other consciousness.[716]

Th. Stcherbatsky observes that the Buddhist conception of the sense organs as composed of matter subtler than the things that become the corresponding objects is reminiscent of the Sāṃkhya view—namely, that matter developed along two different lines, the one with predominance of the translucent intelligence-stuff (*sattva*), the other with predominance of dead matter (*tamas*), resulting in sense objects in their subtle (*tanmātra*) and gross (*mahābhūta*) forms. But the fundamental difference, to which Th. Stcherbatsky himself draws attention, is that in Buddhism, unlike in the Sāṃkhya, the two groups are not conceived "as modifications or appurtenances of an eternal substance."[717]

Moreover, the force of this parallelism tends to fade away because of the circumstance that in most of the schools of Indian thought the sense organs are conceived in more or less similar manner. The Jainas speak of two kinds of sense organs: *dravyendriya*, the physical sense organ, and *bhāvendriya*, its psychical correlate. The former, in turn, consists of two parts: *nivṛtti*, the organ itself, and *upakaraṇa*, the supporting environment. According to Caraka, the sense organs are distinct from their peripheral seats. The Mīmāṃsakas maintain that "the sense organs consist in the faculty of potency (*śakti*) abiding in the sockets." The Śankarite Vedāntin is of the view that the organs of sight, hearing, smell, taste, and touch are composed of the *sāttvic* parts of light, ether, earth, water, and air, respectively.[718]

If the sense organs are a species of sensitive matter, why do they differ in their receptivity to external objects? Most of the Indian schools explain this as a community of interest between the sense organ and the corresponding sense object. The Nyāya-Vaiśeṣika, for instance, holds that each sense organ is sensitive to the quality of that particular elemental substance of which it is composed. The organ of sight is composed of light (*tejas*). Therefore it is sensitive to color, which is the quality of light. The organs of hearing, smell, taste, and touch are the qualities of ether, earth, water, and air, respectively. Therefore they become objects of the organs of sight, hearing, smell, taste, and touch.[719] There is thus a community of interest between the sense organ and the corresponding sense field.

This Nyāya-Vaiśeṣika theory seems to have been accepted by some Buddhists in a modified form. This is shown by Ācariya Buddhaghosa's comments on two similar theories. The first says that among the four great elements that support the organ of sight, heat is in excess. Likewise, in the case of the hearing, smell, and taste organs, air, earth, and water are in excess. As for the organ of touch, there is no difference between the supporting great elements. According to the second theory, the five sense organs (in the order they are mentioned above) have heat, ether (*vivara*), air, water, and earth, respectively, in excess.[720]

The subcommentary to the *Visuddhimagga* says that the first theory was held by some Mahāsāṅghikas and was advocated by one Ācariya Vasudhamma.[721] The Siṃhala *sanne* to the *Visuddhimagga* attributes the second to the Abhayagiri fraternity, the rival sect of the Mahāvihāra.[722] Ācariya Buddhaghosa's critical comments on them are as follows:

> But some give as their reason that it is because these (several sensitivities = sense organs) are (respectively) aided by visible data, and so on, as qualities of fire, and so on. They should be asked: "But who has said that visible data, and so on, are qualities of fire, and so on?" For it is not possible to say of primary elements that remain always inseparable: "This is the quality of this one, that is the quality of that one." Then they may say, "Just as you assume, from excess in such and such material things, the (respective) functions of upholding (*sandhāraṇa*) and so on, for earth and so on, so from finding visibility, and so on, (respectively) in a state of excess in material things that have fire in excess, one may assume that visible data and so on are (respectively) qualities of these." They should be told, "We might assume it if there were more odor in cotton that has earth in excess than in fermented liquor that has water in excess, and if the color of cold water were weaker than the color of hot water that has heat in excess. But since neither of these is a fact, you should therefore give up conjecturing the difference to be in the supporting primary elements."[723]

The Abhidhamma's explanation for the differences between the sense organs is that they come into being through the action of kamma (*kamma-samuṭṭhāna-rūpa*). The desire to see, hear, smell, taste, and touch is the kamma condition responsible for the arising of a physical sense apparatus with diverse functions.[724]

How the sense organs apprehend their respective objects is another issue that needs clarification. As to the senses of touch, taste, and smell, the sensory contact is not difficult to understand. For in these three cases the objects come in actual physical contact with the respective sense organs. In the case of seeing and hearing, how sensory contact takes place is not so evident. On this issue we find two different views within the Theravāda exegesis. Earlier is the one mentioned in the *Sīhala Aṭṭhakathā*, to which we find a reference in a Pāli commentary. It says that all the sense organs apprehend their objects when they come in actual physical contact with them (*sampatta-gocara*).[725] As we shall see, according to this view both color/light and sound travel and directly impinge on the eye organ and the ear organ. The second view is the one introduced by the Pāli commentaries to substitute the first. It says that the organs of smell, taste, and touch apprehend their objects when they come in direct contact with them and that the organs of sight and hearing apprehend their objects at a distance (*asampatta-gocara*).[726] This new interpretation, which replaces the earlier, is in fact the same as the one accepted by the Sarvāstivādins.[727]

According to the role they play in the causality of sense perception, each sense organ becomes a physical base (*vatthu*) as well as a door (*dvāra*) to the consciousness named after it. The eye organ, for example, is the physical base for the occurrence of eye consciousness and its concomitants. As a door it also plays the role of a channel through which eye consciousness and its concomitants reach the object.[728]

Although the sense organ and the sense object play a dual role for sense consciousness to arise, it is the sense organ that is considered as a faculty (*indriya*). A faculty is that which wields power, dominance, or suzerainty (*ādhipacca, issariya*) in its respective domain;[729] in this case, in relation to the sense consciousness. For it is the intensity of the sense organ that decides the intensity of the consciousness. If the former is sharp, strong (*tikkha*), the latter, too, becomes sharp, strong, and if the former is weak (*manda*), the latter too becomes weak. This seems to be the reason why each sense consciousness is named not after its object but after its sense organ.[730]

Sense-Field Matter

"Sense-field matter" (*gocara-rūpa*) is the term used in the Abhidhamma to refer to the five sense fields—namely, the visible (*rūpa*), the audible (*sadda*), smell (*gandha*), taste (*rasa*), and the tangible (*phoṭṭhabba*).

Let us take first the sense field of the visible (*rūpāyatana*). Its earliest Abhidhamma definition is in the *Dhammasaṅgaṇi*. It is an enumeration, first of some examples of color—blue, yellow, red, white, and so on—and then some examples of figure—circular, oval, square, hexagonal, and so on.[731] Thus both color and figure form the objective sense field of the visible.

The commentary observes that the addition of figure is a concession to popular parlance (*vohāra*), because only color constitutes the visible. As to why figure is not visible, the commentary makes two statements. The first is that "the terms 'long,' and so on, are accomplished by mutual reference (*aññam'aññam upanidhāya*), and that the terms 'circular,' and so on, are accomplished by juxtaposition (*sannivesana*). Among them, with reference to what is 'short,' 'long' is so called as higher (*uccatara*) than 'short' and 'short' is so called as being lower (*nīcatara*) than 'long.' With reference to what is 'big,' a thing smaller than that, is 'little,' with reference to which a greater thing is 'big.'"[732] The second statement adds: "Among these expressions, because it is possible to know 'long' and so on, also by touch, but not 'blue-green' and so on, therefore in reality 'long' is not directly (*nippariyāyena*) a visible object; neither is 'short' or similar terms."[733]

The first statement means that our notions of "figure," such as long, short, circular, oval, or square, are relative concepts with no objective counterparts. The second adds proof to this conclusion. While color cannot be known by the sense of touch, it is possible to know (infer) certain instances of figure by touch as well. What both statements mean is that figure (*saṇṭhāna*) is not a part of the visible. Rather, it is a conceptual construct that we "superimpose on the difference of coloration."[734] It is in keeping with this new interpretation that some Pāli subcommentaries began to use the more specific "the sense field of color" (*vaṇṇāyatana*)[735] in place of the older term "the sense field of the visible" (*rūpāyatana*) to mean the sense field of the visual organ.

What led to this new interpretation could perhaps be traced to the Vaibhāṣika-Sautrāntika controversy on the nature of the visible. The Vaibhāṣika position is that both color (*varṇa*) and figure (*saṃsthāna*) combine to constitute the visible. The visible can be color without being figure (*saṃsthāna-nirapekṣam*)—for example, blue, red, yellow, white, shade, sunlight (*ātāpa*), light (*āloka*), darkness (*tamas*). The visible can also be figure without being color (*varṇa-nirapekṣam*)—for example, that part of long, short, and so on that constitutes the bodily intimation (*kāyavijñapti*). Or else it can be, at one and the same time, both color and figure—for example, all other varieties of the visible.[736]

The Sautrāntika position is that color alone is real, that only color constitutes the visible, and that figure is only a mental construct (*mānasaṃ parikalpitam*) with no objective reality (*prajñapti-sat*).[737]

The Sautrāntikas seek to establish their thesis on three main arguments. The first is that one can obtain the notion of "long," "short," and so on by seeing or by touching something. If figure were a real entity, then one would have to admit that it could be cognized by two sense organs. Such a conclusion will go against the canonical definition of the visible as the objective sense field corresponding to only one sense organ—namely, the organ of sight. The counterargument of the Vaibhāṣikas is that when we obtain the idea of, say, "long" by touching something, it is not that we actually cognize it by the organ of touch but that we are reminded of the figure (long) because it is associated with the tangible. It is just as when we see the color (visible) of fire we are reminded of its heat (tangible) or when we smell the odor of a flower we are reminded of its color. The Sautrāntikas contend that this analogy is not of universal validity. If color reminds us of the tangible, and the odor reminds us of the color, it is because there is an invariable association (*avyabhicāra*) between the two things given in each example. But every tangible is not associated with a particular figure. If it were otherwise, then every time we touched something we should be able to know the color associated with it.[738]

The second argument of the Sautrāntikas is that if "figure" were a real and discrete entity, then one would have to concede that there is a plurality of material dharmas occupying the one and the same locus (*ekadeśa*). In a variegated carpet, for instance, there are a large number of figures. If "figure" is a real entity, then the figure that is part of a long line cannot at the same time be a part of a short line. The Vaibhāṣikas contend that if figure is nothing but a certain disposition of color, then the figure can never change if the color is the same. The Sautrāntika answer is that one calls something long and so on when a number of real dharmas are placed in a certain manner or disposition, and that apart from the real dharmas so placed there is no real and discrete entity called "figure." The third argument of the Sautrāntikas is that color is a constituent element of the smallest unit of matter. But the same is not true of figure.[739]

Why the Vaibhāṣikas strongly objected to interpreting figure as a mental construct is perhaps due to the need they felt to establish the reality of bodily intimation (*kāya-vijñapti*). As we shall see, they believe that bodily intimation is a certain figure of the body, known as an object of visual consciousness.[740] They could not deprive it of its reality because, together with vocal intimation (*vacī-vijñapti*), it is closely associated with *avijñapti-rūpa*, a material dharma not recognized either by the Theravādins or by the Sautrāntikas.

The Sautrāntikas, it may be noted here, had a strong tendency to declare as nominal some of the items recognized by other schools as real. It is very likely, therefore, that they were the first to define the visible as consisting of only color. It is equally likely that this new interpretation found its way to Theravāda Abhidhamma during the commentarial period. Whether it was introduced from an outside source, or whether it was developed within Theravāda, it could be easily accommodated in the Theravāda Abhidhamma. For, unlike the Vaibhāṣikas, the Theravādins do not explain bodily intimation as a variety of figure (*saṇṭhāna*), nor do they recognize a material dhamma corresponding to the *avijñapti-rūpa* of the Vaibhāṣikas. Hence they could conveniently relegate figure to the domain of conceptual constructs without thereby undermining the basis of any established doctrine.

The second sense field is sound, the audible (*saddāyatana*). As to how it impinges on the ear, we have briefly referred to the *Sīhala Aṭṭhakathā* view. What it says is that sound travels in an elemental series (*dhātu-paramparā*) and impinges on the sensitive portion of the ear. Of much interest is the example given in support of this view: The bodily movements of men felling trees or of washermen washing clothes are seen (quickly), although they are at a great distance. On the other hand, the sound they make is relatively slow of ascertainment (*vavatthāna*) because it comes in an elemental series and strikes the auditory organ.[741] This *Sīhala Aṭṭhakathā* view, as noted by E. R. Sarachchandra,[742] is similar to the one advanced by the Nyāya-Vaiśeṣikas: "Either sounds reach the ear in concentric circles of waves like the waves of water, or they shoot out in all directions like the filaments of a *kadamba*."[743] However, what is important to note here is that the *Aṭṭhakathā* view provides us with empirical evidence in support of its conclusion. It is also interesting to notice that the *Aṭṭhakathā* view not only recognizes that sound travels and impinges on the ear but that light travels faster than sound. This gets confirmed by another example given: "The color/light of the discs of the moon and sun situated above 42,000 yojanas away strikes the sentient visual organ. That color, although it appears to be far, is known to be in physical contact. Because it has such a range, the eye is said to have attained range contact."[744]

The Pāli commentaries refer to this (earlier) theory of sound only to reject it as unsound. Their main objection is that it cannot adequately account for our knowledge of the direction of sound. If sound comes slowly (gradually), having arisen at a distance, then it will be apprehended after some time. Coming in an elemental series and impinging on the sensitive portion of the ear, the direction it comes from might not be evident.[745] For when one hears a sound one can (fairly accurately) say whether it is a distant sound, or a near sound, or whether it is a sound from the farther bank or from the hither bank.[746] A subcommentary adds that if sound travels toward the ear, then there cannot be the determination of its locus (*desādesa-vavatthāna*). It further notes that when sound is apprehended it continues to remain where it has arisen. As to how an echo arises, it says that although sound remains at a distance, it can become a condition (*paccaya*) for the arising of an echo elsewhere, even as a magnet (*ayo-kānta*) for the movement of iron.[747] It is also observed that our ability to hear the sound of thunder that arises at a distance, and the sound produced within the body covered by the skin, shows that for its apprehension sound need not travel toward the ear and strike its sensitive portion.[748]

This new theory that the Pāli commentaries introduced in place of the earlier is in fact identical with the one accepted by the Sarvāstivāda Abhidharma. For here, too, sound is described as having the characteristic of "nonoccurrence as a series."[749]

With the development of the theory of material clusters (*rūpa-kalāpas*), which is the Theravāda version of atomism, one question that arose concerned the production of sound. As we shall see later, the possibility of atoms coming into immediate contact with one another is denied.[750] If this idea were to be retained, the production of sound could not be attributed to an actual physical collision (*ghaṭṭana*) of the atoms that constitute material aggregates. It became necessary, therefore, to reinterpret physical collision as "the arising of material clusters (atoms) in close proximity to one another due to appropriate conditions."[751] The words "arising in close proximity" are meant to rule out the actual physical contact of the material clusters as well as their movement.

The next two sense fields are smell and taste. Their descriptions are mainly classifications. The *Dhammasaṅgaṇi*, for instance, refers to a variety of smells—the smell of roots, sap, bark, leaves, flowers, and fruit, of putrid smell, pleasant smell, unpleasant smell and "whatever other smell there is."[752] The commentary adds that agreeable smell (*iṭṭha-gandha, sugandha*) and disagreeable smell (*aniṭṭha-gandha, duggandha*) exhaust all varieties of smell.[753] One Buddhist tradition says that there is a variety of smell that is neither agreeable nor disagreeable (*sama-gandha*).[754] The sense field of taste (*rasa*) has the following different types: sour, sweet, bitter, pungent, saline, alkaline, acrid, astringent, nice, nauseous, "and whatever other taste there is."[755] The Sarvāstivādins recognize six basic varieties (*ṣan-mūla-jāti*): sweet, sour, salty, pungent, bitter, and astringent. Their mixtures can give rise to many subvarieties.[756]

As for the sense field of the tangible, as noted earlier, the Theravāda view is that it consists of three of the great material elements—namely, the earth element, the fire element, and the air element. The water element is excluded from the tangible on the ground that it cannot be physically sensed but must be known as an object of inference.

Faculties of Sex

There are two faculties of sex: the faculty of femininity and the faculty of masculinity. The first as defined in the *Dhammasaṅgaṇi* is the physical appearance, marks, traits, and deportment peculiar to a female, or the state of femininity (*ittthatta, itthibhāva*). Likewise, the second is the physical appearance and so on peculiar to a male, or the state of masculinity (*purisatta, purisabhāva*).[757]

Elaborating on these differences, the commentary observes:

> The shape of a woman's hands, feet, neck, breast, and so on is not like that of a man's. The lower body of the female is broad, the upper body is less broad. The hands and feet are small, the mouth is small. The female breast is prominent. The face is without beard or moustache. The dressing of the hair, the weaving of clothes, are also unlike those of a man's. The masculine features are just the opposite. For the shape of the hands, feet, neck, breast, and so on of a man is unlike the shape of those of a woman. For a man's upper body is broad, the lower body is less broad, the hands and feet are large, the face is large, the breast flesh is less full; beard and moustache grow.[758]

Then there are differences as to habits and deportment: "Thus in youth women play with tiny shallow baskets, pestles and mortars, variegated dolls, and weave string with clay fibre. There is a want of assertion in women's walking, standing, lying down, sitting, eating, and swallowing. Indeed, when a man of that description is seen, folk say: 'He walks, stands, and so on, like a woman.' In the case of men there is a marked difference. In youth they play with chariots and ploughs, and so on, make sand banks and dig ponds. There is assertion in their walking, and so on. When a woman is seen taking long strides, and so on, folk say: 'She walks like a man.'"[759]

Although the *Dhammasaṅgaṇi* defines the two faculties to mean the physical features and so on that are peculiar to women and men, the commentary takes a somewhat different position. It says that physical features and so on are not the two faculties. They are what result from them as their causes. Just as a tree grows because of a seed, replete with twigs and branches, even so because of the faculty of femininity there come into being such physical features and so on as are peculiar to a female. With necessary changes this observation applies to the faculty of masculinity as well.[760] Thus the "that" (*yaṃ*) of the *Dhammasaṅgaṇi* is in its commentary understood as "that through which" (*yena*).[761]

According to the commentary the faculty of femininity/masculinity is spread all over the physical body (*sakala-sarīra-byāpaka*) as the faculty of touch is.[762] As to their relative position, it is not correct to say that the faculty of femininity/masculinity is either "located in the space where the organ of touch is located" or "located in the space where that is not located."[763] Both are diffused all over the physical body, yet one is not an aspect of the other. The four great material elements that support the organ of touch are different from those that support the faculty of sex (*bhinna-nissayatā*).[764]

For the Sarvāstivāda, the faculty of femininity/masculinity is not distinct from the organ of touch. "A part of the organ called faculty of touch (*kayendriya*) is the faculty of sex."[765] In this sense, the two faculties cognize the tangible. The Theravādins seem to have had this theory in mind when they say that some entertain the wrong belief that the faculty of sex is only a part of the physical body (*sarīrekadesavutti*).[766] The Theravāda position is that the two faculties do not cognize the tangible. They are not part of the materiality that is impingent (*rūpaṃ sappaṭighaṃ*).[767]

The Material Faculty of Life

As we have already noted, the Theravāda recognizes two life faculties. One is the psychic life faculty (*arūpa-jīvitindriya*). This is the factor that sustains and stabilizes consciousness and mental factors. It is therefore listed as one of the seven universal mental factors (*sabba-citta-sādhāraṇa*). The second is the material life faculty (*rūpa-jīvitindriya*). It is the factor that sustains and stabilizes material factors that come into being as a result of kamma. This refers to all instances of organic matter that enters into the composition of a living being—namely, the physical sense organs, the faculties of sex, the physical base of mental activity, and other material dhammas associated with them. Accordingly, the material life faculty is invariably present in all kamma-originated material clusters.[768]

The Sarvāstivāda, as noted earlier, recognizes only one life faculty. It is not of the nature of matter, nor is it an exclusively mental factor (*caitasika dharma*), although it resembles the latter. For unlike the mental factors, it is not associated with consciousness. It is therefore included in a category called "mental formations dissociated from consciousness" (*cittaviprayukta*). Its inclusion here shows that although it is neither material nor, strictly speaking, mental, it is common to both groups.

Thus as to the faculty of life we find two parallel developments, one recognizing two and the other only one. What led to this situation becomes clear from a controversy recorded in the *Kathāvatthu* where the point at issue is whether there are two life faculties or not. The arguments of the non-Theravādins (Pubbaseliyas and Sammitīyas, according to the commentary) remind us of the position taken up by the Sarvāstivādins. They contend that there is only one life faculty, that it is common to both mind and matter, and that it is nonmaterial (*arūpa*). Its description as nonmaterial suggests only its exclusion from the aggregate of corporeality and not its identity with any of the mental factors. For although they include the life faculty in the aggregate of mental formations, yet they deny that any of the mental formations obtains in the attainment of cessation (*nirodha-samāpatti*). For in the attainment of cessation, the stream of consciousness and its concomitants is temporally arrested though the physical body remains alive. The non-Theravādins' view, therefore, seems to be that although the life faculty could be assigned a place in the aggregate of mental formations, it is certainly not a pure mental factor. It may be recalled here that the Sarvāstivādins include it in the category of mental formations dissociated from consciousness but make it distinct from the mental factors. In fact, the commentary observes that in the opinion of the Pubbaseliyas and Sammitīyas the life faculty is a "nonmental dhamma dissociated from consciousness" (*citta-vippayutta-arūpa-dhamma*).[769]

The Theravādins' claim for the desirability of recognizing two life faculties is based on two main grounds. The first is that it explains satisfactorily that attainment of cessation is not identical with death, because what keeps the physical body of the person who attains "cessation" live is not the mental but the material life faculty. The second is that the absence of mental phenomena in the material sphere (*asañña-bhava*) does not mean that the life principle of matter is not recognized. For in this plane of existence what operates is not the mental but the material life faculty.[770]

As to the recognition of the life faculty, the Sautrāntikas take a different position. In their view karma alone is sufficient and efficient to stabilize and sustain what arises as a result of karma. "Just as the destiny of an arrow and the time it will take to reach its destination are determined at the moment of its shooting, similarly the karma of an individual at the moment of rebirth fixes the destiny (*nikāya-sabhāga*) and the duration of the continuity (*santāna*) of the five aggregates."[771] The postulation of a separate entity called "life faculty" is not only superfluous but it gives rise to, and leaves unexplained, the question of accounting for its own stability and continuity.[772]

Material Nutriment

In Buddhism the term "nutriment" (*āhāra*) is used in a broad sense to denote not only edible material food or its nutritive essence but also three other factors—namely, sensory contact (*phassa*), volition (*mano-sañcetanā*), and consciousness (*viññāṇa*).[773] They are all called nutriment because they sustain and keep going the empiric individuality in the cycle of saṃsāra. Thus what we call the empiric individuality or individual existence is a process of alimentation, a process of nutriment kept going by four kinds of food.

The Pāli expression for edible material food is *kabaliṅkāra-āhāra*. It literally means "food made into a ball" or "morsel-made food." While the Pāli suttas understood it in the general sense of solid food that all living beings take for their sustenance and growth, the Abhidhamma interprets it in a more abstract sense to mean the nutritive aspect of matter, the quality of nutrition. It is of course true that the *Dhammasaṅgaṇi* defines it by citing some examples of food, such as boiled rice, sour gruel, flour, fish, flesh, milk, curds, butter, cheese, and so on.[774] But as the commentary observes, this is a definition given in terms of its embodiment (*vatthu-vasena*).[775] The commentarial observation is supported by the fact that elsewhere in the *Dhammasaṅgaṇi* material food is included in the objective field of mental objects (*dhammāyatana*).[776] This means that it cannot be known by any of the senses other than the mind; it is known by a process of inference. Nevertheless, this definition by way of its embodiment reminds us of its earlier meaning as found in the Pāli suttas.

Quite in contrast is the Sarvāstivāda definition of edible food (*kavaḍīkāra-āhāra*). It consists of three sense fields: odor, savor, and the tangible.[777] Why the sense field of sound is excluded needs no explanation. But as to why the sense field of the visible is excluded, the reason given is that it does not contribute to the actual process of alimentation, although it remains in inseparable association with that which really constitutes edible food.[778] It may be noted here that the three sense fields that make up material food along with the sense field of the visible represent those material dharmas that are inseparable (*avinirbhāga*) and that are said to enter into the composition of all material aggregates. Therefore if we overlook for the moment the exclusion of the sense field of the visible from what constitutes edible food, then this explanation does not amount to a radical departure from its earlier conception. For, it amounts to a case of approaching the subject from the standpoint of the sense fields.

The Physical Base of Mental Activity

As noted earlier, the first-ever allusion to the physical base of mind and mind consciousness is found in the *Paṭṭhāna*. Although this work does not specify what that physical base is, in the commentaries it came to be identified as the heart base (*hadaya-vatthu*). With this identification, the heart base came to be introduced as a separate material dhamma as well. This is how the twenty-seven material dhammas of the Abhidhamma Piṭaka became twenty-eight in the Pāli commentaries.

If the heart base is a separate material dhamma, why is it not mentioned in the *Dhammasaṅgaṇi*? We find this question raised in the subcommentary to the *Visuddhimagga*, and the answer given is this:

> In the section on base dyads (*vatthu-duka*) of the *Dhammasaṅgaṇi* the exposition is made with reference to the physical

> bases of the first five kinds of consciousness, e.g., "there is matter that is the base of visual consciousness, there is matter that is not the base of visual consciousness." If the dyads were stated with reference to mind consciousness as well, as "there is matter that is the base of mind consciousness, there is matter that is not the base of mind consciousness," then the section on base dyads would not fall in line with the section on object dyads (*ārammaṇa-duka*), where the dyads are stated with reference to the objects of the first five types of consciousness. For it is not possible to establish a dyad like: "There is matter that is the object of mind consciousness, there is matter that is not the object of mind consciousness" (because all material dhammas become the objects of mind consciousness). If there were to be inconsistency between the two sections in question, there would not be uniformity in the method of exposition. Here the Teacher's intention was to develop the exposition in a form that has unity (*ekarasa*). Hence the omission in the *Dhammasaṅgaṇi* of the heart base, which is the base of mind and mind consciousness, was unavoidable.[779]

The Pāli commentators' interpretation of what has remained unidentified in the *Paṭṭhāna* as the heart base can neither be supported nor refuted with reference to the original *Paṭṭhāna* passage. For it is an answer to a question left unanswered. An interesting argument in support of the answer is given in the subcommentaries. The first part of this argument is an attempt to find out whether it is possible to identify the alluded material base with any of the twenty-seven material dhammas listed in the *Dhammasaṅgaṇi*.

Attention is first drawn to the situation that the organs of sight, hearing, smell, taste, and touch, which are the physical bases of the five kinds of consciousness named after them, are a variety of *nipphanna-upāda-rūpa* (concretely produced dependent material dhammas). Therefore, so runs the argument, the physical base of mind and mind consciousness, too, should belong to the same category. This eliminates from the field the four great material elements because, although they are *nipphanna*, they are not *upādā-rūpa*. Then are eliminated the ten items that we shall examine in the next chapter because, although they are *upādā-rūpa*, they are not *nipphanna*. Consequently, the field is narrowed down to the thirteen material dhammas that we have already examined in this chapter.

Among them, none of the five physical sense organs can be selected because they are the physical bases of the five kinds of consciousness named after them. As for the four sense fields (the fifth consists of three great elements of matter) and nutriment, they exist not only in the body of a living being but also outside of it. Hence they too have to be eliminated. The two faculties of sex too have to be eliminated because mind and mind consciousness obtain even in those living beings who do not possess the faculty of sex. The faculty of life has its own function to perform. To attribute another is not quite right. Hence it should also be eliminated.[780]

So far it has been a case of elimination and so far two things have been established. One is that what the *Paṭṭhāna* alludes to as the physical base of mind and mind consciousness should be a material dhamma that is *nipphanna* as well as *upādā-rūpa*. The other is that it cannot be identified with, and should therefore be different from, any of the already known thirteen material dhammas that constitute the category of *nipphanna-upādā-rūpa*. This is the justification for the introduction of a separate material dhamma as the seat of mental activity.

The next problem is to find out where it is located. The answer is sought in empirical observation. It is observed that when someone thinks of anything, bringing it to mind intently and directing his whole mind to it, he experiences exhaustion (*khijjana*) in his heart. Therefore it is to be inferred that the location of the seat of mental activity is inside the heart (*hadayabbhantare*).[781]

14

THE NOMINAL DEPENDENT MATTER

IN THE PREVIOUS CHAPTER we examined the fourteen dependent material dhammas that are *nipphanna* (concretely produced)—that is, those that have their own nature as ultimate components of material existence. In the present chapter we propose to examine the opposite category, the *anipphanna* (nonconcretely produced)—that is, those that exist as modalities or attributes of the nipphanna, the real material dhammas. As we have already noted, what come under the category of *anipphanna* are nominal entities with no corresponding objective counterparts. The Pāli commentators observe that it is as a matter of convention (*rūḷhiyā*) that these are called *rūpa-dhammas*.[782] If we, too, keep on referring to them as material dhammas it is in order to conform to this commentarial convention. The *anipphanna* category includes ten items: space element as the principle of material delimitation (*pariccheda-rūpa*), two means of intimation and three special modes of matter (*vikāra-rūpa*), and four characteristics of matter (*lakkhaṇa-rūpa*).[783]

The Space Element

It was noted earlier that in the Pāli suttas sometimes the empiric individuality is analyzed into six basic constituents (*dhātus*), among which one is called *ākāsa-dhātu*, the space element. It was also noted that when the

Saṅgīti Sutta of the *Dīghanikāya* refers to a kind of material phenomenon, which is neither visible (*anidassana*) nor impinging (*appaṭigha*), the reference is most probably to the space element referred to above. It is this same space element that we find listed in the *Dhammasaṅgaṇi* of the Abhidhamma Piṭaka as one of the secondary material dhammas. Its recognition as such carries the implication that it is dependent on the four great material elements.[784]

In explaining why the space element is so recognized, some observe that since space is necessary for the existence and movement of matter, it can well be provided a place under matter.[785] It is very doubtful that this was the reason for its being recognized as a material phenomenon. If that were so, then it ought to have been given a position at least on par with the four great material elements rather than being considered as dependent on and therefore secondary to them.

In the *Vibhaṅga* we find space element defined as follows: the cavities of the ear, of the nose, the mouth door, that through which what is eaten, drank, or chewed is swallowed, that where it is deposited, and that through which it is evacuated are instances of internal (*ajjhattika*) space element. Likewise the cavities and interstices that obtain outside of the body, the cavities in the wall, the door space, and so on, are instances of external (*bāhira*) space element.[786] We find its counterpart in the Sarvāstivāda Abhidharma as well. The cavity of the mouth, of the nose, and so on—this is internal (*ādhyātmika*) space element. The cavity of the door, of the window, and so on—this is external (*bāhya*) space element.[787]

It will thus be seen that what the Abhidhamma means by space element is not space as a kind of receptivity for the existence and movement of matter. Rather, the reference is to void region, the space bound or delimited by matter. Once we have understood the space element as "the void region that delimits," why it is presented as a material phenomenon dependent on the four great material elements should become clear. Our notion of the void is determined by the environing matter and in this sense it is dependent on matter. All matter has the four great material elemens as its necessary base. Therefore, in terms of the elemental analysis, the space element is ultimately dependent on the four great material elements.

This becomes further clear by the commentarial definitions. Space element is the material phenomenon of delimitation (*pariccheda-rūpa*). Delimitation signifies not only that which delimits (*paricchindati*) but also that which is delimited (*paricchijjhati*).[788] Since space element means void region, the space bound by matter, it sets limits to and is itself limited by the surrounding matter. It has the characteristic of delimiting matter; its function is to show the boundaries of matter; it manifests as confines of matter; its proximate cause is delimited matter. It is the space element that serves as a basis for our notions of "below," "above," "across," and so on.[789] By delimiting and separating material objects, it enables us to perceive them as distinct entities.

For the Sarvāstivādins space element is either light (*āloka*) or darkness (*tamas*), and as such it is visible. Therefore it is included in the sense field of the visible.[790] Its inclusion by the Theravādins among the mental objects shows that in their view it is not visible. This gets further confirmed by a *Kathāvatthu* controversy on the visibility of the space element. Some Buddhists argue that one can see the interval between two trees or two posts, the space in a keyhole or in a window, and therefore that space element is visible. The Theravādins' reply is that in the case of an interval between two trees, for instance, one sees with one's eye only the color of the two trees and that the interval as such is known only by the mind.[791]

Why the space element is a nominal material dhamma is clear: it has no own nature and therefore it is not a dhamma. Nor is it of the nature of materiality (*ruppana*). Although space element is defined as the material phenomenon of delimitation, it is nothing but the mere limitation of matter (*rūpa-pariccheda-matta*). Only as a matter of convention (*rūḷhiyā*) is it presented as a conditioned dhamma.[792] What this amounts to is that it is a conceptual construct (*paññatti*) with no objective counterpart.

Means of Intimation

There are two means of intimation or self-expression. One is bodily intimation (*kāya-viññatti*) and the other vocal intimation (*vacī-viññatti*). They refer to the material phenomena involved in communicating one's thoughts or feelings to another.

Let us take bodily intimation first. The best way to understand it is to get ourselves acquainted first with how it is explained in the Sāṃmitīya and the Vātsīputrīya schools of Buddhism. In their view bodily intimation is a movement (*gati*) resulting from a thought that wishes that movement. The movement is that of the body (*kāya*), and it is called bodily intimation because it makes manifest or expresses that thought in response to which it arises. It is included in the sense field of the visible because it is the movement of the body, of matter that is visible. Therefore bodily intimation is said to be apprehended by the organ of sight.[793]

The Theravāda version takes a different form. According to its earliest definition given in the *Dhammasaṅgaṇi*, bodily intimation is "that tension (*thambhana*), that intentness (*santhambhana*), that state of making the body tense (*santhambhitatta*) in response to a thought, kammically wholesome, unwholesome, or indeterminate, on the part of a person who advances or recedes, or fixes the gaze or glances around, or retracts an arm, or stretches it forth."[794] It is called consciousness-originated (*citta-samuṭṭhāna*) because it is set up, given rise to, or conditioned by that thought in response to which it arises.[795] It is described as occurring together with consciousness (*citta-sahabhū*) because it lasts as long as that consciousness. It is also described as following the pattern of consciousness (*cittānuparivatti*) because, as a physical phenomenon, it conforms to that particular consciousness.[796] It is called bodily intimation because it is the means by which that thought, in response to which it arises, is communicated.

What is clear from this brief definition is that bodily intimation is not identical with bodily movements. This is in contrast to how it is defined by the Sāṃmitīyas and the Vātsīputrīyas, for, as we have seen, they define it as bodily movements. But as the above definition shows, in the Theravāda the term is reserved to signify "that tension, that intentness, that state of making the body tense" that occurs in response to a thought. Again unlike the bodily intimation of the Sāṃmitīya-Vātsīputrīya, it is not something visible because in the Theravāda Abhidhamma bodily intimation is included not in the sense field of the visible but in the sense field of mental objects.[797] It is therefore known only as an object of mind consciousness through a process of inference.

However, the above definition does not deny the role of bodily movements in communicating one's thoughts or feelings to another. For, it refers to bodily movements such as "retracting an arm or stretching it forth," which accompany that state of bodily tension. But it is the latter, not the former, that is identified as bodily intimation. The reason for this can be seen in the description of bodily tension as following the pattern of the thought (*cittānuparivatti*). What seems to be intended by this is that the body behaves in conformity with the intent of that particular thought, by which it is conditioned. While thus following the pattern of thought, the intent of the thought causes the body to move in ways that reveal one's intentions.

The above account of bodily intimation is based on its earliest definition as given in the *Dhammasaṅgaṇi*. The commentarial account of the subject falls within its framework and clarifies it further. Here the "state of bodily tension" of the *Dhammasaṅgaṇi* is described as a special mode of the consciousness-originated air element.[798] Since the air element cannot exist independently of the other three great material elements, it is also observed that bodily intimation is a special mode of all four material elements. If it is described as "of the air element" it is because of the circumstance that here the air element is characterized by a higher degree of intensity (*ussada*) or capability (*sāmatthiya*). In the subcommentaries we find this particular physical condition described as resembling the state of effort-making (*ussahana-vikāra*) that appears on the body of a person when with full effort he lifts a heavy stone.[799]

In order to understand how this special mode of the consciousness-originated air element functions as bodily intimation, we need to first familiarize ourselves with how the Abhidhamma explains the occurrence of bodily movements. As explained in a Pāli commentary, when a thought occurs to someone, such as "I will move forward or step back," that particular thought sets up material phenomena consisting of the following eight material dhammas: earth, water, fire, air, color, odor, savor, and nutritive essence.[800] These eight, it may be noted here, are necessarily coexistent and positionally inseparable and constitute the basic foundation of all instances of materiality. Since these eight are set up by or arise in response to a thought, they are called consciousness-originated matter. Among these material dhammas, the air element is more intense and, as the principle of motion, it is this air element that moves the physical body forward or backward. The other material phenomena within the body—that is, those originated by kamma, nutriment, and temperature—too move with it. "Just as dry sticks and grass fallen in the flowing water go with the water or stop with the water, even so the other material phenomena move with the consciousness-originated matter."[801]

How exactly the body moves in response to a thought has to be understood in light of the Abhidhamma theory of cognition. As we have already seen, an act of cognition involves a continuous process of mental events and the most active phase of such a cognitive process is called javana (impulsion). It is at the javana phase that the object comes to be fully cognized and it is also this phase that represents all volitional activities. A full process of javana takes seven mind moments, each occurring one after the other by way of immediate contiguity.[802] Since the javana phase has a cognitive as well as a volitional aspect, the seven javana moments represent the mind's role in all bodily movements. Now when a thought having the intent of moving the body occurs, then in response to each javana moment there arise material phenomena that are called consciousness-originated because they are set up by that javana. Among these material phenomena, the air element, which is the principle of mobility, has more intensity than the others. The material phenomena that are conditioned by the first six javana moments intensify and prepare the body for movement but they do not have the capacity to move the body. The material phenomena set up by the seventh javana moment actually perform the task of moving the body in the ways directed by the mind. In the words of the commentary: "The seventh moment sets up mobility able both to move the body forward and backward and to cause the act of looking straight ahead or obliquely, of bending and extending the limbs. Hence there results an act of going or coming or both; (by repetition more than a thousand times) it enables us to say that a man has gone a yojana, gone as far as ten yojanas."[803]

This situation is illustrated with the simile of a cart having seven yokes: "As when a cart is drawn by seven yokes, the bullocks at the first yoke are able to bear the yoke but not to turn the wheels. And the same with the bullocks yoked to the second . . . and sixth yokes. But by harnessing bullocks to a seventh yoke a clever driver sitting in the forepart of the cart takes the reins and urges the bullocks with the goad, beginning from the foremost of all; then all the bullocks being of united strength steady the yoke, turn the wheels, draw the cart, enabling us to say that it has gone ten or twenty *yojanas.*"[804]

Now, as already noted, bodily movements are not the bodily intimation. Nor are they the consciousness-originated material phenomena, among which the air element has more intensity and capacity. Rather, bodily movements are a special mode of the air element (*ākāra-vikāra*), which is able to "tense, lift, and move" the body.[805] To quote the commentary: "It is called bodily intimation because it is a capacity for communicating. What does it communicate? A certain wish communicable by an act of the body. If anyone stands in the path of the eye, raises his hands or feet, shakes his head or brow, the movements of his hands, and so on, are visible. Intimation, however, is not visible; it is only knowable by mind. For one sees by the eye a color surface moving by virtue of the change of position in hands, and so on. But by reflecting on it as intimation, one knows it by mind-door consciousness, thus: 'I imagine that this man wishes me to do this or that act.'"[806] As the commentary further illustrates, it is just as when people during the hot season tie palm leaves on the top of a tree in a forest with the intention that by this sign others will know that there is water here, and when others on seeing it come to know that there is water here, although they have not actually seen the water. Or it is like our inferring which way the wind is blowing by our observing the movement of the trees, although we do not see the wind.[807]

Thus intimation is so called not only because of communicating (*viññāpana*) but also because of being communicated (*viññāpitatta*). Communication by sign, as the commentary observes, is sometimes intelligible even to animals: "Whenever dogs, foxes, crows and cattle are assembled, and when they see the gesture of striking, on a stick or a stone being seized, they know 'he wishes to strike us' and flee helter-skelter."[808] Another important point raised in the commentary is whether intimation can be called intimation when the person to whom it is intended is not attending to it; in other words, when the message is not communicated. The answer is that even then it should be called so because it had the potentiality to communicate.[809]

The Theravāda version of bodily intimation that we have sketched above closely corresponds to that of the Dārṣṭāntikas. They are of the view that "there exists a certain *rūpa* that is neither color (*varṇa*) nor figure (*saṃsthāna*) but that is produced by thought. This *rūpa* puts into movement the hands and other members."[810] In the *Karmasiddhiprakaraṇa* of Ācārya Vasubandhu we find an almost identical, if not the same, theory attributed to a Buddhist school called Sauryodayikas. According to this theory, bodily movements are due to a rise in the air element by a certain variety of consciousness (*citta-viśeṣād utpannaḥ*). And it is this air element that is identified by the Sauryodayikas as bodily intimation.[811]

The Sarvāstivādins, too, refuse to identify bodily intimation with bodily movements, but for different reasons. They criticize Buddhist schools such as the Sāṃmitīyas and the Vātsīputrīyas for identifying bodily intimation with bodily movements, on the ground that motion is not something that obtains in a real and ultimate sense. Motion is only a name given to the appearance of a series of momentary material dharmas in adjacent locations (*deśāntarotpatti*).[812] If somebody retracted her arm or stretched it forth, in an ultimate sense it is not correct to say that her arm had moved. What actually happened was that the series of momentary material dharmas that constituted what was called the arm arose in adjacent locations in a certain direction. Only the place of the arising of the momentary dharmas had changed, but not a single dharma had moved. Hence to identify bodily intimation with bodily movements is to deprive it of its reality as a dharma having its own nature, and to deprive its position as a real dharma is to undermine the very foundation of their theory of *avijñapti-rūpa*, which is closely connected with *vijñapti-rūpa*—that is, the bodily and vocal intimations. Hence according to the Sarvāstivādins, bodily intimation is not the movements of the body; rather, it is such and such figure or disposition (*saṃsthāna*) of the body, given rise to or conditioned by a volitional thought.[813] This might appear as something corresponding to the bodily intimation of the Theravāda Abhidhamma, but there is this important difference to be noted: what the Sarvāstivādins identify as bodily intimation, unlike the Theravādins, is something visible. As we have seen earlier, according to the Sarvāstivādins visibility constitutes both color and figure. In their view that particular "figure or disposition of the body" that is called bodily intimation can be apprehended independently of the color (of the body) (*kāya-vijñapti-grahaṇaṃ tu varṇa-nirapekṣam*).[814] Therefore in the Sarvāstivāda system bodily intimation is included in the sense field of the visible. As such, it is a real and ultimate dharma having its own nature.

The Theravāda Abhidhamma takes a different position. What is called bodily intimation is not a separate material dhamma. It is a name given to a special mode of the consciousness-originated air element. Apart from the air element, of which it is a special mode, there is no separate material dhamma called bodily intimation. Its description as "occurring together with consciousness" (*citta-sahabhū*) points to the same conclusion. If bodily intimation and the consciousness in response to which it arises occur for the same length of time, this means that their lifespan is the same. But according to Theravāda Abhidhamma, the lifespan of matter is longer than that of mind. There is, however, no contradiction in describing bodily intimation as occurring together with consciousness. If bodily intimation is said to have the same lifespan as that of the consciousness, it is because bodily intimation is not a separate material dhamma but a name given to the air element only when it functions as a means of communicating the thought. In other words, the air element and its concomitant material dhammas do not cease to exist together with the consciousness, in response to which they arise. What comes to an end together with the consciousness is the air element's function as bodily intimation. This should also show that, as defined in the Theravāda Abhidhamma, bodily intimation is not something distinct from and therefore as real as the consciousness-originated air element. This is precisely why it is included in the category of "nominal material dhammas."

It may then be asked why bodily intimation is described as consciousness-originated, because to assign conditions for something's arising is to acknowledge its reality. This question is in fact raised in the commentary itself. The answer given is that since it is a special mode of the consciousness-conditioned air element and its concomitants, for the convenience of description, and solely as a matter of convention, it is also described as consciousness-originated. The commentary refers us to a similar situation in the recurrent statement "decay and death are impermanent." This statement is based on the idea that since decay and death belong to things that are impermanent, decay and death itself is called impermanent.[815]

The other means of communicating one's thoughts or feelings to another is verbal intimation (*vacī-viññatti*). As for its interpretation, there is general agreement among the schools of Sanskrit Buddhism. Voice (*vāc*) or vocal sound (*vāgdhvani*) as a mode of self-expression or as a medium for the communication of one's thoughts or feelings to another is verbal intimation. It is defined as sound that is discourse by its nature, that is, articulate (*varṇātmaka*) sound; as the pronunciation of sounds (*ghosoccaraṇa*); or as the distinct pronunciation of syllables (*vyaktavarṇoccaraṇa*).[816] Since verbal intimation is vocal sound, it is brought under the sphere of the audible.

On the other hand, the Theravāda account of the subject takes quite a different form. Its earliest account, which we find in the *Dhammasaṅgaṇi*, begins first with a definition of vocal expression. Vocal expression (*vācā*) is defined as utterance (*girā*), enunciation (*byappatha*), vocal emission (*udīraṇa*), noise (*ghosa*), act of making noise (*ghosa-kamma*), and broken or articulate voice (*vacībheda*), which arises in response to a thought—kammically wholesome, unwholesome, or indeterminate. Then it is said that the manifestation of that thought (*viññatti*) or the state of its being made known (*viññāpitatta*) through vocal sound is vocal intimation.[817]

At first sight it might appear from this statement that vocal intimation means vocal sound as a medium of thought expression, but its exclusion from the sphere of the audible shows that it is not conceived as a variety of sound as such.[818] However, the fact that vocal sound is referred to suggests that it is closely connected with vocal intimation, even as bodily movements are with bodily intimation.

The commentary explains it as a modal alteration (*ākāra-vikāra*) of the consciousness-originated earth element. Although it is called so, in reality, like bodily intimation, it is a special mode of all the four great material elements and their concomitants. If it is called so it is because in this case it is the earth element, the element representing the principle of solidity and extension, that is characterized by more intensity or capability.[819]

The production of vocal sound involved in vocal intimation is explained thus: When thought arises, "this will I speak, that will I speak," it sets up material phenomena among which the earth element is more intense. This consciousness-originated earth element arises while impinging the physical apparatus (*upādiṇṇaka*) that produces vocal sound. Together with that elemental impact arises vocal sound.[820] It is called consciousness-originated vocal sound as it arises in response to a thought. However, vocal sound is not the vocal intimation. Rather, it is a certain specific mode (*ākāra-vikāra*) of the consciousness-originated earth element. It plays the role of a condition for the earth element's striking against that particular physical apparatus where articulate vocal sounds are produced (*akkharuppattiṭṭhāna*).[821] Just as bodily intimation causes the body to move in ways that reveal one's intentions, even so verbal intimation causes vocal sounds to be produced in ways that become communicative of one's intentions. And just as bodily movements are not the bodily intimation, even so vocal sounds are not the verbal intimation. When we hear the sound of another calling our name, Tissa, Datta, or Mitta, and think of the intimation as "Methinks he wishes me to do this or that act,"[822] this intimation is known through inference as an object of mind consciousness.[823]

The commentary to the *Dhammasaṅgaṇi* refers to another Theravāda interpretation of verbal intimation, the one that was recorded in the *Mahā Aṭṭhakathā*. According to this interpretation, verbal intimation is the subvocal sound produced by the diffusion of initial application (*vitakka-vipphāra-sadda*) when one begins to think, "I will speak this, I will speak that." This *Mahā Aṭṭhakathā* view seems to have a close connection with the view expressed in the Pāli suttas that initial application (*vitakka*) and sustained application (*vicāra*) are verbal determinations (*vacī-saṃkhāra*). This early Buddhist teaching on vocal determinations suggests that some kind of subvocal activity precedes all verbal expressions. According to the *Mahā Aṭṭhakathā*, verbal intimation is the subvocal sound that is inaudible. It implies that audible sound through which the intention is communicated follows the pattern of the subvocal sound and thus communicates the intention. The Pāli commentary, too, recognizes the role of vocal determinations in the production of vocal sound. However, the commentary questions the validity of the *Mahā Aṭṭhakathā's* view because according to it verbal intimation is the inaudible sound produced by the diffusion of initial application (*vitakka-vipphāra*).[824] On the other hand, according to the Pāli commentary verbal intimation is neither the inaudible sound due to the diffusion of initial application nor audible sound following its pattern but, as clarified earlier, is rather a special mode of the consciousness-originated earth element.

A special mode of the consciousness-originated earth element is recognized as verbal intimation because, like bodily intimation, it too has to be coexistent with consciousness (*citta-sahabhū*). Therefore the position of verbal intimation in relation to the earth element should be understood in the same way as that of bodily intimation in relation to the air element. That is to say, apart from the earth element of which it is a special mode, there is no distinct and separate rūpa-dhamma called "verbal intimation." Hence its inclusion in the category of the nominal material dhammas.

The two kinds of intimation described so far are closely related to the Buddhist doctrine of *kamma*. Kamma is volition or volitional activity (*cetanā*). In terms of this definition, kamma is reckoned as one, but according to its manifestation it is threefold as bodily (*kāya-kamma*), vocal (*vacī-kamma*), and mental (*mano-kamma*). In the Abhidhamma the avenues through which kamma is manifested is called *kamma-dvāra* or doors of kamma. The three avenues for the three kinds of kamma are body (*kāya*), speech (*vācā*), and mind (*mano*).[825] In this particular context "body" does not refer to the physical body, nor does "speech" to articulate vocal sound. Bodily intimation and vocal intimation, as we saw, arise in response to a kammically qualifiable thought. It is through volition manifest in bodily intimation and vocal intimation that all bodily and vocal acts are committed. Hence bodily intimation is called "body" or "door of bodily kamma" (*kāya-kamma-dvāra*) and vocal intimation is called "speech" or "door of vocal kamma" (*vacī-kamma-dvāra*).[826] However, as the Pāli commentaries caution, bodily kamma is not the same as the "body" (= bodily intimation). Hence the [ancient] commentators say:

> Work by a needle done is needlework;
> needle and needlework are things distinct.

> Work by a hatchet done is hatchet work;
> hatchet and hatchet work are things distinct.
> Work that by man is done is called man's work;
> the man and the man's work are things distinct.
> An act by body done is body act;
> body and body act are things distinct.[827]

The distinction between vocal intimation and vocal kamma should be understood in the same way.

Nor are the volitions manifest in body door and speech door themselves bodily kamma and vocal kamma, respectively. Bodily kamma is not the volition manifest in body door (= bodily intimation) but are various bodily acts committed through the volition manifest in the body door. In the same way vocal kamma is not the volition manifest in speech door (= vocal intimation) but are various vocal acts committed by that volition manifest in speech door.[828] The commentary in fact refers to a non-Theravāda view that defined bodily kamma and vocal kamma as the two volitions manifest in them. What the Theravāda position is intended to show is that kamma is one as referring to volition or volitional activity (*cetanā*). If it is said to be of three kinds, this means that it "passes" through three doors (*dvāra-cārino*).[829]

Hence the Ancients say:

> Acts pass through doors, not doors through doors; by doors one
> may distinguish well these acts from those.[830]

Another question raised in the commentaries is whether it is possible to maintain a strict distinction between bodily kamma and vocal kamma on the basis of bodily intimation and vocal intimation, for there can be vocal intimation involved in bodily kamma and, likewise, bodily intimation involved in vocal kamma. When, for example, an unwholesome bodily kamma, such as stealing, is committed it could involve verbal intimation as well. Such a possibility is not denied, for the distinction is said to be based on the frequent occurrence (*yebhuyya-vutti*) and great preponderance (*tabbahula-vutti*) of one in relation to the other.[831]

The Special Modes of Matter

By special modes of matter, we mean the three material phenomena called lightness (*lahutā*), malleability (*mudutā*), and wieldiness (*kammaññatā*). The three terms are always preceded by *rūpassa*, that is, "of matter," in order to distinguish them from their counterparts among mental states. The latter, as we saw, consist of six pairs, each containing an identical characteristic made twofold as it extends to both consciousness and its concomitants.[832] The three special modes of matter under consideration refer to three characteristics, not of matter in general but of the matter that enters into the composition of a living being.

As defined in the *Dhammasaṅgaṇi*, the first, which is lightness of matter (*rūpassa lahutā*), is its capacity for changing easily (*lahu-pariṇāmatā*), its lack of heaviness (*adandhatā*). The second is malleability of matter (*rūpassa mudutā*)—it is that plasticity (*maddavatā*) or absence of rigidity (*akakkhaḷatā*) in matter. The third, which is wieldiness of matter (*rūpassa kammaññatā*), is that serviceableness or workable condition of matter.[833]

It is well known that Buddhism emphasizes not only the necessity and desirability of mental health but of physical health as well. The avoidance of the two extremes of self-mortification and sensual indulgence is, in fact, a preparation of both mind and body for purposes of mental culture leading to the realization of the final goal. For Buddhism the physical body is not a bondage to the mind's freedom but a necessary instrument for the mind's development.

All gains, as the *Dhammapada* says, have health as their highest (*ārogya-paramā lābhā*). The Pāli suttas often describe physical health in terms of pliability (*lahu*) and wieldiness (*kammañña*) of the physical body.[834] Overeating renders the body heavy (*garu*) and unserviceable (*akammañña*), feeling like a load of soaked beans. Such a state of the body is not conducive to putting forth energy in the right direction.[835] In the *Theragāthā* we read the Elder Khitaka exulting in the thought that his physical body is light (*lahu*) and wieldy (*kammañña*) and that it "floats" like a piece of cotton in the air.[836] It is against this background that we need to understand why the Abhidhamma has deemed it necessary to incorporate the three items in question in the list of rūpa-dhammas.

The Pāli commentaries observe that these three material characteristics are not found apart from one another (*na aññam aññaṃ vijahanti*).[837] That is to say, they always arise as a triad. And since they represent physical health, their conditioning factors are said to be agreeable food, suitable weather, and a wholesome mind. Hence they come under matter conditioned by nutriment (*āhāra-samuṭṭhāna*), temperature (*utu-samuṭṭhāna*), and consciousness (*citta-samuṭṭhāna*).[838]

Why they are not recognized as real material dhammas may be explained thus. When the physical body is not characterized by lightness, malleability, and wieldiness, it is said to be due to elemental disturbance (*dhātukkhobha*).[839] What is called elemental disturbance is either the disharmony between wind (*vāta*), bile (*pitta*), and phlegm (*semha*), or that of chime and so on (*rasādidhātu*).[840] In either case, in the final analysis it means the same thing: The triad of lightness, malleability, and wieldiness is a certain peculiar position or a special mode of the four great elements and the material dhammas necessarily associated with them.[841] It is this particular position or special mode that the triad represents. Hence together with the two means of intimation, discussed above, the triad of lightness, malleability, and wieldiness are called special modalities of matter (*vikāra-rūpa*).[842] And since they thus represent a certain position of the four great elements and some other material dhammas, there do not exist three separate material dhammas called lightness, malleability, and wieldiness. In other words, they come within the category of nominal material dhammas with no objective counterparts of their own.

Characteristics of Matter

This category includes four characteristics called integration (*upacaya*), continuity (*santati*), decay (*jaratā*), and impermanence (*aniccatā*) of matter (*rūpassa*).[843] Here, too, as in the preceding, the reference is not to matter in general but to the matter that enters into the composition of an individual being. It is of course true that this limitation in their scope is not explicitly stated in the *Dhammasaṅgaṇi*, where they are presented for the first time as four material dhammas. But the way they are described both in earlier and later texts makes it abundantly clear that this was the underlying assumption. And it is only when this fact is taken into consideration that their significance as well as their mutual relationship become increasingly clear.

Let us begin with the first two. In the *Dhammasaṅgaṇi* the first is defined as "that which is accumulation of āyatanas is the integration of matter" (*yo āyatanānaṃ ācayo so rūpassa upacayo*).[844] The term āyatana as used here embraces only material dhammas because the reference here is obviously to matter and certainly not to mind. The commentary in fact observes that the reference is to the "ten-and-a-half material āyatanas" (*aḍḍhekadasa rūpāyatana*). These words are a technical expression for the ten material āyatanas and the sixteen material dhammas included in the objective field of mental objects (*dhammāyatana*).[845] This, in other words, means all the material dhammas that enter into the composition of the individual being. If sound too is included it is in all likelihood to recognize, where necessary, mind-conditioned inner murmurings and vocal sound as well as nutriment- and temperature-conditioned sounds within the physical body.

Integration of matter, which is the first characteristic, is thus defined as accumulation of āyatanas, and the second characteristic is defined as identical with the first, "that which is integration of matter is the continuity of matter" (*yo rūpassa upacayo sā rūpassa santati*).[846]

This indicates that both signify the same phenomenon and yet differ in some respects. For, while one is called integration (*upacaya*), the other is called continuity (*santati*). Here the commentary says that both refer to the genesis of matter, but on two different occasions: integration means the repeated production of matter from the moment of conception until the moment when the body process is complete, with all the basic components of its constitution.[847] These include the five physical sense organs, the heart base, the material faculty of life, and other material dhammas that should necessarily arise together with them. Hence integration of matter is also defined as growth or accumulation of matter (*vaḍḍhi*).[848]

The second characteristic, which is continuity of matter, is the repeated production of matter in the same body process after the first phase called integration is over. It is growth over growth; it is the further growth of those very same material dhammas that came to be produced by way of integration (*upacitānaṃ rūpānaṃ vaḍḍhi*).[849] This kind of growth does not result in the coming into being of any new (additional) kind of material dhammas that are not already there as a result of the first characteristic called integration. All that it does is to produce matter in order to maintain and keep going a process that has been already completed. Thus both integration and continuity mean genesis or production. The first is genesis of matter by way of integration, or toward the completion of the body process—that is, until it is not deficient with any of the basic constituents of the physical body, such as the sense organs. The second is genesis of matter by way of continuity—that is, not toward completion but toward continuing what is already completed. The commentary illustrates their difference thus: Integration is like water issuing from a hole dug in the riverbank until it is full. Continuity is like water when it overflows. As the commentary observes further: "Integration of matter has the characteristic of accumulation, the function of making material things rise at the beginning, the fullness of matter as manifestation. Continuity of matter has the characteristic of continuous occurrence, the function of linking or binding without a break, unbroken series as manifestation."[850]

We may also note here that according to the definition given to the characteristic of integration, the five physical sense organs arise as a gradual process. This gets further confirmed by a *Kathāvatthu* controversy concerning the genesis of the sixfold sense sphere. According to some schools (Pubbaseliyas and Aparaseliyas, according to the commentary), the sixfold sense sphere comes into being all at once (*apubbaṃ acarimaṃ*). The Theravādins reject this view both as illogical and contrary to scripture. In their view only mind and the organ of touch arise at the moment of conception. The other four—namely, the organs of sight, hearing, smell, and taste—arise subsequently in the order they are mentioned here.[851]

From this it should not be concluded that the sense organs could arise independently of some other material dhammas. Since the sense organs are a species of dependent matter, it is implied that the four great material dhammas and the four dependent material dhammas that necessarily arise with them are also present. Again, since the physical sense organs are a species of kamma-conditioned matter and since the stability of kamma-conditioned matter is dependent on the material faculty of life, the presence of the latter too is implied.

The third characteristic of matter is decay (*rūpassa jaratā*). It is "the decay (*jarā*) or the state of decaying (*jīiraṇatā*) of the body, the brokenness of teeth (*khaṇḍicca*), and grayness of hair (*pālicca*), the state of having wrinkles (*valittacatā*), shrinkage in the length of days (*āyuno saṃhāni*), and hypermaturity of the faculties (*indriyānaṃ paripāko*)."[852] One question that arises here is whether "decay of matter" represents a stage in the history of the body process or whether it refers to the fact of decay itself. The above definition cited from the *Dhammasaṅgaṇi* shows that the reference is not to decay as such but to a stage in the history of the body process when there is a plus tendency toward waning away. The phrase "shrinkage in the length of days" points to the same conclusion. This does not imply that decay as a phenomenon cannot arise during the two preceding phases of integration (*upacaya*) and continuity (*santati*). But when life is young, the tendency is toward growth. With the passage of time there is a plus tendency toward decay. Gradually the faculties get matured and the body begins to show signs of maturity and decay. It is this phase that is taken into consideration in defining "the decay of matter."

The fourth characteristic is "impermanence of matter" (*rūpassa aniccatā*). It stands for the breakup of the body at the time of death. It is the moment when the material as well as the mental life faculties cease to function simultaneously.[853]

In the Pāli commentaries these four characteristics came to be further explained in light of the theory of moments. Now the commentaries too recognize the fact that integration of matter and continuity of matter mean the same phenomenon, but on two different occasions. Both are said to represent the birth or genesis of matter (*jāti* or *uppāda*).[854] With the recognition of this fact the four characteristics get reduced to three: genesis of matter (*rūpassa upacaya* and *rūpassa santati*), decay of matter (*rūpassa jaratā*), and impermanence of matter (*rūpassa aniccatā*). These three items, it may be noted, correspond to the three moments recognized in the Abhidhamma exegesis: the moment of origination, the moment of existence (decay), and the moment of cessation. Once this correspondence is established it is easy to approach the subject from the point of view of the theory of moments. The new explanation that has been developed to fall in line with this development is as follows: The nascent phase or the moment of origination of all those material dhammas that enter into the composition of the body series is the genesis of matter (*rūpassa jāti*). (This refers to both integration and continuity, because both mean genesis at two different levels.) Their static phase or the moment of existence, which is also called the decay phase, is the decay of matter (*rūpassa jaratā*). Their cessant phase or the moment of cessation is the impermanence of matter (*rūpassa aniccatā*).[855] Although both integration and continuity refer to genesis, this difference between them is recognized: The nascent phase or the moment of origination of all those material dhammas that constitute the body series from the moment of conception until it is complete, with all the necessary constituents, such as the sense organs, is integration of matter. The nascent phase or the moment of origination of the material dhammas that constitute the body series thereafter, that is, up to the time of death, is called continuity of matter.[856]

It will be seen that according to the commentarial explanation, decay as defined in the *Dhammasaṅgaṇi* becomes irrelevant. However, decay is recognized with a different interpretation, as "evident decay" (*pākaṭa-jarā*). Brokenness of teeth, grayness of hair, and so on, are instances of evident decay. In terms of the dhamma analysis, evident decay is only a peculiar disposition or special modality (*vikāra*) of the momentary material dhammas that constitute the body series. It is to be distinguished from hidden decay (*paṭicchanna-jarā*) in immaterial states that do not show such external evidence.[857]

Why the three items under consideration are not given the status of real material dhammas may now be considered. It will be seen that whether they are understood according to their earlier version in the *Dhammasaṅgaṇi* or according to their commentarial version, they have to be recognized only as a set of characteristics shared by the real material dhammas. When a real material dhamma originates, it is called origination of matter (*rūpassa jāti* = *rūpassa upacaya* and *rūpassa santati*); when it exists immediately before its moment of cessation, it is called decay of matter (*rūpassa jaratā*); when it ceases to be, it is called impermanence of matter (*rūpassa aniccatā*). In addition to the material dhamma that originates, exists (decay phase), and ceases to be, there are no real entities answering to the names origination, decay, and impermanence.

If these characteristics, too, were postulated as real entities, then it would be necessary to postulate another set of secondary characteristics to account for their own origination, existence, and cessation. And these secondary characteristics would in turn require another set of secondary-secondary characteristics to account for their own origination and so on. In this way it would inevitably lead to a process ad infinitum, and it is in order to avoid this problem of infinite regress (*anavaṭṭhāna*) that the characteristics are not recognized as entities distinct from and as real as the things they characterize.[858]

15

THE MATERIAL CLUSTERS

THE THEORY OF MATERIAL CLUSTERS (*rūpa-kalāpa*), which is the Theravāda version of atomism, has apparently no antecedent history in the books of the Abhidhamma Piṭaka, although its basic principles can of course be traced to them. The *Visuddhimagga* and Pāli commentaries seem to be fairly acquainted with the theory, because we find in them a number of technical terms relating to it. However, it is in the subcommentaries and the Abhidhamma compendiums that we get a fully fledged version of the theory. It has its counterpart in the Sarvāstivāda Abhidharma as the theory of atoms (*paramāṇu*). The reference in the **Abhidharmamahāvibhāṣāśāstra* to the views expressed by celebrated acāryas on the question of whether atoms come in contact or not shows that by its time the atomic theory had become well established within the Sarvāstivāda Abhidharma.[859] Is the Theravāda theory then an adoption from the Sarvāstivāda Abhidharma? This is a question that cannot be answered satisfactorily because we cannot ascertain how much of the Theravāda Abhidhamma was developed in the now nonextant Siṃhala commentaries before they were translated into Pāli by Ācariya Buddhaghosa and his successors.

Even if we consider the theory as an introduction from the Sarvāstivāda, it is certainly not a complete replica of the Sarvāstivādins' atomic theory. As we shall soon see, there are some fundamental differences between the two theories. But most of them are unavoidable, stemming as they do from the fundamental differences between the two schools over the analysis of material existence. To give but one example: since the

Theravādins have recognized a comparatively large number of material dhammas, it is but natural that this numerical difference should reflect itself in the theory of material clusters.

One fundamental principle that serves as a basis for this theory can be traced to the Abhidhamma teaching on conditional relations.[860] This principle states that nothing can activate as a single cause, nor can anything arise as a single effect.[861] Both refer to a situation where a plurality of conditions gives rise to a plurality of effects (the conditioned). Thus whether we approach the dhammas, the basic constituents of actuality, as conditions (*paccaya*) or as the conditioned (*paccayuppanna*), the inevitable situation is that we have to reckon with a multiplicity of dhammas. What this, in other words, means is that all dhammas, mental as well as material, arise not as isolated phenomena but as clusters or groups. We saw how this principle works in the domain of mind as a grouping of mental factors by way of constellations around the many kinds of consciousness. A similar situation obtains in the sphere of matter as well, in what we have described as the principle of positional inseparability. According to this principle, the four great material elements and four of the dependent—namely, color, smell, taste, and nutritive essence—are necessarily coexistent in the sense that they always arise together, exist together, and cease together, besides being positionally inseparable in the sense that they cannot be separated from one another.[862]

If these eight are described as positionally inseparable, that does not mean that the other material dhammas are separable from the material dhammas together with which they arise. Then why are only the four great elements and four types of dependent matter described as positionally inseparable? It is because these eight material dhammas are necessarily found in all instances of matter, whether they exist as part of the complex that makes the individual living being or whether they exist outside of it. The presence of one necessarily implies the presence of the other seven. None of them can arise without the concurrent arising of the other seven. In this sense they do not exist in isolation from one another. Although they exist together, their relative position is not one of juxtaposition: they do not exist side by side, nor do they exist one above the other. For the reference here is not to material entities but to material properties. Now in the case of the remaining material dhammas the situation is different. None of them can arise in isolation from the eight "inseparables," because the latter provide the basic foundation for the existence of all instances of matter. When any one of them arises together with the eight "inseparables," then it also becomes inseparable. However, there is this difference to be noted: in the case of the remaining material dhammas, they can arise in separation from one another. The eye sensitivity (*cakkhuppasāda*), for example, can never arise in isolation from the eight "inseparables." However, the eye sensitivity can arise in isolation from, say, ear sensitivity (*sotappasāda*). The two arise in separation from each other in two different material clusters, each cluster having at least the eight "inseparables."

This distinction between two kinds of material dhammas provides the main principle for the Abhidhamma theory of material clusters.

The earliest allusion to the theory is found in two passages of the *Visuddhimagga* where it refers to two ways of looking at the material components of the body. The first passage says that such components of the body as head hair, body hair, and so on should be understood by way of *kalāpas* or clusters. What in common parlance is called head hair is only a cluster/collection of material dhammas—namely, the four great material elements and the four types of dependent matter: color, smell, taste, and nutritive essence. The passage concludes that what is called head hair is, in terms of the dhamma analysis, "a mere cluster of eight dhammas" (*aṭṭha-dhamma-kalāpa-matta*).[863]

The second passage tells us another way of considering the matter that enters into the composition of the body: "In this body the earth element, taken as reduced to fine dust and pounded to the size of atoms (*paramāṇu*), might amount to an average *doṇa* measure full, and that is held together by the water element measuring half as much."[864]

It will be seen that the eight items mentioned in the first passage are the eight "inseparables" that we have been discussing. It will also be seen that the term used to embrace all the eight items in the sense of a group is *kalāpa*. Now in the Abhidhamma subcommentaries where we get the theory of material clusters in its developed form, the term used to designate the smallest unit of matter is *kalāpa*.[865] However, we cannot say that in the *Visuddhimagga* passage, too, the term *kalāpa* is used in this same technical sense. What it says is that head hair, for instance, is a cluster/collection of eight (types) of dhammas. If it had used the term in its technical sense, then it would have said that head hair is an enormous number of kalāpas, each consisting of eight dhammas. The term should occur in the plural and not in the singular. For in its technical sense *kalāpa* means the smallest unit of matter, and as such head hair should consist of an enormous number of *kalāpas*. What the passage intends to refer are the eight kinds of material dhammas that enter into its composition. The term is used in a general sense and not in the technical sense.[866]

On the other hand, it can be shown that what the *Visuddhimagga* calls *paramāṇu* (atom) in the second passage corresponds to kalāpa in its technical sense. As we have already shown, in the Pāli exegesis the names of the four great elements of matter are used in two distinct senses: one in the sense of characteristic (*lakkhaṇa*) and the other in the sense of intensity (*ussada*). In the first sense "earth element" means "solidity" (*kakkhaḷatta*); in the second it means "what is solid" (*kakkhaḷa*). For where the characteristic of solidity is more intense in any material aggregate, it is also called earth element, although in fact it consists of all the four great material elements and their concomitants.

It will be noticed that when the *Visuddhimagga* refers to the atomization of the earth element it uses the term "earth element" in the second sense. In fact, at the beginning of the passage it is said that head hair, body hair, and so on are "earth," and that blood, mucus, and so on are "water." It is also said that they are called so on account of the intensity of each great material element in them. Now, as we have already noted, according to the principle of positional inseparability, the four great material elements and four of the dependent (color, smell, taste, and nutritive essence) are necessarily coexistent and positionally inseparable. It follows then that those components of the human body that, owing to the intensity of the earth element, are conventionally called earth element consist of the selfsame eight material dhammas. Therefore when head hair, body hair, and so on are reduced to the size of atoms, each atom in turn should consist of the same eight inseparable material dhammas. Thus what the *Visuddhimagga* calls *paramāṇu* (atom) turns out to be an aggregate of eight material dhammas. It is exactly identical with *kalāpa*, when the term is understood in its technical sense to mean the smallest cluster of material dhammas.

Thus for the Theravāda Abhidhamma, the ultimate unit of matter is not a unitary dhamma but a collection of unitary dhammas. In the *Visuddhimagga*, where we find the theory introduced for the first time, it is called *paramāṇu* (atom).[867] Whereas in the subcommentaries and Abhidhamma compendiums, where we get the theory in its fully fledged version, the term used is *kalāpa* (cluster).[868] The first term shows that it is the smallest unit of matter. The second term shows that although it is the smallest unit of matter, in the final analysis it is a group of material dhammas, all having a simultaneous origination (*ekuppāda*) and a simultaneous cessation (*eka-nirodha*), and thus all forming a unity.[869] Two other terms used to describe the smallest unit of matter are *piṇḍa* (lump) and *rūpa-samudāya* (compound of material dhammas). They also show that the smallest unit of matter is a plurality.

The basic principle behind the conception is this: what are called dependent material dhammas are always dependent on the great material dhammas. Hence the former do not arise independently of the latter. Nor can a single great material dhamma arise independently of the other three or independently of the four types of dependent matter—namely, color, smell, taste, and nutritive essence. Thus none of the eight material dhammas, whether they are the four great elements or what is dependent on them, can have an independent, isolated existence. They always and necessarily arise by way of groups.[870] Consequently, when a given instance of matter, say a piece of stone, is reduced to smaller pieces, whatever the number of pieces and whatever the size of each piece, the fact remains that each of them is a group of material dhammas. The smallest unit of matter, whether we call it *paramāṇu* (atom), *piṇḍa* (lump), *kalāpa* (cluster), or *rūpa-samudāya* (compound of material dhammas), is no exception to this fundamental law.

In the Sarvāstivāda Abhidharma the theory of atoms (*paramāṇu*) takes a different form. A descriptive definition of the atom, given in the Chinese version of the **Abhidharmamahāvibhāṣāśāstra*, and as translated by Venerable Bhikkhu Dhammajoti in his *Sarvāstivāda Abhidharma*, is as follows:

> An atom (*paramāṇu*) is the smallest *rūpa*. It cannot be cut, broken, penetrated; it cannot be taken up, abandoned, ridden on, stepped on, struck or dragged. It is neither long nor short, square nor round, regular nor irregular, convex nor conclave. It has no smaller parts; it cannot be decomposed, cannot be seen, heard, smelled, touched. It is thus that the *paramāṇu* is said to be the finest (*sarva-sūkṣma*) of all *rūpas*. . . . Seven of these *paramāṇu*-s constitute an *aṇu*. . . . Seven *aṇu*-s constitute a *tāmra-rajas*. . . . Seven *tāmra-rajas*-s constitute an *ap-rajas*. . . . Seven *ap-rajas*-s constitute a *śaśa-rajas*. . . . Seven *śaśa-rajas*-s constitute an *eḍaka-rajas*. . . . Seven *eḍaka-rajas*-s constitute a *go-rajas*. . . . Seven *go-rajas*-s constitute a *vātāyana-rajas* . . . [in this way, the whole physical universe is composed].[871]

While this "doctrine of sevenfold incremental atomic aggregation" is retained in later works, they give more succinct definitions of the atom. Below is the definition given by Acārya Saṃghabhadra, a celebrity of the Vaibhāṣika school, as translated by Venerable Bhikkhu Dhammajoti from the Chinese version of the **Nyāyānusāra*:

> The finest part in a resistant matter which cannot be further divided is called a *paramāṇu*. That is, this *paramāṇu* cannot be further divided into many [parts] by means of another matter [or] the intellect (*buddhi*). This is then said to be the "ultimately small" (*parama-aṇu*) among matter. As there can be no further part, it is called the "ultimately small." In the same way, a *kṣaṇa* is the smallest [unit] of time; it cannot be further analyzed into half-*kṣaṇas*.[872]

This smallest unit of matter, which is not amenable to further analysis, is also called *dravya-paramāṇu*, the unitary atom. However, such an atom does not arise or exist in isolation. It always arises and exists together with other atoms. A number of them having a simultaneous origination and a simultaneous cessation, and thus constituting an inseparable material cluster, is called *saṃghāta-paramāṇu*, a molecule or aggregate atom.

The smallest aggregate is an octad, consisting of the four great material elements and four of the dependent—namely, color, smell, taste, and the secondary tangible (*bhuatika-spraṣṭavya*).[873]

This is a brief statement of the atomic theory of the Sarvāstivāda Abhidharma. It shows that the Theravāda version is different in many important respects. For the Sarvāstivāda, the atom is the smallest unit of a single unitary material dharma, so small that it has no spatial dimensions.[874] For the Theravāda, the atom is an aggregate of a number of unitary material dhammas. This is why it is described not only as "atom" (*paramāṇu*) but also as "cluster of material dhammas" (*rūpa-kalāpa*). It thus corresponds not to the atom of the Sarvāstivāda Abhidharma but to what it calls the "octuple aggregate." The Theravāda term that corresponds to the "atom" of the Sarvāstivāda is *kalāpaṅga*—that is, the constituent of a kalāpa.

The Sarvāstivādins' atomic theory, it may be noted here, came in for criticism on the part of the Sautrāntikas. What made the Sautrāntikas join issue with the Sarvāstivāda conception of the atom was that it was sought to be defined as devoid of parts (*niravayavat*) and exempt from resistance/impenetrability (*pratighāta*), which is the defining characteristic of matter. According to the *Abhidharmakośa-vyākhyā*, the second characteristic is a logical corollary from the first. When there are no parts, there cannot be impenetrability/resistance.[875] To the objection that if the atom is of this nature it escapes the definition of matter, the Sarvāstivādins reply: Certainly the atom is exempt from resistance/impenetrability, but matter in the form of an atom never exists in a state of isolation, and when it is in a state of agglomeration it is susceptible to disintegration and resistance.[876]

But this way of defining the atom, on the part of the Sarvāstivādins, led to further problems. As the *Abhidharmakośabhāṣya* and the *Vyākhyā* point out, if the atom is devoid of parts and exempt from resistance/impenetrability, then the aggregate, too, will be devoid of both characteristics, because the aggregate is ultimately constituted of the atoms. What is lacking in the latter cannot be predicated of the former.[877] The same criticism was voiced by the Idealist school of Buddhism as well. Although this school did not recognize the ultimate reality of matter, as a base for its polemics it provisionally agreed with the objection of the Sautrāntikas that the aggregates are ultimately constituted of and therefore cannot be different from the atoms, the difference between one atom and an aggregate being only one of magnitude.[878] If this oneness (*ekatva*) is overlooked it can lead to many mutually incompatible conclusions and will fail to give a rational explanation to many a phenomenon of day-to-day experience. It is a matter of common experience, for instance, that when the sun rises a given aggregate is found illuminated at its eastern direction and dark at its western direction, or when one sees or touches, say, a wall one does not see or touch its opposite side—two situations that unmistakably point to the conclusion that aggregates have spatial dimensions. This characteristic cannot be predicated of them if the atoms that constitute them do not severally possess it.[879]

It is supposed (by the neo-Sarvāstivādins) that the combination of atoms takes place in such a way that six different atoms occupy six different points in space—east, west, north, south, above, and below. This principle of atomic aggregation carries with it the implication that the atom has at least six sides. On the other hand, if it were contended that the locus occupied by one atom is common to all six, then all six would coalesce into one (the atom being devoid of parts and exempt from resistance/impenetrability), and the difference between the magnitude of one atom and that of the six would vanish—a situation that would lead to the very collapse of the theory of atoms.[880]

Thus the Buddhist atomic theory gave an opportunity for the Buddhist Idealists to add another argument to their theory that matter is not logically admissible. They argued that if the atom has spatial dimensions, this is to admit its divisibility—a situation that goes against its definition as the most subtle (*sarva-sūkṣma*). On the other hand, to deny its spatial dimensions is to deny the spatial dimensions of the aggregates—a situation contradicted by common experience. If anything, the atom should have spatial dimensions. But what is spatially extended is by its very nature divisible and what is divisible cannot be a real entity (*dravyasat*).

Thus the main problem the Buddhist atomists had to face was the definition of the atom. In this situation let us see what the Theravāda position in relation to this problem is. For the Theravādins, as we have already noted, the atom is not "the ultimately small" of a unitary material dhamma but "the ultimately small" of a cluster of unitary material dhammas. But is not a constituent dhamma smaller than the group and is it not more logical to recognize it as the atom (*paramāṇu*) and to define it as the smallest of all (*sabba-pariyantima*)?

According to the Sarvāstivāda, the question will certainly justify an affirmative answer, for in their view it is nothing but logical to define the constituent as the atom, although an atom cannot exist in isolation from seven other atoms. What is more, any aggregate by its very nature admits divisibility, and to describe as the most subtle what admits divisibility is a contradiction in terms.

The Theravāda, on the other hand, seems to have followed a different line of argument. It is true that since the rūpa-kalāpa is an aggregate of material dhammas, each of the constituents that makes up this aggregation is smaller (subtler) than the aggregate itself. But this is only logically so. In reality the constituent of a rūpa-kalāpa, that is, the kalāpaṅga, does not exist by itself but rather in inseparable association with other constituents. With this the Sarvāstivāda Abhidharma, too, agrees. The Pāli commentators observe that although it is possible, for the sake of defining the individuating characteristics (*lakkhaṇa*), to speak of color, taste, smell, and so on as separate dhammas, yet positionally they are not separable from one another. Color, taste, and so on, so runs the argument, cannot be dissected and separated like particles of sand.[881] The color of the mango, for instance, cannot be separated from its hardness (earth element) or from its taste. This situation is equally true of the constituents of a rūpa-kalāpa as well. Hence there is no necessity, other than logical, to postulate the constituent (*kalāpaṅga*) as the smallest of all (*sabba-pariyantima*).

The next question that we need to clarify is whether the atom, as defined in the Theravāda Abhidhamma, has spatial dimensions or not. What we need to remember is that of the four great material elements, the earth element represents the principle of solidity and extension. And since the earth element is one of the constituents that invariably enter into the composition of every atom (*rūpa-kalāpa*) it logically follows that every atom is characterized by solidity, whatever be its degree of intensity (*ussada*) and, by extension, whatever be its extent. Thus unlike the atom of the Sarvāstivāda, what the Theravāda defines as the atom has spatial dimensions. This gets further confirmed by a reference in the Siṃhala *sanne* to the *Visuddhimagga* when it says that ākāsa, the intervening space between two atoms (*rūpa-kalāpas*), "has the function of delimiting the atom, as this is the lower side (*yaṭa*) of the atom and that is the upper side (*uḍa*) of the atom."[882]

That the atom has spatial dimensions is also shown by a table given to determine its size in relation to a (cubic) inch (*aṅgula*). It occurs in the commentary to the *Vibhaṅga*[883] and the term used is *paramāṇu* (atom), which, as we have seen, is another term for *rūpa-kalāpa*. The table is as follows:

36 *paramāṇus*	= 1 *aṇu*
36 *aṇus*	= 1 *tajjāri*
36 *tajjāris*	= 1 *rathareṇu*
36 *rathareṇus*	= 1 *līkhā*
7 *līkhās*	= 1 *ūkā*
7 *ūkās*	= 1 *dhaññamāsa*
7 *dhaññamāsas*	= 1 *aṅgula* (finger-breadth), i.e., (cubic) inch

Thus the size of the atom (*paramāṇu*) in relation to a cubic inch is:

1 / 36×36×36×36×7×7×7 = 1/576,108,288

We find similar tables presented by other schools of Buddhism that resorted to atomism in explaining the constitution of matter. At best they all may be described as attempts to emphasize how almost infinitesimally small the atom, the smallest building block of matter, is. For the atom is so small that in the commentary to the *Vibhaṅga* it is figuratively described as a particle of space (*ākāsa-koṭṭhāsa*).[884] The subcommentary to the *Visuddhimagga* observes that the atom comes only within the range of the divine eye (*dibba-cakkhu*).[885] This is similar to the view expressed in some Jaina works—namely, that the atom can be known only by those who have the highest level of knowledge (*kaivalya-jñāna*).[886]

Another controversial issue among Buddhist schools that adopted atomism was whether atoms can come in contact with one another. Since the Sarvāstivādins maintained that the atom is devoid of parts and exempt from resistance/impenetrability, any conclusion in respect to this issue should in no way contradict this belief. In fact, they take these two characteristics of the atom as the very premise of the expected conclusion. They grant the possibility of two alternatives, both of which they contend are equally inadmissible. The first is to assume that the atoms touch in their totality. If this were to happen, then the atoms, being exempt from resistance/impenetrability, would coalesce into one—that is to say, they all would occupy the same locus. The second is to assume that the atoms touch partially. If this were to happen, it would mean that the partless atoms have parts.[887] Another argument, the one attributed to Ācārya Vasumitra, is based on the theory of moments. If the atoms could touch one another, whether partially or totally, it would mean that they exist for two consecutive moments. That is to say, an atom should arise first (first moment) in order to touch (second moment). This view, if accepted, will go against the theory that all basic factors of existence, whether mental or material, endure but for one single moment.[888]

On the strength of these arguments the Sarvāstivādins conclude that it is not possible for atoms to come in contact with one another and that between atoms there is always an intervening space. In this intervening space there is no light and it is so small that another atom cannot occupy it. If the presence of light is denied it is because, since light is included in the category of matter, to admit its presence is to deny the vacuity between the atoms.[889] If there is an intervening space between atoms, the question arises as to why the aggregates do not get pulverized into atoms owing to the impact of other aggregates, since all aggregates are ultimately constituted of atoms. The answer given is that the attractive force of the air element keeps the atoms together.[890]

The Sautrāntikas, as can be expected, criticize the notion of "atomic noncontact." They contend that if atoms do not come in contact, we cannot explain empirically observable contact between aggregates, because the latter are ultimately constituted of the former.[891] In this regard they refer to the explanation given by Ācārya Bhadanta as the best—namely, that contact is another expression for "absence of interval" or "immediate juxtaposition" (*nirantaratva*).[892] If there is an interval, so they argue, what would prevent the atoms from moving within the interval.[893] They seem to have overlooked the Sarvāstivāda theory that in the case of momentary material dharmas there is no motion. What is momentary disappears wherever it appears.

Let us now consider how the Theravādins responded to this problem. As we have seen, in their view the unitary material dhammas that constitute a rūpa-kalāpa (the smallest unit of matter) are necessarily co-nascent and positionally inseparable. Therefore the possibility of their being separated by an interval does not arise. Hence the question is whether the rūpa-kalāpas can come in contact or not. The answer given is that there is no contact. There is always an intervening space between them. Every rūpa-kalāpa is delimited (*paricchindate*) by the environing space.[894] This space or interval is almost infinitesimally small, so the notion of delimitation is described as "as if delimiting" (*paricchindantī viya*).[895] However, the rūpa-kalāpas do not touch one another, because each rūpa-kalāpa is described as "not touched" (*asamphuṭṭha*) by the other rūpa-kalāpas separated from it.[896] The clear implication is that the vacuity is a fact, although it is almost infinitesimally small. Hence the delimiting space is said to manifest as "untouchedness" (*asamphuṭṭha-paccupaṭṭhāna*).[897] What is sought to be stressed is the separateness of each rūpa-kalāpa, that it is an entity physically separated from the other rūpa-kalāpas. This separation is not possible if there is contact. And it is the delimiting space that prevents the rūpa-kalāpas from mixing together (*asaṃkarabhāva*).[898]

As we have seen, the Sarvāstivāda theory of atomic noncontact is mainly based on the denial of spatial dimensions of the atom. However, for the Theravādins the issue as to the possibility or otherwise of physical contact is a question relating to the rūpa-kalāpas, the spatial dimensions of which are not denied. Hence the Theravāda argument for noncontact between rūpa-kalāpas has to take a different form. This is based on the view that the constituents of a rūpa-kalāpa are positionally inseparable. It is argued that if the rūpa-kalāpas are not physically separated by the delimiting space (*paricchedākāsa*), then this will inevitably lead to one of two alternatives, both of which are equally incompatible with the principle of positional inseparability.

The first alternative is to assume that the constituents of a rūpa-kalāpa are separated by the delimiting space. In such a situation the separateness and independence of each rūpa-kalāpa would vanish, establishing the separateness and independence of each of the constituents of the rūpa-kalāpa. The ultimate unit of matter then would be the constituent (*kalāpaṅga*) and not the aggregate (*rūpa-kalāpa*).[899] For the reasons we have already given, the Theravādins are not prepared to accept such a conclusion, for although it is logically true that each of the constituents should be smaller than their combination, in fact their position within the combination is one of positional inseparability.

The second alternative is to assume that there is no space between two rūpa-kalāpas. Such an assumption means that the characteristic of positional inseparability, which applies only to the constituents of a rūpa-kalāpa, has to be extended to the two rūpa-kalāpas as well. In such a situation the separateness of each rūpa-kalāpa would vanish and both would combine to form a bigger rūpa-kalāpa.[900] If the principle could be extended to two rūpa-kalāpas, then it could also be extended to three or more, and so the process could be indefinitely extended. If a given piece of stone, let us say hypothetically, is composed of one billion rūpa-kalāpas, then those billion rūpa-kalāpas would become one big rūpa-kalāpa precisely as big as that piece of stone. If the piece of stone is one big rūpa-kalāpa, then according to the theory of positional inseparability no part of it can be separated. The moment one breaks the piece of stone into pieces then the theory in question, too, so to say, breaks into pieces. Such an assumption would also go against the view of a plurality of rūpa-kalāpas and would result in a most improbable situation. For if two or more rūpa-kalāpas could combine to form a bigger rūpa-kalāpa, then this principle could be extended to embrace the whole physical world, resulting in a situation where the whole physical world would become one mighty rūpa-kalāpa.

It is interesting to recall here that one of the arguments of the Sarvāstivādins to deny contact between atoms is that if two of them touch in their totality, the atom being nonresistant and devoid of parts, all the atoms would coalesce into one—the whole physical world would coalesce into one atom so small that no spatial dimensions could be predicated of it. The objection of the Theravādins, when its implications are fully unfolded, is that if rūpa-kalāpas could touch each other the whole physical world would become one enormous rūpa-kalāpa, precisely as big as the physical world. The Sarvāstivādin objection is that the world would be reduced to an atom so small that it has no spatial dimensions; the Theravādin objection is that the atom (*rūpa-kalāpa*) would be inflated to the size of the world—two situations literally with a world of difference.

There are in all seventeen different kinds of rūpa-kalāpa. The smallest is an octad consisting of the four great material elements and four of the dependent category—namely, color, taste, odor, and nutriment. This collection of material dhammas, called "the bare octad" (*suddhaṭṭhaka*),[901] corresponds to the smallest aggregate atom (*saṃghāta-paramāṇu*) of the Sarvāstivādins, but for two differences. First, in place of nutriment, the Sarvāstivādin list contains the tangible. The difference is unavoidable. According to the Theravādins, the tangible includes three of the great elements of matter. Hence from the point of view of the Theravāda, it is not necessary to repeat the tangible because it is already represented by the enumeration of the great elements of matter. According to the Sarvāstivādins, the tangible includes "the primary tangible" (*bhūta-spraṣṭavya*)—that is, the four great material elements and "the secondary tangible" (*bhautika-sprasṭavya*). It is in order to represent the latter, the so-called secondary tangible, that the tangible is repeated, although one aspect of it is represented by the four great material elements. A similar situation is responsible for the inclusion of nutriment in the Theravāda list. As we have noted, while the Theravādins postulate nutriment as a separate material dhamma, the Sarvāstivādins consider it as a combination of taste, odor, and the tangible, which three items occur in their list.

The two lists are thus representative of the same items except for the fact that the secondary tangible is not represented in the list of the Theravādins. This is because the latter do not admit that any of the dependent material dhammas come under the object of touch.

The other difference is more significant. It is a Sarvāstivādin principle that each dependent material dharma has a separate tetrad of the great material elements as its support. Those great material elements that serve as a support (*āśraya*) for a given dependent, say, color, do not at the same time serve as a support for another, say, smell.[902] Hence, as the *Abhidharmakośabhāṣya* rightly points out, the smallest aggregate atom (*saṃghāta-paramāṇu*) should consist of not eight but twenty material dharmas. The Sarvāstivādin reply is that the nature (*jāti*) of each of the tetrad of the great material elements that support the dependent material dharmas remains the same and that therefore there is no anomaly in counting them as four, although there are four of each type.[903] In contrast, the Theravādins believe that the four great material elements of the basic octad (*suddhaṭṭhaka*) are the common support (*eka-nissaya*) of the dependent material dhammas.[904]

These, then, are the two main differences between the basic octad (*suddhaṭṭhaka*) of the Theravādins and the octuple aggregate atom (*saṃghāta-paramāṇu*) of the Sarvāstivādins.

The remaining sixteen rūpa-kalāpas are formed according to the same principle as adopted by the Sarvāstivādins in forming the saṃghāta-paramāṇus other than the octad. The (eight) items of the octad are the basic material dhammas; they are present in every instance of matter. Therefore in all the kalāpas these eight material dhammas are present as their basis. The other rūpa-kalāpas are formed by adding one or more, as the situation demands, of the remaining material dhammas (= those other than the eight in question) to the basic octad.

Since we have already examined all the material dhammas, we shall confine ourselves to show how they enter into the composition of the kalāpas.

Next to the basic octad (*suddhaṭṭhaka*) comes the sound nonad (*sadda-navaka*), which, according to both schools, is formed by adding sound to the basic octad.[905]

As to the composition of the five sense-organ kalāpas or saṃghātas, the two schools follow two slightly different methods.

According to the Sarvāstivādins, among the sense-organ samghatas, the one relating to the organ of touch consists of the minimum number of dravya-paramāṇus. It is a nonad consisting of the basic octad and one dravya-paramāṇu of *kāyendriya* (organ of touch) added to it. Each of the other four sense-organ saṃghātas is formed by adding one dravya-paramāṇu of each of them to the kāyendriya nonad. Thus while the kāyendriya-saṃghāta is a nonad, the other sense-organ saṃghātas are decads.[906]

For the Theravādins every sense-organ kalāpa is a decad (*dasaka*). First one kalāpaṅga of *rūpa-jīvitindriya* (material faculty of life) is added to the basic octad to make it organic. The resulting nonad is called *jīvita-navaka*, the vital nonad. The five sense-organ kalāpas are then formed by adding each of the sense-organ kalāpaṅgas to the jīvita-navaka. Thus there are *cakkhu-dasaka* (eye decad), *sota-dasaka* (ear decad), *ghāna-dasaka* (nose decad), *jivhā-dasaka* (tongue decad), and *kāya-dasaka* (body decad).[907]

The Sarvāstivādins add one dravya-paramāṇu of kāyendriya to the other four sense-organ saṃghātas, because the other four sense organs are said to be associated with kāyendriya (*tat-pratibaddha-vṛttitvāt*).[908] They seem to have taken the view that the organs of sight, hearing, taste, and smell are certain modifications of the organ of touch, a view accepted by certain Nyāya-Vaiśeṣikas, too.[909] It is of course true that according to the Theravāda the organ of touch is present in every part of the body (*sabba-sarīra-byāpaka*), existing as it were like oil soaked in cotton.[910] However, there is no possibility of confusion (*saṅkara*) between the sense organs as they are said to differ from each other in respect to their characteristic (*lakkhaṇa*), function (*rasa*), and manifestation (*paccupaṭṭhāna*). Why the Sarvāstivādins, unlike the Theravādins, do not include *jīvitindriya* in the sense-organ *saṃghātas* is understandable. For, as stated earlier, they have recognized only one variety of *jīvitendriya*, which is included in the category of *citta-viprayukta-saṃskāras*.

Since the Theravādins have defined the two faculties of sex as separate material dhammas rather than conceiving them as part of the organ of touch, and since they have postulated the heart base as the seat of mental activity, these three items, too, are explained by way of kalāpas, to which corresponding saṃghāta-paramāṇus are not found in the Sarvāstivāda. The method of their formation is like that of the sense organs. That is to say, one kalāpaṅga of *itthindriya* (faculty of femininity), *purisindriya* (faculty of masculinity), and *hadaya-vatthu* (heart base) is added to *jīvita-navaka*. The resulting three decads are called *itthibhāva-dasaka* (femininity decad), *pumbhāva-dasaka* (masculinity decad), and *vatthu-dasaka* (base decad), respectively.[911]

The kalāpaṅgas or the constituents of the kalāpas that we have considered so far are all *nipphanna-rūpa* (the real). Of the ten *anipphanna-rūpas* (the nominal), only five are recognized as kalāpaṅgas.

The five that are not recognized as kalāpaṅgas are *ākāsa-dhātu* (space element), *upacaya* (growth), *santati* (continuity), *jaratā* (decay), and *aniccatā* (impermanence). Why they are excluded needs hardly any explanation. *Ākāsa-dhātu*, that is, space delimited by matter, is not something that enters into the composition of the kalāpas, rather it is that which intervenes between the kalāpas. That is to say, it sets bounds to, and is itself bounded by, the kalāpas. The other four items are merely indicative of certain phases of matter. As such, they are not material constituents of the kalāpas.[912]

The five anipphanna-rūpas that are recognized as kalāpaṅgas are the two *viññattis* (intimation) and the triad of *lahutā* (lightness), *mudutā* (plasticity), and *kammaññatā* (wieldiness). We have already shown that although the anipphanna-rūpas are called rūpa-dhammas, they do not stand for something distinct from the nipphanna-rūpas. Accordingly, although some anipphanna-rūpas are recognized as kalāpaṅgas, they do not stand for something distinct from the nipphanna-kalāpaṅgas. Let us take one example to clarify the situation.

Kāyaviññatti, it may be recalled here, signifies a particular position or situation (*ākāra-vikāra*) of a set of mind-originated material dhammas (*citta-samuṭṭhāna-rūpa*) that are nipphanna. In the context of the theory of material clusters, kāyaviññatti signifies a particular position or situation of the mind-originated material clusters (*cittasamuṭṭhāna-kalāpa*). For the mind-originated matter (*cittasamuṭṭhāna-rūpa*), too, exists by way of kalāpas. Now, each of these kalāpas, a particular position of which is called *kāyaviññatti*, is indicated by the addition of kāyaviññatti as one of its kalāpaṅgas. Thus the recognition of kāyaviññatti as a kalāpaṅga does not carry the implication that it is something distinct from the nipphanna-kalāpaṅgas. Its purpose is to indicate the type of kalāpa, a particular position of which is represented by the kāyaviññatti. It is in this manner that we should understand the significance of the five kalāpaṅgas that are anipphanna.

Let us now consider those kalāpas, some of the kalāpaṅgas of which are anipphanna-rūpa.

The first, called *kāyaviññatti-navaka* (bodily-intimation nonad), is formed by the addition of one kalāpaṅga of kāyaviññatti to the basic octad. It represents the citta-samuṭṭhāna-kalāpa, a particular position of which is called kāyaviññatti. Next comes *vacīviññatti-dasaka* (vocal-intimation decad), which is formed by the addition of one kalāpaṅga of sound and one kalāpaṅga of vacīviññatti to the basic octad. This represents the cittasamuṭṭhāna-kalāpa, a particular position of which is called vacīviññatti.[913] The addition of sound is necessary because vacīviññatti is intimately connected with vocal sound. Since the Sarvāstivādins treat *kāyavijñapti* as a part of *rūpāyatana*, the sense field of the visible,[914] they do not recognize a separate saṃghāta-paramāṇu corresponding to it. But the same is not true of *vāgvijñapti*. Although it is treated as part of *śabdāyatana*, the sense field of sound,[915] its composition as a saṃghāta is more complex than that of ordinary sound. For the sound that is produced by the great material elements that form part of the organism (*upātta*) does not exist independently of the organs. Hence in the case of the saṃghāta-paramāṇu of vāgvijñapti sound, the usual sound nonad becomes an undecad by the addition of two dravya-paramāṇus of kāyendriya and jiḥvendriya.

The last four kalāpas, to which no corresponding saṃghāta-paramāṇus can be traced in the Sarvāstivāda, with the exception of perhaps one, have as their kalāpaṅgas the usual (eight) inseparables of the basic octad; the triad of lahutā, mudutā, and kammaññatā; and the two viññāttis.[916]

The first, called *lahutādekādasaka* (undecad of material lightness, and so on) consists of the basic octad plus three kalāpaṅgas of lahutā, mudutā, and kammaññatā. It may be recalled here that the last three items, which represent the physical body when it is healthy and efficient, arise always together (*na aññam' aññaṃ vijahanti*).[917] This explains why the three items are included in the same kalāpa rather than establishing three separate kalāpas corresponding to them.

The second and the third, called *kāyaviññatti-lahutādi-dvādasaka* (dodecad of bodily intimation, material lightness, and so on) and *vacīviññatti-sadda-lahutādi-terasaka* (tredecad of vocal intimation, sound, material lightness, and so on), are formed by adding lahutā, mudutā, and kammaññatā to the previously mentioned kāyaviññatti-navaka and vacīviññatti-dasaka, respectively. The occurrence of the two viññattis could be accompanied (facilitated) by the triad of lahutā and so on.[918] It seems that it is in order to explain such situations that these two kalāpas have been postulated.

The last kalāpa is *sadda-lahutādi-dvādasaka* (dodecad of sound and material lightness, and so on). It is the same as the previously mentioned vacīviññatti-sadda-lahutādi-terasaka except for the absence of one constituent—namely, vacīviññatti. Since the triad of lahutā and so on is included here, it certainly concerns itself with a phenomenon associated with the physical body of a living being.[919] And since vacīviññatti is lacking, we may interpret it as representative of vocal sound unaccompanied by vacīviññatti as well as sound produced by other parts of the body. In the *Abhidharmakośabhāṣya* there is reference to a saṃghāta-paramāṇu, called the sound decad, which consists of the basic octad and two dravya-paramāṇus of sound and the organ of touch. It represents the phenomenon of *upātta-mahābhūtika* sound—that is, sound produced, say, by the clapping of hands and so on.[920] Cases like these, it may be observed, are represented by the kalāpa in question. The noninclusion of kāyindriya as a constituent of this kalāpa is understandable, for we have already seen that, unlike the Sarvāstivādins, the Theravādins do not add kāyindriya either to the kalāpas of the first four sense organs or to the kalāpa of vacīviññatti sound.

This brings us to an end of our survey of the seventeen kinds of kalāpa. They all are again classified into four groups on the basis of the four generative conditions (*rūpa-samuṭṭhāna-paccaya*) of matter: kamma, citta, utu, and āhāra. Since we have discussed them elsewhere, here we shall confine ourselves to indicating how the kalāpas are classified accordingly. It should also be noted here that if a kalāpa is conditioned by more than one of the four generative conditions, say, by three (*ti-samuṭṭhāna*), then that particular kalāpa is counted thrice. In this way, although there are seventeen distinct kalāpas, the number is brought up to twenty-one.

Since the eight material *indriyas* and the *hadaya-vatthu* are recognized as coming into being through the action of kamma, the five sense-organ *dasakas*, the two sex *dasakas*, the *jīvita-navaka*, and the *vatthu-dasaka* are brought under *kamma-samuṭṭhāna* (*kamma*-originated). Since the two viññattis represent a particular position (*ākāra-vikāra*) of citta-samuṭṭhāna-rūpa, the four kalāpas—namely, kāyaviññatti-navaka, vacīviññatti-dasaka, kāyaviññatti-lahutādi-dvādasaka, and vacīviññatti-sadda-lahutādi-terasaka—are brought under citta-samuṭṭhāna (mind-originated). The two kalāpas—namely, sadda-navaka and sadda-lahutādi-dvādasaka—are utu-samuṭṭhāna (temperature-originated). These two kalāpas refer to two varieties of sound, the first to sound produced in the body of a living being and the second to sound produced in the insentient (*aviññāṇika*) world. It should be noted here that, although sound arises owing to the concussion (*ghaṭṭana*) of the great material elements, *utu* (temperature of cold and heat) is considered as a special condition for its continuity.

On the other hand, the two kalāpas—namely, lahutādekādasaka and suddhaṭṭhaka—are "three-originated" (*ti-samuṭṭhāna*) in the sense that they are alternatively conditioned by consciousness (*citta*), temperature (*utu*), and nutriment (*āhāra*). The first, which refers to the triad of lahutā and so on, is "three originated" because bodily efficiency that is implied by the triad could be brought about by a wholesome state of mind (*citta*), or by agreeable nutrition (*āhāra*), or by good temperature (*utu*).[921]

When the basic octad consisting of the four great material elements and four of the dependent is brought into relation with consciousness, as in the case of bodily movements arising in response to a thought, it is called mind originated (*citta-samuṭṭhāna*). When it arises conditioned by nutrition or by cold and heat temperatures, it is called nutrition originated (*āhāra-samuṭṭhāna*) and temperature originated (*utu-samuṭṭhāna*), respectively. All matter, other than that which enters into the composition of living beings, what the commentaries call *dhammatā-rūpa* (matter by nature), is ultimately constituted of basic octads and sound nonads, both conditioned only by temperature.[922] For the temperature of cold and heat, according to Theravāda, is an essential factor for the arising, continuity, and changes of all such matter.[923]

Why the basic octad is not kamma originated needs explanation. It is true that the (eight) constituents of this octad enter into the composition of all kalāpas, including those that are kamma originated. It should, however, be recalled here that although some material dhammas come into being, being conditioned by kamma, yet their uninterrupted continuity is said to depend on the rūpa-jīvitindriya.[924] Therefore a kamma-originated kalāpa should at least be a nonad (*navaka*), consisting of the (eight) items of the basic octad and one kalāpaṅga of rūpa-jīvitindriya. An octad in itself can never be kamma- samuṭṭhāna.

COMPOSITION OF THE MATERIAL CLUSTERS

Material Clusters	*The Constituents*
Suddhaṭṭhaka (basic octad)	*(1+2+3+4+5+7+8+9)*
Sadda-navaka (sound nonad)	*(1+2+3+4+5+7+8+9) +6*
Jīvita-navaka (vital nonad)	*(1+2+3+4+5+7+8+9) +15*
Cakkhu-dasaka (eye decad)	*(1+2+3+4+5+7+8+9) +15+10*
Sota-dasaka (ear decad)	*(1+2+3+4+5+7+8+9) +15+11*
Ghāna-dasaka (nose decad)	*(1+2+3+4+5+7+8+9) –15+12*
Jivhā-dasaka (tongue decad)	*(1+2+3+4+5+7+8+9) +15+13*
Kāya-dasaka (body decad)	*(1+2+3+4+5+7+8+9) +15+14*
Itthibhāva-dasaka (decad of femininity)	*(1+2+3+4+5+7+8+9) +15+16*
Pumbhāva-dasaka (decad of masculinity)	*(1+2+3+4+5+7+8+9) +15+17*
Vatthu-dasaka (decad of heart basis)	*(1+2+3+4+5+7+8+9) +15+18*
Kāyaviññatti-navaka (nonad of bodily expression)	*(1+2+3+4+5+7+8+9) +19*
Vacīviññatti-dasaka (decad of vocal expression)	*(1+2+3+4+5+7+8+9) +6+20*
Lahut'ād'ekādasaka (undecad of plasticity)	*(1+2+3+4+5+7+8+9) +21+22+23*
Kāyaviññatti-lahut'ādi-dvādasaka (dodecad of bodily expression and plasticity)	*(1+2+3+4+5+7+8+9) +19+21+22+23*

Vacīviññatti-sadda-lahut'ādi-terasaka (tredecad of vocal expression, sound, and plasticity)	*(1+2+3+4+5+7+8+9) +20+6+21+22+23*
Sadda-lahut'ādi-dvādasaka (dodecad of sound and plasticity)	*(1+2+3+4+5+7+8+9) +6+21+22+23*

ABBREVIATIONS

1 = paṭhavī-dhātu (earth element)

2 = āpo-dhātu (water element)

3 = tejo-dhātu (fire element)

4 = vāyo-dhātu (air element)

5 = rūpa (color)

6 = sadda (sound)

7 = gandha (smell)

8 = rasa (taste)

9 = āhāra (nutriment)

10 = cakkhu (organ of sight)

11 = sota (organ of hearing)

12 = ghāna (organ of smell)

13= jivhā (organ of taste)

14 = kāya (organ of touch)

15 = rūpa-jīvitindriya (material faculty of life)

16 = itthindriya (faculty of femininity)

17 = purisindriya (faculty of masculinity)

18 = hadaya-vatthu (heart base)

19 = kāyaviññatti (bodily expression)

20 = vacīviññatti (vocal expression)

21 = rūpassa lahutā (lightness of matter)

22 = rūpassa mudutā (pliancy of matter)

23 = rūpassa kammaññatā (wieldiness of matter)

16

TIME AND SPACE

THE ABHIDHAMMA THEORY of reality requires that we make a clear distinction between the types of entities that exist in a real and ultimate sense (dhammas) and the types of entities that exist only as conceptual constructs (paññatti). The former refer to those entities that truly exist independently of the cognitive act and the latter to those entities that owe their being to the act of cognition itself. It is in this context that we need to understand the place the Abhidhamma assigns to time and space.

On the subject of time the Abhidhamma Piṭaka is relatively silent, perhaps because here time is not assigned the status of a dhamma. If time is not a dhamma, conditioned or unconditioned, this obviously means that it is a mental construct with no objective reality. This seems to be the position taken up by other Buddhist schools on the nature of time. There is, however, reference to one Buddhist school that took up the opposite position. It maintained that like all other dhammas, time, moment, or "any stroke of time" is something positively produced (*parinipphanna*). Positive production, according to Theravāda, is true of only conditioned dhammas because, unlike mental constructs, they are actually produced by causes and conditions.[925]

The overall Buddhist theory of time is in sharp contrast to that of the substantialist schools of Indian philosophy, where we find time recognized as an eternal, all pervading substance: its existence is said to be inferred from facts of consecution and simultaneity between phenomena. An extreme position on the nature of time was maintained by the eternalist school of Kālavādins. They insisted that absolute time is the primordial cause of everything, an almighty force that brings under its inexorable sway all that exists. We find their theory summarized in a Pāli subcommentary:

> It's time that creates all living beings;
> it's time that destroys them all.
> It's time that's awake while the world is asleep;
> irreversible indeed is the flow of time.[926]

A direct Buddhist response to this we find in the *Mūlapariyāya Jātaka*:

> Time consumes all, including time itself. Who isn't consumed by the all-consumer?—Tell.[927]

It is the arahant, the one who has attained nibbāna, that has consumed the all-consuming time.[928] Hence the arahant is also called "the one who has gone beyond time (*gataddha*), the one who has transcended saṃsāric time (*saṃsāraddham atikkanta*)."[929]

In the Abhidhamma there are at least five technical terms signifying time. These are *kāla* (time, season), *addhan* (length of time, duration), *samaya* ("coming together" = occasion), *santati* (series, continuum), and *khaṇa* (moment). What is interesting to note here is that *kāla* is the term most often used when the objective reality of time is denied. The reason could be Kālavāda, the time doctrine, which, as noted above, asserted the absolute reality of time. *Addhan* is used to mean "stretch, length," not only of time but of space as well.[930] In the sense of time, it means a lifetime or a long period like the beginningless cycle of births and deaths (*saṃsārad-dhāna*).[931] This explains why nibbāna is described as free from addhan.[932] As we shall see, *santati* as series or continuum means perceptible time, the actual experience of a now, in contrast to momentary time, which is not perceptible. *Khaṇa* is used in a general sense to mean a small fraction of time and in a technical sense to mean the briefest temporal unit. It is also used to mean the right occasion, the opportune time (*khaṇo ti okāso*).[933]

Samaya is the term that Buddhism prefers most. In its technical sense it means "the confluence of conditions" (*paccaya-sāmaggi*) or "the coming together of the appropriate causes" (*kāraṇa-samavāya*). This is another way of referring to a particular occurrence.[934] Every occurrence is, for the Abhidhamma, a concurrence, in view of its causal principle that a multiplicity of conditions gives rise to a multiplicity of effects. To clarify where samaya differs from kāla, a Pāli subcommentary cites this sentence. "Perhaps tomorrow we might go there, considering both *kāla* and *samaya*." Here kāla means the arrival time (*yutta-kāla*), whereas samaya means the confluence of conditions (*paccaya-sāmaggi*) necessary for arrival.[935] "Arrival" is not something distinct from "the confluence of conditions." The confluence of conditions is itself the arrival.[936]

There is another important difference to be noted between kāla and samaya: It is kāla in the sense objective time that the Abhidhamma denies. Samaya in the sense of time is in fact not denied, because what it really means is "the coming together of conditions" (*sameti samavetī ti samayo*).[937] In fact, samaya is the Abhidhamma's answer to what the substantialist schools call kāla in the sense of absolute time. An interesting commentarial observation on samaya concerns why it is used in three different cases in the Sutta, Vinaya, and Abhidhamma Piṭaka: A sutta begins with *ekaṃ samayaṃ*, "at one time." Here samaya is used in the accusative case (*upayoga-vacana*). Vinaya begins with *tena samayena*, "at that time." Here samaya is used in the instrumental case (*karaṇa-vacana*). Abhidhamma begins with *yasmiṃ samaye*, "at which time." Here samaya is used in the locative case (*bhumma-vacana*). The use of the term in three different cases, it is claimed, is not accidental but purposefully done. If the suttas use the accusative case, this is to show that the time intended here is nonspecific, nondefinite (*aniyamita*). If Vinaya uses the instrumental case, this is to focus on the factors that are instrumental (*hetubhūtena karaṇabhūtena*) for the promulgation of ecclesiastical rules. If the Abhidhamma uses the locative case, this is to show how time serves as a location, a sort of receptacle for the coming together of consciousness and its concomitants.[938]

As mentioned in chapter 2, there are in all six kinds of concept-as-name (*nāma-paññatti*). The term "time" comes under one of them as an *avijjamāna-paññatti*—that is, a term that refers to a thing that does not exist in a real sense. The notion of "time" is based on the continuous flow of the dhammas.[939] It is the dhammas that arise and perish in continual succession that serve as a base for our construction of the notion of "time." What is denied is not succession, but a distinct entity called time apart from the dhammas succeeding one another. Only the dhammas are real (*paramattha, saccikaṭṭha*); time is a conceptual construct, a product of the interpretative function of our mind (*kappanā-siddha*).[940] Unlike the dhammas, time has no own nature (*sabhāvato avijjamāna*).[941]

That time is determined by events is aptly summarized by the following statement: "Chronological time denoted by reference to this or that event is only a conventional expression" (*taṃ taṃ upādāya paññatto kālo vohāra-mattako*).[942] Temporal sequence is based on eventuation, but there is no time distinct from events (dhammas). Different "times" means not different parts of one and the same time but "times" determined by different events:

> Time is only a concept derived from this or that phenomenon, such as (a) states expressed in such phrases as "temporal (aspect) of mind," "temporal (aspect) of matter"; (b) the phenomenal occurrence expressed by such phrases as "the past" and "the future"; (c) the phenomenal succession in an organism expressed by "the time of seed germination" and "the time of sprouting"; (d) the characteristic marks of phenomena expressed by "the time of genesis" and "the time of decay"; (e) the functions of phenomena expressed by "the time of feeling" and "the time of cognizing"; (f) functions of living beings expressed by "the time of bathing" and "the time of drinking"; (g) the modes of posture expressed by "the time of going" and "the time of stopping"; (h) the revolution of the moon, sun, etc., expressed by "morning, evening, day, and night"; or (i) the grouping of days and nights, etc., into periods expressed by "half-month," "month."[943]

Accordingly, the Pāli commentaries speak of a "plurality of times" (*samaya-nānatta*), and in the same context, of a plurality of causal confluences as well.[944] A causal confluence is the completeness of conditions (*paccaya-sāmaggi*) necessary for the occurrence of an event.[945] All causal confluences, in the final analysis, are causal confluences of mental and physical dhammas. Apart from the dhammas, there is no discrete entity called time (*na hi tabbinimmutto añño koci kālo nāma atthi*).[946]

The question is raised whether any reference to temporal distinctions of past, present, and future implies the recognition of time as a real existent (*addhā nāmāyaṃ dhammo eva āpanno ti?*).[947] The answer given is that there is no such dhamma called time because all temporal distinctions are, in the final analysis, distinctions pertaining to dhammas themselves (*dhammassa pana avatthābhedo*).[948] Although time does not exist in its own nature (*sabhāvena avijjamāno'pi*), yet it is possible to speak of things as belonging to the three divisions of time by considering time as a receptacle (*adhikaraṇa*), as a support (*ādhāra*) for their serial occurrence.[949]

As we have noted in chapter 2, all conceptual constructs (*paññatti*) are time free (*kāla-vimutta*).[950] If time is a conceptual construct, how are we to understand time as time free? What we need to remember here is that time divisions are not divisions of an absolute time. They refer to the dhammas that arise, exist, and dissolve. In other words, time does not exist in time. If time exists in time, then this (second) time will require a third time to exist, and the third a fourth, and thus it will involve what Buddhist exegesis calls a process of interminability (*anupaccheda*) or infinite regress (*anavaṭṭhāna*).

Dhammas become past, present, and future in three different ways: by way of moments, series, and lifespan. According to moments, past means the dhammas that have ceased after going through the three moments of arising, presence, and dissolution (*tayo khaṇe patvā niruddha*); future means the dhammas that have not yet arrived at the three moments (*tayo khaṇe asampatta*); and present means the dhammas that pass through the three moments (*tayo khaṇe sampatta, khaṇattaya-pariyāpanna*).[951] In like manner, we need to understand the other two—by way of series and by way of lifespan.

Strictly speaking, "present" means the momentary present (*khaṇa-paccuppanna*) consisting of the three moments of arising, presence, and dissolution. Obviously this kind of time is not actually perceptible. Serial present (*santati-paccuppanna*) is the answer for perceptible time. As to its definition, we find two different opinions. In illustrating it, Majjhimabhāṇakas, or those who recite the *Majjhimanikāya*, give the following examples: When a person after having sat in darkness goes to the light, material objects do not become manifest to her all at once. The time required for the material objects to become manifest is equal to one or two continua. Similarly, when a person after having walked in the light enters a room, the time that passes until the objects become manifest should be understood as one or two continua. When a person standing afar sees the bodily movements of people washing clothes or beating drums and ringing bells, he does not immediately hear the sound they make. The time that passes until he hears the sound is equal to one or two continua.[952]

On the other hand, Saṃyuttabhāṇakas, or those who recite the *Saṃyuttanikāya*, recognize two kinds of continua: one is material (*rūpa-santati*) and the other mental (*arūpa-santati*). "Material continuity is when the ripples of the water stepped into by one crossing to the bank have not settled down, or when after a journey the heat of the body has not subsided, or when the gloom is not yet dispelled for one coming out of the glare into a room, or when after being occupied with religious exercise in a room one looks out of the window during the day and the quivering of the eyes has not subsided." A mental continuum is equal to two or three cognitive processes (*javana-vīthi*), each lasting seventeen mind moments.[953]

Two or three cognitive processes, as Venerable Nyanaponika Thera observes, appears too brief a time interval to "ascribe actual perceptibility," while "the earlier examples imply a duration too long to convey the idea of 'present.'" However, "still we must suppose that the second division, the 'serial present,' is intended to refer to the actual experience of a now."[954]

The third way of defining the present is with reference to the present life term (*addhā-paccuppanna*). This is according to the teaching of the suttas. It is an exposition of relative validity. The other two ways of defining the present, by way of series and moment, are according to the Abhidhamma. It is an exposition of absolute validity.[955]

On the mutual relationship between time and consciousness, a Pāli commentary says:

Samaye niddisi cittaṃ cittena samayaṃ muni
Niyametvāna dīpetuṃ dhamme tattha pabhedato.[956]

As translated by Venerable Nyanaponika Thera:

By time the Sage described the mind
and by the mind described the time,
in order to show, by such definition,
the phenomena there arranged in classes.[957]

We need to understand this in light of the *Dhammasaṅgaṇi*'s description of the arising of consciousness and its mental factors, to which we referred earlier.[958] Let us recall here that its first part begins with "in which time" (*yasmiṃ samaye*), and the second with "at that time" (*tasmiṃ samaye*). "In which time," as the Pāli commentary says, "is an indefinite locative," "an indefinitely marked time." Its purpose is to identify the time during which consciousness and its mental factors arise (*samaya-niddesa*). On the other hand, "at that time" refers to the time during which all the mental states (both consciousness and mental factors) arise together as a single cognitive act (*dhamma-uddesa*). Now, *samaya* in the phrase *yasmiṃ samaye* is said to occur in the sense of occasion or time, and here time is defined to mean "support" (*ādhāra*) or "locus" (*adhikaraṇa*). It is true that time does not exist in a real and ultimate sense. However, for purposes of description here it is considered as a support (*ādhārabhāvena paññatto*).[959] On the other hand, *samaya* in the phrase *tasmiṃ samaye* (at that time) is used not in the sense of time (support) but in the sense of "aggregation" or "coming together," not one after another but all together. Here the reference is to the causally connected occurrence of consciousness and its mental factors.[960]

It is with reference to samaya in the sense of "time" that samaya in the sense of "coming together" gets delimited. A Pali commentary illustrates this situation as follows: "The person who goes out when the cows are being milked returns when the cows have been milked." Here it is the time of milking the cows (*dohana-kiriyā*) that delimits the time of the man's movement (*gamana-kiriyā*). In the same way, "at which time" delimits the time of the arising of consciousness and such mental factors as sensory contact.[961]

The Pāli commentators interpret "at which time" of the *Dhamma-saṅgaṇi* as "in which moment" and "at that time" as "at that moment." Here the term "moment" (*khaṇa*) is used in its technical sense to mean the briefest temporal unit.[962] In the context of this commentarial interpretation, the moment as the briefest temporal unit becomes definable as equal to the duration of a consciousness and its mental factors. Thus while a consciousness and its mental factors (a cognitive act) determine the measure of the moment as the briefest temporal unit, the moment in turn determines the time during which a consciousness and its mental factors arise.[963]

In concluding this section it is necessary to refer to another meaning that the notion of "time" has assumed in Buddhism. Because "past," "present," and "future" are not entities distinct from the dhammas, therefore as an extension of its meaning "time" came to be reckoned as another expression for the cycle of births and deaths (*saṃsāraddhāna*).[964] When King Milinda asks Nāgasena, "What is time?" the latter explains it as the process of dhammas and *saṅkhāras* (that constitute saṃsāra).[965] If the formula of dependent arising with its twelve factors involves three periods, each period is not distinct from the factors that belong to that particular period.[966] Time comes to an end with the realization of nibbāna. Therefore nibbāna is the transcendence of time through full understanding (*addhāna-pariññā*). Since the three temporal divisions are predicable of the dhammas in the sense that we have examined above, the dhammas came to be described as "belonging to the three times" (*tekālika*). On the other hand, nibbāna is free from time (*kālavimutta*).[967] As mentioned above, one who has attained nibbāna "has gone beyond time" (*gataddha*), "has transcended the cycle of time" (*saṃsāraddhānaṃ atikkanta*),[968] and "has consumed (the all-consuming) time" (*kālaghaso*). We find this same idea in a pre-Abhidhamma work where the arahant is described as one who has transcended time (*kappātīta*).[969]

If time is not elevated to the level of a dhamma, the same situation is true of space as well. In chapter 14 we examined an entity called space element (*ākasa-dhātu*), described as a nominal (*anipphanna*) material dhamma. We saw that strictly speaking it is neither material nor a dhamma. For it does not answer either to the Abhidhamma's definition of matter or to its definition of dhamma.

In the *Milindapañha* we find another kind of space, which it defines as follows: In no way can it be grasped (*sabbaso agayha*); it inspires terror (*santasanīya*); it is infinite (*ananta*), boundless (*appamāṇa*), and immeasurable (*appameyya*). It does not cling to anything (*alagga*), is not attached to anything (*asatta*), rests on nothing (*appatiṭṭha*), and is not obstructed by anything (*apaḷibuddha*).[970] Elsewhere in the same work we are told that two things in this world are not born of kamma (*akammaja*), or of causes (*ahetuja*), or of season (*anutuja*)—namely, nibbāna and space.[971] However, what is important to remember here is this: Although the *Milindapañha* describes space in such a way as to make it appear as something unconditioned, it carefully avoids the use of the term "unconditioned" (*asaṅkhata*) in describing it. What prompted the *Milindapañha* to take this stance seems to be that such a description would elevate space to a level on par with nibbāna.

It is clear that the *Milindapañha* space is not the same as the space element. The latter means not infinite space but spaces (plural) bounded by matter.

The *Milindapañha* space has its counterpart in the Sarvāstivāda Abhidharma as well. It is defined not as space bounded by matter (=*ākāśa-dhātu*, space element) but as that which provides room for the movement of matter (*yatra rūpasya gati*).[972] It is omnipresent (*sarvagata*) and eternal (*nitya*). Its nature is nonobstruction (*anāvaraṇa-svabhāva*). It does not obstruct (*āvṛṇoti*) matter, which freely exists therein; nor is it obstructed (*āvṛyate*) by matter, for it cannot be dislodged by the latter. However, space is not the mere absence of obstruction (*anāvaraṇa-bhāva-mātra*) but something positively real.[973] In view of these characteristics the Sarvāstivāda Abhidharma elevates it to the level of an unconditioned dharma. In this sense it is on par with *pratisaṃkhyā-* and *apratisaṃkhyā-nirodha* (cessation through wisdom, and cessation independent of wisdom). What the Sarvāstivādins call unconditioned space is the space considered as absolutely real and as serving as a receptacle for the existence and movement of material phenomena.[974]

The Sarvāstivādins' space element, as noted earlier, is included in the sense sphere of the visible (*rūpāyatana*), whereas their unconditioned space comes within the sphere of mental objects (*dharmāyatana*).[975]

Thus both in Theravāda and Sarvāstivāda we find two kinds of space—one local and the other infinite. What led to this idea can be traced to the early Buddhist discourses. Here space is sometimes described as referring to cavities, apertures, and interstices. This is what the suttas mean by *ākāsa-dhātu* (space element), when it is counted as one of the six elements (*dhātu*) into which the empiric individuality is analyzed.[976] Sometimes we find space described not as void region but as the ultimate basis, a sort of fulcrum or receptacle for the existence of the physical world. In the *Mahāparinibbāna Sutta*, for instance, the Buddha says: "This great earth, O Ānanda, rests on water, water on air, and air on space."[977] The *Rāhulovāda Sutta* says that space for its part does not rest on anything (*akāso na kattha ci patiṭṭhito*).[978] In fact, the *Milindapañha* cites this same statement in its reference to space as described there. Equally significant is an observation found in the *Abhidharmakośa-vyākhyā* of Ācārya Yaśomitra. It says that when the Vaibhāṣikas (Sarvāstivādins) argue that space is real they base this argument on a sūtra passage where the Buddha declares to a brahmin that the earth rests on the circle of water, the circle of water on air, air on space, and that space for its part does not rest on anything, does not cling to anything.[979]

However, when we come to the *Kathāvatthu* of the Abhidhamma Piṭaka we find the *Milindapañha* version of space in a completely different form. Here, on a controversy as to the nature of space, the Theravādins maintain that space is not something unconditioned. Among the arguments adduced, the main one is that if space is unconditioned, then this will go against the well-established view that there is only one unconditioned reality—namely, nibbāna. If space is something unconditioned, so runs the argument, then this would mean that when a house or a barn is built by enclosing space the unconditioned space gets enclosed; or when a well is dug nonspace becomes unconditioned space; or when an empty well, or an empty barn, or an empty jar is filled, then the unconditioned space disappears. The final conclusion that the Theravādins come to from this controversy is that space is neither conditioned nor unconditioned.[980] The commentary to the *Kathāvatthu* observes that if space is so described, this means that it is a paññatti—that is, a nominal dhamma, a conceptual construct with no objective counterpart.[981] This observation conforms to the view held by the Theravādins that what is neither conditioned nor unconditioned is a conceptual construct. It will be noticed that the *Milindapañha* describes space in such a way as to make it appear something unconditioned, although it cautiously avoids the use of the term "unconditioned" to describe it. This is in contrast to the *Kathāvatthu* space, which, as we have noted, is a conceptual construct.

Thus the Theravādins, too, distinguish between two kinds of space. One is called space element (*ākāsa-dhātu*) and the other space (*ākāsa*). The first means void region that delimits and separates material objects, thus enabling us to perceive them as distinct entities. Hence it is presented as the material principle of delimitation (*pariccheda-rūpa*). As we saw in chapter 14, its description as *anipphanna* means that it is a nominal dhamma with no objective reality of its own.

The other, called space (but not space element), is sometimes described as boundless space (*ajaṭākāsa*).[982] This description highlights its difference from the space element in the sense of bounded space. The use of this term does not mean that "space" is regarded as something real and absolute. The use of another term, "empty space" (*tucchākāsa*),[983] does in fact bring into focus its nature as a conceptual construct. It is of course true that space is sometimes understood in a realistic sense. For instance, matter is defined as that which is extended in space, the principle of extension being represented by the earth element. This seems to suggest that space is a sort of receptacle for the existence of matter. However, the correct position is just the opposite. That is to say, our very idea of space is dependent on matter. If there is no matter, the notion of space does not arise. Space means not the opposite of matter but the very absence of matter. If it is said that matter exists in space, what this really means is that matter exists where there is no matter.

The definition of space in this manner reminds us of the Sautrāntikas. They, too, define it as the mere absence of matter—that is, "the mere absence of the 'substance' that has the characteristic of resistance/impenetrability" (*sapratigha-dravyābhāva-mātra*).[984] The word "mere" (*mātra*) is to emphasize the fact that nonexistence of matter does not mean the existence of anything other than matter. Space means the mere absence of matter.[985]

17

MOMENTARINESS

IT HARDLY NEEDS MENTION that in the Pāli suttas, unlike in the Abhidhamma, the notion of change is not presented either as a doctrine of momentariness or as a formulated theory of moments. This, in fact, is the view held by the Theravāda tradition as well. In introducing the theory, a Pāli commentary says that it is peculiar to the Abhidhamma and not to the Suttanta.[986] What we get in the Pāli suttas is not a doctrine of momentariness but the doctrine of impermanence, the transitory nature of all phenomena. The doctrine finds its classic expression in the well-known formula "All conditioned phenomena are impermanent" (*sabbe saṃkhārā aniccā*), and in the more popular statement "Impermanent, indeed, are conditioned phenomena" (*aniccā vata saṃkhārā*). Both amount to saying that all phenomena brought about by conditions are, by their very nature, subject to change and dissolution.

"There is no moment, no instant, no particle of time when the river stops flowing."[987] This is the simile used to illustrate "the eternal flow of happening, of unbroken continuity of change." *Anicca* (impermanent), *aññathatta* (alteration), *khaya* (waning away), *vaya* (dissolution), *nirodha* (cessation) are the terms often used to stress the instability, impermanence, inconstancy, and transience that all phenomena come to exhibit. The emphatic assertion of impermanence is thus fundamental to Buddhism. It is the Buddhist doctrine that is central to all other Buddhist doctrines. As the first of the three characteristics of sentient existence, it is impermanence that provides the rational basis for the other two characteristics: unsatisfactoriness (*dukkha*) and non-self (*anattā*). Hence an insight into the fact—namely, that whatever is of the nature of arising, all that is of the nature of cessation (*yaṃ kiñci samudaya-dhammaṃ sabbaṃ taṃ nirodha-dhammaṃ*)—is defined as "the eye of wisdom" (*dhamma-cakkhu*).[988] On the other hand, to perceive permanence in impermanence (*anicce nicca-saññā*) is a perversion of perception (*saññā-vipallāsa*), a perversion of thought (*citta-vipallāsa*), and a perversion of the ideological perspective (*diṭṭhi-vipallāsa*).[989]

This early Buddhist doctrine of impermanence, as O. H. de A. Wijesekera observes, "is not the result of any kind of metaphysical inquiry or of any mystical intuition. It is a straightforward judgment arrived at by empirical observation and as such its basis is entirely empirical."[990] On the other hand, as we shall see, the Abhidhamma doctrine of momentariness shows a shift in emphasis from empiricism to rationalism. It is the result of an attempt to understand the process of change through a process of pure reasoning. In the Pāli suttas such characteristics as impermanence and nonsubstantiality are applied to empirically observable things. But in the Buddhist schools such characteristics came to be applied not to the empirically observable things but to the basic constituents into which all such things can be finally resolved; in other words, to the dhammas/dharmas as understood in its technical sense.

Although a doctrine of momentariness is not found in the Pāli suttas, they often use the term *khaṇa*, which is the Pāli for "moment." However, the term occurs without any technical import attached to it, to mean a very small fraction of time. We find it often used in the instrumental (*tena khaṇena*), or in the locative (*tasmiṃ khaṇe*) to mean "at that moment," and as the PTS Dictionary notes, sometimes it is used in the accusative to mean moment as coincidence or concurrence—that is, all at once or simultaneously (*taṃ khaṇaṃ yeva*). The Pāli commentaries explain this sutta usage of *khaṇa* as "moment in the sense of *muhutta*" (*muhutta-saṅkhāta-khaṇa*)—that is, a small fraction of time.[991] This is in order to distinguish it from its technical usage when it means the briefest temporal unit, which is called "moment in the ultimate sense" (*paramattha-khaṇa*).[992]

Another meaning of khaṇa is "the right moment or opportune time." Thus we have *khaṇo ve mā upaccagā*. That is, "Let not the right moment slip away." And, "For those who let the (right) moment slip away come to grief" (*khaṇātītā hi socanti*).[993] This usage of khaṇa brings into focus the brevity and rarity of the right occasion and therefore the urgent need to make the fullest use of it.

What could be described as the earliest allusion, within Theravāda, to a doctrine of momentariness is found in a solitary passage in the *Mahāniddesa*, the canonical commentary to the *Suttanipāta*. The passage goes on to assert that all that we call life, individuality, pain, and pleasure join in one conscious moment that flicks away as soon as it arises. Even the denizens of the heavenly existences, who are supposed to live for 84,000 years, do not live during two conscious moments. One lives only in the present moment, and not in the past and the future moments. The psycho-physical aggregates that have ceased to exist, whether they are of the dead or of the living, are all the same. They have vanished, never to come back.[994] This brief reference in the *Mahāniddesa* to momentariness is in its commentary explained to fall in line with the commentarial version of the theory. However, the commentarial version is a formulated theory of moments that assumes significance only within the framework of the dhamma theory.

When it came to the issue of momentariness one question that divided the early Buddhist schools was whether momentariness could be equally applied to both mind and matter. Some took the position that only mind is momentary, whereas matter has relative duration. As recorded by Ācārya Vasumitra, the Mahāsāṃghikas, for instance, maintained that "the great material elements (*mahābhūta*) and the material faculties (*indriya*) evolve (*pariṇamanti*). [On the other hand] consciousness (*citta*) and its concomitants (*caitta*) do not evolve." Matter has not only a phase of production (*utpāda*) but also a phase of waning away (*kṣaya*). Thus, for example, the substance of milk transforms itself into curd. In contrast, consciousness and its concomitants, having a definite origination and an instantaneous cessation, do not transform themselves from one stage to another. They disappear as soon as they appear.[995] Again, according to Ācārya Yaśomitra, in the opinion of the Ārya-Sāṃmitīyas matter is of longer duration (*kālāntaravasthāyī*), whereas consciousness and its concomitants are characterized by momentary being (*kṣaṇikatva*).[996] Other Buddhist schools, such as the Sarvāstivādins and the Sautrāntikas, not only rejected this distinction but also criticized those who admitted it.

How the Theravādins responded to this issue emerges clearly from two controversies recorded in the *Kathāvatthu* of the Abhidhamma Piṭaka. One controversy is related to the question whether the duration of matter is equal to the duration of a thought moment (*eka-cittakkhaṇika*).[997] The Theravādins' stance is that they are not of equal duration. The opposite view is, in the commentary to the *Kathāvatthu*, attributed to the Buddhist schools known as Pubbaseliyas and Aparaseliyas.[998] Their view is based on the observation that since all conditioned phenomena are impermanent, it is not right to draw a distinction between mind and matter as regards their duration. Among the counterarguments of the Theravādins the one that is most important for our present purpose is that if the lifespan of mind and matter is equal, then it will not be possible to account for the perception of the external world. What it seems to imply is that since the Buddhist theory of perception involves a succession of mental events, if a momentary material object impinges on a momentary sense organ, both will have disappeared by the time the perceptual process is expected to culminate in full perception.[999] It is not clear whether the view rejected here by the Theravādins is identical with the well-known Sautrāntika theory of representative perception (*bāhyārthānumeyavāda*). What interests us here is the fact that according to the Theravādins the life span of matter is longer than that of mind.

The second controversy revolves on the question of whether a single unit of consciousness could last for a comparatively long period of time. The Theravādins' position is that this is not possible. The opposite view, which in the commentary to the *Kathāvatthu* is attributed to a Buddhist school called Andhakas, is based on the apparent continuity of consciousness in higher meditative experiences as in jhāna. Hence they maintain that a single unit of consciousness could last for a comparatively long period, perhaps even for a whole day.[1000] Among the many counterarguments of the Theravādins, the one that is relevant to our discussion is the following. If a single unit of consciousness could persist for a whole day, then one half of the day had to be considered as the moment of its origination (*uppādakkhaṇa*) and the other half as the moment of its cessation (*vayakkhaṇa*).[1001] What this clearly shows is that in the Theravādins' view consciousness is momentary in the sense that it arises in one moment and ceases in the next moment.

This is not the only book of the Abhidhamma Piṭaka where we find allusion to mind's momentariness. In the section *Saṃkhāra Yamaka*, the *Yamaka* often refers to mind's origination moment (*uppādakkhaṇa*) and mind's cessation moment (*nirodhakkhaṇa*).[1002] Thus at least in two books of the Abhidhamma Piṭaka we find mind's momentariness being explicitly recognized. What is important to remember here is that neither of the books mentions mind's static phase or its moment of existence, what the Pāli commentaries call *ṭhitikkhaṇa*. In maintaining why matter is of longer duration the *Kathāvatthu* says that this stance conforms to scriptural authority as well. For in the Pāli suttas it is in respect to mind or consciousness that the rapidity of change is emphasized. The *Aṅguttara-nikāya*, for instance, says that there is no other single thing so quick to change as the mind and that it is no easy thing to even illustrate how quick to change it is.[1003]

What we have observed so far should show the extent to which a theory of momentariness is developed within the books of the Abhidhamma Piṭaka. According to them, while mind is momentary, the duration of matter is not equal to the duration of a single mind moment (*eka-cittakkhaṇika*). Whether this means that matter has relative duration or that matter too is momentary but its duration as a moment is longer than that of a mind moment, we cannot ascertain on the basis of the extant data. It is equally important to remember that according to the Abhidhamma Piṭaka, momentary mental phenomena do not exhibit a static phase. There is only arising and ceasing. It is in the Pāli Buddhist exegesis that the further development of this doctrine can be seen.

Referring to the doctrine of momentariness as found in the Pāli commentaries, Alexander von Rospatt raises the question of whether it originated within the Theravāda or whether it was an adoption from some other Buddhist school on the Indian mainland. He says that in the Theravāda "the doctrine is dealt with as a marginal issue of little significance" and therefore he is "inclined to believe that the theory was adopted from outside and was possibly even introduced by Ācariya Buddhaghosa himself." However, he cautions that this hypothesis "needs to be verified by a systematic examination" of the earlier material, in particular the Siṃhala commentaries that served as the main base for Ācariya Buddhaghosa's Pāli commentaries.[1004]

That within the Theravāda tradition the doctrine of momentariness was dealt with as a marginal issue of little significance is, of course, not adequately borne out by textual data. As we shall see, it plays a vital role in the dhamma theory of the Abhidhamma as it came to be elaborated in the commentarial exegesis. The notion of "momentariness" is, in fact, fundamental to the commentators' analysis of mind as a dynamic reality, as shown from their explanation of an act of cognition as a series of momentary events and from their theory of material clusters (*rūpa-kalāpa*), which is the Theravāda counterpart of the atomic theory. If the earlier distinction between mind and matter as to their relative duration was retained in the theory of momentariness as well, this was because of the need to explain the theory of perception within a realistic framework. For the earlier as well as the later versions of the Theravāda theory of perception are both based on the view that matter is of longer duration than mind. Moreover, as we shall see, two of the conditions in the Theravāda doctrine of conditionality—namely, prenascence (*purejāta*) and postnascence (*pacchājāta*)—are also based on this temporal distinction between mind and matter. Hence this distinction had to be accommodated in the theory of momentariness as well.

As we have noted, reference to a theory of momentariness within the Theravāda tradition is found in three precommentarial works: the *Mahāniddesa*, the *Yamaka*, and the *Kathāvatthu*. Alexander von Rospatt makes note of the *Kathāvatthu* reference but is inclined to believe that that section of the *Kathāvatthu* that deals with this subject "must have been added well after the composition of the core" of this treatise.[1005] Even if this were so, still we have to reckon with the *Yamaka*, which also belongs to the Abhidhamma Piṭaka, where, as we have noted, we find reference made to mind's moments of origination (*uppādakkhaṇa*) and cessation (*nirodhakkhaṇa*). What is more, although the *Paṭṭhāna* of the Abhidhamma Piṭaka does not make specific reference to a theory of momentariness, its theory of conditionality presupposes at least the momentariness of mental phenomena. For the four conditions by way of proximity (*anantara*), immediate contiguity (*samanantara*), absence (*natthi*), and disappearance (*vigata*) clearly imply that the apparently continuous stream of consciousness is in the final analysis a succession of momentary cognitive acts.[1006] Hence it is very unlikely that the commentarial version of the doctrine of momentariness found its way to Theravāda from another Buddhist school on the Indian mainland. It is more to the point to say that it was a further elaboration of the relevant data already found in precommentarial works.

What is more, there is textual evidence to show that the doctrine of momentariness that we find in the Pāli commentaries was, in fact, known to the Siṃhala commentaries (*Sīhala Aṭṭhakathā*) that preceded their Pāli versions. In describing the doctrine of momentariness, one Pāli commentary and two Pāli subcommentaries quote statements from the Siṃhala Commentaries in order to clarify and justify their own statements. The commentary to the *Paṭisambhidhāmagga*, for instance, quotes a statement from a Siṃhala commentary called *Khandhakavagga Aṭṭhakathā* that mentions three moments—the moment of origination (*uppādakkhaṇa*), the moment of duration (*ṭhitikkhaṇa*), and the moment of dissolution (*bhaṅgakkhaṇa*).[1007] As we shall soon see, these are the three moments recognized in the commentarial version of the doctrine of momentariness. The *Abhidhammatthavibhāvinī*, while discussing the topic, says: "Even in the [*Sīhala*] *Aṭṭhakathā* it is said that to each consciousness there are three moments—the moment of origination, the moment of duration, and the moment of dissolution."[1008] Again, in criticizing a nonmainstream view on the Theravāda doctrine of momentariness, the *Saṅkhepavaṇṇanāṭīkā* observes that "when Ācariya Buddhaghosa says that the matter arising at the duration moment of rebirth consciousness ceases at the origination moment of the eighteenth (consciousness) of the same series, he has said so according to what is stated in the (*Sīhala*) *Aṭṭhakathā*" (*Aṭṭhakathā-vacanaṃ nissāya vuttaṃ*).[1009] This clearly shows that the view expressed in the Pāli commentaries—namely, that the duration of a moment of matter is equal to seventeen mind moments—was also known to the Siṃhala commentaries. In another context, but still referring to a fundamental aspect of the doctrine of momentariness, the

Saṅkhepavaṇṇanāṭīkā says that the Mahā-Aṭṭhakathācariyas—that is, those ancient teachers who compiled the great Simhala commentaries—are surely "very wise" (*ati-paññavantā*) and that therefore it is not possible that "they have failed to notice this in the *Yamaka*" (*Na ettakaṃ yamakapāḷiṃ na passanti*).[1010]

These four quotations, one from a Pāli commentary and the other three from two Pāli subcommentaries, show that the Theravāda doctrine of momentariness is not an innovation on the part of the Pāli commentators but a continuation of what was found in the Abhidhamma Piṭaka and in the Siṃhala commentaries. However, this is not to suggest that the Theravāda version of the doctrine developed in splendid isolation. There is strong textual evidence to suggest that the further development of this doctrine, as we find it particularly in the Abhidhamma compendiums and subcommentaries, was due to the impact of the schools of Sanskrit Buddhism on the mainland of India. In fact, the Theravāda version of the doctrine cannot be properly understood unless it is presented against the background of parallel versions in other schools of Buddhism. Therefore in this discussion we intend to refer, where necessary, to parallel versions as well in order to highlight the fundamental features of the Theravāda version of the doctrine of momentariness.

What led to a doctrine of momentariness among Buddhist schools could perhaps be traced to the three characteristics of the conditioned, which we find mentioned in a number of Pāli suttas. In a sutta passage of the *Aṅguttaranikāya*, for instance, we read that whatever is conditioned exhibits three characteristics: origination (*uppāda*), cessation (*vaya*), and change-in-continuance (*ṭhitassa aññathatta*).[1011] This sutta passage, as Louis de La Vallée Poussin has shown, corresponds to the *Trilakṣaṇa Sūtra* of the Chinese version of the *Saṃyuktāgama*.[1012] For early Buddhism, "whatever conditioned" meant all cognizable objects on the empirical level, which are brought about by causes and conditions. But, as we have noted, for the Abhidhamma such cognizable objects are not ultimately real because, being conceptual constructs, they have only consensual reality. What is ultimately real are the dhammas or the basic factors into which all empirical existence can be finally analyzed. In light of this development the three characteristics of the conditioned had to be applied not to composite things but to the elementary dhammas that alone have ontological ultimacy. It is this situation, as we shall see, that gave rise to different versions of momentariness among Buddhist schools.

One immediate question that attracted the attention of Buddhist schools concerned the relationship between the dhammas/dharmas and the three characteristics of the conditioned. On this question we have different explanations. The one attributed to Vibhajyavādins is that while the dharmas are conditioned, the conditioning characteristics are unconditioned (*asaṃskṛta*).[1013] Here the characteristics are elevated to a level higher than that assigned to what is characterized by them. This explanation is justified on the ground that if the characteristics of the conditioned are themselves conditioned, their nature being weak, they will not be able to accomplish their respective functions of causing the dharmas to arise, change, and disappear.[1014] Clearly this is an attempt to show that the conditioning characteristics of all that is conditioned have universal applicability and eternal validity. Everything that is causally dependent and thus conditioned comes under their inexorable sway.

A modified version of this explanation is the one attributed to the Dharmaguptakas. In their view only the characteristic of dissolution (*vyaya*) or cessation (*nirodha-lakṣaṇa*) is unconditioned.[1015] This is an attempt to stress the fact that not only the conditioned dharmas but also the characteristics responsible for their origination and modification are all brought to an end by the all-powerful characteristic of dissolution (*vināśa-lakṣaṇa*). It is the characteristic that is most formidable and therefore it is the one that justifies an elevated status. Even in the Pāli suttas the emphasis is more on the fact of cessation than on the fact of origination, as is seen from the well-known statement that whatever is of the nature of origination is by its very nature subject to cessation (*yaṃ kiñci samudaya-dhammaṃ sabbaṃ taṃ nirodha-dhammaṃ*).[1016]

Another explanation on the relationship between the characteristics and the dharmas is that both are equally conditioned. The well-known protagonists of this theory are the Sarvāstivādins, and its most trenchant critics are the Sautrāntikas and the Theravādins. We find a view similar to this appearing as a controversial issue in the *Kathāvatthu* of the Abhidhamma Piṭaka. The controversial issue is whether the three characteristics of impermanence (*aniccatā*), decay (*jaratā*), and death (*maraṇa*) are *parinipphanna*.[1017] The term *parinipphanna* means "concretely produced" or "fully produced" and is therefore predicable of all real and ultimate factors of existence (dhammas) because, unlike conceptual constructs (paññatti), they are actually and concretely produced by conditions. Hence the term *parinipphanna* is used to qualify all conditioned dhammas.[1018] The controversial issue involved here can therefore be restated as to whether the three characteristics of impermanence, decay, and death are as conditioned as the dhammas they characterize. The protagonists of this theory, according to the *Kathāvatthu* commentary,[1019] are the Andhakas, and it is this same theory that we find in the Sarvāstivāda in a fully developed form.

What led to the view that the conditioning characteristics are as conditioned as what is conditioned by them can be traced to the original sutta passage, which begins with the words: "Monks, there are these three conditioned characteristics of the conditioned."[1020] It will be noticed that the term "conditioned" (*saṅkhata*) is mentioned twice. It seems to give the impression that the characteristics of the conditioned are also conditioned. In fact, the Sarvāstivādins understand the repetition of the term "conditioned" (*saṃskṛta*/*saṅkhata*) as indicating that these characteristics themselves are conditioned and that therefore they exist as discrete entities.[1021]

On the other hand, the Sautrāntikas maintain that the repetition of the term "conditioned" should not be understood in a literal sense. If the sūtra passage repeats the term this does not mean that the characteristics are like signs revealing the presence of what is conditioned, as for example in the case of herons indicating the proximity of water. Rather, these are characteristics that find themselves in certain things, showing thereby that those things are conditioned.[1022]

On this issue the Theravādins, too, take up the same position as the Sautrāntikas. If we go by the Pāli commentary as to why the term "conditioned" is repeated in the sutta passage, it is not because of any idiomatic peculiarity of the language but is absolutely necessary. Now, what is "conditioned" (*saṅkhata*) can have not only the three mentioned but also many more other characteristics, as for example the characteristic of non-self (*anattā*). If the sutta passage were to be rephrased without repeating the term "conditioned" (*saṅkhata*), it would take the following form: "Monks, there are these three characteristics of the conditioned: arising can be discerned, the passing away can be discerned, and change-in-continuance can be discerned." What is wrong with this rephrased sentence is that it gives the wrong impression that what is conditioned has only three characteristics. However, what the sutta passage wants to show is that among many characteristics of that which is conditioned there are three specific characteristics that allow us to identify what is conditioned as conditioned. Hence it is very necessary to repeat the term.

In clarifying this situation one Pāli commentary draws our attention to a similar statement that also occurs in the *Aṅguttaranikāya*, which is as follows: *Tīṇ'imāni bhikkhave paṇḍitassa paṇḍita-lakkhaṇāni*.[1023] Translated literally, this reads: "Monks, there are these three wise characteristics of the wise." Surely, just because the word "wise" is repeated it does not mean that the characteristics of the wise are also wise. They are repeated precisely in order to recognize the wise man as a wise man (*paṇḍitassa paṇḍitato salakkhaṇato*).[1024] For besides the three characteristics that enable us to identify the wise man as wise, the wise man has many more other characteristics.

In this regard, we cannot overlook the fact that in the sutta passage in question even the opposite word "unconditioned" is repeated (= *asaṅkhatassa asaṅkhata-lakkhaṇāni*). Surely this is not intended to show that the characteristics of the unconditioned are also unconditioned.

The Sarvāstivādin argument is that if no distinction is admitted between the characteristic (*lakṣaṇa*) and the characterized (*lakṣya*), both will be identical. If origination, for instance, is not different from what originates, then the use of the genitive expression *saṣṭī-vacana*, "origination of color," cannot be justified, for this will mean the same thing as "color of color." The Sautrāntikas point out that this way of interpreting the characteristics will certainly entail some interminable problems. In order to justify the notion of "nonsubstantiality" (*anātmatva*), for example, it will be necessary to recognize the independent existence of an entity called nonsubstantiality corresponding to it. Or to justify the notions of "number," "extension," "individuality," "conjunction," "disjunction," and "existence," one will have to admit a number of independently existing entities corresponding to them. As to the implication of the genitive expression, the Sautrāntikas contend that it should be understood in the same way as when we say "the own nature of color" (*rūpasya svabhāva*), where "the own nature of color" is not something different from color. Accordingly, when we say "originated," it is only a conceptual construct (*prajñapti-mātra*), made for the purpose of indicating that what has not existed earlier does exist now. There are as many originations as there are things originating. When we want to single out a particular origination, we use the genitive expression "the origination of color" or "the origination of sensation." However, the origination of color is not something different from the originating color, nor is the origination of sensation something different from the originating sensation.[1025]

We find a similar view expressed in the Theravāda sources as well. The subcommentary to the *Abhidhammāvatāra* says: "There is no other origination that is distinct from the dhamma which is in its originating phase" (*uppādāvatthāya ca añño jāti nāma natthi*).[1026] This situation becomes clear from the definition given to "origination of consciousness" (*cittuppāda = cittassa + uppāda*), which is as follows: "It originates, therefore it is called origination. The consciousness itself is the origination. Hence it is called origination of consciousness" (*uppajjatī ti uppādo*; *cittam eva uppādo cittuppādo*).[1027] The two terms in the genitive expression do not correspond to two distinct entities; they refer to one and the same phenomenon.

Another argument adduced by the Sautrāntikas and the Theravādins against the Sarvāstivādin interpretation is as follows: "If origination, for instance, is conditioned and is therefore to be reckoned as a separate entity, then it will require another [a second] origination to account for its own origination, and this second in turn a third and thus it will unavoidably entail a process leading to infinite regression (*anavasthāna*/*anavaṭṭhāna*).[1028] We can trace the beginning of this kind of argument to the *Kathāvatthu* when it says that if impermanence, for instance, is something "concretely produced" (*parinipphanna*), then this impermanence will have to have another impermanence to account for its own impermanence, and thus it will lead to an interminable series of impermanence,[1029] what the commentary calls the fallacy of nontermination (*anupaccheda-dosa*).[1030]

Thus for the Theravādins, as for the Sautrāntikas, the characteristics of the conditioned are neither conditioned nor reckoned as separate entities. They are mere characteristics with no corresponding objective counterparts. They are to be understood as conceptual constructs (*paññatti*), and as such, strictly speaking they are neither conditioned (*saṅkhata*) nor unconditioned (*asaṅkhata*).[1031] However, they are not nonexistent in the same way as imagined sky flowers (*nabha-pupphaṃ viya no natthi*). They manifest only when there is a basis (*nissaya-paṭibaddha-vuttito*), the basis being the (conditioned) dhammas.[1032] The Theravāda explanation of the relationship between the conditioned dhammas and their conditioning characteristics should become clear from the following observation made in the commentary to the *Saṃyuttanikāya*:

> The cow is not the cow characteristic, nor is the cow characteristic the cow. The cow characteristic cannot be known without the cow. Nor can the cow be known without the cow characteristic. It is through the cow characteristics that the cow becomes manifest. In the same way, the conditioned is not the characteristic (*saṅkhāro ca na lakkhaṇaṃ*). Nor is the characteristic the conditioned (*lakkhaṇaṃ na saṅkhāro*). Without the conditioned the characteristics cannot be known. Nor can the conditioned be known without the characteristics. It is through the characteristics that the conditioned become manifest.[1033]

The next question relating to the characteristics of the conditioned concerns their number. As we have seen, the original sutta passage mentions only three characteristics: origination (*uppāda*), cessation (*vaya*), and change-in-continuance (*ṭhitassa aññathatta*). However, the Sarvāstivādins increased the number to four as *jāti* or *utpāda* (origination), *sthiti* (presence or duration), *jaratā* (decay or modification), and *anityatā* or *vyaya* (impermanence or waning away). As will be noticed, the additional characteristic is *sthiti* or duration. It is said that if the sūtra passage omits duration, it was done deliberately in order to create aversion on the part of the people toward all conditioned phenomena because it is duration that stabilizes phenomena. In contrast, the other three characteristics cause the dharmas to be transitory by causing them to traverse in the three divisions of time.[1034] According to the Sarvāstivādin theory of tri-temporal existence (*traikālya*), all conditioned dharmas persist in their substantial nature in all the three divisions of time. While *jāti* (origination) causes the future dharmas to be born in the present, *sthiti* (duration) stabilizes them, *jaratā* (decay) weakens and prepares them to be annihilated in the future, and *vināśa* (dissolution) destroys them by pushing them to the past. On the other hand, *sthiti* (duration) performs only the function of stabilizing the dharmas. It does not play any role in the transition of dharmas from the future to the present and from the present to the past. Again, since the unconditioned (*asaṃskṛta*) persists eternally in its own individual nature (*svalakṣaṇena sthitibhāva*), it is in order to highlight its contrast with what is conditioned that the sūtra passage does not say that the conditioned has even an instant of duration.[1035]

As observed above, for the Sarvāstivādins the four characteristics of the conditioned are also conditioned. Accordingly, these are reckoned as four separate dharmas and are included in a category called *citta-viprayukta-saṃskāra*.[1036] Their inclusion in this category is to show that they apply equally to both mind and matter. And since the four characteristics themselves are conditioned they have, in turn, their own secondary characteristics (*anulakṣaṇa*)—namely, *jāti-jāti* (origination of origination), *sthiti-sthiti* (duration of duration), *jaratā-jaratā* (decay of decay), and *anityatā-anityatā* (impermanence of impermanence). Thus when a dharma arises, together with it arise the four primary and the four secondary characteristics. This rather complex situation is explained as follows: Jāti (origination), which is the first primary characteristic, produces the dharma as well as the other three primary and the four secondary characteristics. When jāti performs this function it does so while being in the future, for according to the theory of tri-temporality, the dharmas persist in all three divisions of time. Although jāti produces the above eight elements, it must also be produced. This means that it must transit itself from the future to the present. This function is performed by jāti-jāti, the first secondary characteristic. Thus although jāti-jāti (origination of origination) is produced by jāti (origination) when the latter is in its future state, it is jāti-jāti (origination of origination) that enables jāti (origination) to transit from the future to the present. The second principal characteristic, which is sthiti (duration), while being stabilized by its own secondary characteristic called sthiti-sthiti (duration of duration), stabilizes the dharma and the other seven items—namely, the remaining three principal characteristics and the four secondary characteristics. Likewise, the third and fourth principal characteristics called *jaratā* (decay) and *vināśa* (dissolution), while being weakened and destroyed by their two secondary characteristics called *jaratā-jaratā* and *vināśa-vināśa*, weaken and destroy the remaining items as they apply to each case. Thus, it is through this explanation, based on the principle of reciprocal conditionality, that the Sarvāstivādins seek to obviate the possibility of infinite regression to which both Theravādins and Sautrāntikas have drawn attention.[1037]

If the four characteristics of the conditioned are coexistent, will this not lead to a situation where a dharma arises, subsists, deteriorates, and ceases at one and the same time? This is one question raised against the Sarvāstivādin theory. The reply is that there is a difference in the time they exercise their activities (*kāritra-kāla-bheda*). The characteristic of *jāti* exercises its activity when it is in the future, whereas the other three characteristics operate their activities simultaneously when the dharma has arisen. This explanation, in turn, gives rise to further problems. If the latter three characteristics operate simultaneously, this means that one and the same dharma stabilizes, deteriorates, and ceases at one and the same time. Since the characteristics are mutually incompatible, how can they accomplish their operation without annulling the respective function of one another? On the other hand, to admit temporal sequence in their operation is to admit that the moment is divisible, a situation that goes against the notion of "momentariness."[1038] However, the Sarvāstivādins insist that for them a moment means the time when the characteristics accomplish their operation.[1039] The basis of the Sarvāstivādin argument is that although the characteristics are opposed to one another, yet their different functions result in a coordinated single fact.

In responding to this Sarvāstivādin interpretation of the characteristics of the conditioned, the Sautrāntikas call this an utterly futile exercise analagous to analyzing empty space. In their opinion the four characteristics cannot be applied to a single momentary dharma. Nor were they intended by the original sūtra passage to be so applied. The use in the passage of the term *prajñāyate/paññāyati*, which means "becomes manifest," in referring to the characteristics clearly shows that these characteristics are empirically observable. We cannot expect such a situation if they are applied to a single momentary dharma.[1040] Hence the Sautrāntikas apply the four characteristics not to a single momentary dharma but to a series of momentary dharmas (*dharma-santati*): "*Jāti* is the origination of a series, *vyaya* is its cessation, *sthiti* (duration) is the series [itself], and the difference between the preceding and succeeding states of that series itself is *sthityanyathātva* (change-in-continuance)."[1041] Thus for the Sautrāntikas duration is not the duration of a momentary dharma, rather it is another expression for a series of momentary dharmas. This interpretation is said to conform to what is found in the Abhidharma texts as well, where duration is defined as "noncessation of the *saṃskāras* that have arisen" (*utpannānāṃ saṃskārānām avināśa*).[1042]

However, the Sautrāntikas grant the possibility of applying the characteristics to a momentary dharma, if it is understood in the following manner. Since a momentary dharma comes into being having not been (*abhūtvā bhāva*), its existence after its nonexistence is its origination (*jāti* or *utpāda*). Since it ceases after having been (*bhūtvā abhāva*), its nonexistence after its existence is its cessation (*vyaya* or *vināśa*). As to duration, the immediately succeeding moment could be considered as the duration (*sthiti*) of the immediately preceding moment (*pūrvasya pūrvasyottara-kṣaṇānubandhaḥ sthitiḥ*), because the former could be regarded as the substitute of the latter. In this sense, and in this sense only, one could say that the preceding moment still exists as duration (*sthiti*) in the succeeding moment. The dissimilarity of the succeeding moment in relation to the preceding could be considered as change-in-continuance (*sthityanyathātva*).[1043] It is maintained that even in an apparently homogeneous series, the succeeding moment does not completely resemble the preceding moment. There has to be some kind of dissimilarity (*visadṛśatva*). An illustration cited is a falling thunderbolt, which according to the theory of momentariness is a series of momentary material dharmas that appear and disappear in continual succession. The dissimilarity of its succeeding moments in relation to its preceding moments is due to the transformation of the great material elements, which is determined by the varying velocity of its fall: in each moment of its fall there is a difference in the great material elements (*mahābhūta*) that constitute the series called the thunderbolt (*mahābhūta-pariṇāma-viśeṣa*).[1044]

As noted above, it is only in a metaphorical sense that the Sautrāntikas attribute *sthiti* (duration) and *jaratā* (deterioration or modification) to a momentary dharma. In their opinion, if a dharma is truly momentary it cannot have time either to endure or undergo change. In recognizing the duration of a momentary dharma, the main argument adduced by the Sarvāstivādins is that it is because of this characteristic that a momentary dharma becomes endowed with causal efficiency. It is by the force of the characteristic called duration that the conditioned dharmas, after having arisen, bear their fruit. If a dharma has no duration it will not have that specific power and efficiency (*śakti-prabhāva-viśeṣa*) that enables it to perform its specific function (activity).[1045] It is also contended that it is due to duration that a dharma exists at least for one moment, and therefore if not for duration that very moment will not obtain.[1046] The Sautrāntika position is that it is not due to duration but to antecedent causes and conditions that the dharmas arise, and therefore the recognition of duration is superfluous.

The Sarvāstivādins contend that a dharma that is brought about by causes and conditions is actually stabilized by duration, and if duration does not perform this function the dharma will not exist.[1047] If that were so, runs the Sautrāntika counterargument, then the function of duration would be not to make the dharma stabilized but to generate—a function already assigned to *jāti* (origination). The conclusion of the Sautrāntikas is that if the notion of "momentariness" is to be meaningful, one should accept that a dharma disappears spontaneously as soon as it appears. The recognition of duration is really an argument against momentariness. What is called duration makes the continuous flow discontinuous and thus leads to the collapse of the theory of instantaneous being.[1048]

Equally controversial was the recognition, on the part of the Sarvāstivādins, of jaratā, decay or modification, as a characteristic of a momentary dharma. It is claimed that the function of jaratā is to reduce the strength (*śakti-hāni*) of a dharma so that it will not perform more than one function and thus will be ready to be destroyed by anityatā, the characteristic of dissolution. Jaratā is likened to an enemy who after weakening the dharma and decimating its strength hands it over to anityatā to be destroyed.[1049] The definition of jaratā as its reduction of strength (*śakti-hāni*) could approach what is called *pariṇāmavāda* or the evolutionary theory of causation, a theory associated with the Sāṃkhya system. It implies the presence of an unchanging substance and changing qualities, a distinction that will not fall in line with the Buddhist doctrine of nonsubstantiality. The Sarvāstivādins were not unaware of this vulnerable situation. Hence they say that the dharma called *jarā* (the characteristic of decay) is different from the *dharmin* (the characterized). Whereas for the Sāṃkhya, *pariṇāma* means that while the *dharmin* (substance) remains permanent, it abandons one characteristic (dharma) and assumes another, where both characteristics are identical with the dharmin (substance, the characterized).[1050]

Another argument of the Sautrāntikas is that the very notion of *jaratā* (decay) implies some kind of change, a transformation of a dharma from one stage to another. A momentary dharma, if it is really momentary, has no time to change but only perishes. If a dharma ceases as it is, then there cannot be change; if it undergoes change, then it is not the same dharma.[1051] The latter argument is based on the fact that a dharma represents a unitary indivisible entity devoid of the dichotomy of substance and quality, and therefore to assume that a dharma has undergone change is to assume that it has become something other than itself. Thus in respect to a single dharma, the notion of "change" is not applicable.

How the Sautrāntikas defined "the moment" should become clear from their criticism of the Sarvāstivādin position. In their opinion, a momentary dharma cannot have the two characteristics of duration and modification. This way of looking at the issue led to their theory of moments as point-instants of time. They have no duration in time, just as geometric points have no extension in space. In a way, what is called appearance is itself disappearance. We could even say that they are, in fact, two ways of looking at the same phenomenon.

It is against the background of this Sarvāstivāda-Sautrāntika controversy on the doctrine of momentariness that we can have a better picture of its Theravāda version, particularly as we find it developed in the Pāli Buddhist exegesis. One problem the Sarvāstivādins and the Sautrāntikas had to face was defining the moment in relation to the characteristics of the conditioned. The former, as we saw, defined the moment as that instant when the four characteristics accomplish their operation. This led to the Sautrāntika criticism as to how mutually incompatible characteristics can activate together without the one cancelling the effect of the other. On the other hand, the Sautrāntika definition of the moment as having the two characteristics of origination and dissolution gives rise to the question of how two mutually exclusive characteristics can activate, as there is no dividing middle phase between them.

The Theravāda definition of the moment, on the other hand, keeps clear of both problems. For according to this definition, the three (not four, according to Theravāda) characteristics of the conditioned do not operate simultaneously. Nor do they operate in temporal succession within one single moment. Rather, there are three separate moments corresponding to them: *uppādakkhaṇa*, the moment of origination; *ṭhitikkhaṇa*, the moment of duration/presence; and *bhaṅgakkhaṇa*, the moment of dissolution. A dhamma arises in the first moment, exists in the second moment, and ceases in the third moment. The three characteristics operate one after the other, each accomplishing its operation in its own moment.[1052] This way of presenting the notion of "momentariness" gets rid of the problem that the Sarvāstivādins and the Sautrāntikas had to face. It also ensures the definition of "the moment" as the briefest temporal unit, because during one moment only one characteristic accomplishes its operation.

The Theravādin exegetes took special care to highlight this situation. The *Paramatthavinicchaya*, an Abhidhamma compendium, says that the three characteristics necessarily involve a temporal sequence (*tividhaṃ bhinna-kālikaṃ*).[1053] The idea that the three characteristics are distinct from one another and that they do not commingle in their operation is emphasized in earlier texts as well, though not in the context of momentariness. Thus we read in the *Paṭisambhidāmagga*: "The characteristic of origination is devoid (*suñña*) of the two characteristics of dissolution and change-in-continuance. The characteristic of dissolution is devoid of the two characteristics of origination and change-in-continuance. The characteristic of change-in-continuance is devoid of the two characteristics of origination and dissolution."[1054] This is what is called *lakkhaṇa-suñña*, the emptiness in relation to characteristics.[1055] The commentary to the *Paṭisambhidāmagga* expands this idea thus: "In the case of a conditioned dhamma, during the moment of its origination there comes to be manifested the fact of being conditioned, the characteristic of origination, and moment as the briefest unit of time. When the origination moment has elapsed, there comes to be manifested the fact of being conditioned, the characteristic of decay, and the moment as the briefest unit of time. When the decay moment has elapsed there comes to be manifested the fact of being conditioned, the characteristic of dissolution, and moment as the briefest unit of time."[1056] Thus what comes to be manifested together are not the three characteristics but a given characteristic, the conditioned nature, and the time instant. The commentary observes further: "Origination itself is the fact of being conditioned and the characteristic of the conditioned." The other two characteristics are to be understood similarly.[1057]

As we have seen, in the Theravāda the moment is defined as that time instant when one of the three characteristics operates. However, sometimes we find the moment being defined in another way to embrace the three moments taken together as one unit. Thus we find one mind moment (*eka-cittakkhaṇa*) defined as "the triad of moments corresponding to origination, presence, and dissolution" (*uppāda-ṭṭhiti-bhaṅga-vasena khaṇattayaṃ*).[1058] Thus the moment comes to be defined in two different ways. In its more general sense it means the time taken by a dhamma to originate, exist, and to dissolve. And in its more specific sense it means the time taken by a dhamma either to originate, or to exist, or to dissolve. In this latter sense the moment becomes a submoment. However, the three submoments should not be understood as three momentary phases—the nascent, static, and cessant—of the moment in its wider sense. The three submoments remain distinct and separate events in their successive occurrence.

It remains to be explained now how the three moments of origination, duration, and dissolution correspond to the three characteristics of the conditioned. This becomes clear from the commentary to the *Aṅguttara-nikāya* when it comments on the sutta passage on the three characteristics of the conditioned. Here it is observed that *uppāda* (origination) is *jāti* (genesis), *vaya* (cessation) is *bheda* (dissolution), and *ṭhitassa aññathatta* (change-in-continuance) is *jaratā* (decay). It then observes that these three characteristics, as they are mentioned here, correspond to the three moments of origination (*uppādakkhaṇa*), dissolution (*bhaṅgakkhaṇa*), and duration/presence (*ṭhitikkhaṇa*).[1059] That origination (*uppāda*) and cessation (*vaya*) correspond to the two moments of origination and dissolution can be easily understood. But what is intriguing here is how jaratā could correspond to the moment of duration. Jaratā means decay, which necessarily involves some kind of change or alteration, and therefore how can it correspond to the moment that represents the static phase? What is more, no other Buddhist school seems to have interpreted jaratā in this manner. For they all take jaratā (decay) and *ṭhiti/sthiti* (duration) as two separate characteristics.

As to why jaratā (decay) is called ṭhiti (duration/presence), we find an interesting explanation given in the *Visuddhimagga* and the *Abhidhammāvatāra*. In identical words, both observe that if the moment of duration/presence is called jaratā, this is because at this momentary stage the dhamma has lost its "newness" (*navabhāva-apagama*). "Newness" is another expression for the moment of origination because it appears earlier than the other two, in fact it is the first to appear. It is the moment when the dhamma is new and fresh. "Oldness" is therefore another expression for the moment of duration/presence because it appears after the moment of origination. In other words, it manifests as "the loss of newness" (*navabhāva-apagama*).[1060] Repeating this same idea, the subcommentaries define jaratā, when it means the moment of duration/presence, as "the collapse of newness" (*abhinava-bhāva-hāni*) or as "lapse of newness" (*navatā-hāya*).[1061] Another reason for describing this particular moment as decay is that it shortens the lifespan of the dhamma (*kāla-haraṇa*) by pushing the dhamma, so to say, toward its own moment of dissolution (*bhaṅgakkhaṇa*), toward its own final moment (*antimakkhaṇa*).[1062] There is another reason why the moment of duration/presence could be called decay. This particular moment is sometimes defined as that time-instant when a dhamma is facing its own dissolution, its own cessation (*bhaṅgassa abhimukhāvatthā, nirodhābhimukhāvatthā*).[1063] The obvious implication is that since the moment of dissolution is the inevitable successor to the moment of duration, during the latter moment a dhamma has no other alternative but to face its own destruction, its own death. And since death is generally preceded by old age, on that analogy, but only as a metaphorical expression, the latter could well be described as old age. The commentary to the *Vibhaṅga* says that if the moment of duration is called decay it is because at this moment a dhamma, so to say, gets fatigued by decay (*ṭhitiyaṃ jarāya kilamanti*).[1064] This statement, however, should not be understood to mean that a dhamma undergoes some kind of change during the moment of duration. As the Siṃhala *sanne* to the *Visuddhimagga* observes, this is only a figurative way of saying that the (initial) moment of origination is now succeeded by the (subsequent) moment of duration (*avasthāntara-prāpti*).[1065]

What all this amounts to is that jaratā, if understood in a direct literal sense, has absolutely no place in the Theravāda version of the doctrine of momentariness. It is only a metaphorical expression for the moment of duration. This is precisely why it is defined as the loss of newness (*navabhāva-apagama*) and not as the loss of own nature (*sabhāva-anapagama*). As we have noted, "own-nature," in the context of the Abhidhamma's dhamma theory, is another expression for the dhamma itself. Therefore to admit that a dhamma has lost its own nature is to admit that it has lost its very existence. This is the reason for the emphatic statement that at the moment of duration a dhamma has lost only its newness (= moment of origination) and not its own nature (*sabhāva*). In illustrating this situation, the *Visuddhimagga* as well as the *Abhidhammāvatāra* observe that it is like new paddy becoming old (*vīhipurāṇabhāvo viya*).[1066] This illustration could give the wrong impression that during the moment of duration a dhamma has undergone some kind of change, as when new paddy becomes old. Hence the subcommentary to the *Abhidhammāvatāra* hastens to prevent such an impression by saying that when a paddy becomes old, there is at least a change in its taste, and so on, but when a dhamma becomes old, that is, when it comes to the moment of duration, it abandons nothing other than its moment of origination.[1067]

According to this same subcommentary, this Buddhist idea of change means two things. One is that what is impermanent (= any conditioned dhamma) has a definite beginning and a definite termination (*ādi-anta-vanta*). This means that its temporal boundaries are clearly demarcated by the two phenomena of origination and cessation (*ādi-anta-vatī ti udayabbaya-paricchinna*).[1068] No dhamma is an evolute or a derivative of another dhamma, nor is it an emergent state of an underlying permanent substance. This is why its temporal boundaries are said to be strictly delimited by a definite beginning and a definite ending. This same idea comes into focus when the subcommentary to the *Visuddhimagga* defines *vipariṇāma* (change) as *sabhāva-vigamana*—that is, as the disappearance of own nature.[1069] Since own nature is another expression for a dhamma, *vipariṇāma* means not the alteration of a dhamma from one stage to another but its disappearance or replacement by another dhamma. And the term "disappearance," it is said, should be understood not as some kind of reappearance [in a different form] (*punarāvatti*) but as complete cessation (*kevalaṃ apunarāvatti-nirodha*).[1070] The other aspect of the Buddhist idea of change, as mentioned in the commentary to the *Paṭisambhidāmagga*, is that it completely dissociates itself from the idea of what is called *mandībhāvakkhaya*—that is, the gradual wasting away or gradual waning away. In popular parlance, it is said, the term *khaya* means "diminishing much" (*pahutassa mandībhāva*). But in Buddhist usage the term *khaya* means not gradual change but complete dissolution of what has arisen.[1071]

Thus as decay (*jaratā*) becomes a figurative expression for momentary duration, in this context it is called *khaṇika-jarā*, "momentary decay."[1072] This kind of decay is commonly shared by both mental and material dhammas. But in the case of material phenomena, there is another kind of decay called *pākaṭa-jarā* or evident decay. "Brokenness of teeth," "grayness of hair," and "wrinkles on the skin" are instances of evident decay.[1073] However, what is called evident decay is, strictly speaking, not decay as such. It is just a concession to the popular notion of "decay." "As a path taken by water or by fire can be known from broken and scattered things, or from the charred grass or trees, but the path itself is not the water or the fire, even so the path of decay becomes known from such instances as brokenness of teeth and so on."[1074] In other words, when we see something exhibiting what in common parlance is called decay, what we actually see is a certain disposition of color, for only color constitutes the sphere of visibility. The rest is interpretation superimposed on the difference of coloration; only the color is visible.[1075] An instance of decay, from the point of view of the dhamma analysis, is a peculiarity (*vikāra*) or a particular modality (*avatthā-visesa*) of the momentary material dhammas that constitute a materiality series.[1076]

Now this new interpretation of decay (*jaratā*) to mean its very denial, as will be noted, upsets the correspondence of the three moments, on the one hand, and the three characteristics of the conditioned, on the other. As to the first two characteristics—origination (*uppāda*) and cessation (*vaya*)—a question does not arise, because they correspond to the moment of origination (*uppādakkhaṇa*) and the moment of dissolution (*bhaṅgakkhaṇa*), respectively. But the question is whether the moment of duration (*ṭhitikkhaṇa*) has the legitimacy to represent the third characteristic, which is change-in-continuance, or the phenomenon of becoming otherwise. For here we cannot overlook the fact that although the moment of duration is called decay (*jaratā*), the term is used only as a metaphorical expression. This gives rise to a situation where the third conditioning characteristic remains nonrepresented by any of the three moments.

The authors of the Pāli subcommentaries were not unaware of this situation. Hence the author of the *Abhidhammatthavikāsinī* raises this very pertinent question: "Why is the moment of duration not mentioned in *pāḷi* (= Pāli Tipiṭaka)?"[1077] This question shows that, strictly speaking, the moment of duration does not represent the characteristic called change-in-continuance, because this latter characteristic is certainly mentioned in the original sutta passage. On the other hand, as we have seen, the commentary to the *Aṅguttaranikāya* says that *ṭhitassa aññathatta* (change-in-continuance) is jaratā (decay) and that jaratā corresponds to the moment of duration.

In recognizing a moment corresponding to duration, the Theravādins part company with the Sautrāntikas, for, as we have seen, according to the latter a truly momentary dharma cannot have duration. Why the Theravādins recognize it can be seen from several definitions given to it. Since this moment occupies a midpoint between origination and dissolution, it is called the moment of presence (*atthikkhaṇa*),[1078] the moment of occurrence (*pavattikkhaṇa*),[1079] the moment of standing (*ṭhānakkhaṇa*),[1080] the moment of existence (*vijjamānakkhaṇa*),[1081] or simply as being (*bhāva*).[1082] It is defined as the moment that is delimited by the rise and fall of a dhamma (*udaya-vyaya-paricchinna*),[1083] or as the moment that obtains in their middle (*ubhinnaṃ vemajjhe*).[1084] It is the moment when the dhamma has given up its newness (*navabhāva-apagama*) and is facing its own dissolution (*bhaṅgābhimukhāvatthā*).[1085] It is the moment that serves as a hiatus between the two characteristics (moments) of origination and dissolution, which two characteristics are defined as mutually opposing (*nirodha-viruddho hi uppādo*).[1086] If not for the moment of duration, origination and dissolution will coincide and nullify the effect of each other, a situation that will lead to the collapse of the theory of momentariness. Hence the moment of duration is also defined as the moment that ensures the absence of dissolution during the moment of origination and the absence of origination during the moment of dissolution (*udayakkhaṇe vayassa vayakkhaṇe udayassa abhāvabodhato . . .*).[1087]

These definitions given to the moment of duration are also intended as a response to those who refused to accept it. For, as can be gathered both from the commentaries and subcommentaries, some Theravādins took up the position that in the case of mental phenomena, that is, consciousness and its concomitants, a static phase in the form of a moment of duration does not obtain. Foremost among the advocates of this dissent view was an ācariya called Ānanda, mentioned in the *Abhidhammatthavikāsinī*. The first reference to such a view is in fact found in an earlier work—namely, the commentary to the *Saṃyuttanikāya*—and this shows that this view had an earlier history.[1088]

Ācariya Ānanda's view that the moment of duration does not apply to mental dhammas is sought to be justified mainly on scriptural evidence. He says that in the *Vibhaṅga* of the Abhidhamma Piṭaka, where, as we have seen, mind is described as existing by way of moments, there is no reference to a moment of duration. Only the two moments of origination (*uppādakkhaṇa*) and cessation (*nirodhakkhaṇa*) are mentioned.[1089] Even in the *Kathāvatthu*, as we have noted, the same situation obtains. The absence of any allusion to a static phase or a moment of duration is conspicuous. Then as to the three characteristics of the conditioned mentioned in the suttas, Ācariya Ānanda says that they should be understood only as applying to a series of dhammas. He argues that if they apply to a momentary dhamma, then the sutta passage will not use the word *paññāyanti* (are known), which verb clearly implies that they are observable. If they are intended to be applicable to a momentary dhamma, then since such a dhamma is not empirically observable, the characteristics themselves will not be observable.[1090] Again, he argues that the third characteristic, change-in-continuance (*ṭhitassa aññathatta*), means the difference between two stages (*pubbāparavisesa*) that cannot be predicated of a momentary dhamma, and the reason given is identical with the one given by the Sautrāntikas for rejecting alteration of a momentary dharma.[1091] It may be argued here that this is the mainstream Theravāda view as well. However, there is this situation to be noted. According to the mainstream view, although the third characteristic (*ṭhitassa aññathatta*) is called decay (= change), it is said to be only a figurative expression for the moment of duration. On the other hand, Ācariya Ānanda dissociates from this interpretation by maintaining that the third characteristic should be understood not in a figurative sense but in its literal sense to mean change-in-continuance."[1092]

It will be noticed that Ācariya Ānanda's view is similar to what the Sautrāntikas, too, say on this matter. The only difference between the two versions is this: the Sautrāntikas deny the static phase of all dharmas whether they are mental or material. On the other hand, Ācariya Ānanda denies the moment of duration only to mental dhammas. The reason for this, as we saw, is that the Theravāda theory of sense perception is based on the view that the lifespan of matter is longer than that of mind. It is this circumstance that seems to have prevented those who held the dissent view from denying the moment of duration to material dhammas as well.[1093]

One subcommentary draws our attention to a criticism of the dissent view, made by Ācariya Jotipāla and Ācariya Dhammapāla, which is as follows. Although a single dhamma is the basis of both origination and dissolution, the moment of origination is different from the moment of dissolution. While the moment of origination has the nascent phase as its basis, the moment of dissolution has the cessant phase as its basis. It is necessary, therefore, to assume that even in a single dhamma the nascent phase is separate (*bhinna*) from its cessant phase. Otherwise it will come to mean that while one dhamma originates some other dhamma comes to cessation. Since there is a cessant phase, there should also be a phase facing cessation (*nirodhābhimukhāvatthā*). This is what we call (the moment of) duration, which may also be called decay (as it manifests itself as the lapse of newness/lapse of the moment of origination).[1094] The question is then raised as to why the moment of duration is not mentioned in the suttas. This we are told is due to a practical reason: it is the practice followed in the suttas to adopt a method of exposition that conforms to the inclinations of the listeners.[1095] This is precisely what the Sarvāstivādins, too, say on this matter: it was in order to create dispassion on the part of the disciples toward all conditioned phenomena that it was deemed proper not to mention duration of any conditioned phenomenon.[1096]

In the subcommentary to the *Abhidhammatthasaṅgaha* we find another argument against the denial of momentary duration (*khaṇikaṭṭhiti*): if there is no moment corresponding to duration, then duration becomes another expression only for the series of momentary dhammas (*santatiṭhiti, pabandha-ṭhiti*)—that is, the series itself as duration. But what is called series is, in the final analysis, not something real and ultimate. It is only a conventional expression for a number of momentary dhammas appearing and disappearing in continual succession. Only the momentary dhammas are real and what is called series is a conceptual construct (*paññatti*) with no corresponding objective counterpart. Therefore to maintain that duration is true only of a series means that it applies not to something conditioned but to a conceptual construct. As such, duration loses its significance as representing a characteristic of the conditioned.[1097]

The latest argument in favor of recognizing the duration/presence moment is by the celebrated Burmese Buddhist scholar monk Venerable Ledi Sayadaw. As explained by Venerable Bhikkhu Bodhi in his *Comprehensive Manual of Abhidhamma*, "he regards the moment of presence as the midpoint between the two phases of arising and falling (*udaya-vaya*), just as when a stone is thrown upwards, a moment is needed before it starts falling downwards."[1098] The opposite view says that conditioned phenomena break up as they arise, just as mustard seeds placed on the tips of needles fall to the ground without abiding even for a moment.[1099]

Although the recognition of the duration moment has become the orthodox Theravādin view, the opposite view has behind it a strong precommentarial tradition. In the *Mahāniddesa*, which, as we saw, has the earliest reference to the notion of "momentariness," there is no mention of duration. All that is asserted is that at every moment the conditioned phenomena emerge and break up in continuous succession. As noted earlier, even in the *Yamaka* and the *Kathāvatthu* of the Abhidhamma Piṭaka that allude to a qualified theory of momentariness, mention is made only of origination and cessation. What is more, though there is no doctrine of momentariness in the Pāli suttas, what is emphasized in them is not duration but origination and cessation. Thus we read, for example: All phenomena are of the nature of arising and ceasing (*uppāda-vaya-dhammino*). Having arisen, they cease to be (*uppajjitvā nirujjhanti*).[1100] Whatever is of the nature of origination is of the nature of cessation (*yaṃ kiñ ci samudaya-dhammaṃ sabbaṃ taṃ nirodha-dhammaṃ*).[1101] This is the kind of reflection that leads to emancipation from all clinging.

In these and in many other statements it is the rise and fall of all conditioned things that is stressed and not their duration or subsistence. That anything can have *ṭhiti* or duration is, in fact, denied (*yassa natthi dhuvaṃ ṭhiti*).[1102] The *Paṭisambhidāmagga*, too, says that it is in the sense of rise and fall that impermanence should be understood (*udaya-vaya-ṭṭhena anicca*).[1103] In fact, as we have noted, one subcommentary admits that duration is not mentioned in the Pāli canonical texts (*pāḷiyaṃ*).

This brings us to the third moment in the Theravāda version of momentariness—namely, the moment of dissolution (*bhaṅgakkhaṇa*). It is also called *nirodhakkhaṇa*, the moment of cessation; *vayakkhaṇa*, the moment of extinction; and *antimakkhaṇa*, the final moment.[1104] Over the recognition of this moment, unlike in the case of the moments corresponding to duration and decay, there is obviously no controversy, since it is a fundamental Buddhist teaching that whatever originates must cease to be. What, however, became controversial is whether cessation is something spontaneous or something that needs causes and conditions for it to take place.

Over this issue we have three different explanations. The first is that while mental phenomena cease spontaneously (*ākasmika*), material phenomena (except sound, flame, and so on) require a concourse of external causes for their dissolution. This is the view held by Vātsīputrīyas and Ārya-Sāṃmītīyas.[1105] For, as we have noted, in their view while mental phenomena are momentary, material phenomena have relative duration. The denial of spontaneous dissolution goes against the generally accepted view that origination is necessarily followed by cessation. For what the former view stresses is not the inevitability of cessation but susceptibility to cessation. Hence we find this view criticized by a number of Buddhist schools.[1106] The second explanation is the one attributed to Sarvāstivādins. In their view, although destruction is not due to external causes, yet it is not uncaused. It is caused by the characteristic of destruction, which, as we saw, arises together with the dharma to be destroyed. The third explanation as to whether destruction is spontaneous or not is the one that is common to both Sautrāntikas and Dārṣṭāntikas. In their view cessation of both mental and material dharmas is necessarily spontaneous. Among the many reasons adduced, the most important is that since cessation is the opposite of existence (*abhāva*), it cannot be reckoned as an effect of a cause.[1107] In this connection, the *Saddarśanasamuccaya*, as shown by De la Vallée Poussin, cites a Sautrāntika sūtra where the Buddha says that all references to caused destruction, as references to past and future, time, space, and person, are only a mere designation, a mere convention.[1108]

On this issue the Theravāda position is identical with that of the Dārṣṭāntikas and Sautrāntikas. Dissolution is not due to causes (*vināsassa hi kāraṇa-rahitattā*).[1109] Whatever originates necessarily ceases (*avassaṃ bhijjanti*).[1110] Origination is certainly caused, but dissolution necessarily follows (*nirodhānugatā jāti*), just as the rising sun is coursing toward its own setting.[1111] That dissolution is not caused is recognized in the Theravāda doctrine of conditionality as well. A condition is always defined as a dhamma that assists another dhamma either to originate (*uppattiyā*) or to exist (*ṭhitiyā*), and never to cease.[1112] However, as one subcommentary observes, one could yet speak of caused origination. For whatever dissolves must first originate. Therefore the cause of origination could well be cited as the cause of dissolution as well.[1113]

At this juncture we need to focus our attention on one important aspect of the Theravāda version of momentariness. This refers to the fact that the notion of "momentariness" is not equally extended to both mind and matter. The lifespan of a moment of matter is longer than that of a mind moment. The most important factor that prevented the assignment of equal duration to both can be traced to the theory of conditionality as presented in the *Paṭṭhāna* of the Abhidhamma Piṭaka. Among the twenty-four conditions mentioned here, two are based on the principle that matter is of longer duration than mind. One is the condition by way of pre-nascence (*purejāta-paccaya*). It refers to something that, having arisen first, serves as a condition to something else that arises later. The other is the condition by way of post-nascence (*pacchājāta-paccaya*). It refers to something that, having arisen later, serves as a condition to something else that has arisen earlier.[1114]

Accordingly, these two principles of conditionality cannot operate where the conditioning and the conditioned things have an identical duration. In the first, the condition is always material and what is conditioned thereby is mental. In the second, the condition is always mental and what is conditioned thereby is material. This, in other words, means that the lifespan of matter, whether it is conceived as momentary or otherwise, is necessarily longer than that of mind. As we saw,[1115] it is on the recognition of this difference that the Abhidhamma theory of cognition is based. Hence this difference had to be accommodated in the doctrine of momentariness as well.

Thus in introducing the doctrine of momentariness the *Visuddhimagga* says that the cessation of matter is slow (*dandha-nirodha*) and its transformation is ponderous (*garu-parivatta*), while the cessation of mind is swift (*lahuparivatta*) and its transformation is quick (*khippa-nirodha*).[1116] Accordingly, the duration of matter in relation to mind is calculated to show that during one moment of matter seventeen mind moments arise and cease. The moments of arising and ceasing are temporally equal for both mental and material dhammas. But in the case of material dhammas the moment of presence is longer.[1117] Nevertheless, the presence moment of material dhammas is exceedingly brief (*ati-ittara*).[1118]

Some Theravādin ācariyas did not accept the view that matter is of longer duration than mind in whichever way their relative duration is calculated. This opposite view is based on the observation that the fact of impermanence is universally applicable and that it cannot have two different ways of manifestation (*aniccādibhāva-sāmañña*).[1119] It is also based on a passage in the *Yamaka* of the Abhidhamma Piṭaka on the arising and ceasing of *saṅkhāras*. As mentioned there, "when *kāya-saṅkhāra* arises, together with it arises *citta-saṅkhāra*, and when *kāya-saṅkhāra* ceases, together with it ceases *citta-saṅkhāra*."[1120] Since *kāya-saṅkhāra* means mind-conditioned inhalings and exhalings of breath, and *citta-saṅkhāra* means feelings and perceptions, here we have two categories, one material and the other mental, recognized as arising and ceasing together. This *Yamaka* statement is cited as providing scriptural evidence to show that both mind and matter are of equal duration (*nāma-rūpāni samānāyukāni*).[1121]

However, the mainstream view seeks to interpret the *Yamaka* passage in a different way. It observes that *kāya-saṅkhāra* (the mind-conditioned inhalings and exhalings of breath) arises only at the origination moment of consciousness and never at its moments of presence and cessation. This is said to be the nature (*dhammatā*) of all mind-conditioned material phenomena. Therefore the *kāya-saṅkhāra* that arises together with mind's moment of origination lasts for seventeen mind moments and comes to cessation with the cessation of the seventeenth mind moment. Thus although matter is of longer duration, in the case of mind-conditioned matter its origination and cessation coincide with the origination and cessation of a series of seventeen mind moments.[1122] This explanation, it hardly needs mention, is based on the assumption that the doctrine of momentariness in the form it came to be developed in the Pāli Buddhist exegesis was recognized by the books of the Abhidhamma Piṭaka as well.

More pertinent, however, is the observation made by a subcommentary that if the *Yamaka* has recognized that mind and matter are of equal duration, then the *Paṭṭhāna*, which also belongs to the Abhidhamma

Piṭaka, will not recognize the two conditions by way of pre-nascence and post-nascence. For as we have already noted, these two conditional relations are based on the principle that matter is of longer duration than mind.

The disparity in the duration of mind and matter has other implications as well. Mental dhammas are strong (*balavā*) at their moments of origination and weak (*dubbalā*) at their moments of duration and dissolution. In contrast material dhammas are strong at their moments of duration and weak at their moments of origination and cessation.[1123] Accordingly, it is only at the moment of origination that a mental dhamma can serve as a condition for the origination of any other dhamma, whether it is mental or material. For it is only at this moment that mind is equipped with that specific ability to generate another dhamma (*janaka-sāmatthi-yoga*).[1124] Thus, for instance, what is called mind-originated matter (*citta-samuṭṭhāna-rūpa*) can arise only when the mind is at its moment of origination.[1125] This does not mean that material dhammas do not arise together with mind when the mind is at its moments of presence and dissolution. It only means that if they do arise at these moments they are not conditioned by mind as their generative factor. As noted above, since matter is strong at the moment of presence, it is at this moment, during a cognitive process, that it can cause itself to be known by mind (*pakāsetabbabhāva*).[1126]

An important conclusion drawn from the momentariness of matter is the denial of motion. What we need to remember here is that according to the dhamma theory all ideas of impermanence, motion, and so on, can be predicated only of the dhammas because, as the basic factors of existence, only the dhammas exist in a real and ultimate sense. Hence, as the commentary to the *Vibhaṅga* observes, in the ultimate sense only the *dhātus* (= dhammas) move (*dhātūnaṃ yeva gamanaṃ*).[1127] However, with the development of the doctrine of momentariness even this idea needed redefinition. Momentariness means that the dhammas have no time to move but can only disappear. Dhammas disappear wherever they appear (*yattha yattha ca dhammā uppajjanti tattha tattheva bhijjanti*).[1128] We find this idea first referred to in the commentary to the *Saṃyuttanikāya*, where the term *niruddha* (ceased) is explained as "ceased there itself without moving to another locus" (*desantaram asaṃkamitvā*).[1129] This seems to be the only reference in a Pāli commentary to this theory before it came to be fully articulated in the Pāli subcommentaries.

In addition to momentary being (*khaṇikatā*) another reason given for the denial of motion is called *abyāpāratā* or "nonpervasiveness."[1130] What this seems to mean is that no dhamma can pervade another dhamma so as to blur its identity. And since all motion is applicable only to material dhammas, what is intended by this particular characteristic has to be understood in relation to the material clusters (*rūpakalāpa*), the ultimate units into which all matter is analyzed. As we have noted, each material cluster has its own boundaries well demarcated and what ensures this demarcation is the intervening space between two material clusters (*paricchedākāsa*).[1131] Therefore to admit that any of the material clusters can move is to deny the vacuity between them and to admit the possibility of their mutual pervading.

If there is no movement, how are we to understand the transition of a thing from one locus in space to another (*desantara-saṅkamana*)?[1132] This kind of question is said to be true only in a conventional sense. Strictly speaking, what takes place instead of movement is the successive arising of momentary material dhammas of a given series in adjacent locations (*desantaruppatti*),[1133] giving rise to our ideas of movement. This theory has an antecedent history in the schools of Sanskrit Buddhism. The classic example given is the light of the lamp. The so-called light of the lamp, it is contended, is nothing but a common designation given to an uninterrupted production of a series of flashing points. When the production changes place one says that the light has changed. But in reality, other flames have appeared in another place.[1134] It is very likely that denial of motion is a theory adopted by the Theravādins from Sanskrit Buddhism, a possibility further confirmed by the similarity of the technical terms used to describe it.

18

THE CONDITIONAL RELATIONS

As we saw in the first chapter, the view of reality the Abhidhamma presents is based on the two complementary methods of analysis and synthesis (*bheda-saṅgaha-naya*). The task of analysis is to show that the objects of our ordinary conceptual thought are not substantial entities or irreducible realities. The task of synthesis is to show that the ultimate factors into which they are reducible (= dhammas) are not distinct entities existing in themselves but interdependent nodes in a complex web of relationships. It is in order to accomplish this latter task that the Abhidhamma proposes a theory of conditional relations, a theory set forth in the last (seventh) book of the Abhidhamma Piṭaka.

In the Theravāda sources we find two versions of the doctrine of conditionality. Earlier is the one called *paṭiccasamuppāda*, the doctrine of dependent origination. The principle of dependent origination is expressed by the dictum: "When this exists, that comes to be; [therefore] with the arising of this, that arises" (*imasmiṃ sati idaṃ hoti, imassa uppādā idaṃ uppajjati*). The opposite process of ceasing is expressed as: "When this does not exist, that does not come to be; [therefore] with the cessation of this, that ceases" (*imasmiṃ asati idaṃ na hoti, imassa nirodhā idaṃ nirujjhati*).[1135]

It is this principle of dependent origination that early Buddhism makes use of to explain the causal structure of individual existence. In the Abhidhamma exegesis this principle is defined as "the arising of effects evenly in dependence on a conjunction of conditions" (*paccaya-sāmaggiṃ paṭicca samaṃ phalānaṃ uppādo*).[1136] This, in other words, means that nothing arises from a single cause and nothing arises as a single effect. It is maintained that if in the suttas only one factor is mentioned as the condition for another, it is in order to focus on the most important condition among many others. And if only one effect is mentioned, it is likewise to single out the most important effect among many others.[1137]

The other doctrine of conditionality within the Theravāda tradition, which we propose to examine here, is the one developed by the Abhidhamma. The causal principle involved here is called *paṭṭhāna-naya*, the method of conditional relations. Its purpose is not to substitute the earlier doctrine of dependent origination but to supplement it. Hence in the *Visuddhimagga* we find a combined treatment of both methods of conditionality. In this work, conditional relations of the Abhidhamma doctrine of conditionality are used to explain the relationship between each pair of factors in the twelvefold formula of dependent origination.[1138]

The doctrine of conditionality of the Abhidhamma is an integral part of the dhamma theory and therefore it assumes its significance within its framework. However, its purpose is not to explain the absolute origin of the series of mental and material dhammas into which our world of experience is analyzed. This situation is fully consonant with the early Buddhist doctrine of causality, whose purpose is not to explain the absolute origin and the ultimate direction of the world but to describe the uninterrupted continuity of the saṃsāric process. According to Buddhist teachings, no temporal beginning of the universe is conceivable. Accordingly, the Abhidhamma doctrine of conditionality dissociates itself from all cosmological causal theories that seek to trace the absolute origin of the world process from some kind of uncaused transempirical reality.

There are three postulates that the Abhidhamma doctrine of conditionality recognizes as axiomatic:

1. Nothing arises without the appropriate causes and conditions. It rules out the theory of fortuitous origination (*adhicca-samuppanna*), the theory that rejects all principles of causality and conditionality.[1139]

2. Nothing arises from a single cause. It rules out all theories of a single cause (*ekakāraṇavāda*).[1140] Their rejection means that the Abhidhamma dissociates itself from all monistic theories that seek to explain the origin of the world from a single cause, whether this single cause is conceived as a personal God or an impersonal godhead. It serves as a critique of all metaphysical theories that attempt to reduce the world of experience to an underlying transempirical principle.
3. Nothing arises as a single, solitary phenomenon (*ekassa dhammassa uppatti paṭisedhitā hoti*).[1141] If we elaborate, this should mean that on the basis of a single cause, or on the basis of a multiplicity of causes, or purely due to fortuitous circumstances, there can never be a single effect or a solitary phenomenon.

It is on the rejection of these three views that the Abhidhamma doctrine of conditionality is founded. Their rejection means:

4. From a plurality of causes a plurality of effects takes place. Applied to the dhamma theory this means that a multiplicity of dhammas brings about a multiplicity of other dhammas.

One clear conclusion that emerges from this situation is that dhammas always arise not as solitary phenomena but as clusters. This is true of both mental and material dhammas. This explains why whenever consciousness arises together with it there must arise at least seven mental factors: contact (*phassa*), feeling (*vedanā*), perception (*saññā*), volition (*cetanā*), one-pointedness (*ekaggatā*), psychic life (*arūpa-jīvitindriya*), and attention (*manasikāra*).[1142] No psychic instance can ever occur with less than eight constituents—that is, consciousness and its seven universal concomitants. We thus can see that even the smallest psychic unit or moment of consciousness turns out to be a complex correlational system. In the same way, the smallest unit of matter, called the basic octad (*suddhaṭṭhaka*), is in the final analysis a cluster of eight material factors—namely, the four great material elements and four items of dependent matter: color, odor, taste, and nutritive essence. None of these material factors arises singly because they are necessarily coexistent and positionally inseparable.[1143]

There are two other basic principles behind the Abhidhamma doctrine of conditionality. The first is that no mental or material dhamma can propel itself into existence by its own power. By their very nature, dhammas are completely devoid of own power or own sway (*dhammānaṃ savasavattitābhimāno paṭisedhito hoti*).[1144] This amounts to the rejection of the principle of self-causation. The other is that no mental or material dhamma can be brought into being by a power external to the dhammas either.[1145] This amounts to the rejection of the principle of external causation. The rejection of these two theories means that dhammas alone help other dhammas to arise and persist in being.

Another thing that merits mention here relates to the relationship between the cause (condition) and the effect (the conditioned). The commentaries emphasize that the cause should not be understood as some kind of potential effect. The cause is not "pregnant with the effect" (*na phalena sagabbho*), as the *prakṛti* of the Sāṃkhya philosophy (*Pakativādīnaṃ pakati viya*).[1146] The allusion is to the evolutionary theory of causation (*satkāryavāda*), according to which the effect remains in a latent form in the cause, and therefore the effect is some kind of evolute of the cause. Hence the commentaries observe further that "the cause is not in the effect" (*phale hetu natthi*),[1147] "the effect is empty of the cause" (*hetu-suññaṃ phalaṃ*).[1148] The same idea seems to be expressed by the use of the term *abyāpāra* to describe the relationship between the cause and the effect.[1149] This is explained to mean: "When the condition exists, there is the arising of the effect; when the condition does not exist, the effect ceases to be. Thus the dhammas become causes by the mere fact of their existence. In this way is manifested the fact of abyāpāra."[1150] What this means is that nothing passes from the cause to the effect. In other words, the cause does not pervade the effect.

The Abhidhamma doctrine of conditionality is based on twenty-four kinds of conditional relation. There are three factors involved when one dhamma is related to another dhamma: the first is the conditioning state (*paccaya-dhamma*), the second the conditioned state (*paccayuppanna-dhamma*), the third the conditioning force (*paccaya-satti*). A condition is defined as a dhamma that is helpful (*upakāraka*) for the origination (*uppatti*) or existence (*ṭhiti*) of another dhamma related to it.[1151] This means that when a particular dhamma is activating as a condition, it will cause other dhammas connected to it to arise, or if they have already arisen, it will maintain them in existence. As we shall see in the sequel, there are some conditions that are helpful only for the existence of other dhammas, as for example the post-nascence condition. Some dhammas are helpful only for the origination of other dhammas, as for example the proximity and contiguity conditions. There are others that help other dhammas in both ways, to originate as well as to exist, as for example the root condition.

It will be noticed that the function of causing the cessation is not attributed to any dhamma. The reason is that a dhamma that arises and exists must necessarily come to cessation without the intervention of any causes or conditions. Only origination and existence require causes and conditions, and not cessation. This position is, in fact, consonant with the early Buddhist doctrine of dependent origination (*paticca-samuppāda*), according to which only origination is due to conditions, and not cessation. This is precisely why we do not have the expression "dependent cessation" (*paṭicca-nirodha*).

A conditioned state (*paccayuppanna-dhamma*) is a dhamma that arises or exists in dependence on conditions. The conditioning force (*paccaya-satti*) is that which has efficacy to bring about or accomplish an effect. The conditioning force cannot exist apart from the conditioning state. It is just as the hotness of chili, which is inherent in the chili and cannot exist apart from it. Thus the force and the state possessing the force are not two distinct entities. A dhamma can, in fact, come to possess more than one conditioning force.[1152]

In what follows we will review the twenty-four conditions in the order they are mentioned in the *Paṭṭhāna*, the Abhidhamma Book of Conditional Relations.

Root Condition (*Hetu-Paccaya*)

In the suttas the term *hetu* is used in its literal and general sense to mean cause or reason. It is also used there as a synonymous expression for *paccaya* in the sense of condition. In the Abhidhamma, however, while *paccaya* is used as a general term for condition, the term *hetu* is exclusively reserved to mean roots (*mūla*), the factors that determine the kammic quality of volitional actions. Thus for the Abhidhamma, hetu in the sense of "root" becomes one of the twenty-four paccayas.

There are in all six roots, among which three—greed, hatred, and delusion—are exclusively unwholesome. The other three—nongreed, nonhatred, and nondelusion—are either wholesome or indeterminate. They are wholesome when they are associated with wholesome consciousness and indeterminate when they arise in resultant and functional consciousness. Their role as conditioning states is compared to the roots of a tree in relation to the tree's existence, growth, and stability. They give rise to the conditioned states and make them firm, steady, and strong. In this case, the conditioned states are consciousness and the mental factors associated with the roots and the co-nascent material dhammas. Here material dhammas mean those born of kamma at the moment of rebirth-linking and those born of consciousness (*citta-samuṭṭhāna*) during the course of existence—that is, those involved in purposeful bodily movements (*kāya-viññatti*) and vocal utterance (*vacī-viññatti*).[1153] However, this does not mean that the material dhammas conditioned by the roots become kammically qualifiable. What it means is that they become firmly established due to the impact of the wholesome or unwholesome roots.

Object Condition (*Ārammaṇa-Paccaya*)

The object condition is so called because it causes the conditioned states to arise, taking it as its object. The reference is to the six kinds of sense objects—the visible, sound, smell, taste, touch, and mental objects. Thus its field of operation is so wide as to embrace not only the fundamental components of actuality, called dhammas, but also conceptual constructs that have only a consensual reality. For the definition of the object condition is not based on whether it is real or unreal but whether it could enter the avenue of sense experience as an object of the cognitive process. While the objects of the first five kinds of consciousness belong to the present moment, the mind consciousness can have as its object anything whatever—mental or material; real or conceptual; past, present, or future; or that which is free from time (*kāla-vimutta*).[1154]

Although, as noted above, conceptual constructs that belong to consensual reality could become conditions by way of object, none of them can become that which is conditioned (*paccayuppanna*) in relation to any kind of conditions (*paccaya*). For, if that were so, they too would become components of actuality.[1155]

Predominance Condition (*Adhipati-Paccaya*)

This condition is of two types as object predominance and co-nascence predominance. The first is an extension of the object condition, where it refers to an object that, as a conditioning state, dominates over the mental states that take it as their object. In this case only those objects that have a strong appeal to the individual can become the conditioning state, because of the domineering influence they have on the mind. The second, the co-nascence-predominance, refers to a relation where the conditioning state exercises a dominant influence on the conditioned states, which arise together with it. The conditioning states in this relation are concentrated intention (*chanda*), energy (*viriya*), consciousness (*citta*), and investigation (*vīmaṃsa*). On a given occasion only one of these factors can activate as a condition.[1156] It will be seen that in the first, which is object predominance, the condition is always an object of consciousness. Therefore the condition as object could belong to the past, present, or future. On the other hand, in the case of the second, which is co-nascence-predominance, the condition and what is conditioned thereby are always co-nascent. For here the reference is not to an object of consciousness but to consciousness itself and three mental factors: concentrated intention, energy, and investigation.[1157]

Proximity Condition (*Anantara-Paccaya*) and Contiguity Condition (*Samanantara-Paccaya*)

These two conditions are identical, a fact recognized in the commentarial exegesis as well. They refer to a relation where the conditioning state causes the conditioned state to arise immediately after it has ceased, so that no other state can intervene between them. The two conditions describe the temporal relationship between mental states that arise one after the other. The consciousness and its concomitants that have just ceased are the conditioning states. The consciousness and its concomitants that arise immediately afterward are the conditioned states. This conditional relation highlights two things. One is that between the preceding and the succeeding mental states there is no gap or interstice (*antara*). This in fact is the idea shown by the very name given to this particular conditional relation, for *anantara* means that there is no intervening gap or interstice. The second is that the preceding unit of consciousness, which serves as the condition, gives rise to the succeeding one in such a way that the latter conforms to the former (*anurūpa-cittuppāda-janana-samattho*).[1158] It is this situation that explains why a given process of cognitive events occurs not in a haphazard manner but always in its proper sequence, strictly following the laws of psychological order (*citta-niyāma*). If the proximity and contiguity conditions ensure the occurrence of consciousness in a linear sequence, this also means that two or more units of consciousness do not arise at one and the same time by way of juxtaposition.

Co-Nascence Condition (*Sahajāta-Paccaya*)

This refers to a conditional relation where the condition causes the conditioned state to arise concurrently with it. Here both the condition and what is conditioned thereby occur together. This kind of phenomenon is compared to the flame of a lamp that on arising causes the light, color, and heat to arise together with it. The co-nascence condition operates in the following instances: (a) each mental state for the other mental states (*citta* and *cetasika*) that are associated with it, (b) each mental state in relation to the material phenomena that arise together with it, (c) each of the four great material elements in relation to the other three, (d) each of the four great material elements in relation to the material factors dependent on them, and (e) at the moment of rebirth, the physical base of mind for the resultant (*vipāka*) consciousness and its concomitants.[1159]

Mutuality Condition (*Aññamañña-Paccaya*)

The mutuality condition is an extension of the co-nascence condition, with this difference: here the conditioning state activates reciprocally. If A is a condition by way of co-nascence to B, then at the same time B is a condition by way of co-nascence to A. Both are on a par, supporting each other simultaneously. This is compared to a tripod where each leg supports the other two legs reciprocally so as to maintain the upright position of the tripod. The mutuality condition operates in three different instances: (a) consciousness and mental factors, (b) the four great material elements, and (c) the physical base of mind and the resultant (*vipāka*) consciousness and its concomitants at the moment of rebirth.[1160]

Support Condition (*Nissaya-Paccaya*)

Here the conditioning state causes the conditioned state to arise by serving as its support. The role of the conditioning state is similar to the way the earth supports trees or a canvas a painting. There are two varieties of this condition. The first is co-nascence support (*sahajāta-nissaya*). It is identical in all respects with the co-nascence condition discussed above. The second is pre-nascence support (*purejāta-nissaya*), and it has two subsidiary types. One is base pre-nascence support (*vatthu-purejāta-nissaya*), where base refers to the five physical sense organs and the physical seat of mental activity. During the course of an individual's existence these six physical bases serve as pre-nascence conditions for the consciousness and its concomitants that take them as the material support for their arising. At the moment of rebirth, however, the physical base of mental activity and the resultant mental states arise simultaneously and support each other as co-nascence and mutuality conditions. Immediately after the moment of rebirth the physical base of mind begins to activate as a pre-nascence condition for the mind, mind consciousness, and their concomitants. The second variety of pre-nascence support is called object pre-nascence support (*vatthārammaṇa-purejāta-nissaya*). This refers to a relational situation where consciousness arises with its physical basis as its support and object as well. Here we find a conditional relation where one and the same thing becomes a base as well as an object in relation to a single unit of consciousness.[1161]

Decisive-Support Condition (*Upanissaya-Paccaya*)

This condition is so called because it supports what is conditioned in such manner that it is a powerful inducement or a decisive means. The commentary says that just as *āyasa* (depression) is called *upāyāsa* (despair), so a strong *nissaya* (support) is called *upanissaya* (decisive support).[1162] However, decisive-support condition is not a subordinate variety of the support condition. The support condition, as we have noticed, refers to a condition either pre-nascent or co-nascent in relation to what is conditioned thereby. On the other hand, decisive-support condition can never be co-nascent.[1163]

This condition is of three kinds. The first is object-decisive support (*ārammaṇūpanissaya*) condition. It is another variety of object condition, but with this qualitative difference: only exceptionally desirable or important objects that cause consciousness and its concomitants to apprehend them are included in this category. The second is called proximity-decisive support (*anantarūpanissaya*) condition. It is identical with the proximity condition that explains the linear succession of mental states, but for this difference: here the preceding mental states cause the immediately succeeding mental states to arise because of their strong dependence on the cessation of the preceding conditioning states. The third is called natural-decisive support condition (*pakatūpanissaya*). It is a wide-ranging relation that could embrace as its conditioning factors all past mental and material dhammas that exercise a strong influence for the arising at a subsequent time of consciousness and its concomitants. This conditional relation seeks to explain the impact of previous desires and tendencies as motivating factors for subsequent acts.[1164]

Pre-nascence and Post-nascence Conditions (*Purejāta-* and *Pacchājāta-Paccayas*)

Pre-nascence condition refers to a relation where something that has arisen earlier becomes a support to something else that arises later, and conversely post-nascence condition refers to a relation where something that, having arisen later, becomes a support to something else that has arisen earlier. The first is like the father who supports the son, and the latter is like the son who supports the father. These two conditions, because of their temporal dissimilarity, can apply only to relations between mind and matter. Since the lifespan of matter is longer than that of mind, a material dhamma that arises earlier can become a pre-nascence condition in relation to a mental dhamma that arises later. Similarly, a mental dhamma that arises later can become a post-nascence condition in relation to a material dhamma that has arisen earlier.

There are two types of pre-nascence condition: base pre-nascence (*vatthu-purejāta*) and object pre-nascence (*ārammaṇa-purejāta*). The former refers to the five physical sense organs in relation to the five kinds of consciousness named after them and the heart base in relation to mind and mind consciousness. If each of them is recognized as a prenascence condition, it is because at the time it becomes a condition it has passed its nascent phase and has reached the static phase. Their special role as conditions is due to their very fact of prenascence, for material dhammas, unlike mental dhammas, have the capacity to become conditions only when they have come to their static phase after passing their nascent phase. As for the heart base at the time of rebirth-linking, its relation to the mental states that arise concurrently with it is not one of pre-nascence, because at this moment the heart base and the resultant consciousness and its concomitants arise simultaneously as co-nascence and mutuality conditions. As for the object-prenascence condition, each of the first five sense objects serves as a condition by way of pre-nascence for the consciousness and its concomitants that arise in a given sense-door cognitive process. The object-prenascence condition does also include the eighteen varieties of real material dhammas when they become objects of consciousness and its concomitants in a mind-door process.[1165]

It will thus be seen that all the material dhammas considered as real (*nipphanna-rūpa*) become pre-nascence conditions in relation to the genesis of consciousness either by way of base (*vatthu*) or by way of object (*ārammaṇa*).

In the conditional relation by way of postnascence, the condition is always mental. Consciousness and its concomitants that arise subsequently become postnascence conditions for the material dhammas of the body that have arisen earlier. The reference here is to material dhammas born of all the four generative conditions: consciousness, kamma, nutriment, and temperature. A moment of mind, unlike a moment of matter, is strong at its nascent phase. Therefore it is at their nascent phase, that is, at the submoment of arising, that mental states become conditions by way of postnascence to material dhammas that have arisen earlier.

The prenascence and postnascence conditions, it may be noted, do not apply to relations between mind and mind. This is because mental dhammas arise either simultaneously or in immediate contiguity. If they arise simultaneously, they must disappear simultaneously; if they arise in immediate contiguity, then the immediately preceding ones have to disappear before the immediately succeeding ones can appear. Therefore a mental dhamma cannot serve as a pre-nascence or post-nascence condition in relation to another mental dhamma.

However, a question may be raised here. If preceding mental states can serve as conditions by way of proximity (*anantara*) and contiguity (*samanantara*) to the succeeding mental states, is it not possible to consider the former as pre-nascence conditions as well in relation to the latter? What should not be overlooked here is that although the pre-nascence condition arises earlier, it is at the present time that it activates as a condition. This is precisely why the commentaries take special care to define the pre-nascence condition as something that, having arisen first, helps something else in the present time (*paṭhamataraṃ uppajjitvā vattamānabhāvena upakārako dhammo purejāta-paccayo*).[1166]

Repetition Condition (*Āsevana-Paccaya*)

The repetition condition refers to a conditional relation that obtains between mind and mind only. Its function is to cause its conditioned states to gain more and more proficiency, so that the succeeding states come to possess greater and greater power and efficiency. "It is just as in learning by heart through constant repetition the later recitation becomes gradually easier and easier."[1167] The conditioning states in this relation are the mental dhammas that occur in the javana moments in a cognitive process. It is at the javana stage of the cognitive process that the object comes to be fully apprehended and it is also at this stage that the kammic quality of the consciousness is determined as wholesome, unwholesome, or indeterminate.[1168] Therefore the energy or proficiency that each succeeding event comes to acquire by way of repetition condition is evaluated in terms of ethical or kammic quality. In this particular conditional relation the last javana moment does not function as a repetition condition because it has no successor to impart its strength, although it remains conditioned by the preceding javana moment. Again, although the first javana moment activates as a repetition condition, since it has no javana as a predecessor it is not conditioned by way of repetition.

Kamma Condition (*Kamma-Paccaya*)

The kamma condition is of two kinds. The first is called co-nascent kamma condition (*sahajāta*) because that which is conditioned by it arises simultaneously with it. The reference here is to *cetanā* or volition, which, as we have noted earlier, is one of the universal concomitants of consciousness. As a kamma condition, volition coordinates and causes the accompanying mental states to perform their respective functions. It also causes to arise together with it material dhammas appropriate to the accompanying mental states. The implication is that the mental states and the material dhammas in question are determined, fashioned, and impelled by the force of volition (*cetanā*). The other kind of kamma condition is called asynchronous (*nānākhaṇika*) because in this case there is a temporal difference between the conditioning state and what is conditioned by it. Here the conditioning state is a past wholesome or unwholesome volition, and the conditioned states are resultant (*vipāka*) consciousness, its concomitants, and the material dhammas born of kamma (*kamma-samuṭṭhāna*).[1169]

Result Condition (*Vipāka-Paccaya*)

The conditioning factors in this conditional relation are the mental states, which arise as the results of kamma. The conditioned factors are the selfsame mental states and the material dhammas that have arisen together with them. The role of the result condition is to exert a tranquilizing influence on the conditioned states and to make them passive and quiescent. For the results of kamma are said to arise effortlessly (*nirussāha*) and not as something propelled by any external force. It should be noted here that while the mental states that arise as results of kamma are result conditions with respect to each other, the co-nascent material dhammas, which are conditioned by them, do not in turn activate as a conditioning factor. The reciprocity is only between the mental states.[1170]

Here the term *vipāka* is used to denote only mental states that arise as results of kamma. On the other hand, material dhammas brought about by kamma are called not vipāka but kamma-originated matter (*kamma-samuṭṭhāna-rūpa*). This restricted meaning of the term *vipāka* appears to be confined to the Theravāda tradition. For we find in the *Kathāvatthu* four controversies where the Theravādins object to extending the denotation of the term *vipāka* beyond the mental states that arise as results of kamma. Thus in response to the Mahāsaṅghikas, who maintain that the sense organs are vipāka, the Theravādins argue thus: "The *vipāka* is a matter of feeling—pleasant, painful or neutral; it is conjoined with feeling of these three kinds; it is conjoined with mental contact, feeling, perception, volition, and thought; it goes with a mental object; [and] with it go adverting, attention, volition, anticipation, and aiming. Are the five sense organs anything of this kind?"[1171] Thus for the Theravādins, vipāka is essentially a subjective experience. However, this does not mean that they object to the recognition of the sense organs as resulting from kamma. It only means that in the terminology of the Theravāda Abhidhamma vipāka is given a restricted denotation. In fact, the commentary observes that the Theravāda argument is meant to show that the usage (*vohāra*) of the term *vipāka* does not apply to rūpa-dhammas resulting from kammic fruition.[1172] This also explains why the Theravādins raise no objection against the Mahāsaṅghikas' statement that manāyatana, the mind base, could be vipāka. It is also in conformity to this tradition that in the *Dhammasaṅgaṇi*, while the four aggregates representing the mental dhammas are described as vipāka, the material dhammas are separately mentioned with the expression *kammassa kaṭattā*.[1173] Most probably it is this expression that later gave rise to *kaṭattā-rūpa*, which in the *Paṭṭhāna* became the standard term for kamma-born materiality (*kamma-samuṭṭhāna-*

rūpa).[1174] It must also be noted here that the materiality that comes into being through the action of kamma does not obtain outside the body of a living being. This is a clear conclusion arising from the fact that among the material dhammas only the first five sense organs, the two faculties of sex, the material life faculty, the heart base, and the other material dhammas inseparably associated with them are recognized as kamma originated.[1175]

Nutriment Condition (*Āhāra-Paccaya*)

The conditioning factors in this relation are the four kinds of nutriment on which all living beings subsist. The four factors are the nutritive essence of material food (*kabaliṅkāra-āhāra*), sensory contact (*phassa*), mental volition (*mano-sañcetanā*), and consciousness (*viññāṇa*). Here the term "nutriment" is used in its widest sense to include both material nutriment (*rūpāhāra*) and mental nutriment (*nāmāhāra*) that govern both biological and mental life. The four factors are called food (*āhāra*) because they nourish, maintain, and keep going the empiric individuality, which thus becomes a nutrimental process, a process of alimentation (*āhāraṭṭhitika*). In their role as conditions, while material nutriment is related to the physical body, mental nutriment consisting of sensory contact, mental volition, and consciousness is related to the mental and material dhammas that arise together with it.[1176]

Faculty Condition (*Indriya-Paccaya*)

The faculty condition is like the predominance condition (*adhipati-paccaya*) in the sense that it exercises a dominating influence over the things related to it. There is, however, this difference to be noted: while the predominance condition wields supreme control over all the co-nascent mental states and material dhammas, a faculty condition's control is restricted to its own respective sphere. The predominance condition "is compared to a king who, as head of state, lords over all his ministers, while the faculties are compared to the ministers who govern their own districts but cannot interfere with the others."[1177] This should explain why there could be more than one faculty activating in a single unit of consciousness while only one predominance condition is present at any given time. There are in all twenty-two faculties. Among them only twenty are elevated to the level of faculty conditions. The first five faculty conditions are the physical sense organs, which function as prenascence conditions for the five kinds of consciousness named after them. Their position as faculty conditions is due to the fact that as five varieties of sensitive material dhammas, receptive and reactive to sense data, they determine the efficiency of the consciousnesses that take them as their bases. That is to say, the relative strength or weakness of the sense organ reflects on the consciousness.

The next two faculties are the faculty of masculinity and the faculty of femininity. Though faculties, these two are not recognized as faculty conditions because of the following reasons. It is true that they are responsible for the manifestation of such differences between the male and the female as regards their physical appearance, marks, traits, and deportment. However, they do not perform any of the three functions of a condition—namely, producing, supporting, and maintaining. Another reason given is that at the initial stages of embryonic development, although these two faculties are present they do not perform their respective functions of bringing about the manifestation of sex distinctions. Since they remain dormant and inactive at this stage they are not entitled to be recognized as faculty conditions, because at no time does a factor that can rightly be called a faculty condition remain dormant and inactive.[1178]

Next in the list is life faculty (*jīvitindriya*). It is twofold as mental (*arūpa*) and physical (*rūpa*). The first is the factor that stabilizes and sustains every type of consciousness and its co-nascent mental factors. It is therefore counted as one of the seven universal concomitants of consciousness and as a condition by way of faculty to all consciousness and their concomitants. The second, the material life faculty, is the factor that stabilizes and sustains kamma-originated matter—namely, the first five sense organs, the two faculties of sex, the physical base of mind and mind consciousness, and all other material dhammas inseparably associated with them. It is in relation to these instances of kamma-originated materiality that this life faculty functions as a faculty condition. The remaining faculties (and the mental life faculty discussed above) are all mental.

The first among them is mind faculty. It is another expression for the whole of consciousness—that is, the eighty-nine classes of consciousness. The next five faculties are the five varieties of feeling: pleasure (*sukha*), pain (*dukkha*), joy (*somanassa*), displeasure (*domanassa*), and equanimity (*upekkhā*). Next come the five spiritual faculties: faith (*saddhā*), energy (*viriya*), mindfulness (*sati*), concentration (*samādhi*), and wisdom (*paññā*). Among the last three faculties, the first is the faculty "I will know the unknown" (*aññātaññassāmītindriya*). It is the knowledge of the path of stream-entry. The second is the faculty of one who has final knowledge (*aññātāvindriya*). It is the knowledge of the fruit of arahantship. The third is the faculty of final knowledge (*aññindriya*). It is the six intermediate kinds of supramundane knowledge. These immaterial faculties are each a co-nascence faculty condition for the mental states associated with them and the material dhammas that arise simultaneously with them.[1179]

Jhāna Condition (*Jhāna-Paccaya*)

Here the word *jhāna* is not used in its usual sense to mean higher reaches of mind attained in meditative absorption. As a conditioning factor jhāna here means close contemplation (*upanijjhāyana*) of an object. It refers to the following seven factors—namely, initial application (*vitakka*), sustained application (*vicāra*), zest (*pīti*), one-pointedness (*ekaggatā*), joy (*somanassa*), displeasure (*domanassa*), and equanimity (*upekkhā*). The above-mentioned seven mental states in their capacity as jhana conditions enable the mind to closely contemplate its object. Among them, while displeasure is invariably unwholesome, the other six could be wholesome, unwholesome, or indeterminate. They all have as their conditioned states the consciousness and the mental factors associated with them and the material dhammas that arise together with them.[1180]

Path Condition (*Magga-Paccaya*)

The path condition is so called because it relates to the conditioned state by causing it to function as a means of reaching a particular destination. There are twelve factors that function as path conditions: right view (*sammā-diṭṭhi*), right intention (*sammā-saṃkappa*), right speech (*sammā-vācā*), right action (*sammā-kammanta*), right livelihood (*sammā-ājīva*), right effort (*sammā-vāyāma*), right mindfulness (*sammā-sati*), right concentration (*sammā-samādhi*), wrong view (*micchā-diṭṭhi*), wrong intention (*micchā-saṃkappa*), wrong effort (*micchā-vāyāma*), and wrong concentration (*micchā-samādhi*). These twelve are called path factors, though not because they lead to the same destination. The first eight lead to the realization of blissful states and the final goal of nibbāna. The last four, in contrast, lead to birth in woeful states. The states conditioned by the path factors are all types of rooted consciousness, the mental factors associated with them, and the material dhammas arising together with them.[1181]

Association Condition (*Sampayutta-Paccaya*)

This is another conditional relation that obtains only among mental states (consciousness and mental factors). It refers to a mental state that causes other mental states to arise together with it in such a way as to remain in inseparable association with them. The mental states so associated necessarily share the following four characteristics: a common physical basis—that is, a common physical sense organ or the physical basis of mental activity; a common object; a simultaneous origination; and a simultaneous cessation. However, this close association between mental dhammas does not mean that they have combined themselves into one (*ekībhāvagata*). The correct situation is that from the ultimate point of view (*paramatthena*), they are separate from one another and yet appear as completely united into one (*ekībhāvagatā viya*).[1182] Material dhammas cannot be related to one another in the same way as mental dhammas because of the obvious reason that they cannot share the four characteristics commonly shared by the mental dhammas. Nor can mind and matter be so related, for a mental dhamma and a material dhamma can have in common only one of the above four characteristics, either simultaneous origination or simultaneous cessation. If they arise simultaneously, that is, at the moment of rebirth-linking, then they cannot cease simultaneously.

If they cease simultaneously, then they could not have arisen simultaneously. This is based on the theory that the lifespan of matter is longer than that of mind.[1183]

Dissociation Condition (*Vippayutta-Paccaya*)

As observed above, the relationship between mind and matter is not one of association (*sampayutta*). Accordingly, their relationship is described as one of dissociation (*vippayutta*). This is in view of the particular characteristics that separate the two categories as "mind" and "matter." The two categories exist together but remain separate, like a mixture of water and oil. However, what is described as "dissociated" (*vippayutta*) is not necessarily a dissociation condition (*vippayutta-paccaya*). Thus although all the material dhammas are dissociated in relation to what is mental, not every one of them is postulated as a condition by way of dissociation in relation to mental dhammas. The dissociation condition functions in three different ways: as co-nascence (*sahajāta*), post-nascence (*pacchājata*), and pre-nascence (*purejāta*). Thus at the moment of rebirth-linking the physical seat of mental activity and the mental states that arise simultaneously with it serve as dissociation conditions to each other by way of co-nascence. At this moment the mental states are a dissociation condition for the other kinds of kamma-born material dhammas as well. In the course of life, consciousness and mental factors function as dissociation conditions for the material dhammas of the body by way of post-nascence. The five physical sense organs and the physical seat of mental activity function as dissociation conditions for the seven consciousness elements by way of pre-nascence. One question that arises here is why the physical objects of consciousness are not so recognized. As an answer to this, it is observed that when consciousness springs up, it springs up as if it were "issuing forth" (*nikkhantā viya*) from within its physical base. Thus there is some kind of close association between consciousness and its physical base, an association not observable between consciousness and its object. This shows that when something is related to something else by way of dissociation, there is in fact a close association between them. However, this kind of association is not so pronounced as the association between mental states.[1184]

Presence Condition (*Atthi-Paccaya*) and Nondisappearance Condition (*Avigata-Paccaya*)

These two conditions refer to the same kind of conditional relation. Here the term "presence" or "nondisappearance" refers to the presence or nondisappearance of both the conditioning and the conditioned states at the time when the former activates as a condition in relation to the latter. It is not necessary for the two states related by this condition to arise together or cease together. All that is necessary is for them to overlap at a time when the conditioning state can support the conditioned state in some way. According to this definition, the presence/nondisappearance condition can embrace the pre-nascence, post-nascence, and co-nascence conditions. For, as we have noted, although pre-nascence condition arises earlier and the post-nascence condition later than the states to be conditioned by them, both activate as conditions at the present moment.[1185]

Absence Condition (*Natthi-Paccaya*) and Disappearance Condition (*Vigata-Paccaya*)

These two conditions also refer to the same kind of relationship. Absence condition is so called because its absence provides an opportunity (*okāsadāna*) for the presence of its conditioned state. Likewise, disappearance condition is so called because its disappearance provides an opportunity for the appearance of its conditioned state. Both conditions describe the linear sequence of consciousness where the immediately preceding one disappears before the emergence of the immediately succeeding one. The states related by these two conditions are thus identical with the states related by the proximity and contiguity conditions.[1186]

This brings us to an end of our survey of the twenty-four conditions. The survey should show that a given thing can become, at one and the same time, a condition to something else in different ways. Thus, for example, the visual organ becomes a condition in relation to visual consciousness by way of support (*nissaya*), pre-nascence (*purejāta*), faculty (*indriya*), dissociation (*vippayutta*), presence (*atthi*), and nondisappearance (*avigata*). We need to remember here that although the pre-nascence condition arises earlier than visual consciousness, it is at the present moment (*vijjamānakkhaṇe*) that it activates as a condition.

In the *Abhidhammatthasaṅgaha* of Ācariya Anuruddha we find these twenty-four conditions arranged into six groups according to the way they structure the relations between the different kinds of dhammas. The six groups include relations between (1) mind and mind, (2) mind and mind-and-matter, (3) mind and matter, (4) matter and mind, (5) mind-and-matter and concepts and mind, (6) mind-and-matter and mind-and-matter.

There are six conditions that operate exclusively in relations between mind and mind: proximity, contiguity, absence, disappearance, repetition, and association. The first four, as we have seen, explain the conditionality of mental states that arise in linear sequence, the preceding yielding place to the succeeding, without leaving any gaps between them. The fifth shows how they arise in the same way, but while imparting greater proficiency to the succeeding mental states. The sixth explains the conditionality of mental states that arise simultaneously to constitute a cognitive act having a common basis, a common object, a simultaneous origination, and a simultaneous cessation. These six kinds of conditional relations, as we have shown, cannot activate either between mind and matter or between matter and matter.

There are five conditions that operate in relations between mind on the one hand and mind-and-matter on the other. They are roots, jhāna, path, kamma, and result. Here, except for the asynchronous kamma condition (the second kamma condition), in the conditional relations mind becomes a conditioning state to mind-and-matter when they are co-nascent. In the case of the asynchronous kamma condition, there is a temporal gap between the condition and the conditioned.

There is only one condition where mind becomes the conditioning state exclusively in relation to matter—namely, the condition by way of postnascence. This is because of the difference in duration between mind and matter. Since the duration of matter is longer than that of mind, in any relationship established by the postnascence condition the conditioning state has to be the mind and the conditioned state has to be matter.

Similarly, there is only one condition where matter becomes the conditioning state exclusively in relation to mind—namely, the condition by way of prenascence. This is, again, because of the relative duration of mind and matter. Since the lifespan of mind is shorter than that of matter, in any relationship established by the pre-nascence condition the conditioning state has to be matter and the conditioned state has to be mind.

There are only two ways in which mind-and-matter and concepts (*paññatti*) operate as conditions in relation to mind. These are the two conditions by way of object and decisive support. The object condition, as noted earlier, can embrace not only mental and material dhammas but also mental constructs as concepts (*paññatti*).

Although the decisive-support condition has three types—object-decisive support, proximity-decisive support, and natural-decisive support—it is only as object-decisive support that concepts can become conditions in relation to mental states. The object-decisive support, it may be repeated here, is an extension of the object condition. It will thus be seen that although concepts have no objective reality, they can enter conditional relations only as object conditions. They cannot become a condition in any other way. Nor can they become the conditioned in relation to any kind of condition.

There are nine ways in which mind-and-matter become conditions in relation to mind-and-matter: by way of predominance, conascence, mutuality, support, nutriment, faculty, dissociation, presence, and nondisappearance.[1187]

Another division of the twenty-four conditions is the one based on the time of their occurrence. On this basis there are four groups. The first group includes those that function as conditions simultaneously with the conditioned (*samāna-kāla*), in other words, those that activate in the present (*paccuppanna*). This group includes fifteen conditions: roots, conascence, mutuality, support, prenascence, postnascence, result, nutriment, faculty, jhāna, path, association, dissociation, presence, nondisappearance. The inclusion of prenascence and postnascence in this group is because of the following reason. Although they arise at a time before or after what is to be conditioned by them arises, yet they activate as conditions in the present moment. At the time they activate as conditions, the conditions as well as the conditioned coexist. The second group refers to those conditions that arise and activate in the past (*atīta*). This group includes five conditions: proximity, contiguity, repetition, absence, and disappearance. These five conditions refer, in one way or another, to the linear sequence of mental states, where the immediately preceding disappears, yielding place to the immediately succeeding. The third group, if it can be called a group, includes only one: the kamma condition. As conascent kamma condition, it activates in the present in relation to what is conditioned by it. As asynchronous kamma condition, it is always a past wholesome or unwholesome volition that becomes the conditioning state. The fourth group includes those conditions that belong to the three divisions of time—past, present, and future (*tekālika*)—as well as those that are independent of time (*kāla-vimutta*). Here, those that belong to the three divisions of time are the mental and material dhammas that become objects of consciousness. While the objects of the first five kinds of consciousness are always present, the objects of mind consciousness can belong to any of the three periods of time. The conditions that are independent of time are nibbāna and mental constructs (*paññatti*). Both become objects of mind consciousness. Since nibbāna is the unconditioned dhamma, it transcends time. Mental constructs are independent of time because, unlike dhammas, they are not brought into being by conditions and as such they have no objective counterparts of their own.[1188]

Our review of the twenty-four conditions should show that some conditions are repeated under different names. We refer here to the three pairs: (1) proximity and contiguity, (2) presence and nondisappearance, and (3) absence and disappearance. Each of these pairs, as we have noted, contains two identical conditions. If we eliminate what is repeated we are left with twenty-one conditions. Why the number was increased to twenty-four could perhaps be explained in the context of the schematic order of exposition followed in the *Paṭṭhāna* in presenting the doctrine of conditionality. The number twenty-four, unlike the number twenty-one, is easily amenable to divisions, classifications, and combinations. Therefore it is very likely that the number of conditions was increased from twenty-one to twenty-four in order to facilitate their schematic presentation.

APPENDIX

THERAVĀDA AND VIBHAJJAVĀDA

Strangely enough, the terms *theravāda* and *vibhajjavāda* occur in the Pāli suttas, which were compiled long before there emerged a school of Buddhist thought that came to be known by these two terms. We find the term *theravāda* in the Pāli suttas that relate the bodhisatta's meeting with Ālāra the Kālāma and Uddaka the son of Rāma. After having learned the teaching imparted by them, the bodhisatta declared his mastery of their teaching by using the two words *ñāṇavāda* and *theravāda*.[1189] Obviously in this particular context the term *theravāda* does not occur in the sense of "doctrine of the elders." It occurs in a sense that according to its commentarial gloss means "profession of certainty of conviction" (*theravādan ti thirabhāva-vādaṃ*).[1190] In the same way the other word *ñāṇavāda*, which occurs together with *theravāda*, means "profession of knowledge" (*ñāṇavādan ti jānāmī ti vādaṃ*). Here both terms are used to emphasize the bodhisatta's thorough grasp of what was taught by Ālāra the Kālāma and Uddaka, the son of Rāma.

On the other hand, the term *vibhajjavāda* occurs in a more technical sense to mean a qualified answer, an analytical explanation, or a statement of conditional assertion. It is often contrasted with *ekaṃsavāda*, which means an unqualified answer or a categorical statement either in the affirmative or in the negative.[1191] But as another name for Theravāda, what does Vibhajjavāda really mean? Under what historical circumstances, due to what doctrinal reasons, if any, and in which period in the history of Buddhist thought did these two terms become mutually convertible?

Now the identification of Theravāda with Vibhajjavāda can be traced to the traditional accounts of the Third Buddhist Council as presented in the *Mahāvaṃsa* and the two commentaries to the *Vinaya* and the *Kathāvatthu*, and not to its earlier version as recorded in the *Dīpavaṃsa*.[1192] The accounts given in the three works mentioned first are more or less the same in content and are couched in more or less the same language. They all begin with a continuous narration of a series of episodes culminating in the main event. These involve a detailed account of the life of the Venerable Moggaliputta Tissa Thera, who presided at the Council; the conversion of King Asoka to Buddhism and his many acts of beneficence and lavish gifts to the Saṅgha; the entry into the Dispensation (*sāsana*) of heretics who masqueraded as Buddhist monks, declaring their own doctrines as the true word of the Buddha; the postponement of the *Uposatha* ceremony for a period of six years because of the heretics within the Saṅgha; and the king's abortive attempt at reconciliation through his minister Mahādeva, as well as the remorse felt by the king over this act, his meeting with the Venerable Moggaliputta Tissa Thera, who declares that the king has no moral responsibility over this act, and the Thera's instruction to the king on the teaching of the Buddha for seven consecutive days at the Royal Park.

> On the seventh day the King Asoka had the community of monks assembled at Asokārāma. He got an enclosure of screens prepared and took his seat within this enclosure. Getting the monks to group themselves according to the divergent views they professed, the King summoned each group of monks in turn and asked this question: "What was the Perfectly Enlightened One a teacher of" (*Kiṃvādī Sammā Sambuddho*)? In response to this question, those who believed in eternalism replied that the Buddha was an advocate of eternalism. Those who believed in qualified eternalism replied that the Buddha was an advocate of qualified eternalism. Likewise, those who propounded theories of finiteness and infinitude, the eel-wrigglers, casuits, those who professed theories of conscious existence, nonconscious existence, neither conscious nor nonconscious existence, annihila-

> tionists and those who professed nibbāna of this life also replied according to the views they held. It was not difficult for the King, who had already learnt the Dhamma, to realize that they were not Buddhist monks but heretics who belonged to other persuasions. The King gave them white garments and expelled them, all sixty thousand, from the community of monks. Next the King summoned the remaining monks and asked the same question: "What was the Perfectly Enlightened One a teacher of?" They said in reply: "Great King, He was *Vibhajjavādī*." Receiving such a reply, the King, for confirmation, asked the Venerable Moggaliputta Tissa Thera: "Was the Perfectly Enlightened One *Vibhajjavādī*?" "Yes, great King," replied the Thera. Thereupon King Asoka told Venerable Moggaliputta Tissa Thera: "Venerable Sir, the Dispensation is now pure, let the fraternity of monks perform the *Uposatha*." At this assembly, numbering sixty thousand monks, the Venerable Moggaliputta Tissa Thera recited the treatise called *Kathāvatthu* in order to refute the heretical views. Even as the Elders, Kassapa the Senior, and Yasa the son of Kākandaka rehearsed the Dhamma and Vinaya, he, too, selected a thousand monks from those numbering sixty thousand who were well versed in the learning of the threefold knowledge and rehearsed the Dhamma and Vinaya. Thus rehearsing the Dhamma and Vinaya, he purified the Dispensation of all stains and held the Third Council.[1193]

It will be seen that the most important, in fact the very pivotal, word in this account is *vibhajjavādī*, which we have left untranslated. A proper interpretation of this word will not only show why the Theravāda came to be called Vibhajjavāda but would also shed much light on the actual causes that led to the Third Council.

The first-ever rendering of *vibhajjavāda* into English could perhaps be traced to George Turnour's translation of the *Mahāvaṃsa* (1868), where we find it rendered as "the religion of investigated truth."[1194] In *A Dictionary of the Pāli Language* (1875), R. C. Childers explained the term as the "religion of logic or reason." Childers also took into consideration its earlier rendering into English by George Turnour, for he observes that this latter rendering is not inappropriate.[1195] One of the earliest to endorse Childers's interpretation was Wilhelm Geiger, who in his *Mahāvaṃsa* translation observes that it renders the sense of the term very appropriately.[1196] Since then we find this interpretation recognized and sometimes developed on to mean that the Buddha always followed the analytical method and therefore Buddhism could rightly be called a doctrine of analysis.[1197]

In this appendix we propose to show that this particular interpretation of Vibhajjavāda, when it stands as another name for Theravāda, does not appear to be corroborated either by textual evidence or by historical data. Its fallacy, it seems to us, stems from the failure to take into consideration the textual and doctrinal context in which this term assumes its significance. For, the term does not lend itself to a correct interpretation when it is sought to be explained in isolation from its proper frame of reference.

As already noted, we can trace the reasons that led to the use of the term *vibhajjavāda* as another expression for Theravāda to the traditional account of the Third Council. It is strange, however, that a word of such significance should have been left unexplained in the works where this account occurs. This situation is perhaps responsible for there being more than one explanation in the Pāli subcommentaries as to why the Buddha is *vibhajjavādī*. The subcommentary to the *Mahāvaṃsa* explains it as: "[The Buddha is] *vibhajjavādī* because he analyzes [the individual being] into aggregates" (*khandhānaṃ vibhajjakattā vibhajjavādī*).[1198] We are not sure whether this refers to the analysis of the individual being into aggregates or to the analysis of the aggregates, in turn, into dhammas, the basic factors of empirical reality as presented in the Abhidhamma. In whichever way we interpret it, it is on the importance of analysis that the emphasis is laid.

It is of course true that analysis plays an important role in the Buddhist teachings both of the Pāli suttas and of the Abhidhamma. However, it is equally true that no less important a role is played by synthesis as well. If the early Buddhist teachings on the *khandhas*, *āyatanas*, and *dhātus* and the Abhidhamma teaching on the dhammas represent the analytical aspect of Buddhism, the Buddhist principles of causality and conditionality highlight the importance attached to synthesis. Let us also recall here that the dhamma theory of the Abhidhamma is based not only on analysis (*bheda*) but on synthesis (*saṅgaha*) as well. Therefore to represent Buddhism as a doctrine of analysis is to overlook the importance attached to synthesis in the Buddhist methodology.

The *Sāratthadīpanī*, a Vinaya subcommentary, says that the Buddha is called *vibhajjavādī* because he follows the method of qualified explanation whereby he is able to avoid such extremist views as eternalism and annihilationism.[1199] On the other hand, according to *Vimativinodanī*, another subcommentary to the Vinaya, the Buddha is "*ekanta-vibhajjasīla*."[1200] This seems to suggest that the Buddha always maintains the *vibhajjavāda* standpoint. Both explanations, it seems to us, fail to give a satisfactory explanation for the presence in the discourses of the Buddha of categorical statements (*ekaṃsavāda*) as well.

This whole situation will become clear if we refer here to the well-known Buddhist classification of questions into four groups, which is as follows:

1. *pañho ekaṃsa-vyākaraṇīyo*, a question that should be answered categorically, either in the affirmative or in the negative
2. *pañho vibhajja-vyākaraṇīyo*, a question that should be answered analytically, in other words, a question to which a qualified answer should be given
3. *pañho paṭipucchā-vyākaraṇīyo*, a question that should be answered by raising a counterquestion, the need for the counterquestion being due to the ambiguities in the original question
4. *pañho ṭhapanīyo*, a question that should be set aside, a question to which no answer should be given

It will be seen that the four kinds of questions imply four corresponding kinds of answers as well. It will also be seen that among them one kind of answer is not considered superior or inferior to any other kind of answer. The sequence of their enumeration does not in any way imply a theory as to their degrees of validity. Each kind of answer, when apposite, is equally valid and equally commendable. What determines the validity of the answer is whether it belongs to the same class to which the question belongs. Hence the Buddha says that a person who does not answer categorically a question that ought to be answered categorically, who does not answer analytically a question that ought to be answered analytically, who does not answer with a counterquestion a question that ought to be answered by raising a counterquestion, and who does not set aside a question that ought to be set aside—such a person is indeed not fit to discuss with (*akaccha*).[1201]

It is in conformity with this situation that we find in the Pāli suttas statements that can be cited as examples for all the four modes of explanation. A typical example of an *ekaṃsavādī* or categorical statement is the recurrent formula *sabbe saṅkhārā aniccā* (all conditioned phenomena are impermanent) or *sabbe dhammā anatttā* (all things are devoid of a self-entity).

Before we come to the second kind of question, let us take the third and the fourth. A good example for the third is the answer given by the Buddha to the question whether consciousness is one thing and the soul another. Before the Buddha answers it he raises a counterquestion in order to clarify what the interlocutor takes to be the soul.[1202] The best example for the fourth category is the Buddha's setting aside of ten questions without providing answers to them. These relate to whether the world is finite or not in terms of time and space, whether the life principle and the physical body are identical or not, and whether the Tathāgata, the one who has gained emancipation, exists after death, or does not exist, or both exists and does not exist, or neither exists nor nonexists.

Now let us take the second mode of explanation in the fourfold classification, which we postponed to be considered last. This refers to questions to which qualified or analytical answers/explanations should be given. An example for this is found in the *Subha Sutta* of the *Majjhimanikāya*, which records a conversation between the Buddha and Subha, the young man. When Subha asks the Buddha for his opinion on the proposition that it is a householder and not a recluse who would succeed in obtaining what is right, just, and good, the Buddha says in reply: "Here (*ettha*), O young man, I give an analytical explanation; I do not make here (*ettha*) a categorical assertion" (*Vibhajjavādo'ham ettha māṇava, nāham ettha ekaṃsavādo*).[1203] For, as the Buddha says, the answer to the question raised by Subha depends not on whether the person is a layman or a monk but on the person's conduct, whether the conduct is good or bad. It will be seen that the use of the adverbial form *ettha* in the answer given by the Buddha is of great significance. It means "here,"' "herein," "in this respect," or to be more precise, "in relation to the question raised by Subha." Its significance lies in the fact that it clearly indicates the specific context in which the Buddha gives his answer following the *vibhajjavāda* method. If we were to overlook this context-indicating term *ettha*, as is sometimes done,[1204] it would give the incorrect impression that the Buddha always follows *vibhajjavāda* in preference to *ekaṃsavāda*; in other words, that he endorses only analytical statements and not universal propositions. But the use of the term *ettha* prevents us from drawing such a conclusion.

Another instance of the Buddha following the *vibhajjavāda* mode of explanation is recorded in the *Aṅguttaranikāya*: "Sir, the Blessed One blames what is blamable, praises what is praiseworthy. Sir, by blaming what is blamable and praising what is praiseworthy, the Blessed One speaks after analyzing. Here, the Blessed One does not speak categorically" (*Gārayhaṃ kho bhante Bhagavā garahati pāsaṃsiyaṃ pasaṃsati. Gārayhaṃ kho bhante Bhagavā garahanto pāsaṃsiyaṃ pasaṃsanto vibhajjavādo Bhagavā. Na so Bhagavā ettha ekaṃsavādo*).[1205] It is this quotation, more than the one already referred to, that is often cited in modern writings to show that the Buddha is always an advocate of the *vibhajjavāda* mode of explanation and therefore that the term *vibhajjavāda* could rightly be used as another expression for early Buddhism. Such a conclusion does not follow because of the simple reason that although the context-indicating term *ettha* does not occur immediately before or after the words *vibhajjavādo Bhagavā*, it does certainly occur in the last sentence of the quotation: *Na so Bhagavā ettha ekaṃsavādo*. Here, too, the use of the term *ettha* is intended to show that if the Buddha does not make a categorical assertion on this issue it is because the context does not warrant it. Again the clear implication is that the Buddha resorts to both *vibhajjavāda* (noncategorical) and *ekaṃsavāda* (categorical) modes of explanation.

It is in consonance with this situation that when Poṭṭhapāda, the wandering ascetic, tells the Buddha, "We do not know of any categorical doctrines preached by the Buddha," the Buddha in reply says, "I have taught and laid down doctrines of which it is possible to make categorical assertions and I have taught and laid down doctrines of which it is not possible to make categorical assertions."[1206] Thus the truth of the matter is that according to Buddhism a categorical statement is no less valid or no less logical than an analytical statement just because it is categorical. Likewise an analytical statement is no less valid or no less logical than a categorical statement just because it is analytical. What matters is not whether a given statement is categorical or analytical but the context in relation to which the statement is made. It follows therefore that *vibhajjavāda*, which refers to analytical or qualified explanations, has no special claim to be more logical or rational than *ekaṃsavāda*, which refers to categorical statements. Therefore on the basis of early Buddhist discourses it is not possible to support the view that the use of the term *vibhajjavāda* is intended to show that Buddhism endorses only analysis, and that by extension this means Buddhism is the religion of analysis.

Now this situation that we have just clarified poses an important problem in relation to the traditional account of the Third Council to which we have already referred. It may be recalled here that in this account it is maintained that the Buddha is *Vibhajjavādī* without in any way qualifying this statement, in other words, without specifying the relevant context. It therefore gives the impression that the Buddha always maintained the *vibhajjavāda* standpoint. Clearly this is at variance with the situation that obtains in the early Buddhist texts, where, as we have noticed, no such claim is made. It is very unlikely that in the account of the Council the term *vibhajjavādī* is used in a different sense either. How, then, are we to reconcile these two situations is the question that arises here.

As an answer to this question, Mrs. Rhys Davids suggests that although each kind of explanation is, "when apposite, equally commendable, yet it is easy to discern that whether established generalizations were being arraigned by criticism or whether as in the Asokan age errors arising from uncritical interpretations of doctrine were to be expunged, the path to purity of views and the hallmark of sagacious exposition lay chiefly in the *distinguo* or the *vibhajjavāda* method of explanation."[1207] However, as Mrs. Rhys Davids herself observes, a universal predication (*ekaṃsavāda*) is no less logical than an analytical statement (*vibhjjavāda*).[1208] Hence this gives rise to the question of why only the *vibhajjavāda* standpoint should have been singled out as the hallmark of sagacious exposition.

It is of course not impossible to give a broad interpretation to the term *vibhajjavāda* so as to include within it all four modes of explanation. For it may be argued, although this argument may appear rather ingenious, that when one is asked for his opinion on a proposition, the most rational position she should take up before she gives her own explanation is to make a preliminary analysis of the proposition so as to find out to which of the four categories it belongs. Since this preliminary exercise involves the *vibhajjavāda* methodology, the term *vibhajjavāda* could be used as a generic term to denote all four categories. In such a situation, of course the term would stand for the genus as well as for one of its species. Although the possibility of such an interpretation cannot be completely ruled out, its probability is very much doubtful. Even in the Buddhist texts where this fourfold classification occurs, no indication is given in support of such an interpretation.

In solving the problem of why in the account of the Third Council the Buddha is represented as *vibhajjavādī*, we may do well to focus our attention on the following facts. It will be observed that in this account the term *vibhajjavādī* is used in such a way as to distinguish the teaching of the Buddha from such theories as eternalism and annihilationism. The obvious implication is that more than any other term it brings into focus the essential nature of the Buddha's teaching, the distinctive characteristic of Buddhist thought. However, as Mrs. Rhys Davids observes, it is rather surprising why this particular term was selected for this purpose when a term such as *anattāvādī* (one who advocates non-self), or *aniccavādī* (one who advocates impermanence) could have served the same purpose in a better way.[1209] Besides, the selection of such a term would not give rise to the kind of problem that the use of the term *vibhajjvādī* has given rise to. We cannot certainly say that the authors of this account were not aware of the true import of this term either. What both these circumstances suggest is that there was an important historical reason for retaining the term. Behind the use of this term there seems to lie a nucleus of historical truth that is unwittingly expressed here.

What this nucleus of historical truth is will become clear if we take into consideration the parallel data in the literary sources of other schools of Buddhist thought as well. In the *Abhidharmakośabhāṣya*, for instance, we read: "Those who maintain, after having analyzed, that some things exist—namely, the present and the past *karma* that has not borne its fruit—and that some things do not exist—namely, the past (*karma*) that has borne its fruit and the future—are called Vibhajyavādins."[1210] Here the reference is to the Buddhist doctrinal controversy on the tri-temporality of the dharmas and here the Vibhajyavādins are identified as Kāśyapīyas. As to the names of other Buddhist schools that came to be known as Vibhajyavādins, the texts differ. Among the names cited are Kāśyapīyas, Mahāsāṃghikas, Ekavyavahārikas, Lokottaravādins, Kaukkuṭikas, and Prajñaptivādins.[1211]

In this connection, Louis de La Vallée Poussin observes that in all probability the Theravādins, too, came to be known as Vibhajjavādins because of the position they took in respect to this selfsame controversial issue.[1212] There is in fact much indirect evidence in the literary sources of the Theravādins themselves, which we propose to adduce in support of this conclusion.

As we have noted in our first chapter, the Theravādins' response to the controversial issue is that only the dhammas in the present phase of time exist, whereas the dhammas in the past and future phases of time do not exist. This explanation, too, follows the *vibhajjavāda* method, although of course it does not fall on all fours with that of the Kāśyapīyas. The similarity is only in the mode of explanation and not in the explanation itself. For here, too, there is neither unconditional assertion nor unconditional negation. While the existence of the dhammas in the present phase of time is asserted, the existence of the dhammas in the past and future phases of time is negated. It is very likely, therefore, that it is in the context of this controversial issue that the Theravādins, too, came to be known as Vibhajjavādins.

Another question that we wish to raise here is whether the doctrinal controversy that we have been referring to served as the major factor that led to the Third Council. According to its traditional account, of course what led to the Council was a different state of affairs. It was the entry into the Saṅgha of members from other religious persuasions who proclaimed their own views as the word of the Buddha, which resulted in the postponement of the *Uposatha* ceremony for six consecutive years. With the intervention of King Asoka, a purification of the *sāsana* was brought about, at the end of which it was decided by the assembly of monks headed by the Venerable Moggaliputta Tissa Thera to convene a Council. The discord within the Saṅgha that led to the intervention of King Asoka could be accepted as a historical fact, for the king himself alludes to it in his Minor Pillar Edicts of *Sārnāth*, *Kausambi*, and *Sāñci*. What appears rather unlikely, however, is that it also led to the Third Council. The traditional account of the Council, it appears to us, is a mix of both history and legend where we could detect a confusion between two events, both of which are historically true. One is the Buddhist controversy on the tri-temporality of the dhammas, which, we believe, led to the summoning of the Council. The other is the disunity and the resulting state of turmoil within the Saṅgha that led to the intervention of King Asoka.

If, as suggested by its traditional account, the Council was summoned to refute the type of speculative views, such as eternalism and annihilationism, that the non-Buddhist members within the Saṅgha put forward as the word of the Buddha, then in the *Kathāvatthu*, the treatise compiled at the Third Council, we should expect a refutation of those selfsame views. But what we get in this treatise instead is a formal refutation of views held by Buddhists other than the orthodox Theravādins. Besides, the arguments and the counterarguments of the Buddhist sects involved in this doctrinal controversy are very well recorded in it. Its sixth chapter, "Does All Exist" (*sabbam atthīti kathā*), contains a refutation, from the Theravāda perspective, of the Sarvāstivāda theory, and its eighth chapter, "Does Some Exist" (*ekaccaṃ atthīti kathā*), contains a refutation of the modified version of the theory held by the Kassapikas-Kāśyapīyas.

In fact, the very title (= *Kathāvatthu*) of the treatise compiled at this Council, either by accident or by design, reminds us of the Buddhist controversy on the tri-temporality of the dhammas. For in the *Saṅgīti Suttanta* of the *Dīghanikāya* we read that there are three kinds of *kathāvatthu*, topics of discussion, corresponding to the three divisions of time—the past, present, and future.[1213] Since the treatise called *Kathāvatthu*, too, deals, among others, with the existence or otherwise of the dhammas in the three divisions of time, one cannot fail to notice the resemblance it presents to the three kinds of *kathāvatthu* mentioned in the Pāli suttas.

An indication of the main event that led to the Third Council is also given in the *Vijñānakāya* of the Sarvāstivādins' Abhidharma Piṭaka, whose authorship is attributed to the arahant Devaśarman. What interests us here is the fact that its first chapter is called "Maudgalyāyana-skandhaka," and as Louis de La Vallée Poussin observes, it is extremely likely that the reference here is to the Elder Moggaliputta Tissa, who is said to have convened the Third Council.[1214] The answer to why a chapter of a book belonging to the Sarvāstivādins should be named after a celebrated Elder of the Theravādins is not far to seek. For what we get here is a criticism of the views expressed by the Elder Moggaliputta Tissa in rejecting the theory of tri-temporality. Thus the "Does All Exist" of the *Kathāvatthu* and the "Maudgalyāyana-skandhaka" of the *Vijñānakāya* represent the two opposite positions taken up by the Theravādins and the Sarvāstivādins over an issue that separated them from each other in the third century BCE.

One question often raised by historians who do not believe in the historicity of the Third Council is why no reference is made to it in any of the edicts of King Asoka. According to our understanding of the situation, the question does not arise. For as we have already suggested, what in all likelihood led to the Council was the Buddhist controversy on the notion of the tri-temporality of the dhammas, an issue that did not warrant the intervention of King Asoka. What is more unlikely than the temporal head of the state intervening in the settlement of a metaphysical problem, the abstruse implications of which only the erudite monks would have understood? Even according to the traditional account of the Council, it was not King Asoka but the assembly of monks headed by the Venerable Moggaliputta Tissa Thera who decided to convene a Council after the purification of the *sāsana* by the intervention of King Asoka.

Another question often raised is why, unlike the first two Councils, the third does not find mention in the literary sources of the other schools of Buddhist thought. One observation made in this regard is that it was a "party meeting" confined to the Theravādins and therefore it was ignored by others.[1215] If this were so, then even the first two Councils would not be much different from the third, in the sense that we do not hear of a Buddhist Council participated by more than one school of Buddhist thought. As an answer to this question, we would like to offer the following explanation.

If a number of Buddhist sects, or for that matter even if all of them, refer to the First Council it is because at the time it was held there were no Buddhist sects, and hence we could expect it to be recorded by the Buddhist sects that emerged subsequently as an event connected with their own history, without being prevented from recording it so by any sectarian feelings. Similarly, all those Buddhist sects that broke away from the Theravāda sometime after the Second Council could be expected to record it, because it was an event that took place before they branched off into different schools of Buddhist thought. But in the case of the Third Council, the situation is somewhat different. For, we are not aware of Theravāda undergoing a schism in India after the Third Council. In fact, its history in India after its introduction to Sri Lanka is shrouded in mystery. For we know that it was in Sri Lanka that the Theravāda split into three fraternities: the Mahāvihāra, the Abhayagiri, and the Jetavana. Now there is nothing to suggest that any of these fraternities doubted the historicity of the Third Council, for they all could refer to it as part of their common history. In view of this situation that is peculiar to the Third Council, one could understand why all information pertaining to it is confined to the literary sources of Sri Lanka's Theravāda tradition.

What we have observed so far is an attempt to explain why the Theravāda came to be known as Vibhajjavāda. In this connection, it must also be mentioned here that contrary to what has been observed in some Pāli subcommentaries, there is sufficient evidence to suggest that the Pāli commentators were not unaware of the doctrinal context in which this term becomes meaningful as another expression for Theravāda. Hence it is that in introducing the Buddhist doctrine of causality in the *Visuddhimagga*,

Ācariya Buddhaghosa says that he will give a full exposition of it "by delving into the *Vibhajjavādi-maṇḍala* (the circle of the Vibhajjavādins)."[1216] Since the rejection on the part of the Theravādins of the Sarvāstivāda theory of tri-temporality has a direct relevance to the Buddhist doctrine of causality, it is nothing but proper that this fact should be taken into consideration in any exposition that seeks to bring out its true implications. This also explains why a similar idea finds expression in the colophon of the commentary to the *Paṭṭhāna* where we get the Abhidhamma doctrine of conditional relations.[1217]

In concluding this appendix, we would like to mention here that no other event in the history of Buddhist thought seems to have exerted so much influence on its subsequent history than the Buddhist doctrinal controversy that we have been referring to. At its very outset, as we saw, it precipitated a crisis within the Theravādin fraternity that not only led to the summoning of the Third Council but also resulted in the emergence of a new school of Buddhist thought called Sarvāstivāda. It was again this controversy that occasioned the emergence, this time, from among the ranks of the Sarvāstivādins themselves of yet another school of Buddhist thought called Kāśyapīyas. What is called *sarvam-asti-vāda*, or the "all exists theory," which came into vogue as a result of this controversy, played a very decisive role in determining the history of Buddhist thought in the centuries that followed. In fact, among the post-Asokan Buddhist schools it became one of the hotly debated issues, resulting in a bewildering mass of arguments and counterarguments that find mention in a host of literary works belonging to a number of Buddhist traditions. After the Buddhist Council said to be held in Jalandhara under the patronage of King Kaniṣka, the Vaibhāṣikas of Kāśmīr became the chief exponents of this theory. Its main critics were the Sautrāntikas. What provoked much opposition to this theory was that it was said to lead to some kind of substantialism that was radically at variance with the Buddhist teaching on the nonsubstantiality of all phenomena. A detailed statement of the theory, together with its critique on the part of the Sautrāntikas, is found in Ācārya Vasubandhu's *Abhidharmakośabhāṣya*. However, since his presentation of the subject was made against the background of its Sautrāntika criticism, it did not get a sympathetic response from the Vaibhāṣikas. It was in order to meet Ācārya Vasubandhu's criticism of this and other subjects pertaining to the Vaibhāṣika Abhidharma that Ācārya Saṃghabhadra composed his well-known treatise the **Nyāyānusāra*, a work that has come down to us only in its Chinese translation. Among the Mahāyānists it was mainly the Mādhyamikas who maintained a sustained criticism against the "all exists theory" of the Sarvāstivādins. This is not to suggest that the Mādhyamikas were in sympathy with the position taken up by the Theravādins and the Sautrāntikas. For in their opinion the so-called basic factors of empirical reality (dhammas/dharmas) are not real even in the present phase of time.

ABBREVIATIONS

A.	Aṅguttaranikāya
AA.	Aṅguttaranikāya Aṭṭhakathā
AbhD.	Abhidharmadīpa (with Vibhāṣāprabhāvṛtti)
AbhMṬ	Abhidhamma-Mūla-Ṭīkā
Abhvk.	Abhidhammatthavikāsinī
Abhvt.	Abhidhammāvatāra
ADSS.	Abhidharmārthasaṃgrahasannaya
ADVṬ.	Abhidhammattha-Vibhāvinī-Ṭīkā
AKB.	Abhidharmakośabhāṣya
AKB(FT).	*L'Abhidharmakośa de Vasubandhu*, trans. Louis de La Vallée Poussin
AKvy.	Abhidharmakośavyākhyā (Sphuṭārthā) of Yaśomitra
BCA.	Bodhicaryāvatāra
BCA-P.	Bodhicaryāvatāra-Pañjikā
BPS	Buddhist Publication Society, Kandy, Sri Lanka
CMA.	*A Comprehensive Manual of Abhidhamma*, trans. Bhikkhu Bodhi
CNdA.	Cūla-Niddesa Aṭṭhakathā
CPM.	Candrakīrti Prasannapadā Madhyamakavrtti
D.	Dīghanikāya
DA.	Dīghanikāya Aṭṭhakathā
Dhp.	Dhammapada
Dhs.	Dhammasaṅgaṇi
DhsA.	Dhammasaṅgaṇi Aṭṭhakathā

DK.	Dhātukathā
Dkp.	Dukapaṭṭhāna
DṬ.	Dīghanikāya-Ṭīkā
ItiA.	Itivuttaka Aṭṭhakathā
KSP.	Karmasiddhiprakaraṇa (*Le traité de la démonstration de l'acte*, trans. Lamotte)
Kvu.	Kathāvatthu
KvuA.	Kathāvatthu Aṭṭhakathā
M.	Majjhimanikāya
MA.	Majjhimanikāya Aṭṭhakathā
MLS.	*Middle Length Sayings* (Majjhimanikāya translation), Pali Text Society
MNd.	Mahāniddesa
MNdA.	Mahāniddesa Aṭṭhakathā
Mil.	Milindapañha
MilṬ.	Milinda-Ṭīkā
MV.	Mohavicchedanī
Netti.	Nettippakaraṇa
NRP.	Nāmarūpapariccheda
NRS.	Nāmarūpasamāsa
PaṭṭhānaA.	Paṭṭhāna Aṭṭhakathā
Peṭ.	Peṭakopadesa
PPS.	Pitāputrasamāgama-sūtra
Psm.	Paṭisambhidāmagga
PsmA.	Paṭisambhidāmagga Aṭṭhakathā
PTS	Pali Text Society, London.
PTSD	*Pali-English Dictionary* of the Pali Text Society
PugP.	Puggalapaññatti
PugPA.	Puggalapaññatti Aṭṭhakathā
PV.	Paramattha Vinicchaya
RRV.	Rūpārūpavibhāga.
S.	Saṃyuttanikāya
SA.	Saṃyuttanikāya Aṭṭhakathā
Sn.	Suttanipāta
SnA.	Suttanipāta Aṭṭhakathā

SS.	Saccasaṃkhepa
Therag.	Theragāthā
Tkp.	Tikapaṭṭhāna (with commentary)
Triṃś.	Triṃśikā (Vijñaptimātratāsiddhi)
UdA.	Udāna Aṭṭhakathā
Vbh.	Vibhaṅga
VbhA.	Vibhaṅga Aṭṭhakathā
Viṃś.	Viṃśatikā (Vijñaptimātratāsiddhi)
VS.	Vaiśeṣika Sūtras of Kaṇāda
Vsm.	Visuddhimagga
VśmS.	Viśuddhimārgasannaya
VsmṬ.	Visuddhimagga Ṭīkā
Yam.	Yamaka
YamA.	Yamaka Aṭṭhakathā

NOTES

1 CMA. 14.

2 DhsA. 330.

3 Dhs. 340.

4 See AKB. 75ff.; AKvy. 171ff.

5 A. I, 152.

6 PsmA. 462.

7 A. I, 102.

8 See, e.g., D. II, 58; M. I, 51; S. II, 3.

9 AKvy. 11.

10 Dhs. 139.

11 DhsA. 317.

12 AKB. 164–65; AKvy. 26.

13 AbhMṬ. passim.

14 See, e.g., VbhA. 405; ADVṬ. 321.

15 CMA. 123.

16 AKB. 244; AKvy. 305.

17 AKB. 244; AKvy. 305.

18 *The Path of Purification* (*Visuddhimagga*), trans. Bhikkhu Ñāṇamoli, 599 n.6.

19 See, e.g., Sarachchandra, *Buddhist Psychology of Perception*, 89–96.

20 *Le traité de la démonstration l'acte* (*Karmasiddhiprakaraṇa*), trans. Lamotte, 250.

21 *Le traité de la démonstration l'acte*, 250 n.116.

22 See VsmṬ. 542–46 for some critical observations on *Sassatavāda, Ucchedavāda, Akiriyavāda, Issaranimmāṇavāda, Kālavāda, Yadicchāvāda, Kāpilā* (*Sāṃkhya*), *Sabhāvavāda, and Samavāyavāda*. See also Abhvk. 320.

23 See, e.g., VsmṬ. 445.

24 Mil. 3.

25 See S. II, 77; ItiA. 178; DṬ. 123.

26 S. II, 17, 77.

27 S. IV, 54.

28 AbhMṬ. 121: *Dhammo ti sabhāvo*; see also DhsA. 126; MhNdA. 261.

29 Abhvk. 414; PsmA. 18; Mvn. 6: *Paccayehi dhārīyantī ti dhammā.*

30 VsmṬ. 138: *Yathāpaccayaṃ pavattamānānaṃ sabhāva-dhammānaṃ natthi kāci vasavattitā.*

31 A. II, 60.

32 A. II, 60.

33 M. I, 396–425.

34 M. I, 396–410.

35 MV. 266.

36 VsmṬ. 225; PV. v. 1066.

37 S. III, 158: *Katamañ ca bhikkhave dukkhaṃ ariyasaccaṃ? Pañcupādānakkhandhā ti'ssa vacanīyaṃ.*

38 D. III. 216; S. IV, 259.

39 M, I, 90.

40 S. III, 203ff.

41 S. IV, 359–61.

42 AA. I, 54–55; DA. I, 251–52.

43 AA. I, 55.

44 ADVṬ. 4.

45 Abhvk. 156.

46 VsmṬ. 484.

47 S. II, 60 ff.

48 In Sanskrit Abhidharma, *saṣṭī-vacana*; see AKB. 78.

49 Kvu. 584ff.

50 KvuA. 89–90.

51 PV. v. 1111.

52 KvuA. 89–90.

53 VsmṬ. 461–62; Abhvk. 228; KvuA. 135.

54 AKB(FT). 33ff.

55 AKB(FT). 33ff.

56 In this study only the dhammas that constitute the conditioned reality will be taken into consideration.

57 See, e.g., Dhp. v. 279. That nibbana too is a dhamma is clear from A. II, 34: *Yāvatā bhikkhave dhammā saṅkhatā vā asaṅkhatā vā virāgo tesaṃ aggam ak-*

khāyati yadidaṃ . . . nirodho nibbānaṃ.

58 See, e.g., Sn. v. 1036; S. I, 35; MhNd. 435; Miln. 49.

59 S. II, 3–4: *Katamañ ca bhikkhave nāma-rūpaṃ. Vedanā saññā cetanā phasso manasikāro. Idaṃ vuccati nāmaṃ. Cattāro ca mahābhūtā catunnañ ca mahābhūtānaṃ upādāya rūpaṃ. Idaṃ vuccati nāma-rūpaṃ.*

60 See, e.g., D. II, 56.

61 See, e.g., S. III, 47, 86–87; M. III, 16.

62 See, e.g., S. II, 248; S. III, 231.

63 See, e.g., D. II, 302; D. III, 102, 243; A. III, 400; A.V, 52.

64 See, e.g., S. II, 140; D. I, 79; D III, 38; A. I, 255; A III, 17.

65 See, e.g., S. III, 49.

66 M. I, 265: *Aññatra paccayā natthi viññāṇassa sambhavo.*

67 See Dhs. 5ff.

68 Ven. Nyanaponika Thera, *Abhidhamma Studies*, 42.

69 NRP. v. 208.

70 VsmṬ. 6, 95, 137.

71 Abhvk. 22; ADVṬ. 5: *Vibhāgavantānaṃ dhammānaṃ sabhāva-vibhāvanaṃ vibhāgena vinā na hoti.* Also VsmṬ. 430: *Vibhāgavantānaṃ pana sabhāva-vibhāvanaṃ vibhāga-dassana-mukhen'eva hoti.*

72 Abhvk. 66: *Dhamma-sabhāva-sāmaññena hi ekībhūtesu dhammesu yo nānattakaro viseso so añño viya katvā upacarituṃ yutto. Evaṃ hi attha-visesāvabodho hoti.*

73 ItiA. 178: *Atidhāvantī ti paramatthato bhinnasabhāvānam pi sabhāvadhammānaṃ yvāyaṃ hetuphalabhāvena sambandho, taṃ agahetvā nānattanayassā'pi gahaṇena tattha tattheva dhāvanti. Tasmā ucchijjati attā ca loko ca na hoti parammaraṇāti ucchede vā bhavanirodhapaṭipattiyā paṭikkhepadhammataṃ atidhāvanti atikkamanti.*

74 Cf. DṬ. 123: *Yathā hetu-phala-bhāvena pavattamānānaṃ sabhāvadhammānaṃ sati' pi ekasantānapariyāpannānaṃ bhinna-santati-patitehi visese hetuphalānaṃ paramatthato bhinnasabhāvattā bhinnasantatipatitānaṃ viya accanta-bheda-sanniṭṭhānena nānattanayassa micchāgahaṇaṃ ucchedābhinivesassa kāraṇaṃ.*

75 Cf. DṬ. 123: *Evaṃ hetuphalabhūtānaṃ dhammānaṃ vijjamāne'pi sabhāvabhede ekasantatipariyāpannatāya ekattanayena accantaṃ abhedagahaṇam'pi kāraṇam eva.*

76 S. II, 17, 77.

77 S. II, 77.

78 VsmṬ. 510.

79 VsmṬ. 548.

80 See chapter 18, "Conditional Relations."

81 Kvu. 2ff.

82 For a detailed study, see *L'origine des sectes bouddhiques d'après Paramārtha*, trans. Demiéville, 1:57ff.; *Origin and Doctrines of Early Indian Buddhist Schools*, trans. Masuda, 53–57; Conze, *Buddhist Thought in India*, 122ff.; Warder, *Indian Buddhism*, 289ff.

83 Kvu. 16.

84 S. III, 25; cf. AKvy. 706: *bhāraṃ ca vo bhikṣavo deśayiṣyāmi bhār'ādānaṃ ca bhāra-nikṣepaṇaṃ ca bhāra-hāraṃ ca. tac chṛṇuta sādhu ca suṣṭhu ca manasi-kuruta bhāṣiṣye. bhāraḥ katamaḥ. paṃcopādāna-skaṃdhāḥ. bhār'ādānaṃ katamat. tṛṣṇā paunarbhavikī nandī-rāga-sahagatā tatra-tatrābhinandinī. bhāra-nikṣepaṇaṃ katamat. yad asyā eva tṛṣṇāyāḥ paunarbhavikyā nandī-rāga-sahagatāyāḥ tatra-tatrābhinandinyāḥ aśeṣa-prahāṇaṃ pratiniḥsargo vyantī-bhāvaḥ kṣayo virāgo nirodho vyupaśamo'staṃgamaḥ. bhāra-hāraḥ katamaḥ. pudgala iti syād vacanīyaṃ.*

85 See, e.g., D. III, 83, 97; S. I, 71.

86 S. IV, 81–82.

87 A. I, 60; Netti. 21.

88 Cf. S. IV, 189: *Suñño loko suñño loko ti bhante vuccati. Kittāvatā nu kho bhante suñño loko ti vuccati? Yasmā ca kho Ānanda suññaṃ attena vā attaniyena vā tasmā suñño loko ti vuccati.*

89 BCA. 455.

90 Cf. ItiA. 179: *Paccaya-sambhūtattā paramatthato vijjamānattā bhūtan ti vuccati.*

91 See, e.g., Sn. vv. 68, 219 (*paramattha-dassī*); MNd. 409 (*paramatthaṃ vuccati amataṃ Nibbānaṃ*).

92 This becomes clear from the definition given in the Theravāda and the Sarvāstivāda to *samanantara-paccaya/pratyaya*, the condition by way of immediate contiguity; see chapter 18, "Conditional Relations."

93 Cf. MNdA. 277: *Na hi sakkā ten'eva cittena taṃ cittaṃ jānituṃ. Yathā na sakkā ten'eva asinā so asi chinditun ti. Purimaṃ purimaṃ pana cittaṃ pacchimassa pacchimassa cittassa tathā uppattiyā paccayo hutvā nirujjhati.*

94 M. III, 187.

95 A. I, 26, 465.

96 See M. III, 188.

97 See, e.g., M. 556; Psm. 53.

98 Ibid.

99 VsmṬ. 462: *Yaṃ kiñcī ti anavasesa-pariyādāna-dīpaka-padadvayaṃ*. See also VbhA. 2.

100 Vbh. 92.

101 Vbh. 114.

102 Vbh. 93.

103 Kvu., chap. 6.

104 Kvu. 115ff.

105 This gives further evidence to establish the historicity of the elder who presided at the Third Buddhist Council and his authorship of the *Kathāvatthu*.

106 S. III, 71–73; *Connected Discourses of the Buddha* (*Saṃyuttanikāya*), trans. Bhikkhu Bodhi, 905–6.

107 Based on *Points of Controversy or Subjects of Discourse* (*Kathāvatthu*), trans. Aung and Rhys Davids, 85-86.

108 CNdA. 106–7.

109 CNdA. 106–7. Cf. VsmṬ. 512: *Pubbantāparantesu avijjamāna-sarūpattā udayato pubbe kuto ci nāgacchanti, vayato ca uddhaṃ na kattha ci gacchanti*; VbhA. 68: *Atha kho pubbe udayā appaṭiladdhasabhāvāni uddhaṃ vayā paribhinnasabhāvāni pubbāparantavemajjhe paccayāyattavuttitāya avasani pavattanti*.

110 VbhA. 68. Cf. PsmA. 371: *Imesaṃ khandhānaṃ [dhammānaṃ] uppattito pubbe anuppannānaṃ rāsi vā nicayo vā natthi. Uppajjamānānam' pi rāsito vā nicayato vā āgamanaṃ nāma natthi. Nirujjhamānānam' pi disāvidisāgamanaṃ nāma natthi. Niruddhānaṃ vā'pi ekekasmiṃ ṭhāne rāsito nicayato nidhānato avatthānaṃ nā'pi natthi*.

111 Vsm. 410; Abhvk. 417.

112 Abhvk. 417.

113 Vsm. 410; VbhA. 33.

114 Cf. VsmṬ. 516: *Pubbanto vā sabhāvadhammassa udayo tato pubbe avijjamānattā. Aparanto vayo tato paraṃ abhāvato. Tasmā pubbantāparanta-vivittato ti pāgabhāva-viddhaṃsābhāvato ti vuttaṃ hoti*.

115 Abhvk. 417.

116 VsmṬ. 510.

117 See, e.g., Abhvk. 417; VbhA. 516; Vsm. 541; CNdA. 105ff.

118 Cf. AbhD. 259; AKB. 293.

119 AKB. 294.

120 DṬ. 108ff.

121 DṬ. 108ff.

122 DṬ. 123.

123 AbhMṬ. 113.

124 SA. III, 285–86.

125 Cf. AbhD. 259–60; AKB. 293.

126 Stcherbatsky, *The Central Conception of Buddhism and the Meaning of the Word "Dharma,"* 65.

127 Stcherbatsky, *Central Conception of Buddhism*, 65.

128 Abhvk. 393.

129 VsmṬ. 397: *Na ca sabhāvo aññathā hotī ti na hi iddhibalena dhammānaṃ kena ci lakkhaṇaññathattaṃ kātuṃ sakkā*. See also VśmS. IV, 258.

130 MV. 69: *Na hi sabhāvā kena ci sahabhāvena saṃ sabhāvaṃ jahanti, abhāvappattito.*

131 VsmṬ. 197: *Na hi kālabhedena dhammānaṃ sabhāvabhedo atthi.*

132 Cf. AbhD. 260; AKB. 293.

133 Stcherbatsky, *Central Conception of Buddhism*, 66; Ven. Dhammajoti, *Sarvāstivāda Abhidharma*, 147ff.

134 DṬ. 673. Cf. VsmṬ.: *Svāyaṃ kattuniddeso pariyāyaladdho dhammato aññassa kattunivattanattho*. See also DṬ. 28; Abhvk. 16–17; PsmA. III, 600.

135 Cf. AbhD. 260; AKB. 293; Ven. Dhammajoti, *Sarvāstivāda Abhidharma*, 147ff.

136 See AKB. 294; AbhD. 260.

137 Psm. II, 211.

138 Netti. 79.

139 See, e.g., MNdA. 370; DhsA. 121–22; VśmS. V, 6.

140 See, e.g., ADVṬ. 4.

141 Abhvk. 156.

142 Cf. Abhvk. 117: *Paramatthato ekasabhāvo'pi sabhāvadhammo pariyāyavacanehi viya samāropitarūpehi bahūhi pakārehi pakāsīyati. Evaṃ hi so suṭṭhu pakāsito hoti.* Abhvk. 16: *Sakasakakiccesu hi dhammānaṃ attappadhānatā-samāropaṇena kattubhāvo, tadanukūlabhāvena tatsampayutte dhammasamūhe kattubhāva-samāropaṇena (paṭipādetabbassa) dhammassa karaṇatthañ ca pariyāyato labbhati.*

143 DṬ. 28.

144 Abhvk. 16: *Cittacetasikānaṃ dhammānaṃ bhāvasādhanam eva nippariyāyato labbhati.*

145 AbhMṬ. 21: *Na ca sabhavā añño dhammo nāma atthi.*

146 AbhMṬ. 70: *Dhammamattadīpanaṃ sabhāvapadaṃ.*

147 AbhMṬ. 21–22: *Na ca dhāriyamānasabhāvā añño dhammo nāma atthi. Na hi ruppanādīhi aññe rūpādayo kakkhaḷādīhi ca aññe paṭhavi-ādayo dhammā*

vijjantī ti. Aññathā pana avabodhetuṃ na sakkā ti nāmavasena viññātāviññāte sabhāvadhamme aññe viya katvā attano sabhāvaṃ dhārentī ti vuttaṃ.

148 DṬ. 76: *Bodheyyajanānurodhavasena.*

149 DṬ. 673: *Dhammato añño kattā natthī ti dassetuṃ.* AbhMṬ. 66: *Dhammato aññassa kattu-nivatthanatthaṃ dhammam eva kattā ti niddisati.* Abhvk. 16–17: *Sakasaka-kiccesu hi dhammānaṃ attappadhānatā-samāropaṇena kattubhāvo, tadanukūlabhāvena taṃsampayuttena dhammasamūhe kattubhāva-samāropaṇena (paṭipādetabba-dhammassa) karaṇatthañ ca pariyāyato labbhatī ti tathā tathā niddisanaṃ pana dhamma-sabhāvato aññassa kattādino abhāvaparidīpanatthan ti veditabbaṃ.* See also Vsm. 484; VśmS. V, 184.

150 Vsm. 513: *Nāmarūpato uddhaṃ issarādīnaṃ abhāvato.*

151 VsmṬ. 482.

152 Abhvk. 393.

153 Abhvk. 392; VsmṬ. 482.

154 Abhvk. 123.

155 Psm. 211.

156 DhsA. 39; PsmA. 26–27; Mvn. 6; Abhvk. 414.

157 AbhMṬ. 21–22: *Na ca dhāriyamānasabhāvā añño dhammo nāma atthi.*

158 VsmṬ. 462: *Yathā-paccayaṃ hi pavattimattam etaṃ sabhāvadhammo.* See also VśmS. V, 132; Abhvk. 116.

159 PsmA. III, 634: *Attano eva vā bhāvo etasmiṃ natthī ti sabhāvena suññaṃ.*

160 Cf. VsmṬ. 138: *Yathāpaccayaṃ pavattamānānaṃ sabhāvadhammānaṃ natthi kā ci vasavattitā ti vasavattibhāvanivāraṇatthaṃ vitakkanaṃ vitakkatī ti vuttaṃ.* See also VśmS. VI, 122.

161 VsmṬ. 345.

162 PsmA. 632.

163 *The Connected Discourses of the Buddha*, trans. Bhikkhu Bodhi, 1163–64 (S. IV, 54).

164 See, e.g., NRP. v. 1569.

165 NRP., v. 632.

166 NRP., vv. 632ff.

167 PsmA. 634–35: *Avijjamānassa ca suññan ti vacanaṃ . . . loka-vacanena ca bhagavato vacanena ca naya-sadda-gantha-vacanena ca virujjhati. Anekāhi' pi yuttīhi virujjhati.*

168 VbhA. 64: *Attano lakkhaṇaṃ dhārentī ti dhammā.* See also VśmS. V, 273; VsmṬ. 359.

169 VsmṬ.: *Yathā hi nīlapītādibhedena anekadhā binnassāpi rūpāyatanassa*

sanidassanattaṃ lakkhaṇaṃ, nīlādibhedena bhinnassāpi sanidassanabhāvaṃ anatikkamanato. See also PsmA. 24; VsmṬ. 23.

170 SA. 276–77; Vsm. 520.

171 VsmṬ. 321.

172 Cf. VsmṬ. 362: *Nanu ca kakkhaḷattam eva paṭhavīdhātu? Saccam etam. Tathā' pi abhinne' pi dhamme kappanāsiddhena bhedena evaṃ niddeso kato. Evaṃ hi atthavisesāvabodho hoti.*

173 See PsmA. 632.

174 See AbhMṬ. 21–22.

175 VsmṬ. 362.

176 Abhvk. 250; VsmṬ. 354; AbhMṬ. 23–24.

177 AbhMṬ. 21–22: *Dhārīyantī ti upadhārīyanti, lakkhīyantī ti attho.* Abhvk. 25: *Lakkhīyati anenā ti lakkhaṇaṃ.*

178 See, e.g., VsmṬ. 24; SA. 276; DT. 105.

179 VsmṬ. 24.

180 Cf. MV. 67–68: *Na hi jāti jāyati, jarā jīrati, maraṇaṃ mīyatī ti voharituṃ yuttaṃ, anavaṭṭhānato.* See also Abhvk. 288; AKB. 238; AKvy. 211; CP. Mdhy. Vrt. 110, 273; 126–27.

181 SA. I, 35–36; PsmA. 35–36.

182 See SA. 56; PsmA. 35–36; Abhvk. 392.

183 SA. 56.

184 ADSS. 3.

185 *The Path of Purification* (*Visuddhimagga*), trans. Bhikkhu Ñāṇamoli, 421.

186 VsmṬ. 159.

187 VsmṬ. 227; Mvn. 258; ItiA. 142.

188 See Abhvk. 445.

189 Abhvk. 4; VsmṬ. 225: *sa-lakkhaṇa-saṅkhāto aviparīta-sabhāvo.*

190 Mvn. 69.

191 VsmṬ. 197; ADVṬ. 123.

192 Cf. Abhvk. 117: *Tathā gahetabbākāro bodhaneyya-janānurodha-vasena pana paramatthato ekasabhāvo'pi...sabhāvadhammo pariyāyavacanehi viya samāropitarūpehi bahūhi pakārehi pakāsīyati. Evaṃ hi so suṭṭhu pakāsito hotī ti.*

193 Gethin, "Bhavaṅga and Rebirth according to the Abhidhamma," 27.

194 Griffiths, *On Being Mindless*, 53–54.

195 Gethin, "Bhavaṅga and Rebirth according to the Abhidhamma," 27–28.

196 M. I, 480.

197 *The Questions of King Milinda*, trans. T. W. Rhys Davids, 97 (Mil. 58–59).

198 For other illustrations, see DhsA. 316; MA. 345; Abhvk. 293.

199 Dhs. 270.

200 See VśmS. 389.

201 Abhvk. 292.

202 VsmṬ. 510.

203 See, e.g., Abhvk. 200.

204 Mil. 58–59.

205 See chapter 18, "Conditional Relations."

206 DhsA. 61–62.

207 See CMA. 78–79.

208 See chapter 12, "The Great Elements of Matter."

209 The importance of the category of *paññatti* to the Abhidhamma is shown by KvuA. when it says that the Buddha is "*sabba-paññatti-kusala*" (1)—that is, the Buddha is skillful in the whole range of *paññattis*.

210 In the Nettippakarana (8–9) *paññatti* is listed as one of the eighteen *hāras*: *Ekaṃ Bhagavā dhammaṃ paññattīhi vividhāhi deseti. So ākāro ñeyyo paññatti nāma hāro ti*. Here it means elucidation, further explanation, elaboration, or interpretation (*etass'eva atthassa saṃkāsanā pakāsanā vivaraṇā vibhajanā uttanīkammaṃ paññatti*).

211 D. I, 202.

212 D. I, 202.

213 S. III, 71ff.

214 Dhs. 226: *Yā tesaṃ tesaṃ dhammānaṃ saṅkhā sāmaññā paññatti vohāro nāmaṃ nāmakammaṃ nāmadheyyaṃ nirutti vyañjanaṃ abhilāpo*. Translation by Mrs. Rhys Davids, *Buddhist Manual of Psychological Ethics* (*Dhammasaṅgaṇi*), 340.

215 DhsA. 392.

216 DhsA. 392.

217 *The Expositor*, 500 (DhsA. 392). See also SA. 121.

218 S. I, 39.

219 *The Connected Discourses of the Buddha*, 136. Cf. SA. 121: *Nāmaṃ sabbaṃ anvabhavī ti nāmaṃ sabbaṃ abhibhavati, anupatati. . . . Nāmena mutto satto vā saṅkhāro vā natthi*.

220 See Abhvk. 445.

221 Abhvt. 84: *Paramattho ca paññatti, tatiyā koṭi na vijjati. / Dvīsu ṭhānesu kusalo, paravādesu na kampati*.

222 NRP. 53.

223 YamA. 60: *Ettha ye paññatti-nibbāna-saṅkhatā dhammā khandhā na honti*.

224 Abhvk. 346.

225 See KvuA. 181–82.

226 Cf. PsmA. 95: *Saṅkhāre upādāya satto ti paññatti-matta-sambhavato vā phalopacāreṇa saṅkhārā 'sattā' ti vuttā ti veditabbā. Na hi koci satto paccayaṭṭhitiko atthi aññatra saṅkhārehi. Vohāra-vasena pana evaṃ vuccati.*

227 AbhMṬ. 114ff.

228 AbhMṬ. 116.

229 VsmṬ. 210.

230 Cf. ADVṬ. 36: *Vinasābhāvato atīta-kālādi-vasena na vattabbattā nibbānaṃ paññatti ca kālavimuttā nāma.*

231 MA. II, 360.

232 PaṭṭhānaA. 29.

233 Cf. KvuA. 92: *Saṅkhatāsaṅkhata-lakkhaṇānaṃ pana abhāvena na vattabbā saṅkhatā ti vā asaṅkhatā ti vā.*

234 VsmṬ. 225.

235 ADVṬ. 53.

236 ADVṬ. 151; Abhvk. 317ff.; MilṬ. 7–8.

237 ADVṬ. 151; SS. vv. 37ff.; PV. v. 1066.

238 ADSS. 53.

239 ADSS. 159.

240 ADSS. 54.

241 VsmṬ. 218: *Sabhāvadhammo hi gambhīro, na paññatti.*

242 Cf. ADSS. 159: *Mehi karma sādhana prajñapti śabdayen rūpādi-dharmayange 'samūha-santānādi avatthāvisesādi bheda' eti saṃvṛti satya nam vū upādā prajñapti saṅkhyāta artha prajñapti darśanaya, kartṛsādhana prajñapti śabdayen saṃvṛti-paramārtha dharmayange abhidhāna yayi kiyana lada nāma prajñaptiya ukta yayi data yutu.*

243 Cf. VsmṬ. 351: *Paññatti-samatikkamanato ti yā ayaṃ paṭhavīdhātū ti ādikā paññatti, taṃ atikkamitvā lakkhaṇesu eva cittaṃ ṭhapetabbaṃ. Evaṃ paññattiṃ vijahitvā kakkhaḷatta-lakkhaṇādisu eva manasikāraṃ pavattentassa lakkhaṇāni supākaṭāni suvibhūtāni hutvā upaṭṭhahanti. Tass'evaṃ punappunaṃ manasikāravasena cittaṃ āsevanaṃ labhati. Sabbo rūpakāyo dhātumattato upaṭṭhāti, suñño nissatto nijjīvo.*

244 AbhMṬ. 85: *Aniccatā dukkhatā anattatā ti hi visuṃ gayhamānaṃ lakkhaṇaṃ paññattigatikaṃ, paramatthato avijjamānaṃ. Na vijjamānattā eva parittādivasena na vattabba-dhammabhūtaṃ. Tasmā visuṃ gahetabbassa lakkhaṇassa paramatthato abhāvā aniccaṃ dukkhamanattā ti saṅkhāre sabhāvato sallakkhento va lakkhaṇāni sallakkheti nāmā ti.*

245 KvuA. 89–90: *Na sā [dhammaniyāmatā = paṭiccasamuppāda] aññatra*

avijjādīhi visuṃ ekā atthi. Avijjādīnaṃ pana paccayānaṃ yev' etaṃ nāmaṃ. Uppanne'pi hi Tathāgate anuppanne'pi avijjāto saṅkhārā sambhavanti, saṅkhārādīhi ca viññāṇādīni. See also VśmS. VI, 124–25.

246 Kvu. 322ff.

247 KvuA. 91–92.

248 *Points of Controversy or Subjects of Discourse* (*Kathāvatthu*), trans. Aung and Rhys Davids, 338 (Kvu. 584).

249 Kvu. 584ff.

250 CMA. 326.

251 Govinda, *The Psychological Attitude of Early Buddhist Philosophy and Its Systematic Representation according to Abhidhamma Tradition*, 171.

252 Abhvk. 401: *Samūhekatta-gahaṇa-vasena satto ti pavatto sammoso sattasammoso.*

253 MNdA. I, 47: *Na hettha yathāvutta-samūha-vinimmutto kāyo vā itthī vā puriso vā añño vā koci dhammo dissati.*

254 VsmṬ. 346.

255 Based on Ven. Ñāṇamoli Thera's translation of the relevant passages in the subcommentary to *The Path of Purification* (*Visuddhimagga*), 256, n.11. See also PugPA. 1ff.

256 ADVṬ. 55.

257 VsmṬ. 539: *Na hi abhāvassa koci sabhāvo atthi.*

258 MV. 67–68; Abhvk. 288.

259 PV. v. 1111.

260 See PugPA. 2.

261 PV. v. 1107: *Tabbohāranimittānaṃ abhāve'pi pavattito abhinivesa-paññatti nāma titthiya-kappitā.*

262 Ibid., v. 1111.

263 ADSS. 160: *Santāna prajñaptiya tīrthakayan visin guṇī dravya yayi kalpanā karaṇu labeda e prajñapti yayi seyi. Samūha prajñaptiya yam prajñaptiyak tīrthakayan visin saṃyogaya, avayavaya, avayavī yayi kiyā kalpanā karaṇu lebeda e prajñapti yayi seyi. Diśā prajñapti, kāla prajñapti yam prajñaptiyek tīrthakayan visin diśā dravyaya, kāla dravyaya yi kalpanā karaṇu lebeda e prajñapti yayi seyi. Ākāśa prajñaptiya yam prajñaptiyak tomo tīrthakayan visin ākāśa dravyaya yi kalpanā karaṇu lebeda e prajñapti yayi seyi.*

264 See, e.g., AbhMṬ. 128ff.; UdA. 15; DṬ. 29; PV. vv. 1132–38; SS. vv. 382–87; MV. 110–11; CMA. 327–28.

265 Cf. PugPA. 5: *Yā taṃ taṃ dhamma-sabhāvaṃ apekkhitvā paṭhavī tejo kakkhaḷatā uṇhatā'ti ādikā paññāpanā ayaṃ tajjā-paññatti nāma.* See also MA.

V, 96: *Tajjaṃ tajjan ti taṃ sabhāvaṃ taṃ sabhāvaṃ*; MV.: *Taṃ taṃ sabhāvanissitā paṭhavādikā tajjā-paññatti nāma.*

266 See MV. 110–11.

267 See CMA. 328.

268 CMA. 328.

269 CMA. 328.

270 CMA. 328.

271 A. II, 60.

272 A. II, 60.

273 AA. II, 118.

274 Edgerton, *Buddhist Hybrid Sanskrit Grammar and Dictionary*, see *nītārtha.*

275 D. III, 226.

276 Cf. Sn. v. 897: *Yā kāc'imā sammutiyā puthujjā sabbā va etā na upeti vidvā* and its corresponding version in *Bodhisattvabhūmi*, 48: *Yaḥ kaścana saṃvṛtayo hi loke sarvā hi tā muni nopaiti.*

277 Duve *saccāni akkhāsi sambuddho vadataṃ varo, / sammutiṃ paramatthañ ca tatiyaṃ nūpalabbhati*—AA. I, 54; KvuA. 34; DA. I, 251–52; SA. II, 77.

278 *Satya ime duvi lokavidūnam diṣṭa svayam aśruṇitva paresam saṃvṛti ya ca tatha paramārtho satyu na sidhyati kiṃ ca tṛtīyu*—quoted in PPS. 171.

279 See AA. I, 54; KvuA. 34; DA. 251; SA. II, 77; SS. v. 3.

280 AKB. 335.

281 AKvy. 524.

282 *Documents d'Abhidharma: La controverse du temps; les deux, les quatre, et les trois verities,* trans. de La Vallée Poussin, 5:34–40.

283 Jayatilleke, *Early Buddhist Theory of Knowledge*, 364.

284 AA. I, 54–55; DA. I, 251–52; SA. II, 77.

285 DA. I, 251; see also SA. II, 72.

286 SA. I, 51.

287 KvuA. 103.

288 VsmṬ. 346; KvuA. 103: *Atthi puggalo ti vacana-mattato abhiniveso na kātabbo.* Cf. AA. I, 54–55: *Lokasammutiñ ca Buddhā Bhagavanto nappajahanti, lokasamaññāya lokaniruttiyā lokābhilāpe ṭhitā yeva dhammaṃ desenti.*

289 SA. I, 51.

290 Cf. MA. I, 125: *Tasmā vohāra-kusalassa lokanāthassa satthuno, / sammutiṃ voharantassa musāvādo na jāyati.*

291 DA. I, 251–52.

292 DA. I, 351.

293 Abhvt. 88: *Na ca daḷhaṃ mūlhagāhinā bhavitabbaṃ.*

294 See SS. vv. 367ff.; PV. vv. 1062ff.; NRP. vv. 847ff.

295 Abhvt. 88: *Tasmā dve'pi sammuti-paramattha-saccāni asaṅkarato ñātabbāni. Evaṃ asaṅkarato ñatvā koci kārako vā vedako vā nicco dhuvo attā paramatthato natthī ti. . . .*

296 See, e.g., AA. I, 54; DA. I, 251; Abhvk. 324.

297 Sn. v. 884.

298 Jayatilleke, *Early Buddhist Theory of Knowledge*, 364.

299 Cf. DhsA. 32: *Suttapiṭakaṃ vohārakusalena Bhagavatā vohārabāhullato desitattā vohāradesanā; abhidhammapiṭakaṃ paramatthakusalena paramatthabāhullato desitattā paramatthadesanā ti vuccati.*

300 Mil. 188; see also MilṬ. 391.

301 MV. 266.

302 M. I, 256: *Aññatra paccayā natthi viññāṇassa sambhavo.*

303 M. I, 256.

304 S. III, 67–68. Translation by Ven. Nyanatiloka Mahāthera, *Fundamentals of Buddhism*, 21.

305 S. III, 67–68.

306 M. I, 259.

307 *Connected Discourses of the Buddha* (S. III, 53), trans. Bhikkhu Bodhi, and quoted in Ven. Nyanatiloka Mahāthera, *Fundamentals of Buddhism*, 890.

308 D. II, 62–63: *Viññāṇa-paccayā nāma-rūpaṃ; nāma-rūpa-paccayā viññāṇaṃ.* See also S. II, 6, 8, 12; S. III, 102.

309 See, e.g., S. II, 3–4.

310 S. II, 3–4.

311 *Connected Discourses of the Buddha* (*Saṃyuttanikāya*), trans. Bhikkhu Bodhi, 596.

312 The beginning of the distinction between *citta* and *cetasika* can be traced to the *Cullavedalla Sutta* in M., where we read that *saññā* and *vedanā* are *cetasikā dhammā* and that they are *cittapaṭibaddhā* (conjoined with consciousness).

313 Stcherbatsky, *Central Conception of Buddhism*, 13ff.

314 M. I, 298: *Imesaṃ kho āvuso pañcannaṃ indriyānaṃ nānāvisayānaṃ nānāgocarānaṃ na aññamaññassa gocaravisayaṃ paccanubhontānaṃ mano paṭisaraṇaṃ mano ca nesaṃ gocaravisayaṃ paccanubhoti* (quoted in DhsA. 221).

315 AKB. 22; AKvy. 39: *Yad-yat samanantara-niruddhaṃ vijñānaṃ tat-tan mano-dhātur iti.*

316 AKB. 22ff.; AKvy. 39 ff.

317 ADVṬ. 4: *Cittaṃ pana kena ci cetasikena vinā'pi ārammaṇe pavattatī ti taṃ cetasikam'eva cittāyattavuttikaṃ nāma.*

318 AbhMṬ. 51: *Mano tesaṃ dhammānaṃ paṭhamaṃ uppajjatī ti sahajāto'pi mano sampayutte saṅgahitvā adhipatibhāvena pavattamāno paṭhamaṃ uppanno viya hotī ti evaṃ vutto.*

319 Mil. 58–59.

320 Kvu. 337.

321 CMA, 76.

322 See the section on "Means of Intimation" in chapter 14, "The Nominal Dependent Matter."

323 AbhMṬ. 28–29; Abhvk. 107; ADSS. 14.

324 PV. v. 352.

325 AKB. 62.

326 Kvu. 337; KvuA. 94–95 attributes the dissent view to Rājagirikas and Siddhatthikas.

327 Kvu. 337ff.

328 See Tkp. 4ff.; CMA. 292 ff.

329 Ven. Nyanaponika Thera, *Abhidhamma Studies*, 46.

330 See Tkp. 4ff.; CMA. 305.

331 MhNA. 277: *Aniruddhamhi paṭhame na uppajjati pacchimaṃ. Nirantaruppajjanato ekaṃ viya pakāsati.*

332 See chapter 15, "The Material Clusters."

333 MhNA. 195; MA. IV, 89.

334 MhNA. 277.

335 ADVṬ. 4: Cf. *Cintetī ti cittaṃ. Āramma ṇaṃ vijānātī ti attho. Yathāha: visaya-vijānana-lakkhaṇaṃ cittan ti.*

336 ADVṬ. 5: *Cittaṃ ārammaṇikaṃ nāma.*

337 ADVṬ. 4: *Sati hi nissaya-samanantara-paccaye na vinā ārammaṇena cittaṃ uppajjatī ti tassa tā lakkhaṇatā vuttā. Etena nirālambaṇavādimataṃ paṭikkhittaṃ hoti.*

338 See, e.g., NRP. 9; VśmS. V, 184.

339 NRP. 9; ADVṬ. 4; VśmS. V, 184. (*Sammohavinodanī Atthayojanā*, 42, adds two more *sādhanas*. One is *kammasādhana*, or object denotation; the other *adhikaraṇa-sādhana*, or locative denotation.)

340 ADVṬ. 4; Abhvk. 6: *Cittacetasikānaṃ dhammānaṃ bhāvasādhanam'eva nippariyāyato labbhati*. See also VśmS. V, 184.

341 VsmṬ. 462: *Yathāpaccayaṃ hi pavattimattam etaṃ sabhāvadhammo*. See also Abhvk. 116; VśmS. V, 132.

342 AbhMṬ. 66; DṬ. 673; VsmṬ. 484.

343 See, e.g., DṬ. 325–26; PsmA. I, 14.

344 CMA. 29.

345 For two detailed accounts of the Buddhist teaching on mind-body relationship, see Harvey, "The Mind-Body Relationship in Pāli Buddhism: A Philosophical Investigation"; and Suwanda, "The Whole Body, Not Heart, as Seat of Consciousness: The Buddha's View."

346 AKB. 22.

347 AKB. 22.

348 M. II, 17.

349 Tkp. 4.

350 C. A. F. Rhys Davids, *Buddhist Psychology*, 71.

351 Bareau, *The Buddhist Sects of the Lesser Vehicle*, pt. 1, 64.

352 *The Path of Purification* (*Visuddhimagga*), trans. Bhikkhu Ñāṇamoli, 696–97.

353 See chapter 18, "Conditional Relations."

354 *Compendium of Philosophy* (*Abhidhammatthasaṅgaha*), trans. Aung, ed. Mrs. Rhys Davids, 278.

355 VsmṬ. 449.

356 See, e.g., Vsm. 493; see AKvy. 96, where a similar explanation is given.

357 Vsm. 596–97.

358 C. A. F. Rhys Davids, *Buddhist Psychology*, 34.

359 Vbh. 87–88, 144.

360 Abhvk. 271: *Aṭṭhikatvā manasikatvā sabbaṃ cetasā samannāharitvā kiñci cintentassa hadayappadesassa khijjanato tatthedaṃ tiṭṭthatī ti viññāyati.*

361 AKvy. 39.

362 See CMA. 28, Table 1.1.

363 See CMA. 28ff.

364 CMA. 34.

365 CMA. 32.

366 The term *upekkhā* usually refers to one of the four *Brahmavihāras*, when it means the quality of equanimity in the highest sense. Here it means neutral feeling—that is, "neither painful nor pleasant feeling" (*adukkhamasukhā vedanā*).

367 CMA. 36.

368 CMA. 37.

369 Abhvt. 85.

370 AKB. 252: *Na hi punar vipākād vipākāntaraṃ janmāntareṣu pravardhate / yadi hi pravardheta mokṣo na syāt.* See also AKvy. 211.

371 See DhsA. 546.

372 CMA. 40.

373 CMA. 42ff.

374 See chapter 10, "The Cognitive Process."

375 CMA. 44–45; see also introductory essay, *Compendium of Philosophy* (*Abhidhammatthasaṅgaha*), trans. Aung, ed. Mrs. Rhys Davids, 22ff.

376 DhsA. 63: ... ārogyaṭṭhena anavajjaṭṭhena kosalla-*sambhūtaṭṭhena ca kusalaṃ*.

377 See ADS. 46.

378 *Expositor*, 83–84 (DhsA. 63).

379 DhsA. 63: *Nippariyāyena pana ñāṇasampayuttaṃ ārogyaṭṭhena anavajjaṭṭhena kosallasambhūtaṭṭhenā ti tividhenā'pi kusalan ti nāmaṃ labhati, ñāṇavippayuttaṃ duvidhen'eva.*

380 S. (Buddha-Jayanti ed.), 544: *Rāgo kho bhante pamāṇakaraṇo, doso pamāṇakaraṇo, moho pamāṇakaraṇo. Te khīṇāsavassa bhikkhuno pahīṇā ucchinnamūlā tālāvatthukatā anabhāvakatā āyatiṃ anuppādadhammā.*

381 S. (Buddha-Jayanti ed.), 544: *Rāgo kho bhante nimittakaraṇo, doso nimittakaraṇo, moho nimittakaraṇo....*

382 Sn. vv. 484, 795.

383 S. II, 173; III, 31.

384 Ven. Nyanatiloka Mahathera, *Buddhist Dictionary*, 102 (A. V, 193).

385 DhsA. 209–10.

386 Ven. Nyanaponika Thera, "Buddhism and the God-Idea," in *The Vision of Dhamma*, 294–300.

387 Ven. Nyanaponika Thera, "Buddhism and the God-Idea," in *The Vision of Dhamma*, 294–300.

388 Dhs. 3.

389 DhsA. 168–69.

390 See CMA. 65ff.

391 CMA., 65ff.

392 See, e.g., Vsm. 589 (here *cittaṭṭhiti* occurs instead of *ekaggatā*; both terms mean the same); CMA. 77.

393 AbhD. 68.

394 See the section "Material Faculty of Life" in chapter 13, "The Real Dependent Matter."

395 See Jaini, "Origin and Development of the Theory of *Viprayuktasaṃskāras*," pt. 3, as to why there are two different traditions pertaining to life faculty.

396 See, e.g., S. II, 3–4; Mil. 49: *Aññamaññaṃ upanissitā ete dhammā, ekato'va uppajjanti.*

397 S. II, 114.

398 D. II, 63–64.

399 DhsA. 134, 251, 310.

400 Ven. Nyanaponika Thera, *Abhidhamma Studies*, 49.

401 D. II, 308–9.

402 S. II, 247.

403 M. II, 27.

404 Netti. 15.

405 Ven. Nyanaponika Thera, *Abhidhamma Studies*, 52.

406 AKvy. 127.

407 Mil. 59.

408 Abhvk. 112.

409 See, e.g., M. I, 111: *Cakkhuñ c'āvuso paṭicca rūpe ca uppajjati cakkhuviññāṇaṃ, tiṇṇaṃ saṅgati phasso.*

410 S. IV. 68: *Yā kho bhikkhave imesaṃ tiṇṇaṃ dhammānaṃ saṅgati sannipāto samavāyo ayaṃ vuccati bhikkhave cakkhusamphasso.*

411 DhsA. 109–10: *Ayaṃ hi tattha tattha tiṇṇaṃ saṅgati phasso ti evaṃ kāraṇass'eva vasena pavedito ti imassa ca suttapadassa tiṇṇaṃ saṅgati phasso ti ayaṃ attho; na saṅgatimattam eva phasso ti evaṃ paveditattā pana tenevākārena paccupaṭṭhā ti sannipātapaccupaṭṭhāno ti vutto.*

412 Cf. AKB. 143: *Ṣaṭṣaṭko dharmaparyāyaḥ katamaḥ/ ṣad ādhyātmikāny āyatanāni/ ṣaṭ bāhyāny āyatanāni/ ṣaṭ vijñānakāyāḥ/ ṣaṭ sparśakāyāḥ/ ṣaṭ vedanākāyāḥ/ ṣaṭ tṛṣṇākāyā iti/ atra hīndriyārthavijñānebhyaḥ sparśakāyāḥ pṛthag deśitāḥ/.*

413 AKB. 143ff.

414 Netti. 28.

415 Mln. 60.

416 Sarachchandra, *Buddhist Psychology of Perception*, 15.

417 DhsA. 16–17: *Yathā vā 'cakkhunā rūpaṃ disvā' ti ādisu cakkhuviññāṇādīni cakkhu ādi nāmena vuttāni, evaṃ idhā'pi tāni cakkhu ādi nāmena vuttānī ti veditabbāni.*

418 DhsA. 108: *Ayaṃ hi arūpadhammo'pi samāno ārammaṇesu phusanākāreṇ'eva pavattatī ti phusanalakkhaṇo.*

419 DhsA. 108.

420 DhsA. 108.

421 Abhvk. 113–14.

422 *Compendium of Philosophy* (*Abhidhammatthasaṅgaha*), trans. Aung, ed. Mrs. Rhys Davids, 40.

423 Dhs. 146–47.

424 DA. II, 500: *Paṭighasamphasso ti sappaṭighaṃ rūpakkhandhaṃ vatthuṃ*

katvā uppajjanakaphasso.

425 DA. II, 500: *Cattāro khandhe vatthuṃ katvā manodvare adhivacana-samphassa-vevacano manosamphasso uppajjati.*

426 AKvy. 305: *Adhyucyate'nenety adhivacanaṃ/ vāṅ nāmni pravartate nāmārthaṃ dyotayatīty adhivacanaṃ nāma.*

427 AKB. 244: *Manaḥsaṃsparśaḥ ṣaṣṭhaḥ so'dhivacanasaṃsparśa ity ucyate/ kiṃ kāraṇaṃ adhivacanam ucyate nāma/ tat kilāsyādhikamālambanamayo'dhiva cana'saṃsparśa iti/ yathoktaṃ 'cakṣur-vijñānena nīlaṃ vijānāti no tu nīlaṃ manovijñānena nīlaṃ vijānāti nīlam iti ca vijānāti' ti.*

428 AKB. 244: *Apare punar āhuḥ/ vacanam adhikṛtyārthesu manovijñānasya pravṛttir na pañcānām/ atas tad evādhivacanam/ tena samprayuktaḥ sparśo'dhivacanasaṃsparśar it y eka āśrayaprabhāvito dvitīyaḥ saṃprayogaprabhāvitaḥ/.*

429 CMA. 123.

430 CMA. 297.

431 CMA. 80.

432 *Expositor*, 145–46 (DhsA. 109–10).

433 DhsA. 546: *Cakkhudvārādisu hi catusu upādārūpam eva upādārūpaṃ ghaṭṭeti, upādārūpe yeva upādārūpaṃ ghaṭṭente paṭighaṭṭananighaṃso balavā na hoti, catuṇṇaṃ adhikaraṇīnaṃ upari cattāro kappāsapicupiṇḍe ṭhapetvā picupiṇḍen'eva pahaṭakālo viya phuṭṭhamattam'eva. Kāyadvāre pana bahiddhā mahābhūtārammaṇaṃ ajjhattikaṃ kāyappasādaṃ ghaṭṭetvā pasādapaccayesu mahābhūtesu paṭihaññati. Yathā adhikaraṇimatthake kappāsapicupiṇḍaṃ ṭhapetvā kūṭena paharantassa kappāsapicupiṇḍaṃ bhinditvā kūṭaṃ adhikaraṇiṃ gaṇhāti, nighaṃso balavā hoti.*

434 Vsm. 461.

435 *Expositor*, 146 (DhsA. 110–11).

436 Ven. Nyanaponika Thera, *Abhidhamma Studies*, Appendix 2, 119ff.

437 DhsA. 111–12.

438 DhsA. 111–12.

439 See chapter 18, "Conditional Relations."

440 *Expositor*, 156 (DhsA. 119).

441 DhsA. 124.

442 DhsA. 133.

443 *Expositor*, 175 (DhsA. 133).

444 DhsA. 133.

445 M. I, 190: *Ajjhantikañ ce āvuso cakkhuṃ aparibhinnaṃ hoti, bāhirā ca rūpā na āpāthaṃ āgacchanti no ca tajjo samannāhāro hoti neva tāva tajjassa viññāṇabhāgassa pātubhāvo hoti.*

446 For a detailed account, see Ven. Dhammajoti, *Sarvāstivāda Abhidharma*, 288ff.

447 *A Buddhist Manual of Psychological Ethics* (*Dhammasaṅgaṇi*), trans. Mrs. Rhys Davids, 10–11.

448 DhsA. 115.

449 *Expositor*, 151 (DhsA. 115).

450 *Expositor*, 152 (DhsA. 115).

451 *The Middle Length Discourses of the Buddha: A Translation of the Majjhima Nikāya*, trans. Bhikkhu Ñāṇamoli and Bhikkhu Bodhi, 363–64 (*Pubbe kho āvuso Visākha vitakketvā vicāretvā pacchā vācaṃ bhindati, tasmā vitakka-vicārā vacīsaṅkhāro*). See also S. IV, 293.

452 For a detailed account of the close connection between *vicāra* and *papañca*, see Ven. Ñānananda, *Concept and Reality in Early Buddhism*.

453 See AKvy. 140; see also Stcherbatsky, *Central Conception of Buddhism*, 87–88.

454 Vsm. 453.

455 See AKB. 61: "*Vāksaṃskārā vitarka-vicārāḥ sūtra uktāḥ / 'vitarkya vicārya vācaṃ bhāṣate nāvitarkyāvicārye' ti / tatra ye audārikās te vitarkāḥ ye sūkṣmās te vicārāḥ /*."

456 *Expositor*, 175 (DhsA. 115).

457 AKB(FT). 54 n.5.

458 AKB(FT). 54 n.5.

459 AKB(FT). 54 n.5.

460 AKvy. 128ff.

461 M. III, 25.

462 Vbh. 165.

463 AKB. 55.

464 See AKB(FT) 160 n.3.

465 AKB. 56: *kauśīdyaṃ cetaso nābhyutsāho vīrya-vipakṣaḥ*.

466 *A Buddhist Manual of Psychological Ethics* (*Dhammasaṅgaṇi*), trans. Mrs. Rhys Davids, 15–16.

467 *Expositor*, 159; DhsA. 121–22: *Sammā āraddhaṃ sabbāsaṃ sampattīnaṃ mūlaṃ hotī ti veditabbaṃ*.

468 DhsA. 116.

469 DhsA. 116–17.

470 CMA. 57.

471 CMA. 57.

472 DhsA. 133.

473 ADS. 274.

474 CMA. 320.

475 CMA. 95.

476 DhsA. 250; Abhvk. 132.

477 DhsA. 250–51, Vsm. 468: *Moho . . . sabba-akusalānaṃ mulan ti daṭṭhabbo.*

478 DhsA. 248; Vsm. 468.

479 A. I, 51: *Dve'me bhikkhave sukkā dhammā lokaṃ pālenti. Katame dve? Hiri ca ottappañ ca.*

480 A. I, 51 (*Book of Gradual Sayings*, vol. 1, 46).

481 *Expositor*, 334 (DhsA. 261); Abhvk. 133.

482 AKB. 56.

483 *Expositor*, 332 (DhsA. 250); Vsm. 468.

484 DhsA. 250.

485 DhsA. 252.

486 See, e.g., D. III, 230; Dhs. 212–13.

487 Ven. Nyanatiloka Mahāthera, *Buddhist Dictionary*, 47.

488 See, e.g., Vsm. 684.

489 See, e.g., Vsm. 683; DhsA. 253–54.

490 AKB. 29.

491 AKB. 283.

492 CMA. 95: *Diṭṭhi catūsu diṭṭhigatasampayuttesu. Māno catūsu diṭṭhigatavippayuttesu.*

493 *A Buddhist Manual of Psychological Ethics* (*Dhammasaṅgaṇi*), trans. Mrs. Rhys Davids, 299.

494 See, e.g., D. III, 216; S. I, 12; Sn. v. 842: *seyyo'ham asmi, sadiso'ham asmi, hīno'ham asmi.*

495 Vsm. 469; DhsA. 256; Abhvk. 133.

496 Vbh. 350.

497 AKB. 61.

498 CMA. 95.

499 *A Buddhist Manual of Psychological Ethics* (*Dhammasaṅgaṇi*), trans. Mrs. Rhys Davids, 282.

500 *Expositor*, 472 (DhsA. 367–68).

501 *A Buddhist Manual of Psychological Ethics* (*Dhammasaṅgaṇi*), trans. Mrs. Rhys Davids, 299.

502 DhsA. 258.

503 *A Buddhist Manual of Psychological Ethics* (*Dhammasaṅgaṇi*), trans. Mrs. Rhys Davids, 299–300. The etymological definition of *macchariya* given at VbhA. 513 is "*Idaṃ acchariyaṃ mayhaṃ eva hotu, mā aññassa acchariyaṃ*

hotū ti pavattattā macchariyan ti vuccati."

504 DhsA. 258; see also 373ff.

505 DhsA. 376.

506 DhsA. 258.

507 DhsA. 377: *Mayham eva hontu mā aññassā ti sabbā'pi attano sampatti yo byāpetuṃ icchatīti viviccho. Vivicchassa bhāvo vevicchaṃ; mudu-macchariyass'etaṃ nāmaṃ, kadariyo vuccati anariyo, tassa bhāvo kadariyaṃ; thaddha-macchariyass'etaṃ nāmaṃ.*

508 See DhsA. 384.

509 AKB. 57–58; AKvy. 132–33.

510 *A Buddhist Manual of Psychological Ethics* (*Dhammasaṅgaṇi*), trans. Mrs. Rhys Davids, 313.

511 *Expositor*, 492 (DhsA. 384: *Uppajjamānaṃ pana kukkuccaṃ āraggam iva kaṃsa-pattaṃ manaṃ vilikhamānam eva uppajjati. Tasmā manovilokho ti vuttaṃ*).

512 AKB. 58: *Katamat kaukṛtyaṃ kuśalam/ yat kuśalam akṛtvā tapyate akuśalaṃ ca kṛtvā/ viparyayād akuśalaṃ kaukṛtyam/.*

513 DhsA. 385: *Na taṃ nīvaraṇaṃ. . . .* Nīvaraṇa-*patirūpakaṃ pan'etaṃ kappati na kappatīti vīmaṃsanasaṅkhātaṃ vinayakukkuccaṃ nāma.*

514 DhsA. 256.

515 Vsm. 469; DhsA. 256.

516 Vsm. 469; DhsA. 256.

517 *Expositor*, 484 (DhsA. 378).

518 CMA. 97.

519 DhsA. 378.

520 Abhvk. 284.

521 Vsm. 450; DhsA. 378ff.

522 DhsA. 378ff.

523 *A Buddhist Manual of Psychological Ethics* (*Dhammasaṅgaṇi*), trans. Mrs. Rhys Davids, 116.

524 MA.

525 Vsm. 471; DhsA. 269.

526 See, e.g., DhsA. 301.

527 Vsm. 471: *Vicikicchāya abhāvena pan'ettha adhimokkho uppajjati.*

528 DhsA. 355.

529 *Expositor*, 157 (DhsA. 119).

530 AKB(FT). 156 n.3.

531 DhsA. 119, 145.

532 *Expositor*, 161 (DhsA. 146).

533 DhsA. 146.

534 *The Questions of King Milinda*, trans. T. W. Rhys Davids, 58 (Mil. 59).

535 DhsA. 123.

536 CMA. 83.

537 PugP. 79–80 (trans. Ven. Nyanatiloka Mahāthera, *Buddhist Dictionary*).

538 DhsA. 125–26.

539 DhsA. 125–26.

540 See, e.g., D. II, 80; D. III, 245; S. II, 70; S. V, 343.

541 DhsA. 129–30.

542 *Expositor*, 166 (DhsA. 127).

543 A. I, 51.

544 Ven. Nyanaponika Thera, *Abhidhamma Studies*, 69; see also *The Vision of Dhamma*, 117ff.

545 DhsA. 128.

546 DhsA. 128.

547 DhsA. 128.

548 DhsA. 193.

549 Mainly based on the *Expositor*, 167ff. (DhsA. 128ff.).

550 DhsA. 129.

551 *The Path of Purification* (*Visuddhimagga*), trans. Bhikkhu Ñāṇamoli, 166.

552 Vsm. 318.

553 *The Path of Purification* (*Visuddhimagga*), trans. Bhikkhu Ñāṇamoli (Vsm. 318).

554 Dhs. 131.

555 *Expositor* (DhsA. 133). With minor edits for clarity.

556 DhsA. 131; Vsm. 465–66.

557 DhsA. 151; Vsm. 465–66.

558 DhsA. 151; Vsm. 465–66.

559 DhsA. 151; Vsm. 465–66.

560 DhsA. 151; Vsm. 465–66.

561 DhsA. 151; Vsm. 465–66.

562 Ven. Nyanaponika Thera, *Abhidhamma Studies*, 77ff.

563 AKB. 55; AKvy. 128ff.

564 Abhvk. 281.

565 DhsA. 193; Vsm. 318.

566 DhsA. 193; Vsm. 318.

567 *Expositor*, 161 (DhsA. 149).

568 *Expositor*, 162 (DhsA. 149).

569 DhsA. 460.

570 DhsA. 564.

571 Cf. Mil. 299.

572 See, e.g., CMA. 149ff.

573 CMA. 149ff.

574 Sarachchandra, *Buddhist Psychology of Perception*, 88.

575 See CMA. 153.

576 CMA. 153.

577 CMA. 153.

578 See VbhA. 356ff.

579 AbhMṬ. 96.

580 Vsm. 458–59; see *Compendium of Philosophy* (*Abhidhammatthasaṅgaha*), trans. Aung, ed. Mrs. Rhys Davids, 248ff.

581 DhsA. 559.

582 See, e.g., Vsm. 613; VbhA. 25.

583 VbhA. 25–26.

584 VbhA. 25: *Rūpaṃ garupariṇāmaṃ dandhanirodhaṃ; arūpaṃ lahupariṇāmaṃ khippanirodhaṃ*. See also Vsm. 613.

585 VbhA. 25.

586 For a detailed account, see Ven. Dhammajoti, "The Sarvāstivāda Doctrine of Simultaneous Causality."

587 *Abhidharmadīpa* (with *Vibhāṣāprabhāvṛtti*), ed. Jaini, 79.

588 *Abhidharmadīpa* (with *Vibhāṣāprabhāvṛtti*), ed. Jaini, 82.

589 See Ven. Dhammajoti, *Abhidharma Doctrine and Controversy on Perception*, 69, 96.

590 Abhvk. 169: *Iminā pana idaṃ vuttaṃ hoti: ye rūpādayo pañca ārammaṇā santatta-ayogule patitaṃ jalabindu viya parittakkhaṇikā, dibbacakkhunā'pi asakkuṇeyyagahaṇā, paramāṇu viya parittavatthukā, tato ca sakasakaviññāṇassa āpāthaṃ na gacchanti; kevalam pana manoviññāṇasseva gocarāni, te dhammārammaṇaṃ nāmā ti yesaṃ laddhi, te yesaṃ vā dhammārammaṇaṃ nāmā ti eten'eva ca atītānāgatabhāvena, atidūra-accāsannabhāvena, kuḍḍādi antaritabhāvena ca āpāthaṃ anāgacchantānam'pi rūpādīnaṃ saṅgaho kato hotī ti.*

591 Abhvk. 169–70.

592 DhsA. 573.

593 Based on Ven. Dhammjoti, *Abhidharma Doctrine and Controversy on Perception*, 14 ff.

594 Vsm. 17; VsmṬ. 40: *Cakkhunā rūpaṃ disvā ti ettha yadi cakkhu rūpaṃ passeyya*

aññaviññāṇasamaṅgino'pi passeyyuṃ. Na c'etam atthi. Kasmā? Acetanassa cakkhussa. Tenāha: cakkhu rūpaṃ na passati, acittakattā ti. Atha viññāṇaṃ rūpaṃ passeyya tirokuḍḍādigatam'pi naṃ passeyya appaṭighabhāvato. Idam'pi natthi. See also Abhvk. 256.

595 Vsm. 17.

596 VsmṬ. 40.

597 Abhvk. 256: *Yassa cakkhu passatī ti mataṃ, tassā pi na sabbaṃ cakkhu passati, atha kho viññāṇādhiṭṭhitam eva. Yassa pana viññāṇaṃ passatī ti mataṃ, tassā pi na sabbaṃ viññāṇaṃ passati, atha kho cakkhunissitam eva.*

598 Cf. Abhvk. 256.

599 Ven. Dhammajoti, *Abhidharma Doctrine and Controversy on Perception*, 74ff.

600 Ven. Dhammajoti, *Abhidharma Doctrine and Controversy on Perception*, 74ff.

601 Cf. VsmṬ. 472: *Sa cāssa indriyādhīnavuttikassa ārammaṇasabhāvupaladdhi na ekakalāpagatavaṇṇavasena hoti. Nāpi katipayakalāpagatavaṇṇavasena.*

602 Cf. VsmṬ. 472: *Atha kho ābhogānurūpaṃ āpāthagatavaṇṇavasenā ti anekam eva rūpaṃ saṃhaccakāritāya viññāṇassa paccayo hotī ti dassento Bhagavā "rūpe cā" ti bahuvacanena niddisi. . . . Na c'ettha samudayārammaṇatā āsaṅkitabbasamudayābhogasseva abhāvatā. Samuditā pana vaṇṇadhammā ārammaṇa-paccayo hoti.*

603 Cf. VsmṬ. 472.

604 See Ven. Dhammajoti, *Abhidharma Doctrine and Controversy on Perception*, 74.

605 VsmṬ. 472: *Visuṃ visuṃ asamatthānaṃ sivakāvāhanādisu samatthatāya dassanato. Kesādīnañ ca yasmiṃ ṭhāne ṭhitānaṃ paccekaṃ vaṇṇaṃ gahetuṃ na sakkā, tasmiṃ yeva hi samuditānaṃ vaṇṇaṃ gahetuṃ sakkā ti bhiyyo pi tesaṃ saṃhaccakāritā paribyattā. Etena "cakkhuviññāṇassa paramāṇurūpaṃ ārammaṇaṃ udāhu taṃsamudayo ti" adikā codanā paṭikkhittā ti veditabbā.*

606 CMA. 152.

607 DhsA. 575.

608 CMA, 17.

609 ADVṬ. *Tattha cakkhudvārikacittānaṃ sabbesam'pi rūpam eva ārammaṇaṃ, tañ ca paccuppannaṃ, tathā sotadvārikacittādīnam'pi saddādīni, tāni ca paccuppannāni yeva. Manodvārikacittānam pana chabbidham'pi paccuppannaṃ atītaṃ anāgataṃ kālavimuttañ ca yathārahaṃ ālambanaṃ hoti.*

610 ADVṬ. 163ff.

611 ADVṬ. 163ff.

612 DhsA. 74.

613 Based on Sarachchandra, *Buddhist Psychology of Perception*, 63ff.; *Compen-*

dium of Philosophy (*Abhidhammatthasaṅgaha*), trans. Aung, ed. Mrs. Rhys Davids, 37ff.

614 Sarachchandra, *Buddhist Psychology of Perception*, 54.

615 See, e.g., UdA. 42; VbhA. 3-4; PsmA. I, 79; Abhvk. 315.

616 CMA. 234.

617 CMA. 235 (S. III, 86).

618 Abhvk. 245: *Ruppatī ti sītuṇhādīhi vikāraṃ āpajjati, āpādīyatī ti vā attho. Vikāruppatti ca sītādi-virodhappaccaya-sannidhāne visadisuppatti yeva. Na hi yathāsakaṃ paccayehi uppajjitvā ṭhitadhammānaṃ aññena kena ci vikārāpādanaṃ sakkā kātuṃ; tasmā purimuppanna-rūpasantati viya ahutvā pacchā uppajjamānānaṃ visabhāga-paccaya-samavāyena visadisuppatti yeva idha ruppanan ti daṭṭhabbaṃ.*

619 See, e.g., VśmS. VI, 51: *Mihi ruppana nam kimayat? Sītādivirodhapratyaya sannniddhyayehi visadṛśotpattiyayi.*

620 On the denial of motion, see chapter 17, "Momentariness."

621 Abhvk. 245; see also VśmS. V, 52.

622 DhsA. 328; Vsm. 449.

623 DhsA. 328; Vsm. 449.

624 AKB. 21; AKvy. 24. That the Theravādins were aware of this Sarvāstivāda definition is shown by DṬ. 665: *Paṭighāto ruppanan ti apare.*

625 AKvy. 56.

626 See chapter 12, "The Great Elements of Matter."

627 See chapter 15, "The Material Clusters."

628 See chapter 15, "The Material Clusters."

629 Cf. VsmṬ. 459–60: *Svāyaṃ rūpasaddo rūḷhiyā ataṃsabhāve'pi pavattatī ti aparena rūpasaddena visesetvā vuttaṃ rūpa-rūpan ti.*

630 They are a species of sensitive matter; see chapter 13, "The Real Dependent Matter."

631 See AKB. 5; AKvy. 29.

632 See chapter 13, "The Real Dependent Matter."

633 *Yaṃ kiñci rūpaṃ atītānāgatapaccuppannaṃ ajjhattaṃ vā bahiddhā vā oḷārikaṃ vā sukhumaṃ vā hīnaṃ vā paṇītaṃ vā yaṃ dūre santike vā, sabbaṃ rūpaṃ . . .* See, e.g., M. III, 16; S. III, 47; S. IV, 382.

634 See Dhs. 148.

635 See DhsA. 337; ADVṬ. 116; Abhvk. 294.

636 See DhsA. 337; ADVṬ. 116; Abhvk. 294.

637 AKvy. 294.

638 AKB. 36; AKvy. 44.

639 AKB. 36; AKvy. 44.
640 Vbh. 2, 3.
641 See AKB. 36–37; AKvy. 44–45.
642 D. III, 217.
643 See Dhs. 147.
644 See Dhs. 147; DhsA. 264.
645 See, e.g., M. I, 421; S. V, 204; A. IV, 57; D. III, 228, 276; S. II, 11, 98; M. I, 48.
646 A. IV, 57.
647 See AKvy. 57.
648 See chapter 16, "Time and Space."
649 Kvu. 459–62; 626–27.
650 See, e.g., DhsA. 343.
651 Cf. ADVṬ. 112: *Kammādīhi paccayehi nipphannattā nipphannarūpaṃ nāma.* See also Abhvk. 291.
652 ADVṬ. 112.
653 Vsm. 381.
654 CMA. 237.
655 ADVṬ. 112.
656 ADVṬ. 112: *Sabhāven'eva upalabbhamānato lakkhaṇattayāropaṇena sammasituṃ arahattā sammasanarūpaṃ.*
657 See, e.g., SS.
658 See Tkp. 3, 4, 6, 7.
659 ADVṬ. 110: *Yaṃ hi mahābhūte upādiyati sayañ ca aññehi upādiyati na taṃ upādārūpaṃ; yaṃ pana upādiyateva na kena ci upādiyati tad eva upādāya rūpan ti.*
660 See Bhaduri, *Studies in Nyāya-Vaiśeṣika Metaphysics*, chap. 3.
661 See *Pañcastikāyasāra*, ed. and trans. Chakravartinayanar, 79.
662 See, e.g., D. III, 274; M. I, 431.
663 See, e.g., M. III, 31; A. I, 176.
664 See, e.g., M. I, 421ff.
665 Vsm. 296.
666 Cf. VsmṬ. 362–63: *Nanu ca kakkhaḷattam eva paṭhavīdhātū ti? Saccam etam. Tathā'pi viññātāviññāta-saddatthatā-vasena abhinne'pi dhamme kappanā-siddhena bhedena evaṃ niddeso kato. Evaṃ hi atthavisesāvabodho hotī ti.*
667 DhsA. 286.
668 Vsm. 287; Abhvt. 64.
669 *Compendium of Philosophy* (*Abhidhammatthasaṅgaha*), trans. Aung, ed. Mrs. Rhys Davids, 155 n.1.

670 Vsm. 289; see also DhsA. 332; Mvn. 58; Abhvk. 240.

671 AKvy. 3.

672 Vsm. 289; DhsA. 336; Abhvk. 250; Mvn. 58.

673 *Expositor*, 435; DhsA. 335: *Ayapiṇḍi-ādīni āpodhātu ābandhitvā thaddāni karoti, tāya ābaddhattā tāni thaddhāni nāma honti. Pāsāna-pabbata-tālaṭṭhi-hatthidanta-gosiṅgādīsu'pi es'eva nayo. Sabbāni h'etāni āpodhātu eva āband-hitvā thaddhāni karoti, āpodhātuyā ābaddhattā va thaddhāni honti.*

674 AKvy. 33.

675 AKvy. 33.

676 *The Vaiśeṣika Sūtras of Kanāda*, 59.

677 ADVṬ. 111: *Kiñcāpi hi sītatā phusitvā gayhati, sā pana tejo yeva. Mande hi uṇhatte sītabuddhi, sītasaṅkhātassa kassa ci guṇassa abhāvato. . . . Tathā hi ghammakāle ātāpe ṭhatvā chāyaṃ paviṭṭhānaṃ sītabuddhi hoti, tatth'eva ci-rakālaṃ ṭhitānaṃ uṇhabuddhi.* See also VsmṬ. 459; VśmS. V, 75.

678 DhsA. 332.

679 Dhs. 177; see also Vbh. 84.

680 VsmṬ. 359; Abhvk. 249; ADVṬ. 110.

681 VsmṬ. 359; ADVṬ. 110.

682 Vsm. 346: *Sabbāsam'pi dhātūnaṃ salakkhaṇādito nānattaṃ. Aññāni eva hi paṭhavīdhātuyā lakkhaṇa-rasa-paccupaṭṭhānāni, aññāni āpodhātu-ādīnaṃ.*

683 DhsA. 336.

684 See chapter 17, "Momentariness."

685 *The Path of Purification* (*Visuddhimagga*), trans. Bhikkhu Ñāṇamoli, 402 (Vsm. 391).

686 Vsm. 381.

687 *The Path of Purification* (*Visuddhimagga*), trans. Bhikkhu Ñāṇamoli, 401.

688 VsmṬ. 364: *Yadi hi imā dhātuyo aññam'aññassa anto ṭhitā na sakiccakarā si-yuṃ. . . . Atha bahiṭṭhā vinibbhuttā siyuṃ. Tathā sati avinibbhuttavādo hāy-eyya. Tasmā na niddisitabbaṭṭhānā.* See also Abhvk. 248.

689 *The Path of Purification* (*Visuddhimagga*), Bhikkhu Ñāṇamoli, 403 (Vsm. 452).

690 AKvy. 33: *Pṛthivī-dravye saṃgraha-pakti-vyūhana-darśanāc cheṣāṇāṃ jala-tejo-vāyūnām astitvam anumīyate. apsu nau-saṃdhāraṇoṣṇateraṇa-karma-darśanāt pṛthivī-tejo-vāyūnām astitvaṃ. agni-jvālāyāṃ sthairya-sampiṇḍana-calana-darśanāt pṛthivyudaka-vāyūnām astitvaṃ. vāyau saṃdhāraṇa-śītoṣṇa-sparśa-darśanāt pṛthivy-ap-tejasām astitvam iti Vaibhāṣikāḥ.*

691 See Bhaduri, *Studies in Nyāya-Vaiśeṣika Metaphysics*, chap. 4.

692 VsmṬ. 450ff.; Abhvk. 273ff.

693 VsmṬ. 451; Abhvk. 273ff.

694 See AKvy. 124.

695 See VsmṬ. 451; Abhvk. 273.

696 DhsA. 333: *Kim pana etāni tīṇi mahābhūtāni ekappahāren'eva āpātham āgacchanti udāhu no ti? Āgacchanti. Evaṃ āgatāni kāyappasādaṃ ghaṭṭentī ti? Ghaṭṭenti. Ekappahāren'eva tāni ārammaṇam katvā kāyaviññāṇaṃ uppajjati n'ūppajjatī ti? N'ūppajjati. Kasmā? Ābhuñjitavasena vā hi ussadavasena vā ārammaṇakaraṇaṃ hoti.*

697 *Expositor*, 434 (DhsA. 333–34).

698 *Expositor*, 434 (DhsA. 333–34).

699 AKB. 53.

700 AKB. 53.

701 See Vsm. 357; Abhvk. 274.

702 *Compendium of Philosophy* (*Abhidhammatthasaṅgaha*), trans. Aung, ed. Mrs. Rhys Davids, 155 n.6.

703 DhsA. 179.

704 See Seal, *Positive Sciences of the Ancient Hindus*, chap. 1.

705 Seal, *Positive Sciences of the Ancient Hindus*, chap. 1.

706 Cf. *Pañcastikāyasāra*, ed. and trans. Chakravartinayanar, 28: *Adesamattamutto dhāducatukkassa kāraṇaṃ jo du, so neo paramāṇo pariṇāmaguṇo sayamasaddo.*

707 See Bhaduri, *Studies in Nyāya-Vaiśeṣika Metaphysics*, chap. 3.

708 See chapter 15, "The Material Clusters."

709 Cf., e.g., M. I, 111–12, 190, 259; S. IV, 39–40, 67ff.

710 *A Buddhist Manual of Psychological Ethics* (*Dhammasaṅgaṇi*), trans. Mrs. Rhys Davids, 173 n.1.

711 AKvy. 24.

712 AKvy. 68: *Na hīndriyāṇi dvi-dhā bhavanti chinnasyāṃgasya kāyād apagatasya nirindriyatvāt. idam api kathaṃ gamyate. nirindriyaṃ tad aṃgaṃ yac chinnaṃ kāyād apagatam iti. yasmāt tat pratītya spraṣṭavy'ādikaṃ ca kāy'ādi-vijñānānupapattiḥ.*

713 AKvy. 68: *Kathaṃ tarhi chinnena punar lagnena nasikā'greṇa kāyavijñānotpattiḥ. nāsikā-mūla-saṃbandhena punaḥ kāyendriyotpatter adoṣaḥ. katham iha gṛhagodhik'ādīnāṃ pucchāni chinnāni spandante yadi tatra kāyendriyaṃ nāsti. vāyu-dhātor eṣa vikāro.*

714 DhsA. 306–7.

715 Translation mainly based on Ven. Ñāṇamoli's *The Path of Purification* (*Visud-*

dhimagga) (Vsm. 445–46; DhsA. 307ff.).

716 Vsm. 444; DhsA. 312.

717 Stcherbatsky, *Central Conception of Buddhism*, 12.

718 Sinha, *Indian Psychology: Perception*, chap. 1.

719 See Bhaduri, *Studies in Nyāya-Vaiśeṣika Metaphysics*, 152ff.

720 Vsm. 376: *Keci pana tejādhikānaṃ pasādo cakkhu, vāyu-paṭhavī-āpādhikānaṃ bhūtānaṃ pasādo sota-ghāna-jivhā, kāyo sabbesan ti vadanti. Apare tejādhikānaṃ pasādo cakkhu, vivara-vāyu-āpa-paṭhavādikānaṃ sota-ghāna-jivhā-kāyā ti vadanti.* See also DhsA. 312–13. That *bhūtānaṃ* means "among the supporting great elements" is supported by the rest of the passage in Vsm. and by VśmS. V, 56–57.

721 VsmṬ. 431.

722 VśmS. V 57.

723 *The Path of Purification* (*Visuddhimagga*), trans. Bhikkhu Ñāṇamoli, 491–92 (Vsm. 444–45; see also DhsA. 312–13).

724 DhsA. 312.

725 DhsA. 317.

726 See Vsm. 445; DhsA. 313; Abhvt. 67; Abhvk. 262.

727 AKvy. 83.

728 See CMA. chap. 4.

729 See Vsm. 491ff.

730 See Vsm. 493ff.; AKB. 107–8; AKvy. 96.

731 Dhs. 139.

732 DhsA. 317: *Dīghādīni hi aññam' aññaṃ upanidhāya siddhāni, vaṭṭādīni sannivesena. Tattha rassaṃ upanidhāya tato uccataraṃ dīghaṃ, taṃ upanidhāya tato nīcataraṃ rassaṃ, thūlaṃ upanidhāya tato khuddakataraṃ aṇukaṃ, taṃ upanidhāya tato mahantataraṃ thūlaṃ.*

733 DhsA. 317: *Tattha yasmā dīghādīni phusitvā' pi sakkā jānituṃ, nīlādīni pan'eva na sakkā tasmā na nippariyāyena dīghaṃ rūpāyatanaṃ; tathā rassādīni.*

734 DhsA. 317.

735 AbhMṬ. 106; Abhvk. 254; ADVṬ. 49.

736 AKB. 165; AKvy. 26.

737 See AKvy. 26: *Na hi cākṣuṣam etat saṃsthāna-grahaṇaṃ. mānasaṃ tv etat parikalpitaṃ. varṇa-saṃniveśa-viśeṣa eva hi saṃsthānaṃ. na saṃsthānaṃ nāma dravyaṃ kiṃcid asti. varṇāgrahaṇe saṃsthāna-grahaṇābhāvāt.* See also *Le traité de la démonstration de l'acte*, 209ff.

738 AKB. 195ff.

739 AKB. 195ff.

740 See chapter 14, "The Nominal Dependent Matter."

741 *Expositor*; DhsA. 313: *Dūre rukkhaṃ chindantānam pi rajakānañ ca vatthaṃ dhovantānaṃ dūrato va kāyavikāro paññāyati. Saddo pana dhātuparamparāya sotaṃ ghaṭṭetvā saṇikaṃ vavatthānaṃ gacchatī ti.*

742 Sarachchandra, *Buddhist Psychology of Perception*, 34.

743 Sinha, *Indian Psychology: Perception*, 22.

744 DhsA. 314. Thus according to the *Sīhala Aṭṭhakathā*, all the sense organs are *sampatta-gocara*—that is, they apprehend their objects when the latter come in contact with them. On the other hand, according to the Pāli commentators only the organs of smell, taste, and touch are *sampatta-gocara*. However, in the Pāli commentaries the term *sampatta-gocara* is sometimes used in respect to all the sense organs. It seems that *sampatta* is used as referring not only to the physical contact between the organ and the object but sometimes to the apprehension of the object by the organ as well. See AKB(FT). 87 n.1, where de La Vallée Poussin cites a *Vibhāṣā* passage according to which *prāpta*, which in this context corresponds to Pāli *sampatta*, occurs in the same two senses.

745 DhsA. 314: *Saddo pi sace saṇikaṃ āgaccheyya dūre uppanno cireṇa sūyeyya, paramparāghaṭṭanāya ca āgantvā sotaṃ ghaṭṭento asukadisāya nāmā ti na paññāyeyya.*

746 DhsA. 314.

747 VsmṬ. 446–47.

748 ADVṬ. 114.

749 AKvy. 69.

750 See chapter 15, "The Material Clusters."

751 VsmṬ. 452.

752 Dhs. 141.

753 DhsA. 320.

754 AKvy. 27.

755 Dhs. 142.

756 AKvy. 27.

757 Dhs. 142; see also Vbh. 122–23.

758 *Expositor*, 419ff. (DhsA. 321–22).

759 *Expositor*, 419ff. (DhsA. 321–22).

760 DhsA. 321: . . . *itthiliṅgādi pana na itthindriyaṃ...yathā bīje sati bījaṃ paṭicca rukkho vaḍḍhitvā sākhāviṭapasampanno ākāsaṃ pūretvā tiṭṭhati. Evam eva itthibhāvasaṅkhāte itthindriye sati itthiliṅgādīni honti. Bījaṃ viya hi itthindriyaṃ.*

761 DhsA. 321: . . . *yan ti kāraṇavacanaṃ. Yena kāraṇena*. . . .

762 Vsm. 378; Abhvk. 269; ADVṬ. 111.

763 Vsm. 378: *Na ca kāyappasādena ṭhitokāse ṭhitan ti vā aṭṭhitokāse ṭhitan ti vā vattabbaṃ.*

764 Vsm. 448; Abhvk. 269: *Na ca tassa kāyappasādena saṅkaro lakkhaṇabhedato nissayabhedato vā.*

765 AKvy. 97.

766 VsmṬ. 448.

767 See Dhs. 147.

768 See chapter 15, "The Material Clusters."

769 Kvu. 394ff.; KvuA. 112.

770 Kvu. 394ff.

771 Jaini, "Origin and Development of the Theory of *Viprayuktasaṃskāras*," 100–102.

772 AKB. 53.

773 See, e.g., D. III, 228, 276; M. I, 48; S. II, 11, 93.

774 Dhs. 144.

775 DhsA. 330.

776 Dhs. 340.

777 See AKB. 152.

778 See AKB. 152.

779 Based on *The Path of Purification*, trans. Bhikkhu Ñāṇamoli, 497 n.26 (VsmṬ. 449–50); see also Abhvk. 271, ADSS. 154–55, and VśmS. VI, 64–65, where the same explanation is repeated.

780 See VsmṬ. 449; VśmS. V, 64–65.

781 Abhvk. 271: *Aṭṭhikatvā manasikatvā sabbaṃ cetasā samannāharitvā kiñci cintentassa hadayappadesassa khijjanato tatthedaṃ tiṭṭhatī ti viññāyati.*

782 Cf. DhsA. 226; VsmṬ. 459–60.

783 DhsA. 227

784 Vbh. 84.

785 See, e.g., A. B. Keith, *Buddhist Philosophy in India and Ceylon*, 189.

786 Vbh. 84–85.

787 AKvy. 15, 57.

788 Vsm. 379; MV. 65; Abhvt. 70.

789 MV. 65: *Yāya paricchinnesu rūpesu idaṃ ito uddhaṃ, adho, tiriyan ti ca hoti.*

790 AbhD. 13: *ākāśa-dhātus tu cākṣuṣo rūpāyatana-saṃgṛhītaḥ, āloka-tamaḥsabhāvo varṇaviśeṣo . . .*

791 Kvu. 330–31; KvuA. 142.

792 Abhvk. 279.

793 See KSP. IV, 212–13; AKB(FT). 4; *La Siddhi de Hiuan Tsang* (*Vijñaptimātratāsiddhi*), trans. de La Vallée Poussin, vol. 1, 48.

794 *A Budddhist Manual of Psychological Ethics* (*Dhammasaṅgaṇi*), trans. Mrs. Rhys Davids, 186 (Dhs. 143).

795 Dhs. 147.

796 Dhs., 148.

797 Dhs. 179.

798 See DhsA. 83, 343; Vsm. 448; Abhvk. 273ff.

799 Abhvk. 274–75: . . . *mahantaṃ pāsānaṃ ukkhipantassa sabbatthāmena gahaṇakāle sarīrassa ussahanavikāro viya . . . labbhamāno eko ākāravikāro kāyaviññatti nāmā ti vuttaṃ hoti*. See also ADVṬ. 13.

800 DhsA. 96.

801 Expositor, 112 (Dhs. 96).

802 See chapter 10, "The Cognitive Process."

803 Expositor, 110 (DhsA. 96).

804 Expositor, 110 (DhsA. 96).

805 DhsA. 95–96.

806 Expositor, 110–11 (DhsA. 97).

807 DhsA. 96ff.

808 Expositor, 110ff. (DhsA. 97).

809 DhsA. 98.

810 *La Siddhi de Hiuan Tsang* (*Vijñaptimātratāsiddhi*), vol. 1, 48.

811 KSP. IV, 219ff.

812 KSP. IV, 219ff.

813 AKvy. 26; KSP. IV, 207–9.

814 AKvy. 26.

815 DhsA. 96.

816 AKvy.: *Yathā kāya-vijñaptiḥ saṃsthānātmikā na tathā vāg-vijñaptiḥ. kiṃ tarhi. vāg-ātmako dhvanir varṇ'ātmakaḥ śabda ity arthaḥ*. See also CPM. 307; KSP. IV, 156, 260.

817 Dhs. 143–44, 148.

818 Both *kāya-viññatti* and *vacī-viññatti* are included in *dhammāyatana*, the sphere of mental objects.

819 VsmṬ. 452.

820 Abhvk. 277; Mvn. 65.

821 Abhvk. 277; Mvn. 65.

822 Expositor, 115–16 (DhsA. 87).

823 DhsA. 87.

824 DhsA. 87.

825 DhsA. 85–86.

826 DhsA. 85–86.

827 Expositor, 113 (DhsA. 86).

828 DhsA. 85ff.

829 DhsA. 85.

830 Expositor, 112 (DhsA. 85).

831 DhsA. 86.

832 See chapter 9, "The Beautiful Mental Factors."

833 See Dhs. 144.

834 Cf., e.g., D. I, 67; M. II, 187.

835 Cf. the description of the eight *kusītavatthus*, bases of indolence, in A. IV, 332ff.

836 *Theragāthā*, 15.

837 Abhvk. 281.

838 See ADSS. 165.

839 See DhsA. 326–27; Vsm. 448–49.

840 VsmṬ. 453: *Dhātukkhobho*: *vāta-pitta-semhappakopo*; *rasādidhātūnaṃ vā vikārāvatthā*.

841 VsmṬ. 453: *Dvidhā vutto'pi atthato paṭhavi-ādi-dhātūnam yeva vikāro daṭṭhabbo*.

842 CMA. 240.

843 Dhs. 153.

844 Dhs. 153.

845 DhsA. 328; see chapter 11, "The Analysis of Matter."

846 Dhs. 153.

847 DhsA. 282.

848 DhsA. 282.

849 DhsA. 282.

850 Expositor, 427 (DhsA. 282).

851 See Kvu. 493ff.

852 Dhs. 144.

853 KvuA. 113: *cutikkhaṇasmiṃ dve'pi jīvitāni sah'eva bhijjanti*.

854 DhsA. 282: *Atthatohi ubhayampetaṃ jātirūpasseva adhivacanaṃ; ākāra-nānattena pana veneyyavasena ca upacayo santatī ti uddesadesanaṃ*. . . .

855 See chapter 17, "Momentariness."

856 Cf. Vsm. 449–50; DhsA. 327; Abhvk. 282ff.

857 Vsm. 449; DhsA. 328.

858 Cf. Mvn. 67–68: *Na hi jāti jāyati, jarā jīrati, maraṇaṃ mīyatī ti voharituṃ yuttaṃ, anavaṭṭhānato.* See also Abhvk. 288; AKvy. 211; CPM. 110 n.273.

859 See AKB(FT). 90 n.1; McGovern, *Manual of Buddhist Philosophy*, 126ff.

860 See chapter 18, "Conditional Relations."

861 That things can arise from a single cause (*ekakāraṇavāda*) and that a thing can arise as a single, solitary effect (*ekassa dhammassa uppatti*) are both rejected (DhsA. 59–60).

862 See ADS. 28; VśmS. 389; CMA. 244.

863 See Vsm. 364: *Kalāpato ti yā ayaṃ kesa-lomā ti ādinā nayena vīsatiyā ākārehi paṭhavīdhātu, pittaṃ semhan ti ādinā nayena dvādasākārehi āpodhātu niddiṭṭhā. Tattha yasmā: 'vaṇṇo gandho raso ojā catasso cā'pi dhātuyo aṭṭhadhammasamodhānā hoti kesā ti sammuti tesaṃ yeva vinibbhogā natthi kesā ti sammuti.' Tasmā kesā'pi aṭṭhadhammakalāpamattam eva.*

864 Vsm 365: . . . *imasmiṃ hi sarīre majjhimena pamāṇena parigayhamānā paramāṇubhedasañcuṇṇā sukhumarajabhūtā paṭhavīdhātu doṇamattā siyā, sā toto upaḍḍhappamāṇāya āpodhātuyā saṅgahitā.*

865 See, e.g., ADS. 29; ADSS. 156; ADVṬ. 58; SS. 4; NRS. 19.

866 This conclusion gets further confirmed by VśmS. IV, 136, where it is stated that *aṭṭha-dhamma-kalāpa* refers to the eight kinds of *rūpa*, which in their combination is called head hair: (*aṭṭhadhammakalāpamattam eva*) *yanudu keśa-prajñaptiyaṭa kāraṇa vū varṇādīn ekatvayen gena kīha. Ovun aṣṭadharmamātra noveyi data yutu.*

867 Vsm. 365.

868 See, e.g., VsmṬ. 453; ADVṬ. 98; Abhvk. 279; VśmS. V, 67.

869 CMA. 252.

870 ADVṬ. 58: . . . *etāni rūpāni kammādito uppajjamānāni'pi ekekaṃ va na samuṭṭhahanti, atha kho piṇḍato' va samuṭṭhahanti.* See also ADSS. 166.

871 Ven. Dhammajoti, *Sarvāstivāda Abhidharma*, 260.

872 Ven. Dhammajoti, *Sarvāstivāda Abhidharma*, 260.

873 See AKvy. 123ff.

874 AKvy. 85: *Tad etad dig-bhāga-bhedavattvaṃ necchanti Vaibhāṣikāḥ. dig-bhāga-bhedo hi saṃghāta-rūpāṇām eva kalpyate.*

875 AKvy. 85.

876 AKvy. 85.

877 AKvy. 85ff.

878 Cf. Viṃś. 7: *Naiva hi paramāṇavaḥ saṃyujyante niravayavatvāt. mā bhūd eṣa doṣaprasaṅghaḥ. saṃhatās tu parasparaṃ saṃyujyanta iti kāśmīravaibhāṣikāsta idaṃ praṣṭhavyāḥ. yaḥ paramāṇūnāṃ saṃghāto na sa tebhyo'rthān-*

taram iti. See *La Siddhi de Hiuan Tsang* (*Vijñaptimātratāsiddhi*), vol. 1, 39ff.

879 *La Siddhi de Hiuan Tsang* (*Vijñaptimātratāsiddhi*), vol. 1, 40; cf. Viṃś. 7: *Chāyāvatī kathaṃ vā yady ekaikasya paramāṇor digbhāgabhedo na syād ādityodaye katham anyatra chāyā bhavaty anyatrātapaḥ. na hi tasyānyaḥ pradeśo'sti yatrātapo na syāt. āvaraṇaṃ ca kathaṃ bhavati paramāṇoḥ paramāṇvantarena yadi digbhāgabhedo neṣyate. na hi kaścid api paramāṇoḥ parabhāgo'sti yatrāgamanād anyenānyasya pratighātaḥ syāt.*

880 Cf. Viṃś. 7: *ṣaṭkena yugapadyogāt paramāṇoḥ ṣaḍaṃśatā. ṣaḍbhyo digbhyaḥ ṣaḍbhiḥ paramāṇubhir yugapadyoge sati paramāṇoḥ ṣaḍaṃśatāṃ prāpnoti. ekasya yo deśas tatrānyasya saṃbhavāt. ṣaṇṇāṃ samānadeśatvāt piṇḍaḥ syād aṇumātrakaḥ. atha ya evaikasya paramāṇor deśaḥ sa eva ṣaṇṇāṃ. tena sarveṣāṃ samānadeśatvāt sarvaḥ piṇḍaḥ paramāṇumātraḥ syāt.*

881 DhsA. 311.

882 VśmS. V, 68: *ākāśadhātu . . . me uḍaya me yaṭa yayi kalāpayange paryantaya pahaḷa kirīma kṛtya koṭa ettīyi.*

883 VbhA. 343; see also *Abhidhānappadīpikā-sūci*, ed. Ven. Subhūti, 138ff.

884 VbhA. 343.

885 VbhA. 286.

886 See, e.g., *Pañcastikāyasāra*, ed. and trans. Chakravartinayanar, 84.

887 AKB. 33.

888 AKB. 33.

889 AKvy. 85: *Yan madhye nāsti kiṃcid iti bruvāṇā Vaibhāṣikā madhye ālok'ādi necchanti. anya-paramāṇu-praveśānavakāśaṃ tu na bruvate*; see also AKB. 32.

890 AKvy. 84ff.

891 AKvy. 85; see also Viṃś. 7.

892 AKvy. 85.

893 AKvy. 85.

894 See VsmṬ. 453; ADVṬ. 98; Abhvk. 279; VśmS. V, 67; cf. ADSS. 156: (*ākāsadhātu), karmādi eki ekī pratyayen samurthita vū cakśur-daśakādi kalāpayan kalāpantaraya hā saṃkara novana heyin pirisindinā sabhāva vū ākāśadhātu tomo*; (*pariccheda-rūpaṃ nāma*) *paricchedarūpa nam ve.*

895 VsmṬ. 453.

896 VsmṬ. 453.

897 VsmṬ. 453: (*Rūpa-mariyāda-paccupaṭṭhānā*) *ti yasmiṃ kalāpe bhūtānaṃ paricchedo teh'eva asamphuṭṭha-bhāva-paccupaṭṭhānā.*

898 Abhvk. 279; ADSS. 156.

899 Cf. VśmS. V, 68.

900 Cf. VśmS. V, 68: *Ekkalāpayakama rū ven ven koṭa pirisindiyen. Me ese vuvahot*

ek kalabuyehi rū da nānā kalāpayehi rū seyin ma vinirbhogabavaṭa peminena bevin he da no menava.

901 See Abhvk. 297. See also ADS. 29; SS. 5; NRP. 39.

902 Cf. AKvy. 126: *Yad bhūta-catuṣkam āśraya ekasyopādāya-rūpasya nīlasya pīta-sya vā. na tad evānyasyopādāya-rūpasya gandhasya rasasya v'āśrayaḥ. kiṃ tarhi. anyad eva bhūta-catuṣkaṃ tasy' āśraya iti Vaibhāṣika-siddhāntaḥ.*

903 AKvy. 126.

904 ADSS. 166; cf. Abhvk. 297.

905 See AKvy. 123; ADS. 29; SS. 5.

906 Cf. AKB. 22.

907 See ADS. 29; SS. 4; NRP. 38.

908 AKvy. 123.

909 See Bhaduri, *Nyāya-Vaiśeṣika Metaphysics*, chap. 3.

910 See DhsA. 311; Vsm. 432.

911 CMA. 252ff.

912 CMA. 254: *Kalāpānaṃ pariccheda-lakkhaṇattā vicakkhanā na kalāpaṅgam icc'āhu ākāsaṃ lakkhaṇāni ca.*

913 See the section on "Means of Intimation" in chapter 14, "The Nominal Dependent Matter."

914 See the section on "Means of Intimation" in chapter 14, "The Nominal Dependent Matter."

915 See the section on "Means of Intimation" in chapter 14, "The Nominal Dependent Matter."

916 See CMA. 253.

917 Abhvk. 281.

918 See the section "The Special Modes of Matter" in chapter 14, "The Nominal Dependent Matter."

919 See the section "The Special Modes of Matter" in chapter 14, "The Nominal Dependent Matter."

920 See AKB. 33.

921 Cf. ADSS. 165: *Laghutādi-traya*; (*utucittāhārehi*) *satprāya ṛtuya prasanna cit-taya satprāya āhāraya yana meyin* (*sambhoti*) *vanneyi.*

922 CMA. 254: *Tattha suddhaṭṭhakaṃ saddanavakañ cāti dve utu-samuṭṭhā-na-kalapā bahiddhā'pi labbhanti. Avasesā pana sabbe'pi ajjhattam evā ti.*

923 See DhsA. 342ff.

924 See the section "The Material Faculty of Life," in chapter 13, "The Real Dependent Matter."

925 Kvu. 511ff.

926 VsmṬ. 543: *Kālo karoti bhūtāni kālo saṃharatī pajā / kālo suttesu jāgarati kālo hi duratikkamo ti kālavādino.* The Pāli for "die," *kālaṃ karoti*, "he does his time" = "he has fulfilled his time" (PTSD), indicates that death is due to the irreversible flow of time. Cf. *kālaṃ kaṅkhati*, "to await the appointed time." UdA. 52: *Kaleti satte khepetī ti kālo, maraṇam. Taṃ kato patto ti kālaṅkato; kālena vā maccunā kato naṭṭho adassanaṃ gato ti kālaṅkato.* SA. II, 13: *Kālo nāma antako; tassa kiriyā ti kālakiriyā.*

927 PTS. 181, Jātaka (Pāli) II, 260: *Kālo ghasati bhūtāni sabbān'eva sah'attanā / yo ca kālaghaso bhūto so bhūtapacaniṃ pacī ti.* The translation was modified for clarity.

928 MA. I, 29: *Yo ca kālaghaso bhūto ti ettha khīṇāsave* [*bhūtasaddo*].

929 MNdA. 85.

930 VsmṬ. 259: *Ayaṃ hi addhāna-saddo kālassa desassa ca vācako.*

931 SA. III, 119; MNdA. 59.

932 DhsA. 56; ItiA. I, 41.

933 DṬ. 32.

934 AbhMṬ. 47.

935 DhsA. 57–58; AbhMṬ. 47: *Appeva nāma sve'va upasaṅkameyyāma kālañ ca samayañ ca upādāyā ti ettha kālo nāma upasaṅkamanassa yutta-payutta-kālo. Samayo nāma tass'eva paccayasāmaggi.*

936 DhsA. 57–58. A free translation of: *Sace amhākaṃ sve'va gamanassa yuttakālo bhavissati kāye balamattā c'eva . . . gamanapaccayā ca añño aphāsuvihāro na bhavissati, athetaṃ kālañ ca gamana-kāraṇa-samavāya-saṅkhātaṃ samayañ ca upadhāretvā api eva nāma sve āgaccheyyāmā ti.*

937 DṬ. 32.

938 UdA. 30ff.

939 DhsA .59.

940 DṬ. 32.

941 DhsA. 59.

942 DhsA. 59.

943 *Expositor*, 78 (DhsA. 59).

944 DhsA. (SHB. vol. 42), 76.

945 DhsA. (SHB. vol. 42), 76; DṬ. 272; UdA. 19.

946 Abhvk. 407.

947 DṬ. 679.

948 DṬ. 679.

949 AbhMṬ. 47: *Kālo'pi hi citta-paricchinno sabhāvato avijjamāno'pi ādhārabhāven'eva saññāto adhikaraṇan ti vutto.* DṬ. 32: *Dhammappavatti-*

mattatāya atthato abhūto'pi hi kālo dhammappavattiyā adhikaraṇaṃ; karaṇaṃ viya ca kappanā-matta-siddhena rūpena vohariyatī ti.

950 See chapter 2, "The Nominal and the Conceptual."

951 VbhA. 12; PsmA. 20, 28–29, 361–62; VsmṬ. 496.

952 DhsA. 420ff.

953 DhsA. 420ff.

954 Ven. Nyanaponika Thera, *Abhidhamma Studies*, 106–7.

955 VbhA. 10–11; VśmS. 233ff.

956 DhsA. (SHB. vol. 42), 76.

957 Ven. Nyanaponika Thera, *Abhidhamma Studies*, 93.

958 See chapter 4, "The Analysis of Mind."

959 UdA. 31: *Tathā kālo sabhāva-dhamma-pavattimattāya paramatthato avijjamāno'pi ādhārabhāvena paññatto.*

960 UdA. 31: *Adhikaraṇaṃ hi kālattho* (*kāla* means "support" or "location"); *samūhattho ca samayo* (*samaya* means "aggregation").

961 UdA. 31: *Yathā hi gāvīsu duyhamānāsu gato, duddhāsu āgato' ti, ettha gāvīnaṃ dohana-kiriyāya gamana-kiriyā lakkhīyati.*

962 See, e.g., DhsA. 167; DṬ. 32: *Khaṇo eva ca samayo. Yo khaṇo ti ca samayo ti ca vuccati so ekovāti hi attho.*

963 See Ven. Nyanaponika Thera, *Abhidhamma Studies*, 93ff.

964 SA. III, 156–57; MNdA. 122.

965 Mil. 49–50.

966 ADSS. 151.

967 SA. III, 155.

968 MNdA. 85.

969 Sn. v. 373.

970 Mil. 387–88.

971 Mil. 268.

972 AKB. 3.

973 AKvy. 15.

974 As pointed out by Stcherbatsky in *Buddhist Logic* (1:85 n.3), this way of defining space and elevating it to the level of an unconditioned dharma provoked Kamalaśīla (as recorded in Pañjikā to *Tattvārthasaṃgraha*, 140) to say that since the Vaibhāṣikas (Sarvāstivādins) admit the reality of space they do not deserve to be called Buddhists—*na Śākya-putrīyāḥ*.

975 AbhD. 13.

976 See, e.g., M. I, 231; M. II, 47.

977 D. III, 107.

978 M. I, 424.

979 AKvy. 15; AbhD. 13–14: *Uktaṃ hi Bhagavatā "pṛthivyapsu niśritā / āpo vāyau / vāyur ākāśe / ākāśaṃ tu nityatvāt svapratiṣṭhitam" iti.*

980 Kvu. 328–30.

981 KvuA. 93.

982 See, e.g., KvuA. 92–93; Abhvk. 279.

983 KvuA. 92.

984 AKvy. 57.

985 This is the Madhyamaka position as well. BCA-P. 220 says that since space is devoid of own nature, and free from all activities, it is a mere concept (*prajñapti-san-mātram*).

986 VbhA. 7.

987 A. IV, 137.

988 See, e.g., Vin. I, 33, 41, 57.

989 A. II, 52; Netti. 85.

990 Wijesekera, *Three Signata*, 1.

991 PsmA. (SHB) vol. 3, 612.

992 PsmA. (SHB) vol. 3, 612.

993 Sn. v. 333; Dhp. v. 315.

994 MhNd. I, 117–18:

Jīvitaṃ attabhāvo ca sukhadukkhā ca kevalā
ekacittasamāyuttā, lahuso vattatikkhaṇo.
Cullāsītisahassāni kappā tiṭṭhanti ye marū
na tv'eva te'pi jīvanti dvīhi cittehi samāhitā.
Ye niruddhā marantassa tiṭṭhamānassa vā idha
sabbe'va sadisā khandhā gatā appaṭisandhikā.
Anantarā ca ye bhaṅgā ye ca bhaṅgā anāgatā
tadantare niruddhānaṃ vesammaṃ natthi lakkhaṇe.
Anibbattena na jāto, paccuppannena jīvati
cittabhaṅga-mato loko, paññatti-paramatthiyā.

995 *Origin and Doctrines of Early Indian Buddhist Schools*, trans. Masuda, 34; see also *Documents d'Abhidharma: La controverse du temps,* trans. de La Vallée Poussin, 136ff.

996 Cf. AKvy. 179: *Yo'py āha nikāyāṃtarīya iti ārya-Sāṃmatīyaḥ. sa ghaṭ'āder mudgar'ādi-kṛto vināśa iti manyate. kālāṃtarāvasthāyi hi tasya rūpaṃ. citta-caittānāṃ tu kṣaṇikatvaṃ.*

997 Kvu. 620ff.

998 KvuA. 196.

999 See chapter 10, "The Cognitive Process."

1000 Kvu. 204–8; see also 458–59; 620–21.

1001 Kvu. 207: *upaḍḍhadivaso uppādakkhaṇo upaḍḍhadivaso vayakkhaṇo.*

1002 Yam.: *Saṃkhāra Yamaka,* passim.

1003 A. I, 10.

1004 Rospatt, *The Buddhist Doctrine of Momentariness,* 34ff.

1005 Rospatt, *The Buddhist Doctrine of Momentariness,* 19.

1006 See chapter 18, "Conditional Relations."

1007 PsmA. (SHB.) vol. 3, 425: *Tattha saṅkhatānaṃ uppādakkhaṇe saṅkhatā'pi uppādalakkhaṇam'pi kālasaṅkhāto tassa khaṇo'pi paññāyati. Uppāde vītivatte saṅkhatā'pi jarālakkhaṇam pi kālasaṅkhāto tassa khaṇo'pi paññāyati. Bhaṅgakkhaṇe saṅkhatā'pi bhaṅgalakkhaṇam pi kālasaṅkhāto tassa khaṇo'pi paññāyatī ti Khandhakavaggaṭṭhakathāyaṃ vuttaṃ.*

1008 ADVṬ. 57: *Evañ ca katvā vuttaṃ aṭṭhakathāyam'pi ekekassa cittassa uppādaṭṭhitibhaṅgavasena tayo tayo khaṇā ti.* (When the Pāli commentaries and subcommentaries mention the term *aṭṭhakathā* without any qualification, the reference is to the *Sīhala Aṭṭhakathā.*)

1009 ADVT. 27: *Tāni pana sattarasa cittakkhaṇāni rūpadhammānaṃ āyū ti idaṃ paṭisandhicittena sahuppannaṃ rūpaṃ tato paṭṭhāya sattarasamena saddhiṃ nirujjhati, paṭisandhicittassa ṭhitikkhaṇe uppannaṃ aṭṭharasamassa uppādakkhaṇe nirujjhatī ti Buddhaghosācariyena vuttaṃ. Aṭṭhakathāvacanaṃ nissāya vuttaṃ.*

1010 ADVṬ. 28: *Kāyasaṅkhāro ti cittasamuṭṭhāno assāsapassāsavāto. So cittassa uppādakkhaṇe yeva uppajjati, na ṭhitikkhaṇe vā bhaṅgakkhaṇe vā. Esa cittasamuṭṭhānarūpassa dhammatā ti niyamato cittasaṅkhārena saddhiṃ ekabhaṅgakkhaṇe yeva nirujjhanato āmantā ti vuttan ti. Mahā-aṭṭhakathācariyā'pi atipaññavantā. Na ettakaṃ Yamakapāḷiṃ na passanti; passantā'pi evaṃ vadantī ti.*

1011 A. I, 152.

1012 AKB (FT). 223 n.2.

1013 Bareau, "Les sectes bouddhiques du Petit Véhicule et leurs Abhidharmapiṭaka," 116.

1014 Bareau, "Les sectes bouddhiques du Petit Véhicule et leurs Abhidharmapiṭaka," 116.

1015 Bareau, "Les sectes bouddhiques du Petit Véhicule et leurs Abhidharmapiṭaka," 116.

1016 See, e.g., Vin. I, 33, 41, 57.

1017 Kvu. 460–61.

1018 See Kvu. 459–62; 626–27.

1019 KvuA. 134–35.

1020 A. I, 152.

1021 See AKvy. 174ff.

1022 AKvy. 174 ff.

1023 A. 102.

1024 PsmA. 462.

1025 Cf. AKB. 78: *Jātam ityeva tu na syād asatyāṃ jātau ṣaṣṭhīvacanaṃ ca rūpasyotpādaḥ iti yathā rūpasya rūpam iti / . . . tena tarhy anātmatvam apyeṣṭavyam anātmabuddhisiddhyarthaṃ / saṃkhyā-parimāṇa-pṛthakva-saṃyoga-vibhāga-paratvāparatva-sattādayo'pi tīrthakara-parikalpitā abhyupagantavyā . . . / eṣā ca ṣaṣṭhī kathaṃ kalpyate / rūpasya sabhāva iti / tasmāt prajñaptimātram evaitad abhūtvābhāva-jnāpanārthaṃ kriyate jātam iti / sa cābhūtvābhāvalakṣaṇa utpādo bahuvikalpaḥ / tasya viśeṣaṇārthaṃ rūpasyotpāda iti ṣaṣṭhīṃ kurvanti yathā rūpasaṃjñaka evotpādaḥ pratīyeta mā'nyaḥ pratyāyīti /.*

1026 Abhvk. 282ff.

1027 ADSS. 73.

1028 Cf. VsmṬ. 461–62: *Uppattimantānaṃ hi rūpāyatanādīnaṃ jāti-ādīni lakkhaṇāni vijjanti, na evaṃ jāti-ādīnaṃ. Tasmā viññātabbam etaṃ jāti-ādīni na jāyantī ti. Siyā panetaṃ jāti-ādīnam'pi jāti-ādīni lakkhaṇāni vijjanti? Taṃ na. Kasmā? Tathā sati anavaṭṭhānāpattito. Yadi hi jāti-ādīni jāti-ādimantāni siyuṃ, tāni'pi jāti-ādimantāni, tāni'pi jāti-ādimantānī ti anavaṭṭhānam eva āpajjati.* See also Abhvk. 288; ADVṬ. 115.

1029 Kvu. 460–61.

1030 KvuA. 135.

1031 KvuA. 92: *Saṅkhatāsaṅkhata-lakkhaṇānaṃ pana abhāvena na vattabbā saṅkhatā ti vā asaṅkhatā ti vā.*

1032 Abhvt. vv. 21, 22, 23.

1033 SA. (SHB) vol. 2, 266; see also PsmA. III. 596.

1034 AKB. 77.

1035 AKB. 77.

1036 For a detailed analysis of this category, see Ven. Dhammajoti, *Sarvāstivāda Abhidharma*, 371ff.; Jaini, "Origin and Development of the Theory of *Viprayuktasaṃskāras*," 531–47.

1037 AKB. 76.

1038 AKB. 78.

1039 AKB. 78.

1040 AKB. 77.

1041 AKB. 77: *Jātir ādiḥ pravāhasya vyayaś chedaḥ sthitis tu saḥ / sthityanyathātvaṃ tasyaiva pūrvāparaviśiṣṭatā //.*

1042 AKB. 77.

1043 AKB. 77.

1044 AKB. 77.

1045 AbhD. 105.

1046 AKvy. 176.

1047 AKvy. 176.

1048 AKvy. 175–76.

1049 AbhD. 106.

1050 See AbhD.: *Anya eva hi no jarākhyo dharmo, anyaś ca dharmī / sāṃkhyasya tv avasthitasya dharminaḥ svātmabhūtasya dharmāntarasyotsargaḥ svātmabhūtasya cotpādaḥ pariṇāma iti /.*

1051 AKB. 78.

1052 See, e.g., VbhA. 10ff., 36ff.

1053 PV. v. 98. Cf. PsmA. 462: *Uppādo eva saṅkhatan ti lakkhaṇan ti saṅkhatalakkhaṇam. Evaṃ itaradvaye'pi attho veditabbo. Iminā uppādakkhaṇe sesaṃ dvinnaṃ, ṭhitikkhaṇe sesaṃ dvinnaṃ, bhaṅgakkhaṇe ca sesaṃ dvinnaṃ abhāvo dassito.*

1054 Psm. (SHB), vol. 2, 179: *Uppāda-lakkhaṇaṃ vaya-lakkhaṇena ca ṭhitaññathatta-lakkhaṇena ca suññaṃ. Vaya-lakkhaṇaṃ uppāda-lakkhaṇena ca ṭhitaññathatta-lakkhaṇena ca suññaṃ. Ṭhitaññathatta-lakkhaṇaṃ uppāda-lakkhaṇena ca vaya-lakkhaṇena ca suññaṃ.*

1055 Psm. (SHB), vol.2, 179.

1056 Psm A. 425: *Tattha saṅkhatānaṃ uppādakkhaṇe saṅkhatā'pi uppādalakkhaṇam'pi kālasaṅkhāto tassa khaṇo'pi paññāyati. Uppāde vītivatte saṅkhatā'pi jarālakkhaṇam'pi kālasaṅkhāto tassa khaṇo'pi paññāyati. Bhaṅgakkhaṇe saṅkhatā'pi bhaṅgalakkhaṇam'pi kālasaṅkhāto tassa khaṇo'pi paññāyati.*

1057 Psm A. 462.

1058 ADS. 153: *Uppāda-ṭṭhiti-bhaṅga-vasena khaṇattayaṃ ekacittakkhaṇaṃ nāma.*

1059 AA. II, 252.

1060 Vsm. 449; Abhvt. 71.

1061 Abhvk. 283; NRP. v. 53; Pv. 97.

1062 NRP. v. 53.

1063 Abhvk. 305; ADVṬ. 112.

1064 VbhA. 68.

1065 VśmS. VII, 221.

1066 Vsm. 469; Abhvt. 71.

1067 Abhvk. 284: *Vīhipurāṇabhāvo tāva rasādiṃ apaneti. Ayam pana kevalaṃ uppādāvattham eva apaneti.*

1068 Abhvk. 699.

1069 VsmṬ. 310: *Vipariṇatan ti sabhāva-vigamanena vigataṃ.*

1070 PsmA. 177.

1071 PsmA. 177.

1072 VsmṬ. 280, 455, 529; Abhvk. 283.

1073 DhsA. 328.

1074 DhsA. 328.

1075 See the section on the "Sense-Field Matter" in chapter 13, "The Real Dependent Matter."

1076 Abhvk. 283.

1077 Abhvk. 120: *Kasmā pāḷiyam ṭhitikkhaṇo na vutto ti?*

1078 Mvn. 64.

1079 Abhvk. 120.

1080 NRP. v. 94.

1081 Abhvk. 94.

1082 NRP. v.1527.

1083 VsmṬ. 236; DṬ. 699; UdA. 392: *Uppādanirodhābhāvato c'eva tadubhayaparicchinnāya ṭhitiyā. . . .*

1084 ADVṬ 57.

1085 VsmṬ. 455; Abhvk. 305; ADVṬ. 112.

1086 Abhvk. 418.

1087 Abhvk. 266.

1088 SA. (SHB) vol. 2, 266: *Apare pana vadanti: arūpadhammānaṃ jarākhaṇo nāma na sakkā paññāpetuṃ. Sammāsambuddho ca 'vedanāya uppādo paññāyati vayo paññāyati ṭhitāya aññathattaṃ paññāyatī' ti vadanto arūpadhammānam'pi tīṇi lakkhaṇāni paññāpeti. Tāni abhikkhaṇam upādāya labhantī ti vatvā:*
Atthitā sabbadhammānaṃ ṭhiti nāma pavuccati;
tass'eva bhedo maraṇaṃ sabbadā sabbapāṇinan' ti imāya ācariyagāthāya tamatthaṃ sādhenti.

1089 Abhvk. 304–5: *Ānandācariyo pana cittassa ṭhitikkhaṇam eva natthī ti āha. Vuttaṃ hi tena. Yo cettha cittassa ṭhitikkhaṇo vutto, so ca atthi natthī ti vicāretabbo. Cittayamake hi uppannaṃ uppajjamānan ti etassa Vibhaṅge 'bhaṅgakkhaṇe uppannaṃ, no ca uppajjamānan' ti ettakam eva vuttaṃ, na vuttaṃ ṭhitikkhaṇe bhaṅgakkhaṇe cāti. Tathā nuppajjamānaṃ nuppannan ti ettha 'bhaṅgakkhaṇe nuppajjamānaṃ no ca nuppannan ti ettakam eva vuttaṃ, na vuttaṃ ṭhitikkhaṇe bhaṅgakkhaṇe vāti. Evaṃ niruddhaṃ nirujjhamānan ti etesaṃ paripuṇṇavissajjane uppādakkhaṇe anāgatan cāti vatvā ṭhitikkhaṇe avacanaṃ. Atikkantakālavāre ca bhaṅgakkhaṇe cittaṃ uppādakkhaṇṇaṃ vītivattan ti vatvā ṭhitikkhaṇe ti avacanaṃ ṭhitikkhaṇābhāvaṃ cittassa dīpeti.* See also ADSV. 27–28; ADVṬ. 57–58.

1090 Abhvk. 304: *Sutte'pi ṭhitassa aññathattaṃ paññāyatī ti tasseva ekassa aññathattabhāvato yassa aññathattaṃ paññāyati tassa sā santati-ṭhitī ti.*

1091 Ācariya Ānanda's argument as given in Abhvk. 305: "*Api ca yathābhūto dhammo uppajjati, kiṃ tathābhūtova bhijjati, udāhu aññathābhūto? Yadi tathābhūtova bhijjati na jaratāya sambhavo. Aññathābhūto añño eva so' ti sabbathā'pi ṭhitikkhaṇassa abhāvo yeva*" is identical with the following given in the AKB. (II, 79): *Tathātvena jarā'siddhir anyathātve'nya eva saḥ; / Tasmān naikasya bhāvasya jarā nāmopapadyate.*

1092 Abhvk. 304.

1093 That mental dhammas do not have a static phase was a view shared by the Abhayagiri fraternity as well. See AbhMṬ. 140; VsmṬ. 424.

1094 AbhMṬ. 140; VsmṬ. 424: *Ācariya-Jotipāla-Dhammapālattherānaṃ panetaṃ nakkhamati. Te hi ekadhammādhārabhāve'pi uppāda-nirodhānaṃ añño uppādakkhaṇo añño nirodhakkhaṇo, uppādāvatthaṃ hi upādāya uppādakkhaṇo nirodhāvatthaṃ upādāya nirodhakkhaṇo, uppādāvatthāya bhinnā nirodhāvatthā ti ekasmiṃ yeva ca sabhāvadhamme yathā icchitabbā. Aññathā añño yeva dhammo uppajjati, añño nirujjhatī ti āpajjeyya. Evaṃ nirodhāvatthāya viya nirodhābhimukhāvatthāyā'pi bhavitabbaṃ. Sā ṭhiti jaratā cāti sampaṭicchitabbam etaṃ.*

1095 AbhMṬ. 140; VsmṬ. 424.

1096 AKB. 76; cf. AbhD. 104–5.

1097 ADVṬ. 57–58.

1098 CMA. 156.

1099 VśmS. VII, 268.

1100 See, e.g., D. II, 157, 199; S. I, 5; II, 193.

1101 See, e.g., Vin. I, 33, 41, 57.

1102 Dhp. v. 47.

1103 Psm. I, 191.

1104 See NRP, v. 54.

1105 *Le traité de la démonstration de l'acte*, 214ff.

1106 See, e.g., AKB. 263ff.

1107 Cf. AKB. 193: *ākasmiko hi bhāvānāṃ vināśaḥ / kiṃ kāraṇam / kāryasya hi kāraṇaṃ bhavati / vināśaś cābhāvaḥ / yaś cābhāvas tasya kiṃ kartavyam/.*

For original sources on *nirhetukavināśavāda*, see *Abhidharmadīpa* (with *Vibhāṣāprabhāvṛtti*), ed. Jaini, 107 n.1.

1108 *Documents d'Abhidharma: La controverse du temps*, trans. de La Vallée Poussin, 148 n.1: *Pañcemāni bhikṣavaḥ saṃjñāmātraṃ pratijñāmātraṃ saṃvṛtimātraṃ vyavahāramātram / katamāni pañca / atīto'dhvā anāgato'dhvā sahetukavināśaḥ ākāśaṃ pudgala iti.*

1109 ItiA. II, 50.

1110 Vsm. 530.

1111 NRP. v. 103.

1112 Abhvk. 226: *Yo dhammo yassa dhammassa ṭhitiyuppattiyā'pi ca upakārako hi so tassa paccayo ti vuccati.* See also NRP. v. 48.

1113 Abhvk. 307.

1114 See chapter 18, "Conditional Relations."

1115 See chapter 10, "The Cognitive Process."

1116 Vsm. 526; VbhA. 36.

1117 Vsm. 526; ADSV. 27–28.

1118 DṬ. 177: *Ati-ittaro rūpadhammānam pi pavattikkhaṇo.*

1119 ADSV. 28.

1120 See Yam. (Sankhara-Yamaka), 233–34.

1121 ADSV. 29–30.

1122 ADSV. 28.

1123 See the section "Means of Intimation" in chapter 14, "The Nominal Dependent Matter."

1124 VbhA. 36; YamA. 83; ADVṬ. 113.

1125 ADSV. 28: *Kāyasaṅkhāro ti cittasamuṭṭhāno assāsa-passāsa-vāto. So cittassa uppādakkhaṇe yeva uppajjati, na ṭhitikkhaṇe vā bhaṅgakkhaṇe vā. Esa cittasamuṭṭhānarūpassa dhammatā.*

1126 DṬ. 177.

1127 MA. I, 261.

1128 VsmṬ. 397.

1129 SA. II, 279.

1130 VsmṬ. 453; Abhvk. 279; ADSS. 156; VśmS. V, 68.

1131 Vsm. 397.

1132 Vsm. 397.

1133 VsmṬ. 451; Abhvk. 251; AbhMṬ. 254.

1134 See Stcherbatsky, *Buddhist Logic*, 1:99.

1135 See *Nidāna Saṃyutta* of the *Saṃyuttanikāya*.

1136 See, e.g., PsmA. 251: *Paccaye paṭicca nissāya samā saha vā uppannattā paṭiccasamuppannaṃ.*

1137 Vsm. XVII, 66ff.

1138 Vsm. XVII.

1139 D. I, 28; Ud. 69.

1140 DhsA. 60; AbhMṬ. (46) says that here the term *ekakāraṇavāda* refers either to Sāṃkhya philosophy or the theory of divine creation (*ekakāraṇavādo ti pakatikāraṇavādo issarakāraṇavādo vā*).

1141 DhsA. 79.

1142 See CMA. 77.

1143 CMA. 253ff.

1144 DhsA. 61.

1145 Cf. Vsm. 513: *Nāmarūpato uddhaṃ issarādīnaṃ abhāvato.*

1146 PsmA. 140.

1147 VsmṬ. 546.

1148 VsmṬ. 546; see also PsmA. 140.

1149 See, e.g., PsmA. 251.

1150 VśmS. VII, 301.

1151 NRP. 48; Abhvk. 226.

1152 See CMA. 293–94.

1153 For more details, see Y. Karunadasa, *Buddhist Analysis of Matter*, 69ff.

1154 *Kāla-vimutta*, "independent of time," includes the unconditioned reality of nibbāna and paññatti—that is, mental constructions with no corresponding objective counterparts.

1155 See chapter 2, "The Nominal and the Conceptual."

1156 CMA. 316–17.

1157 CMA. 316–17.

1158 ADVṬ. 111; ADSS. 153.

1159 CMA. 317.

1160 CMA. 317–18.

1161 CMA. 318–19.

1162 CMA. 315–16.

1163 CMA. 315–16.

1164 CMA. 315–16.

1165 CMA. 314.

1166 PatthanaA. (SHB) vol. 2, 262; Abhvk. 449.

1167 Ven. Nyanatiloka Mahāthera, *Buddhist Dictionary*; see *Āsevana-paccaya*.

1168 See chapter 10, "The Cognitive Process."

1169 CMA. 312.

1170 CMA. 313.

1171 *Points of Controversy or Subjects of Discourse* (*Kathāvatthu*), trans. Aung and Rhys Davids, 267 (Kvu. 467ff.).

1172 KvuA. 136.

1173 Dhs. 211.

1174 Tkp. 6; Dkp. 16–17.

1175 CMA. 246ff.

1176 CMA. 319.

1177 CMA. 316.

1178 Tkp. 50.

1179 CMA. 320.

1180 CMA. 272, 312.

1181 CMA. 272, 312.

1182 ADVṬ. 143; ADSS. 154.

1183 See chapter 17, "Momentariness."

1184 ADSS. 154.

1185 Abhvk. 453.

1186 VśmS. VI, 167; Abhvk. 454.

1187 See CMA. 305ff.

1188 See Paṭṭhāna Aṭṭhakathā (SHB), vol. 2, 266; Abhvt. 136.

1189 M. I, 164: *So kho ahaṃ bhikkhave tāvataken'eva oṭṭhapahatamattena lapitalāpanamattena ñāṇavādañ ca vadāmi theravādañ ca, jānāmi passāmīti ca paṭijānāmi ahañ ceva aññe ca.*

1190 MA. II, 171. Ms. I. B. Horner's translation of *theravāda*, as it occurs in this particular context as "the doctrine of the elders," does not seem to represent its correct meaning. However, in a footnote she refers to its commentarial gloss as *thirabhāvavāda* (see MLS I, 208 and n.2). PTSD explains the term *theravāda* as "the doctrine of the Theras, the original Buddhist doctrine," and refers to the term's occurrence at M. I, 164. This gives the incorrect impression that in the suttas, too, the term is used in the sense of "the doctrine of the elders."

1191 See, e.g., M. II, 197; A. V, 190.

1192 *Mahāvaṃsa*, chap. 5; VA. 60ff.; KvuA. 5ff.; *Dīpavaṃsa*, 58–59.

1193 Translation mainly based on Jayawickrama, *The Inception of Discipline and the Vinaya Nidāna*.

1194 *Mahāvaṃsa*, trans. Turnour, 22.

1195 Childers, *A Dictionary of the Pāli Language*; see *vibhajati*.

1196 Geiger, *The Mahāvaṃsa or the Great Chronicle of Ceylon*, 59 n.1.

1197 See, e.g., Grimm, *The Doctrine of the Buddha*, 49 ("The teaching of the Buddha is therefore a religion of reason; moreover, in the Canon it is characterized directly by the epithet *vibhajjavāda*, a word which is translated in Childers's Pali Dictionary as 'religion of logic or reason.'"); Winternitz, *A History of Indian Literature*, 62; Law, *A History of Pali Literature*, 12; Rhys Davids and Stede, *Pali-English Dictionary*, see *vibhajati*; Rahula, *History of Buddhism in Ceylon*, 50 n.2; Jayawickrama, *The Inception of Discipline and the Vinaya Nidāna*, 22.

1198 *Vaṃsatthappakāsinī Mahāvaṃsa-Ṭīkā*, 1:240.

1199 *Sāratthadīpanī*, ed. Ven. Devarakkhita Thera, 125.

1200 *Vimativinodanī*, ed. Ven. Dhammadhara Thera, 27.

1201 A. I, 197.

1202 D. II, 185.

1203 M. II, 197.

1204 See, e.g., Ven. Nyanatiloka Mahāthera, *Buddhist Dictionary*, 172.

1205 A. X, 94.

1206 D. I, 191.

1207 *Points of Controversy or Subjects of Discourse* (*Kathāvatthu*), trans. Aung and Rhys Davids, xl–xli.

1208 *Points of Controversy or Subjects of Discourse* (*Kathāvatthu*), xli n.1.

1209 *Points of Controversy or Subjects of Discourse* (*Kathāvatthu*), xli, 12.

1210 AKB. 296.

1211 See AKB(FT). Introduction, LV; IV. 23, n.3; *L'origine des sectes bouddhiques d'apres Paramārtha*, trans. Demiéville, 1:49.

1212 AKB (FT). Introduction, XXXIII.

1213 D. III, 220.

1214 AKB (FT). I, 33ff.

1215 See Kern, *Manual of Indian Buddhism*, 110.

1216 Vsm. 522: *vibhajjavādi-maṇḍalaṃ otaritvā.*

1217 Tkp. 366; see also VbhA. 130.

BIBLIOGRAPHY

Primary Sources

Abhidhammatthasaṅgaha and Abhidhammattha-Vibhāvinī-Ṭīkā. Edited by Saddhātissa Hammalawa. PTS, 1989.

Abhidhammatthavikāsinī. Edited by A. P. Buddhadatta. Colombo, 1961.

Abhidhammāvatāra. Edited by A. P. Buddhadatta. Buddhadatta's Manuals 1, 1–142. PTS, 1915.

Abhidhānappadīpikā-sūci. Edited by Ven. Subhūti. Colombo, 1938.

Abhidharmadīpa (with *Vibhāṣāprabhāvṛtti*). Edited by P. S. Jaini. Patna, India, 1959.

Abhidharmakośabhāṣyam of Vasubandhu. Edited by P. Pradhan. Patna, India, 1975.

Abhidharmakośavyākhyā (*Sphuṭārthā*) *of Yaśomitra*. Edited by U. Wogihara. Tokyo, 1932–36.

Abhidharmārthasaṃgrahasannaya included in *Abhidhammatthasaṅgaha*. Edited by Paññāmoli Tissa. Ambalangoda, Sri Lanka, 1926.

Aṅguttaranikāya, vols. 1–4. Edited by R. Morris, E. Hardy, and C. A. F. Rhys Davids. PTS, reprinted 1999.

Aṅguttaranikāya-Aṭṭhakathā (*Manorathapūraṇī*), vols. 1–5. Edited by M. Walleser and H. Kopp. PTS, reprinted 1973–77.

Candrakirti Prasannapada Madhyamakavrtti. Paris, 1959.

Davvasaṅgaha (with a commentary by Brahmadeva). Edited and translated by S. C. Ghoshal. Sacred Books of the Jainas 1. Allahabad, India, 1917.

Dhammasaṅgaṇi. Edited by E. Muller. PTS, reprinted 2001.

Dhammasaṅgaṇi-Aṭṭhakathā (*Atthasālinī*). Edited by E. Muller. PTS, reprinted 1979.

Dhātukathā-Pakaraṇa and Its Commentary. Edited by E. R. Gooneratne. PTS, reprinted 1995.

Dīghanikāya, vols. 1–3. Edited by T. W. Rhys Davids and J. E. Carpenter. PTS, reprinted 1995–2001.

Dīghanikāya-Aṭṭhakathā (*Sumaṅgalavilāsinī*), vols. 1–3. Edited by T. W. Rhys Davids, J. E. Carpenter, and W. Stede. PTS, reprinted 1968–71.

Dīghanikāya-Ṭīkā (*Dīghanikāya* subcommentary), vols. 1–3. Edited by Lily de Silva. PTS, 1996.

Dukapaṭṭhāna. Edited by Mrs. Rhys Davids. PTS, reprinted 1996.

Itivuttaka-Aṭṭhakathā, vols. 1–2. Edited by M. M. Bose. PTS, reprinted 1977.

Kathāvatthu, vols. 1–2. Edited by A. C. Taylor. PTS, reprinted 1999.

Kathāvatthuppakaraṇa-Aṭṭhakathā. Edited by N. A. Jayawickrama. PTS, 1979.

Mahāniddesa, vols. 1–2. Edited by Louis de La Vallée Poussin and E. J. Thomas. PTS, reprinted 2001.

Mahāniddesa-Aṭṭhakathā (*Niddesavaṇṇanā = Saddhammappajjotikā*), vols. 1–2. Edited by A. P. Buddhadatta. PTS, reprinted 1980.

Majjhimanikāya, vols. 1–3. Edited by V. Trenkner, R. Chalmers, and Mrs. Rhys Davids. PTS, reprinted 2002–4.

Majjhimanikāya-Aṭṭhakathā (*Papañcasūdanī*), vols. 1–4. Edited by J. H. Woods, D. Kosambi, and I. B. Horner. PTS, reprinted 1976–77.

Milindapañha. Edited by V. Trenckner. PTS, reprinted 1997.

Milinda-Ṭīkā. Edited by Padmanabh S. Jaini. PTS, reprinted 1997.

Mohavicchedanī. Edited by A. P. Buddhadatta and A. K. Warder. PTS, 1961.

Nāmarūpapariccheda. Edited by A. P. Buddhadatta. *Journal of the Pali Text Society* (1914): 1–114.

Nāmarūpasamāsa. Edited by P. Dhammarama. *Journal of the Pali Text Society* (1916): 1–19.

Niyamsara. Edited and translated by U. Sain. Sacred Books of the Jainas 9. Lucknow, India, 1931.

Nettippakaraṇa. Edited by E. Hardy. PTS, reprinted 1995.

Pañcastikāyasāra. Edited and translated by A. Chakravartinayanar. Sacred Books of the Jainas 3. Allahabad, India, 1920.

Paṭisambhidāmagga, vols. 1–2. Edited by A. C. Taylor. PTS, reprinted 2003.

Paṭisambhidāmagga-Aṭṭhakathā (*Saddhammappakāsinī*), vols. 1–3. Edited by C. V. Joshi. PTS, 1933–47.

Patthana-Atthakatha, Pancappakaranatthakatha (SHB), vols. 1–2. Colombo, reprinted 2012.

Peṭakopadesa. Edited by Arabinda Barua. PTS, reprinted 1982.

Pitaputrasamagama-sutra in the Siksasamuccaya of Santideva. Edited by Cecil Bendall and W. H. D. Rouse. Andesite Press, 1922, reprinted 2014.

Puggalapaññatti. Edited by R. Morris. PTS, reprinted 1997.

Puggalapaññatti-Aṭṭhakathā. Edited by G. Landsberg and Mrs. Rhys Davids. *Journal of the Pali Text Society* (1914): 170–254.

Rūpārūpavibhāga. Edited by A. P. Buddhadatta. Buddhadatta's Manuals 1, 149–59. PTS, 1915.

Saccasaṃkhepa. Edited by P. Dhammarama. *Journal of the Pali Text Society* (1917–19): 1–25.

Samayasara. Edited and translated by J. I. Jaini. Sacred Books of the Jainas 8. Lucknow, India, 1930.

Saṃyuttanikāya, 3 vols. Edited by H. Dhamminda, W. Amarasiha, and G. Saranankara. Buddha Jayanti edition. Sri Lanka, 1960.

Saṃyuttanikāya, vols. 1–5. Edited by L. Feer and Mrs. Rhys Davids. PTS, reprinted 1994–2001. (Citations are to this edition unless otherwise noted.)

Saṃyuttanikāya-Aṭṭhakathā (*Sāratthappakāsinī*), vols. 1–3. Edited by F. L. Woodward. PTS, reprinted 1977.

Sāratthadīpanī. Edited by Ven. Devarakkhita Thera. Colombo, 1933.

Suttanipāta. Edited by D. Anderson and H. Smith. PTS, reprinted 1997.

Suttanipāta-Aṭṭhakathā (*Paramatthajotikā*, vol. 2), vols. 1–3. Edited by H. Smith. PTS, reprinted 1989–97.

Tattvasaṃgraha of Śāntarakṣita with Pañjikā of Kamalaśīla, vols. 1–2. Edited by Embar Krishnamacharya. Gaekwad's Oriental Series 30–31. Baroda [Vadodara], India, 1926.

Theragāthā. Edited by K. R. Norman and L. Alsdorf. 2d ed. PTS, 1966.

Tikapaṭṭhāna (with commentary), vols. 1–2. Edited by Mrs. Rhys Davids. PTS, reprinted 1996.

Udāna-Aṭṭhakathā (*Paramatthadīpanī*). Edited by F. L. Woodward. PTS, reprinted 1977.

The Vaiśeṣika Sūtras of Kaṇāda. Edited and translated by N. Sinha. Allahabad, India, 1911.

Vaṃsatthappakāsinī Mahāvaṃsa-ṭīkā. Edited by G. P. Malalasekara. PTS, 1936.

Vibhaṅga. Edited by Mrs. Rhys Davids. PTS, reprinted 2003.

Vibhaṅga-Aṭṭhakathā (*Sammohavinodanī*). Edited by A. P. Buddhadatta Thero. PTS, reprinted 1980.

Vijñaptimātratāsiddhi: *Deux traités de Vasubandhu*. Edited by S. Lévi. Paris, 1925.

Vimativinodanī. Edited by Ven. Dhammadhara Thera. Colombo, 1935.

Visuddhimagga, vols. 1–2. Edited by C. A. F. Rhys Davids. PTS, reprinted 1975.

Visuddhimagga-Ṭīkā (*Paramatthamañjūsā*). Edited by M. Dhammananda. Colombo, 1928.

Viśuddhimārgasannaya, vols. 1–6. Edited by M. Dharmaratne. Colombo, 1890–1917.

Yamaka, vols. 1–2. Edited by C. A. F. Rhys Davids. PTS, reprinted 1995.

Yamakappakaraṇa-Aṭṭhakathā. Edited by C. A. F. Rhys Davids. *Journal of the Pali Text Society* (1910–12): 51–107.

Primary Sources Translated into Modern Languages

L'Abhidharmakośa de Vasubandhu, vols. 1–4. Translated by Louis de La Vallée Poussin. Edited by Étienne Lamotte. New edition by the Institut Belge des Hautes Études Chinoises. Brussels, 1971.

The Book of Analysis (*Vibhaṅga*). Translated by P. A. Thiṭṭila (Seṭṭhila). PTS, 2002.

The Book of Gradual Sayings (*Aṅguttaranikāya*), 5 vols. Translated by F. L. Woodward. PTS, 1951–55.

A Buddhist Manual of Psychological Ethics (*Dhammasaṅgaṇi*). Translated by Mrs. Rhys Davids. Oriental Translation Fund, New Series 12. London, 1923.

Compendium of Philosophy (*Abhidhammatthasaṅgaha*). Translated by S. Z. Aung. Revised and edited by Mrs. Rhys Davids. PTS, 1910.

A Comprehensive Manual of Abhidhamma: *The Abhidhammattha Saṅgaha of Ācariya Anuruddha*. Translated by Bhikkhu Bodhi. BPS, 1993.

Conditional Relations (*Paṭṭhāna*), vols. 1–22. Translated by U. Nārada, assisted by Thein Nyun. PTS, 1997–98.

The Connected Discourses of the Buddha (*Saṃyuttanikāya*). Translated by Bhikkhu Bodhi. Somerville, MA: Wisdom Publications, 2000.

The Debates Commentary (*Kathāvatthu-Aṭṭhakathā*). Translated by B. C. Law. PTS, 1940.

Designation of Human Types (*Puggalapaññatti*). Translated by B. C. Law. PTS, 1924.

Dialogues of the Buddha (*Dīghanikāya*), vols. 1–3. Translated by T. W. Rhys Davids. Sacred Books of the Buddhists 2–4. London, 1899–1912.

Discourse on Elements (*Dhātukathā*). Translated by U. Nārada, assisted by Thein Nyun. PTS, 1962.

Dispeller of Delusion (*Sammohavinodanī* = *Vibhaṅga Aṭṭhakathā*), vols. 1–2. Translated by Bhikkhu Ñāṇamoli. Revised by L. S. Cousins, Nyanaponika Mahāthera, and C. M. M. Shaw. PTS, 1987–92.

Documents d'Abhidharma: *Textes relatifs au nirvāṇa et aux asaṃskṛtas en général*. Translated by Louis de La Vallée Poussin. Bulletin de l'École Française de l'Extrême-Orient. Hanoi, 1930.

Documents d'Abhidharma: *La controverse du temps*; *les deux*, *les quatre*, *et les trois vérités*, vol. 5. Translated by Louis de La Vallée Poussin. Melanges Chinoise et Bouddhiques, l'Institut Belge des Hautes Études Chinoises. Brussels, 1936–37.

Elders' Verses, 2 vols. Translated by K. R. Norman. PTS, 1969–71. [Translation of the *Theragāthā* and *Therigāthā*].

The Expositor (*Atthasālinī = Dhammasaṅgaṇi-Aṭṭhakathā*), vols. 1–2. Translated by Maung Tin. Edited by Mrs. Rhys Davids. PTS, 1920–21.

The Guide according to Kaccāna Thera (*Nettippakaraṇa*). Translated by Bhikkhu Ñāṇamoli. PTS, 2008.

The Mahāvaṃsa. Translated by George Turnour. Colombo, 1868.

The Middle Length Discourses of the Buddha: A Translation of the Majjhima Nikāya. Translated by Bhikkhu Ñāṇamoli and Bhikkhu Bodhi. Somerville, MA: Wisdom Publications, 2001.

Middle Length Sayings (Majjhima-Nikāya), vols. 1–3. Translated by I. B. Horner. PTS, 1954–59, reprinted 2007.

Origin and Doctrines of Early Indian Buddhist Schools [Hsuan-Chwang version of Vasumitra's treatise]. Translated by J. Masuda. Asia Major 2. Leipzig, 1925.

L'origine des sectes bouddhiques d'après Paramārtha, vol. 1. Translated by P. Demiéville. Mélanges Chinois et Bouddhiques, l'Institut Belges des Hautes Études Chinoises. Brussels, 1932.

The Path of Discrimination (*Paṭisambhidāmagga*). Translated by Bhikkhu Ñāṇamoli. PTS, 1992.

The Path of Purification (*Visuddhimagga*). Translated by Bhikkhu Ñāṇamoli. Colombo, 1956.

Points of Controversy or Subjects of Discourse (*Kathāvatthu*). Translated by S. Z. Aung and Mrs. Rhys Davids. PTS, 1915.

The Questions of King Milinda. Translated by T. W. Rhys Davids. Delhi 1965, reprinted.

La Siddhi de Hiuan Tsang (*Vijñaptimātratāsiddhi*), vols. 1–2. Translated by Louis de La Vallée Poussin. Paris, 1928–29.

Le traité de la démonstration de l'acte (*Karmasiddhiprakaraṇa*), vol. 4. Translated by É. Lamotte. Mélanges Chinoises et Bouddhiques, l'Institut Belge des Hautes Études Chinoises. Brussels, 1936.

Trois traités sur les sectes bouddhiques attibués à Vasumitra, Bhavya et Vinītadeva. Translated by A. Bareau. *Journal Asiatique* 242 (1954): 229–66.

Secondary Sources

Abhidharma and Indian Thought. Published by the Committee for the Felicitation of Professor Doctor Jun Sho Kato's Sixtieth Birthday. Tokyo, 2000.

Aung, S. Z. "Abhidhamma Literature in Burma." *Journal of the Pali Text Society* (1910–12): 112–32.

Bapat, P. V. *Vimuttimagga and Visuddhimagga: A Comparative Study*. Poona [Pune], India, 1937.

Bareau, A. *The Buddhist Sects of the Lesser Vehicle*. Translated from the French by G. M. Chodron. N.p., 2005. https://suvacobhikkhu.wordpress.com/buddhist-sects/. Accessed August 9, 2018.

———. "Les sectes bouddhiques du Petit Véhicule et leurs Abhidharmapiṭaka." *Bulletin de l'École Française de l'Extrême-Orient* 44 (1951): 1–110.

Bastow, D. "The *Mahāvibhāṣā* Arguments for Sarvāstivāda." *Philosophy East and West* 44.3 (1994): 489–500.

———. "Debates on Time in the *Kathāvatthu*." *Buddhist Studies Review* 13.2 (1996): 109–32.

Bhaduri, S. *Studies in Nyāya-Vaiśeṣika Metaphysics*. Poona [Pune], India, 1947.

Bronkhorst, J. "Dhamma and Abhidhamma." *Bulletin of the School of Oriental and African Studies* 48 (1985): 305–20.

Brown, Jason W. "Microgenesis and Buddhism: The Concept of Momentariness." *Philosophy East and West* 49.3 (1999): 261–77.

Childers, R. C. *A Dictionary of the Pāli Language*. London, 1875. Reprint, Delhi, 1975.

Conze, E. *Buddhist Thought in India*. London, 1962.

Cousins, L. S. "Dhammapāla and the Ṭīkā Literature." *Religion: Journal of Religion and Religions* 2 (1972): 159–65.

———. "The *Paṭṭhāna* and the Development of the Theravādin Abhidhamma." *Journal of the Pali Text Society* 9 (1981): 22–46.

Cox, C. "On the Possibility of a Nonexistent Object of Consciousness: Sarvāstivādin and Dārṣṭāntika Theories." *Journal of the International Association of Buddhist Studies* 11.1 (1988): 31–87.

———. *Disputed Dharmas: Early Buddhist Theories on Existence—An Annotated Translation of the Section on Factors Dissociated from Thought from Saṃghabhadra's Nyāyānusāra*. Tokyo, 1995.

Dhammajoti, K. L. "The Sarvāstivāda Doctrine of Simultaneous Causality." *Journal of Buddhist Studies* 1 (May 2003): 200–250

———. *Abhidharma Doctrine and Controversy on Perception*. Centre of Buddhist Studies, The University of Hong Kong. Hong Kong, 2007.

———. *Sarvāstivāda Abhidharma*. Centre of Buddhist Studies, The University of Hong Kong. Hong Kong, 2009.

Edgerton, F. *Buddhist Hybrid Sanskrit Grammar and Dictionary*, 2 vols. New Delhi, 2004.

Frauwallner, E. *Studies in Abhidharma Literature and the Origins of Buddhist Philosophical Systems*. English translation by Sophie Francis Kidd under the supervision of Ernst Steinkellner. New York, 1995.

Galmangoda, S. *An Introduction to Theravāda Abhidhamma*. Singapore, 1998.

———. *Reality and Expression*. Singapore, 1999.

———. *Abhidhammic Interpretations of Early Buddhist Teachings*. Singapore, 2005.

Geiger, Wilhelm. *The Mahāvaṃsa or the Great Chronicle of Ceylon*. Colombo, 1912.

Gethin, R. "Bhavaṅga and Rebirth according to the Abhidhamma." *The Buddhist Forum* 3 (1994): 11–35.

———. *The Foundations of Buddhism*. Oxford, 1998.

Godakumbura, C. E. "References to Buddhist Sanskrit Writers in Sinhalese Literature." *University of Ceylon Review* 1 (1943): 86–93.

Gorkom, Nina van. *Abhidhamma in Daily Life*. Dhamma Study and Propagation Foundation. Bangkok, 1989.

Govinda, Lama Anagarika. *The Psychological Attitude of Early Buddhist Philosophy and Its Systematic Representation according to Abhidhamma Tradition*. London, 1969.

Griffiths, P. J. *On Being Mindless: Buddhist Meditation and the Mind-Body Problem*. Bibliotheca Indo-Buddhica Series no. 196. Reprint, Delhi 1986.

Grimm, George. *The Doctrine of the Buddha: The Religion of Reason and Meditation*. Berlin, 1958.

Guenther, Herbert V. *Philosophy and Psychology in the Abhidharma*. Berkeley, 1976.

Hamilton, S. *Identity and Experience: The Constitution of the Human Being according to Early Buddhism*. London, 1996.

Harvey, P. "The Mind-Body Relationship in Pāli Buddhism: A Philosophical Investigation." *Asian Philosophy* 3.1 (1993): 29–41.

———. *The Selfless Mind: Personality, Consciousness and Nirvana in Early Buddhism*. Surrey, UK, 1995.

Hirakawa, A. "The Meaning of 'Dharma' and 'Abhidharma.'" In *Indianisme et Bouddhisme: Mélanges offerts à Mgr Étienne Lamotte*, 159–75. Louvain, Belgium, 1980.

Horner, I. B. "Abhidhamma Abhivinaya." *Indian Historical Quarterly* 17 (1941): 548–60.

Jaini, P. S. "Origin and Development of the Theory of *Viprayuktasaṃskāras*." *Bulletin of the School of Oriental and African Studies* 22 (1959): 531–47.

———. "The Vaibhāṣika Theory of Words and Meanings." *Bulletin of the School of Oriental and African Studies* 22 (1959): 95–107.

Jayasuriya, W. F. *The Psychology and Philosophy of Buddhism: An Introduction to the Abhidhamma*. Kuala Lumpur, 1976.

Jayatilleke, K. N. *Early Buddhist Theory of Knowledge*. London, 1963.

Jayawickrama, N. A. *The Inception of Discipline and the Vinaya Nidāna*. PTS, 1961.

Kajiyama, Y. "Realism of the Sarvāstivāda School." In *Buddhist Thought and Asian Civilization: Essays in Honor of Herbert V. Guenther on His Sixtieth Birthday*, edited by Leslie S. Kawamura and Keith Scott, 114–31. California, 1977.

Kalupahana, D. J. "The Buddhist Conception of Time and Temporality." *Philosophy East and West* 24 (1974): 181–91.

———. *The Principles of Buddhist Psychology*. New York, 1987.

Karunadasa, Y. *Buddhist Analysis of Matter*. Reprint, Singapore, 1989.

Karunaratna, W. S. *The Buddhist Theory of Causality*. Colombo, 1974.

———. *Buddhist Psychology: Citta, Cetasika, Cetanā, Consciousness*. Encyclopaedia of Buddhism Extract, no. 4. Colombo, 1995.

Kasyap, J. *The Abhidhamma Philosophy*, vols. 1–2. Benares, 1943.

Kern, H. *Manual of Indian Buddhism*. Reprint, Delhi, 1968.

Law, B. C. *A History of Pali Literature*. London, 1933.

Ledi Sayadaw. *Paramatthadīpanī-saṅgaha-mahā-ṭīkā*. Rangoon, 1907.

———. "Some Points in Buddhist Doctrine." *Journal of the Pali Text Society* (1913–14): 115–63.

———. "On the Philosophy of Relations." *Journal of the Pali Text Society* (1915): 21–53.

Malalasekara, G. P. *The Pali Literature of Ceylon*. Reprint, BPS, 1994.

McGovern, William M. *Manual of Buddhist Philosophy*. UK, 1923.

Ñānananda, Katukurunde. *Concept and Reality in Early Buddhism*. Colombo, 1966.

Nyanaponika Thera. *Buddhism and the God-Idea*. Wheel no. 47. BPS, 1981.

———. "Buddhism and the God-Idea." In *The Vision of Dhamma*, n.p.

———. *The Vision of Dhamma: Buddhist Writings of Nyanaponika Thera*. Edited, with an introduction by Bhikkhu Bodhi. Foreword by Erich Fromm. BPS, 1994.

———. *Abhidhamma Studies: Buddhist Explorations of Consciousness and Time*. BPS in collaboration with Wisdom Publications. Boston, 1997.

Nyanatiloka Mahāthera. *Guide through the Abhidhamma Piṭaka*. Kandy, 1971.

———. *Buddhist Dictionary: Manual of Buddhist Terms and Doctrines*. Colombo, 1972.

———. *The Fundamentals of Buddhism*. BPS, 1994.

Paranavitana, S. "Mahayanism in Ceylon." *Ceylon Journal of Science* 2 (1928): 35–71.

Pieris, Aloysius. *Studies in the Philosophy and Literature of Pāli Ābhidhammika Buddhism*. Colombo, 2004.

Potter, Karl H., ed. *Abhidharma Buddhism to 150 A.D.* Delhi, 1996.

Poussin, Louis de La Vallée. "Notes bouddhiques II: Le Vijñānakāya et le Kathāvatthu." *Académie Royale de Belgique, Bulletin de la Classe des Lettres* (*5e série*) 8.11 (1922): 516–20.

———. "La controverse du temps et du pudgala dans le Vijñānakāya." In *Études asiatiques poubliées à l'occasion de 25e anniversaire de l'École Française d'Extrême-Orient*, vol. 1, 343–76. Paris, 1925.

———. "Notes sur le moment ou kṣaṇa des bouddhistes." In *Rocznik Orjentalistyczny*, vol. 8, 1–9. Brussels, 1931.

Prasad, C. S. "Theravāda and Vibhajjavāda: A Critical Study of the Two Appellations." *East West New Series* 22.1–2 (1972): 101–13.

———. "The Concept of Time in Pāli Buddhism." *East West* 38.1–4 (1988): 107–36.

———. *Essays on Time in Buddhism*. Delhi, 1991.

Rahula, Walpola. *History of Buddhism in Ceylon*. Reprint, Colombo, 1956.

Rhys Davids, C. A. F. *Buddhist Psychology*. London, 1914.

Rhys Davids, T. W. "Kathāvatthu." *Journal of the Royal Asiatic Society* (1892): 1–37.

Rhys Davids, T. W., and W. Stede. *Pali-English Dictionary*. PTS, 1925.

Rospatt, A. von. *The Buddhist Doctrine of Momentariness: A Survey of the Origins and Early Phase of This Doctrine up to Vasubandhu*. Stuttgart, 1995.

Sarachchandra, E. R. *Buddhist Psychology of Perception*. Colombo, 1958.

Sasaki, G. *Linguistic Approach to Buddhist Thought*. Delhi, 1992.

Seal, B. N. *Positive Sciences of the Ancient Hindus*. Delhi, 1925.

Shoten, H. *Early Buddhism and Abhidharma Thought*. Japan, 2002.

Sinha, T. N. *Indian Psychology: Perception*. London, 1934.

Skilling, Peter. "Vimuttimagga and Abhayagiri: The Form-Aggregate according to the Saṃskṛtāsaṃskṛta-Viniścaya." *Journal of the Pali Text Society* 20 (1994): 171–210.

Stcherbatsky, Th. *The Central Conception of Buddhism and the Meaning of the Word "Dharma."* Prize Publication Fund, vol. 7. London, 1923.

———. "The 'Dharmas' of the Buddhists and the 'Guṇas' of the Sāṃkhyas." *Indian Historical Quarterly* 10 (1934): 737–60.

———. *Buddhist Logic*, vols. 1–2. Delhi, 1993.

Suwanda, H. J. Sugunasiri. "The Whole Body, Not Heart, as Seat of Consciousness: The Buddha's View." *Philosophy East and West* 45.3 (1995): 409–30.

Suzuki, D. T. "The Analytic and the Synthetic Approach to Buddhism." *Middle Way* 24 (1954): 102–4.

Takakusu, J. "The Abhidharma Literature of the Sarvāstivādins." *Journal of the Pali Text Society* (1904–5): 67–146.

Tatia, N. "Sarvāstivāda." *Nava Nālandā Mahāvihāra Research Publication* 2 (1960): 75–138.

Thatcher, Cynthia. *Just Seeing: Insight Meditation and Sense-Perception*. BPS, 2008.

Venkataramanan, K. "Sāmmitīyanikāya Śāstra." *Visva Bharati Annals* 5 (1953): 153–243.

Warder, A. K. *Indian Buddhism*. Delhi, 1980.

Wijesekera, O. H. de A. "Canonical References to Bhavaṅga." *University of Ceylon Review* 15 (1959): 1–25.

———. *Three Signata: Anicca, Dukkha, Anatta*. Wheel Publication no. 20. Kandy, 1982.

Willemen, C., et al. *Sarvāstivāda Buddhist Scholasticism*. Leiden, 1998.

———. *The Essence of Scholasticism Abhidharmahṛdaya*, T no. 1550. Delhi, 2006.

Williams, Paul. "Buddhadeva and Temporality." *Journal of Indian Philosophy* 4 (1977): 279–94.

———. "On the Abhidharma Ontology." *Journal of Indian Philosophy* 9 (1981): 227–57.

Winternitz, M. *A History of Indian Literature*, vol. 2. Calcutta, 1933.

INDEX

A

Abhayagiri fraternity, 151, 178, 215, 353, 404n1093
Abhidhamma (Skt. Abhidharma)
  development of, x–xi, 2–4
  suitability for studying, xiv
  three major systems of, xi–xii
  See also Sarvāstivāda Abhidharma; Theravāda Abhidhamma
Abhidhamma exegesis
  on conceptual constructs, 58–60
  consciousness defined in, 93–94
  on dependent origination, 317–18
  on dhamma theory, 18
  on dhammas as own nature, 40–41
  parallel interpretations in Abhidharma (Skt.), 7
  paramattha used in, 48
  proper understanding of, 1–2
  in Sutta Piṭaka, 3–4
  three moments in, 246–47
Abhidhamma Piṭaka, 4, 249
  analysis and synthesis in, 23
  on bodily movement, 233
  classification lists in, 22
  commentaries on, purpose of, 2
  on conditional relations, 317–18
  on consciousness, 93, 118
  on doors of kamma (*kamma-dvāra*), 240
  early dhamma theory in, 18
  hadaya used in, 99
  on material existence, 187–88
  on material nutriment, 225–26
  momentariness, development in, 286–87, 290
  paññatti used in, 56–58, 369n209
  on *saṅkhāras*, 313
  on sense organs, differences between, 215
  technical terminology in, 81
  on time, 271, 273
  on tri-temporality, 32
  twenty-eight material dhammas in, 190
  ultimate categories in, 80–81
  See also *Kathāvatthu*; *Paṭṭhāna*
Abhidhammatthasaṅgaha (Anuruddha), xii, xiii, 3, 18, 67, 309, 337
Abhidhammatthasaṅgaha (*Siṃhala Sanne*), 67
Abhidhammatthavibhāvinī, 289
Abhidhammatthavikāsinī, 3, 24, 294, 304–5, 306, 307
Abhidhammāvatāra, 3, 51, 58, 78, 303–4. See also *Abhidhammatthavikāsinī*
Abhidharmakośabhāṣya (Vasubandhu), 354–55
  on *adhivacana*, 128–29
  on atoms, 255, 263
  on mahābhūtas as objects of touch, 209
  on *saṃvṛti-sat*, 74
  on sound decad, 267
  on Vibhajyavādins, 350
  on vipāka, 107

Abhidharmakośavyākhyā (Yaśomitra), 7, 74, 100, 135, 136, 212, 255, 280, 285
Abhidharmamahāvibhāṣāśātra, 179, 249, 253–54
abstinences (*virati*), 166–67
accessory locution (*sasambhāra-kathā*), 180
activity denotation (*bhāva-sādhana*), 94, 181. *See also* nature denotation (*bhāva-sādhana*)
actual being (*bhūtattha*), 33, 48, 50
agency definition (*kattu-sādhana*), 14, 41, 42, 43, 44, 60, 93, 94, 181
aggregates (*khandhas*), five, 10, 21, 79, 128, 330, 344
 as devoid of own nature, 40, 43–45
 exclusions from, 59
 of grasping/clinging, 12–13, 117
 mental factors and, 85
 momentariness of, 285
 person as, 27, 28
 purpose of analysis of, 20, 30
 rebirth and, 225
 relationship between, 84
 totality of, 193
 tri-temporality and, 32, 34–35
 universal characteristics of, 47–48
aggregation of basic factors (*samūha*), 37
air element (*vāyo dhātu*), 188, 190
 alteration (*vikāra*) of, 212
 in atoms, 259
 bodily intimation as special mode of, 233–35, 236, 237, 240
 defining, 204
 in human body, 202
 other mahābhūtas and, 207
 in tangible sense field, 221
Ālāra the Kālāma, 341
ālaya-vijñāna (storehouse consciousness), 8
all exists theory (*sarvam-asti-vāda*), 9, 354–55
alteration, 37, 303, 308
 aññathatta, 38, 39, 283 (*see also* change-in-continuance [*ṭhitassa aññathatta*])
 modal (*ākāra-vikāra*), 235, 238, 239, 265, 268
 vikāra, 187–88, 212, 247, 306
analogies and examples
 bamboo bundles, two, 123
 blind man and cripple, 99
 boatman and boat, 99
 cane syrup, 38
 carpet, variegated, 218
 cart with seven yokes, 234–35
 children playing with kahapana (coin), 178–79
 chili, hotness of, 321
 cows, 277–78, 295
 dialects, use of, 13, 76
 falling thunderbolt, 298–99
 father and son, 326
 for feeling, 130
 for five hindrances, 113
 flavors, distinguishing, 87
 gem, 212
 gold, 38
 golden pot, 37
 herons, 292
 ice, 207
 king and ministers/retinue, 87, 140, 331
 lamps, 168, 177, 315, 324
 monkey grabbing branches, 85
 new paddy becoming old, 304–5
 prince and four nurses, 213
 river flowing, 283
 sky flowers, 295
 space, analyzing empty, 298
 sticks producing fire, 83–84
 sword's inability to cut itself, 91
 trees, 322
analysis (*bheda*), 9
 in distinguishing dhammas, 52, 54
 knowledge of (*paricchede ñāṇa*), 72
 and synthesis, combined use of, 54, 317, 344–45
 time and, 23
 See also *vibhajjavāda*
Ānanda, 11, 45
Ānanda, Ācariya, 307–8
Ancients, 180, 240–41
Andhakas, 33–34, 286, 292
Aṅguttaranikāya, 5, 6, 71, 78, 287, 290, 293, 346

Aṅguttaranikāya Aṭṭhakathā, 72, 76, 303, 306
animal kingdom, 162, 235
annihilationism (*ucchedavāda*), 25, 144–45, 147, 342–43, 345, 349, 351
Anupada Sutta, 124
Anuradhapura, 4
Anuruddha, Ācariya. See *Abhidhammatthasaṅgaha*
Aparaseliyas, 245, 286
application
  initial (*vitakka*), 113, 114, 117, 133–35, 167, 239–40, 333
  sustained (*vicāra*), 113, 114, 117, 133–35, 239, 333
arahants, 333
  conditioning factors, transcending, 111–12
  neutral kiriya consciousness of, 108–9, 114, 115
  supramundane consciousness of, 117, 118
  as transcending time, 272, 278
arising. See *uppāda*
Ārya-Sāṃmitīyas, 285, 311
Asoka, King, 342–43, 351, 352
assumption of distinction where there is no such distinction (*abhede bheda-parikappaṇā*), 42
atoms (*paramāṇu*), 178, 181, 189, 210
  aggregate (*saṃghāta-paramāṇu*), 75, 254–55, 256, 262, 263, 266
  contact between, variant views on, 259–62
  delimiting space (*paricchedākāsa*) and, 258, 260–61
  and *kalāpa*, correspondence between, 252–53
  and material clusters (*rūpa-kalāpa*), comparisons between, 249–55, 257–58, 260–64, 266
  non-Buddhist views on, 210
  sevenfold incremental aggregation doctrine, 254
  size of, 258
  as smallest unit of matter, 253, 255
  spatial dimensions of, 255, 256, 257–58, 260, 262
  unitary (*dravya-paramāṇu*), 75, 254, 263, 264
  See also material clusters (*rūpa-kalāpa*)
attention (*manasikāra*)
  mindfulness and, 157, 158
  in nāma, 19, 84, 123, 124
  restless and, 143
  as universal mental factor, 53, 122, 124, 133, 319
  unwise, 141
  and vitakka, distinction between, 134
  See also deliberate attention (*ābhūñjita-vasena*)
audible sense field (*saddāyatana*), 216, 219–21, 238, 266
Aung, S. Z., 98, 210
avarice (*macchariya*), 141, 148, 149, 380n503
aversion (*dosa*), 12, 104–5
  allaying of, 161, 168
  in cognitive process, 174
  four unwholesome factors occurring with, 148–50
  as hatred, 106
  toward conditioned phenomena, 295–96
  as unskillful, 109
avijjamāna-paññatti, 68, 273–74
avijjamānena-avijjamāna-paññatti, 69
avijjamānena-vijjamāna-paññatti, 68
avijñapti-rūpa, 191, 192, 193, 219
āyatanas, twelve (bases of cognition), 10, 20, 21, 79, 85–86, 126, 190–92, 344–45. *See also* sense fields

B

Bahuvedanīya Sutta, 11
balance of mind (*tatramajjhattatā*), 129
Bañña, 34
bare consciousness (*citta*), 85–86, 87, 93, 122
bare mind-door process (*suddha-mano-dvāra-vīthi*), 172, 183
base of infinite consciousness (*viññāṇañcāyatana*), 115
base of infinite space (*ākāsānañcāyatana*), 115

base of neither perception nor non-perception (*n'evasaññānāsaññāyatana*), 115
base of nothingness (*ākiñcaññāyatana*), 115
basic octad (*suddhaṭṭhaka*), 53, 262–63, 268, 269, 319–20
beautiful consciousness (*sobhana-citta*), 119, 155–56, 160
beautiful mental factors, 122
  abstinences (*virati*), 166–67
  list of, 155–56
  pairs of kāya and citta, 164–66
Bhadanta, Ācārya, 259–60
Bhārahāra Sutta, 28
bhāva-anyathātva (change in mode of being) theory, 37–38
bhavaṅga consciousness
  and *ālāya-vijñāna*, relationship between, 8
  arrest of (*bhavaṅga-upaccheda*), 173, 175
  function of, 169–70
  in mind-door process, 183
  past (*atīta-bhavaṅga*), 175, 176
  vibration of (*bhavaṅga-calana*), 173, 175
bhūta-rūpa, 204
births and deaths, beginningless cycle of (*saṃsāraddhāna*), 272, 278
bliss, 151–52, 334
Bodhi, Ven. Bhikkhu, 7, 104, 139. See also *Comprehensive Manual of Abhidhamma*
Bodhisattvabhūmi (Asaṅga), 80
bodily intimation (*kāya-viññatti/vijñapti*), 88, 190, 192, 219, 231
  as bodily movements, refutation of, 232–34, 235, 236
  composition of (*kāyaviññatti-navaka*), 265–66, 268, 269
  as consciousness-originated, 232, 237–38, 392n818
  definitions of, 232–33
  intentions and, 239
  kamma and, 240–41
  root condition and, 322
  as special mode of air element, 234–35, 236, 237, 243
  Theravādin and Sarvāstivādin distinctions between, 236–37
  See also *kāyaviññatti-lahutādi-dvādasaka*
body, physical (*rūpassa*)
  attainment of cessation (*nirodha-samāpatti*) and, 224
  and bodily actions, as distinct, 240–41
  Buddhist view of, 242–43
  consciousness and, 96
  decay of, 246
  elemental disturbance of, 243
  as empty and impersonal, 62
  and feeling, strength of impact on, 130
  four elements in, 201–2
  health of, 166, 266
  impermanence of, 246
  material clusters of, 251, 252
  movements of, 232–35, 268
  sex faculties and, 223
  torpor of, 151–52
body consciousness (*kāya-viññāṇa*), 95, 107, 108
body decad (*kāya-dasaka*), 264, 269
body sensitivity (*kāya-prasāda*), 212, 213
Brahma heavens, 163
Brahman (cosmic soul), 68
brahmavihāra. *See* four divine abodes (*brahmavihāra*)/four illimitables (*appamaññā*)
Buddha, ix
  on language, 56
  neutral kiriya consciousness of, 108–9, 114, 115
  paññattis of, 369n209
  questions not answered by, 14
  as skilled in expression, 77, 80
  as *vibhajjavādī*, 343–48
Buddhadeva, Bhadanta, 40
Buddhaghosa, 151–52, 169, 214, 215, 249, 287–88, 289. See also *Visuddhimagga* (Buddhaghosa)
Buddhism
  as doctrine of analysis, refutation of, 344–48, 408n1197
  fundamental doctrines of, 21, 283
  health in, 242–43

mind as preeminent in, 95
other Indian schools and, 213–15
three councils of, 353 (*see also* Third Buddhist Council)
Buddhist hybrid Sanskrit, 72
Burmese tradition, xii, xiii, 3, 184–85, 309–10

C
capability (*sāmatthiya*), 208–9, 233
Caraka, 99, 214
categorical statement (*ekaṃsavāda*), 341, 345, 346, 347–48, 349
causal efficiency (*kāritra*), 39
causality/causation, 52, 290, 299, 311, 345
conditioning characteristics and, 291
in consciousness and mental factors, 277–78
evolutionary theory of (*pariṇāmavāda*), 300
hetu and *paccaya*, distinction between, 41
rejection of, 34
simultaneous (*sahabhū-hetu*), 176–77
See also conditional relations (*paṭṭhāna-naya*)
cause and effect, 250, 318, 320, 394n861
cessation (*nirodha*), 283
attainment of (*nirodha-samāpatti*), 224
cause of, 321
as caused or spontaneous, controversy on, 311–12
characteristic of, 291
motion and, 315
simultaneous cessation (*eka-nirodha*), 88, 89
cetasikas. *See* mental factors (*cetasikas*)
Chachakka Sutta, 126
chanda. *See* desire to act (*chanda*)
change-in-continuance (*ṭhitassa aññathatta*), 47, 290, 295, 298–99, 302, 303, 306, 308
characteristic that separates from other characteristics (*asādhāraṇa-lakkhaṇa*), 46
characteristics (*lakkhaṇa*)
characterized (*lakṣya*) and, 126, 202, 293–94
of consciousness, 94
emptiness in relation to (*lakkhaṇa-suñña*), 302
individual (*paccatta*), 46, 47, 50, 62
intrinsic (*āveṇika*), 46
lakṣaṇa-anyathātva (change-in-characteristics) theory, 38–39
loss of, 38
of matter, four, 243–48
of sense organs, 213, 264
types of, 46
universal (*sāmañña*), 47, 62–63
See also own characteristic (*salakkhaṇa*)
Childers, R. C., *Dictionary of the Pāli Language*, 343–44
Chinese tradition, xi, xii, 4, 16, 253–54, 290, 355
citta-niyāma. *See* psychological order (*citta-niyāma*)
cognition
bodily movement and, 234
causality of, controversy on, 176–78
conditionality and, 312
definitions of, 41–42
single unit of, 89–91
tri-temporality and, 31
two levels of reality and, 58
cognitive acts (*dhamma-uddesa*), 337
analysis of, 85
dhammas and, 50, 58, 271
momentariness and, 288, 289
time and, 90–91, 277, 278
universal mental factors in, 122, 129, 133, 157
cognitive process, 7, 128
attraction in, 174
mindfulness in, role of, 157
object condition and, 322, 323
repetition condition and, 328–29
sense-door, 327
stages of, 173–75, 179, 324
time and, 276
variant endings of, 174–75
cohesion (*bandhanatta*), 53, 188, 204, 207, 212

coincidence (*saṅgati*), 83, 125, 128, 284
cold, 187, 188, 209–10
  fire element and, 189
  Theravāda and Sarvāstivāda differences in defining, 138, 203–4
collective concepts (*samūha-paññatti*), 64–65, 67
color
  in basic octad (*suddhaṭṭhaka*), 262, 319–20
  and material dhammas, inseparability of, 52, 253, 255, 257
  organ of sight and, 214, 216
  own characteristic of, 46
  own nature of, 294
  sense field of (*vaṇṇāyatana*), 7, 217
  visible sense field and, 217–19
commonsense realism, 18, 55
compact contact (*paṭigha-samphassa*), 128
compassion (*karuṇā*), 156, 164, 167–68
Comprehensive Manual of Abhidhamma (Bodhi), xii–xiii, 1–2, 309–10
co-nascence (*sahajāta*)
  of citta and cetasikas, 87, 88
  kamma condition, 329
  predominance condition, 323
  reciprocal (*aññamañña-sahajāta*), 90, 205, 206
  See also under conditions (*paccaya*)
conceit (*māna*), 141, 147–48, 165
concentration. See *samādhi* (concentration)
concept-as-meaning (*attha-paññatti*), 12, 60–62, 64–67, 78
concept-as-name (*nāma-paññatti*), 12, 60–62, 67–69, 78, 81, 273–74
concepts established through adherence to wrong views (*abhinivesa-paññatti*), 67
concepts of continuity (*santāna-paññatti*), 64–65, 67
conceptual constructs (*paññatti*), 15, 62, 63–64, 77, 183
  apositional (*upanidhā*), 66
  conditioning characteristics as, 294, 295
  as conditions, 338
  definitions of, 56–60, 369n210
  dhammas and, 271
  noncollective concepts (*asamūha*), 65
  object condition and, 322
  purpose of, 55–56, 369n209
  serial dhammas as, 309
  space as, 231, 281
  as time-free (*kāla-vimutta*), 275, 339, 406n1154
  See also concept-as-meaning; concept-as-name
conceptual proliferations, 32
conceptual thought, 30, 49, 60, 62, 78, 317
concomitance (*sahagata*), 26, 87, 88, 89, 91, 177
concomitants (*caitta*). *See* mental factors (*cetasikas*)
concurrence (*sannipāta*), 83, 125, 273, 284
conditional relations (*paṭṭhāna-naya*)
  basic principles of, 53, 250, 318–20, 394n861
  purpose of, 318
  twenty-four kinds, 320–21 (*see also* conditions)
conditionality, 52, 311–12, 314, 345
  of citta and cetasikas, 90–91
  co-nascent and asynchronous, 132
  paññattis' lack of, 59
  reciprocal, 297
  temporal distinction between mind and matter in, 288
conditioned dhammas/dharmas, 302, 305
  consciousness as, 100
  duration of, 299
  number of, 10, 198
  positive production (*parinipphanna*) of, 197, 271, 292
  space as, convention of, 231
  three characteristics of, 197, 291–95
  tri-temporality of, 33, 296
conditioned existence, 30, 43, 47–48, 59, 210
conditioned genesis (*paccayākāra-naya*), 26. *See also* conditions (*paccaya*)
conditioned phenomena, 283–84, 286, 296, 309, 310, 346

conditioned state (*paccayuppanna-dhamma*), 90, 132, 320–21, 322, 323–24, 325, 328, 329, 330, 333, 336, 338
conditioning characteristics
  four, 295–97
  secondary characteristics of, 296–97
  temporal sequence of, 301–2
  three, 5–6, 290–95, 301–3, 306, 308
  See also change-in-continuance (*ṭhitassa aññathatta*); *uppāda*; *vaya*
conditioning force (*paccaya-satti*), 320–21
conditioning state (*paccaya-dhamma*), 90, 132, 206, 320–21, 322, 323–25, 326, 328, 329, 336, 337–38, 339
conditions (*paccaya*), 250
  absence (*natthi*), 91, 289, 336, 337, 339
  association (*sampayutta*), 90, 334–35, 337, 338
  causal confluence of, 274–75
  co-nascence (*sahajāta*), 90, 98, 198, 324, 325, 327, 335, 336
  contiguity (*samanantara*), 90–91, 93, 96, 234, 289, 321, 323–24, 328, 336, 337, 339, 364n92
  decisive-support (*upanissaya*), 325–26, 338
  definitions of, 311–12, 320–21
  disappearance (*vigata*), 91, 289, 336, 337, 339
  dissociation (*vippayutta*), 335–36, 337, 338
  faculty (*indriya*), 331–33, 337, 338
  immediate, 94, 130
  jhāna, 333, 337, 338
  kamma, 132, 215, 245–46, 329, 337, 339
  mutuality/reciprocity (*aññamañña*), 90, 324–25, 327, 338
  nondisappearance (*avigata*), 90, 336, 337, 338–39
  nutriment (*āhāra*), 331, 338
  object (*ārammaṇa*), 93, 322–23, 327, 338
  path (*magga*), 333–34, 337, 338
  post-nascence (*pacchājāta*), 288, 312, 314, 321, 326, 327–28, 335, 336, 338
  predominance (*adhipati*), 323, 331–32, 338
  pre-nascence (*purejāta*), 98, 288, 312, 314, 325, 326–27, 328, 332, 335, 336, 337, 338
  presence (*atthi*), 90, 336, 337, 338
  proximity (*anantara*), 90–91, 289, 321, 323–24, 326, 328, 336, 337, 339
  repetition (*āsevana*), 328–29, 337, 339
  result (*vipāka*), 329–31, 337, 338
  root (*hetu*), 321–22, 337, 338
  support (*nissaya*), 90, 93, 96–97, 198, 325, 326, 337, 338
  three functions of, 332
  ways of categorizing, 337–40
confluence (*samavāya, sāmaggi*), 83, 125, 177, 179, 272–73, 274–75
consciousness (*citta*), 22, 124, 373n312
  bodily intimation and, 232, 237
  classes of, criteria for, 101–2
  definitions of, 93–94
  determining (*votthapana*), 108, 173, 175
  emotional value in classifying, 103, 105, 109
  as generative condition of matter, 197, 267–68, 327–28
  initial descent of (*cittassa paṭhamābhinipāto*), 127
  and mental factors, conascence (*sahajāta*) of, 53, 87–89, 121, 319
  origination of, 294
  partial experience by, 130
  predominance condition and, 323
  process (*vīthi-citta*) and process-free (*vīthi-mutta*), 170–71, 173, 175
  rectitude of (*cittujjukatā*), 156, 165
  sickness of (*citta-gelañña*), 150–51
  three special modes of matter and, 243
  time and, 31, 276–78
  two senses of, 100
  verbal intimation and, 240
  See also bare consciousness (*citta*); fine-material sphere (*rūpa-bhava*); immaterial sphere (*arūpa-bhava*); sense sphere (*kāma-bhava*)
consciousness (*viññāṇa*), 124
  dependency of, 20
  doors (*dvāra*) and bases (*vatthu*) of, distinctions between, 95, 216
  and nāma-rūpa, reciprocal conditionality of, 19, 84, 123, 124

as nutriment, 225, 331
and other mental dhammas, as blended, 51
storehouse (*ālaya-vijñāna*), 8
See also sense consciousnesses; six kinds of consciousness
consciousness-originated matter (*citta-samuṭṭhāna-rūpa*), 88, 232, 233–35, 237–38, 265, 314, 322, 392n818
consensual (*sammuti*) truth/reality, 11, 30, 290
object condition and, 323
paññatti and, 55, 62, 68
of person, 27, 77
as *sammuti* or *saṃvṛti*, distinctions between, 72–73
two kinds of existence in, 74–75
See also two truths
constituents (*kalāpaṅgas*), 255, 257, 261, 264, 265–66, 269
contact (*phassa*), 83
and "correlation of three," variant views on, 124–27
feeling and, 129
in *nāma*, 19, 84, 123
as nutriment, 225, 331
partial experience by, 130
and *pasāda-ghaṭṭana*, distinction between, 127
sense organs and, 215–16, 220, 390n744
six types, 126, 128
as universal mental factor, 53, 122, 124, 319
convention (*vohāra*), 42, 48, 77, 315
cosmology, Buddhist, 60, 101, 318
covetousness (*abhijjā, kadariya*), 143, 149
craving, 118, 126, 136, 144, 145, 161–62
creation, divine, 406n114. *See also* God
Cullavedalla Sutta, 373n312

D

Dārṣṭāntikas, 177, 179, 192, 236, 311
Dasuttara, 2–3
death, 145, 246, 292, 397n926
death consciousness (*cuti-citta*), 170–71
decay (*jaratā*), 295, 296, 299–300, 305
of decay (*jaratā-jaratā*), 296–97
evident (*pākaṭa-jarā*), 188, 247, 305–6
as figurative expression, 303–10
incessant (*avici-jarā*), 188
of matter (*rūpassa jaratā*), 190, 243, 246, 247–48, 265
as *parinipphana*, controversy on, 292
definitions, 14–15, 41–42, 46, 50, 93–94, 202
definitive meaning (*nītattha*), 11, 28, 71
deliberate attention (*ābhūñjita-vasena*), 208–9
delimitation, material (*pariccheda-rūpa*), 230–31, 281
delusion (*moha*), 103, 111, 112
arising of, 106
classes of consciousness rooted in, 105, 145–46
sheer (*momūha*), 105
as unskillful, 109
as unwholesome mental factor, 141–42, 144
in wholesome consciousness, absence of, 110
dependent matter (*upādā-rūpa*), 53, 198–99, 227–28, 253, 319–20, 324
dependent origination (*paṭiccasamuppāda*), 10, 15, 26, 63, 83–84, 117, 317–18, 321. *See also* twelve-factored formula of dependent arising
designation (*adhivacana*), 56–57, 128–29. *See also* conceptual constructs (*paññatti*)
desire, 31–32, 138, 144, 326
for eternal life (*bhava-taṇhā*) and death (*vibhava-taṇhā*), 145
greed and, 143
sensual (*kāmacchanda, kāma-rāga*), 113, 118, 139, 166
desire to act (*chanda*), 136, 323
as occasional mental factor, 133, 139–40
as universal mental factor, 122, 137–38
detachment, 117, 161
determination. *See* resolve (*adhimukti/adhimokṣa*)
determining consciousness (*votthapana-citta*), 108, 173, 175

deva heavens, 163
Devaśarman, Ven., 34, 352
Dhamma
direct knowledge of (*dhamme ñāṇa*), 72
inductive knowledge of (*anvaye ñāṇa*), 72
multiplicity of presentations of, 11–14, 71, 76–77, 78, 81
and non-Dhamma, distinguishing, 12
dhamma theory, 51–52
absolutist interpretation, refutation of, 29–30
analysis and synthesis in, 9, 345
antecedents of, 19
conditionality in, 53, 318, 319, 320–21
denial of motion and, 314–15
development of, 14–15
as dhamma realism, 15, 55
emptiness and, 10
knowledge of analysis and, 72
misunderstandings about, 22–25
momentariness and, 285, 288
person concept in, 26–30
phassa as "union of three" and, 126–27
purpose of, 17–18, 48, 187
tri-temporality and, 30–40, 193, 275–76, 278
Dhammajoti, K. L., 179, 253–54
Dhammapada, 242
Dhammapāla, Ācariya, 308–9
dhammas (Skt. *dharmas*)
as basic factors, 37, 49, 94
classification of, 50–51
and conceptual constructs, distinction between, 57, 58–60, 271
conditionedness (*sappaccayatā*) of, 51, 53
and conditioning characteristics, relationships between, 291–94, 296–97
as conditions or conditioned, 250
displacement of (*bhāva-vigamana*), 38
expressions for, 49–50
and function of, lack of distinction between, 39–40
general meaning of, x
impersonal, 181
as interconnected but distinguishable, 25–26
knowable (*ñeyya-dhamma*), 49, 58
momentary (*santati-ṭhiti, pabandha-ṭhiti*), 236, 298–300, 307, 308, 309
nāma-paññatti assigned to, 61–62, 68
nonpervasiveness (*abyāpāratā*) of, 315
old age of, 304
ontological status of, 33
as own characteristic, 45–48, 62
as own nature, 33, 40–45, 62, 68, 196, 304
own power, as devoid of, 320
"person" and, 27
shift in meaning of term, 17
stabilizing, 296
technical meaning of, 22
time as continuous flow of, 273–75
two truths and, 73–74
as ultimate existents, 48–49, 290–91
See also conditioned dhammas/dharmas; dhamma theory; material dhammas; mental dhammas
Dhammasaṅgaṇi, 3
analytical method in, 23
on bodily intimation in, 232, 233
on characteristics of matter, 243–44, 246, 247
classification lists in, 22
commentarial tradition and, 2
commentary to, 161–63, 222–23, 239
on consciousness and mental factors, 277
on doubt, 152
on first fine-material jhāna, 116–17
on five aggregates, 330
heart base, omission of in, 226–27
on material dhammas, inseparability of, 52
on material food, 225–26
mental factors absent from, 136, 139
on middha and kāya, 151–52
on paññatti, 56–57
phassa-pañcaka in, 124
on sex faculties, 221–22
on smell, 221
on space element, 230
on special modes of matter, 242

on time, 278
on visible sense field (*rūpāyatana*), 216–17
visual field in, 6–7
on vocal expression, 238
wholesome energy (*viriya*) in, 138
dhammatā-rūpa (matter by nature), 268–69
dhammāyatana (Skt. *dharmāyatana*), 2, 86, 126, 191–92, 195–96, 226
dhammāyatana-rūpa, 191, 193, 195–96
Dharmaguptaka school, xi, 5, 291
Dharmaskandhaśāstra, 5
Dharmatrāta, Bhadanta, 37–38, 179
Dhātukathā, 3
Dhātukāyaśāstra, 5
dhātus, eighteen (elements of cognition), 10, 20, 21, 32, 79, 85, 86–87, 344–45
dhātus, six (elements), 20, 21
dichotomization, three principals of, 103–4, 109
Dīghanikāya, 2–3, 25, 56, 123. See also *Saṅgīti Sutta*
Dīpavaṃsa, 342
discourse (*desanā*), 80, 81
"Discourse on the Bearer of the Burden" (*Bhārahāra Sutta*), 28
disgust, absence of (*ajigucchana*), 142. *See also* moral shamelessness (*ahirika*)
Dispensation (*sāsana*), 342–43, 351, 352
displeasure (*domanassa*), 105, 106, 110, 131, 148–49, 333
dissimilarity, genesis of (*visadisuppatti*), 187–88
dissolution (*bhaṅga*), 59, 197
moment dhamma is facing own (*bhaṅgābhimukhāvatthā*), 307
See also *vaya*
distension (*thambhitatta*), 189, 204, 206, 207
divine eye (*dibba-cakkhu*), 258, 284
dominance (*adhipatibhāvena, ādhipacca*), 87, 216
doubt (*vicikicchā*), 105, 113, 135, 141, 145, 152–53, 166
drowsiness (*paccalāyikā*), 152
duration (*sthiti*), 295–97
as decay (*jaratā*), 303–4
duration of (*sthiti-sthiti*), 296–97
interpretations of, 298–99
momentariness and, 300

E

ear consciousness (*sota-viññāṇa*), 7, 86, 95, 99, 173
ear decad (*sota-dasaka*), 264, 269
ear sensitivity (*sotappasāda*), 251
early Buddhism, 348
and Abhidhamma, differences between, 17, 30
on analysis, modes of, 79
āyatanas as rūpa in, 191
cognition in, 169–71
conditioned phenomena in, 290
dependent origination in, 317–18, 321
dhammāyatana-rūpa links in, 192–94
emptiness in, 29, 45
energy in, 137
explicit and implicit meaning in, 28
four material properties in, 202
four truths in, 63
heterogeneous unity of dhammas in, 51
impermanence in, 284
middle doctrine of, 25–26
on mind, analysis of, 83–85
momentariness in, divided views on, 285–87
perception in, 134–35
person concept in, 27
on space, 280
on speculative views and beliefs, 144, 145
and Theravāda Buddhism, distinctions between, 4
totality (*sabba*) in, 32
on two truths, antecedents to, 30, 71–72
earth element (*paṭhavī dhātu*), 188, 190
characteristic and intensity of, 252
characteristics of, 43
as constituent of atoms, 257–58
defining, 46, 202–3, 204
in human body, 201

other mahābhūtas and, 206
space and, 281
in tangible sense field, 221
vocal intimation as special mode of, 238–40
echos, 220
Edgerton, F., 72
edible food (*kabaḷīkāra-āhāra*), 195, 225–26, 331
effect described though its cause (*phalūpacāra*), 152
effort-making (*ussahana-vikāra*), 233
eightfold path, 138, 158, 166–67, 333–34
Ekavyavahārikas, 350
elemental disturbance (*dhātukkhobha*), 243
elemental series (*dhātu-paramparā*), 219–20
elements, four material (*mahābhūtas*), 29–30, 38, 53, 319–20
bodily intimation and, 233
in Buddhism, primary position of, 210
characteristics and intensity of, 204–5, 208–9, 252
co-nascence condition and, 324
and dependent matter, relationship between, 198–99, 227–28, 250, 253
duration of, 285
equal presence of (*tulya-bhūta-sadbhāva*), 208, 209
extrusion of one mahābhūta over others (*ussadavasena*), 208, 209
five sense organs and, 214–15
mind and, 84, 85
mutual conditionality of, 205–6, 325
in physical body, 96, 251
positional inseparability (*padesato avinibhoga*) of, 206–8
Sāṃkhya view of, 213
in serial dhammas, 299
sex faculties and, 223
and space element, relationship between, 201, 230
special modes of matter and, 243
as support (*āśraya*), 198, 263
Theravādin definitions of, 188–89
verbal intimation and, 238
embryonic development, 332
empiric individuality, 19–21, 20, 75–76, 84, 225, 229–30, 280, 331
empirical existence, 6, 17–18, 29, 43, 48, 49, 54, 55, 81, 290–91
emptiness (*suññatā*), 10, 28–29, 44–45, 62
energy (*viriya*), 133, 136, 137–38, 139–40, 323, 333
envy (*issā*), 141, 148, 149
equanimity (*upekkhā*), 333
in consciousness rooted in delusion, 105
in consciousness rooted in greed, 105, 375n366
consciousnesses associated with, 106, 107, 108, 110
as feeling (*vedanā*), 131
illimitable, 167
jhāna factor of, 113, 114, 115
and neutrality, distinction between, 129, 163–64
equanimity-neutrality (*tatramajjhattupekkhā*), 164
eternalism (*śāśvatavāda*), 25, 144, 145, 147, 342, 345, 349, 351
ethics
and Buddhist psychology, affinity between, 109
in classifying consciousness, 101
javana and, 174
mindfulness in, 158
social, mental factors that protect, 159–60
wholesome energy (*viriya*) in, 138
exhaustion (*khijjana*), 99–100
existence, 37
actual and verifiable (*saṃvijjamānatā*), 49
four spheres of (*catubhūmaka-dhammesu nipatati*), 57, 59–60
objective (*paramatthato vijjamānatā*), 49
See also empirical existence; individual existence
experience-based processes (*diṭṭhavāra*), 184
eye consciousness (*cakkhu-viññāṇa*), 83, 88, 95
contact (*phassa*) and, 126, 127

as mere seeing (*dassana-matta*), 7, 173
and mind consciousness, relationship between, 173
eye decad (*cakkhu-dasaka*), 264, 269
eye of wisdom. *See* divine eye (*dibba-cakkhu*)
eye sensitivity (*cakkhuppasāda*), 251
eye sphere, 32–33

F
factors of awakening (*bojjhaṅga*), 138, 158
faculties (*indriya*)
condition (*paccaya*), 331–33, 337, 338
definition of, 216
duration of, 285
hypermaturity of (*indriyānaṃ paripāko*), 246
See also sense organs (*indriya*)
faith (*saddhā*), 155, 156, 165, 333
far/near (*dūre/santike*), pair of, 192–94
feeling (*vedanā*), 11, 109
aggregate of, 139
characteristic of, 47
direct experience by, 130
as faculty (*indriya*), 130–31
and feelingness, distinction between, 15, 64
in nāma, 19, 84, 123
and other mental dhammas, as blended, 51
six kinds, 126
three affective tones of, 129
as universal mental factor, 53, 122, 124, 319
feminine faculty (*itthindriya*), 152, 190, 192, 195, 221–23, 228
composition (*itthibhāva-dasaka*) of, 264–65, 268, 269
faculty condition and, 332
kamma-originated, 331
fetters, ten, 32, 118
figure (*saṇṭhāna*), 6–7, 217–19, 236–37
fine-material sphere (*rūpa-bhava*), 101, 112, 115
beautiful consciousness in, 119
consciousness in, fifteen types, 114
first jhāna, analysis of, 116–17
jhāna in, five factors of, 113
jhāna in, five stages of, 113–14
supramundane consciousness and, 118
fire element (*tejo dhātu*), 188, 190, 202, 203–4, 207, 208, 221
five mental hindrances (*nīvaraṇa*), 113, 135, 139, 150, 165, 166
five sense-door adverting consciousness (*pañca-dvāra-āvajjana-citta*), 108, 173, 175
five-door processes (*pañca-dvāra-vīthi*), 172, 182, 183–84, 327
fluidity (*davatā*), 188, 203, 209–10
fortuitous origination (*adhicca-samuppanna*), 318
four divine abodes (*brahmavihāra*)/ four illimitables (*appamaññā*), 160, 161, 167, 375n366
four extreme philosophical positions, 9–10
four noble truths, 12, 32, 63–64, 79
fruition consciousness (*phala-citta*), 117, 118
full understanding as abandoning (*pahāna-pariññā*), 48
full understanding as the known (*ñāta-pariññā*), 47–48
functional (*kiriya*) consciousness, 101, 118, 122
beautiful consciousness and, 119
beautiful mental factors in, 155, 160
in fine-material sphere, 114
in immaterial sphere, 115
with roots, 111–12
three types, 106, 108–9
three wholesome roots in, 160

G
Gandhāra, xi
Geiger, Wilhelm, 344
generosity, 109. *See also* nongreed (*alobha*)
genitive expression (*sāmi-vacana*), 15
Gethin, Rupert, 50, 51
Ghoṣaka, Bhadanta, 38–39, 179
God, 43, 116, 319
godhead, impersonal, 116, 319
Govinda, Lama Anagarika, 65

grasping
of belief in self (*attavāda-upādāna*), 144
collective concepts and, 65
of views (*diṭṭhi-upādāna*), 144
greed (*lobha*), 103, 106, 111, 112
and chanda, difference between, 139
classes of consciousness rooted in, 104, 141
conceit and, 147
delusion accompanying, 105–6
and hatred, mutual exclusion between, 106, 142
mindfulness and, 158
as unskillful, 109
as unwholesome mental factor, 141, 143–44
wrong view and, 144, 145
Griffiths, P. J., 50
gross/subtle (*oḷārika/sukhuma*), pair of, 192–94
growth (*upacaya*), 265. *See also* integration (*upacaya*)
guardians of the world (*lokapālā dhammā*), mental factors as, 142, 160

H

happiness, 13, 99, 113, 114. *See also* pleasure (*sukha*)
hatred (*dosa*), 103, 106, 111, 112
classes of consciousness rooted in, 104–5, 141
delusion accompanying, 105–6
and greed, mutual exclusion between, 106, 142
as unwholesome mental factor, 141, 144, 148–49
health, 162, 165, 166, 242–43, 266. *See also* mental health (*ārogya*)
hearing, 133
function of (*savaṇa-kicca*), 173
memory revival of, 184, 185
mere (*savaṇa-matta*), 7, 173
organ of (*sota*), 190, 211, 213, 214, 227, 245, 264, 270
sensory contact and, 215–16
heart base (*hadaya-vatthu*), 88, 97–100, 190, 226–28
base pre-nascence (*vatthu-purejāta*) and, 327
composition (*vatthu-dasaka*) of, 264–65, 269
integration and continuity of, 244
kamma-originated, 268, 331
heat, 138, 187, 188, 189, 204
heretics, 29, 342, 343
higher knowledge, six kinds (*chaḷabhiññā*), 114

I

iddhi, 138
idealism, 5
Idealist school, 8, 255–56
ideation processes, 172, 174, 179, 182–83, 184
ignorance (*avijjā*), 118, 142. *See also* delusion (*moha*)
ill will (*vyāpāda*), 113, 161, 166
immaterial plane (*arūpa-loka*), 100, 112–13
immaterial sphere (*arūpa-bhava*), 115–17, 119
impermanence (*aniccatā,* Skt. *anityatā*), 283, 305, 313
of body, 96
as conceptual construct, 63
of consciousness, 83
dhamma theory and, 37, 314
of dhammas, 33
empirical basis of, 284
of impermanence (*anityatā-anityatā*), 296–97
of matter (*rūpassa aniccatā*), 190, 243, 246, 247–48, 265
nongreed and, 162
own nature and, 10, 44
as *parinipphana*, controversy on, 292, 294–95
reification of, 15
suffering and, 13
inclination/predilection. *See* desire to act (*chanda*)
Indian Buddhism, xi, xii, 5
Indian medical tradition, 99
Indian philosophy
on mahābhūtas, 201, 210

on nonexistence, 66
substantialist view of existence in, 29–30, 56
on time, 271–72
See also Sāṃkhya system; Vaiśeṣika system
indifference (*upekkhā*), 106. *See also* equanimity (*upekkhā*)
individual existence, 12–13, 170, 225, 317, 325
individual nature (*āveṇika-sabhāva*), 59
indolence (*kosajja*, Skt. *kauśīdya*), 137, 138
inferability of external objects (*bāhyārthānumeyavāda*), 177, 178
inference, 31, 191, 193, 221, 226, 232, 235, 239
infinite regress (*anavaṭṭhāna*), 15, 47, 66, 248, 275, 294, 297
information-based processes (*sutavāra*), 184
inseparability
actual (*saṃsaṭṭhatā, avinibhogatā*), 51
positional (*padesato avinibhogatā*), 52, 189, 206–8, 250–51, 252, 261
insight (*vipassanā*), x, 114, 197
instantaneous being, 299
instrumental definition (*karaṇa-sādhana*), 14, 41–42, 93–94
integration (*upacaya*), 243, 244, 245, 246
intellectual faculty (*paññāya dubbali-karaṇa*), 113
intensity (*ussada*), 38, 208–9, 233, 252, 257
interminability (*anupaccheda*), 15, 275
invariable association (*avyabhicāra*), 218
investigating consciousness (*santīraṇa-citta*), 107, 108, 173, 175
investigation (*vimaṃsa*), 323
Itivuttaka, commentary to, 24–25

J

Jainism, 37, 201, 210, 214, 258
Jalandhara, 354
Japan, xii
jāti. See *uppāda*
javana (running swiftly), 173–75, 179, 234, 328–29
Jayatilleke, K. N., *Early Buddhist Theory of Knowledge*, 75
jealousy (*usūyana*), 149
Jetavana fraternity, 353
jhāna
as analyzable, 116–17
Buddhist and non-Buddhist understandings of, 115–16
in classifying consciousness, 101
condition (*paccaya*), 333, 337, 338
as conditioned experience, 117
fifth, as foundation, 114, 115
pīti in, 139
single unit of consciousness in, 286
as suffering, 13
vitakka and vicāra in, 135
See also fine-material sphere; immaterial sphere
Jñānaprasthānaśāstra, 4–5
Jotipāla, Ācariya, 308
joy (*somanassa*), 105, 106, 108, 110, 333
joy, appreciative (*muditā*), 156, 164, 167, 168
juxtaposition (*sannivesana*), 66, 217

K

kalāpa, uses of term, 251–53
Kālavādins, 271–72
kāla-vimutta (independent of time), 59–60, 183, 275, 322, 339, 406n1154
Kamalaśīla, 398n974
kamma (Skt. *karma*)
basic octad and, 269
bodily material phenomena and, 234
in classifying consciousness, 101–2
determining quality of, 328–29
four classes of, 100–102
as generative condition of matter, 197, 245–46, 267–68, 327–28, 330–31, 332, 335
heart base and, 98
and intimation, two kinds, 240–41
material clusters originated from, 267, 268
material life faculty and, 223, 225
results of, effortlessly arising, 330
root condition and, 322
sense organs and, 215, 245–46

space as *akammaja*, 279
threefold, 240
tri-temporality and, 31, 33
See also volition (*cetanā*)
kammic determinism, refutation of, 107
kammic order, transcending (*kamma-niyāma*), 111, 112
Kaṇāda, 9
Kaniṣka, King, 354
Kāpilā, 9
Kashmir, xi
Kassapa the Senior, 343
Kassapikas (Skt. Kāśyapīyas), 33, 350, 351, 354
Kathāvatthu, 3, 4, 343, 351–52, 365n105
on citta and cetasikas, 87, 89, 374n326
on conditioning characteristics, 291–92, 308
duration, lack of mention in, 310
on impermanence as concretely produced, refutation of, 294–95
on life faculties, 224
meaning of name, 352
on momentariness, 285–86, 287, 288
parinipphanna used in, 197
on personalism, refutation of, 28
on reification, 63
on Sarvāstivāda tri-temporality, critique of, 16, 34–35
on sixfold sense sphere, arising of, 245
on space, 231, 280–81
on thusness, 15
on *vipāka*, controversies about, 330
Kathāvatthu Aṭṭhakathā, 281, 286, 342, 369n209
Kaukkuṭikas, 350
kāyaviññatti-lahutādi-dvādasaka, 267, 268, 269
Khandhakavagga Aṭṭhakathā, 289
khandhas, five. *See* aggregates (*khandhas*), five
Khemappakaraṇa, 3
knowledge (*ñāṇa*, Skt. *jñāna*)
consciousness associated with (*ñāṇa-sampayutta*), 109, 110, 111, 168
consciousness disassociated with (*ñāṇa-vippayutta*), 109, 110, 168
of decease and survival of beings (*cutūpapāta-ñāṇa*), 114
of destruction of defiling impulses (*āsavakkhaya-ñāṇa*), 114
four kinds, 72
resolve (*adhimokṣa*) and, 136
supramundane, 333

L

La Vallée Poussin, Louis de, 16, 34, 290, 311, 350, 352
lahutādekādasaka, 266, 268, 269
Lamotte, Étienne, 8
language and linguistic conventions, 12, 14–15, 56, 57, 61, 72, 77, 129, 181
latent proclivities (*anusaya*), 146
let-than. *See* little finger manuals (*let-than*)
liberation (*vimutti*), ix, x, 23, 118
life faculty, 98, 122–23, 224–25, 228, 332. *See also* material life faculty; psychic life faculty
lifespan
decay and, 303–4
of gods, 285
of mind and matter, comparisons of, 88, 98, 172, 176, 178, 237, 286–87, 288, 289–90, 308, 312–13, 335, 338
tri-temporality and, 275–76
light, 214, 216, 220, 259
lightness
of consciousness (*citta-lahutā*), 155, 165
of matter (*rūpassa lahutā*), 166, 190, 242–43, 265 (see also *lahutādekādasaka*)
of mental factors (*kāya-lahutā*), 155, 165
little finger manuals (*let-than*), 3, 18
living beings, 76, 84, 331
material clusters in, 250–51, 267, 268
material life faculty in, 223–25
matter in, four characteristics of, 243–46
matter in, three characteristics of, 242–43
naming (*nāma*), 57–58
as object of four immeasurables, 161, 164

self-entity of, 65, 68, 78
six components of, 195
time and, 272, 274
local concepts (*disā-paññatti*), 64–65, 67
locative denotation (*adhikaraṇa-sādhana*), 14, 374n339
logical abstractions. *See* conceptual constructs (*paññatti*)
Lokottaravādins, 350
loving-kindness (*mettā*), 109, 160, 161, 167

M

Madhupiṇḍika Sutta, 134–35
Madhyamaka, xii, 8, 18, 29, 355, 399n985
Mahā Aṭṭhakathā, 239–40
Mahā Aṭṭhakathācariyas, 290
Mahānidāna Sutta, 123
Mahāniddesa, 288, 310
Mahāparinibbāna Sutta, 280
Mahāsāṃghika school, 4, 8, 97, 125, 214, 285, 330, 350
Mahāsatipaṭṭhāna Sutta, 124
Mahāvaṃsa, 342, 343, 344
Mahāvedalla Sutta, 51
Mahāvihāra fraternity, 215, 353
Mahāyāna, xii, 7–8, 355
Mahīśāsaka school, 8, 63
Majjhimabhāṇakas, 276
Majjhimanikāya, 11, 126, 276, 346
malleability (*mudutā*)
of consciousness (*citta-mudutā*), 155, 165
of matter (*rūpassa mudutā*), 166, 190, 242–43, 265
of mental factors (*kāya-mudutā*), 155, 165
masculine faculty (*purisindriya*), 152, 190, 192, 195, 221–23, 228
composition (*pumbhāva-dasaka*) of, 264–65, 268, 269
faculty condition and, 332
kamma-originated, 331
material aggregates, 207, 208–9, 221, 224, 226, 252
material clusters (*rūpa-kalāpa*), 53, 91, 181, 182, 319
composition of, 263–67, 269–70
four elements in, 210
generative conditions of, 265, 267–68
material life faculty in, 223
momentariness and, 288
nipphanna and anipphanna division of, 265–66
nonpervasiveness (*abyāpāratā*) of, 315
and Sarvāstivādin atomism, comparisons between, 249–55, 257–58, 260–62
separateness of, 260–62
and sound production, variant views on, 220–21
See also atoms (*paramāṇu*)
material dhammas (*rūpa-dhammas*), 22, 69, 334
in Buddhism, primacy of, 210
concretely produced dependent (*nipphanna-upāda-rūpa*), 227–28
conditioned by roots, 322
as conditions, capacity for, 327
coordinate factors of, 196
definitions of, 189–90
evident decay of, 305–6
four elements and dependent matter division of, 198–99, 253
four generative conditions of, 197, 267–68, 327–28
heart base and, 226–27
heterogeneous unity of, 52
inseparable (*avinirbhāga*), eight, 226, 233, 251
kamma condition and, 329
kamma-originated, 330, 335
life faculty of, 122
mind-originated, 265, 322
momentariness of, 187–88
nipphanna and anipphanna division of, 196–98, 211, 229
in same locus (*ekadeśa*), 218
in *Saṅgīti*, three groups of, 194–96
in sense organs and objects, 130, 227–28
strength of, 314
Theravādin and Sarvāstivādin distinctions in, 262–63
twenty-eight, list of, 190

two truths and, 73–75
material food. *See* edible food (*kabaḷīkāra-āhāra*)
material life faculty (*rūpa-jīvitindriya*), 190, 223, 224–25, 269
composition of (*jīvita-navaka*), 264, 269
integration and continuity of, 244, 246
kamma-originated, 331
material matter (*rūpa-rūpa*), 197–98
material sphere (*asañña-bhava*), 224–25
materiality (*rūpa*), 84
characteristic of, 47
components of, 192–94
impinging (*sappaṭigha*), 128, 173, 194–95, 220, 239
nonimpinging (*appaṭigha*), 194, 195, 230
tri-temporality and, 32
matter (*rūpa*)
to be comprehended by insight (*sammasana-rūpa*), 197
conceptual constructs and, 59
consciousness-originated, 88, 232, 233–35, 237–38, 265, 314, 322, 392n818
continuity of (*rūpassa santati*), 190, 243, 244–45, 246, 265
decay of (*rūpassa jaratā*), 190, 243, 246, 247–48, 265
definitions of, 91, 187–89, 255–56
four elements, presence in, 208–9
having its own characteristic (*salakkhaṇa-rūpa*), 197
kamma-originated, 197, 245–46, 267–68, 327–28, 330–31, 332, 335
lightness of (*rūpassa lahutā*), 166, 190, 242–43, 265
malleability of (*rūpassa mudutā*), 166, 190, 242–43, 265
and materiality, distinction between, 15, 64
and mind, reciprocal dependence of, 84–85
and mind, relative duration of moments, 88, 98, 172, 176, 178, 237, 286–87, 288, 289–90, 308, 312–13, 335, 338
mind-conditioned, 313
momentariness of, 285–87
movement of, 279
mutability of (*ruppana*), 43, 47, 187, 196, 231
by nature (*dhammatā-rūpa*), 268–69
nutriment as generative condition of, 197, 267, 268, 327–28
past bhavaṅga and, 176
resistant (*appaṭighabhāvato*), 180
as rūpa, 123
space and, 281
special modalities of (*vikāra-rūpa*), 242–43
temperature as generative condition of, 197, 267–68, 327–28
wieldiness of (*rūpassa kammaññatā*), 190, 242–43, 265
See also dependent matter (*upādā-rūpa*); material dhammas (*rūpa-dhammas*)
measurements
of consciousness, single unit of, 286–87
cubic inch (*aṅgula*), 258
doṇa, 251
of matter, smallest unit, 53, 189, 210, 251–52, 253, 255, 319
table of, 258
of time, briefest unit of (*khaṇa*), 272, 278, 284, 301, 302
meditation, 18, 62. *See also* insight (*vipassanā*); *samādhi* (concentration)
memory, 31, 131, 157, 184
mental advertence. *See* attention (*manasikāra*)
mental calm (*vūpasama*), 143
mental consciousness, 7, 20, 128–29, 181. *See also* mind consciousness (*mano-viññāṇa*)
mental constructs (*mānasaṃ parikalpitam*), 47, 182, 192, 195, 218–19, 271. *See also* conceptual constructs (*paññatti*)
mental culture, 32, 48, 153, 156, 161, 166, 242
mental dhammas, 404n1093
arising of, 53, 91, 319, 328

as contact (*phassa*), 127–28
decay of, 305
momentariness of, 289, 307–9
psychic life faculty of, 122
relationship between, 51, 334
repetition condition and, 328–29
strength of, 314
mental factors (*cetasikas*), 22, 69, 121, 285
arising with consciousness, 19, 84, 93, 250
and consciousness, relationship between, 87–90
distinguishing from mind, 85, 373n312
predominant (*adhipati*), 140
rectitude of (*kāyujjukatā*), 156, 165
sickness of (*cetasika-gelañña*), 150, 151
See also individual mental factor
mental formations (*saṅkhāra*), 20, 21, 22, 117, 139
mental formations dissociated from consciousness (*cittaviprayukta*), 224
mental health (*ārogya*), 109, 111, 143, 150–51, 165, 242
mental impediments (*nīvaraṇas*), 143, 150, 152, 153
mental intoxicants (*āsava*), 146
mental life faculty. *See* psychic life faculty (*arūpa-jīvitindriya*)
mental objects, 20, 108, 183, 209, 231, 322, 330
mental objects, sphere of (*dhamma-dhātu/dhammāyatana*), 32, 86, 226, 232, 244, 280, 392n818
mental purity (*anavajja*), 109, 111
mental states
arising of, 277
conditional relations and, 323–24, 325, 326, 328, 333, 334, 335–36
heart base and, 327
and kamma, conditional relationships to, 329–31
linear sequence of, 337, 339
phassa-pañcaka, 124
relationship between, 89–91, 323–24
middle doctrine, 25–26
Milinda, King, 51, 278
Milindapañha, 9
bhavaṅga in, 8, 170
on contact (*phassa*), 127
on mental factors, heterogeneous unity of, 51–52
on nippariyāya method, 81
on space, 279, 280, 281
on time, 278
on universal mental factors, 124
Mīmāṃsakas, 214
mind (*manas*, *buddhi*), 88, 91, 99
constructs of (*buddhi-parikappita*, *paññatti*), 46, 59 (*see also* conceptual constructs [*paññatti*])
in early Buddhist psychology, 83–84
interpretative and synthesizing function of (*kappanā*), 60, 68
and matter, reciprocal dependence of, 84–85
matter originated from (*see* consciousness-originated matter [*citta-samuṭṭhāna-rūpa*])
momentariness of, 169, 285–87, 288
origination and cessation of, 287, 288–89
physical base of, 96–97, 99, 226–27, 226–28, 324, 325, 332, 335 (*see also* heart base [*hadaya-vatthu*])
as self-substance, refutation of, 85
static phase of, 287
transcendence of conceptual level of, 62
two levels of reality and, 58
unification and refinement of, 116, 117
mind base (*manāyatana*), 85–86, 191, 330
mind consciousness (*mano-viññāṇa*), 86, 95, 99, 173, 226–28, 239
mind contact (*mano-samphassa*), 128, 130–31
mind door, 131, 171, 172, 235. *See also* mind-door adverting consciousness (*mano-dvāra-āvajjana-citta*); mind-door process (*mano-dvāra-vīthi*)
mind element (*mano-dhātu*), 86–87, 97, 98
mind faculty (*manendriya*), 86–87, 333
mind moment (*eka-cittakkhaṇika*), 172, 319, 327–28
in cognitive process, 175–76
lifespan of, 88, 98, 172, 176, 178, 237, 286–87, 288, 289–90, 308, 312–13, 335, 338

as triad of moments, 302
mind-door adverting consciousness (*mano-dvāra-āvajjana-citta*), 108
mind-door process (*mano-dvāra-vīthi*), 172, 179, 182–85, 327
mindfulness (*sati*, Skt. *smṛti*), 122, 155, 333
as beautiful mental factor, 157
four foundations of, 157–58
right and wrong, 158
in Sarvāstivāda system, 158
misconceptions, three basic, 48
misconduct
bodily and verbal, 142, 158–59
sexual, 167
mixed-door process (*missaka-dvāra-vīthi*), 172
mobility (*samudīraṇa*), 53, 189, 206, 207, 208–9, 212, 234
Moggaliputta, Tissa Thera (Moggallāna), 16, 34, 342, 343, 351, 352, 365n105
Mohavicchedanī, 3
momentariness
and air element, defining, 204
and atoms, contact between, 259, 260
bodily intimation and, 236–37
cognitive process and, 172, 176–78, 234
development of theory, 286–90
earliest allusion to, 285
four characteristics of matter and, 246–48
of material dhammas, 187–88
of mind and matter, distinctions between, 312–14 (*see also* lifespan)
movement and, 314–15
parallel versions of, 290–95
rationalism of, 284
Sarvāstivāda-Sautrāntika controversy on, 296–301
temporal sequence and, 297, 301–2
momentary being (*khaṇikatā*), 315
momentary present (*khaṇa-paccuppanna*), 275
moments (*khaṇa*), 272, 275–76, 278, 284–85
of cessation (*nirodhakkhaṇa*), 287, 288, 308
of decay (*khaṇika-jarā*), 305–10
of dissolution (*bhaṅgakkhaṇa*), 289, 301, 303, 306, 309, 310–11, 314
of duration (*ṭhitikkhaṇa*), 287, 289, 301, 303, 306, 307, 309–10
of existence (*vijjamānakkhaṇa*), 307
of occurrence (*pavattikkhaṇa*), 307
of origination (*uppādakkhaṇa*), 287, 288, 289, 301, 303, 306, 307–8, 309, 314
of presence (*atthikkhaṇa*), 307, 309–10, 313, 314
of standing (*ṭhānakkhaṇa*), 307
ubhinnaṃ vemajjhe, 307
udaya-vyaya-paricchinna, 307
monism, 9, 25–26, 54, 84–85, 319
moral evil, 142, 143. *See also* three roots of moral evil
moral fear (*ottappa*), 142, 155, 158–59
moral fearlessness (*anottappa*), 141, 142, 159–60
moral governance, 160
moral shame (*hiri*), 142, 155, 158–59
moral shamelessness (*ahirika*), 141, 142, 159–60
moral training, 165
motion (*samudīraṇa*), 204, 314–15
Mūlapariyāya Jātaka, 272
mutual reference (*aññam'aññam upanidhāya*), 66, 217

N

Nāgārjuna, 8
Nāgasena, 51–52, 278
nāma and rūpa, 19, 21, 58–59
Nāmacāradīpaka, 3
nāma-rūpa, 19, 84, 94, 96
Nāmarūpapariccheda, 3, 23, 58–59
naming, 57. *See also* concept-as-name (*nāma-paññatti*)
Ñāṇamoli, Ven. Bhikkhu, ix, 7
nature denotation (*bhāva-sādhana*), 14, 42, 94, 181
neo-Sarvāstivādins, 256
Nettippakaraṇa, 3, 40–41, 124, 126, 369n210
neutrality of mind (*tatramajjhattatā*), 155, 163–64, 167

newness (*navabhāva-apagama*), 303, 304–5, 307, 309
neyyattha (meaning to be drawn out), 11, 28, 71–72, 78–79
nibbāna, 13, 183, 279, 280
as dhamma, 17, 362n57
in early Buddhism, 30
as excluded from aggregates, 59
as *kamma-nirodha*, 111
as non-self, 45
realization of, 6, 100, 334
supramundane consciousness and, 117
as time free (*kāla-mutta/vimutta*), 33, 272, 339, 406n1154
as without limit (*appamāṇa*), 111–12, 278
nihilism, 9, 25. *See also* annihilationism (*ucchedavāda*)
Nikāyas, ix
Niruttipatha Sutta, 34, 56
nītattha (drawn out meaning), 11, 28, 71–72, 78–79
nominal entities, 190, 229. *See also* dependent matter (*upādā-rūpa*)
nondelusion (*amoha*), 106, 109, 111–12, 156, 160, 162–63, 168
nonexistence, 35, 37, 282
absolute (*sabbena sabbaṃ natthi*), 36
concept of (*abhāva-paññatti*), 66
of dhammas, 39, 298
as emptiness, refutation of, 45
nongreed (*alobha*), 106, 109, 111–12, 155, 160–63, 168
nonhatred (*adosa*), 106, 109, 111–12, 155, 160, 167, 168
nonpervasiveness (*abyāpāratā*), 315, 320
nonreturning (*anāgāmi*), 117, 118
non-self (*anattā*), 5, 10, 17, 41, 45, 116, 283, 292–93
nonsubstantiality (*anātmatva*), 284, 293, 300, 354
nontermination, fallacy of (*anupaccheda-dosa*), 295
nonvisible and impinging (*anidassana-sappaṭigha*) materiality, 194–96
nonvisible and nonimpinging (*anidassana-appaṭigha*) materiality, 194–96
nose consciousness (*ghāna-viññāṇa*), 95
nose decad (*ghāna-dasaka*), 264, 269
nutriment (*āhāra-rūpa*), 2, 190, 192, 225, 228, 244, 253, 320
bodily material phenomena and, 234
four kinds, 331
as generative condition of matter, 197, 267, 268, 327–28
Theravādin and Sarvāstivādin distinctions in, 262
three special modes of matter and, 243
See also under conditions (*paccaya*)
Nyanaponika, Ven. Bhikkhu, 22–23
Abhidhamma Studies, xiii–xiv
on beautiful mental factors, twofold, 166
on conditional relationships, 90
on false interpretations of jhāna experience, 116
on memory, 131
on nondelusion (*amoha*), 160
on phassa-pañcamā, 124
on time, 276, 277
**Nyāyānusāra* (Saṃghabhadra), 254, 355
Nyāya-Vaiśeṣika school, 210, 214, 219–20, 264

O

object denotation (*kamma-sādhana*), 14, 44, 60, 374n339
objects
of concentration (*ārammaṇātikkama*), 115
of mind cognition, 191, 385n630
of perception, variant views on, 181–85
of process-free consciousness, 170–71
of touch, 130, 203–4, 208, 209, 262
once-returning (*sakadāgāmi*), 117, 118
one-pointedness (*ekaggatā*)
as jhāna factor, 115, 333
right concentration and, 167
as universal mental factor, 53, 122, 124, 132, 319
origination. See *uppāda*
origination of origination (*jāti-jāti*), 296–97
other nature (*parabhāva*), 41, 43

own characteristic (*salakkhaṇa*), 45–48, 50, 62, 94
own nature/being (*sabhāva*), 10, 50
 of consciousness, 94
 dhammas as, 33, 40–45, 62, 68, 196, 304
 dhammas without (*asabhāva-dhamma*), 59
 disappearance of, 305
 in Jaina sevenfold predication, 37
 lack of, 66
 as nipphanna, 197
 own characteristic and, 45–46
 time's lack of, 274, 275
 tri-temporality and, 35–36, 39
 as ultimate, 48
own sway (*vasavattitā*), 10, 44, 320

P

Pacceka Buddhas, 108–9, 114, 115
pain (*dukkha*), 105, 107, 117, 129, 130–31, 285, 330, 333
Pakativādino, 9
Pāli Buddhist literature, 4
Pāli exegesis and commentaries
 on air element, 204
 on *bhavaṅga*, 170
 bhāvaññathatta used in, 38
 on change-in-characteristics (*lakṣaṇa-anyathātva*), 38–39
 on characteristics, defining, 257
 on citta and cetasikas, 88–89
 on conceptual constructs, 57
 on delusion, 142
 on dhammas, 8–9, 26, 41, 50
 on four elements, 205, 252
 on heart base, 97–100, 227
 on material clusters, 249
 on mere seeing, 129
 on mind and matter, 91
 on momentariness, 287–88, 313
 on moments (*khaṇa*), 284
 parinipphanna used in, 197
 on right energy, 138
 on sound, 220
 on time, 33, 35–36, 274–75
 on time and consciousness, relationship between, 276–78
 on totality (*sabba*), 32
 two truths in, 73, 75–76
 universal mental factors in, 122
 vicikicchati and *na adhimuccati* in, 152
Pāli language, xii
Pāli Suttas
 and Abhidhamma, relationship of, 2–4
 adhimokkha used in, 136
 chanda used in, 139
 conceptual constructs in, 56
 on consciousness and nāma-rūpa, 96
 on contact (*phassa*), 125, 128
 conventional terms in, 80–81
 dhamma, use of term in, 17
 early Buddhism in, 4
 on edible food, 225, 226
 emptiness in, 45
 energy in, 137
 on five material organs, 211
 four modes of explanation in, 346
 hetu used in, 321
 on impermanence, 283–84
 kathāvatthu, three kinds in, 352
 language in, 14
 on mahābhūtas, 201–2
 on material dhammas, 195
 on mental change, rapidity of, 287
 on moral shame and fear, 142
 on origin and cessation of dhammas, 291, 310
 pariyāya-desanā used in, 81
 phassa-pañcamā in, 124
 on physical health, 242, 393n835
 practical method of exposition in, 309
 on right and wrong mindfulness, 158
 on space element, 230–31
 theravāda and *vibhajjavāda* used in, 341, 407n1190
 on three conditioning characteristics, 290
 on threefold conceit, 147
 on twofold passaddhi, 166
 on universal mental factors, 123
 on vitakka-vicāra, 134–35
 on vocal determinations, 239
Pañcappakaraṇaṭṭhakathā, 3
paññatti. *See* conceptual constructs (*paññatti*)

papañca, 135
Paramatthavinicchaya, 3, 67, 301
parinipphanna. *See under* production
path
  condition (*paccaya*), 333–34
  consciousness (*magga-citta*), 117–18
  eightfold, 138, 158, 166–67
  three divisions of, ix–x
Path of Purification (Ñāṇamoli), ix
Paṭisambhidāmagga, 3, 43, 44, 45, 301–2, 310
Paṭisambhidāmagga Aṭṭhakathā, 289, 305
Paṭṭhāna, 3
  bhavaṅga used in, 8, 170
  on conditionality, 288–89, 312, 313–14, 321, 339–40
  on heart base, 226, 227, 228
  on kamma-born materiality, 330–31
  on mahābhūtas and dependent matter, 198
  on physical base of mind and consciousness, 96–97, 98
  on six conditional relations, 90
  synthetical method in, 23
Paṭṭhāna Aṭṭhakathā, 354
perception, 308
  agent of, variant views on, 179–81
  correct, 18
  direct, 178–79, 181
  in early Buddhism, 134–35
  as inference, 31
  momentariness and, 288
  perversion of (*saññā-vipallāsa*), 284
  representative (*bāhyārthānumeyavāda*), 286
  representative (*sākāra-jñāna-vāda*), 177
  as succession of mental events, 286
  three conditions for, 133
  See also sense perception
perception (*saññā*)
  mindfulness and, 157–58
  in nāma, 19, 84, 123
  and other mental dhammas, as blended, 51
  partial experience by, 130
  solid (*thira*), 157
  as universal mental factor, 53, 122, 124, 131, 319
permanence (*niccatā*), 35, 36–37, 48, 56, 83, 94, 144–45, 284, 300, 305
person (*puggala*), 27–29, 77
personalism (*pudgalavāda*), 28–29
Peṭakopadesa, 3
petas, sphere of, 162
physical base, common (*eka-vatthuka*), 88
Pitāputrasamāgama Sūtra, 73
pīti. *See* zest
plasticity. *See* malleability (*mudutā*)
pleasure (*sukha*), 108
  feeling and, 129, 131, 333
  as jhāna factor, 113, 114, 117
  and zest (*pīti*), difference between, 138–39
pluralism, 9, 22–25, 26, 54
plurality
  of causes, 319–20
  of dhammas, 51, 52, 54
  of material clusters, 261–62
  of material dhammas in same locus, 218
  principle of (*nānatta-naya*), 9, 25
  of smallest unit of matter, 253
positional inseparability (*padesato avinibhogatā*), 52, 189, 206–8, 250–51, 252, 261
potency to project results (*phalākṣepa*), 39
Poṭṭhapāda Sutta, 56, 348
prajñā (understanding), 122, 135, 146–47, 179
Prajñaptiśāstra, 5
Prajñaptivādins, 350
Prakaraṇapādaśāstra, 5
presence (*ṭhiti*), 59, 197. *See also* change-in-continuance (*ṭhitassa aññathatta*)
present life term (*addhā-paccupanna*), 276
primordial nature (*pakati*, Skt. *prakṛti*), 9, 48, 67, 68, 210, 320
process consciousness (*vīthi-citta*), 170, 171, 173
process-free consciousness (*vīthimutta*), 170–71, 175

production
of matter (*rūpassa upacaya*), 190
positive (*parinipphannatā*), 59, 197, 271, 292–95
proficiency of consciousness (*citta-paguññatā*), 156, 165, 166
proficiency of mental factors (*kāya-paguññatā*), 155–56, 165, 166
proximate cause (*padaṭṭhāna*), 94
of sense organs, 213
of various mental factors, 129, 135–36, 141, 142–43, 149
psychic life faculty (*arūpa-jīvitindriya*), 53, 122, 124, 132–33, 223, 246, 319, 332
psycho-kinesis (*iddhividha*), 114
psychological order (*citta-niyāma*), 169, 324
psychology, Buddhist, 83–85, 109, 158
Pubbaseliyas, 63, 224, 245, 286
Pudgalavādins, 27–28, 29, 30, 48
Puggalapaññatti, 3
Puggalapaññatti Aṭṭhakathā, 65
purgatories, 162

Q
questions, fourfold classification of, 345–48, 349

R
radical separateness (*accanta-bheda*), 25
Rāhula Saṃyutta, 124
Rāhulovāda Sutta, 280
Rājagirikas, 374n326
range contact, 220, 390n744
realism, 5, 9, 18, 55
rebirth, 83, 170–71, 225, 289, 324, 325, 334
rebirth-linking consciousness (*paṭisandhi-citta*), 98, 170, 171, 322, 327, 334–35
receiving consciousness (*sampaṭicchana-citta*), 107, 173, 175
reducibility (*bheda*), two kinds, 74–75
registration (*tadārammaṇa*), 174–75
resistance (*pratighāta-lakṣana*), 128, 135, 188, 189, 255, 256, 259, 282
resolve (*adhimukti/adhimokṣa*), 122, 133, 135–36, 152
restlessness (*uddhacca*), 105, 141, 142–43, 145, 150, 158, 166
restlessness and worry (*uddhacca-kukkucca*), 113
resultant (*vipāka*) consciousness, 122, 160
beautiful consciousness and, 119
beautiful mental factors in, 155, 160
bhavaṅga and, 170
conditional relations and, 324, 325, 327, 329
fifteen types, 106–8
in fine-material sphere, 114
in immaterial sphere, 115
mutuality condition and, 325
with roots, 111
volition in, 132
retrocognitive knowledge of past existences (*pubbenivāsānussati-ñāṇa*), 114
retrospective cognition (*pubbenivāsānussati-ñāṇa*), 31
Rhys Davids, Caroline, 97, 99, 201, 211–12, 348–49
right action (*sammā-kammanta*), 156, 166–67, 334
right concentration (*sammā-samādhi*), 167, 334
right effort (*sammā-vāyāma*), 137, 138, 167, 334
right endeavor (*sammappadhāna*), 137
right livelihood (*sammā-ājīva*), 156, 166–67, 334
right mindfulness (*sammā-sati*), 167, 334
right speech (*sammā-vācā*), 156, 166–67, 334
right thought/intention (*sammā-saṃkappa*), 167, 334
right view (*sammā-diṭṭhi*), 167, 333–34
Royal Park, 342
rūpa-dhammas. *See* material dhammas (*rūpa-dhammas*)
rūpa-loka/rūpajjhāna, 112–13. *See also* fine-material sphere (*rūpa-bhava*)
Rūpārūpavibhāga, 3

S

Saccasaṃkhepa, 3
sadda-lahutādi-dvādasaka, 267, 268, 270
Saddarśanasamuccaya, 311
samādhi (concentration), 122, 167, 333, 334
samaya, uses of term, 272–73, 277–78, 398n960
Saṃghabhadra, Ācārya, 136, 254. *See also* **Nyāyānusāra*
Saṃgītiparyāyaśāstra, 5
Saṃkhāra Yamaka, 287
Sāṃkhya system, 9, 37, 210, 213, 300, 320, 406n114
Sāṃmitīya school, 224, 232, 236. *See also* Ārya-Sāṃmitīyas
Sammohavinodanī, 3
Saṃyuktāgama, 290
Saṃyuttabhāṇakas, 276
Saṃyuttanikāya, 12, 13, 34, 56, 57–58, 276, 295, 307
Saṃyuttanikāya Aṭṭhakathā, 314–15
Saṅgha, x, xi, 4, 342, 351. *See also* Dispensation (*sāsana*)
Saṅgīti Sutta, 2–3, 72, 194, 195, 230, 352
Śankarite Vedātins, 214
saṅkhata (conditioned), use of term, 5–6
Saṅkhepavaṇṇanāṭikā, 289, 290
Sanskrit Buddhism, 72, 212, 238, 290, 315
Sarachchandra, E. R., 127, 171, 184–85, 219–20
Sāratthadīpanī, 345
Śāriputrābhidharmaśāstra, xi, 5
Sarvāstivāda Abhidharma, xi–xii, xiii, 16, 309
  all exists theory (*sarvam-asti-vāda*) of, 354–55
  analytical emphasis of, 9
  atomic theory in, 249–51, 253–56, 257, 259, 260
  on avijñapti-rūpa, 191, 192, 193, 219
  on bodily intimation, 236
  on citta and cetasikas, 89
  on conditioning characteristics, production of, 291–92
  on contact, 125–26, 127
  on destruction, cause of, 311
  dhamma theory in, 18
  on edible food, 226
  on energy, 137
  on four characteristics of the conditioned, 289–99, 295–97
  on four elements, 203, 207
  on gross and subtle (*oḷārika* and *sukhuma*), 193
  on indeterminate mental factors, 133–34
  on kaukṛtya (P. *kukkucca*), 150
  on life faculty, 122–23, 224
  on mada and māna, 148
  on mano-dhātu, 86–87
  on matter as resistant (*pratighāta*), 188–89, 385n624
  on mindfulness, 158
  on momentariness, critiques of, 285
  on personalism, 28–29
  on physical bases of consciousness, 95–96
  on restlessness, 143
  and Sautrāntika, distinctions between, 5–6, 7
  on sense objects and organs, relationship between, 216
  seven treatises of, 4–5
  on sex faculties, 223
  on six basic tastes, 221
  on sound, 220
  on space, 195, 230, 231, 279–80, 398n974
  on two truths, 74–75
  twofold passaddhi parallel in, 166
  universal mental factors in, 122–23, 136, 140, 142, 143
  on wrong views, 146–47
  See also under tri-temporality (*traikālya*)
Sarvāstivāda Abhidharma (Dhammajoti), 253–54
Sarvāstivāda Abhidharma Piṭaka, 16, 34, 352
Ṣaṭṣaṭka Dharmaparyāya, 126
Sauryodayika school, 236
Sautrāntika school, 5, 285

on agent of perception, 180–81
on āyatanas, 192
on causality of cognition, 176–78
on cessation, 311
on characteristics, 293, 295
on contact (*sparśa*), 126
on duration, 306–7
on empirical existence, 6–7
on intensity of mahābhūtas, 209
on life faculty, 225
on material dhammas, four components of, 194
on mental factors as sequential, 125
on momentary dharmas, 308
on objects of perception, 181
on real and nominal, distinguishing, 219
on representative perception, 177, 286
on resolve (*adhimokṣa*), 136
on Sarvāstivāda, critiques of, 255, 256, 259–60, 294, 297–99, 300, 301, 354
on space, 195, 281–82
on two truths, 75
on visible, nature of, 218–19
on vitarka and vicāra, 135
Sayadaw, Ven. Ledi, 309–10
Sayadaw, Ven. Rewata Dhamma, xii
scriptural authority, 28, 48
secondary tangible (*bhautika-spraṣṭavya*), 254
seeing, 180, 182, 235
function of (*dassana-kicca*), 173, 179
memory revival of, 184, 185
mere (*dassana-matta*), 7, 129, 173
sensory contact and, 215–16, 218
See also sight
self-entity (*atta*), 68, 86
analysis of, 24
cognitive process and, 94, 169
concept of, 67
emptiness of, 10
erroneous belief in, 6
grasping to belief in (*attavāda-upādāna*), 144
grasping to belief in (*satta-sammosa*), 65
obtainment of (*atta-paṭilābha*), 56
substantial (*attavāda*), 26, 79
self-infatuation (*mada*), 148
selflessness (*anattatā*), 63, 162
self-mortification, 163, 242
self-substance (*sabhaṃ ekattaṃ*), 26
sense consciousnesses, 7
adverting consciousness and, 108
cognition and, 175, 176–78
contact (*phassa*) and, 125, 126, 127
ideal revival and, 184–85
as mere awareness of object, 173
and sense organs, relationship between, 86, 96–97, 98–99, 216, 332
as unwholesome resultant consciousness, 107
sense fields, 190, 191, 195, 211, 228
audible (*saddāyatana*), 216, 219–21, 238, 266
sense organs and, 214
smell (*gandhāyatana*), 216, 221, 226, 253, 255, 257, 262, 319–20
tangible (*phoṭṭhabbāyatana*), 221, 226, 262
taste (*rasāyatana*), 221, 226, 253, 255, 257, 262, 320
visible (*rūpāyatana*), 6–7, 194, 216–19, 226, 231, 232, 266, 280
sense objects
cognition and, 169, 176–78
as conceptual (*prajñapti-sat*), 182
contact (*phassa*) and, 125, 126, 127, 128
corporeal components of, 193
four grades of, 172
object condition and, 322
perception and, 133
and sense organs, relationship between, 214
sense organs (*indriya*), 108, 216
cognition and, 169, 176–78
composition of, Theravādin and Sarvāstivādin distinctions in, 263–64
and consciousness, relationship between, 171, 172–73
contact (*phassa*) and, 125, 126, 127, 128, 215–16, 390n744
feeling and, 130
heart base and, 98–99, 227–28
manifestation (*paccupaṭṭhāna*) of, 213, 264

as vipāka, refutation of, 330
sense organs, five physical, 88, 191, 211, 385n630
base pre-nascence (*vatthu-purejāta*) and, 327
corporeal components of, 193
dissociation condition and, 335
faculty condition and, 331
five door cognitive process and, 171–72
five internal āyatanas and, 190–91
gradual arising of, 245
integration and continuity of, 244, 247
kamma-originated, 267, 268, 331
peripheral (*sasambhāra*) and sentient (*pasāda*), difference between, 212–15
support condition and, 325
tranquility of, 166
sense perception, 32, 75–76, 130, 177, 211, 216, 308
sense sphere (*kāma-bhava*), 100–101, 168
beautiful consciousness in, 119
consciousness with roots in, 111–12
rootless consciousness in, 106–9
unwholesome consciousness in, 103–6
sense sphere (*kāmāvacara*), 51
sense-field matter (*gocara-rūpa*), 216–21. *See also* sense fields
sensitive matter (*pasāda-rūpa*), 211–13
sensory contact/sense impression. *See* contact (*phassa*)
sensual indulgence, 13, 163, 242
sensual plane. *See* sense sphere (*kāma-bhava*)
sensual pleasure, 13, 211, 212
sentient existence, 147
in early Buddhism and Abhidhamma, comparisons of, 27–29
five modes of analyzing, 21
three characteristics of, 63, 116, 197, 283–84
serenity (*sampasāda*), 152
serial dhammas, 275, 298–99, 308, 309, 315
serial present (*santati-paccuppanna*), 275–76
sevenfold predication (Jaina theory), 37
Siddhatthikas, 374n326
sight
faculty of, 133
organ of, 124, 182, 190, 194, 211, 213, 214, 216, 218, 227, 232, 245, 264, 270
sign concepts (*nimitta-paññatti*), 64–65
Sīhala Aṭṭhakathā, 215–16, 219–20, 289–90, 390n744
Siṃhala commentaries, 67, 214–15, 249, 258, 288, 289–90, 304
single cause (*ekakāraṇavāda*), 53, 250, 318, 319, 394n861, 406n1140
single effect, 53, 250, 318, 319
six kinds of consciousness, 20, 86–87, 95–96
skillful (*kusala*) and unskillful (*akusala*), 109, 111
sleep, 150, 152, 170
sloth (*thīna*), 141, 150–51, 165, 166
sloth and torpor (*thīna-middha*), 113, 135
smell
memory revival of, 184, 185
organ of, 190, 211, 213, 214, 216, 227, 245, 264, 270, 390n744
positional inseparability (*padesato avinibhogatā*) and, 52
See also dependent matter (*upādā-rūpa*)
smell sense field (*gandhāyatana*), 216, 221, 226, 253, 255, 257, 262, 319–20
smile-producing consciousness (*hasituppāda-citta*), 108–9
solidity (*kakkhaḷatta*), 46, 53, 62, 188, 189, 203, 204, 206, 207, 238, 252, 257
soul theory (*ātmavāda*), 28–29
souls (*purisa*), 48, 49, 67, 68
sound
within physical body, 244
travel of, 216, 219–20
tri-temporality and, 36
vocal intimation and, 238, 239, 266
See also audible sense field (*saddāyatana*); *vacīviññatti-sadda-lahutādi-terasaka*
sound nonad (*sadda-navaka*), 263, 268, 269

space
as absence of matter, 281–82, 399n985
boundless (*ajaṭākāsa*), 281
concept of (*ākāsa-paññatti*), 67
empty (*tucchākāsa*), 281
as noncollective concept, 65
two kinds, 279–80
as unconditioned, 279, 398n974
space element (*ākāsa-dhātu*), 190, 192, 195–96, 229, 280
between atoms/material clusters, 258, 259, 260, 265, 315
internal and external, 230
as material delimitation (*pariccheda-rūpa*), 230–31, 281
as nominal (*anipphanna*) dhamma, 278–79
variant views of, 201
space particle (*ākāsa-koṭṭhāsa*), 258
spaces (bounded by matter), 279
spatial extension (*āvaraṇa-lakṣana*), 188, 202–3
spatial location of genesis (*uppatti-desa*), 91
spiritual avarice (*dhamma-macchariya*), 149
spiritual faculties, five, 138, 156, 158, 333
spiritual powers (*bala*), five, 138, 156, 158
Sri Lanka, xii, xiii, 1, 8, 16, 100, 353
Śrīlāta, Bhadanta, 75, 182, 194
static phase, 247, 287, 303, 307, 308, 327, 404n1093. *See also* duration (*sthiti*)
Stcherbatsky, Th., 86, 213, 398n974
stream-entry (*sotāppati*), 13, 117, 118, 333
Subha Sutta, 346–47
submoments, 176, 302, 328
substance
analysis of, 24
in dhammas, refutation of, 29, 44
in mind, refutation of, 169
mistaken notions on, 42, 89
person as, 27
time and, 37, 39, 271–72
substance and quality (*ādhāra-ādheya*)
denial of distinction between, 26, 52, 55, 79, 89–90, 189, 196, 300
dichotomy between, 15
suchness, 64
suffering (*dukkha*)
beautiful mental factors that pacify, 161–62, 164, 166
as conceptual construct, 63–64
conditioned experience as, 13
in jhāna experience, 117
noble truth of, 12
See also pain (*dukkha*)
superimposition, 50, 73–74, 182
support (*nissaya, ādhāra*)
four elements as, 198, 263
and supported (*ādhāra-ādheya-bhāva*), 26
time as, 275, 277
See also under conditions (*paccaya*)
supramundane (*lokuttara*) consciousness, 100, 117–18
supreme effort (*sammappadhāna*), 138
Suśruta, 99
Suttanipāta, 80, 285
synthesis (*saṅgaha*), 9, 23, 53, 54, 317, 344–45

T
Taiwan, xii
Tāmraparṇīyā, 8, 100
tanmātras (subtle matter), 210, 213
taññānatā, rejection of, 31, 91
taste
memory revival of, 184, 185
organ of, 190, 211, 213, 214, 216, 227, 245, 264, 270, 390n744
positional inseparability (*padesato avinibhogatā*) and, 52, 257
See also dependent matter (*upādā-rūpa*)
taste sense field (*rasāyatana*), 221, 226, 253, 255, 257, 262, 320
telepathic knowledge (*cetopariya-ñāṇa*), 114
temperature (*utu*), 188–89, 244
bodily material phenomena and, 234
as generative condition of matter, 197, 267–68, 327–28
three special modes of matter and, 243
temporal concepts (*kāla-paññatti*), 64–65, 67

tentative attribution (*samāropaṇa*), 42
Thailand, xiii
Theragāthā, 124, 242
Theravāda Abhidhamma, xii–xiii
on agent of perception, 179–80, 181
analysis and synthesis in, 9
on atoms, 256–58, 260
on *bhāva-vigamana*, 37–38
on bodily intimation, 232–36, 237–38
on change in characteristics (*lakṣaṇa-anyathātva*), 39
on cognitive process, 129
on cold and fire element, relationship between, 203–4
on conceptual constructs, 15, 60–62, 64, 67
on conditioned dhammas and conditioning characteristics, 295
on conditioning characteristics, critiques of, 291, 292–93
on consciousness, duration of single unit of, 286–87
on contact as distinct mental factor, 125, 126, 127
dhamma analysis in, 22
on dhammāyatana-rūpa, 192–94
on direct perception, 178–79
on dissolution, 310–12
on energy, 137–38
historical development of, 1–3
on ideal revival, 185
on life faculties, two types, 122, 224–25
on mano-dhātu, 87
on material clusters, 249, 251–53
on matter, 188–89, 385n624
on mental states, relationship between, 89
on mind and matter, lifespan of, 286–87
on mindfulness, 158
misunderstandings about, 22–25
on momentariness, 288–90
on moments, two definitions of, 301–2
on objects of perception, 182
on physical base of mind and mind consciousness, 96–100
on pīti, 139
on resolve (*adhimokkha*), 136
Sarvāstivāda influence on, 40
on self-infatuation (*mada*), 148
on sense of touch, 209–10
on sense organs, arising of, 245
on sex faculties, 223
on space, 231, 280–81
systematization of, 4
on *vinaya-kukkucca*, 150
vipāka, restricted meaning in, 330
on vocal intimation, 238–40
Theravāda Abhidhamma, approach of, xiii, 1, 362n56
Theravāda exegesis
on javana, divergent views, 174
on mental factors, simultaneity of, 125
on momentariness, 301–2
on pluralism, 24–25
on sensory contact and sense organs, divergent views, 215–16
on visual consciousness, 219
Theravāda tradition, ix
and early Buddhism, distinctions between, 4
"person" in, 28
on relative truth, distinct understanding of, 72–73
and Sarvāstivāda, differences between, 16, 33–36, 294
Sautrāntika influence on, 6–7
in Sri Lanka, 8, 100
theravāda, translations and meanings of, 341, 407n1190
Third Council and, 351, 353
three fraternities of, 353
on tri-temporality, 35–36
on two truths, 75–78, 79
as Vibhajjavāda, identification with, 342–43, 350, 353–54
Third Buddhist Council, 16, 34, 342–43, 344, 348, 349, 351–53, 354, 365n105
thought moment. *See* mind moment (*eka-cittakkhaṇika*)
thoughts, perversion of (*citta-vipallāsa*), 284
Three Jewels, 156

three roots of moral evil, 103, 111, 112, 141, 322
three signs (marks) of sentient existence (*tilakkhaṇa*), 63, 116, 197, 283–84
three wholesome roots (*kusalamūla*), 160, 161–63, 168, 322
thusness, 15
Tibetan monastic universities, xii
time, 56
  Abhidhamma terms for, 272–73, 397n926
  asynchronous kamma condition and, 132, 329, 337, 339
  as beginingless, 318
  briefest unit of (*khaṇa*), 272, 278, 284, 301, 302
  and consciousness, mutual relationship of, 276–78
  as cycle of births and deaths, 272, 278
  days, shrinkage in length of (*āyuno saṃhāni*), 246
  dhammas and, 23
  in five-door and mind-door processes, distinctions between, 183
  as mental construct, 271, 273–74
  as noncollective concept, 65
  See also *kāla-vimutta* (independent of time); tri-temporality (*trai-kālya*)
tongue consciousness (*jivhā-viññāṇa*), 95
tongue decad (*jivhā-dasaka*), 264, 269
torpor (*middha*), 113, 135, 141, 150–52, 165, 166
totality (*sabba*)
  of material phenomena (*sabbaṃ rūpaṃ*), 193
  tri-temporality and, 32
touch
  mahābhūtas and object of, variant views on, 207–8, 209–10
  memory revival of, 184, 185
  mere, 7, 130
  organ of, 190, 211, 213, 214, 216, 223, 227, 245, 263–64, 266, 267, 270, 390n744
  tactile sensation, 130, 208, 212, 223
  tangible sense field (*phoṭṭhabbāyatana*), 221, 226, 262
trainees (*sekha*), 114, 115
tranquility of consciousness (*citta-passaddhi*), 155, 164, 166
tranquility of mental factors (*kāya-passaddhi*), 155, 164, 166
transcendence of conceptual level (*paññatti-samatikkamana*), 62
Trilaksaṇa Sūtra, 290
tri-temporality (*trai-kālya*), 16
  conditional relations and, 322, 323, 338–39
  dhammas and, 30–40, 193, 275–76, 278
  paññattis and, 59
  Sarvāstivāda theories on, 33–40, 49, 296, 350, 351, 352
  in Theravāda and Sarvāstivāda positions, controversy between, 33–36, 350, 351, 352, 354, 355
true existent (*saccikaṭṭha*), 50
truth as characteristic (*lakkhaṇa-sacca*), 63
truth as concrete base (*vatthu-sacca*), 63
Turnour, George, 343, 344
twelve-factored formula of dependent arising, 19, 278, 318
two truths
  conceptual constructs and, 55–56, 58, 81
  of dhammas and person, 27, 30
  distinguishing, 73–75, 78–79
  early Buddhist antecedents to, 30, 71–72
  relative status of, variant views on, 10–11, 71–72, 75–78, 79–81
  significance of, 13–14

U

Uddaka, 341
ultimate (*paramattha*), 27, 29–30, 48–49, 50, 55, 58
ultimate point of view (*nippariyāyena*), 110–11
ultimate truth (*paramattha-sacca*), 11, 77. *See also* two truths
unconditioned (*asaṃskṛta*), 291, 296
unconditioned dhammas/dharmas, 112, 279, 339, 398n974

understanding, 47–48. *See also* prajñā (understanding)
unity principle (*ekatta-naya*), 9, 51, 54
universal mental factors (*sabba-citta-sādhāraṇa*), 53, 223
  faculty condition and, 332
  theory of, antecedents to, 123–25
  Theravāda and Sarvāstivāda differences in, 122–23
universal predication. *See* categorical statement (*ekaṃsavāda*)
unsatisfactoriness (*dukkha*), 283. *See also* suffering (*dukkha*)
unwholesome consciousness, 122
  four universal unwholesome mental factors in, 141–43, 159
  and mindfulness, variant views on, 158
  resultant (*akusala-vipāka-citta*), 107
  three classes and twelve types (sense sphere), 103–6
upādā-rūpa. *See* dependent matter
Uposatha ceremony, 342, 343, 351
uppāda (Skt. *utpāda*, "arising, origination"), 47, 59, 88, 89, 197, 246, 247–48, 290, 293–94, 295, 296, 299, 302–3, 305, 306, 310, 312, 317
Uttarāpathakas, 64

V

vacīviññatti-sadda-lahutādi-terasaka, 267, 268, 270
Vaibhāṣika school, 176–78, 254, 354–55
  on perception, 179, 181–82
  on space, 280, 398n974
  on visible, nature of, 217–19
  See also Nyāya-Vaiśeṣika school
Vaiśeṣika system, 9, 29–30, 66, 203, 207
Vassa, 34
Vasubandhu
  Abhidharmakośa, xii, 149
  Karmasiddhiprakaraṇa, 8, 236
  Pañcaskandhaprakaraṇa, 124
  See also *Abhidharmakośabhāṣya* (Vasubandhu)
Vasudhamma, Ācariya, 214
Vasumitra, 39, 259, 285
Vātsīputrīya school, 232, 236, 311
vaya (Skt. *vyaya*, "cessation, dissolution"), 47, 283, 290, 291, 295, 296, 298, 302, 303, 305, 306–7, 310
Vedānta, 210, 214
verbal/designation contact (*adhivacana-samphassa*), 128
vibhajjavāda
  four modes of explanation and, 349
  interpretations and translations of, 343–44, 408n1197
  purpose of using, 349–50
Vibhajjavāda (Skt. *Vibhajyavāda*, "Doctrine of Analysis"), 15–16, 291, 350
Vibhaṅga, 3, 32, 136, 148, 194, 230
Vibhaṅga Aṭṭhakathā, 258, 304, 314
vicāra. *See under* application
vijjamāna-paññatti, 67–68
vijjamānena-avijjamāna-paññatti, 68
vijjamānena-vijjamāna-paññatti, 69
Vijñānakāya, 16, 28–29, 352
Vijñānakāyapāda, 34
Vijñānakāyaśāstra, 5
Vimativinodanī, 345
Vinaya Piṭaka, ix, 343
  commentary to, 342
  as distinctly Theravāda, 4
  paññatti in, 56
  subcommentaries to, 345
  transgressions of (*vinaya-kukkucca*), 150
vipāka, restricted meaning of, 330
viriya. *See* energy (*viriya*)
visayappavatti, 171
visible and impinging (*sanidassana-sappaṭigha*) materiality, 194–96
visible sense field (*rūpāyatana*), 6–7, 194, 216–19, 226, 231, 232, 237, 266, 280
visual consciousness, 46, 179, 213, 337
Visuddhimagga (Buddhaghosa), ix, 353–54
  on dhammas as actual state, 48–49
  on four elements, 205, 206
  on heart base, 97–98
  on jaratā (decay) as ṭhiti (duration), 303
  on loss of newness, 304–5
  on material clusters, 249, 251–53
  momentariness in, 312
  Siṃhala *sanne* to, 214–15, 258, 304
  subcommentary to, 7–8, 24, 61–62, 214, 226–27, 305

Theravāda Ābhidamma in, 3
on vicikicchā and adhimokkha, 152
vitakka. *See under* application
vitakka-vicāra combination, 134–35, 167
vital nonad (*jīvita-navaka*), 264, 268, 269
vocal intimation (*vacī-viññatti/vijñapti*), 88, 190, 192, 219, 231, 236, 392n818
composition of (*vacīviññatti-dasaka*), 265, 266, 268, 269
consciousness-originated, 239–40
as inaudible sound, 239–40
kamma and, 240–41
root condition and, 322
sound and, 238
three special modes of matter and, 243
vitakka-vicāra in, 134–35
as vocal sounds, refutation of, 239
See also *vacīviññatti-sadda-lahutādi-terasaka*
volition (*cetanā*)
bodily intimation and, 236
in body and speech doors, 241
javana and, 174, 234
as kamma and universal, distinctions between, 132
kamma condition and, 329
mental (*mano-sañcetanā*), 331
in nāma, 19, 84, 123
as nutriment, 225
partial experience by, 130
as universal mental factor, 53, 122, 124, 131, 319
vitakka and, 135
von Rospatt, Alexander, 287, 288

W

waning away (*khaya,* Skt. *vyaya*), 283, 295, 296, 305
water element (*āpo dhātu*), 188, 190, 192, 195
defining, 203, 204
in human body, 201
as object of inference, 221
other mahābhūtas and, 206–7, 208
"What Does Not Belong to You" (*Na Tumhākaṃ Sutta*), 28
wholesome consciousness, 122
beautiful consciousness and, 119
beautiful mental factors in, 155
in fine-material sphere, 114
in immaterial sphere, 115
resultant, 107–8
of sense sphere, 109–11, 168
supramundane consciousness and, 118
three wholesome roots in, 160
wieldiness
of consciousness (*citta-kammaññatā*), 155, 165
of matter (*rūpassa kammaññatā*), 166, 190, 242–43, 265
of mental factors (*kāya-kammaññatā*), 155, 165
wisdom (*paññā*), ix, x, 109, 110, 168, 333
wise people, 159, 293
worldly consent (*lokasaṅketa-nimmitā*), 60
worldly usage (*lokavohārena siddhā*), 60
worry (*kukkucca*), 141, 148, 149–50, 166
wrong effort (*micchā-vāyāma*), 137, 334
wrong view (*diṭṭhi*), 334
Buddhism's concern with, 146
in classifying consciousness, 103–4
and conceit, as mutually exclusive, 147
concepts established through adherence to (*abhinivesa-paññatti*), 67
in consciousness rooted in greed, 105
as excluded from consciousness motivated by delusion, 145–46
five kinds, 147
greed and, 144–45
hatred and, 105
malleability and, 165
unwholesome mental factor of, 141

Y

Yamaka, 3, 287, 288, 290, 310, 313
Yasa, 343
Yaśomitra, 255, 256. See also *Abhidharmakośavyākhyā*
Yogācāra, xii, 73. *See also* Idealist school

Z

zest (*pīti*), 133, 138–39, 333

ABOUT THE AUTHOR

Y. Karunadasa is professor emeritus at the University of Kelaniya and a former director of its Graduate Institute of Pali and Buddhist Studies. He has served as a visiting professor at the University of London's School of Oriental and African Studies, the University of Toronto, and the University of Hong Kong, and as the Numata Chair at the University of Calgary. He lives in Colombo, Sri Lanka. He is the author of *Early Buddhist Teachings: The Middle Position in Theory and Practice* and *The Buddhist Analysis of Matter*.

WHAT TO READ NEXT FROM WISDOM PUBLICATIONS

Early Buddhist Teachings
Y. Karunadasa

A clear, elegant exploration of the basic teachings of early Buddhism, ideal for both general readers and scholars.

Abhidhamma Studies
Buddhist Explorations of Consciousness and Time
Nyanaponika Thera
Edited and Introduced by Bhikkhu Bodhi

". . . one of the most profound and lucid interpreters of Buddhist psychology in our time."—Daniel Goleman, author of *Emotional Intelligence*

Manual of Insight
Mahasi Sayadaw
Forewords by Joseph Goldstein, Daniel Goleman

"The teachings of Mahasi Sayadaw formed the essential context in which I learned, practiced, and studied meditation. That context is beautifully expressed in this book. I believe, as a Western laywoman who has been able to access the liberating teachings of the Buddha in a direct and pure form, I owe an inexpressible debt to Mahasi Sayadaw's scholarship, understanding, and courage of transmission. It is a great gift to have this translation available."—Sharon Salzberg, author of *Lovingkindness*

About Wisdom Publications

Wisdom Publications is the leading publisher of classic and contemporary Buddhist books and practical works on mindfulness. To learn more about us or to explore our other books, please visit our website at wisdompubs.org or contact us at the address below.

Wisdom Publications
199 Elm Street
Somerville, MA 02144 USA

We are a 501(c)(3) organization, and donations in support of our mission are tax deductible.

Wisdom Publications is affiliated with the Foundation for the Preservation of the Mahayana Tradition (FPMT).